SONGS OF FELLOWSHIP

songs of
fellowship

VOLUME THREE

MUSIC EDITION

KINGSWAY MUSIC
EASTBOURNE

First published 2003

ISBN 1 84291 131 7
Combined words edition (1, 2 & 3) ISBN 1 84291 132 5

Front cover title logo design by Julia Evetts.

Music setting by STM Publishing.

Cover design and print production by
Bookprint Creative Services, P.O. Box 827, BN21 3YJ, England for
KINGSWAY COMMUNICATIONS LTD
Lottbridge Drove, Eastbourne, East Sussex, BN23 6NT, UK.
Printed in Great Britain.

Contents

Important notes

Order of songs

The songs appear in alphabetical order by first line (letter by letter), not necessarily by author's title, for easy use in praise and worship meetings. An index of titles and first lines is included at the back, along with other useful indexes and chord charts (see Contents page).

To further facilitate the use of this book, most two-page songs and hymns appear on facing pages to avoid turning over, while maintaining the alphabetical order.

Numbering of songs

The songs are numbered from 1151 to 1690, continuing the numbering sequence from the companion Songs of Fellowship 2 Music Edition. This numbering and song order is also reflected in the Combined Words Edition, and the enclosed computer disk (see below).

Scripture references

References – listed in biblical order – are to the key Bible passages quoted or echoed in the songs, and to some passing references. In many cases the whole Bible passage will repay further exploration, beyond the verses listed. A full index to the Scripture references is provided at the back of the book.

Computer Disk

The computer disk contains the words to all 540 hymns and songs in Songs of Fellowship 3. For instructions on how to install the disk on your computer, please read the label on the disk itself, and refer to the 'Using The Computer Disk' pages at the back of this book.

1151. Above all

*2 Kings 19:15; Ps 97:9; Is 53:4;
Mk 15:46; Eph 1:21; Col 1:15-17*

Lenny LeBlanc
& Paul Baloche
Slow 4
Verse
E/D D Esus4 E A A/C♯
1.A-bove all pow - ers, a-bove all kings, a-bove all
king - doms, a-bove all thrones, a-bove all
E/D D Esus4 E A A/C♯
na - ture and all cre-a - ted things; a-bove all
won - ders the world has e - ver known; a-bove all
F♯m Amaj7/E D A/C♯
wis - dom and all the ways of man,
wealth and trea - sures of the earth,
1.
Bm7 D/A E/G♯ A A/C♯
You were here be-fore the world be-gan. 2. A-bove all

2.
Bm7
D/A
C♯sus4/G♯
C♯
there's no way to mea - sure what You're worth.
Chorus
A
Bm7
E/G♯
A
Cru - ci-fied, laid be-hind the stone; You
Bm7
E/G♯
A
A/G♯
lived to die, re - jec-ted and a-lone; like a rose,
F♯m
Amaj7/E
D
A/C♯
tram-pled on the ground, You took the fall,
Bm7
A/C♯
Dsus2
D
Esus4
E
A
Asus4
A
and thought of me, a-bove all.

1152. Again and again

Ps 31:3; 40:2; Jer 29:11; 1 Cor 2:9

Steadily

Dave Bilbrough

A
Verse
E/G♯
D
1. A-gain and a gain, You have re vealed Your love to me.
Esus4 E
A
E/G♯
A-gain and a gain grace has shone through.
D
Esus4 E
A
You've al - ways been there
E/G♯
D
Esus4 E
for me when I have come to You:
F♯m
D
Esus4
You are the Rock on which I stand.

E
Chorus
D
C♯m
You're won - der-ful, You're mar - vel-lous, You're ev-
Bm
A
D
'ry thing to me. Your stead - fast and un-chang-
A/C♯
Bm
Esus4 E
ing love are all I'll e - ver need. What peace
D
C♯m
Bm
and what se - cu - ri-ty can be found in know - ing You,
Last time to Coda
D.C.
A
Bm
G
Esus4 E
my Hea - ler, De - li - ve-rer.

D
Bridge
You've been my for - tress through the shift -
A
ing sands of time; in change and ad - ver-si-ty
Bm
You have
G
an-swered my prayer to guide me.
Esus4
E
D.S. al Coda
You're won -
Coda
Esus4
E
A
rit.

2. There is no limit to this never-ending stream
That's entered the castle of my soul.
You give me a hope and future
Beyond my wildest dreams.
Your love is greater than I know.

1153. A humble heart

(Won't let go)

Gen 32:26; 51:17; 55:17; 74:10; 126:6

Brian Houston

Country rock feel

G C D C
1. A hum-ble heart You have yet to de-spise,
G C D G
and so I hum-ble my-self in this place.
C D C
If they that sow in tears shall reap in joy,
G C D G
let a mil-lion tears or more roll down my face.
D C G
If You don't an-swer me to-day, Lord,

D C G
I'm gon-na be right here to-mor - row.
D C G
If You don't an - swer when I pray from the morn-
Am/E C/E
ing to the eve - ning, 'cause it's You I do be-lieve in, I will say,
D
Chorus
ev-'ry day I'm gon - na say that I
G C D
won't let go till You bless me, Lord. No, I

G
C
D
G
won't let go till You bless me, Lord. And I will cry
Em
D
C
out to You till I can't cry no more. And I
G
C
1.
D
G
2.
D
G
won't let go till You bless me, Lord. me, Lord.

2. Where can I go if You don't bid me go?
And I have no hope if You are not my hope.
And I have no peace if You don't give me peace,
And I have no faith if You don't help me to believe.
If You don't answer me today
Will the heathen nations mock Your name
And say You're made of wood or clay?
Ah, but I've seen You provide for me,
I've kissed Your lips and felt You heal my pain.
Hey, can You do it once again?

'Cause I won't let go till You bless me, Lord...

1154. All around Your throne

(Brighter than the sun)

Ps 2:1; Mt 24:29; Phil 2:11; 1 Pet 3:22; Rev 1:16; 4:3, 5, 8

Paul Oakley

Intensely
C♯m Verse
E
F♯
mf
1. All a-round Your throne, rain-bow co-lours fly through light,
A/E
C♯m
E
(v.2)
and hea-vy thun-der rolls, and the
F♯
A
G♯/D♯
F♯/C♯
light-ning blinds, so bright. Liv-ing
A/E
E
E/D♯
C♯m
C♯m/B
(v.2)
crea-tures cry "Ho-ly is the Lord," as they
F♯
1. A/E
2.,3. A/E
Chorus
try to hide their eyes. 'Cause

E
E/D♯
C♯m
C♯m/B
F♯
f You shine bright-er than the sun, on-ly Ho-ly One, and You
Am/E
E
E/D♯
C♯m
C♯m/B
shine on — me. Oh, — Je-sus, on-ly ri-sen Son, seat-ed on Your
F♯
Am/E
E
throne, would You shine on — me to-day? —
C♯m
E/B
F♯
A
D.C. (v.3)
To end
E

2. Rulers of this world
   Only join in vain as one.
   There's no other power
   Could ever overthrow Your Son.
   Principalities and powers
   Know that You are Lord
   And they try to hide their eyes.

3. There will be a day
   When the stars will leave the sky,
   Heaven and earth will shake,
   And the moon will give no light;
   While every tongue will cry
   "Jesus Christ is Lord,"
   Some will try to hide their eyes.

1155. All creation cries to You

(God is great)

Capo 2 (A)

Hab 3:3; Jn 4:23; Rev 4:8; 5:13

Marty Sampson

Strongly

B(A) Verse E(D) F♯sus4(E)
1. All cre - a - tion cries to You,
F♯(E) B(A) E(D)
wor-ship-ping in spi - rit and in truth.
F♯sus4(E) F♯(E) G♯m7(F♯m)
Glo-ry to
(v.3)
that all may hear,
E(D) F♯sus4(E) G♯m7(F♯m) F♯(E) E(D)
the Faith - ful One, Je-sus Christ, God's Son.

and all may see.
F♯(E)
E(D)
1.
F♯(E)
2.,3.
F♯(E)
Chorus
B(A)
E(D)
God is great, and His praise fills the earth,
F♯(E)
E(D)
B(A)
fills the heavens, and Your name will be praised
G♯m7(F♯m)
F♯sus4(E)
F♯(E)
through all the world. God is
B(A)
E(D)
F♯(E)
great, sing His praise all the earth, all the hea-

Last time to Coda
E(D)
G♯m7(F♯m)
E(D)
vens, 'cause we're liv - ing for the glo - ry of Your name,
F♯sus4(E)
F♯(E)
E(D)
the glo - ry of Your name.
G♯m7(F♯m)
F♯sus4(E)
F♯(E)
1st time D.C.
Bridge
B(A)
'Ho - ly
E(D)
F♯sus4(E)
F♯(E)
G♯m7(F♯m)
is the Lord', the whole earth sings,
E(D)
F♯sus4(E)
1. - 3.
F♯(E)
4.
F♯(E)
D.S. al Coda
the whole earth sings. God is

Coda

F♯sus4(E)
F♯(E)
G♯m7(F♯m)
'cause we're liv - ing for the glo -

E(D)
F♯sus4(E)
F♯(E)
ry of Your name, the glo - ry of Your name.

B(A)
E(D)
F♯sus4(E)
E(D)

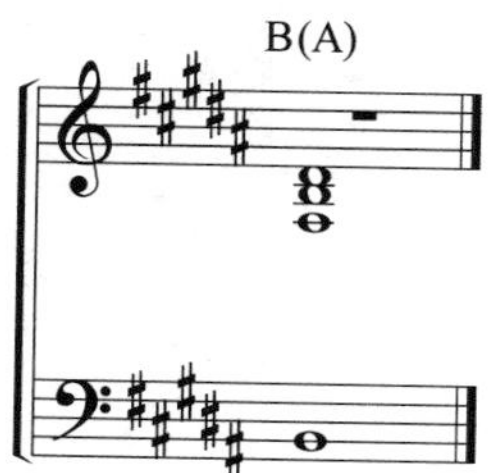
B(A)

2. All creation gives You praise,
You alone are truly great;
You alone are God who reigns
For eternity.

3. All to you, O God we bring.
Jesus teach us how to live.
Let your fire burn in us
That all may hear,
And all may see.

1156. Alleluia, alleluia
(Jesus is the Lord)

Jn 8:12; 14:6

Tony Ryce-Kelly
& Rónán Johnston

Worshipfully

E
A/E
E
A/E
Al - le - lu - ia, al - le -

E
A
lu - ia, Je - sus is the Lord,

1.
F♯m9
E
A/E
E
A/E
He's the Lord of all my heart.

2.
F♯m9
E
A/E
E
the Lord of all my heart.
He's the way,

SoF3

B
A
E
A/E
He's the truth,
He's the life.
E
B
A
He's the way,
He's the truth,
He's the life.
E
A/E
To repeat
E
D.C.
Last time
E
You're the way,
B
A
E
A/E
E
You're the truth,
You're the light.

1157. All glory, laud and honour

Mt 21:9

Tune: ST THEODULPH

Melchior Teschner (1584-1635)
Harmony from Johann Sebastian Bach (1685-1750)

C G C F G/D C G Am F G C
All glo - ry, laud and ho - nour to Thee, Re-deem-er, King, to
F E/G♯ Am F Dm7 C/G G C
(Fine)
whom the lips of chil - dren made sweet ho - san - nas ring. Thou
Am D/F♯ C/E Dsus4 D G G/F C/E G/D C D G G/B
art the King of Is - rael, Thou Da-vid's ro - yal Son, who
C C/B♭ F/A C♯dim Dm Am C/B♭ F/A C/G D7/F♯ G C
in the Lord's name com - est, the King and bles-sèd One.

2. The company of angels
Are praising Thee on high,
And mortal men and all things
Created make reply.
The people of the Hebrews
With psalms before Thee went;
Our praise and prayer and anthems
Before Thee we present.

3. To Thee before Thy passion
They sang their hymns of praise;
To Thee now high exalted
Our melody we raise.
Thou didst accept their praises;
Accept the prayers we bring,
Who in all good delightest,
Thou good and gracious King.

4. All glory, laud and honour
To Thee, Redeemer, King,
To whom the lips of children
Made sweet hosannas ring.

Theodulph of Orleans (c750-821)
Tr. John Mason Neale (1818-66)

1158.
All my days
(Beautiful Saviour)
Is 9:6; Ps 18:6; 36:8-9; Jn 14:6; 1 Cor 15:54; Heb 10:22; Rev 5:12; 11:15; 22:16
Capo 3 (D)
Stuart Townend
Steadily
Verse
Dm7(Bm) E♭2(C) F(D) B♭/D(G) E♭(C) B♭(G)
1. All__ my days I will sing this song of glad - ness,
2. I__ will trust in the cross of my Re - dee - mer,
Dm7(Bm) E♭2(C) F(D) B♭/D(G) E♭(C) Cm7(Am) E♭maj7(C)
give__ my praise to the Foun - tain of de - lights; for in my
I__ will sing of the blood that ne - ver fails; of sins for -
F(D) E♭(C) B♭/D(G) F(D) Cm7(Am) E♭maj7(C)
help - less - ness You heard my__ cry, and waves of
giv - en, of con - science__ cleansed, of death de -
Dm7(Bm) 1. G/B(E) C(A)
mer - cy poured__ down on my life.__
fea - ted and__ life with - out
2.3. C/E(A) Dm7(Bm) C(A) C/B♭(A) Chorus F/A(D) B♭(G)
end.__ Beau - ti - ful Sa - viour, Won - der - ful
Lamb!__

C(A) C/E(A) F(D) Gm(Em)
Coun - sel - lor, clothed in ma-jes-ty, Lord of
Gm/F(Em) C/E(A) Dm7(Bm) C(A) C/B♭(A) F/A(D)
his-to-ry, You're the Way, the Truth, the Life. Star of the Morn-ing,
B♭(G) C(A) C/E(A) F(D) Gm(Em)
glor-ious in ho - li - ness, You're the Ri-sen One, hea-ven's
Gm/F(Em) C/E(A) Dm7(Bm) C(A) Dm7(Bm)
Cham-pi-on, and You reign, You reign o-ver_ all!
E♭2(C) F(D) (Fine)
(3. I)

3. I long to be where the praise is never-ending,
Yearn to dwell where the glory never fades;
Where countless worshippers will share one song,
And cries of 'worthy' will honour the Lamb!

1159. All my life

(True surrender)

Jn 3:30

Liz Holland

Steadily
Verse
E
E/D♯
E/G♯
1. All my life, all my will, ev-'ry day I
A
Bsus4
E
E/D♯
lay it all be-fore You. All my life, all my will,
E/G♯
A
Bsus4
1.
E
ev-'ry day I lay it all be-fore You now.
2.3.
E
Chorus
A
And Je-sus, take us to the place of
E
Bsus4
A
true sur-ren-der, where we be-come less and

SoF3

E
Bsus4
A
You be-come great - er; and Your ho-ly ways in-to our
E
Bsus4
F♯m7
lives will en-ter, and all that we are, and
A
Bsus4
E
D.C. (fine)
all that we have be-come Yours.

2. All my pain, all the fears, every tear,
I lay them all before You.
All my pain, all the fears, every tear,
I lay them all before You now.

1160. All of me

Gal 2:20

Gareth Robinson

Worshipfully
Verse
C2
Cmaj7
C7
F
All of me, all of me I give to You,
More of You, more of You I long for,
G
C
Bb2
F/A
only You, Jesus.
1.
2.
Chorus
For this life I live for You;
Em
Am
I truly worship You, all of my days,
F
F/A
G/B
in ev-'ry way, I will praise You.

C
Em
Am
In thought and word and deed,
pow'r'd by Your life in me,
Em
Am
Em
all of my days,
in ev - 'ry way,
F
G
F/A
G/B
C
I will praise You, Lord.

1161. All of You

(Enough)

Gen 15:1; Is 55:1-2; Mt 13:45-46

Chris Tomlin & Louie Giglio

Moderately
Chorus
A D2/F♯ Esus4 D2
All of You is more than e-nough for all of me,
A D2/F♯ Esus4 D2 A D2/F♯
for e-v'ry thirst and e-v'ry need. You sa-tis-fy
Esus4 D2 A/C♯ D2
3rd time to Coda
me with Your love, and all I have in You
Esus4
(Last time fine)
A D2/F♯ Esus4 D2
is more than e-nough.
A D2/F♯ Esus4 D2 A D2
Verse
1. You're my sup-ply,

Esus4
A/C♯
D2
my breath of life;
still more awe -
Bm7
Esus4
A
D2
some than I know.
You're my re-ward,
Esus4
A/C♯
D2
worth liv - ing for;
still more awe -
Bm7
Esus4
some than I know.
And all of You
Coda
Esus4
A
D2
Esus4
D2
More than all I want,
more than all I need,

A/C♯
D2
Esus4
You are more than e-nough for me.
A
D2
Esus4
D2
More than all I know, more than all I can,
A/C♯
D2
1.
Esus4
You are more than e-nough.
2.
D.S. al fine
Esus4
than e-nough. And all of You

2. You're my sacrifice
   Of greatest price;
   Still more awesome than I know.
   You're my coming King,
   You are everything;
   Still more awesome than I know.

1162. All the way my Saviour leads me

Neh 9:15;
Ps 48:14; Mt 11:28; Jn 6:35;
1 Cor 10:4; 15:53; Heb 4:9

Worshipfully

Music: Rich Mullins

Verse
mf
D
G
A
1. All the way my Saviour leads me, what have I to ask beside?
Can I doubt His tender mercy, who through life has been my guide?
Heavenly peace, divinest comfort, here by faith in Him to dwell,
for I know

F♯m7 G 1. A
what-e'er be-fall me, Je-sus do-eth all things well.
D
2. All the way
2. A D Chorus G
f
spring of joy I see. And all the way my Sa - viour leads
A F♯m7 Em7
me, oh the ful - ness of his love. Per-fect
D G A
rest to me is pro - mised in my Fa-ther's house a - bove.

D
G
And when my spi - rit clothed im-mor - tal wings its
A
F♯m7 Em7
D
flight to realms of day, this my song through end-less a-
G
A
D
- ges, Je - sus led me all the way.

2. All the way my Saviour leads me,
Cheers each winding path I tread.
Gives me grace for every trial,
Feeds me with the Living Bread.
Though my weary steps may falter
And my soul athirst may be,
Gushing from a Rock before me,
Lo! a spring of joy I see.

Fanny Crosby (1820-1915)

1163. All to Jesus I surrender
(I surrender all)

Winfield Scott Weedon (1847-1908)
Arr. Stuart Townend

Tenderly
Verse
D G/D D A2/C♯ F♯ F♯/A♯ Bm Bm/A G D/F♯ Em7 A D G/D
1. All to Je-sus I sur-ren-der, all to Him I free-ly give;
D G/D D C♯m7♭5 F♯ F♯/A♯ Bm Bm/A G D/F♯ Em7 A D
I will e-ver love and trust Him, in His pre-sence dai-ly live.
Chorus
D/F♯ G D/F♯ Em7 A D G/A A
I sur-ren-der all, I sur-ren-der all,
D G/D D D/F♯ Daug5/F♯ G D/A Bm7 Em7 A7 D
all to Thee, my bles-sèd Sa-viour, I sur-ren-der all.

2. All to Jesus I surrender,
Humbly at His feet I bow;
Worldly pleasures all forsaken,
Take me Jesus, take me now.

3. All to Jesus I surrender,
Make me, Saviour, wholly Thine;
Let me feel the Holy Spirit,
Truly know that Thou art mine.

4. All to Jesus I surrender,
Lord, I give myself to Thee;
Fill me with Thy love and power,
Let Thy blessing fall on me.

5. All to Jesus I surrender,
Now to feel Thy sacred flame;
O, the joy of full salvation!
Glory, glory to His name!

Judson W. Vande Varter (1855-1939)

1164. All who are thirsty

Ps 42:7; Is 55:1; Rev 22:20

Brenton Brown
& Glenn Robertson

Not too fast
G
Bm7
All who are thir-sty, all who are weak,
C2
Am G/B
come to the foun - tain, dip your heart in the stream of
C C/D G Bm7
life. Let the pain and the sor - row be washed a - way
C2
Am G/B
in the waves of his mer-cy, as deep cries out to
C C/D G Am/G G C2
deep. (We sing) Come, Lord Je - sus, come.

G Am/G G C2 G Am/G
Come, Lord Je - sus, come. Come, Lord
G C2 G Am/G G
Je - sus, come. Come, Lord Je - sus,
C2
1. D.C.
2.
G Am/G G
come. All who are Ho - ly Spi - rit,
C2 G Am/G G C2
come. Ho - ly Spi - rit, come.
G

1165. Almighty God

Mark Vargeson

Worshipfully
A
D/A
A
Al - migh - ty God, faith - ful and
Un - chang - ing God, for - e - ver the
D/A
D
A/E
true, in my wor - ship
same, it's You I wor - ship,
D/F♯
1. E
2. E
I want to meet with You.
to know Your heart a -
gain. And I fall
A
E
down on my knees a - gain, as You show
F♯m7
D2
me what grace means; and You love

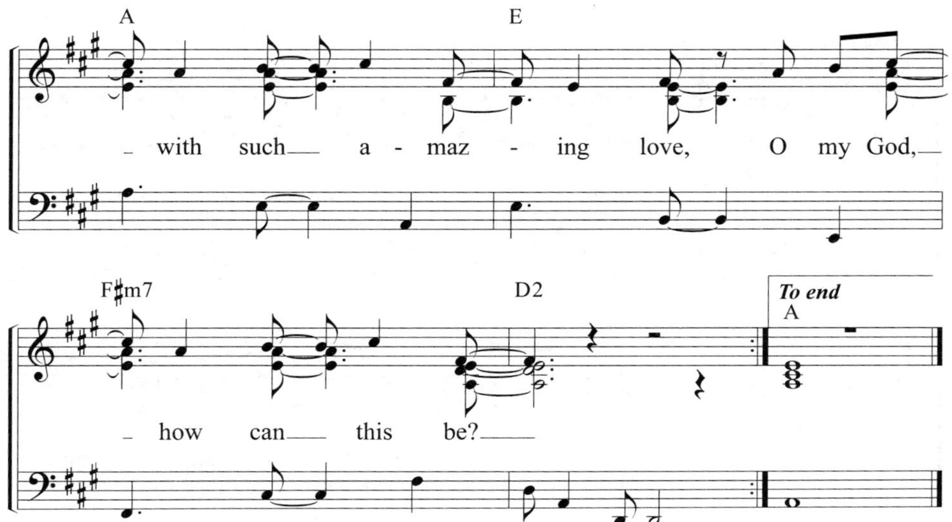
A
E
with such a - maz - ing love, O my God,
F♯m7
D2
To end
A
how can this be?

1166.
Almighty God, Holy One
Is 61:10; 1 Pet 2:24; Rev 5:12; 7:9-10
Rhys Scott
Capo 3(D)
Worshipfully
F2(D)
Csus4(A)
Al-migh-ty God, Ho - ly One.
Lamb, who bore our sin.
Cm7(Am)
Eb(C)
Who can stand be - fore You, who can
Who de - serves such mer - cy, gra - cious
Csus4(A)
1.
2.
F2(D)
come? Per - fect I come
King?
(Em) (D)
Gm F/A
Gm(Em)
Csus4(A)
to Your throne of grace, I'm stand - ing in
F2(D)
Gm7(Em)
Christ, I'm clothed in His right - eous -

Csus4(A)
Dm2(Bm)
B♭(G)
ness. To know Your pre-sence,
Csus4(A)
Dm2(Bm)
Gm7(Em)
to seek Your face. Fa-ther, I de-light
Last time to Coda
Csus4(A) C7sus4/G (A)
1. F2(D)
2. F2(D)
in Your em-brace. And I
Gm7(Em)
Csus4(A)
D.C.
Coda F(D)
Al-migh-ty

1167. Almighty God, to whom all hearts are open

Music: A. Piercy, D. Clifton
& C. Groves
Words: The Alternative Service Book (1980)

Quietly
G
Am7
D
C/G
G
Al-migh-ty God, to whom all hearts are o - pen,
Am7
D
all de-sires known, and from whom no se-crets are
C/G
G
F
Em
B7
hid - den: cleanse the thoughts of our
C
G/B
A7
G/D
D7sus4
D7
hearts by the in-spi-ra - tion of Your Ho-ly

G
F
3
Spi - rit, that we may per - fect - ly love You,
C/E
3
G
and wor - thi - ly mag - ni - fy, that we may
F
3
C/E
3
G
per - fect - ly love You, and wor - thi - ly mag - ni - fy Your
D
Em
D
Am7
C
ho - ly name; through Christ our Lord, a - men.
Em
D
Am7
C/D
G
Gsus4
G
Through Christ our Lord, a - men.

1168. Amazing grace

Ps 33:20-22; 142:5; Mt 18:13; 21:9; Lk 15:4, 24; Jn 1:16; 9:25; Phil 2:9; Rev 14:3

Strongly

Music: Nathan Fellingham

Verse
G F C/E G/B C2 Dm7(addG)
1. A - ma - zing grace, how sweet the sound that
Am7 G Gsus4 G Gsus4 G F
saved a wretch like me; I once was
C2/E G/B C2 Dm7(addG) Am7 G Gsus4
lost, but now am found, was blind, but now I see.
G Dm7 Bridge Dm7/C Gsus4 G Gsus4 G Dm7
A - ma - zing love has
Dm7/C Gsus4 G Chorus C
come to me. I lift up my voice to the hea-

F
C/E
F
Am7
- vens, lift up my hands to the King, and I cry 'ho - san - na, ho-
G
C/E
F
C
san - na in the high - est.' Je - sus my Lord is ex - al -
F
C/E
F
Am7
ted far a - bove e - v'ry name, and I cry 'ho - san - na, ho-
G
C/E
F
To end
G
san - na in the high - est.'

2. 'Twas grace that taught my heart to fear,
And grace my fears relieved;
How precious did that grace appear,
The hour I first believed!

3. The Lord has promised good to me,
His word my hope secures;
He will my shield and portion be
As long as life endures.

John Newton (1725-1807) adapt. Nathan Fellingham

Sing to the Lord, for He has done glorious things; let this be known to all the world.

ISAIAH 12:5

1169. And after all
(Unashamed)

Capo 3(G)

Ps 56:11; Is 53:3, 5; Rom 1:16; 1 Cor 1:18; Phil 2:7-8; 3:7

Paul Oakley

With energy

Verse
Chorus
Bb(G)
F/A(D)
Gm(Em)
Eb(C)
F(D)
1. And af - ter all, ev - 'ry - thing I once held dear just proved to be so vain.
To lose it all, and find a Friend who's al - ways near could on - ly be my gain.
And when I think of what You've done for me, to bring me to the Fa - ther's side:
Un - a - shamed and un - a - fraid,
Un - a - shamed and un - a - fraid,

Gm(Em)
Eb(C)
Bb(G)
I will choose to wear Your name, in a world so full
I will love You all my days, I don't care what peo-
F/A(D)
1.3.
Gm(Em)
Eb(C)
Bb/D(G)
of hate, I will al - ways live Your
ple say, I'm un - a - shamed and un - a -
2nd time to Mid section
Cm(Am)
Cm7/Bb(Am)
F(D)
Cm(Am)
Cm7/Bb(Am)
way.
fraid.
F(D)
D.C.
2.4.
Gm(Em)
Eb(C)
D.S.
I will al - ways live Your way.
5.
Gm(Em)
Eb(C)
Bb(G)
F/A(D)
un - a - shamed and un - a - fraid.
shamed.)

Gm(Em)
E♭(C)
B♭(G)
Fine
(I'm un - a -
Mid section
Cm(Am)
Cm7/B♭(Am)
F(D)
I know some will say it's fool-ish-ness:
You can't make a blind - man see.
But I know that there is pow - er in the cross
3
to save those who be - lieve.
D.S.

2. Could it be
That You should put on human flesh,
Your glory laid aside?
Bruised for me,
Majesty upon the cross,
Forsaken and despised.
When I think of what it cost for You,
To bring me to the Father's side:

1170. And I'm forgiven

(You are my King)

Is 53:3, 5; Lk 19:38; Acts 2:32-33

Billy James Foote

Worshipfully

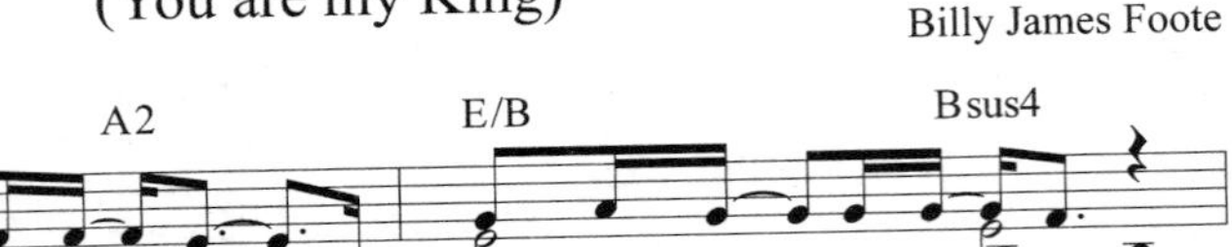

Verse
E2/G♯
A2
E/B
Bsus4

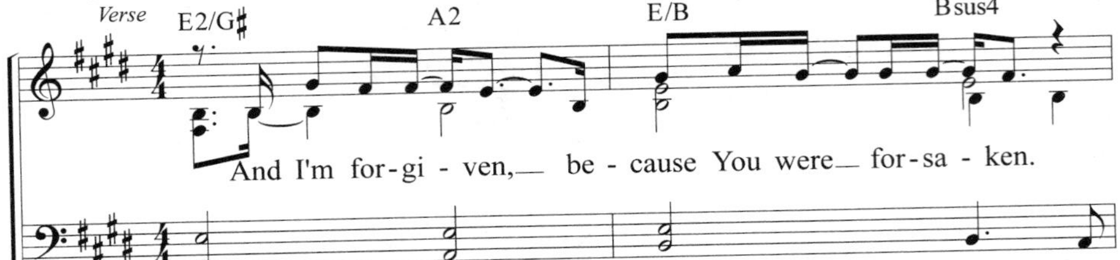

And I'm for-gi - ven, be - cause You were for-sa - ken.

E2/G♯
A2
E/B
Bsus4
And I'm ac-cep - ted: You were con-demned.

E2/G♯
A2
E/B
Bsus4
And I'm a-live and well, Your Spi-rit is with-in me, be-

A2
Bsus4
E
E
Chorus
cause You died and rose a-gain. A-ma-zing love, how

A
E
can it be that You, my King, would die for me?

Bsus4
B
A/B
E
A
A-ma-zing love, I know it's true;
E
Bsus4
B
now it's my joy to ho - nour You. In all I
A2
Bsus4
E
(Fine)
do, I ho - nour You. You are my
King, You are my King, Je - sus,
D.S. al Fine
You are my King, You are my King.

1171. Angels bow

1 Chron 29:11; Heb 1:6

Capo 3 (D)

Keith Getty

With wonder

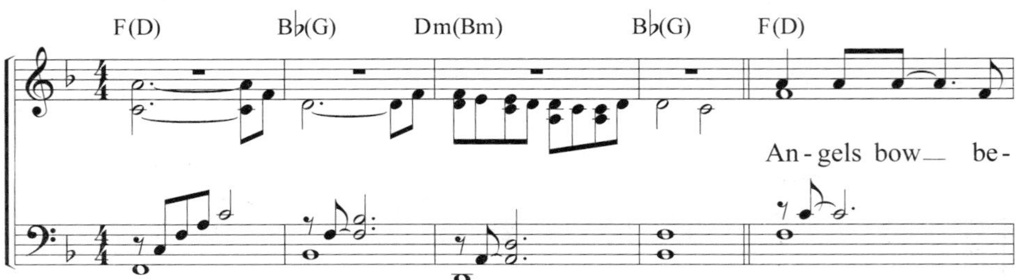
F(D)
B♭(G)
Dm(Bm)
B♭(G)
F(D)
An - gels bow be -

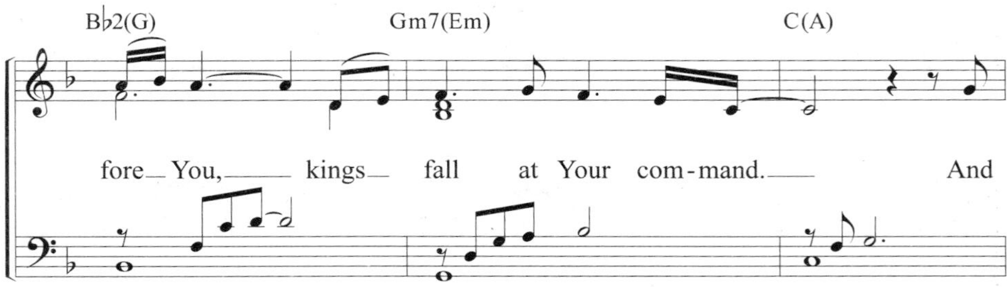
B♭2(G)
Gm7(Em)
C(A)
fore You, kings fall at Your com - mand. And

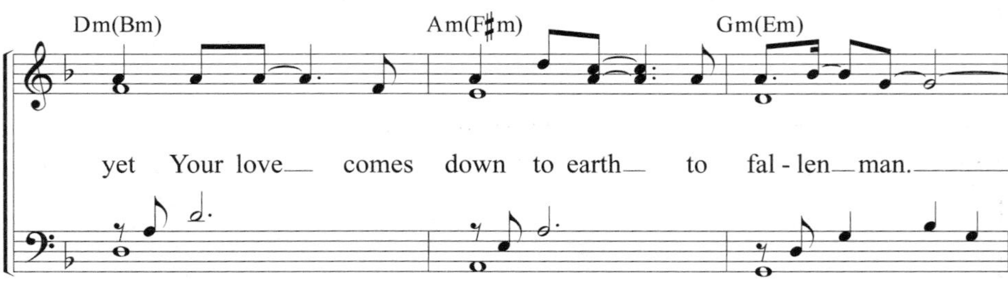
Dm(Bm)
Am(F♯m)
Gm(Em)
yet Your love comes down to earth to fal - len man.

C(A)
Dm(Bm)
B♭(G)
How can I know Your work - ings, e -

Gm7(Em) F/A(D) C(A) Dm(Bm)
ter - nal my - ste-ry? I must bow down and
Am(F♯m) Gm(Em) A(F♯) Dm(Bm) C2/E(A)
give my life, must fol-low You. And I love You,
F(D) B♭(G) F2/A(D)
Lord, e-v'ry-thing be-longs to You, is known by You, and
Gm7(Em) C7(A) Dm(Bm) C2/E(A)
made for Your e - ter - nal glo - ry. You, my
F(D) B♭(G) (A) Csus4 (A) C F(D)
Lord, re-ceive the praise of my thank - ful heart.

1172. A refuge for the poor
(This is our God)

Capo 1 (E)

Ps 35:10; 55:8; 68:5; Is 25:9; 54:5; Joel 2:25; Lk 2:25; Jn 4:14; 14:1, 27; 1 Pet 5:6; Rev 4:10; 7:17

With awe

Chris Tomlin
& Jesse Reeves

F(E)
B♭(A)
1. A re - fuge for the poor, a shel - ter from the storm:
F(E)
B♭(A)
F(E)
this is our God. He will wipe a - way your tears
B♭(A)
F(E)
and re - turn your was - ted years: this is our
B♭(A)
Gm7(F♯m7)
B♭(A)
God. Oh, mmm, this is our

F(E)
Gm7(F♯m7)
B♭(A)
God. Oh, mmm, this is our
F(E)
1.
2.,3.
God.
B♭2(A2)
Dm7(C♯m7)
This is the One we have wait-ed for,
B♭2(A2)
Dm7(C♯m7)
this is the One we have wait-ed for,
B♭2(A2)
Dm7(C♯m7)
Gm7(F♯m7)
this is the One we have wait-ed for, oh, mmm,

B♭(A)
F(E)
1.
D.C.
2.
this is our God.

2. A Father to the orphan,
A healer to the broken:
This is our God.
He brings peace to our madness
And comfort in our sadness:
This is our God.

3. A fountain for the thirsty,
A lover for the lonely:
This is our God.
He brings glory to the humble
And crowns for the faithful:
This is our God.

"Come to me, all you who are weary and burdened, and I will give you rest."

MATTHEW 11:28

1173. Are the prayers of the saints?

(The prayers of the saints)

Rev 5:8

Matt Redman

With awe
D
1. Are the prayers of the saints like
D2
sweet smel-ling in-cense, are the
D
prayers of the saints like
D2
sweet smel-ling in-cense to Your
G
heart, to Your
D
heart?
Em7
Let these prayers of the saints
D/F♯
be
G
sweet smel-ling in-cense, let these
Em7
prayers of the saints
D/F♯
be

G
1.
D
D.C.
Dsus2
sweet smel-ling in-cense to Your heart.
2.
D.S.
D
Last time
D
Dsus2
heart.
heart.

2. Are the songs of the saints
Like sweet smelling incense,
Are the songs of the saints
Like sweet smelling incense to Your heart,
To Your heart?
(Repeat)

Let these songs of the saints
Be sweet smelling incense,
Let these songs of the saints
Be sweet smelling incense to Your heart.

1174. Around You such beauty

(I bow down)

1 Kings 8:27; Ps 95:6; Is 1:18; 6:5; Rev 4:8

Steve & Vikki Cook

Gently
Verse
E Esus4/2 A/E E Esus4/2
1. A - round You such beau - ty, Your ma-jes-ty could
A/E E Amaj9 F♯m
fill an end - less sky: ho - ly are You, Lord.
E Esus4/2 A/E E Esus4/2
Tran - scen - dent, ex -
A/E E Esus4/2 A/E E
al - ted, the hea - vens can - not con-tain Your pre -
Amaj9 F♯m E Esus4/2
sence: ho - ly are You, Lord.

A/E E B C♯m B C♯m A2
And as I be-hold Your glo-ry
E2 E2/G♯
I'm un-done. I bow down
Chorus
A2 E2/G♯ A2
at Your feet, I bow down at Your feet,
E2/G♯ B/D♯ C♯m
I bow down at Your feet for You are my God,
B 1. Asus2 2. A2/C♯ B D.S. al fine
my God. 2. You I bow down

3.
Asus2
Esus2
Fine

2. You saved me, the sinner,
With crimson red You washed me white as snow:
How I love You, Lord.
You loved me, the mocker,
With kindness You won my heart forever:
How I love You, Lord.
And as I behold this mercy
I'm undone.

Therefore, there is now no condemnation for those who are in Christ Jesus.

ROMANS 8:1

1175. As for me and my house

Josh 24:15

Moderately

Jim Bailey

E A E B
As for me and my house, as for me and my family,
E A 1. E B E
as for me and my children, we will serve the Lord.
2. E B (Fine) E A
we will serve the Lord. In this family, we're gonna do things
E B
properly, read God's word ev'ry day and then we'll
E E/G♯ A
try to pray; although we get it wrong, we will still

E
B
car - ry on,
make Je - sus
num-ber one
in this
D.C. al fine
place.
In this place
we're gon - na say grace.

1176. As sure as gold is precious

(Revival)

Lam 5:21; Jer 31:17; 33:7

Robin Mark

Steadily
E
1. As sure as gold is precious and the
dream - er dream - ing in her
A B
ho - ney sweet, so You
dead - end job; ev - 'ry
E A E
love this ci - ty and You love these streets.
dri - ver dri - ving through the rush hour mob.
Ev - 'ry child out play - ing by their
I feel it in my spi - rit, feel it
A B
own front door; ev - 'ry
in my bones, You're going to

E
A
E
ba - by lay - ing on the bed - room floor.
send re - vi - val, bring them all back home.
1.3.
2.,4.
2. Ev - 'ry
I can
Chorus
A
B
E
A
B
hear that thun - der in the dis - tance like a train on the edge of town;
C♯m
C♯m/B
A
B
C♯m
I can feel the brood - ing of Your Spi - rit:
A
B
C♯m
C♯m/B
A
B
E
'Lay your bur - dens down, lay your bur - dens down.'

D.C.
1.
2.
3. From the
Re - vive
B/E
us,
re - vive
C♯m
B/C♯
C♯m
E/B
us,
re - vive
A
F♯m7/A
us
with
Your
E2
E
1.
2.
Fine
fire!
Re - vive

3. From the preacher preaching when the well is dry
To the lost soul reaching for a higher high.
From the young man working through his hopes and fears,
To the widow walking through the vale of tears.

4. Every man and woman, every old and young;
Every father's daughter, every mother's son.
I feel it in my spirit, feel it in my bones,
You're going to send revival, bring them all back home.

1177. As we bring our songs

(How long?)

Rev 6:9-11; Phil 3:7-8; Heb 12:1

Graham Kendrick

Building in strength
Verse
D
Em7
A7sus4
D
1. As we bring our songs of love to-day, do you
It's a har-mo-ny of cost-ly praise from the
Em7
A7sus4
D
hear a sound more glo-ri-ous? Like the
lips of those who suf-fer, of
Em7
A7sus4
Bm7
migh-ty roar of o-cean waves, ma-ny
sighs and tears and mar-tyrs' prayers un-
D/F#
Em7
A7sus4
D Dsus4
1. D Dsus4
D.C.
wit-nes-ses sur-round us.
til this age is o-ver.

Chorus
2.
D
A
A/G
D/F♯
G
How long,
Lord, till You come?
How long
How long
till the earth
is filled
with Your song?
How long
till the whole
world hears
and the work
is done,
Em7
G/A
A
2nd time D.S.
(2nd chorus)
un-til Your jus - tice shines
like the sun?
un-til at last
we see
Your re-turn?
How long,
D
Dsus4
Lord, till You come?
How long
till the earth
is filled
with Your song?
How long?
How long?

1.
Gmaj7/B
D
Gmaj7/B
D.C.

2.
Gmaj7/B
D
(x3)
Gmaj7/B
How
long?
How

D
long?

2. Lord, help us to live worthy of
Our sisters and our brothers
Who love You more than their own lives,
Who worship as they suffer:
To embrace the scandal of the cross,
Not ashamed to tell Your story,
To count all earthly gain as loss,
To know You and Your glory.

1178. As we come today

(Holy moment)

Ps 100:4; 134:2; Heb 4:16

Matt Redman

Steadily
F♯m7
E/G♯
1. As we come to-day, we re-mind our-selves of what
A2
F♯m7
we do; that these songs are not just songs,
E/G♯
D2
F♯m7
E/G♯
but signs of love for You. This is a ho-ly mo - ment now,
A2
F♯m7
E/G♯
A2
some-thing of hea - ven tou - ches earth, voi-ces of
F♯m7
E/G♯
A2
Bsus4
an-gels all re-sound, we join their song.

Chorus
F♯m7
E/G♯
A2
Come, come, come, let us wor - ship
run, run, run through Your gates, O
Bsus4
1.
F♯m7
E/G♯
God with our hands held high, and our
God, with a
D2
2.
F♯m7
hearts bowed down. We will
shout of love,
Last time to Coda
E/G♯
D2
D.C. al Coda
with a shout of love.
2. Lord, with con -
Coda
D2
3
F♯m7
E/G♯
shout of love. Let this be a ho - ly mo - ment now.

To repeat
A2
3
To end
A2
Fine
Let this be a

2. Lord, with confidence
We come before Your throne of grace.
Not that we deserve to come
But You have paid the way.
You are the holy King of all,
Heaven and earth are in Your hands,
All of the angels sing Your song,
We join them now.

1179. As we lift up Your name

(Revival fire, fall)

Brightly, with feeling

Ps 85:4-7; Joel 2:23; Mt 6:9-10; Acts 2:2-3

Paul Baloche

Verse

(Leader - Echo)

A D2 A G D2 A G A D2 A G D2 A G

1. As we lift up — Your name, (as we lift up — Your name,) let Your fi - re fall. (let Your fi - re fall.) Send Your wind and — Your rain, (Send Your wind and — Your rain) on Your wings — of love. (on Your wings — of love.)

D/F♯ Em7

(All)

Pour out — from hea - ven — Your pas - sion — and pre - sence, —

A D/A A Chorus D D/F♯ G Em7
bring down Your burn - ing de - sire. Re - vi - val fi - re,
Asus4 A D D/F♯ G Em7 Asus4 A
fall! Re - vi - val fi - re, fall!
Bm F♯m7
Fall on us here in the pow'r of Your Spi - rit;
G D/A A D D/F♯ G Em7
Fa - ther, let re - vi - val fi - re fall. Re - vi - val fi - re,
Asus4 A D D/F♯ G Em7 Asus4 A
fall! Re - vi - val fi - re, fall!

Bm
F♯m7
Let the flame consume us with hearts a-blaze for Je-sus;
G
A
D
Fa-ther, let re-vi-val fi-re fall!

2. As we lift up Your name, *(Leader - Echo)*
Let Your kingdom come,
Have Your way in this place,
Let Your will be done,
Pour out from heaven Your passion and presence, *(All)*
Bring down Your burning desire.

1180. At the foot of the cross

Jn 19:25; Rom 8:19; Phil 3:7; Rev 22:2

Tré Sheppard

Thoughtfully

Verse
D
D/F♯
Gsus2
1. At the foot of the cross where I kneel in a - do - ra - tion, and I lay my bur - dens down
I ex - change all my sin for the pro - mise of sal - va - tion, and Your name a - cross my brow.
(D.C. after v.1 only)
2. At the

Last time to Coda
Bm
Chorus
Asus4+2
Gsus2
I will wait here at the cross.
1.-3.
Bm
4.
Gsus2
D.C.
Coda
Gsus2
I will
3. At the

2. At the foot of the cross
I give up my vain ambition,
And I leave my selfish pride.
In the peace that is there
Will You restore my vision
In all the places I am blind?
I will wait here at the cross. (x4)

3. At the foot of the cross
There is healing for this nation,
There is rest for those who wait;
And the love that we find
Is the hope of all creation,
We are stunned by what You gave.
We will wait here at the cross. (x4)

4. We will wait at the cross,
A hungry generation,
With our broken hearts and lives.
Will You hear, will You come,
Will You fill our desperation?
O God, let this be the time.
We will wait here at the cross. (x4)

This is how we know what love is: Jesus Christ laid down His life for us.

1 JOHN 3:16

1181. At this table we remember

Jn 6:33; 1 Cor 11:26-29; Rev 19:9

Capo 3 (D)
Tune: STUTTGART

German melody
arr. Christian Friedrich Witt (c.1660-1716)

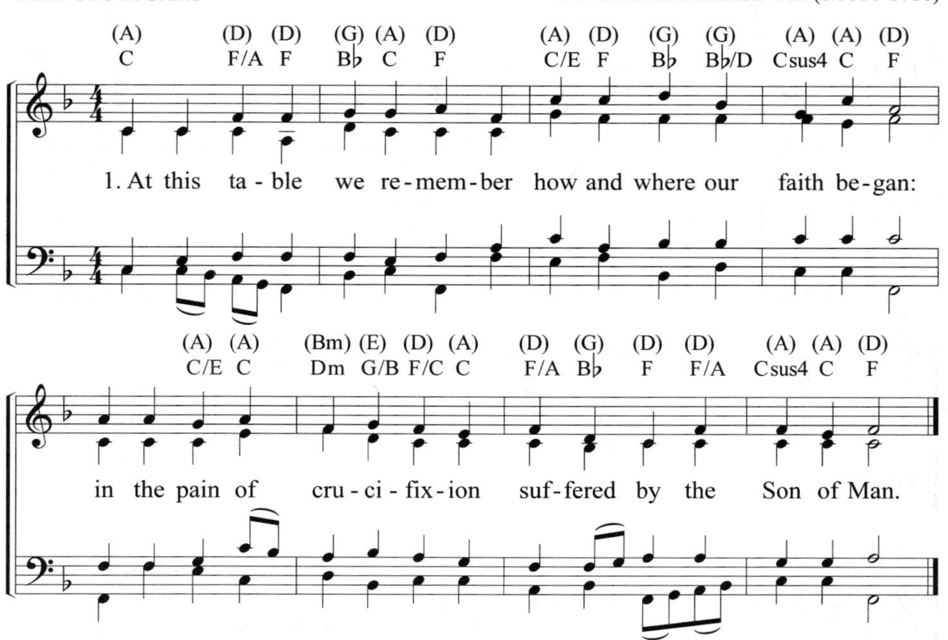

(A) (D) (D) (G) (A) (D) (A) (D) (G) (G) (A) (A) (D)
C F/A F B♭ C F C/E F B♭ B♭/D Csus4 C F
1. At this ta - ble we re - mem - ber how and where our faith be - gan:
(A) (A) (Bm) (E) (D) (A) (D) (G) (D) (D) (A) (A) (D)
C/E C Dm G/B F/C C F/A B♭ F F/A Csus4 C F
in the pain of cru - ci - fix - ion suf - fered by the Son of Man.

2. Looking up in adoration
Faith is conscious - He is here!
Christ is present with His people,
His the call that draws us near.

3. Heart and mind we each examine:
If with honesty we face
All our doubt, our fear and failure,
Then we can receive His grace.

4. Peace we share with one another:
As from face to face we turn
In our brothers and our sisters
Jesus' body we discern.

5. Bread and wine are set before us;
As we eat, we look ahead:
We shall dine with Christ in heaven
Where the kingdom feast is spread.

6. Nourished by the bread of heaven,
Faith and strength and courage grow -
So to witness, serve and suffer,
Out into the world we go.

Martin E. Leckebusch (b.1962)

1182.
Awake, awake, O Zion
(Our God reigns)
Capo 3 (D)
Is 52:1; 52:7-9; Mt 1:23; Heb 10:19; 12:2
Nathan Fellingham
With strength
Verse
B♭(G) C(A) Dm7(Bm) B♭(G) C(A)
1. A - wake, a - wake, O Zi - on, and clothe your - self with
you have been re - deemed by the pre - cious blood of
Dm7(Bm) B♭(G) C(A)
1. Dm7(Bm) C/E(A)
strength, shake off your dust and fix your eyes on
Je - sus, and now you sit en -
Fsus4(D) F(D)
2. Dm7(Bm) C/E(A) Fsus4(D)
Him. For throned with Him.
F(D) Chorus F(D) C/E(A) B♭2(G)
Our God reigns, He is King of all the
and sing a song of
Last time to Coda
Csus4(A) C(A) F(D) C/E(A) B♭2(G)
earth, our God reigns, and He's seat - ed on the
praise, our God reigns, the awe - some Lord most

1.
Csus4(A) C(A) Dm7(Bm)
2.
Csus4(A)
1. to verse 2
D.S.
C(A)
throne. Lift your voice high. 2. How
2. to bridge
C(A)
Bridge
B♭(G) C(A) Dm7(Bm) B♭(G) C(A)
Em - ma - nu - el, Em-ma - nu -
Dm7(Bm) B♭(G) C(A) Dm7(Bm) C/E(A)
el, our God is with us
Fsus4(D) F(D) D.S. al Coda
now. 3. The
Coda
Csus4(A) C(A) F(D) Fine
high.

2. How beautiful the feet are
Of those who bring good news,
For they proclaim the peace that comes from God.
Rise up you holy nation,
Proclaim the great salvation,
And say to Zion "Your God reigns".

3. The watchmen lift their voices,
And raise a shout of joy,
For He will come again.
Then all eyes will see the
Salvation of our God,
For He has redeemed Jerusalem.

Shout for joy to the Lord, all the earth. Worship the Lord with gladness; come before Him with joyful songs.

PSALM 100:1-2

1183. Awake, my soul

(Rise up)

1 Chron 16:32-33; Ps 57:8; 90:14; Is 55:12; 60:1; Lk 19:40

Strong beat

Owen Hurter

Am G Am Dm Am G Am Dm
1. A -

Am G Am F Am G
wake, my soul, rise up from your sleep - ing; do not slum-ber or

Am F Am G Am F
sleep a - ny-more. Raise your wea - ry head to a new — day;

Am G F
1. (to v.2) 2.
lift your shout, let your voice be — heard. — — Rise up, —

C
F/C
C
my soul, and sing. Rise up, my soul, and sing.
F/C
C
F/C
C
Rise up, my soul, and give glo - ry to the Lord.
1.
F/C
2.
D.S.(v.3)
F/C
G
Fmaj7
Rise up,
I don't want to sleep a-ny-more, but
Dm
G
I'll a-wake the dawn with sing - ing. Hear this cry - ing heart
Fmaj7
Dm
1.
G
2.
of mine, as I lift up my song. Lift it up,

lift it up, lift it up. Rise up,
C
F/C
C
my soul, and sing. Rise up, my soul and sing.
F/C
C
F/C
C
Rise up, my soul, and give glo - ry to the Lord.
1.
F/C
2.
F/C
C
Rise up

2. Rocks will cry out if we are silent,
Trees will clap their hands and rejoice;
The mighty ocean roars with a new song,
Mountains bow down to honour Your name.

3. Let the song of a bride in blooming
Thunder clap through the heavens above.
Rising up in true adoration,
Arise and shine for Your light has come.

1184. Beautiful Lord

(The Potter's hand)

Ps 4:3; Jer 18:6

Darlene Zschech

Gently

G D/F♯
Beau - ti - ful Lord,___ won - der - ful Sa - viour,
You gent - ly call___ me in - to Your pre - sence,

C Cm6/E♭
I know for sure,___ all of my days___ are
guid - ing me by___ Your Ho - ly Spi - rit.

Em7 Asus4 A/C♯ Am7/D
held in Your hand,___ craf - ted in - to___ Your per - fect___
Teach me, dear Lord, to live all of my life___ through Your___

D Em D/F♯
plan.___ I'm cap - tured by___ Your ho - ly cal - ling,
eyes.___

G C/G G D/F♯
set me a - part___ I know You're draw - ing me___

Em
Asus4
A
Am7/D
to Your-self;
lead me, Lord,
I
pray.
Dsus4
D
G
D/F♯
Am7
Take me,
mould me,
use me,
Call me,
guide me,
lead me, walk be-
D/E
Em
F
C/E
fill me;
side me;
I give my life
to the Pot - ter's hand.
1.
Am7
Dsus4 D
2.
Am7
G/B
Dsus4
D
G
D/G
Oo,
Em
D/E
G/F
F
D
To end
G
oo,
oo.

1185.

Because of You

(Sing for joy)

Ps 40:3; 71:23

Dave Bilbrough

Latin feel

Chorus

B7 E B7 E B7 C#m C#m/B A B7sus4 E

Be-cause of You, I can be free;
be-cause of You, I can be me.
Since that day when love broke through,
my life was changed be-cause of You.
Be-cause of

Last time to Coda 1. 2.

Verse

Bm7 E Bm7 E Bm7

You fill my heart with me - lo - dy,
sal-va-tion is my song.
The way was o-pened up

A
E
F♯m7
E/G♯
A
D.S. al Coda
– for me – to know You as – my God. – Be-cause of
Coda
E
Bm7
– So I will sing for – joy, – sing for – joy, –
A
E
sing for – joy – to You. Yes, I will sing for – joy, –
Bm7
1.
A
E
sing for – joy, – sing for – joy – to You. Yes, I will
2.
A
E
sing for – joy – to You.

1186. Before one ever came to be

(Book of days)

Ps 118:24; 139:15-16; Eph 5:20; 1 Thess 5:18

Capo 3 (D)

Lara Martin

Fast 4

F(D) Bb(G)

Be-fore one e - ver came to be, all the days

Dm(Bm)
or-dained for me were writ-ten in Your book of days.
Bbmaj7(G)
F(D)
You are the One who fa - shioned me,
Bb(G)
Dm(Bm)
the One I praise con-ti - nual-ly, so per-

Bb(G)
Gm7(Em)
fect are Your ways. I will re-joice

Lara Martin (Abundant Life Ministries, Bradford, England)

F/A(D)
B♭(G)
Gm7(Em)
and be glad.
And in all things
F/A(D)
E♭(C)
C(A)
F(D)
I give thanks.
This is the day
B♭(G)
You have made, I will re-joice,
I will
C(A)
B♭maj9(G)
C(A)
re-joice:
in You I boast.
(in my God)
F(D)
B♭(G)
This is the day
You have made, I will re-joice,
I will
C(A)
B♭(G)
C(A)
F(D)
re-joice:
in You I boast.

1187. Before the throne of God above

Jn 8:58; Acts 7:55; Rom 3:25; 8:1-2; Col 3:3; Heb 4:14; 7:25; Rev 5:9

Majestically
Music: Vikki Cook
D G/D D
1. Be-fore the throne of God a - bove I have a strong, a per-fect
F♯m D/F♯ G D/F♯ A Bm
plea, a great High Priest whose name is Love, who ev - er
G6 Em7 G/A D F♯m7 G D/F♯ D
lives and pleads for me. My name is gra - ven on His
A D/F♯ F♯m7 G D/F♯ G A Bm Bm/A
hands, my name is writ - ten on His heart; I know that
G D/F♯ A Bm2 Bm Bm/A G6 Em7 G/A
while in heav'n He stands no tongue can bid me thence de -

Bm
Bm/A
G2
Em7
G/A
D
part, no tongue can bid me thence de - part.

2. When Satan tempts me to despair,
   And tells me of the guilt within,
   Upward I look and see Him there
   Who made an end to all my sin.
   Because the sinless Saviour died,
   My sinful soul is counted free;
   For God the Just is satisfied
   To look on Him and pardon me,
   To look on Him and pardon me.

3. Behold Him there! The risen Lamb,
   My perfect, spotless righteousness;
   The great unchangeable I AM,
   The King of glory and of grace!
   One with Himself I cannot die,
   My soul is purchased with His blood;
   My life is hid with Christ on high,
   With Christ, my Saviour and my God,
   With Christ, my Saviour and my God.

Charitie L Bancroft (1841-92)

1188. Befriended

Prov 18:24; Jn 15:15

Matt Redman

Verse
Em7
A7sus4
1. Be - friend - ed, be - friend - ed by the King a - bove all
D
Em7
kings. Sur - ren - dered, sur -
A7sus4
1.
D
ren - dered to the Friend a - bove all friends. 2. In -
2.3.
D
Chorus
G
Em7 A7sus4
seen. This will be my sto - ry, this will be my
D
G
Em7
song. You'll al - ways be my Sa - viour, Je -

A7sus4
Last time to Coda
D
1.
sus, You will al-ways have my heart.
3. A-
2.
Bm7
A7sus4
4. De-ter-mined, de-ter-mined now to live this life for
D
Bm7
You. You're so wor-thy, my
A7sus4
D.S. al Coda
Coda
D
D
great-est gift would be the least You're due.
heart.

2. Invited, invited deep into this mystery.
Delighted, delighted by the wonders I have seen.

3. Astounded, astounded that Your gospel beckoned me.
Surrounded, surrounded, but I've never been so free.

1189. Behold the Lamb of glory comes

(In majesty He rides)

Ps 24:8; 45:4; 68:1; Is 62:6; Mal 4:2; Rev 5:5; 6:2

Triumphant march

Robert Critchley

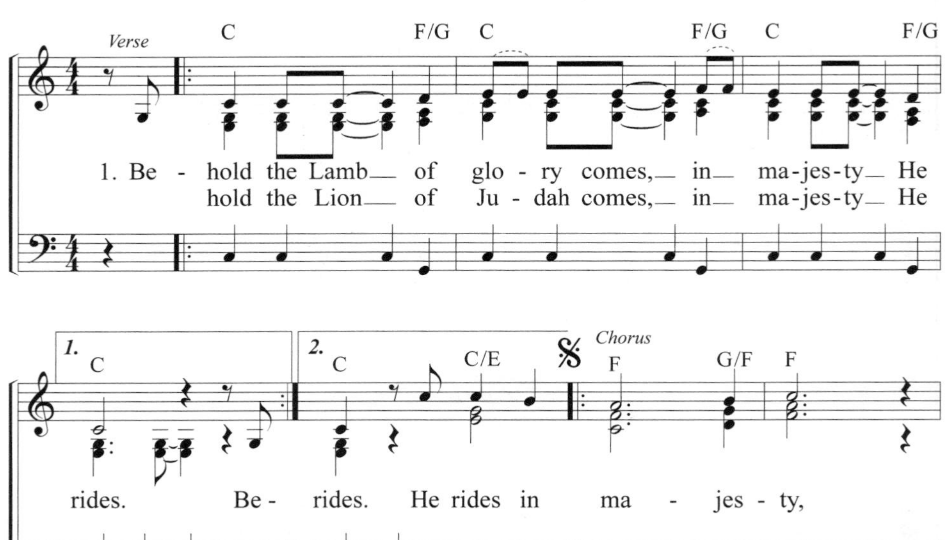

Verse
C F/G C F/G C F/G
1. Be - hold the Lamb of glo - ry comes, in ma-jes-ty He
hold the Lion of Ju - dah comes, in ma-jes-ty He
1. C
2. C C/E
Chorus
F G/F F
rides. Be- rides. He rides in ma - jes - ty,

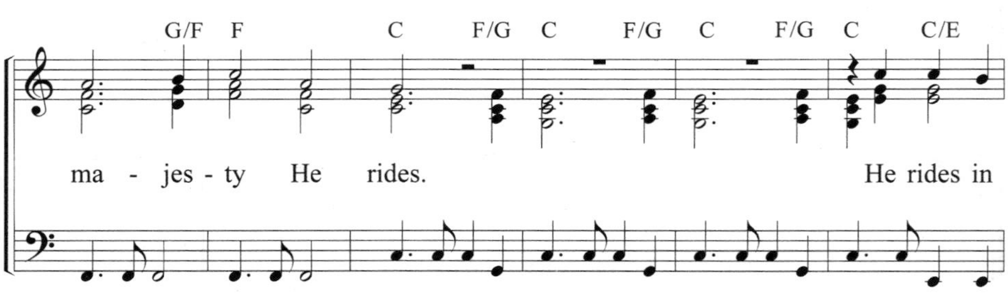

G/F F C F/G C F/G C F/G C C/E
ma - jes - ty He rides. He rides in

F G/F F G/F F C F/G
ma - jes - ty, ma - jes - ty He rides.

1.3.
2.4. (Fine)
C F/G C F/G C F/G C
2. Be -
3. The
And when the
Mid section
G Am/G G Am/G G Am/G
Lord goes to bat - tle, who can stand a-gainst
G C F/G C F/G C F/G
His awe - some might?
C C B♭ C B♭ C B♭
Let God a - rise and His e - ne-mies be
C B♭ C B♭ C B♭ C B♭
scat-tered. Whoa - o - o, whoa - o - o -

1.
C
B♭
2.
C
C/E
D.S.
o.
Let
o.
He
rides
in

2. Behold the Sun of Righteousness,
   On a white horse He rides.
   His cavalry is following Him,
   An army from on high.

3. The watchmen on the tower
   Are interceding for the land.
   The saints proclaim God's victory,
   He stretches forth His hand.

Sing to the Lord a new song,
His praise from the ends of the earth.

ISAIAH 42:10

1190. Be lifted up

1 Chron 16:29-31; Ps 95:6

Paul Oakley

Slow 4
E
B
Be lif - ted up,
be lif - ted up.
A
1.
B
E
As we bow down,
be lif - ted up.
2.
B
E
Be lif - ted
be lif - ted up.
(Fine)
A
E
Let the hea-vens re-joice,
let the na-tions be glad.
A
E
Let the whole earth trem - ble,
for You are God.

A
C♯m7
Come and wor - ship the Lord in the beau - ty of ho -
B
A
B
li - ness. As we bow down, be lif - ted
E
A
B
up. As we bow down, be lif - ted
E
D.S. al Fine
up, be lif - ted

1191. Belovèd and Blessèd

Ps 23:1; 103:8; Song 2:16; 6:3; Mal 4:2; Mt 3:17; 17:5; Jn 4:14;6:33; 15:15; 1 Cor 1:30;2 Cor 1:3; Eph 1:6; 1 Tim 2:6;Heb 10:22; 13:8; Jas 4:8; 1 Jn 1:1; 4:18; Rev 5:5-6

Stuart Townend

Steadily
Verse
C G C/E F G
1. Be - lov - èd and Bles - sèd, the Fa-ther's pure de-light.
C F/G C G C/E F G
Re - dee-mer, Sus - tai - ner, You're my pas-sion and my prize.
1. C F/G 2. C Chorus G/B Am D/F♯
2. My You're un - chang - ing, You're mag -
G G/F C/E F Gsus4 G C G/B
ni - fi-cent, You are all I could de-sire. You're my
Am D/F♯ G G/F C/E
Breath of life, Sun of right - eous-ness, You're the

F
C/E
1.
Gsus4
G
D.C.
2.
Gsus4
G
D.S.
Love that sa - tis-fies.
3. There's
(Ch 2) You're the
3.
Gsus4
G
Dm7
C/F G
Dm7
C/F G
Be - lov - èd.
My Be - lov - èd.
Repeat as required
C
(Be -)

2. My Brother, my Comforter,
My Shepherd and my Friend.
My Ransom, my Righteousness,
You're the Stream that never ends.

3. There's kindness, compassion
For those who will draw near;
Acceptance, forgiveness,
And a love that conquers fear.

(Chorus 2.)
You're the Word of life,
You're the Bread of heaven,
You're the Lion and the Lamb.
All within me cries,
'Lord be glorified
By everything I am.'

1192. Blessèd are the poor

(The Beatitudes)

Mt 5:3-10, 12

David Lyle Morris
& Pat Youd

Steadily

Verse

C F C F C
1. Bles-sèd are the poor in spi - rit, for theirs is the king - dom of

G C F C
heav'n. Bles - sèd are the mourn - ing hearts,

F C G Am
com - fort to them — will be — giv'n. Bles - sèd are the

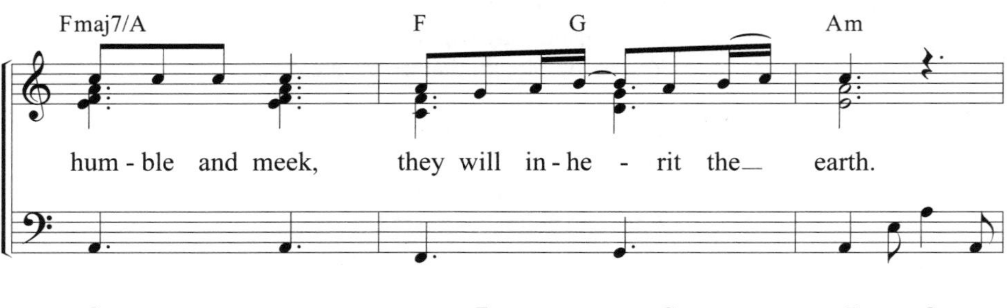

Fmaj7/A F G Am
hum - ble and meek, they will in - he - rit the — earth.

C F C F C
Bles - sèd are those who hun - ger and thirst for righ - teous -

G
G7
C
Chorus
Am
(v.2)
ness, for they will be filled. Re - joice and be — glad, for
Fmaj7
G
great your re-ward — in hea - ven. — Re-
Am
Fmaj7
G
joice and be — glad, for great your re-ward — in hea - ven. —
To end
C

2. Blessèd are the merciful,
For mercy to them will be shown.
Blessèd are the pure in heart,
For they will see their God.
Blessèd are the makers of peace,
They will be called sons of God.
Blessèd are those who suffer for Christ
And righteousness,
Theirs the kingdom of heaven.

Final Chorus:
Give glory to God,
For He's our reward in heaven.
Give glory to God,
For He's our reward in heaven.

Rejoice and be glad,
Give glory to God in heaven.
(Repeat)

1193.

Blessèd be Your name

Job 1:21; Is 35:1, 6; Phil 4:11

Capo 2 (A)

Beth & Matt Redman

Verse
B(A)
F♯(E)
Bles - sèd be Your name in the
And bles - sèd be Your name when I'm
G♯m7(F♯m7)
E(D)
land that is plen - ti - ful, where Your
found in the de - sert place, though I
B(A)
F♯(E)
streams of a - bun - dance flow,
walk through the wil - der - ness,
bles - sed
E(D)
be Your name.
B(A)
E - v'ry bles - sing

SoF3

F♯(E)
G♯m7(F♯m7)
E(D)
You pour out I'll turn back to praise.
B(A)
F♯(E)
G♯m7(F♯m7)
And when the dark - ness clo - ses in, Lord, still I will
E(D)
Chorus
B(A)
say: Bles - sèd be the name of the Lord,
F♯(E)
G♯m7(F♯m7)
E(D)
bles - sèd be Your name. Bles - sèd be the
B(A)
F♯(E)
name of the Lord, bles - sèd be Your

G♯m7(F♯m7)
F♯(E)
E(D)
1.
D.C. (v2)
Last time to Coda
glo - ri - ous name.
2.
B(A)
F♯(E)
You give and take a - way, You
G♯m7(F♯m7)
E(D)
B(A)
give and take a - way. My heart will choose to
F♯(E)
G♯m7(F♯m7)
1. E(D)
say, 'Lord, bles - sèd be Your name, You
2. E(D)
D.S. al Coda
Coda
B(A)
name.' Bles - sèd be the

2. Blessèd be Your name
When the sun's shining down on me,
When the world's 'all as it should be,'
Blessèd be Your name.
And blessèd be Your name
On the road marked with suffering,
Though there's pain in the offering,
Blessèd be Your name.

1194. Born in the night

(Mary's child)

Tune: MARY'S CHILD

Lk 2:7; Jn 1:9; 8:12; 14:6; Acts 1:11

Geoffrey Ainger

G Em C Cm G Bm7 Em
1. Born in the night, Ma-ry's child, a long way from Your

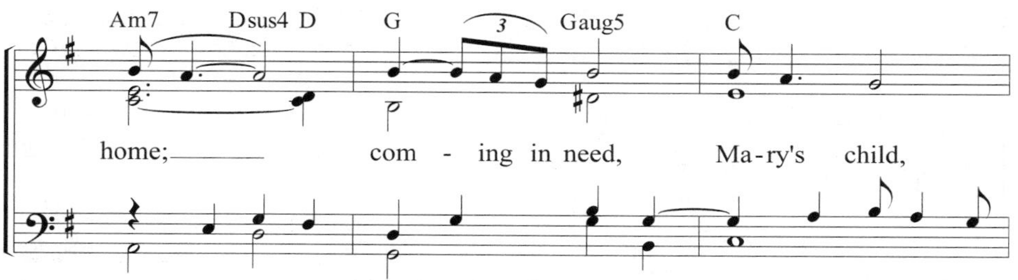

Am7 Dsus4 D G Gaug5 C
home; com - ing in need, Ma-ry's child,

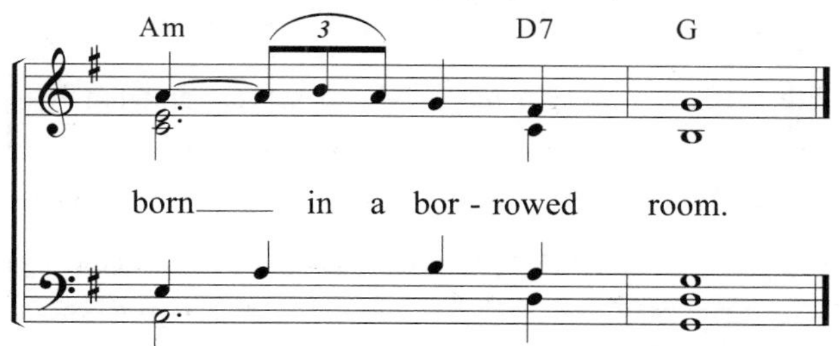

Am D7 G
born in a bor - rowed room.

2. Clear shining light,
   Mary's child,
   Your face lights up our way;
   Light of the world,
   Mary's child,
   Dawn on our darkened day.

3. Truth of our life,
   Mary's child,
   You tell us God is good:
   Prove it is true,
   Mary's child,
   Go to Your cross of wood.

4. Hope of the world,
   Mary's child,
   You're coming soon to reign:
   King of the earth,
   Mary's child,
   Walk in our streets again.

1195. Breathe on me

Is 6:8; Jn 20:22; Heb 12:1

Capo 1(D)
With intensity
Andrea Lawrence
& Noel Robinson
E♭2(D2) Gm7(F♯m7) A♭2(G2) A♭/B♭(G/A)
Breathe on me, O wind of change, a -
E♭(D) Gm7(F♯m7) A♭2/C(G2) B♭9/D(A9) E♭(D) B♭m7(Am7)
noint me with fresh oil from Your throne. Lord, re - store
D♭/E♭ (C/D) A♭(G) Gm7(F♯m7) Cm7(Bm7) B♭m7(Am7)
me with new life, so I'm rea - dy to serve and I'm rea-
A♭(G) Gm7(F♯m7) Cm7(Bm7) A♭2(G2) Gm7(F♯m7)
dy to go, rea - dy to do Your will. So I'm rea-
Cm7(Bm7) B♭m7(Am7) A♭(G) Fm7(Em7) (G/A) A♭/B♭ B♭(A) E♭(D)
dy to serve and I'm rea - dy to go, rea - dy to do Your will.

SoF3

C♭maj7(B♭maj7) B♭m7(Am7) E♭2/G (D2) A♭m7(Gm7)
Lord, help me to run this race and to live by Your grace,
C♭maj7(B♭maj7) D♭(C) E♭2(D2)
all I want to do is Your will.
C♭maj7(B♭maj7) B♭m7(Am7) E♭2/G (D2) A♭m7(Gm7)
Rea-dy to serve, rea-dy to go, rea-dy to do, rea-dy to be,
C♭maj7(B♭maj7) D♭(C) E♭2(D2)
(Fine)
rea - dy to do Your will.

1196. Bring Your best to their worst

Is 42:3; 61:3

Quietly

John L. Bell

All
Em
Bring Your best to their worst, bring Your
Cmaj7
Am/C
Am
Bm7
D/E
Em
(Fine)
peace to their pain, God of love, heal Your peo - ple.

Leader
D.C.
1. That none who cry a - loud may cry in vain:

2. That those who fear may never walk alone:

3. That those near death may see the light of day:

4. That guilty folk may find themselves forgiven:

5. That those who doubt may find a deeper faith:

6. That broken folk may know they will be whole:

1197. Calling all nations

Ps 86:9; Rev 14:3; 15:4

Noel Richards & Wayne Drain

Rock style
Chorus
A G D G
Call - ing all na - tions, hear the sto - ry
A G D G A G
of God's a - ma-zing grace. Call-ing all na-tions,
D G A G D
Last time to Coda
come and wor - ship, fill the earth with praise.
E Verse F♯m
1. Ev - 'ry wo-man, ev-'ry man, rich and poor,
D E
old and young, hea-ven's love is com-ing down to

F♯m
G
D.C. al Coda
wipe all your tears a - way.

Coda
A

2. There's a bell to be rung,
There's a song to be sung.
Sweeter music yet to play
When we gather on that day.

1198.

Celebrate in the Lord

(Dancing on holy ground)

Lev 25:10; Ps 103:12; Gal 5:1

Evan Rogers

Brightly
C
F
C
G7
Verse
1. Ce-le-brate in the Lord, He is the rea-son we re-joice; for
He has cast our sins a-way, for-got-ten now, for-e-ver and al-ways,
al-ways, al-ways, yes, al-ways,
al-ways, al-ways.

Chorus
C F C G7
f
This is where the par - ty is, this is where the joy of heav'n a-bounds.
C F C G
In His pre-sence we are free to praise, to shout a-loud.
Am D Am F/G
This is where the par - ty is, sing-ing with the an-gels, hear the sound.
C F C G
This is where the par - ty is, we are dan - cing on ho-ly ground,
C F C G
ho-ly ground, ho-ly ground, ho-ly ground,

Last time to Coda
C
F
C
G
ho - ly ground.
C
(Fine)
F
C
G
D.S. al Coda
3. For
Coda
F
C
G
C
ho-ly ground,
ho-ly ground.
Si-ya-vu
- ya,
F
C
1. G
2. G
si-ya-vu - ya,
si-ya-vu - ya.
Si-ya-vu - ya.
Ja-bu-la-
Repeat, then
D.S.S. al fine
C
F
C
G
- ni,
ja-bu-la - ni,
ja-bu-la - ni.
(Ja-bu - la-)

2. This is our jubilee,
No debt, no bondage, we are free.
We're free to give Him everything
For we have nothing, now it is all His,
All His, all His, it's all His,
All His, all His.

3. For freedom You have set us free,
No longer bound to slavery,
You've broken every chain that binds;
You've conquered sin forever and all time.
All time, all time, yes, all time,
All time, all time.

1199. Christ is made the sure foundation

1 Cor 3:11; 1 Pet 2:5-7; Rev 21:2

Tune: WESTMINSTER ABBEY

Henry Purcell (1659-95)

G D/F♯ G C/E Am/C D G/B D7/A
1. Christ is made the sure Foun - da - tion, Christ the
G A7/E D Asus4 A7 D A/C♯ D
Head and Cor - ner - stone, cho - sen of the
G/B D7/A G C/E Bm/D Am/C Baug5 Am B7
Lord and pre - cious, bind - ing all the Church in
Em E E/D A/C♯ D D/C G/B
one; ho - ly Zi - on's help for e - ver,

C
Am
D7
G
Dsus4
D7
G
and her con - fi - dence a - lone.

2. All within that holy city
 Dearly loved of God on high,
 In exultant jubilation
 Sing, in perfect harmony;
 God the One-in-Three adoring
 In glad hymns eternally.

3. We as living stones invoke You:
 Come among us, Lord, today!
 With Your gracious loving-kindness
 Hear Your children as we pray;
 And the fullness of Your blessing
 In our fellowship display.

4. Here entrust to all Your servants
 What we long from You to gain -
 That on earth and in the heavens
 We one people shall remain,
 Till united in your glory
 Evermore with You we reign.

5. Praise and honour to the Father,
 Praise and honour to the Son,
 Praise and honour to the Spirit,
 Ever Three and ever One:
 One in power and one in glory
 While eternal ages run.

From the Latin, John Mason Neale (1818-66)

Praise the Lord. Praise God in His sanctuary; praise Him in His mighty heavens. Let everything that has breath praise the Lord.

PSALM 150: 1, 6

1200. Christ, whose glory fills the skies

Ps 8:1; Mal 4:2; Mk 9:24; Lk 1:78-79; Jn 8:12

Tune: RATISBON

Melody from J. G. Werner's *Choralbuch,* Leipzig, 1815
Arr. William Henry Havergal (1793-1870)

D D/F♯ G A/E D A Bm A/C♯ D G A D
1. Christ, whose glo - ry fills the skies, Christ, the true, the on - ly light,
A D G/B A7/C♯ D Bm F♯ G Em6 F♯ Bm
Sun of righ-teous - ness, a - rise, tri - umph o'er the shades of night:
G A Bm Em F♯ Bm/D Bm A/C♯ D G A D
Day-spring from on high, be near; Day-star in my heart ap-pear.

2. Dark and cheerless is the morn
Unaccompanied by Thee;
Joyless is the day's return,
Till Thy mercy's beams I see;
Till they inward light impart,
Glad my eyes, and warm my heart.

3. Visit then this soul of mine;
Pierce the gloom of sin and grief;
Fill me, radiance divine;
Scatter all my unbelief;
More and more Thyself display,
Shining to the perfect day.

Charles Wesley (1707-88)

1201. Come all you people

(Uyai mose)

Alexander Gondo
arr. John L. Bell

Energetically

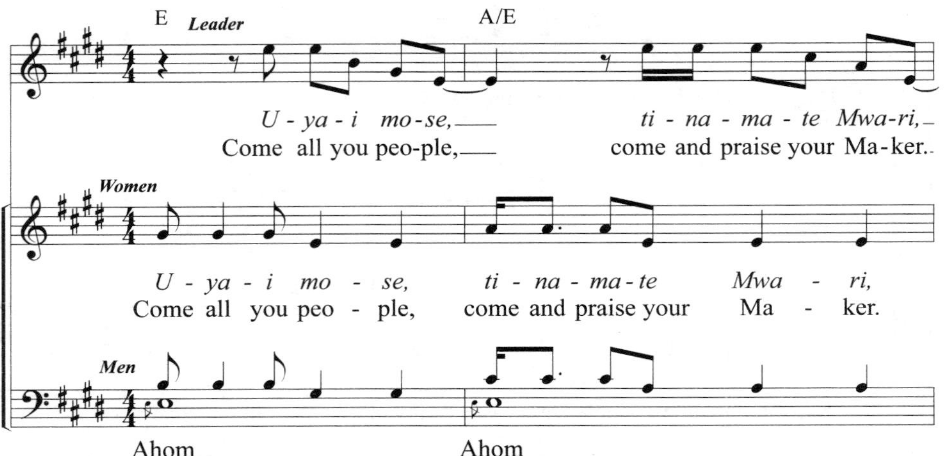
E
Leader
A/E
U - ya - i mo-se, ti - na - ma - te Mwa-ri,
Come all you peo-ple, come and praise your Ma-ker.
Women
U - ya - i mo - se, ti - na - ma - te Mwa - ri,
Come all you peo - ple, come and praise your Ma - ker.
Men
Ahom
Ahom

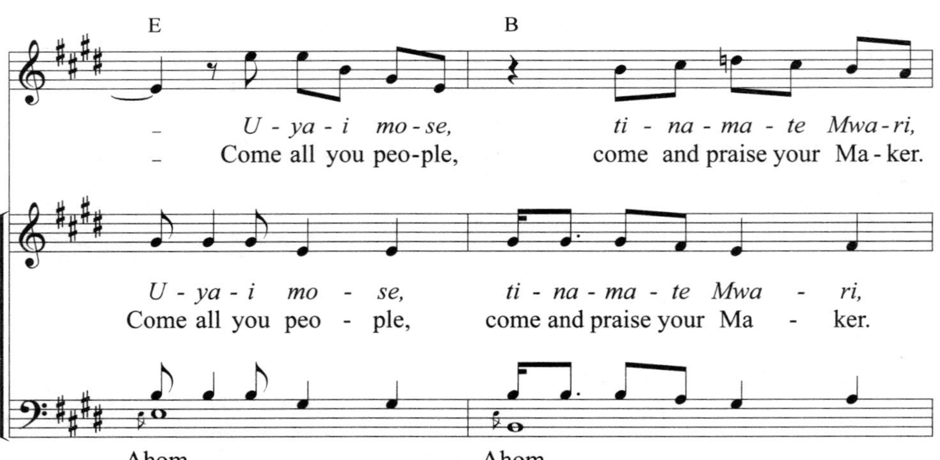
E
B
U - ya - i mo-se, ti - na - ma - te Mwa-ri,
Come all you peo-ple, come and praise your Ma - ker.
U - ya - i mo - se, ti - na - ma - te Mwa - ri,
Come all you peo - ple, come and praise your Ma - ker.
Ahom
Ahom

E
A/E
U - ya - i mo - se, ti - na - ma - te Mwa - ri,
Come all you peo - ple, come and praise your Ma - ker.
U - ya - i mo - se, ti - na - ma - te Mwa - ri,
Come all you peo - ple, come and praise your Ma - ker.
Ahom
Ahom
E
B
E
[except last time]
U - ya - i mo - se zvi - no. ti - na - ma - te - Mwa - ri.
Come now and wor - ship the Lord. Come and praise your Ma - ker.
U - ya - i mo - se zvi - no.
Come now and wor - ship the Lord.
Ahom
Ahom
Ahom

1202. Come down, O Love divine

Ps 63:1; 84:2; 110:105; Lk 18:13; Jn 1:4; 14:16-17; Acts 2:3; Gal 5:24-25; Jas 4:10

Tune: DOWN AMPNEY

Ralph Vaughan Williams (1872-1958)

D A/C♯ D Asus4 A G D A/C♯
1. Come down, O Love di - vine, seek Thou this
Bm A/C♯ Esus4 E A D G A G/B D Em/G D/F♯ G Em7
soul of mine and vi - sit it with Thine own ar - dour
Asus4 A7 D Bm F♯m G D F♯m E/G♯ A
glow - ing; O Com - for - ter, draw near,
C/E D/F♯ G D Em D/F♯ G A A/G D/F♯ G A G/B
with - in my heart ap - pear, and kin - dle it, Thy

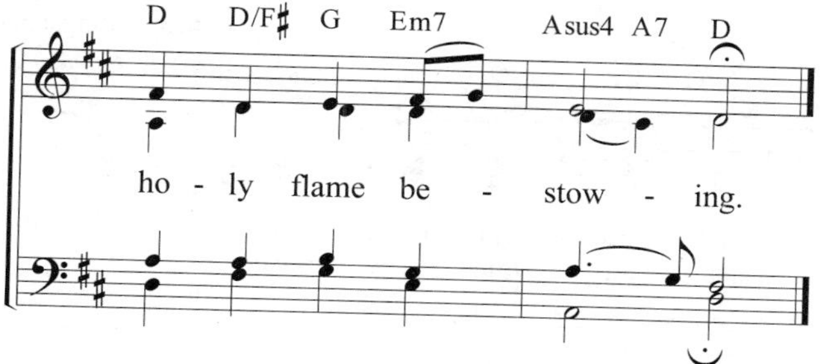
D D/F♯ G Em7 Asus4 A7 D
ho - ly flame be - stow - ing.

2. O let it freely burn,
Till earthly passions turn
To dust and ashes, in its heat consuming;
And let Thy glorious light
Shine ever on my sight,
And clothe me round, the while my path illuming.

3. Let holy charity
Mine outward vesture be,
And lowliness become my inner clothing;
True lowliness of heart,
Which takes the humbler part,
And o'er its own shortcomings weeps with loathing.

4. And so the yearning strong,
With which the soul will long,
Shall far outpass the power of human telling;
For none can guess its grace,
Till he become the place
Wherein the Holy Spirit makes His dwelling.

After Bianco da Siena (d.1434)
Richard F. Littledale (1833-90)

1203. Come, let us worship

1 Kings 8:10; Ps 25:1; Jn 8:58; 17:21; Heb 4:16; Rev 5:12; 17:14; 19:16

Nathan Fellingham

With strength

Verse

C F/C C G C F C G Am7 F G Am7 F C/E G C

Come, let us wor - ship the King of kings, the Cre - a - tor of all things. Let your soul a - rise to Him, come and bless the Lord our King.

Lord, my heart and voice I raise, to praise Your won - drous ways, and with con - fi - dence I come to ap - proach Your heav'n - ly throne.

F C/E F G C/E F

Come and fill this place with Your glo - ry, come and cap - ti - vate our gaze; come and fill us with Your fire,

Am7
Dm7
Gsus4
G
that the world might know Your name. For You are
Chorus
C
C/E
F
G
God, and You're wor - thy to be praised, and You are
C
C/E
F
G
good, for Your love will ne - ver end: the great I
Am
Em/G
Dm7
1.
Gsus4
G
Am, You are faith - ful in all of Your ways. You are
2.
Gsus4
G
D.C.
Last time
C
ways.

"If anyone is thirsty, let him come to me and drink. Whoever believes in me, as the Scripture has said, streams of living water will flow from within him."

JOHN 7:38

1204. Come near to me

Ps 42:1-2; Jn 7:37;
Rom 5:2, 5; Eph 3:19; Jas 4:8

With a rhythmic feel

Alan Rose

Verse
Bm7 Asus2 Gsus2 Asus2 Bm7 Asus2
1. Come near to me, as I come near to You;
Gsus2 Asus2 Bm7 Asus2 Gsus2 D/F♯
pour out Your mercy and Your
Em7 Asus4 A Bm7 Asus2
grace. I need Your
(v.2)
Gsus2 Asus2 Bm7 Asus2 Gsus2 Asus2
love, I need Your ten-der-ness;
Bm7 Asus2 Gsus2 D/F♯ Em7
I'm long-ing for Your sweet em-brace.

F♯7
G
Chorus
D
My heart cries out for more of
E7
G
A7sus4
You, Lord; I'm so hun - gry for Your pre - sence.
G
D
Em7
Your love is wa-ter to my soul.
A
G
D
I will be sa - tis - fied with You,
E7
G
A7sus4
Em7
Lord; You ful-fil my deep-est long - ing. Pour out Your

1. D.C.
2.
D/F♯ G F♯7 Asus4 A
Spi-rit once a-gain.
G D/F♯ Em7
I've felt Your pre-sence, Lord, I've tas-ted of Your love.
D/F♯ G D/F♯ Em7
Now all I am cries out for more of You,
D/F♯ G D/F♯ G
I want more of You; more of Your Spi-rit
D/F♯ Em7 F♯7 D.S.
poured from a-bove, more of Your pow-er, more of Your love.

2. Draw close to me, as I draw close to You.
Release Your power from above.
I'm dry and thirsty, Lord, come and fill me up;
I'm waiting for Your touch of love.

1205. Come, now is the time

Ps 95:1-2; Phil 2:10-11

Steadily

Brian Doerksen

Verse
D
G/D
Come, now is the time to wor - ship.
Come, just as you are to wor - ship.
D
A
Come, now is the time to give
Come, just as you are be - fore
Em
G
D
Last time repeat to finish
(Fine)
your heart. Come.
your God.
Chorus
G
D
One day ev - 'ry tongue will con - fess You are God.
G
D
One day ev - 'ry knee will bow.

G
Bm
Still, the great - est trea - sure re - mains for those who glad -
Em7
A
Asus4
A
D.C.
- ly choose You now.

1206. Come, praise the Lord

(Every breath)

Ps 139:12; 142:1; 150:6; Mt 9:13; Jn 1:4; 10:10

Kristyn Lennox
& Keith Getty

Brightly
Verse
E B A
1. Come, praise the Lord, He is life in all its full - ness;
E B A E B
will you lift your voice? Come, praise the Lord, He is light
A E B
that shat - ters dark - ness; we have come to re - joice.
A F♯m7 B
All a - round the world He is call - ing
F♯m7 B
peo - ple who would take up His call and fol - low Him.

Chorus
E A/C♯ B C♯m
E - v'ry breath be praise, e - v'ry heart be raised
A E/G♯ F♯m7 A B7sus4
to the King of all cre - a - tion.
E A/C♯ B C♯m
E - v'ry breath be praise, e - v'ry heart be raised
A B E E/D♯ A2/C♯ E C♯m7 E/B A2
to the Lord of all.
D.C. E

2. Come, praise the Lord,
He is love that welcomes sinners;
Will you give your life?
Come, praise the Lord,
He is great above all others;
All His ways are right.
All around the world He is calling
People who would take up His call
And follow Him.

1207. Come, see the Lord

Is 53:3; Jn 1:1; 20:20; Acts 2:31; Eph 4:8; Phil 2:7; Heb 10:21; Rev 1:17; 5:12-13

Tune: EPIPHANY

Joseph Francis Thrupp (1827-1867)

D A/C♯ Bm A/C♯ D
1. Come, see the Lord in His breath-tak-ing splen-dour:
A/G D/F♯ A7/E D G Em A
gaze at His ma-je-sty- bow and a-dore!
D/F♯ D A A7 Bm E/G♯ A
En-ter His pre-sence with won-der and wor-ship-
D/F♯ G6 D/A A7 D
He is the King, and en-throned e-ver-more.

SoF3

2. He is the Word who was sent by the Father,
Born as a baby, a child of our race:
God here among us, revealed as a servant,
Walking the pathway of truth and of grace.

3. He is the Lamb who was slain to redeem us -
There at the cross His appearance was marred;
Though He emerged from the grave as the victor,
Still from the nails and the spear He is scarred.

4. He is the Lord who ascended in triumph -
Ever the sound of His praises shall ring!
Hail Him the First and the Last, the Almighty:
Jesus, our Prophet, our Priest and our King.

5. Come, see the Lord in His breathtaking splendour:
Gaze at His majesty - bow and adore!
Come and acknowledge Him Saviour and Sovereign:
Jesus our King is enthroned evermore.

Martin E. Leckebusch (b.1962)

1208. Come, see this glorious Light

(Blessing and honour)

Capo 1 (D)

Steadily

Is 53:5; 55:1; Hag 2:7; Jn 20:20; 1 Pet 2:24; 1 Jn 2:2; Rev 1:17; 5:11-13; 7:9; 15:3; 19:11; 22:12

Stuart Townend

Verse
E♭(D)
Fm/E♭(Em)
E♭(D)
Fm/E♭(Em) E♭(D)
1. Come, see this glo - ri - ous Light as it shines on
Come, see these wounds of love, scars that make you
B♭(A)
Cm/B♭(Bm) B♭(A) Fm7(Em)
Cm7(Bm)
B♭(A)
you, bring - ing grace and peace to the depths of your soul.
whole, blood that paid the price for the sins of the world.
Fm7(Em)
B♭(A)
Fm7(Em)
He is the Light e - ver - last - ing, He is the
D♭(C)
B♭/D(A)
E♭(D)
Chorus
First and the Last.
Bles - sing and ho - nour and
Jus - tice and truth are the marks
Fm7(Em)
E♭/G(D)
glo - ry and pow'r, bles - sing and ho - nour and
of Your reign, an - gels a - dore You, the

A♭(G)
B♭(A)
Cm7(Bm)
glo - ry and pow'r, bles - sing and ho - nour and
Lamb who was slain, they're cry - ing 'ho - ly' a -
D♭(C)
A♭(G)
glo - ry and pow'r to You Lord, You're the King
gain and a - gain, Lord Je - sus, You're the King
1.
Cm7(Bm)
B♭(A)
2.
Cm7(Bm)
B♭(A)
E♭(D)
Fm/E♭(Em)
of the A - ges. of the A - ges.
E♭(D)
Fm/E♭(Em)
D.C.
Last time
E♭(D)

2. Come, all you thirsty and poor,
Come and feast on Him,
That your souls may live
And be satisfied.
Come from the ends of the earth,
Every tribe and tongue,
Lift your voice and praise
Your eternal Reward.
He's the Desire of the nations,
He is the Faithful and True.

1209. Come to the table

1 Cor 11:25; Rev 19:9

Dave Bilbrough

Steadily
G
Come to the ta - ble, drink from His cup;
come to the ta - ble, you can ne - ver get e - nough of His
C
G
love for you, of His love for you.
Em
C
G
Oh, such pre - cious love.
Em
C
G
Turn your face to Him.

Em
C
G
Let the feast be - gin.
Em
C
D
With the an - gels sing:
C
D
C
hal - le - lu - jah,
hal - le - lu - jah
D
C
G
(Fine)
D.C.
to the Lord.
2. We will

2. We will come to the table,
Drink from Your cup;
Come to the table,
We can never get enough
Of the love You give,
Of the love You give.
Oh, such precious love,
Oh, such precious love.

1210. Come, wounded Healer

Is 53:5; Jn 15:18-19; 2 Cor 8:9; 1 Pet 2:24

Capo 1 (D)
Tune: SLANE

Irish Traditional Melody
Arr. David Ball

Eb (D) Ab (G) Bb7 (A) Eb (D) Eb/G (D) Bb (A) Ebsus4 (D) Eb Eb/G
1. Come, woun - ded Hea - ler, Your suf - f'rings re - veal - the
Bbsus4 (A) Bb Bb2 Bb Eb (D) Gm (F#m) Ab (G) Eb/G (D) Cm7 (Bm) Bbsus4 (A) Bb Eb7 (D)
scars You ac - cep - ted, our an - guish to heal. Your
Ab (G) Ab/Eb Ebmaj7 (D) Bb6/D (A) Cm7 (Bm) Eb/G (D) Bb2 (A) Bb Ab2 (G) Ab Bb7 (A)
wounds bring such com - fort in bo - dy and soul to
Eb (D) Gm/D (F#m) Cm (Bm) Eb/Bb (D) Ab6 (G) Ab Ab/Bb Eb (D)
all who bear tor - ment and yearn to be whole.

2. Come, hated Lover, and gather us near,
Your welcome, Your teaching, Your challenge to hear:
Where scorn and abuse cause rejection and pain,
Your loving acceptance makes hope live again!

3. Come, broken Victor, condemned to a cross —
How great are the treasures we gain from Your loss!
Your willing agreement to share in our strife
Transforms our despair into fullness of life.

Martin E. Leckebusch (b.1962)

1211. Create in me

(Pure, pure heart)

Ps 51:7, 10; Is 64:8; Jer 18:6

Prayerfully

Matt Redman

Verse
Em
1. Cre-ate in me the pur - est of hearts, ac-cord-
D/F♯
Em
ing to Your un - fail-ing love. Re-new a stead - fast spi-
D/F♯
- rit with-in, and wash a-way my sin. And make
Em7
D/F♯
A
Em7
D/F♯
me like the snow, but e - ven whi - ter still.
A
Chorus
3
etc...
Em
I just want to have a pure heart,

D/F♯
I just want to have a pure, pure heart.
D
Em
I just want to have a pure heart.
D/F♯
I just want to have a pure, pure heart.
D
(Fine)
2. I'm clay

2. I'm clay within the Potter's hand
Where tenderness meets discipline,
I need it all, Lord, come and form
Your holiness in me.
And make me like the snow,
But even whiter still.

1212. Day after day

Ps 24:4-5; 96:2; Song 1:4; 1 Cor 13:12

Tim Hughes

Simply
Verse
E F♯m D
1. Day af - ter day, I'll search to find You;
E F♯m D
day af - ter day, I'll wait for You. The
E F♯m D E F♯m
deep-er I go, the more I love Your name.
D Chorus A E Bm
So keep my heart pure, and my ways true, as I
A E D A E
fol - low You. Keep me hum - ble, I'll stay

Bm
A
E
D
1.
mind - ful of Your mer - cies, Lord. 2. I'll

2.

2. I'll cherish Your word,
I'll seek Your presence,
I'll chase after You with all I have.
As one day I know
I'll see You face to face.

1213. Do not be afraid

Is 43:1-2; Jn 14:18, 21

Gerard Markland

Gently
Chorus
C
C
Dm7
G7
Do not be a - fraid, for I have re-
C
Am
D7
Dm7
G7
deemed you. I have called you by your name; you are
C
(Fine)
Verse
Am
Am/G
Mine. 1. When you walk through the wa-ters I'll be
D/F♯
F/G
G7
C
D.S.
with you; you will ne - ver sink be-neath the waves.

2. When the fire is burning all around you,
   You will never be consumed by the flames.

3. When the fear of loneliness is looming,
   Then remember I am at your side.

4. When you dwell in the exile of the stranger,
   Remember you are precious in My eyes.

5. You are Mine, O my child; I am your Father,
   And I love you with a perfect love.

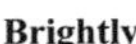
1214.

Don't build your house

(Sandy land)

Ex 17:6; 33:22; Mt 7:24-27; 1 Cor 10:4

Karen Lafferty

Brightly

C
Don't build your house on the san - dy land,

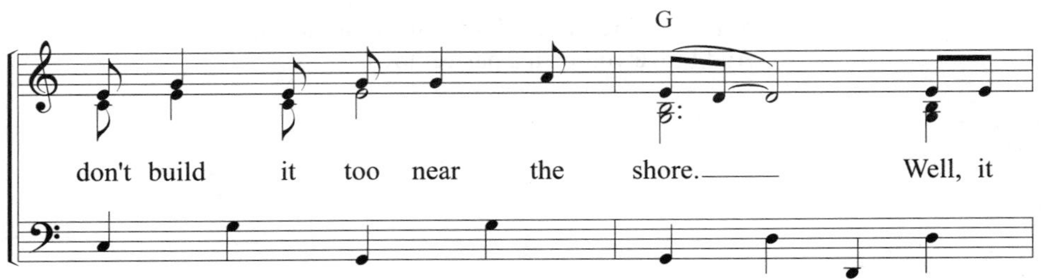
G
don't build it too near the shore.
Well, it

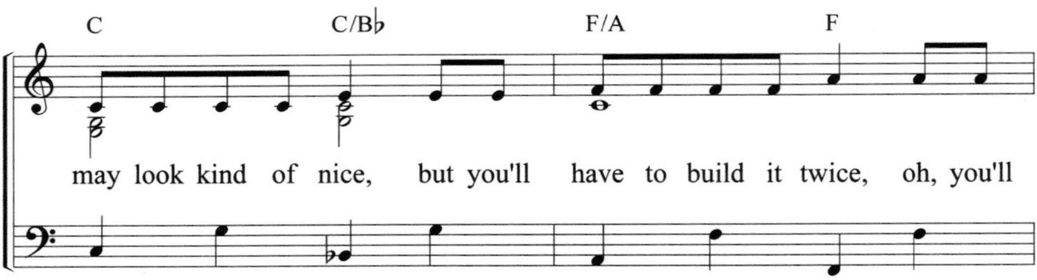
C
C/B♭
F/A
F
may look kind of nice, but you'll have to build it twice, oh, you'll

C
G7
C
have to build your house once more.
You bet - ter

(Descant)
Rock of a - ges,
*
build your house___ up - on a rock, make a
cleft for me,___ let me
G C C/B♭
good foun - da - tion on a so - lid spot.___ Oh, the storms may
hide my - self in___ Thee.___
F/A F C G7 C
come and go,___ but the peace of God you will know.

*(This song can be sung as a round. Group 2 begins when Group 1 reaches *)*

1215. Do you love to praise the Lord?

Ps 134:2; 149:3

(Dance)

Capo 3 (G)
Noel Richards, Wayne Drain,
Neil Costello, Bradley Mason
& Wayne Freeman
Rock 'n' roll style
F(D)
Do you love to praise the Lord? (Do you love
to praise the Lord. (We have come
to praise the Lord?) Do you love to praise the Lord?
to praise the Lord.) We have come to praise the Lord.
(Do you love to praise the Lord?) Lift your voi-
(We have come to praise the Lord.) Lift our voi-
B♭(G)
ces high, raise your hands to the sky.
ces high, raise our hands to the sky,
1.,3.
F(D)
Make a joy - ful noise!
Make a joy - ful noise!

2.,4.
F(D)
Do you love___ (and) e - v'ry - bo - dy dance!
We have come___ Then we're gon - na dance!
B♭(G)
Praise___ Him in___ the dance,
F(D)
e - v'ry-bo-dy dance.___
Praise_
B♭(G)
_ Him in___ the dance,___
e-
F(D)
Last time to Coda
D.S. al Coda
v'ry-bo - dy dance.___
We have come_

Coda
C(A)
we love to praise the Lord;
Gm(Em)
it's what we're made for.
C(A)
We love to praise
the Lord;
Gm(Em)
it's in our na - ture.
C(A)
We love to praise
the Lord,
Gm(Em)
it's deep with-in us.
C(A)
We love to praise
the Lord with
Gm7(Em)
e - v'ry - thing that's in us, with

e - v'ry - thing that's in us, with e - v'ry - thing that's in
spoken
F(D)
us we will dance!
B♭(G)
(Last time rall...)
F(D)

1216. Draw me closer

1 Kings 19:12; Is 43:2; Mt 5:3; Jn 10:10; 1 Cor 9:27; Phil 3:14; Heb 6:19; Heb 10:22; Jas 4:8

Ian Hannah

Simply

D Em/D D

1. Draw me clo - ser, pre - cious Sa - viour, near - er

D/F♯ G Em7 G/A A

to Your ho - ly throne; let me know Your cleans - ing

D G Asus4 A D Em/D

po - wer, as I wait on You a - lone. I am no - thing with - out

D G
You, Lord, I am na - ked, weak and poor; but in

Em7 G/A A D G G/A
You I find a full - ness, no-thing else can give me

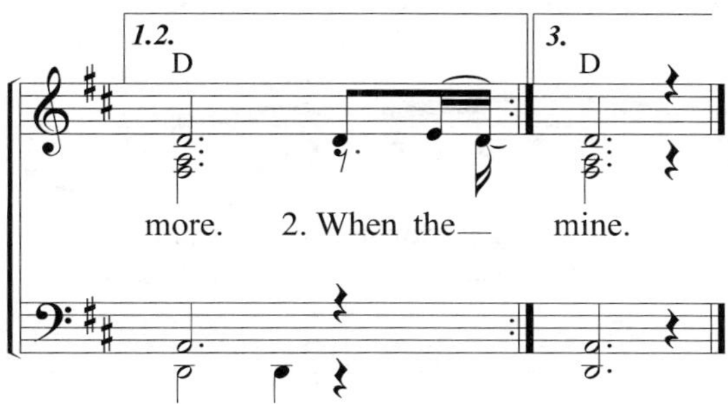
1.2.
D
3.
D
more. 2. When the mine.

2. When the waters of destruction
Try to sweep me far away,
Jesus, You are still my anchor;
I need never be afraid.
I will cling to You, my master,
Holding on with surety.
Pressing onward, looking upward,
Until Jesus, You I see.

3. Help me listen to Your whisper,
Help me live obediently.
Give me courage in the battles,
Strength to face uncertainty.
Help me never to deny You,
But to cross that finish line.
Moving forward, never backward,
To claim the prize as mine.

1217. Draw me close to You

Capo 3 (G)

Ps 73:25; Jn 15:15; Jas 4:8

Kelly Carpenter

Steadily
A
Verse
D/A
E/A
2nd time
Draw me close to You, never let me go.
You are my desire, no one else will do,
A
E2/G♯
D/F♯
I lay it all down again,
'cause nothing else could take Your place,
F♯m
F♯m/E
Dmaj7
to hear You say that I'm Your friend.
to feel the warmth of Your embrace.
A/E
D/E
E
Help me find the way, bring me back to You.
A
D/E
E
A
Chorus
E/A
D/A
You're all I want,

A E/G♯ D/F♯ Esus4 E A E/A
You're all I've ev - er need - ed. You're all I want,
D/A Esus4 E A
help me know You are near.

1218. Draw me near to You

(Draw me near)

Ps 23:4; Lk 24:15, 40; Jn 20:20; Jas 4:8

Dave Doran

With intensity
Verse
E(no3rd)
D
1. Draw me near to You;
can I come so close
that I can hear Your song of love that heals my bro - ken heart?
C♯m7
Bsus4
A(no3rd)
B(no3rd)
A2
Chorus
E
And I will walk with You,

A(no3rd)
a-no-ther foot-step now. Can we walk on a-gain,
E
A(no3rd)
a - no-ther foot - step now?
C♯m7
I've walked in fields of pain, I've shel-tered in Your love;
A
C♯m7
in the val-ley of death's sha-dow, I will fear no
A
C♯m7
e - vil, for You are here with me.

A(no3rd)
D Dmaj7
My com-fort be,
my com-fort be.
1.
E(no3rd)
2.
E(no3rd)
2. Draw me near

2. Draw me near to You,
Even closer still,
So I can see Your scars of love
That saved my wounded soul.

1219. Draw me to Your side

(Hold me)

2 Sam 6:22; Song 5:13; Is 61:1; Mt 27:51; Jn 13:25; 20:22; 1 Cor 2:16

Brian Houston
& Tom Brock

With a Cajun feel

Verse
D A G D A G
1. Draw me to Your side, Lord, let me feel Your breath, the
D A G D A G
ve - ry breath of life, Lord, rest my head up - on Your chest. And
(v.2)
A G A G
hold me in Your arms, Lord, wrap me in Your em - brace,—
(v.2)
A
close e - nough that I can feel Your breath up - on my face. When
(v.2)

Chorus
D A G D A G
I cry out in pas-sion, to love You more than this, re-
D.S.S. to repeat chorus (last time)
Bm A G D G A D G
new me in Your pre-sence and re - fresh me with Your kiss. (When)
(Fine)
D A D G D A D G D A D G A
D A G D A
3. Well, the curse has been bro-ken, I know the cur-tain is torn in
G D A G
two, no child, no man or wo-man need be

D
A
G
D.S.
se - pa - ra - ted from You. The

2. Far too long I've begged You
For Your sweet release,
To be lost in Your presence
And to know the taste of Your lips.
And for a heart like Yours, God,
And for the mind of Christ
To know no shame and no restraint
In my worship sacrifice.

3. Well, the curse has been broken,
I know the curtain is torn in two,
No child, no man or woman
Need be separated from You.
The lonely and the broken,
Rejected and despised
Run through the gates of grace by faith,
Into the arms of Christ.

1220. Drawn from every tribe

Ps 23:4; Rev 7: 9-17; 12:11

Capo 1(D)

David Lyle Morris
& Faith Forster

Steadily
Verse Eb(D)
1. Drawn from e-v'ry tribe, e-v'ry tongue and na-tion,
Ab(G)
Bb(A)
ga-thered be-fore the throne.
Eb(D)
Cast-ing down their crowns, they fall at His feet and
(v.2)
(v.3)
Ab(G)
Bb(A)
Fm(Em)
wor-ship the Lord a-lone.
(v.3)
What a glo-rious sight,
(vv.2&3)
Cm7(Bm)
Ab(G)
dressed in robes of white,
(vv.2&3)
washed by the blood of the Lamb.
(vv.2&3)

B♭(A)
Chorus
Fm7(Em)
B♭(A)
Sing-ing praise and glo - ry, wis-dom and thanks,
E♭(D)
A♭(G)
Fm7(Em)
ho-nour, pow - er and strength be to our God, for-e-
B♭(A)
A♭(G) B♭6(A)
1.2.
E♭(D)
- ver and e - ver, a - men.
A♭(G)
B♭(A)
3.
A♭(G)
Fm7(Em)
men. All glo-ry and
e - ver and
E♭/G(D)
A♭(G)
1.2.3.
B♭sus4(A)
B♭(A)
4.
B♭sus4(A)
B♭(A)
ho-nour and pow-er to Je - sus, all for - e - ver, a -
e - ver and e - ver and e - ver, for-

E♭(D)
Fm7(Em)
E♭/G(D)
A♭(G)
A♭/B♭(G)
men.
A -
E♭(D)
Fm7(Em)
E♭/G(D)
A♭(G)
E♭(D)
men.
A - men.

2. We are those who follow,
   Through scenes of fiery trial,
   Drawing from wells of grace.
   Through the darkest valley
   From the depths of pain,
   We'll come to that holy place.
   We will overcome
   By looking to the Lamb
   And worshipping face to face.

3. Never will we hunger,
   We'll no longer thirst,
   There's shade from the heat of day.
   Led to springs of life,
   Jesus, our Shepherd,
   Will wipe every tear away.
   Our God upon the throne
   Will shelter all His own
   Who worship Him night and day.

1221. Eat this bread

Lk 22:19-20; Jn 4:14; 6:35;
1 Cor 11:23-25

Taizé
Jacques Berthier (1923-1994)

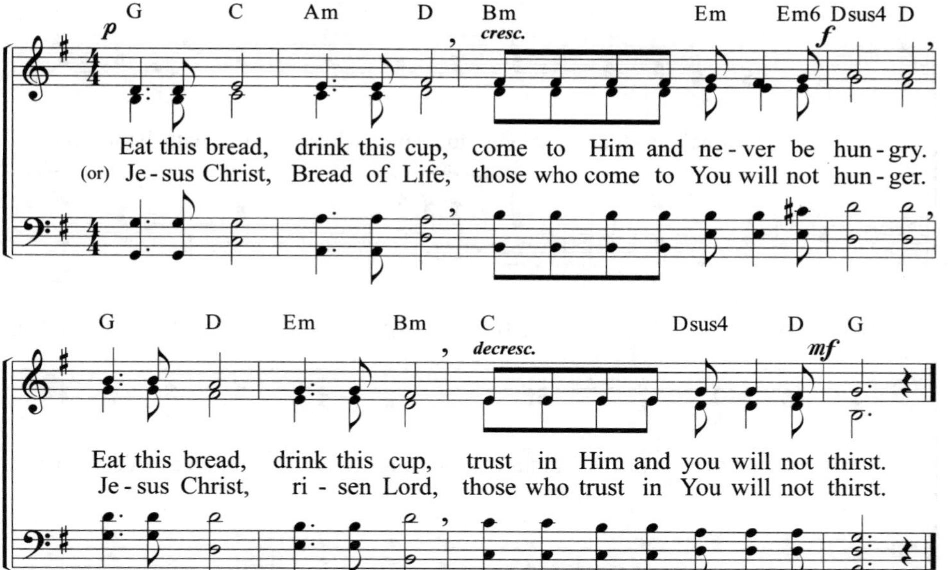

G C Am D Bm Em Em6 Dsus4 D
p cresc. f
Eat this bread, drink this cup, come to Him and ne - ver be hun - gry.
(or) Je - sus Christ, Bread of Life, those who come to You will not hun - ger.
G D Em Bm C Dsus4 D G
decresc. mf
Eat this bread, drink this cup, trust in Him and you will not thirst.
Je - sus Christ, ri - sen Lord, those who trust in You will not thirst.

1222. Eternal Father, strong to save

Gen 1:2; Job 38:8; Ps 89:9; Prov 8:29; Is 43:2; Mt 14:25; Mk 4:39

Tune: MELITA

John Bacchus Dykes (1823-76)

C F C G/B Am D G G/B
1. E - ter - nal Fa - ther, strong to save, whose arm hath bound the
Dsus4 D G G7/B C A7/C♯ D B7/D♯
rest - less wave, who bidds't the migh - ty o - cean deep its
Em B7/F♯ Em/G Am Em/B B Em C7 F
own ap - poin - ted li - mits keep: O hear us when we
D7 G G7/B C D/F♯ C/G G7 C
cry to Thee for those in pe - ril on the sea.

2. O Christ, whose voice the waters heard,
And hushed their raging at Thy word,
Who walkedst on the foaming deep,
And calm amid the storm didst sleep:
O hear us when we cry to Thee
For those in peril on the sea.

3. O Holy Spirit who didst brood
Upon the waters dark and rude,
And bid their angry tumult cease,
And give, for wild confusion, peace:
O hear us when we cry to Thee
For those in peril on the sea.

4. O Trinity of love and power,
Our brethren shield in danger's hour;
From rock and tempest, fire and foe,
Protect them wheresoe'er they go:
Thus evermore shall rise to Thee
Glad hymns of praise from land and sea.

William Whiting (1825-78)

1223. Everlasting

2 Cor 1:20; Phil 3:8; Rev 5:13

Sue Rinaldi
& Caroline Bonnett

Steadily

Verse
D
C
D
1. E - ver - last - ing, e - ver_ true,_ all cre - a-tion_
C
D
C
sings to You._____ E - ver faith-ful, liv - ing_ Lord,_
D
C
Chorus
G
D
Let the sound of praise be heard._ Je sus,___ You are_
G
Em7
C
D
_ all___ that I am liv-ing for_ and all that I be-lieve is in You,_

G D G Em7
– Je-sus, all that I am liv-ing for, and
C D G
all that I be-lieve is in You.

2. Never changing, awesome God,
Sing the glory of the Lord.
Ever loving, holy One,
I will praise what You have done.

1224. Every breath I breathe

(You are my God)

Ps 139:2-6, 17; 146:2; Phil 2:9; Rev 11:15

Lara Martin

Moderately
G/A D A G
E-v'ry breath I breathe comes from You,
D A G D A
I'll ne-ver take it for gran-ted. All that I have,
Bm7 A G D/F♯ Em7
all I've e - ver need - ed, You have pro-vi -
A D A G
ded. You know when I sit, You know when I rise,
D A G D A
You know my thoughts com - plete - ly. You hem me in be -

Bm7
A
G
D/F♯
Em7
fore and be-hind: such love is hard to de-
A
G/A
D/F♯
G
A
D/F♯
scribe. You are my God, You are my
G
A
G
God. As long as I have breath,
D/F♯
Em7
A
D/F♯
I will sing of Your great - ness. You are my
G
A
D/F♯
G
A
source, my all in all, my

Bm7
Bm/A G
first love, the One I love,
Last time to Coda
A
Bm7 A G
A Bm7 A G
A
You are my God.
D
A
G
Precious to me are Your thoughts, O God; no
D
A
G
D
A
wis-dom or know - ledge is grea - ter. Praise be to You,
Bm7
A
G
Name a - bove all names: who

G
A
F♯m7
Bm7
G
A
reigns for-e-ver, e-ver and e-ver, who reigns for-e-ver,
reign for-e-ver, e-ver and e-ver, You reign for-e-ver,
F♯m7
Bm7
G
A
F♯m7
Bm7
e-ver and e-ver, who reigns for-e-ver, e-ver and e-ver, who
e-ver and e-ver, You reign for-e-ver, e-ver and e-ver, You
D.S. al Coda
G
1.
Asus4
A
2.
Asus4
A
D/F♯
reigns for - e-ver more. You You are my
reign for - e-ver more.
Coda
D

1225. Every day

(The eyes of my heart)

Ps 123:2; 2 Cor 3:18

Matt Redman

Rhythmically

C
Verse
Csus4
C
Csus4
Am7
1. Ev-'ry day, I see more of Your

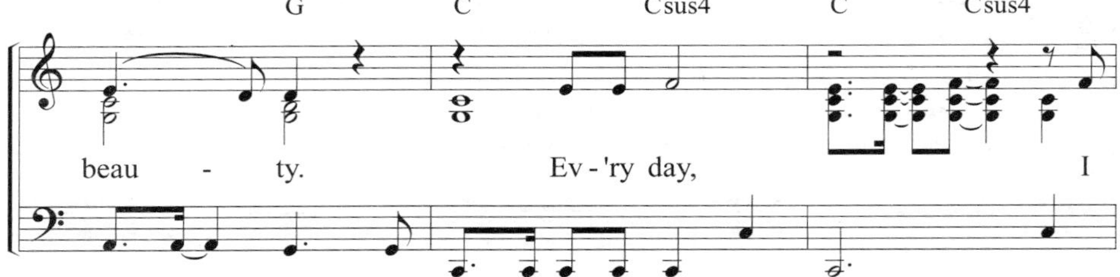
G
C
Csus4
C
Csus4
beau - ty. Ev-'ry day, I

Am7
G
B♭sus2
know more of my frail - ty, Lord. And I can on-ly

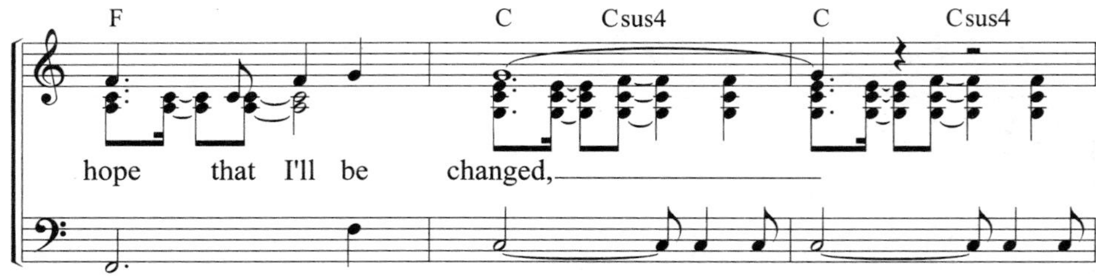
F
C
Csus4
C
Csus4
hope that I'll be changed,

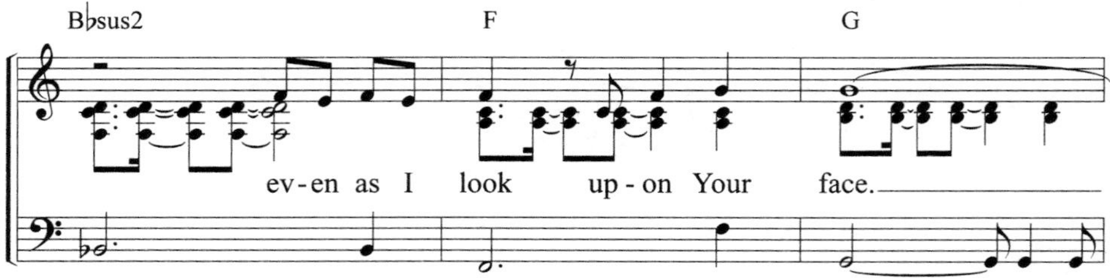
B♭sus2
F
G
ev-en as I look up-on Your face.

Chorus
C
For the eyes of my
Am7
heart,
B♭
they are on You for - ev - er,
F
they are on You for - ev - er.
1.
Yes, the eyes
2.
D.C.
To end
C

2. Every day, I see more of Your greatness.
Every day, I know more of my weakness, Lord.
And I can only hope that I'll be changed,
Even as I look upon Your face.

1226. Every day He is watching

Song 3:2-3; 5:10;
Mt 9:36; 18:12; Lk 15:4, 20
Robin Mark
Steady 4
C
1. E-v'ry day He is watch - ing from the
F
hea-vens and the skies.
C
And He scans the ho-ri-
zon,
F
look-ing for the sign
Am
of a son or a daugh-
C
ter
Am
with a pro-di-gal
F
heart,
C
com-ing back to the
F
Fa -
G
ther of
C
life.
(To v2)

F
C
Oh, His compas - sion is for e-v'ry-one.
(Your)
F
C
F
Yes, for the lost and the a - fraid. And
C
if you lis - ten you can hear His voice, hear Him
(I) (I) (Your) (You)
Am
F
Gsus4
G
D.C.(v3)
call-ing, hear Him call-ing your name.
(You) (my)
To end
C

2. And the Shepherd is searching
For the sheep who's gone astray,
Though there's ninety and nine safe,
At the closing of the day.
His pursuit is relentless, His obsession divine;
It's the heart of the Father of life.

3. Have you seen my belovèd?
He is radiant and most fair.
In the evening He calls me,
I can see His shadow there.
I will rise up to meet Him,
I will run to His side;
To the Son of the Father of Life.

1227. Every morning

Ps 5:3; 61:3; 63:6; 92:2; 141:2

Noel Richards
& Wayne Drain

Slow 4

Chorus
E
F♯m
E - v'ry morn - ing I will praise You,

A
e - v'ry mo-ment I am Yours.

E
F♯m
E - v'ry eve - ning I will wor-ship,

A
A/B
E
(Fine)
e - v'ry day I love You more.

A
Verse
G♯m E
1. I re - vel in Your mer - cy,
A
G♯m E
I mar - vel at Your grace.
A
G♯m C♯m
I need a thou - sand life - times
2nd time D.C. al fine
F♯m7
Bsus4 B
to give You all my praise.

2. At night, when I am sleeping,
In every waking hour,
I know You will protect me,
My God, my strong high tower.

1228. Falling

I Sam 3:9; Job 13:15; Ps 34:8; Is 55:2

Dave Wellington
With awe
Verse
G
D/F♯
Em7
Fal - ling, mov - ing clo - ser,
Wait - ing, list - 'ning, hop - ing
C
G
D/F♯
deep in - to You. Feast - ing, drink - ing
here's where You are. Crav - ing, cal - ling
Em7
1.
C
B♭6
my fill, tast-ing of You.
Your name,
F/A
2.
C
B♭
I need You more.
F/A
Chorus
C
With strength
I will hold on, hold through the fire,

G/B
Am7
Dsus4 D
G/B
C
cling through the rain,
I long to hear
You. I need You here,
G/B
Am7
all that You are,
on - ly Your touch
will sa - tis - fy
C/D
1.3.
D
G/B
C
(Fine)
Am7
D.C.
2.
D
G/B
C
D.S.
me.
me.
I will hold on

1229. Father, hear the prayer we offer

Ex 17:6; Jn 5:17;
1 Cor 10:4; 2 Cor 6:4; Phil 4:11-13

Tune: SUSSEX

English traditional melody
Adapt. & arr. by Ralph Vaughan Williams (1872-1958)

G D Em Bm Em C C/E G D
Fa - ther, hear the pray'r we of - fer: not for ease that
Em G/B D G G/B C D G/B Em D C
pray'r shall be, but for strength, that we may e - ver
G/B D7/A G/B C D G
live our lives cou - ra - geous - ly.

2. Not for ever in green pastures
Do we ask our way to be:
But by steep and rugged pathways
Would we strive to climb to Thee.

3. Not for ever by still waters
Would we idly quiet stay;
But would smite the living fountains
From the rocks along our way.

4. Be our strength in hours of weakness,
In our wanderings be our Guide;
Through endeavour, failure, danger,
Father, be Thou at our side.

5. Let our path be bright or dreary,
Storm or sunshine be our share;
May our souls, in hope unweary,
Make Thy work our ceaseless prayer.

Love Maria Willis (1824-1908)

1230. Father, into Your courts I will enter

(All the earth)

Ps 96:6-9, 11-12

Andrew Ulugia
& Wayne Huirua

Capo 3 (G)

With feeling

B(G)
F♯/A♯(D)
Fa - ther, in - to Your courts I will en - ter,
Glo - ry, glo - ry in Your sanc - tu - a - ry,
G♯(E)
C♯m7(Am)
1. (Em) (Am)
G♯m/C♯ C♯m7
Ma - ker of hea - ven and earth, I trem - ble
splen - dour and ma - je - sty, Lord, be -
(D)
F♯sus4 F♯ F♯sus4 F♯ F♯sus4 F♯
2. (Em) (Am)
G♯m/C♯ C♯m7
F♯7sus4(D)
in Your ho - ly pre - sence. fore You; all life a-
F♯sus4 F♯
(G)
B C♯m7(Am)
(G)
B/D♯ F♯sus4(D) F♯
dores You. All the earth will de - clare that Your love

(Em)
G♯m F♯(D) Emaj7(C) B/D♯(G)
is e - v'ry - where. The fields will ex - alt,
B/E F♯sus4(D) F♯ F♯sus4 F♯ F♯sus4 F♯
seas re - sound. Hear the trees'
(G)
B(G) C♯m7(Am7) B/D♯ F♯sus4(D) F♯ G♯m7(Em) F♯(D)
joy - ful cry, prais - ing You and so will I.
Emaj7(C) B/D♯(G) C♯sus4(A) C♯
A new song I'll sing, Lord, I will
1.
Emaj7(C) F♯(D)
(G) (Am) (G)
B C♯m7 B/D♯ F♯7sus4(D)
glo - ri - fy and bless Your ho - ly name.

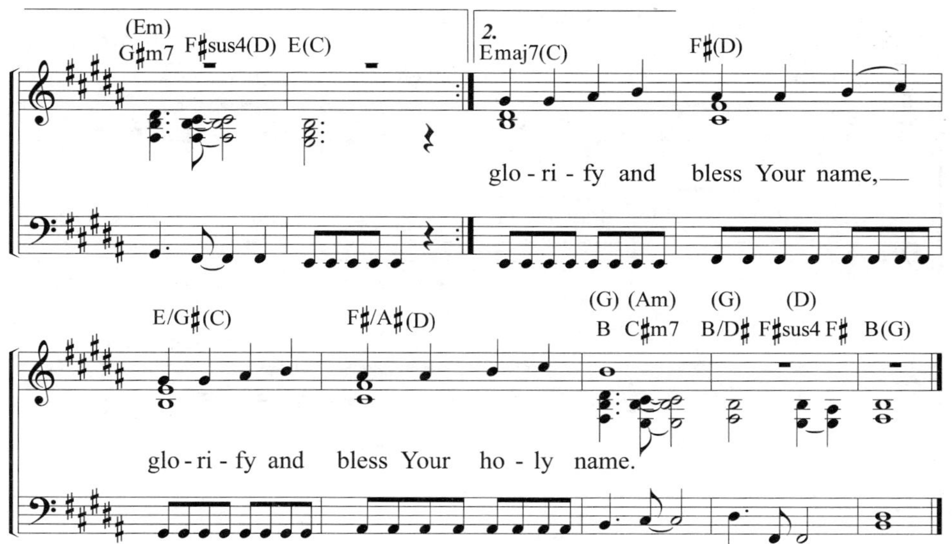
(Em)
G♯m7
F♯sus4(D)
E(C)
2.
Emaj7(C)
F♯(D)
glo - ri - fy and bless Your name,
E/G♯(C)
F♯/A♯(D)
(G) (Am)
B C♯m7
(G)
B/D♯
(D)
F♯sus4 F♯
B(G)
glo - ri - fy and bless Your ho - ly name.

1231. Father of life, draw me closer
(Let the peace of God reign)

Capo 3 (D)

Ps 3:3; Jn 14:16-17; Eph 5:18; Col 3:15; Heb 12:1-2; Jas 4:8

Darlene Zschech

Steadily

Verse
F(D) B♭/F(G) Dm(Bm) C/E(A) F(D)
1. Fa - ther of life, draw me clos - er, Lord, my heart is set on
E♭2(C) B♭/D(G) (A) Csus4 C(A) B♭(G) F/A(D)
You: let me run the race of time with Your
B♭(G) C(A) Dm(Bm) 3 G/B(E) C(A) 3
life en-fold - ing mine, and let the peace of God, let it
1. B♭(G) Gm7 (Em) F(D) 2. B♭(G) Gm7 (Em) F(D)
reign. reign.
Chorus
C(A) Dm(Bm)
O Lord, I hun - ger for
B♭(G) F(D) C(A) Dm(Bm) 3
more of You; rise up with-in me, let me

G/B(E) C(A) B♭(G) C(A) Dm(Bm)
know Your truth. O Ho - ly Spi - rit, sa - tu -
Gm7 Am7 Dm
(Em) (F♯m) (Bm) G/B(E) C(A) F/A(D) B♭(G)
rate my soul, and let the life of God fill me now, let Your
G/B(E) C(A) F/A(D) B♭(G)
heal - ing pow'r breathe life and make me whole, and let the
G/B(E) C(A)
1. B♭(G) Gm7 (Em) F(D) D.C.
2. B♭(G) Gm7 (Em) F(D)
peace of God, let it reign. reign.
3

2. O Holy Spirit,
Lord, my comfort;
Strengthen me, hold my head up high:
And I stand upon Your truth,
Bringing glory unto You,
And let the peace of God,
Let it reign.

1232. Father, we have sinned against You

Is 9:2; 53:6; Lk 15:18

Geoff Twigg

Unhurried
A
Em
D
Fa - ther, we have sinned a - gainst You, failed to do what's
Fa - ther, we have run a - way from what we know is
A
C
right; we have walked a - lone in dark - ness,
true; now we turn a - round, and we are
1. D
A
2. D
A
hid - ing from the light.
com - ing home to You. We have
A
C
sinned, we have bro - ken - Your
(We have sinned)

G
A
law, we're re - turn - ing once more home to You;
C
we have sinned, we are seek - ing Your
(We have sinned)
G
A
face, we re - turn by Your grace home to You.

1233. Find rest, all the earth

Ps 62:1-2; Mt 5:16

Kristyn Lennox
& Keith Getty

With a lilting feel

Verse
C F G C Dm/C C
1. Find rest, all the earth, in God a - lone. We
F C
find our on - ly hope from hea-ven's throne. Our
G C F C F
Rock, our Sal - va - tion, no, we shall not be sha - ken. Find
C Am7 F G
rest all the earth in God a - lone.
1.
C Am F G C Am
Am

F
G
2.3.
C
C (Fine)
B♭
2. His
storm.
lone.
Tell of the One
who lif-ted Your soul,
F
C
share all His
good - ness.
Chil-dren of light
B♭
Dm
Gsus4
G
D.S. al fine
de-clar-ing the truth,
that all may
know.
1. Find

2. His peace holds you firm in the storm.
His love brings new life forever more.
Our Rock, our Salvation,
No, we shall not be shaken.
His peace holds you firm in the storm.

1234. For the fruits of His creation

Gen 8:22; Mt 25:40; Gal 5:22-23

Tune: AR HYD Y NOS

Welsh trad. melody
Arr. R. Vaughan Williams (1872-1938)

G G/B C G/B Am Am/C D G/B C D7 G
1. For the fruits of His cre - a - tion, thanks be to God!
for His gifts to e - v'ry na - tion, thanks be to God!
C/E G C/E G/B C Dm C/E G Am G/B Am/C Em Am Am/C Dsus4 D
for the plough - ing, sow - ing, reap - ing, si - lent growth while we are sleep - ing;
G/B C G/B Am Am/C D G/B C D7 G
fu - ture needs in earth's safe - keep - ing, thanks be to God.

2. In the just reward of labour,
God's will is done;
In the help we give our neighbour,
God's will is done;
In our worldwide task of caring
For the hungry and despairing,
In the harvest we are sharing,
God's will is done.

3. For the harvests of His Spirit,
Thanks be to God!
For the good we all inherit,
Thanks be to God!
For the wonders that astound us,
For the truths that still confound us;
Most of all, that love has found us,
Thanks be to God.

F. Pratt Green (1903-2000)

1235. For the healing of the nations

Ps 121:8; Jn 10:10; 1 Cor 2:16; 2 Cor 3:18; Jas 2:8-9; Rev 22:2

Tune: ALLELUIA DULCE CARMEN

Samuel Webbe (1740-1816)

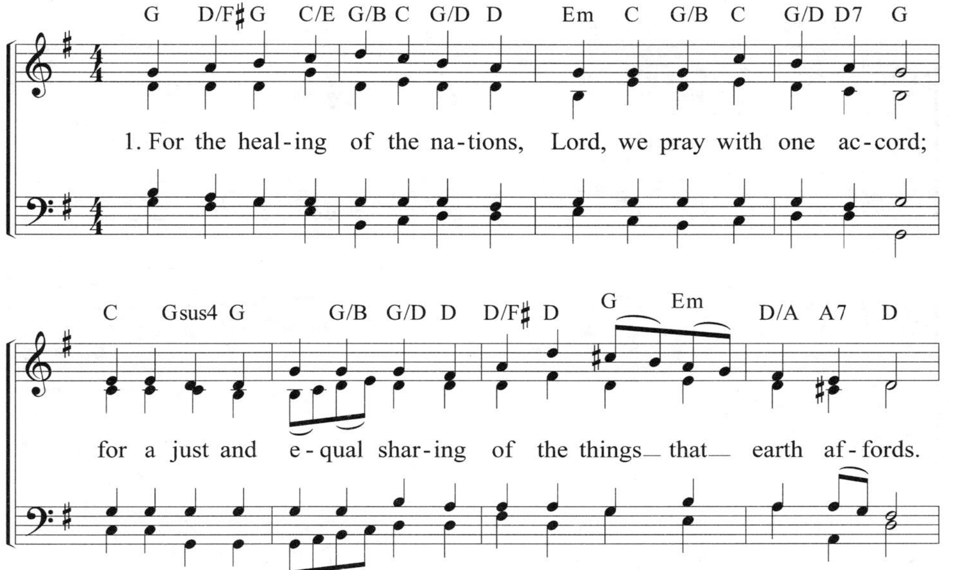
G D/F♯ G C/E G/B C G/D D Em C G/B C G/D D7 G
1. For the heal-ing of the na-tions, Lord, we pray with one ac-cord;
C Gsus4 G G/B G/D D D/F♯ D G Em D/A A7 D
for a just and e-qual shar-ing of the things that earth af-fords.

D/C G/B G C B Em D G G/B C Am7 G/D D7 G
To a life of love in ac-tion help us rise and pledge our word.

2. Lead us forward into freedom;
From despair Your world release,
That, redeemed from war and hatred,
All may come and go in peace.
Show us how through care and goodness
Fear will die and hope increase.

3. All that kills abundant living,
Let it from the earth be banned;
Pride of status, race or schooling,
Dogmas that obscure Your plan.
In our common quest of justice
May we hallow life's brief span.

4. You, Creator-God, have written
Your great name on humankind;
For our growing in Your likeness
Bring the life of Christ to mind;
That by our response and service
Earth its destiny may find.

Fred Kaan (b.1929)

1236. For the Lord is good

Ps 136:1; 145:13; Lam 3:22-23

Lynn DeShazo & Gary Sadler

Brightly

Chorus
D E A
For the Lord is good, and His love
D E A D E
endures forever; He's a faithful God
F♯m Dsus2 Esus4 E
to all generations. For the Lord
D E A D E
is good, and His mercies will not fail
A D E F♯m
us; they are new each day, O, lift

D
E
A
Dsus2
your voice and say, "the Lord is good!"
Last time to Coda
F♯m
E
Verse
A
D/A
E/A
(Leader) Great is Your faith - ful - ness, O Lord.
A
D/A
E/A
A
(Leader) Your lov - ing kind-
(Echo) Great is Your faith - ful - ness, O Lord.
D/A
Bm7
E
ness fills our (All) hearts to o - ver - flow - ing.
A
D/A
E/A
F♯m
(Leader) Songs of re - joic - ing and sweet praise,
(Echo) Songs of

Dsus2
(Leader) they fill our hearts,
praise! (Echo) They fill our hearts, (All) they fill
E
our days.
D.C.
Coda
A

1237. Forth in Thy name, O Lord, I go

Eccles 2:24-25; Mt 11:30; 25:21; Lk 21:36; Rom 12:2; 1 Cor 2:2; Col 3:17

Tune: ANGELS SONG

Orlando Gibbons (1563-1625)

F C F/A Gm C7/G F B♭/D C C/E
1. Forth in Thy name, O Lord, I go, my dai-ly la - bour

Dm7/F G C F B♭/D Cm B♭ Am/C B♭/D C7/E F
to pur - sue, Thee, on - ly Thee, re - solved to

C C/B♭ F/A B♭ F C C7 Dm F/A Csus4 C F
know in all I think, or speak, or do.

2. The task Thy wisdom has assigned
O let me cheerfully fulfil;
In all my works Thy presence find,
And prove Thy acceptable will.

3. Thee may I set at my right hand,
Whose eyes my inmost substance see;
And labour on at Thy command,
And offer all my works to Thee.

4. Give me to bear Thy easy yoke,
And every moment watch and pray,
And still to things eternal look,
And hasten to Thy glorious day.

5. For Thee delightfully employ
Whate'er Thy bounteous grace hath given,
And run my course with even joy,
And closely walk with Thee to heaven.

Charles Wesley (1707-88)

1238. From the rising of the sun

Ps 113:3-4; Rev 7:11

Capo 3 (D)
Viola Grafström
Steadily
Chorus
F(D) F/E♭(D) F/A(D)
From the ri-sing of the sun, e - ven to its go-
B♭(G) C7sus4(A)
ing down, shall Your name be great. Through
F(D) F/E♭(D) F/A(D)
all the earth, a - mong the na - tions, we give
B♭(G) Dm(Bm) C(A) B♭(G) C7sus4(A)
You praise; Your name is high a-bove all o-ther
F(D) F/E♭(D) F/A(D) B♭(G)
(Fine)
gods.
Verse
F(D) F/A(D)
(v.2)
1. Je - sus, Lo-ver of my

B♭(G)
F/A(D)
Gm7(Em)
soul, You a-lone are King, wor-thy of my
(v.2)
C7sus4(A)
F(D)
F/A(D)
praise. My wor - ship I'll give to on-ly
B♭(G)
F/A(D)
Gm7(Em)
one; O Lord, my heart I'll bring when to
(v.2)
1st time D.C.
Last time D.C. al Coda
E♭(C)
B♭/D(G)
C7sus4(A)
You I come. From the
Coda
F(D)

2. Holiness, Majesty and King,
Let Your will be done
When we worship bring.
Eternal, Your love will remain;
Before Your throne we bow,
With our voices sing.

1239. From the squalor of a borrowed stable

(Immanuel)
Is 42:3; 53:5; Mt 1:18-23; 11:19; Lk 1:34-35; 2:7-13; 4:1; 22:48 1Thess 4:16; Heb 2:9, 14; 4:15-16; 7:25; Rev 20:15; 21:2
Gently building
Stuart Townend
D(no3rd)
1. From the squa - lor of a bor - rowed sta - ble,
Bm
Em7 D/G A7sus4 D(no3rd)
by the Spi - rit and a vir - gin's faith; to the an - guish and the
Bm
A7sus4
shame of scan - dal came the Sa - viour of the hu - man
D(no3rd)
D/F♯ G
race! But the skies were filled with the praise of heav'n,
D
Asus4 A
D
shep - herds lis - ten as the an - gels tell of the Gift of God come

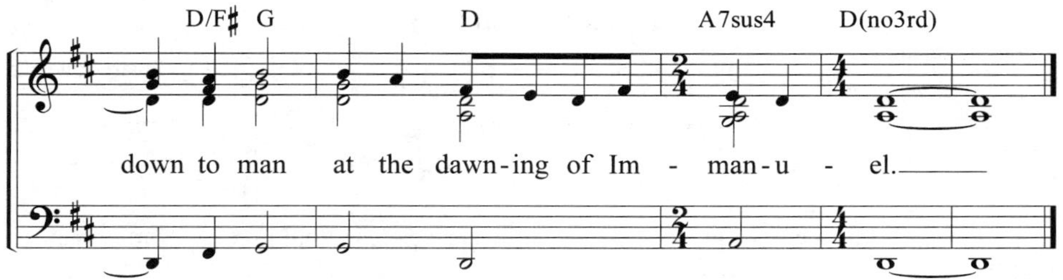
D/F♯ G
D
A7sus4
D(no3rd)
down to man at the dawn-ing of Im - man-u - el.

2. King of heaven now the Friend of sinners,
Humble servant in the Father's hands,
Filled with power and the Holy Spirit,
Filled with mercy for the broken man.
Yes, He walked my road and He felt my pain,
Joys and sorrows that I know so well;
Yet His righteous steps give me hope again -
I will follow my Immanuel!

3. Through the kisses of a friend's betrayal,
He was lifted on a cruel cross;
He was punished for a world's trangressions,
He was suffering to save the lost.
He fights for breath, He fights for me,
Loosing sinners from the claims of hell;
And with a shout our souls are free -
Death defeated by Immanuel!

4. Now He's standing in the place of honour,
Crowned with glory on the highest throne,
Interceding for His own belovèd
Till His Father calls to bring them home!
Then the skies will part as the trumpet sounds
Hope of heaven or the fear of hell;
But the Bride will run to her Lover's arms,
Giving glory to Immanuel!

1240. Giver of grace
(You are good to me)

Ps 13:6; 61:3; 62:2; 119:72; Ezek 34:26; Jn 1:17; Eph 1:7-8, 14; 2:6

Stuart Townend

Gently rhythmic

Verse
A/E E A/E E
1. Giv - er of grace, how price - less Your love for me,
A/C♯ E/B F♯/A♯ B A/E E
pur - er than sil - ver, more cost - ly than gold. Giv - er of life,
A/E E A/C♯ E/B
all that I'll ev - er need, strength for my bo - dy and
F♯/A♯ B Chorus A F♯m7 E
food for my soul. Oh, You are good, so
B E A F♯m7 E B E
good to me. Yes, You are good, so good to me. Oh, You are

A F♯m7 E
B E
A F♯m7 E
good, so good to me. Yes, you are good, so
B E
(Fine)
Bm7
A
good to me.
I've ne-ver known a love so
E B D A A/E
per-fect in its faith-ful-ness; it lifts me up to the high-
E Bm7 A
-est place. A glimpse of hea-ven and a
E B D A Bsus4
taste of my in-he-ri-tance, I know that one day I'll be
D.C. al fine
B
with You.

2. Giver of hope, Rock of salvation,
Tower of refuge, yet there in my pain.
Now I'm secure, loved for eternity,
Showered with blessings
And lavished with grace.

1241. Give thanks to the Lord

(Forever)

Ps 113:3; 136:1, 12; Jn 3:3

Chris Tomlin

Steadily, with a strong rhythm
Verse
A
1. Give thanks to the Lord, our God and King: His
love en - dures for - e - ver.
D
For He is good, He is a -
bove all things. His love en - dures for - e - ver. Sing
A
E
praise, sing praise.
1. D2/F♯
2. D2/F♯
E
D/F♯
praise, sing praise, sing praise.

Chorus
A
For - e - ver God is faith - ful, for - e -
F♯m
- ver God is strong.
E
For - e - ver God is with
D
1.
2.
us, for - e - ver, for - e - for - e -
A
D.S.
To end
- ver.

2. With a mighty hand and an outstretched arm,
His love endures forever.
For the life that's been reborn.
His love endures forever.
Sing praise, sing praise.
Sing praise, sing praise.

3. From the rising to the setting sun,
His love endures forever.
By the grace of God, we will carry on.
His love endures forever.
Sing praise, sing praise.
Sing praise, sing praise.

Trust in the Lord with all your heart and lean not on your own understanding; in all your ways acknowledge Him, and He will make your paths straight.

PROVERBS 3:5-6

1242. Giving it all to You

1 Pet 5:7

Geraldine Latty

Slow 4
Em7 A F♯m7 Bm7
Giv-ing it all to You, giv-ing it all to You, no more
Gmaj7 Em7 A
hid-den a-gen-da, giv-ing it all to You. Lay-ing my bur-
Gmaj7 A F♯m7 Bm7
dens down, bow-ing in full sur-ren-der, kneel-ing be-fore
Gmaj7 A7sus4 D
Your cross, giv-ing it all to You.

1243. God gave us His Son
(I am not ashamed)

Rom 10:14; 2 Cor 3:18; 5:19, 21; 6:2; Phil 2:15-16; 2 Tim 1:12

Capo 3 (D)

Kate & Miles Simmonds

Steadily
Verse
Dm(Bm)
Bb(G)
1. God gave us His Son, the sin-less One to be sin for us, that we might be the right-eous-ness of God.
Your king-dom has come, we're be-ing changed in-to Your like-ness; chil-dren of light, it's our time to a-rise.
C(A)
Chorus
F(D)
I am not a-shamed,

Dm(Bm)
Bb(G)
I know whom I've believed, for God Himself has come
F/A(D)
Gm(Em)
Gm/C(Em)
F(D)
to me, now Jesus is my destiny. I know
Dm(Bm)
I am changed, and all You've given me, this hope,
Bb(G)
F/A(D)
Gm(Em)
this love, this life, I can't deny Your pow'r within
Gm/C(Em)
Bb(G)
F/A(D)
Gm(Em)
Gm/C(Em)
F(D)
me. So here I am, send me.

1.
2.3.
(Fine)
Bridge
Dm(Bm)
2. Now
Pu - ri - fy us, Lord, so we're
B♭(G)
spot - less and pure as we hold out Your word
Dm(Bm)
to this ge - ne - ra - tion.
How can they hear,
and how can they be - lieve, how can they
call on Your name un - less we tell them?
2nd time D.S. al fine

2. Now we are in You,
And You have given us Your message
To tell the world: be reconciled to God.
Your favour is here
In this day of salvation.
Now is the time, let Your glory arise!

1244. God is good all the time

Ps 23:4; 40:3; 135:3; 139:12; Jer 29:11; Lam 3:22; Mt 28:20; Mk 10:18; Acts 1:8; Rom 5:8

Don Moen
& Paul Overstreet

Brightly
Chorus
Amaj7/B E C♯m7
God is good all the time! He put a song
A E/G♯ F♯m7 B
of praise in this heart of mine. God is
E C♯m7
good all the time! Through the dark-
A E/G♯ F♯m7 B7 A
est night His light will shine: God is good, God is
3rd time to Coda
B7 E A/E E A/E E
(Fine)
Verse
good all the time. 1. If you're

B
C♯m
walk - ing through the val - ley and there are
A
C♯m
B
G♯m7
sha - dows all a-round, do not fear, He will
C♯m
A
guide you, He will keep you safe and
B7
F♯m7
sound; 'cause He has pro-mised to ne - ver leave
B7
F♯m7
A
B
D.S.
you nor for - sake you, and His word is true. God is

Coda
E
A/E
E
Bridge
C♯m
G♯m7
Though I may not un - der - stand all the
Bm7
F♯m7
C
plans You have for me, my life is in Your
D.S. al fine
G
F♯m7(add4)
E/G♯
A
A/B
hands, and through the eyes of faith I can clear-ly see: God is

2. We were sinners, so unworthy,
Still for us He chose to die:
Filled us with His Holy Spirit,
Now we can stand and testify
That His love is everlasting
And His mercies, they will never end.

1245. God is our Father

(Kingdom of heaven our goal)

Mt 6:9, 25-26, 28-30, 33

David Lyle Morris
& Nick Wynne-Jones

Capo 1 (D)
Gently

Verse
Eb(D)
Ab(G)
Eb(D)
1. God is our Fa-ther in hea-ven a - bove, and He
Ab(G)
Bb(A)
Cm(Bm)
cares for His chil-dren with in-fi-nite love. Our wor-ries are
Ab(G)
Eb(D)
Bb(A)
Ab(G)
Eb(D)
need-less; look up in the sky where care-free and sing-ing the
Bb7(A7)
Eb(D)
Bridge
Ab(G)
birds free - ly fly. Their Ma - ker who
Eb/G (D/F#)
Ab(G)
Bb(A)
Fm(Em)
knows them, sup - plies all their food; how much more is our

E♭/G (D/F♯) A♭(G) B♭sus4(Asus4) B♭(A)
Fa - ther con - cerned for our___ good?
Chorus
A♭(G) E♭(D) A♭(G) B♭(A)
For our Fa-ther in hea-ven knows all of our needs; He will
Fm7(Em) E♭/G (D/F♯) A♭(G) B♭(A)
care for us al-ways. We sur - ren - der our_ all, and make the
Fm(Em) B♭(A) E♭(D)
king-dom of hea-ven our goal.

2. Look at the lilies
And see how they grow:
They are clothed by God's goodness
In beautiful show.
Our Father in heaven
Who cares for each flower,
Provides for us always,
So great is His power.

(Bridge 2)
The kingdom of heaven
And His righteousness
We will seek with a passion
So all may be blessed.

1246. God of mercy

(Prayer song)*

2 Chron 6:19; Ps 34:4; 48:14; 116:15; Rom 8:26; Phil 1:21

With feeling

Louise Fellingham

C G/B C G/B C F
1.3. God of mer - cy, hear our — cry, turn Your — hand to - day.
2. God of mer - cy, hear our — cry, heal their — souls to - day.
C G/B C G/B C F
Bring re - lief from their — pain, be their — com - fort. —
Give them peace from their — fears, be their — hope, Lord. —
And
G C G C
e - v'ry day they're gi - ven — breath, give them strength to
F G C G C
live. And as their wea - ry bo - dies — fail, fight - ing is o - ver,

* *This song was originally written as a prayer for AIDS orphans in Africa.*

G Am F F/G
flesh gives way, be their {light / star} to guide them
C Csus4 1. C 2.3. C (Fine) Am
home. Some - times I don't know what
F G
to ask for, some - times I don't know what to say, but I
Am C/E Dm7
know that You are watch - ing o - ver them. Some-
Am F
times I don't know what to pray for, some - times I don't know how

G
Am
C/E
to give, but I know that You are watch - ing o - ver them,
Dm7
C/E
F
Gsus4
and their life is not in vain.
G
D.C. al fine
So

1247. God of restoration
(I am Yours)

Capo 3 (D)

Ps 23:3; 71:2; Is 42:3; 53:5; 1 Pet 2:24

Matt Redman

With life

F(D) F2/E(D) B♭/D(G)
1. God of re-stor-a - tion, my hope is in the life
God of my sal-va - tion, with sav-ing love You came
F/E(D) F(D) F2/E(D)
You bring to me. Heal-er of my wounds, I thank
to res - cue me. Heal-er of my soul, I thank
B♭/D(G) F/E(D) B♭(G) F/A(D) Csus4(A)
You, oh I thank You. to-day and ev-'ry day.
You, oh I thank You,
C(A) F(D) C2/E(A)
I am Yours, I am Yours, ev-'ry
B♭/D(G) C/E(A) F(D)
breath that I breathe, ev-'ry mo-ment that's lived. I am Yours, I am

Last time to Coda
C2/E(A)
B♭/D(G)
C/E(A)
Yours, You're the rea - son to breathe, You're the rea - son to live. And now
C(A)
D/F♯(B)
B♭(G)
F/A(D)
ev-'ry-one that You have saved will come to be Your praise,
Csus4(A)
C(A)
1.
F(D)
C/E(A)
B♭/D(G)
F(D)
C/E(A)
B♭/D(G)
D.C.
2.
F(D)
I am Yours.
Yours.
B♭(G)
F/A(D)
And if my food is to do Your will, then I'm hun -
C(A)
F/A(D)
B♭(G)
gry, still hun - gry; there's so much more that I need to give

1.
F/A(D)
C(A)
F/A(D)
to thank You, to thank You. Yes, if my food

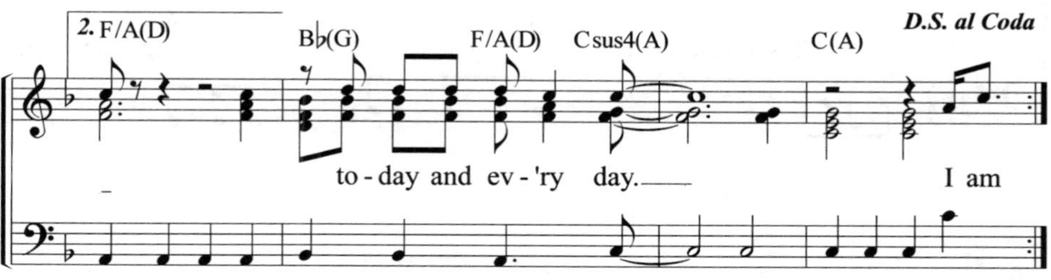
2. F/A(D)
B♭(G)
F/A(D)
Csus4(A)
C(A)
D.S. al Coda
to-day and ev-'ry day. I am

Coda
C/E(A)
F(D)
rea-son to live, I'm Yours.

2. Singing of a love now,
You taught this broken heart to sing again.
Every day I'll come, to thank You, oh, to thank You.
Singing of a life now,
You taught this wounded soul to live again.
Every day I'll live to thank You, oh, to thank You,
Today and every day.

1248. God of the mountains

(Creation praise)

Ps 24:1-2; Prov 18:24; Jn 8:12; 1 Cor 1:30; Gal 5:1; Eph 2:14; Rev 19:6

Moderately

Sue Rinaldi, Caroline Bonnett & Steve Bassett

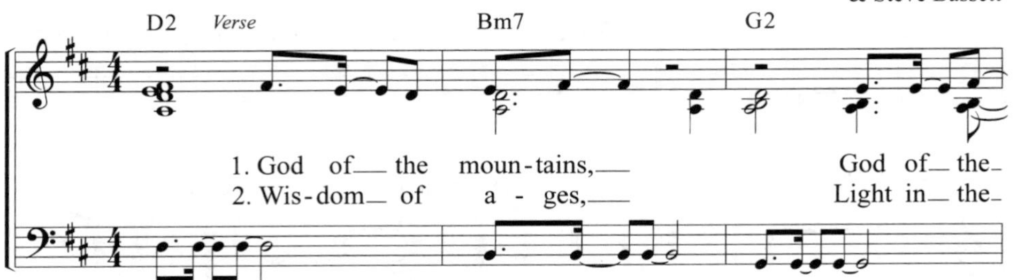
D2
Verse
Bm7
G2
1. God of the mountains, God of the
2. Wis-dom of ages, Light in the

D2
Bm7
sea; God of the heavens,
dark; home for the outcast,

G2
Bm7
of e-ter-ni-ty. God of the
peace for the heart. Friend of the

A/C♯
G2
fu-ture, God of the past;
lone-ly, strength for op-pressed;

Bm7
A/C♯
G2
God of the present, God of all
Voice of the voiceless, God of all
Chorus
D/F♯
Bm7
hi - sto - ry.
li - ber - ty.
Cre - a - tion praise will thun - der to You,
Asus4
A
G2
thun - der to You, thun - der to You. Cre -
D/F♯
Bm7
a - tion praise will thun - der to You. I'm
Asus4
A
D
lost in the won - der, lost in the won - der of You.

1249. God, You are good

Ps 136:1; Prov 3:34; Mal 4:2; Mt 23:37; Lk 1:52; Jn 11:35; 15:15

Gently

Brian Houston

Verse
Em7
D
Em7
D
Em7
D
1. God, You are good,
God, You are kind.
God, You are sun,
God, You are shine.
God, You are truth,
God, You are pure.

Em7
You've mel-ted my heart,
and now I am Yours.
D
Chorus
Em7
I'm hap-py to be a friend of
D
Em7
God.
I'm hap-py that God's a friend to
1.
D
2. (Fine)
D
me.
2. You're burst-ing with love
me.
F♯m
Bm
F♯m
And You love me so much
that You weep for my pain,

Bm
F♯m
Bm
and You guide with Your touch. For it is
Em
G
Em
not Your heart to see me fall, or let my sin re-main.
A
D.S. al fine
For God, You are good,

2. You're bursting with love
For the ones that You made.
You're happy to bless
Every one of their days.
You humble the proud
But You raise up the low.
You cry for the lost
But You eat with the poor.

1250. Good and gracious

Gen 1:1; Ps 93:4; 103:13; Rom 5:1-2; 1 Cor 15:55; Heb 2:14-15; Rev 4:8, 11

Gareth Robinson

Steadily
Verse
A G6 D
Good___ and gra - cious,___ att - ri - butes___ of a
E A G6
lo - ving Fath - er, You're high___ and migh - ty,___ but
D E F♯m
hum - ble all the same.___ You have made the hea - vens and___
B D E
___ the earth,___ and You made us___ in Your im - age, Lord.___
Chorus
A2 G D E
Ho - ly, ho - ly, ho - ly is___ the___ Lord Al - migh - ty, and

A2 G D E
we re - joice in You a-lone, for You are wor-thy and
F♯m B F♯m
You have gi-ven life to me, and I love to wor-ship at
B D E
Your feet, and I love to love You just for who You are.
A (Fine) G2 Cmaj7
I'm so grate-ful for the things that
G2 C2 G2
You have gi-ven me: Your love, Your grace, Your

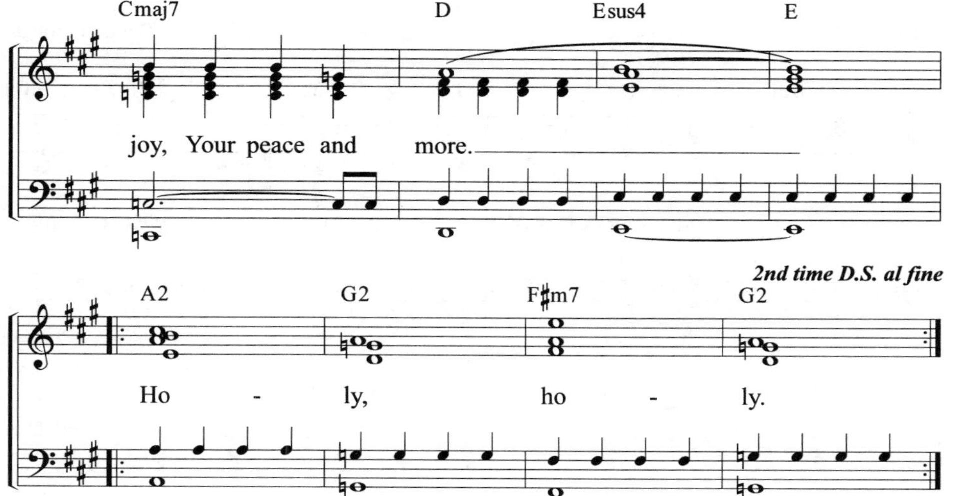
Cmaj7
D
Esus4
E
joy, Your peace and more.
2nd time D.S. al fine
A2
G2
F♯m7
G2
Ho - ly, ho - ly.

2. Death and hell are now no longer things I fear because
You have saved me and I'm grateful to the core.
I'm Your child because of Jesus' blood,
And Your Spirit leads me, guides me, fills me.

1251. Grace and mercy

Phil 4:19

Slowly
Dave Bilbrough
Bm7 A/C♯ D G A Bm7 A/C♯
Grace and mer - cy wash o - ver me, cleanse my
D G Asus4 A G A D Bm A
soul with Your heal - ing stream. Here I stand with this
D G A Bm A G A/C♯
pray'r with - in my heart. Take me deep - er in the ri - ver that
Last time to Coda
D/G A/E A A/C♯ D A/C♯
flows with Your love. Thank You, thank

D Bm A Bm Am Bm A G A
You, oh what rich - es are mine in Christ Je - sus.
A/C♯ D A/C♯ D Bm A Bm A Bm
Thank You, thank You, Your for - give - ness is
A G A D.C. al Coda
so un - de - served.
Coda
D

1252. Great and marvellous

Jer 10:6-7; Rev 7:9; 15:3-4

Ian Hannah

Very rhythmic

D

1. Great and mar-v'llous are Your deeds, Lord; just and true are

Am7 C D

all of Your ways. Who would dare to ne-ver fear You,

Am7 C D Gm

or bring glo-ry to Your name. For no-thing com-

Am7 Gm/B♭ C 1. D

pares to You.

Gm/D

Omit these bars after verse 3....

2.,3. D Gm

You. No, no-thing

Am7 Gm/B♭ C
D
D/C
compares to You.
E - v'ry na - tion
D5/B♭ (or D(no3rd)) D5/A
D5/G
D5/F
D5/E
rise and sing prai - ses to our glo - rious
Asus4 A
D5
D5/E
D5/F
D5/G
King. E - v'ry tongue in one ac - cord
D5/A
D5/B♭
D5/C
D5/A
D5
cry out and con - fess: "Je-sus is Lord!"
Gm/D
D.C.(v.3)
D5

2. You are worthy to receive all
Of the glory, honour and power.
By You all things were created
And by You all things are sustained.
For nothing compares to You.

3. "Hallelujah" cry Your servants,
"We will worship" both great and small.
King of all kings, Lord of all lords,
You will reign for evermore.
For nothing compares to You.
No, nothing compares to You.

1253. Great and marvellous

Jer 10:6-7; Phil 2:11; Rev 4:11; 7:9; 15:3-4; 17:14; 19:16

Geraldine Latty
& Carey Luce

In a latin style

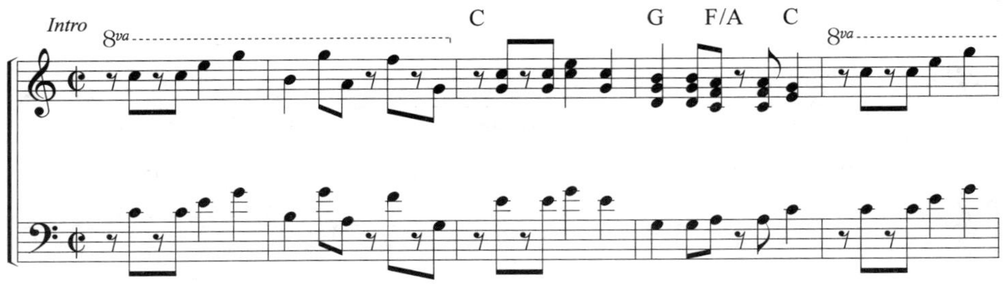
Intro
8va
C
G F/A C
8va

(8va)
C
G F2/A C
Verse
C
1. Great and mar - vel-lous are

Em7 F
Your deeds, O God, sov'-reign o - ver all,

C
Em7
just and right - eous in e - v'ry way. Great King for all time

F E/G♯ Am G Fmaj7 Em7
e-ter - nal. Who shall not fear You, Lord?
Am G Fmaj7 Dm Am7 G Fmaj7
Who shall not ho - nour Your name? Who shall not fear
Em7 Dm7 F Gsus4
You, Lord? There is none the same.
G
Chorus
C Em7 F G
All the na - tions, e - v'ry race,
C Em7 F G Dm7 Em7
com-ing now to seek Your face. Sing-ing to the Ho-

F
Am7
Dm/G G
ly One, Je - sus Christ, God's on - ly Son.
C
Em7
F
G
C
Em7
F
All the peo - ple in this place, thank-ing You for sav -
G
Dm7
Em7
ing grace, bur-dens rolled to Cal - va - ry,
NC
F/G
C
once in chains but now set free.

2. Great and marvellous are Your deeds,
O, Lord, how we long to see Your
Plan in our time revealed:
Hearts longing to worship Jesus.
And we will fear You, Lord;
And we will honour Your name.
Yes, we will fear You, Lord:
There is none the same.

1254. Great is He

Rev 4:11; 17:14; 19:16

With strength

Author unknown
Arr. Stuart Townend

Women 1
Great is He who's the King of kings and the Lord of lords, He is won - der-ful!
Women 2
Al - le - lu - ia, al - le - lu - ia, al-le-lu - ia, He is won - der-ful!
Men
Al-le-lu - ia, sal - va-tion and glo - ry, ho-nour and pow - er, He is won - der-ful!
A A/C♯ D Bm7 E E/D C♯ C♯7/E♯
F♯m F♯m/A Bm7 Esus4 E A (Asus4)

1255. Hallelujah, hosanna

(Halala Ngo 'Jesu)

Mt 21:9; Phil 2:9-11

Capo 3 (D)

Victor S. Masondo
& Malcolm du Plessis

Brightly
Chorus
F(D) B♭(G) F(D) C(A)
Hal - le - lu - jah, ho - san - na, hal - le - lu - jah, hos - san - na,
F(D) B♭(G)
hal - le - lu - jah, ho - san - na, hal - le - lu - jah,
1. Dm(Bm) C(A) F(D)
ho - san - na! Hal - le - lu - jah
2. Dm(Bm) C(A) F(D)
2nd & last time to Coda
ho - san - na!
Verse
F(D) B♭(G)
God has ex - al - ted Je - sus to the high - est place,
Gm(Em)
and gi - ven Him the name that is a - bove

F/C(D)
C(A)
F(D)
e - v'ry name,
that at the name of Je-
B♭(G)
sus e - v'ry knee shall bow
and
F/C(D)
C(A)
F(D)
e-v'ry tongue con-fess that He is Lord. (Hal-le-lu, hal-le-
D.S.
Coda
F(D)
lu.) Hal-le-lu-jah
Hal-la - lan - go Je - su,
B♭(G)
Gm(Em)
hal-la-lan - go Je - su,
hal-la-lan - go Je - su,

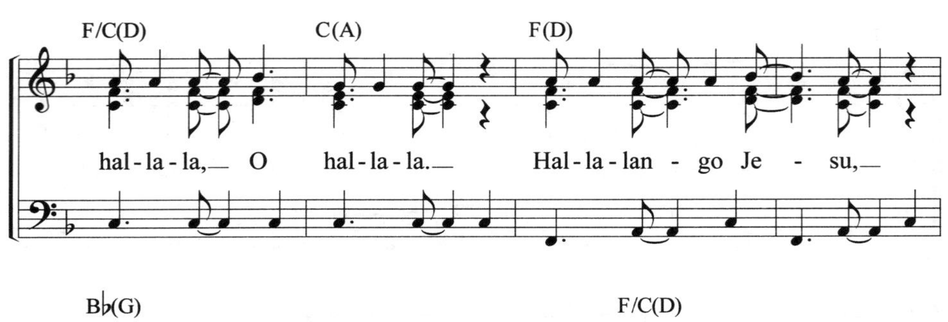
F/C(D)
C(A)
F(D)
hal - la - la, O hal - la - la. Hal - la - lan - go Je - su,

B♭(G)
F/C(D)
hal - la - lan - go Je - su, hal - la - lan - go Je -
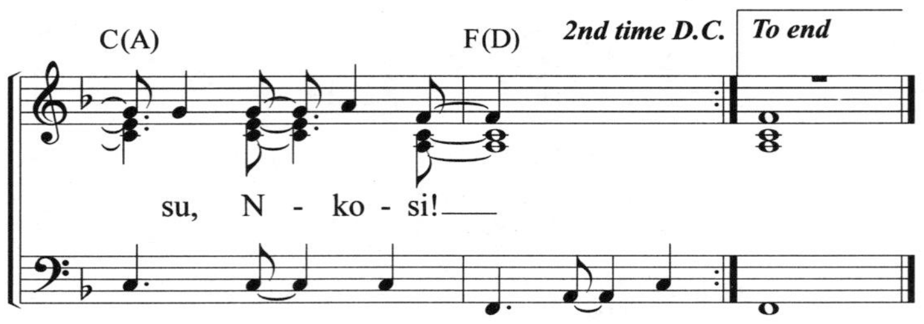
C(A)
F(D)
2nd time D.C.
To end
su, N - ko - si!

1256. Have I not been faithful?

(Waiting for the blessing)

Jer 12:1, 3; Ps 37:7; 51:9; 94:3; 139:23

Brian Houston

Country rock
Verse
Chorus
1. Have I not been faith - ful to You, Lord?
Have I not of - fered up my pray - ers and
tried to fol - low Your word?
Lord, will You search me,
show me where I'm wrong?
I've been wait - ing for the bles - sing for far to long,
D G A D G D G A D D/C♯ Bm F♯m G D D Em A

Bm D Em
I've been wait - ing for the bles - sing for
Last time to Coda
1. (to v.2)
2.
A D G D A
Bridge
far too long.
Do not be
G D A
an - gry with me, O my God,
Please don't
G D A
hide Your face a way.
I'm like a child,
G D
and I'm down on my knees
And I'm beg -

Em
A
D.C.(v.3)
ging for You just to bless me to-day.
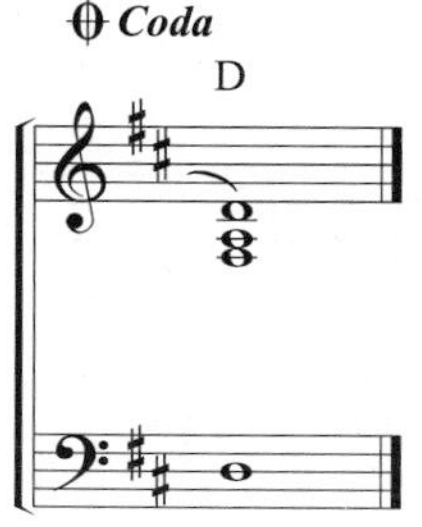
Coda
D

2. Now Lord, forgive me,
For speaking this right out.
But I see the wicked prosper
While the godly go without.
No, I can't read human hearts,
But do You know where I'm coming from?
I've been waiting . . .

3. Lord, up ahead You know
I see a lonely road.
Got this burden on my back,
It's such a heavy load.
These days I've questions,
But there's no answers in my songs.
I've been waiting . . .

1257. Have we forgotten?

(Saviour and Friend)

Rom 5:9; 6:23; Eph 1:7; 1 Pet 1:2

Andy Ferrett

G
Verse
Have we for-got-ten the price that's been paid?
It was my life He paid with His pain,
D2/F#
Have we re-mem-bered the wage of our ways?
suf-fered at the hands of those He had made.
Em7(addA)
Can we dis-miss what He's done on the cross as
Can we con-si-der what He once went through to be
Asus4
A
Am
fool-ish-ness? Oh, thank You, oh,
with us?
C
Dsus4
D
Chorus
C
G
thank You. O Sa-viour and Friend,

C G G/F♯
Re-deem - er of ma-ny, You
Em Asus4 A C
poured out Your blood to me, and gave up Your life for me.
A7 1. Am7 D2 D
Oh, thank You.
2. Am7 C Am7
how can I re-pay such a love? Oh, how can I re-pay such a
C Am7 C D
love? How can I re-pay such a love? Oh,

G
C
G
C
G
thank You.
O Sa-viour and Friend,
C
G
C
G
Re-deem-er of ma-ny.
Sa-viour and Friend,
rit.
C
G
Re-deem-er of ma-ny.

1258. Hear all creation

Capo 1(D)

Ps 98:8; Lk 19:40; Eph 2:8; Rev 17:14; 19:16

Margaret Becker
& Keith Getty

Brightly
E♭(D) A♭/E♭(G) B♭/E♭(A) A♭/E♭(G) E♭(D) A♭/E♭(G)
B♭/E♭(A) A♭/E♭(G)
Verse
E♭(D) A♭/E♭(G)
(v.2)
1. Hear all cre - a - tion
B♭/E♭(A) A♭maj7/E♭(G) E♭(D) A♭/E♭(G)
lift its voice, the moun - tains sing and the
B♭/E♭(A) E♭(D) E♭maj7/G(D) A♭(G)
ri - vers re - joice for the name of Je - sus,
E♭(D) A♭/E♭(G)
for His name. And

E♭(D) A♭/E♭(G) B♭/E♭(A) A♭maj7/E♭(G)
(v.2)
we His peo - ple saved by grace, we
E♭(D) A♭/E♭(G) B♭/E♭(A) A♭maj7/E♭(G)
bow our hearts and we bring our praise to the
A♭(G) E♭(D)
sweet Re - deem - er, for His name.
Cm7(Bm) E♭/G(D)
So with ev - 'ry - thing we are, and
Cm7(Bm) E♭/G(D) A♭(G) (G) A♭/B♭ B♭(A) E♭(D) E♭/G(D)
ev - 'ry - thing we have we pour out our of - fer - ings. And if

A♭(G) B♭(A) Cm7(Bm) E♭/G(D)
e - ver we_ should fail, the rocks will_ rise up and
A♭(G) A♭/B♭(G) B♭ (A) E♭(D) A♭/E♭ (G)
crown Him_ the King of kings.
B♭/E♭ (A) A♭/E♭ (G) E♭(D) A♭/E♭ (G)
1. B♭/E♭ (A) A♭/E♭(G)
2. He
2. B♭/E♭(A) A♭/E♭(G) A♭/E♭ (G) E♭(D)

2. He mends our hearts, He keeps our ways:
He lights our nights and He leads our days,
All for His glory, for His name.
There's nothing greater than to be His,
To bring Him glory and to fully live
For the name of Jesus,
For His name.

1259. Hear my confession

(Take my whole heart)

Is 48:17; Ps 32:8; 84:10; Mt 6:33; 10:39; 16:25

Brian Houston

Steadliy, with a strong rhythm

Verse
E A E A
1. Hear my con-fes - sion in Your com-pas - sion;

C♯m7 G♯m B
could You lead me in the way that I should go?

E Emaj7 A E Emaj7 A
If I lose my life for You, I know I'll find it;

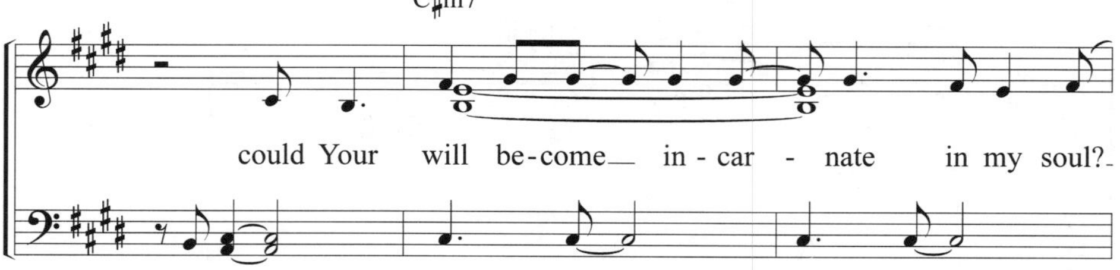

C♯m7
could Your will be-come in - car - nate in my soul?

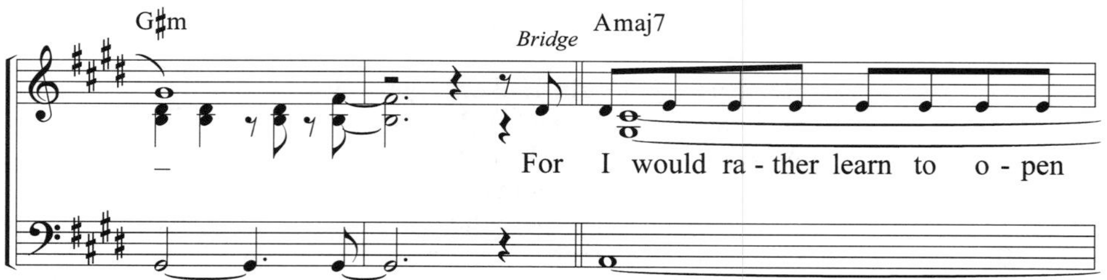

G♯m
Bridge
Amaj7
For I would ra - ther learn to o - pen

C♯m7
doors in Your house, than spend the rest of my days was-ted
Amaj7
some-where else. For I could ne-ver be free or feel Your peace till I sur-
G♯m
B
Chorus
E
Emaj7
A
ren - der to Your love. Take my whole heart;
E
Emaj7
A
I won't hold back the least part. I wan-na fall face
C♯m7
G♯m
B
for-ward in-to the arms of grace. Oh,

E Emaj7 A
may my pas - sion be-come so un - di - vi -
E Emaj7 A C♯m7
ded that I won't be sa - tis-fied with no-thing less,
G♯m G♯m7 Bsus4 B Emaj7 Amaj7
no-thing less than You.
Emaj7 Amaj7
1. D.S. 2. Emaj7
2. Could You give me a hun -

2. Could You give me a hunger for Your kingdom,
That my own desires would all take second place?

1260. Hear my mouth speak

Mt 5:16; Jn 8:12; 2 Cor 3:18

Gareth Robinson

Rhythmically
Verse
E A E A
1. Hear my mouth speak, see my mind think,
E A E A
know my spi - rit tries to pray.
E A E A
Lord, we're long - ing to see You mov - ing,
E A E A
help us as we pray to - day.

G D E A
Words don't seem e-nough to tell You our de-sire,
E A G D
to see Your king - dom come and Your light shine.
(v.2)
E Esus4 E
(v.2)
Chorus
A E/G♯ F♯m F♯m/E
Light of the world, would You
F G E/G♯ A E/G♯
shine on me? Light of the world,
1st time D.C.
2nd time D.S.
F♯m F♯m/E F G E/G♯
would You shine on me?

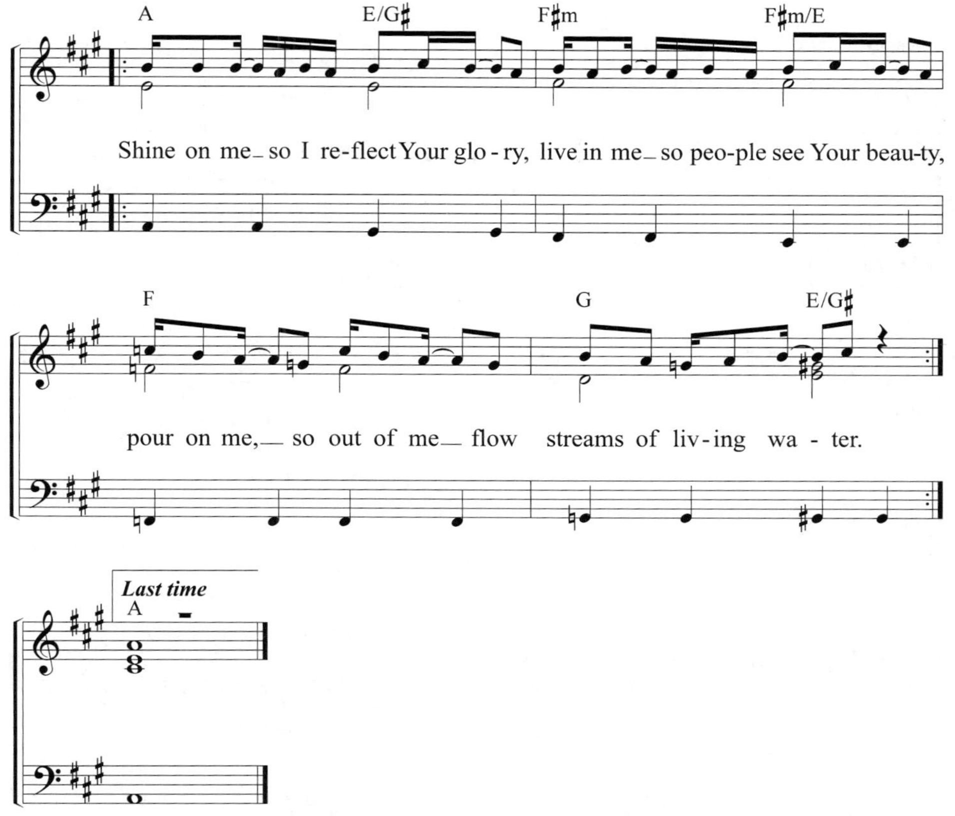
A
E/G♯
F♯m
F♯m/E
Shine on me so I re-flect Your glo - ry, live in me so peo-ple see Your beau-ty,
F
G
E/G♯
pour on me, so out of me flow streams of liv-ing wa - ter.
Last time
A

2. Now I trust You, and I ask You,
   Let Your will be done in me.
   May Your light shine in all the earth and
   Let it draw us all to You.
   Now Your glory shines throughout Your holy church,
   'Cause You're our only hope, Saviour of the world.

1261. Hear my prayer, O Lord

Ps 61:1-4

Steadily

Debbie Owens

E B/E A/E E E/G♯ A E
Hear my pray'r, O Lord, from the ends of the earth
E/G♯ A F♯m B/D♯ C♯m A E/G♯
I cry. Your peace will lead me to the
F♯m7 Bsus4
1. E (Fine) E/A
Rock that is high - er than I.
2. E E2/G♯
For You have been my
A A/B E E2/G♯
strength in times of trou - ble, a tow-er a-bove

A
A/B
C♯m7
E/G♯
F♯m7
my e - ne-mies. And Lord, I will a - bide with You for-e-
E/G♯
1.
A
Amaj7
- ver in the shel - ter of Your wings.
Bsus4
E2/G♯
2.
A/B
D.C. al fine
E
For You have been my - ter of Your wings.

1262. Hear our cry

2 Chron 7:14

Dave Bilbrough

Steady 4
Em Am7 B7 Em
Hear our cry__ for the na-tions, O Lord__ of the hea-vens.__Hear our
G Bsus4 B Em Am7
pray'r__ for this fal - len world.__ Come__ by Your Spi-rit,
B7 Em C B7 1. Em 2. Em
pour__ out Your mer-cy on this earth. Hear our earth.

2. Hear our cry for this nation,
   O Lord of the heavens.
   Hear our prayer as we gather here.
   Come by Your Spirit,
   Pour out Your mercy,
   Heal this land.

1263. Hear our prayer
(Our Father)

Is 11:9; Mt 6:9, 12; Lk 11:2, 4; Heb 12:1; Rev 4:8

With feeling

Don Moen

Verse
D2 D G D
1. Hear our pray'r, we are Your chil - dren, and we've
as it ri - ses to hea - ven, may Your
G2 A2 A Bm G2 A2 A
ga - thered here to - day. We've ga - thered here to pray.
glo - ry fill the earth as the wa - ters co - ver the sea.
D D2 D G D
Hear our cry, Lord, we need Your mer - cy and
See our hearts and re - move a - ny - thing that is
G2 A2 A Bm G2 A2 A
we need Your grace to - day, hear us as we pray.
stand - ing in the way of com - ing to You to - day.

D
Chorus
A
Bm
G
Our Fa - ther, who art in hea - ven,
D
A
D
A
Bm
hal - lo - wed be Thy name. Our Fa - ther,
Last time to Coda
1.
G
D
A
D
hear us from hea - ven, for - give our sins, we pray.
2.
D
Bridge
2. Hear our song And though we are few,
A
Bm
G
we're sur - round - ed by ma - ny who have

D
A
D
crossed that ri - ver be - fore
and this is the song
A
Bm
G
D
A
we'll be sing - ing for - e - ver:
ho - ly is the Lord,
Bm7
G
A
Bm7
G
A
ho - ly is the Lord,
ho - ly is the Lord,
Bm7
G
A
D
D.S. al Coda (v.1)
ho - ly is the Lord.
1. Hear our pray'r
Coda
D

1264. Hear our prayers

Ps 86:6; 90:13

Gareth Robinson
& Joannah Oyeniran

Gently rhythmic and building

Am G F G
Hear our pray'rs and hear our long - ing,
Am G F G Am G
hear our cry, O Lord. Save the peo - ple,
F G Am G F G
bro-ken, hurt - ing, lost with-out Your love.
F E Am D F E
How long will it be, O Lord, how long will it be?

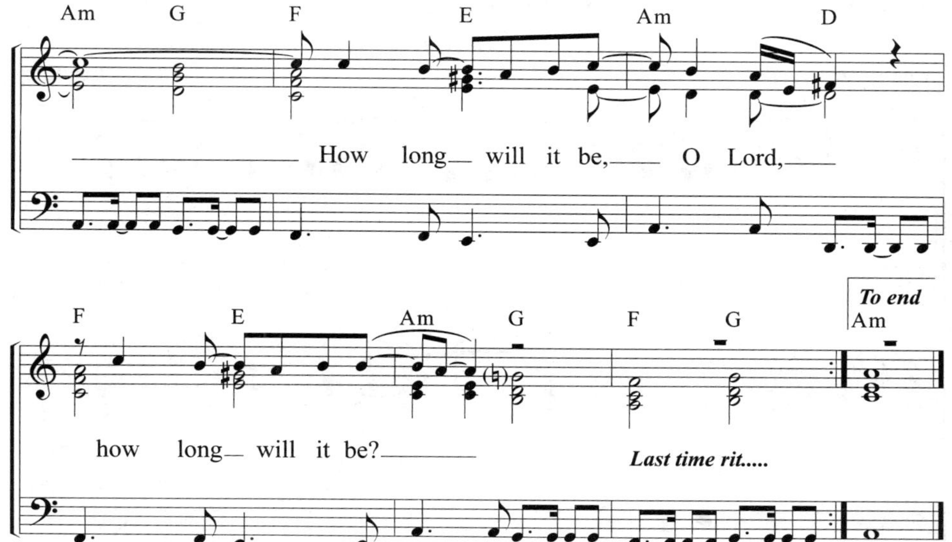
Am
G
F
E
Am
D
How long will it be, O Lord,
F
E
Am
G
F
G
To end
Am
how long will it be?
Last time rit.....

1265. Heaven opened
(Praise)

Lk 21:31; Jn 4:24; Rom 8:15; 12:1; 2 Cor 5:21

With energy

Ken Riley

A
E
Bm
D
Verse
F♯m
1. Heav - en o - pened and You came to
2. You have ri - sen from the grave for-
D2
save me. You were bro - ken and be - came
e - ver, through e - ter - ni - ty I'll praise
sin for me. No death, no hate, no shame, no
my Sa - viour.
slave a - gain to fear; new life, new

Bm
hope, new love, Your king - dom's com - ing near.
Chorus
D
And I give You praise,
A
E
and I lift
Bm
D
A
my hands to You, all of my days
E
Bm
D
I will bring my love to You. I will give
A
E
Bm
Last time to Coda
my life as an off - er - ing, as a sac - ri - fice to the com -

D
A
E
G
ing King_ of grace.___ Je - sus,__
1. To verse 2
D/F♯
2. To bridge
D
F♯m
D
I love and_ a - dore_ You,_ and
B
E
F♯m
D
live for_ Your praise.__ In truth and_ in spi - rit_ I
B
E
D
long_ for You,___ my King.___
A
E
Bm
To chorus
D.S. al Coda
D
_ And I give_ You praise_

Coda
D/F♯
A
E
- ing King. I will give my life as an off - er - ing, as a sac-
G
D/F♯
- ri - fice to the com - ing King: I will give
A
E
Bm
my life to You, Lord, Yeah, yeah, O yeah,
D
A
E
I will give my life as an off - er - ing of praise,
G
praise, praise, praise,
A
and I'll give You praise.

1266. He died for my sake

Rom 5:8

Dave Bilbrough

Gently
G2
Am7
D
C
G
He died for my sake, though I was a sin - ner;
G2
Am7
D
re-deemed me by His grace, to know His love for
C
G
C2
e - ver. With e-v'ry breath that I take, and e-v'ry
G/B
G
G/D
D
beat of my heart I live to give Him wor-ship, and to

C2 Gmaj7/B
1. G C2 Dsus4 D
make His glo - ry known. With e - v'ry
2. C2 D G2 C2 G2 C2
D.C.
glo - ry known.
Last time
G

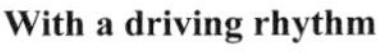
1267.

He is holy, holy, holy
(Holy, holy, holy)

Is 9:6; Mk 14:62; Jn 8:58; Rev 4:8; 5:12; 17:14; 19:7, 16

Ken Riley

With a driving rhythm

Chorus
Bm
D
He is ho - ly, ho - ly, ho - ly, my Lord is

G
Asus4
A
ho - ly, ho - ly, ho - ly, Je - sus. Give

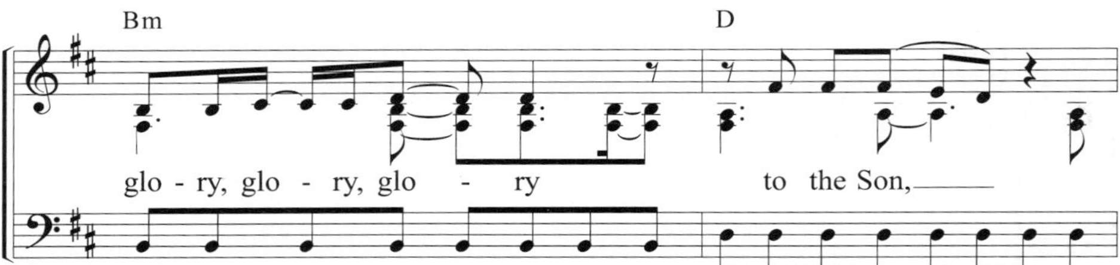
Bm
D
glo - ry, glo - ry, glo - ry to the Son,

G
Asus4
3rd time to mid section
Last time to Coda
glo - ry, glo - ry, glo - ry to Je - sus!

A
Verse
Bm
1. We're gon - na give Him praise, and His

(v.2)
D
G
name we'll raise as we ce - le-brate with
(v.2)
Asus4
A
Bm
Je - sus. Let our voi - ces sing to the
D
G
Asus4
King of kings, who was and is to come.
Mid section
A
D.C.
A
Asus4
Now, He is to Je - sus.
A
G
He's the God of grace, and if we

D
Bm
Asus4
A
seek His face He'll de-mon-strate His pow - er. On the
G
D
Bm
fi-nal day un-to the bride He'll say: "At My side you'll stay for-
Asus4
A
Asus4
A
D.C.
e - ver and e - ver." He is
Coda
A
Asus4
A
Bm7
to Je - sus.

2. He's the Prince of Peace
And He will release
All the chains that keep you down.
He's the Son of Man,
He's the Great I Am,
He's the mighty Lamb of heaven!

1268. He once was dead, but now He lives

Rev 1:17-18

(The First, the Last, the Living One)

David Lyle Morris
& Nick Wynne-Jones

Steadily, with a strong rhythm

Verse
D
A
D
1. He once was dead, but now He lives: the First,
A
D
A/D
Bm
the Last, the Liv - ing One. He holds the keys of death
F♯m
Bm
G/D
D2
A
Last time rit.....
and hell: the First, the Last, the Liv - ing One.
2nd & 3rd time to Chorus
D
(Fine)
Bridge
D
More love, our hearts
the One

G D G
on fire. More pow'r, so faith stands strong. More life,
who knows us. You, Lord, the love that calls us. You, Lord,
A D G
both real and pure. More faith that holds
have pow'r to keep us. You, Lord, speak words
A D A G D
the truth. More, Lord, of You with-in Your church.
of pro-mise. You, Lord, the life vic-to-ri-ous.
You, Lord,
A G D.C.
are King most glo-ri-ous.
2. We hear
3. You once
D Chorus A G D
The First, the Last, the Liv-ing One. Lord, by

A
G
D
Bm
Your word we o - ver-come. We live our lives to You
G
A
a-lone: the First, the Last, the Liv - ing One.
D
1.
D.S.
2.
D.C.
You, Lord,
4. You once

2. We hear Your voice, we come to You:
The First, the Last, the Living One.
We will obey and follow You:
The First, the Last, the Living One.

3./4. You once were dead, but now You live:
The First, the Last, the Living One.
You hold the keys of death and hell:
The First, the Last, the Living One.

1269. Here am I, a sinner free

Capo 3 (G)

Ps 8:4; 23:1; Is 9:6; Zeph 3:17; Mk 1:42; Lk 4:18; 15:6; Gal 5:13; 1 Jn 1:7

With energy
Matt Redman
Verse
B♭(G)
1. Here am I, a sinner free,
Holy King upon the throne, You've
pardoned by Your majesty, Your
made this heart Your very own. I
E♭2(C)
B♭(G)
love has led me into liberty.
feel like the leper who's been healed.
Chorus
E♭2(C)
Lost and dirty, yet You found me:
B♭/D(G)
stained by sin but You have cleansed me,

Cm7(Am)
B♭(G)
can it be I'm pre - cious in Your sight?
E♭2(C)
B♭/D(G)
What is man, and who am I? A child of God, my Fa - ther's pride.
Cm7(Am)
Cm/F(Am)
B♭(G)
what a joy to be the Lord's de - light.

2. I have known a love so sweet,
A saving love that brings relief,
A healing love that makes the blind eye see.
King of Love and Prince of Peace,
Your Shepherd's love is tending me,
A love that satisfies my deepest needs.

1270. Here I am, O God

(Complete)

Ps 123:1; 2 Cor 5:7; Heb 12:2

Andrew Ulugia

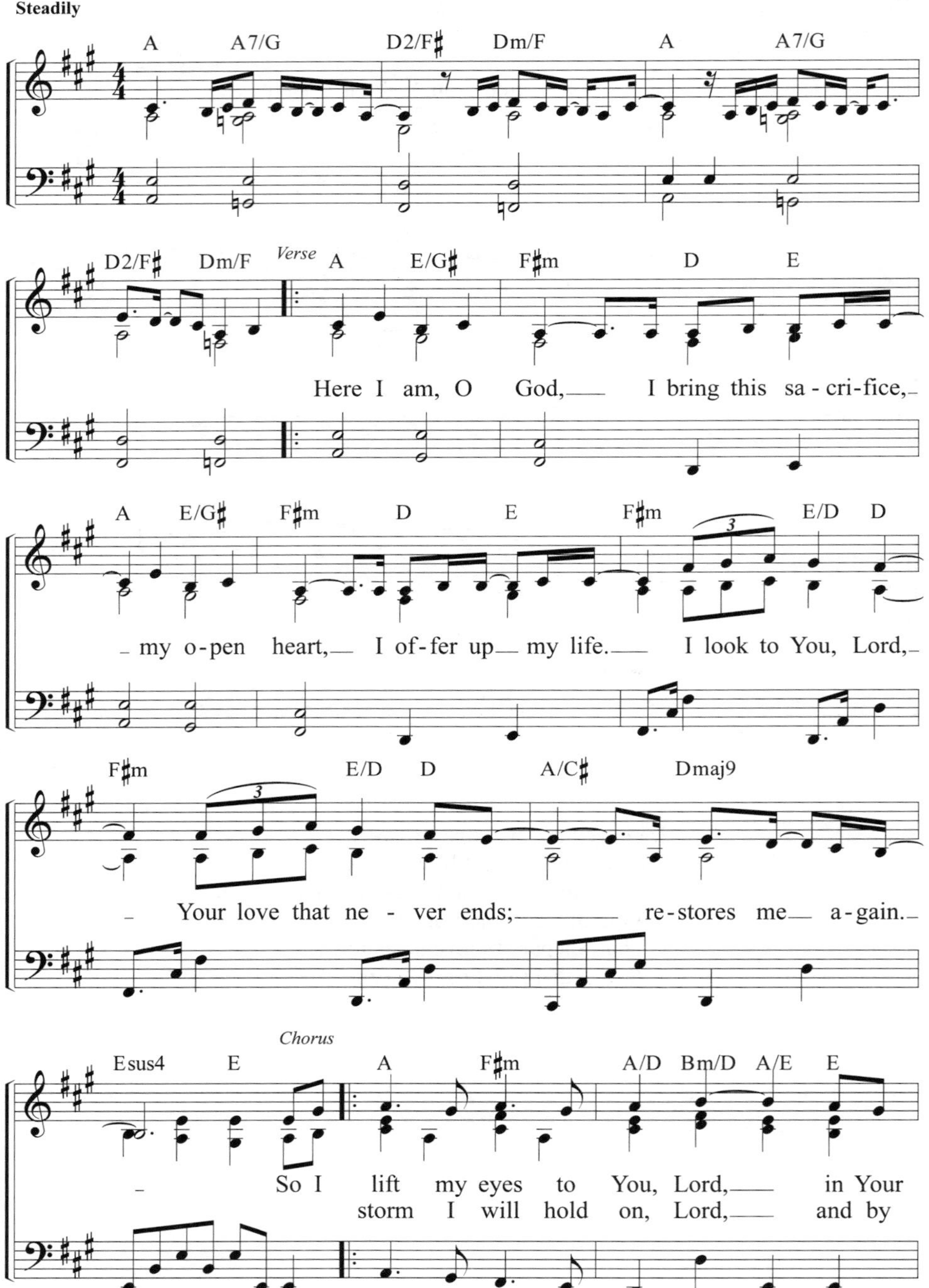
Steadily
A A7/G D2/F♯ Dm/F A A7/G
D2/F♯ Dm/F Verse A E/G♯ F♯m D E
Here I am, O God, I bring this sa-cri-fice,
A E/G♯ F♯m D E F♯m E/D D
my o-pen heart, I of-fer up my life. I look to You, Lord,
F♯m E/D D A/C♯ Dmaj9
Your love that ne - ver ends; re-stores me a-gain.
Esus4 E Chorus A F♯m A/D Bm/D A/E E
So I lift my eyes to You, Lord, in Your
storm I will hold on, Lord, and by

A F♯m A/D Bm/D A/E Fdim
strength will I break through, Lord. Touch me
faith I will walk on, Lord, then I'll
F♯m E/G♯ A A/C♯ D A/C♯
now, let Your love fall down on me. I
see be - yond my Cal - va - ry one day, and
1. Bm7 A/C♯ D Esus4 E
know Your love di - spels all my fears. Through the
2. Bm7 D/E E A
I will be com - plete in You.

1271. Here I am waiting

(Eagles' wings)

Ps 17:8; 42:1; Is 40:31; Jn 15:4; 20:22

With feeling

Reuben Morgan

Am7 Am/C Dsus4 D G G/B C G/B
Here I am wait - ing, a - bide in me I pray,
Am7 Dsus4 D G C/G G
here I am long - ing for You.
Am7 Am7/C Dsus4 D G G/B C G/B
Hide me in Your love, bring me to my knees,
Am7 Dsus4 D G C/D D C/D
may I know Je - sus more and more.

G C/G G C G/B Am7 Am7/C
Come, live in me all my life, take o -
Dsus4 D D/F♯ G C/G G C G/B
ver. Come, breathe in me and I will rise
Am7
1. G/D D
2. G/D D G
on ea - gles' wings. ea - gles' wings.

1272. Here in Your arms

Jn 10:28

With feeling
Ken Riley
Verse
C2
F/C
mf
1. Here in Your arms, I am lost
2. Here, face to face, I am lost
Dm
G
C2
in Your love.
in praise.
Hold - ing me close, ne - ver let
Love's hun - ger grows, burn - ing stron -
Dm
G7
Am
Chorus
me fall.
ger still.
f
I
F
C
G
will wor - ship You, I

F C G E
will wor - ship You, oh I, I
Am F Fm C
will wor - ship You, Lord.
F/C C

Wake up, O sleeper, rise from the dead, and Christ will shine on you.

EPHESIANS 5:14

1273. Here I stand

Rev 3:20

Moderately

Words: Rev 3.20
Paraphrase & Music: John L. Bell

Em C D D/G C F♯7 B
Here I stand at the door and knock, and knock.
Here I stand at the door and knock, and
Em C D D/G Am7 B7 Em
I will come and dine with those who ask me in.
knock. I will dine with those who ask me in.

1274. Here I stand
(In love with God)

Ps 89:1; Jn 10:3; Heb 4:16; 10:20

James Gregory

With energy
Verse
C2
1. Here I stand, long-ing to meet with God; I have
am, fall-ing be-fore Your throne, for my
come, bring-ing a grate - ful heart. And I will
King, lay-ing down a - ny crown, and I will
Am11
Dsus4
sing of this a-maz - ing love a - gain.
sing of this a-maz - ing love a - gain.
1.
D
D.C.
2. Here I
2.
D
Chorus
C2
I am in love with God,
G
C2
G
I am in love with God, I

SoF3

Am7
Em7
hear You call my name, I give my heart a - gain.
I'm on my knees a - gain.
Last time to Coda
Dsus4
1. D
D.S.
I am in love
2. D
D.C.
2. Here I
3. D
Bridge
C2
D
C/E
You have won my heart and I can say that I could find no
D/F#
Am11
C2
o - ther way. Now I am Yours, and here I'll stay to
D Dsus4
D
D.S. al Coda
of - fer up this praise. I am in love

Coda
D
C6
G/B
I'm in love with
1.
C2
G2/B
You.
Last time
Am11
G
You.

2. Here I am before Your throne of grace,
I can come, for You have made a way,
And I'll sing of this amazing love again.
Here I am, so overwhelmed by You;
I come near, for I belong to You,
And I'll sing of this amazing love again.

1275. Here I wait beneath the cross

Ps 134:2; Jn 4:24; 19:25; Acts 4:12; Heb 13:8; 17:14; 19:16

Capo 1 (D)

With quiet intensity

Tim Sherrington

Verse
E♭(D)
A♭maj7/C (Gmaj7)
1. Here I wait be-neath the cross,
2. Here I come to give my all, my
A♭2(G2)
(Asus4) B♭sus4
B♭(A)
(Asus4) B♭sus4
rest - ing in the pre-sence of Your love.
hands reach up in ho-ly praise to You.
E♭(D)
A♭maj7/C (Gmaj7)
Here I wait to know Your heart, as I
Here I cast all chains a - side to
A♭2(G2)
(Asus4) B♭sus4
B♭(A)
(Asus4) B♭sus4
wor-ship You in spi-rit and in truth. For

A♭(G)
E♭2/G (D2)
A♭(G)
You are my God,
You are my King,
E♭2/G (D2)
A♭/C(G)
A♭(G)
You re - veal deep with - in to my ve - ry soul.
(Asus4)
B♭sus4
B♭(A)
(Asus4)
B♭sus4
B♭(A)
E♭2/G (D2)
Chorus
For You a - lone are Je -
A♭2(G2)
E♭2/G (D2)
sus, there's no o - ther name, Je -
A♭2(G2)
Cm(Bm)
B♭sus4(Asus4)
sus, e - ter - nal - ly the same, Je - sus, the King of kings.

A♭(G)
E♭2/G(D2)
Je -
A♭(G)
E♭2/G (D2)
sus, Re - deem - er, Sa - viour, Friend, Je -
A♭(G)
Cm(Bm)
B♭sus4(Asus4)
sus, faith-ful till the end, Je - sus, the King of kings.
D.C.
To end
A♭(G)
E♭2(D2)

1276. Hey Lord, O Lord

Kevin Prosch

Lively
E/G♯
Hey, Lord,
A
O, Lord,
Leader:
Response: Hey, Lord,
O, Lord,
E/G♯
Hey, Lord,
B/D♯
Hey, Lord,
You know what we need.
E/G♯
Hey, Lord,
A
O, Lord,
Hey, Lord,
O, Lord,
E/G♯
Hey, Lord,
B
E
Hey, Lord,
You know what we need.
Chorus
E
A
Na na na na na na na na na na na na na na

SoF3

Last time to Coda
E
B
E
Je - sus,
na na na na na na na na.
Je - sus,
A
You're the One,
E
You set my heart
on
You're the One,
You set my heart
B
fi-re.
E
Je-sus,
A
You're the One,
You
on fi-re.
Je-sus,
You're the One,
E
set my heart
B
D.S. al Coda
You set my heart on fi - re.
Coda
B
E
You know what we need!

1277. Holy, holy

Ps 40:2; Lk 24:3;
Jn 14:6; 8:12; 8:58; Rev 4:8-11; 5:12

Robin Mark

Simply
(v.2)
(v.3)
D
Bm7
G
(v.3)
1. Ho-ly, ho - ly, ho-ly, ho - ly is the Lord God al-migh-
Asus4
D
Bm7
ty. Ho-ly, ho - ly, ho-ly, ho - ly is the song
G
Asus4
G
a-round the throne. Where the an - gels and the el-
Bm7
G
D/F♯
Asus4
ders ga - ther there in sweet as-sem - bly sing-ing ho-
D
Bm7
G2
G/A
(Fine)
D
1.
ly, sing-ing ho - ly is the Lord our God. 2. Wor-thy wor -

SoF3

2.
Chorus
Bm
F♯m7
Bm
The Way, the Truth, the Life, the Light,
F♯m7
Bm
F♯m7
A
the King, the Great I AM.
Bm
F♯m7
Bm
My life, my all, my e - v'ry breath,
F♯m7
Bm
F♯m7
Asus4
A
D.S. al fine
the Rock on which I stand.
3. Oh Je

2. Worthy, worthy, worthy, worthy
Is the Lamb who was slain for me.
Worthy, worthy, worthy, worthy
Is the song within my heart.
I could choose to spend eternity
With this my sole refrain:
Singing worthy, singing worthy
Is the Lord our God.

3. Oh Jesus, oh Jesus,
How You suffered and died for us.
Oh Jesus, oh Jesus,
But that tomb is empty now.
And I long to gaze upon Your throne
And all Your risen glory:
Singing Jesus, singing Jesus
Is the Lord of all.

The twenty-four elders and the four living creatures fell down and worshipped God, who was seated on the throne. And they cried: "Amen, Hallelujah!"

REVELATION 19:4

1278. Holy, holy

Rev 4:8; 5:6, 12

Dave Bilbrough

Steadily
E A B E A
Ho - ly, ho - ly is the Lord our God;
D E A B C♯m
who was and is and is to come, and
A B E (Fine) A
e - ver - more shall be. With a grate - ful heart I will
B E A B
give my praise to the Lamb up - on the throne;
E A B C♯m A B E D.C. al fine
King of a - ges, Lord of life, ex - al - ted o - ver all.

SoF3

1279. Holy, holy are You, Lord

(All the heavens)

Ps 72:19; 117:1; Jn 17:23-24

Reuben Morgan

Gently
C G/B F/A C/G
Ho - ly, ho - ly are You, Lord, the
F C/E Dm7 C G/B C G/B
whole earth is filled with Your glo - ry. Let the na - tions
F/A C/G F C/G Esus4 E
rise to give ho - nour and praise to Your name.
Am D/F♯ G G/F C/E C C/E F C/E Dm7
Let Your face shine on us, and the world will know You
Gsus4 G C Am
live. All the hea - vens shout Your praise,

F
Dm7
G
Em
beau - ti-ful is our God. The u - ni - verse will sing
Am
G
F
Am/G
G
1.
F/A
G/B
F/C
C
F
hal - le - lu - jah to You, our King.
Gsus4
G
2.
C

1280. Holy, holy, God Almighty

(Holy)

Rev 4:8, 11; 5:12; 7:12; 15:3

Brenton Brown

With drive

D
Ho - ly, ho - ly, God Al - migh - ty,
God of glo - ry, You're so wor - thy,
1.
Dmaj7
who was and is to come.
2. Last time to Coda
All the saints bow
D
down.
Chorus
Ho - ly is Your name
A
G2
in all the earth.
D
Right - eous are Your ways,
A
G2
so mer - ci - ful.

D
A
G2
E - v'ry - thing You've done is just and true.
D
G
A
1.3.5.
D
Ho - ly, ho - ly God are You. Ho - ly, ho -
3rd time to Bridge
G
A
D(no3rd)
- ly God are You.
D.C.
2.4.
D
D.S.
You. Ho - ly is Your name.
Bridge
Bm
A
G
All bless - ing, all ho - nour be - longs to You.

D
Dsus4
D
Bm
A
All pow - er, all wis-dom is
1.
D
Dsus4
D
Yours.
2.
D
Dsus4
Yours.
D
D.S.
Ho-ly is Your name
Coda
Dmaj7
down.
D
God of glo - ry, You're so wor - thy, all the saints bow
1.2.3.
down.
4.
down.

1281. Holy, holy, holy

Rev 4:8

Tune: SANTO, SANTO

Argentinian trad.
Arr. Geoff Weaver

C G Am F G/F
Ho - ly, ho - ly, ho - ly, my heart, my heart a -
F/C C F G C Am
dores You! My heart is glad to say the words:
Dm7 G7 C
You are ho - ly, Lord.

Santo, santo, santo
Mi corazón adora!
Mi corazón te sabe decir:
Santo eres Señor.

1282.

Holy, holy, holy Lord

(Forgiven)

2 Chron 20:6; Jer 16:21; Rom 3:25; 1 Cor 13:12; Eph 2:8, 19; 3:6; Phil 3:20; 1 Jn 2:2; Rev 4:8

Capo 1 (D)

Keith Getty, Emma Vardy & Noel Robinson

Hymn style

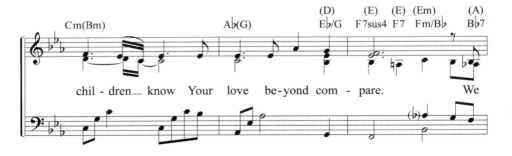

Verse
E♭2(D) Fm7(Em) Gm7(F♯m) Cm7(Bm) Fm7(Em) B♭(A)
1. Ho - ly, ho - ly, ho - ly Lord, God of po-wer and
E♭(D) (Em) Fm7(+4) B♭7(A) E♭(D) Fm7(Em) Gm7(F♯m) Cm7(Bm)
might. Earth and hea - ven wor - ship You, Your
F7sus4(E) F7(E) B♭7sus4(A) B♭(A) Dm7(C♯m) G(F♯)
ma - je-sty so bright. Yet we, Your fal - len
Cm(Bm) A♭(G) (D) E♭/G (E) F7sus4 (E) F7 (Em) Fm/B♭ (A) B♭7
chil - dren know Your love be-yond com - pare. We

E♭2(D) (Em) Fm7(+4) Gm7(F♯m) Cm7(Bm) Fm7(Em) (G) A♭/B♭ B♭7(A)
lift our hands, sur - ren - der to grace so un - de -
E♭sus4(D) E♭(D)
Chorus
B♭m7(Am) (D) E♭13 E♭7
served. Be - fore You Lord, for - gi - ven, we
A♭2(G) Adim(G♯dim) E♭2(D) Cm7(Bm) A♭maj7(G) (G) A♭/B♭ B♭7(A)
bow be-fore Your throne. At Your cross, we
G7(F♯) Cm7(Bm) E♭/F(D) F7(E) A♭/B♭(G) B♭7(A)
find in You our righ - teous-ness re-stored. Be-
E♭(D) B♭m7(Am) (D) E♭13 E♭7 A♭2(G) G7(F♯)
fore You, Lord, for - gi - ven, we stand in Your great

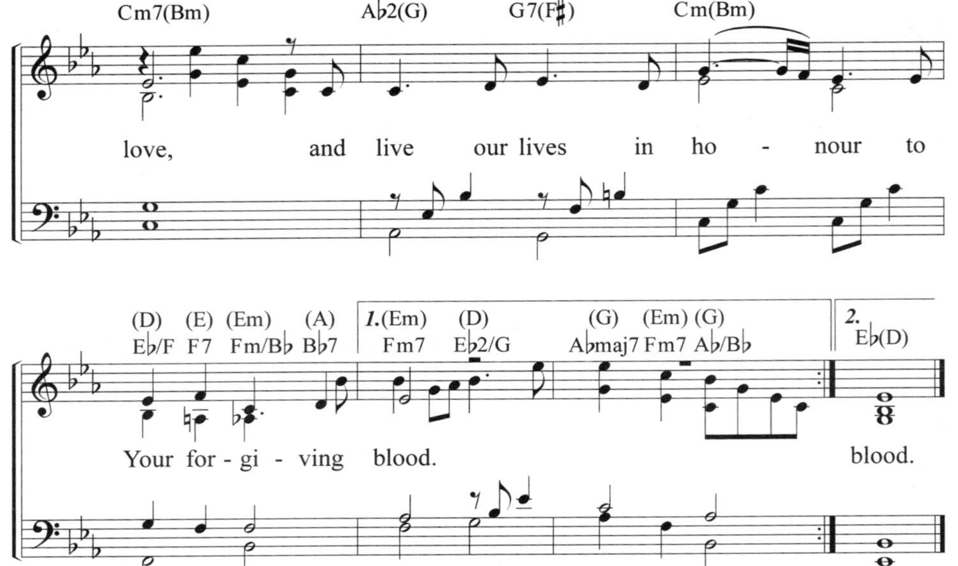
Cm7(Bm) Ab2(G) G7(F#) Cm(Bm)
love, and live our lives in ho - nour to
(D) (E) (Em) (A) 1.(Em) (D) (G) (Em) (G) 2.
Eb/F F7 Fm/Bb Bb7 Fm7 Eb2/G Abmaj7 Fm7 Ab/Bb Eb(D)
Your for - gi - ving blood. blood.

2. Living in Your presence, Lord,
Sin and guilt atoned;
Citizens of heaven,
Heirs unto Your throne.
To be with You in glory,
To see You face to face,
At last home with the Father,
Our holy dwelling place.

To Him who is able to keep you from falling and to present you before His glorious presence without fault and with great joy – to the only God our Saviour be glory, majesty, power and authority, through Jesus Christ our Lord, before all ages, now and for evermore! Amen.

JUDE: 24-25

1283. Holy One

Is 53:5; Mt 18:33; Jn 20:22

Capo 2 (D)
Steadily
Andrew Ulugia
Verse
E(D) F♯m(Em) B/D♯(A) E(D) F♯m(Em) B/D♯(A)
1. Ho - ly One, right - eous King,
Bro - ken One, bruised for me,
E(D) F♯m(Em) B/D♯(A) E(D) A/C♯(G) A(G) B(A) E(D)
mer - ci - ful You are: mer - ci - ful I'll be.
in Your death, O Lord, You have set me free.
1.,3. (Fine)
2. Chorus
B/D♯(A) A/C♯(G)
Be - cause Your Fa - ther loved me so,
E(D) Esus4(D) E(D) F♯m(Em) E/G♯(D) B/D♯(A)
You came to me,
A/C♯(G) G♯/B♯(F♯) G♯(F♯) C♯m(Bm)
Lord Je - sus, so that I would know

A(G)
B/A(A)
G♯m(F♯m)
love un-con-di - tion-al and life e - ter - nal,
A2(G) E/G♯(D)
F♯m(Em) E(D)
D(C)
Bsus4(A)
O my Lord, my God, my all.
B(A)
D.C.

2. Risen One, Majesty,
Restoration, come
Breathe new life in me.
(Repeat)

Blessed are those who hunger and thirst for righteousness, for they will be filled.

MATTHEW 5:6

1284. Holy Spirit, how I love You

Jn 14:16, 26; 15:15; Rom 8:26; Phil 4:7

Peter Brooks, Stuart Townend & Kate Simmonds

Slowly, with feeling
D D/F♯ G A
Ho - ly Spi - rit, how I love You; Ho - ly Spi - rit, flood my
D D/F♯ G
soul. Ho - ly Spi - rit, take me o - ver;
A D (Fine) G
Ho - ly Spi - rit, lead me on. You're the Strength that helps me in my
D G Em7 A D/F♯
weak - ness, You're the Friend who comes to walk be - side; You're the
D.C. al fine
G Bm Em Asus4 A
peace that pas - ses un - der - stand - ing, as You reign in my life.

1285. Holy Spirit, rain down

Capo 3 (D)

Joel 2:23, 28; Mal 3:10; 1 Cor 2:9

Russell Fragar

Gently

B♭/C(G) F(D) E♭/F(C) E♭/B♭(C)
Ho-ly Spi-rit, rain down, rain
B♭(G) Gm7(Em) F/A(D)
down. O Com-for-ter and Friend, how we
B♭maj7(G) Csus4(A) C(A) B♭/C(G) F(D)
need Your touch a-gain. Ho-ly Spi-rit, rain
E♭/F(C) E♭/B♭(C) B♭(G)
down, rain down. Let Your
F/C(D) A7/C♯(F♯)
pow-er fall, let Your voice be heard, come and

Dm(Bm)
Bbm6/Db(Gm)
F/C(D)
change our hearts, as we stand on Your word. Ho-ly Spi -
C(A)
Bb/F(G)
1.
F(D)
2.
F(D)
(Fine)
Bbmaj7(G)
rit, rain down.
No eye has seen,
A7(F#)
Dm7(Bm)
no ear has heard, no mind can know what
Cm7(Am)
(G#m7b5)
Bm7b5
Bbmaj7(G)
God has in store. So o-pen up hea - ven,
A7(F#)
Dm(Bm)
o-pen it wide o - ver Your church, and
1. Cm7(Am)
(G#m7b5)
Bm7b5
2. Bb/C(G)
D.C. al fine
o - ver our lives. o - ver our lives.

In the same way, let your light shine before men, that they may see your good deeds and praise your Father in heaven.

MATTHEW 5:16

1286 . Hope has found its home within me

(For this cause)

Capo 3 (D)

1 Cor 13:12; Phil 3:9

Joel Houston

Steadily
Dm7(Bm) Verse Bb2(G) F(D)
1. Hope has found its home with - in me,
Dm7(Bm) Bb2(G) F(D)
now that I've been found in You.
Dm7(Bm) Bb2(G) F(D)
Let all I am be all You want me to be,
Eb2(C) Bb2(G) F(D)
'cause all I want is more of You,
Eb2(C) Bb2(G) C2(A) Csus4(A)
all I want is more of You.

Chorus
F(D)
B♭2(G)
I'm living for this cause, I lay down my life
Dm7(Bm)
B♭2(G)
C(A) F(D)
into Your hands. I'm living for the truth,
B♭2(G)
Dm7(Bm)
Last time to Coda
the hope of the world, in You I'll stand.
1. B♭2(G)
Dm7(Bm) B♭2(G) F(D) Dm7(Bm) B♭2(G)
All I want is You.
F(D)
D.C.
2. 4.
B♭2(G)
3.
B♭2(G)
Bridge 1
All I want is You.

F(D)
C/E(A)
Dm7(Bm)
All I want is You.
1.
B♭2(G)
All I want is You.
2.
B♭2(G)
Bridge 2
F(D)
All I want is,
C/E(A)
Dm7(Bm)
B♭2(G)
B♭2(G)
all I want is You, Jesus.
D.C. al Coda
Coda
B♭2(G)
F(D)
All I want is You.
C/E(A)
Dm7(Bm)
1.
B♭2(G)
2.
B♭2(G)
All I want is You.
All I want is You.

2. Let Your presence fall upon us,
I want to see You face to face;
Let me live forever lost in Your love,
'Cause all I want is more of You,
All I want is more of You.

1287. Hover o'er me

(Fill me now)

Gen 1:2; Acts 2:4; Eph 5:18

Music: John R. Sweney (1837-99)

Verse freely building to chorus
Verse
D Em/D D G/D D G/D D Em/D D G/D
1. Ho - ver o'er, me Ho - ly Spi - rit, bathe my
D G/D D G/D D Asus4 A D Em/D D G/D
tremb - ling heart and brow; fill me with Thy
D G/D D Em/D D G/D Bm7 Asus4 A7sus4
hal - lowed pre - sence, come, O come and fill me
D A Chorus D
now. Fill me now, fill me now,
G D/F♯ D G/D D Asus4 A D Em/D
Je - sus, come and fill me now. Fill me

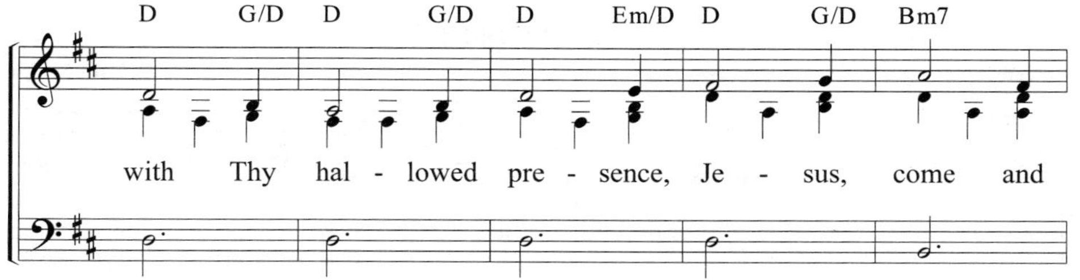
D G/D D G/D D Em/D D G/D Bm7
with Thy hal - lowed pre - sence, Je - sus, come and

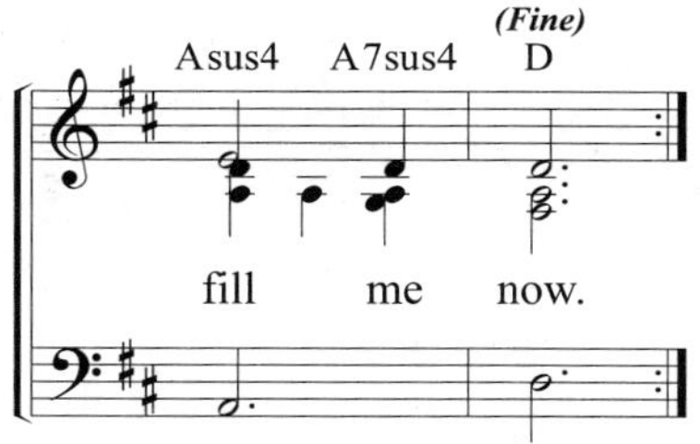
(Fine)
Asus4 A7sus4 D
fill me now.

2. Thou can fill me, gracious Spirit,
Though I cannot tell Thee how;
But I need Thee, greatly need Thee,
Come, O come and fill me now.

3. I am weakness, full of weakness,
At Thy sacred feet I bow;
Blest, divine, eternal Spirit,
Come with power, and fill me now.

Elwood R. Stokes (1815-95)

1288. How can I not praise You?

(Hallelujah)

Ps 8:3; 18:1, 3, 16

Steady 4

Lara Martin

Verse

G C2 D

1. How can I not praise You, when I con-si-der all
How can I not wor-ship when I con-si-der who

Bm7 Em7 C2 1. Am7

You've done? God of cre-a-tion, all suf-fi-
You are? You are my Ma-ster, the

D 2. Am7 C2 D

cient One. One who has my heart.

Chorus

G/B C2

Hal-le-lu-jah, praise the Lord,

D C2

O my soul. Hal-le-lu-jah, it is You
I am saved! Hal-le-lu-jah, free to praise

D
C2
G/B
Am7
– I a - dore. Hal - le - lu - jah, hal - le - lu - jah, hal -
– Your name. Hal - le - lu - jah, hal - le - lu - jah, hal -
C2
1. D
C2
2. D
le - lu - jah. Hal - le - lu - jah, I am saved!
le - lu - jah.
Cmaj7
Gsus2
Cmaj7
Gsus2
Cmaj7
Gsus2
D
D.C.
G

2. How can I not love You,
When Your love reached deep down to me?
Love so amazing, what a mystery.
How can I not give my all,
When You gave heaven's best to me?
Jesus, my treasure for all eternity.

1289. How can I repay You?

Gal 6:14; Eph 2:8-9

Geraldine Latty

With feeling
Intro
Am9
Em7addA
mp
(vv.2&3)
Verse
1. How can I repay You, Lord, for all You've done for me?
Nothing I can say or do will ever be enough.
Chorus
C
I will live for You, walking in
G
Your way,
Am7
lifting high Your name,
F
holding close

G6
C
G
— the cross. — Not in words — a - lone, — but in what — I do, — I will live
Am
Em/G
F
1.,2.
3.
my life — for — You.

2. Dear Lord, Your heart is drawing me,
A calling from Your throne.
And in my brokenness I come
And whisper to You, Lord.

3. It's not by works, but by Your grace,
I'll never earn Your love.
You loved me first, You'll love me last,
Your cross, my only hope.

1290. How good You have been to me

Capo 3 (G)

(How amazing)

Ex 20:3; Ps 119:140; 139:18; 145:13; Jn 10:3; 20:22

Rhythmically

Lara Martin

Verse

B♭(G) E♭2(C) B♭(G) E♭2(C)

1. How good You have been to me, for - e - ver

B♭(G) E♭2(C) B♭(G) E♭2(C) B♭(G) E♭2(C) B♭(G) E♭2(C)

faith - ful. How true are Your pro - mi - ses, ne - ver

B♭(G) E♭2(C) B♭(G) E♭(C) F(D) E♭(C)

sha - ken. You are the Light of my life,

F(D) Cm7(Am) B♭/D(G) E♭(C)

You are the rea - son I live.

Chorus B♭(G) F/A(D) Gm7(Em) E♭(C)

I live for You, I place no one a - bove You.

B♭(G) F/A(D) Gm7(Em) E♭(C)
I'll walk with You, always, always.
B♭(G) F/A(D) Gm7(Em)
To talk with You, and feel Your breath on my
E♭(C) Gm7(Em) Gsus2+4(Esus4) Gm(Em)
face, how amazing, how ama-
E♭(C) F(D) B♭(G) E♭2(C) B♭(G) E♭2(C) B♭(G) E♭2(C)
-zing You are!
1. B♭(G) E♭2(C)
2. How rich
2. B♭(G)

2. How rich is Your word, O Lord,
At work within me.
How soft is Your voice I hear,
That gently calls me.
Each day I wake to Your love;
I know that I am blessed of God.

1291. How great are You, Lord

Ps 36:5, 7; 135:5

Lynn DeShazo

Thoughtfully

Verse

C / Dm7 / F / G/B / Csus2 / G / C / Dm7 / F / G / C *(Fine)*

How great are You, Lord,
how great is Your mercy,
how great are the things that You have done for me.
How great are You, Lord,
Your loving kindness is filling my heart as I sing,
how great are You, Lord.

Chorus
G/B
Am
F
How great is Your love, it reach - es to the hea - vens;
C
G/B
Am
how great is the heart that sought
F
C/E
Dm7
C
G/B
D.C.
and res - cued me.
How great are You, Lord,

1292. How shall I find?

(You are the strength in my heart)

Zech 4:6; Phil 4:13

Capo 1 (G)

Neil Bennetts

Simply

Verse
Ab(G) Db(C) Ab(G)
1. How shall I find my place of rest, true wis-dom and the
Db(C) Bbm(Am) Bbm/Ab (Am) Eb/G(D)
hand of God? Not by my own un-der-stand-ing,
Bbm(Am) Bbm/Ab (Am) 1. Eb(D) 2.3. Eb(D)
but by Your Spi-rit in me. 2. How For
Chorus
Ab(G) Db(C) Eb(D)
You are the strength in my heart, so
Ab(G) Db(C) Eb(D)
faith-ful when o-ther loves fail me. For

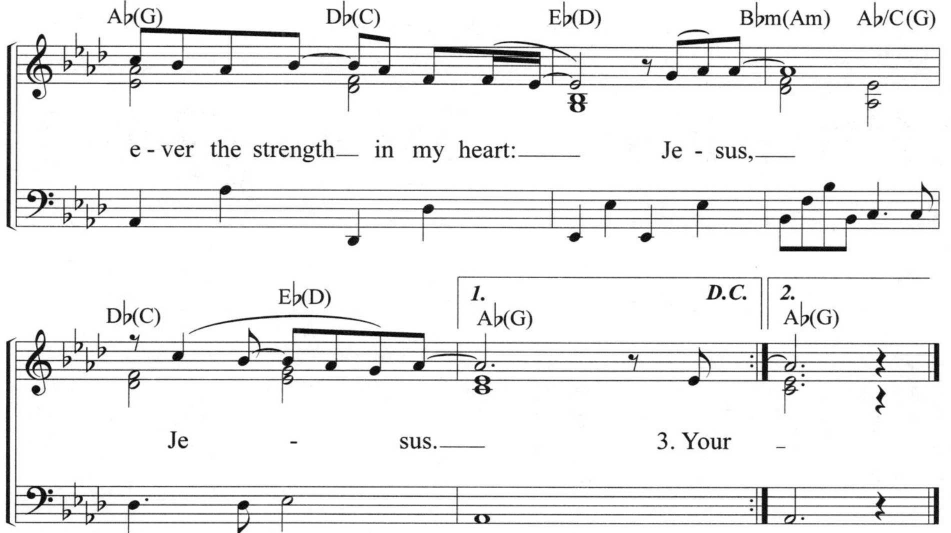
A♭(G)
D♭(C)
E♭(D)
B♭m(Am)
A♭/C(G)
e - ver the strength in my heart: Je - sus,
D♭(C)
E♭(D)
1.
D.C.
2.
A♭(G)
A♭(G)
Je - sus. 3. Your

2. How shall I know the kind of love
   That cannot fade, that cannot fail?
   Not from this world's empty treasure,
   But by the promise of God.

3. Your river flows, it covers me,
   Its blessing fills my life always,
   And sets my eyes on Your beauty
   And fills my heart with a song.

1293. # Hungry, I come to You

(Falling on my knees)

Lk 6:21; 15:20; Rom 12:1

Gently
Kathryn Scott
Verse
C Am7
1.3. Hun - gry, I come to You, for I know
G F C
You sa - tis - fy. I am emp - ty, but
Am7 G F
I know Your love does not run dry. So I
G F/A G/B
wait for You, so I wait for You.
F
Chorus
C Fmaj7
I'm fall - ing on my knees, of - fer-

C
Fmaj7
C
3
- ing all of me.
Je - sus, You're all this heart

Last time to Coda
Fmaj7
1.2.
C
Am7
G
F2
D.C.
is liv - ing for.

3.
C
F
D.S.
I'm fall
Coda
C

2. Broken, I run to You,
For Your arms are open wide;
I am weary, but I know
Your touch restores my life.
So I wait for You,
So I wait for You.

1294. I am amazed

(Your grace covers me)

Is 53:4; Eph 2:8; 1 Jn 3:5

Lara Martin

Slowly

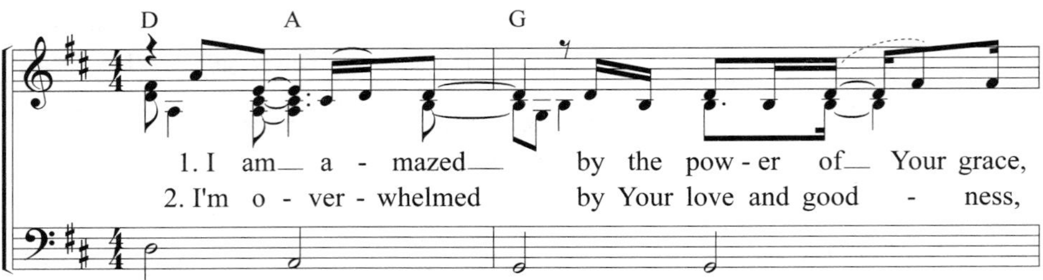
D A G
1. I am a - mazed by the pow - er of Your grace,
2. I'm o - ver - whelmed by Your love and good - ness,

D A G
I am a - mazed that You took my sin and shame;
I'm o - ver - whelmed that You took my bro - ken - ness:

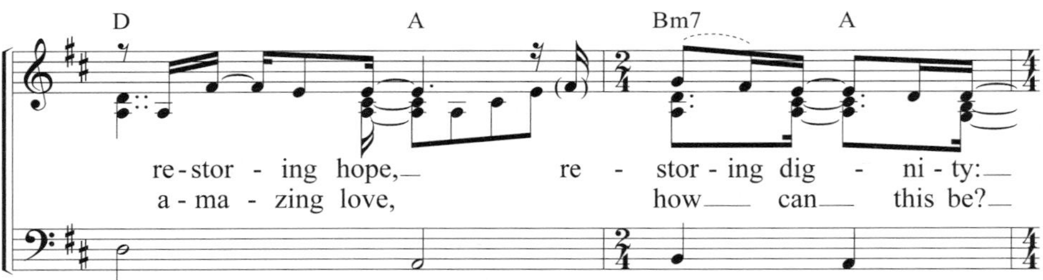
D A Bm7 A
re - stor - ing hope, re - stor - ing dig - ni - ty:
a - ma - zing love, how can this be?

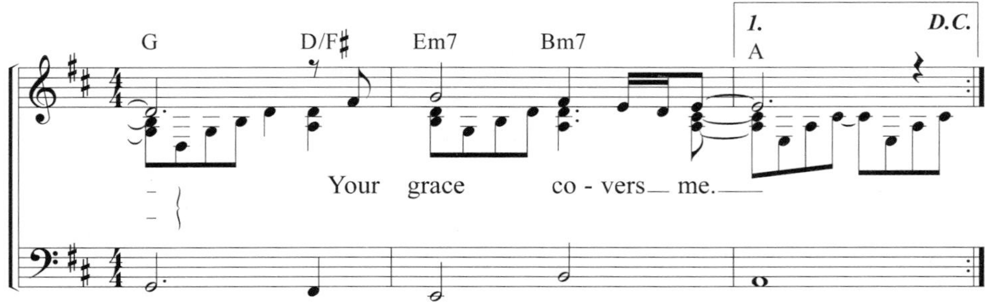
G D/F♯ Em7 Bm7 1. A D.C.
Your grace co - vers me.

2.
A
D/F♯
G
D
G
A
Your grace co - vers me, oh.
Chorus
D
A
G2
D
A
Sav - ing grace, wash-ing o - ver me; sav - ing grace,
G2
D
A
that made a way for me: I was lost un -
Bm7
A
G
A
til You res - cued me, Your grace co -
D
A
Gsus2
D
A
(Fine)
Gsus2
vers me.

1295. I am helplessly in love with You

(I can only give my heart)

Song 2:5; 7:10; Mt 7:7; Lk 15:20

Worshipfully

Sue Rinaldi, Caroline Bonnett & Steve Bassett

E
Verse
F♯m/E
E
1. I am help - less-ly in love with You. I am lost
F♯m/E
E
in some-thing pre - cious. I am drown-
A
E
ing in the sea of You. I am found
A
F♯m7
Bridge
a - mongst Your trea - sures. And I don't know why You
B7sus4
F♯m7
give Your-self, And I can't ex - plain why

B7sus4
A
C♯m7
You should care. When all hea - ven sings Your glo - ry, I'm
F♯m7
Bsus4
B
hum - bled that You hear my pray'r.
Chorus
E
B
F♯m
E
B
I can on - ly give my heart to You, I can on - ly give my
F♯m
E
B
F♯m
heart. I can on - ly give my heart to You,
E
B
F♯m
Last time to Coda
I can on - ly give my heart.

A
F♯m7
A
It's like brea-thing strange new air, walk-ing on some
F♯m
A
dis-tant moon. I'll sing a song from the
F♯m
A/B
B
depths of my soul: seek-ing, find-ing, com-ing home.
A/B
B
D.C. al Coda
Coda
E
Seek-ing, find-ing, com-ing home.

2. I am helplessly devoted to You;
I am scorched by strange new fire.
I am running deeper into You.
I am high upon the wire.

1296. I am the one with the unclean lips

(Wash me clean)

Ps 18:2; 51:7; Is 6:5; Mt 18:34; Lk 17:17

Brian Houston

Rhythmically
G
Verse
1. I am the one with the un - clean lips,
C
I am the one whose mind is ja-ded.
G
I am the one with the im - pure heart,
C
and all my in - no-cence has fa-ded.
Chorus
Am
Wash me
C
G
clean in Your ri-ver of mer-cy.

D
C
G
Re-store my soul by a clear blue stream, yeah.
Am
G/B
C
G
Wash me clean in Your ri-ver of mer-cy,
Last time to Coda
Am
C
re-store my soul, re-new me a-gain.
G
(To v2)
D
You are the Lord who is my
C
D
C
for-tress, You are the Lord who is my hope.

D
C
You are the Lord who is my re-fuge,
1st time D.C.
2nd time D.S. al Coda
Coda
D
C
G
the on-ly safe place for my soul. (So)

2. I am the one whose walk is faithless,
I am the one who walks away.
I am the one whose debts are many
And I am the one who cannot pay.

1297. I behold Your power and glory
(Irresistible)

1 Chron 16:29; Lam 3:22-23

Moderately

Darlene Zschech

Verse
A G A
I be-hold Your pow'r and glo-ry, bring an off-'ring,
G Em7 D/F♯ G
come be-fore You; wor-ship You, Lord, in the
Em7 D/F♯ 1. A 2. A Chorus D
beau-ty of Your ho-li-ness. When-e-ver I
G2 Bm7 A/C♯ D
call, You're there, Re-deem-er and Friend; che-rished be-
G2 Bm7 A/C♯ D
yond all words, this love ne-ver ends.

F2
B♭maj7
C
Morn-ing by morn - ing Your mer-cy a-wa - kens my soul.
D
G2
I lift up my eyes to see the
Bm7
A/C♯
D
G2
won-ders of hea - ven o-pen-ing o-ver me, Your
Bm7
A/C♯
D
F2
good-ness a - bounds; You've tak-en my breath a - way with Your
B♭maj7
C
D
ir - re - sis - ti - ble love.

1298. I believe

Jn 8:32; 14:6; 15:4

James Taylor

Steadily
Verse
G
D/F♯
I be - lieve in ev 'ry - thing You do, all You
some-thing in my life great - er
Em7
A7
have to say. I've come to re - a - lise You're the on -
than be - fore, Your truth has set me free and I love
Csus2
D
ly way, oh I be-lieve in You.
You, Lord,
Csus2
1.
2. 3.
Chorus
I've re-ceived Let the an -
Em7
D/F♯
G
Csus2
gels sing of the Lord's great love,

G
G/F♯
Em7
well, it's shin - ing down like the heav'ns
D/F♯
G
Csus2
G
G/F♯
a - bove.
Let the na -
Em7
D/F♯
C
G/B
tions bow to the liv - ing God and know Your
D
NC
1.
G
Csus2
G
Csus2
truth, I be - lieve in You.
G
Csus2
G
Csus2
2. 3.
G
I be - lieve

G2
G
I be-lieve, I be-lieve, I be-lieve,
D/F♯
Em7
1.2.3.
D/F♯
I be-lieve in You.
I be-lieve,
4.
D/F♯
Last time to Coda
G
Csus2
G
Csus2
G
Csus2
G
G/F♯
D.S.
Coda
G
Let the an -

For God so loved the world that he gave his one and only Son, that whoever believes in him shall not perish but have eternal life.

JOHN 3:16

1299. I believe in God the Father

(Apostles' Creed)

Gen 1:1; Jn 1:10; Acts 2:32-33; 1 Cor 15:3-4, 21-23, 28; Phil 2:8-11; 1 Thess 4:16; Heb 1:3; 2:10; 1 Pet 4:5; 1 Jn 2:12; Jude 14-15

Steadily

Stuart Townend
& Keith Getty

A E F♯m/E E B B/D♯
1. I be - lieve in God the Fa - ther, Ma-ker of heav'n and
E A E F♯m/E E C♯m
earth. I be - lieve in Christ the Sa - viour, Lord of
B B/D♯ E E/G♯ A E/G♯
all, Son of God. Born to Ma - ry, lived and
E/B B E/G♯ A E/G♯ Bsus4 B A
suf - fered at the hands of those He'd made. Cru-ci-

E
F♯m/E
E
B
B/D♯
fied,— was dead and bu - ried, and de - scen - ded to the
E
G♯/B♯
C♯m
F♯/A♯
B
E/G♯
A
F♯m7
E
grave.

2. I believe that Jesus rose again,
 And ascended into heaven
 Where He sits with God the Father,
 And will come to judge all men.
 I believe in God the Spirit,
 In His church that stands forgiven;
 Resurrection of the body,
 And eternal life to come.

1300. I call on You, Almighty Lord

Ps 40:1; Mt 28:20; Jn 9:25; Eph 5:8; 1 Pet 2:9; Rev 5:11-12

Simply

Johnny Parks

Chorus

E E/D♯

I call on You,___ Al - migh - ty Lord;___ I

wor ship You,___ Al - migh - ty Lord;___ I

A2/C♯ **1.** E/D♯ **2.** E/D♯ ***To Coda***

call on You,__ Al-migh-ty Lord.___ I ___ 1. I

wor-ship You,__ Al-migh-ty Lord._

Verse E E/D♯

come to You__ and stand be-fore__ Your___ throne.___ I__

A2/C♯ E/D♯

lift my voice in wor-ship here once___ more.______ You

E E/D♯

turned the dark - ness in me in - to___ light.___ You

A2/C♯
E/D♯
took my blin - ded soul and gave me sight. As I
E
E/D♯
sank down to the depths You heard my cry, You
A2/C♯
E/D♯
lif - ted me and taught me how to fly. You
E
E/D♯
pro - mised me You're al - ways here to stay, so
A2/C♯
Last time D.S. al Coda
E/D♯
as I stand be-fore You, Lord, I want to say. I
Coda
E

2. The heavenly host are captured by the love
Of the One who laid His life down at the cross.
We lift the name of Jesus to the skies,
So all might see and know that there is life.
And where there's hatred let me bring Your love.
And where there's sorrow let me bring Your joy.
As I stand before You, will You lift Your face
And bring resurrection power to this place?

"No eye has seen, no ear has heard, no mind has conceived what God has prepared for those who love Him"

1 CORINTHIANS 2:9

1301. I can do all things

Phil 4:13

Jim Bailey

Brightly
Chorus
G D/F♯ Em
1.
C D
I can do all, (all!) all, (all!) all things through Christ who streng-thens me.
G D
2.
C D
(Fine)
G
Verse
D
I can do Christ who streng-thens me.
1. Go to school:
Em C
(vv 2&3.)
D B7
(vv 2&3.)
all things. O-bey the rules: all things. Keep my cool:
Em C D
D.S. al fine
all things through Christ who streng - thens me. I can do

2. Make new friends: all things.
   Give and lend: all things.
   Make amends: all things
   Through Christ who strengthens me.

3. Pray and sing: all things.
   Love our King: all things.
   Everything: all things
   Through Christ who strengthens me.

1302. I can feel Your arms surrounding

Deut 33:27

Ken Riley

Gently

Verse
D
A
G
I can feel Your arms sur-round-ing, trea-sur-ing my
Lead me to Your place of won-der, show-er me with
Bm
G
D
soul. Draw me e-ver clos-er in-to Your
grace. Ho-ly God, for-give my un-right-eous
Em7
1.
F♯ F♯7
2.
F♯ F♯sus4 F♯7
love, in-to Your love. Oh I
ways, un-right-eous ways.
Chorus
Bm
A G
D/F♯
love You, Lord, all I am is Yours, as Your

Em7
F♯
F♯7 F♯sus4 F♯7
mer - cy pours in - to my heart. You're my
Bm
A G
D/F♯ Em7
faith - ful King, o - ver e - v'ry - thing, hear my spi - rit sing
Asus4 A
A
3
D Dsus4
D Dsus2
(Fine)
that Je - sus is Lord.

1303. I come as I am
(Closer)

Rom 8:38-39; Jas 4:8

Capo 3 (D)

Worshipfully

Ken Riley

Intro
F2(D)
F2♭5(D)
B♭/F(G)
1.
F2(D)
mp
2.
F2(D)
Verse
F2(D)
F2♭5(D)
1. I come as I am, baring all
B♭/F(G)
F2(D)
of my shame. Surround me with love
F2♭5(D)
B♭/F(G)
F2(D)
and ac-cep - tance a-gain.
Chorus
B♭(G)
C7sus4(A)
F2(D)
Come clo - ser, Lord,

B♭(G)
C7sus4(A)
F2(D)
F/E♭(D)
come and re-store;
B♭/D(G)
D♭(B♭)
C7sus4(A)
F2(D)
To Coda
1.
F2♭5(D)
come clo - ser, Lord.
B♭/F(G)
F2(D)
2.
F2(D)
D.S. al Coda
Coda
F2(D)
rit.

2. Nothing I bring
Is too great to forgive,
Though each time Your grace
Is betrayed by my sin.

1304.
I come running
(Only You)
Capo 1 (D)
With pace
Ex 20:3; Ps 42:2; 143:1, 6; Jn 4:14
Paul Oakley
E♭(D) D♭(C) A♭(G)
mf 1. I come run-ning to You, Fa - ther,
try - ing to find a se - cret place with You.
My soul cry-ing out, just to hear Your voice, oh,
I must have You.
2. I come run-ning to You, Je - sus,
I'm so hun-gry for Your truth.
(v.3)

E♭(D) D♭(C) A♭(G)
I've found ma-ny trea - sures hid-den in Your word, but I
E♭(D) D♭(C) A♭(G) Chorus E♭(D) D♭(C)
must have You. On-ly You, Lord, will I wor-
A♭(G) E♭(D) D♭(C) A♭(G)
- ship, on-ly You will I serve. And my hope
E♭(D) D♭(C) A♭(G) E♭(D) D♭(C)
lies in You, Lord, on-ly You can make me whole.
A♭(G) Fm(Em) D♭(C) E♭(D)
And I will say 'I love You.'

A♭(G)
Fm(Em)
D♭(C)
E♭(D) D♭(C)
Yes, I___ will sing_______ to You,___
A♭(G)
E♭(D)
D♭(C)
A♭(G)
To end
E♭(D)
to You.___

3. I come longing for You, Spirit,
So dry I need to know Your touch.
I know living waters deep within me,
But I must have more of You.

Worship the Lord your God,
and serve Him only.

MATTHEW 4:10

1305. I come to bow down

(Heart and soul)

Ps 42:1, 7, 9, 11; 2 Cor 1:3

Kate Simmonds

Capo 4 (G)

Tenderly
B(G)
1. I come to bow down, I come to hear You speak. I wait before You where deep can call to deep.
2. My heart will praise You; in praises You dwell. I long to be with You and come away with You.
(v.2)
D♯7(B)
Be my life, be my all; heart and
E(C)
C♯m7(Am)
B(G)
D♯7(B)

E(C)
C♯m7(Am)
B(G)
soul
I seek You,
Lord.
G♯m7(Em)
F♯/A♯(D)
A/B(F)
E/B(C)
Won - der of hea - ven, joy of my heart;
Rock of sal - va - tion, love of my life;
C♯m7(Am)
G♯m7(Em)
F♯(D)
1.
strength of my be - ing, I love You.
God of all com - fort, draw near.
2.
E(C)
C♯m7(Am)
B(G)
Heart and soul
I seek You, Lord;
D♯7(B)
E(C)
C♯m7(Am)
B(G)
heart and soul
I seek You, Lord.

1306. # I come to You
(Here with me now)

Ps 139:7; 143:8; Is 9:6; Jas 4:8

Capo 3 (D)

Matt Parker & Paul Oakley

Lilting

Verse
Dm(Bm) C/E(A) B♭2(G)
Dm(Bm) C/E(A) B♭2(G)
1. I come to You, Lord of all hope, gi - ver of life, re - vive my soul. I wait for me.
You, Prince of all peace, King of all love, draw near to
Dm(Bm) C/E(A) B♭2(G)
Dm(Bm) C/E(A)
1. B♭2(G)
2. B♭2(G)
Gm(Em)
B♭(G)
It feels some-times like You're far a-way, yet I know You are with me. And I know I can-not go from Your pre-sence, O Lord, but I need to feel You here with me. What can I do just to draw
C7sus4(A)
F(D)
C7sus4(A)
Dm7(Bm)
Gm7(Em)
F(D)

C7sus4(A) Dm7(Bm) Gm7(Em)
near to You? Oh, I need to know You here with me
1. Dm(Bm) C/E(A) B♭2(G) Dm(Bm) C/E(A) B♭2(G)
now. 2. Come to me
2. F(D) C7sus4(A) Dm7(Bm)
Where can I go just to find You, O God? Oh, I long to feel
Gm7(Em) F(D) C7sus4(A)
You hold-ing me. Know that I seek You with all of my heart. Oh, I
Dm7(Bm) Gm7(Em) (Bm) (A) Dm C/E B♭2(G) (Bm) (A) Dm C/E B♭2(G)
need to find You here with me now.
rit. . . .

2. Come to me now, Lord of my heart,
I need to know unfailing love.
Consuming flame, passion and power,
Come let Your fire burn in me now.

1307. I come to You
(Your love)

Jn 20:20; 1 Cor 13:12

Louise & Nathan Fellingham

Tenderly

(v.2)
D
Verse
D/F♯
G
1. I come to You, to sit at Your feet, I hear You call,
A♯°
Bm7
I'm long - ing to meet You. I lift my face
E7
G
A
to You, and catch Your eye, oh how You sa - tis - fy.
(v.2)
D
Chorus
D
D/C
G/B
Em7
D
D/C
Je - sus, Your love sur - rounds me.
G/B
Em7
D
D/C
G/B
Em7
Je - sus, Your love com-

Last time to Coda
2nd time D.S.
Strongly
D D/C G/B Em7 Bm A G♯° G
pletes me. There's no-thing like it,
Bm7 A G Em7 Bm A G♯° G
there's no-thing like it, there's no-thing like the love of God.
D Dsus4 D D D7 Bm/D D+5
Quietly
No lon-ger search - ing, I've found the One,
D D7 Bm/D D+5 D D7
just touched the sur - face, on-ly be-gun; this love goes deep-
D.S. al Coda
Bm/D D+5 D D7 Bm/D D+5
er than a-ny I've known.
Coda
D

2. Now looking closer, I see the scars,
Stories of love,
You paid the greatest price,
So that I may have life.
Thank You, my Friend,
You're showing me once again.

1308. I come, wanting just to be with You

Jn 4:14; 14:6; Col 1:20
Capo 1 (D)
(Just to be with You)
Paul Booth
Gently, building in strength
Eb(D) Db2(C) Ab2/C(G) Fm7(Em) Eb(D)
I come, want-ing just to be with You;
come, want-ing just to give to You,
Db2(C) Fm7(Em)
Last time to Coda
1.
to - day let me hear Your voice. I
to say, You are ev - 'ry - thing.
2.
Eb(D) Bb(A)
Don't ev - er let my heart grow cold,
Fm7(Em) Eb(D) Bb(A)
don't ev - er let me lose sight of Your
Fm7(Em) Eb(D) Bb(A) Fm7(Em)
truth. Draw near that I may drink from e-ter-nal wa - ter.

B♭(A)
Fm(Em)
E♭/G(D)
You are the Foun - tain of all life,
- ly Son of God,
A♭(G)
Fm(Em)
E♭/G(D)
You are the peace un - to my soul.
You gave up Your life to save my soul.
A♭(G)
Fm(Em)
E♭/G(D)
You are the Way, the Truth, the Light;
You have re-deemed me through the cross;
A♭(G)
1.
Fm(Em)
Je - sus, in - to Your arms I run.
Je - sus, with thank -
B♭(A)
2.
Fm(Em)
B♭(A)
D.C.
B♭sus4(A)
You are the ho - - ful - ness I come.
Coda
E♭(D)
Fine

1309. I count as nothing every earthly treasure

Rom 8:32; Phil 3:7

Worshipfully

Neil Bennetts

E Amaj9

I count as no - thing ev - 'ry earth - ly trea - sure, Je - sus;
Why would I look for a - ny world - ly plea - sure, Je - sus,

E Amaj9

what You have shown me is that You are the source ___ of my life. ___
when I have all things in You? And just a ___ heart-beat a - way. ___

B C♯m A2

___ So what else can ___ I do ___ but stay ___
___ So what else can ___ I do ___ but stay ___

1. B F♯m7/B B 2. B A/B E

here? here with You? ___

B7sus4 F♯m7 B7sus4

You're all ___ that I need, ___ You're all ___ that I need, ___

F♯m7
B7sus4
C♯m7
E/B
so here I'll stay
and give my praise

A2
E
to You.

1310. I danced in the morning

(Lord of the dance)

Mt 4:21; 12:12-13; 27:26, 28, 35, 59-60; Lk 2:4; Jn 1:3; 5:9, 16; 15:4

Sydney Carter

Am/C D7 G (Fine) Verse G Em
1. I danced in the morn-ing when the
Bm Em Am/C
world was be-gun, and I danced in the moon and the
Am D G Em
stars___ and the sun, and I came down from hea-ven and I
Bm Em Am/C D7 G
danced on the earth: at Beth-le-hem I had my birth.

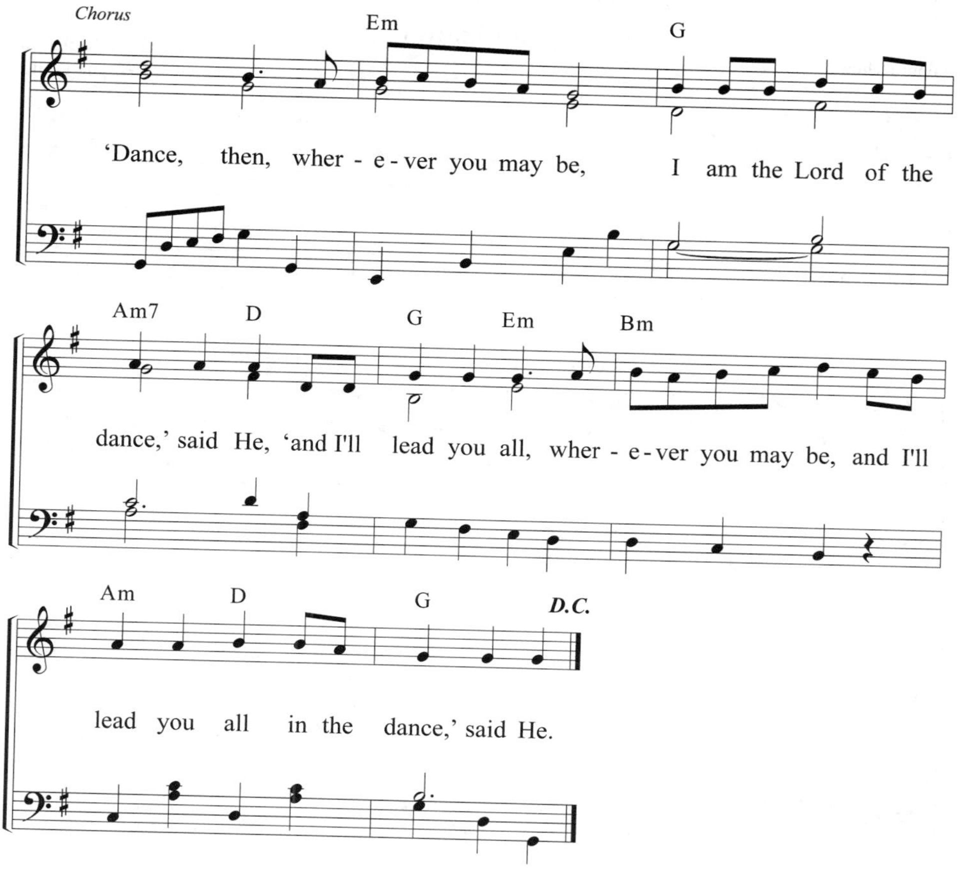
Chorus
Em
G
'Dance, then, wher - e - ver you may be, I am the Lord of the
Am7
D
G
Em
Bm
dance,' said He, 'and I'll lead you all, wher - e - ver you may be, and I'll
Am
D
G
D.C.
lead you all in the dance,' said He.

2. 'I danced for the scribe and the pharisee,
But they would not dance and they wouldn't follow Me.
I danced for the fishermen, for James and John -
They came with me and the dance went on.'

3. 'I danced on the Sabbath and I cured the lame;
The holy people said it was a shame.
They whipped and they stripped and they hung Me on high,
And they left Me there on the cross to die.'

4. 'I danced on a Friday when the sky turned black;
It's hard to dance with the devil on your back.
They buried My body and they thought I'd gone,
But I am the dance, and the dance goes on.'

5. 'They cast Me down and I leapt up high;
I am the life that'll never, never die.
I'll live in you if you live in Me;
I am the Lord of the dance,' said He.

1311.

I don't know why
(All I know)

1 Jn 1:7

Noel & Tricia Richards
& Wayne Drain

With feeling
Verse
D
A/C♯
1. I don't know why, I can't see
G2
Asus4 A
D
how Your pre-cious blood
A/C♯
G2
Asus4 A
could cleanse me now; when all this
Bm Bm/A G D/F♯ Asus4
time I've lived a lie,
A Bm Bm/A G D/F♯ Asus4
with no ex-cuse, no a-li-bi.

Chorus
A G Asus4 A D D/F♯
All I know is I find mer - cy; all my shame
G A Bm Bm/A G Asus4 A
You take from me. All I know, Your cross has pow -
D Em7 D/F♯ Asus4 Bm Bm/A
- er, and the blood You shed clean - ses me.
G D/F♯ Asus4 A
D.C.
Last time
D

2. It's way beyond what I can see,
How anyone could die for me.
So undeserved, this precious grace;
You've won my heart, I'll seek Your face.

1312. I enter in

Ps 118:19; Phil 2:9; Heb 13:15

Capo 3 (D)
Bethan Stevens
Gently
F2(D)
(G) B♭sus2(addG)
F2(D)
I— en - ter in— be-fore— You now,- I—come to You- with an
Csus4(A)
C(A)
F2(D)
(G) B♭sus2(addG)
o - pen heart.- I— lift my voice- to wor - ship You,- I—
F2(D)
B♭maj7(G)
C(A)
Last time to Coda
love You, Lord,— and I could stay in Your pre - sence - for-
F2(D)
1st time only
B♭/F(G)
2.3.
B♭(G)
C(A)
F(D)
B♭(G)
e-ver.— I— Lord— God, I come be-
C(A)
Gm7(Em)
F(D)
C(A)
fore You— with my sa - cri - fice— of praise.— I am

F(D) B♭(G) C(A) Gm7(Em) F(D)
hum-bled in Your pre-sence, Je-sus, Name a-bove all
1. C(A) B♭2/F(G) D.C. 2. C(A) B♭2(G)
names. I names.
F/A(D) B♭2(G) 1. C(A) Csus4(A) 2. Csus4(A) Gm7(Em) F/A(D)
Je-sus, Name a-bove all
Csus4(A) C(A) Gm7(Em) F/A(D) 1. Csus4(A) C(A)
names. Je-sus, Name a-bove all names. Je-sus,
2. Csus4(A) C(A) B♭2/F(G) D.C. al Coda
names. I
Coda
F(D)
e-ver.

1313. # If I seek You

(Pure heart)

Ps 17:6; 51:10; Lk 11:9

Capo 3 (Em)

Noel Richards
& Wayne Drain

Simply

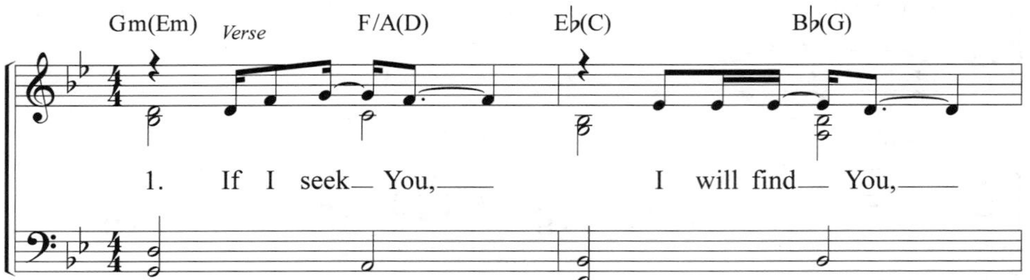
Gm(Em)
Verse
F/A(D)
E♭(C)
B♭(G)
1. If I seek_ You,_ I will find_ You,_

Gm(Em)
F(D)
E♭(C)
Gm(Em)
F/A(D)
but I need_ to take_ the time._ If I call_ You,_

E♭(C)
B♭(G)
Gm(Em)
F(D)
E♭maj7(C)
You will an - swer,_ but I need_ to take_ the time._

Chorus
Gm(Em)
E♭maj7(C)
Gm(Em)
F(D)
Give me a pure heart, give me a pure heart, I'm call-ing to You._

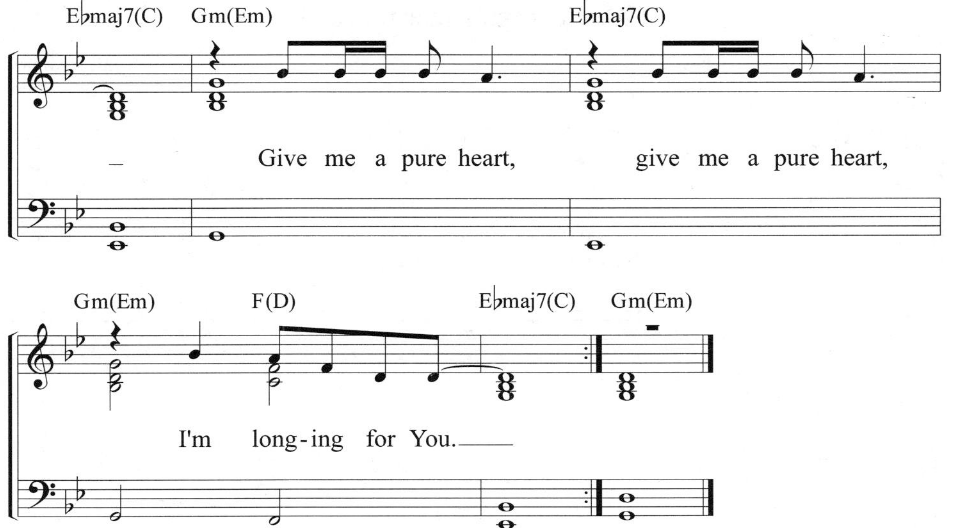
Ebmaj7(C)
Gm(Em)
Ebmaj7(C)
Give me a pure heart,
give me a pure heart,
Gm(Em)
F(D)
Ebmaj7(C)
Gm(Em)
I'm long-ing for You.

2. If I listen, I will hear You,
But I need to take the time.
If I follow, You will lead me,
But I need to take the time.

1314. If it wasn't for Your mercy

(Where angels fear to tread)

Capo 2 (D)

2 Cor 1:21; Eph 6:13; Heb 10:19; 1 Jn 1:7; Rev 6:17

Matt Redman
& Tom Lane

Steadily

Verse A(G)

1. If it was - n't for Your mer - cy, if it
(2.) was - n't for Your clean - sing, if it

E(D) A(G)

was - n't for Your love, if it was - n't for Your kind - ness,
was - n't for Your blood, if it was - n't for Your good - ness,

E(D) *1.*

how could I stand?___ 2. If it
how could I stand?___

2. *Chorus* E/G♯(D/F♯) A(G)

And yet I find my - self___ a - gain___ where e - ven
(And I)

E/B(D/A)
A(G)
an - gels fear to tread, where I would
E/G♯(D/F♯)
A(G)
ne - ver dare to come, but for the
2nd & 3rd times to Coda
E/B(D/A)
F♯m7(Em7)
clean - sing of Your blood. 3. With
A(G)
You there is for - give - ness, and
E/G♯(D/F♯)
A(G)
there - fore You are feared. Je - sus, it's Your lov - ing kind - ness

E/G♯(D/F♯)
D.S. al Coda
that brings me to my knees. And I
Coda
F♯m7(Em7)
E/G♯(D/F♯)
A(G)
In the beau-ty of Your ho - li-ness, in the
E/B(D/A)
A/C♯(G/B)
beau - ty of Your ho - li - ness, in the
E/G♯(D/F♯)
A(G)
beau - ty of Your ho - li - ness, in the
E/B(D/A)
F♯m7(Em7)
1. D.S. al Coda
2. E(D)
beau-ty of Your ho - li-ness. And I

Let us then approach the throne of grace with confidence, so that we may receive mercy and find grace to help us in our time of need

HEBREWS 4:16

1315. If My people

(If)

2 Chron 7:14

Moderately
Ken Riley
C Fmaj7
mf If My peo-ple, who are called by My name,
C Fmaj7
will hum-ble them-selves and pray,
Am G F
and will seek My face,
Am G 1. F 2. F
and turn from their wic-ked ways. Then I will hear
C Am G C
f from hea-ven and for-give their sin. Yes, I will hear

Am
G
C
Am
from hea-ven and for-give their sin. Yes, I will hear from hea-ven and
G
C
Am
G
F
for-give their sin, and will heal their land,
Am
G
F
C
Fmaj7
C
yes, I will heal their land.
1.
Fmaj7
D.C.
2.
Fmaj7
Repeat, building each time
C
Am
p
Will You hear from hea-ven and
Last time
G
C
C
Am
G
C
Fine
for-give my sin? Oh, will You hear from hea-ven and for-give my sin?

1316. If we died with Christ

Mt 19:29; Lk 10:25, 28; Rom 6:8; 2 Tim 2:11-13

David Lyle Morris & Faith Forster

Lightly
Verse
E
1. If we died with Christ, we'll al - so
C♯m7
Bsus4
live with Him, and if we en - dure, we'll al - so reign with Christ.
A2
If we de - ny Him,
E
C♯m7
He will dis - own us,
Bsus4
(v.2)
but if we're faith - less, faith - ful He re - mains.

A2
Chorus
E
A faith - ful Sa -
suf - f'ring Ser -
viour and un - end - ing in mer - cy is our
vant, and our con - quer - ing He - ro are You,
C♯m7
Bsus4
God, the on - ly true God.
God, for - e - ver true God.
1.
2.
The
You are wor - thy to re -
ceive our lives.
2. If we
D.C.

2.
C♯m7
Bsus4
Cleansed from sin and a - live to Christ.
A2
E

2. If we please the Lord
In this present world,
We will inherit eternal life to come.
For He has promised
To raise us from the dead
If we walk worthily of Christ the risen One.

But because of His great love for us, God, who is rich in mercy, made us alive with Christ even when we were dead in transgressions – it is by grace you have been saved.

EPHESIANS 2:4-5

1317. I give my heart to what I treasure

(Treasure)

Ps 72:19; Mt 6:21; Rev 22:2

Wayne Drain
& Noel Richards

Slow 4 with a ♩. ♪ feel
Verse
C G F C G/B
1. I give my heart to what I trea - sure;
Am Em7 F G
my de-vo - tion, e - v'ry-thing I am.
C G F C G/B
Like a dia - mond, You treat me like I'm pre - cious;
Am Em7 F G
to be Yours is more than I de-serve. (oh)
Chorus
C G
Je-sus,
F C G/B Am Em7
You are my trea - sure; Je - sus,

F G C G F C G/B
no-thing less will do. Je-sus, I am Yours for-e-ver;
Am Em7 F
Je - sus, I want to live, (I want to live) I
F/G C G Dm7 F
want to live for You.
C G Dm7 F C(no3rd)

2. We are a people holy to our Saviour;
For this moment He has gathered us
To bring hope and healing to the nations,
Till His name is known in all the earth.

1318.
I have come home
(All I want is You)
Lam 3:22-23; Is 53:5;
Lk 15:20; Jn 10:3; 15:15
Capo 3 (D)
Noel & Tricia Richards
Gently
F(D)
F/A(D)
B♭2(G)
1. I have come home, I'm here a-gain, worn feet
B♭/C(G)
F(D)
and rag - ged heart. Was-ted my time,
F/A(D)
B♭(G)
B♭/C(G)
wan-dered from ways that are best.
Gm7+4(Em)
F(D)
Gm7+4(Em)
I don't de-serve from You mer-cy that falls
Last time to Coda
F(D)
C(A)
(Bm) (A) (G)
Dm7 C B♭2
F(D)
a - new ev-'ry day: all I want is You.

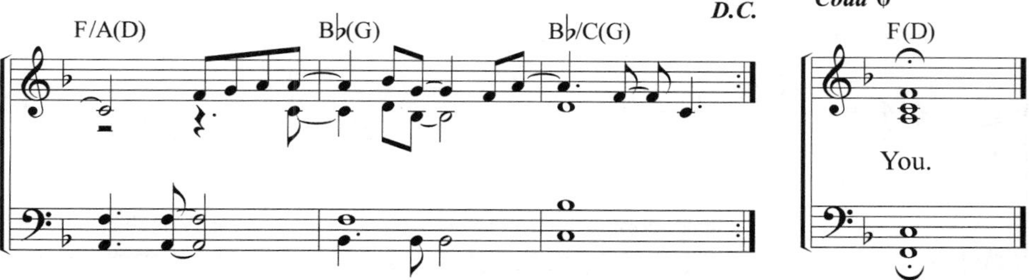
D.C.
Coda
F/A(D)
B♭(G)
B♭/C(G)
F(D)
You.

2. You know my name,
Call me Your friend,
You draw me to Your side.
Though I have failed,
Fallen so far,
Still You care.
Grace covers all my shame.
Jesus, You took the blame, this is love:
All I want is You.

3. I am restored,
Where I belong,
At one with You again.
With all my heart
I choose to walk
In Your ways.
Held in Your strong embrace,
No one will take Your place in my heart:
All I want is You.

1319. I have come to love You

Ps 18:1; Is 42:3; Mt 5:16; Lk 11:2; Jn 4:24; 14:27; 2 Cor 12:10

With a driving rhythm

Martin Cooper & Paul Oakley

E
Verse
A
1. I have come to love You, for You have won
C♯m
E/B
my heart when You re-vealed Your love to me.
(v.2)

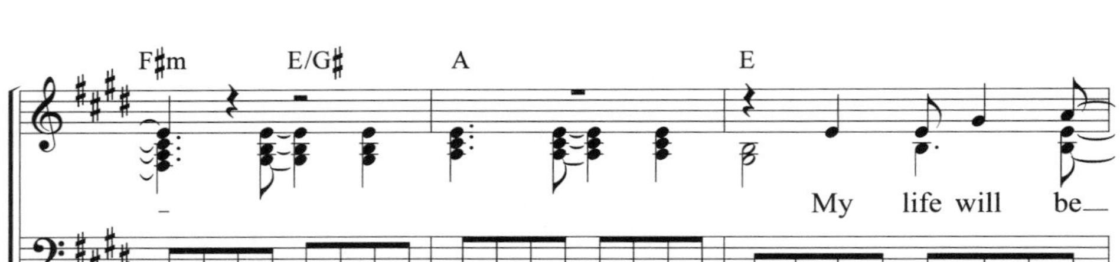
F♯m
E/G♯
A
E
My life will be

A
a wit-ness of such love and such for-give-ness,

C♯m
E/B
F♯m
E/G♯
for You have gi-ven me Your peace,

A
Bsus4
and You're ev - 'ry - thing I need.
Chorus
E
A
I love to sing Your name, to speak
I long to wor - ship You in spi -
C♯m
- a - bout Your fame, You're wor -
- rit and in truth, it's all
Last time to Coda
E/B
F♯m
E/G♯
1.3.
A
- thy of my praise.
I want to do.
2.
A
D.C.
4.
A
G♯m
Mid section
As I come
Fill me with

A
be - fore You now, let Your Spi - rit touch me;
Your love and pow'r and Your com - pas - sion,
C♯m
1.
B
Bsus4
I will make this gos - pel known.
through me let Your king - dom come.
B
2.
F♯m
E/G♯
A
F♯m
E/G♯
Bsus4
D.S.
Coda
A
E
Fine

2. You have come to love me
And heal my broken heart,
Now I am reaching out to You.
Your strength is in my weakness,
I'm clinging to Your promise,
So let Your work in me shine through
In everything I do.

1320. I have come to realise

2 Cor 2:14; 4:7; Eph 1:12

Andrew Rogers

Rhythmically
E
Emaj7
I have come to re - a-lise the glo-ry of the Lord re-sides
F♯m7/E
Bsus4
in this jar of clay. And
E
Emaj7
if my world is going to see the glo-ry of the Lord re-vealed,
F♯m7/E
Bsus4
A
then my pride must break. Then the fra-grance of
E/G♯
Bsus4
B
Bsus4
B
Je - sus will be re - leased,

A
E/G♯
F♯m7
E/G♯
and the glo-ry of God will be re-vealed in
A
Bsus4
B
C♯m7
all my world. Je-sus, let
A
E
B
C♯m7
Your name be fra-grant in me, like per-fume that's
Last time to Coda
A
E/G♯
B
A
poured from this ves-sel of clay. (And) I will live
E/G♯
F♯m
B
all my days to be the praise, and

A
E/G♯
F♯m
I will live all my days to be the praise
B
E
D.S. al Coda
of Your glo - ry.
Coda
Bsus4
E
clay.

1321. I have heard so many songs
(The Father's song)
Zeph 3:17; 1 Cor 13:8; Col 2:2
Capo 1 (D)
Matt Redman
Gently
E♭(D) B♭/D(A) E♭/D♭(D)
I have heard so many songs, listened to a
The Father's song, the Father's love, You sung it over
A♭/C(G) Fm7 (Em) 1. B♭7sus4 (A) B♭7 (A)
thousand tongues, but there is one that sounds above them all.
me and for eternity it's
Cm(Bm) B♭/D(A) A♭2 (G) 2. B♭7sus4 (A) B♭7(A) E♭(D)
written on my heart.
Chorus
A♭/C (G) B♭/D (A)
Heaven's perfect melody, the Creator's
E♭/G (D) A♭2 (G) Fm7(Em)
symphony, You are singing over me

B♭sus4 (A)
Cm(Bm)
B♭/D (A)
E♭/G(D)
the Fa - ther's song.
Hea - ven's per-fect
A♭(G)
B♭/D (A)
E♭/G (D)
mys-te-ry,
the King of love has sent for me,
A♭2(G)
Fm7 (Em)
B♭7(A)
E♭(D)
and now You're sing-ing o - ver me
the Fa-ther's song.
D.C.
Last time
E♭(D)
B♭/D (A)
E♭/D♭ (D)
The Fa-ther's song, the Fa-ther's love,
You sung it o-ver
A♭/C (G)
Fm7 (Em)
B♭7sus4(A)
B♭7 (A)
E♭ (D)
me and for e - ter-ni-ty it's writ-ten on my heart.

1322. I have His word

Mt 16:18; Acts 17:31; Rom 1:17; 8:38-39; 1 Cor 2:9; 13:12; Eph 5:32; Heb 12:2; 1 Jn 3:2; Rev 7:9; 21:3

Brightly

Lex Loizides

D
G
A
1. I have His word, His great and precious promises.
D
D/C♯
Bm
G
He took my sin, His righteousness is mine.
A
I am in Christ, secure for all eternity:
no pow'r can sever me, nor cast me off from His a-
Bm/A

Bm/A
G
A7sus4
D
bun - dant, free
and sov-'reign love.
G
Asus4 A
D
G
Asus4 A
To end
D

2. I have His word,
The Master Builder will succeed.
The gates of hell,
They never will prevail.
Throughout the earth
The joy of Jesus is His church;
She is the mystery
That stirred His heart,
Drawing Him out of heaven
To shed His blood.

3. I have His word,
A day is fixed when all the world
In sudden awe
The Son of God shall see.
And in that day
Our eyes shall see His majesty;
What then of sufferings?
What then of tears?
We shall see perfectly
When He appears!

4. I have His word
That every race shall reign with Him,
We'll reach our home,
The New Jerusalem.
The Triune God
Shall dwell with man eternally,
More joys than eye has seen
Or ear has heard
Wait for us certainly,
I have His word.

1323. I just want to love
(I'll always love You)

Ps 42:2; Jn 4:14, 24

Tim Hughes

With life
Verse
A E F♯m
1. I just want to love, I just want to
D A E
sing to the One a - bove who has
F♯m
touched this thirs-ty soul.
1. (Repeat verse) D
2. D
And now I'll
Bm
ne-ver be the same.
A Chorus
I'll al-ways love
E F♯m D
You, I'll al-ways sing to You, Je-sus.

A
E
F♯m
I long to wor - ship You in spi - rit and in truth.
1.3.
D
2.
D
D.C.
(Fine)
4.
D
Bm
C♯m
D
And with this song we'll lift the name of Je - sus
Bm
C♯m
high - er. And with a shout we'll raise up one
D
D.S. al fine
voice.

2. Every day I'll come,
Spend my life with You,
Learning of Your heart,
And what You're calling me to do.
(Repeat)
My every breath belongs to You.

1324. I know He rescued my soul

(My Redeemer lives)

Job 19:25; Mt 11:30; Acts 2:31; 1 Thess 4:16; Heb 13:11-12; 1 Jn 1:7

Reuben Morgan

With energy
E7
Verse
A7
E7
I know He re-scued my soul, His blood has
My shame He's ta-ken a-way, my pain is
A7
E7
co-vered my sin, I be-lieve,
healed in His name, I be-lieve,
A7
1.
E7
A7
I be-lieve.
2.
E7
A7
Bsus4
I'll raise a ban-ner;
Asus2
Bsus4
Chorus
E
my Lord has con-quered the grave. My Re-dee-mer lives,

A
C♯m7
Bsus4
E
my Re - dee - mer lives;
my Re - dee - mer lives,
A
C♯m7
1.,3.
Bsus4
D.C.
Last time
Bsus4
E
Fine
my Re - dee - mer lives.
2.
Bsus4
D
A/C♯
You lift my bur - den,
I'll rise with You:
E/B
F♯m7
I'm dan-cing on this moun - tain-top to
E/G♯
Bsus4
D.S. al fine
see Your king - dom come.
My Re -

1325. I know not why God's wondrous grace

Mt 24:36; Jn 16:8; 1 Thess 4:16-17; 2 Tim 1:12

Reflectively

Music: Stuart Townend

Verse
D A Bm
1. I know not why God's won-drous grace to
2. I know not how this sa-ving faith to
D D/F♯ G G2/B D/A D G D/F♯ D
me hath been made known; nor why, un-wor-thy
me He did im-part; or how be-liev-ing
Em Bm A D D/F♯ G2 G
Chorus
as I am, He claimed me for His own. But I
in His word wrought peace with-in my heart.
A A7/C♯ Dsus2/4 D D/F♯ A A7/C♯ D D/F♯
know whom I've be-lie-vèd; He's a-ble now to save what

G D/F♯ D Em Bm A D G6 G2/B D
I've com-mit-ted un-to Him un-til that fi-nal day.

3. I know not how the Spirit moves,
   Convincing men of sin;
   Revealing Jesus through the word,
   Creating faith in Him.

4. I know not what of good or ill
   May be reserved for me,
   Of weary ways or golden days
   Before His face I see.

5. I know not when my Lord may come;
   I know not how or where,
   If I shall pass the vale of death,
   Or meet Him in the air.

D.W. Whittle (1840-1901) (adapt. Stuart Townend)

1326. I know You love an offering

(A life of love)

Capo 5 (Am)

2 Sam 24:24; Amos 5:23-24; Lk 10:27, 37; Jn 12:7; Rom 12:3; Phil 2:3

David Gate

Thoughtfully

Dm(Am)
Verse
F(C)
1. I know You love an offering that's costly,
B♭maj7(F)
outreaching, touching Your
Dm(Am)
C(G)
Dm(Am)
heart for the poor. The songs we sing as our
F(C)
offerings are more fragrant in Your
B♭maj7(F)
Dm(Am)
C(G)
presence, if we live a life of love.

F(C)
Chorus
C/F(G) C/E(G)
And as we fol - low Your heart, we are led to the lost,
Dm(Am) Dm/C(Am)
find - ing there a place of praise, no mat -
Dm/B(Am) (G) Csus4 C(G) F(C)
ter what the cost. So we will stand with the weak,
C/F(G) C/E(G)
give our most to the least, serv-
Dm(Am) Dm/C(Am)
ing You with all we have, Your king -

Last time to Coda
Dm/B(Am)
Csus4 (G)
1.
C(G)
2.
C(G)
dom God, we seek.
Instrumental section
Dm(Am)
Dm/B (Am)
B♭ (F)
1.
C (G)
2. D.S. al Coda
C(G)
Coda
Csus4 (G)
C (G)
Dm(Am)
Fine

2. Now I see what You command;
Be faithful and humble, putting selfish hopes aside,
So change my heart that I may love,
My neighbour as my brother and to live a life of love.

But we have this treasure in jars of clay to show that this all-surpassing power is from God and not from us.

2 CORINTHIANS 4:7

1327. I lift You high

(You must increase)

Capo 2 (E)

Jn 3:30

Matt Redman

Steadily
F♯2(E2)
A♯m7(G♯m7)
I lift You high, and bow down low, how
D♯m7(C♯m7)
B2(A2)
F♯2(E2)
high can You be? How low can I go? I lift You high, and
A♯m7(G♯m7)
D♯m7(C♯m7)
bow down low, how high can You be? How
1. first time only
B2(A2)
F♯2(E2)
2.
B2(A2)
low can I go, O Lord? I low can I go,
D2(C2)
C♯m7(Bm7)
B2(A2)
You must in-crease, I must de-crease, Lord.

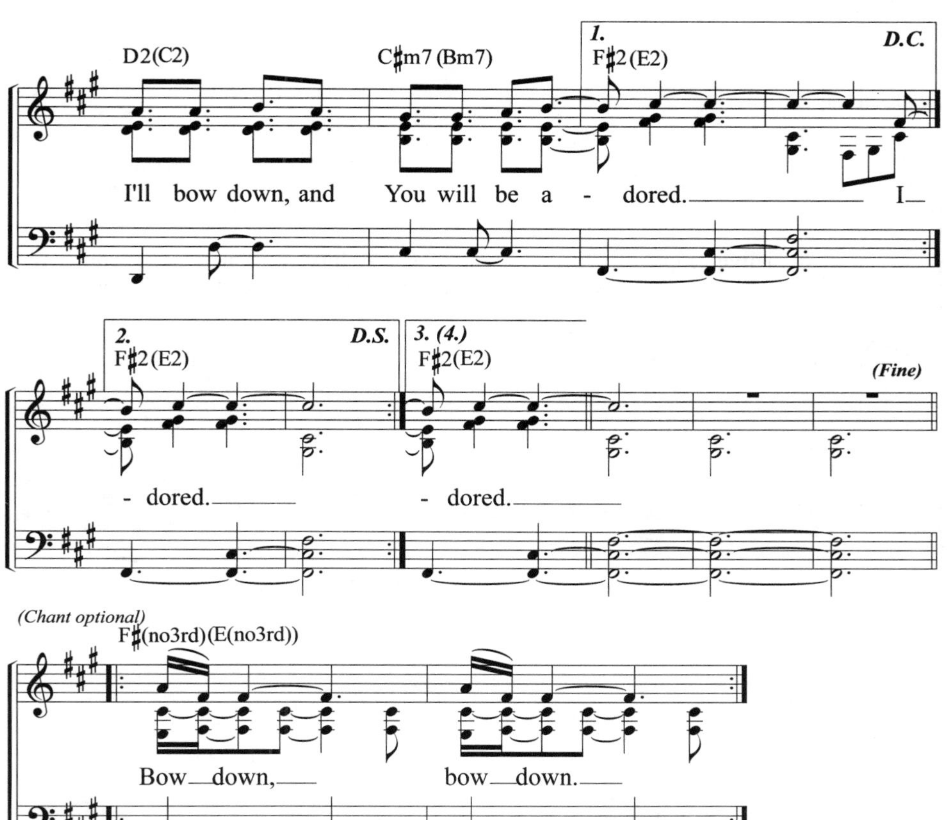
D2(C2)
C♯m7 (Bm7)
1.
D.C.
F♯2 (E2)
I'll bow down, and You will be a - dored. I
2.
D.S.
F♯2 (E2)
3. (4.)
F♯2 (E2)
(Fine)
- dored.
- dored.
(Chant optional)
F♯(no3rd)(E(no3rd))
Bow down, bow down.

1328. I live my life to worship You

Ps 27:4

Capo 1 (Em)

Gareth Robinson

With intensity

Verse

Fm7(Em) D♭maj7(C) Fm7(Em) D♭maj7(C) A♭(G) E♭/G(D) Fm7(Em) 1. D♭maj7(C) 2. D♭(C) A♭(G) E♭/G(D) Fm7(Em)

I live my life to worship You, I spend my days serving You, and now I come, I come. I want to

spend some time with You, to steal away and be with You, so now I come, I come.

Just to be with You, just to know more of Your love;

D♭(C)
A♭(G)
E♭/G(D)
D♭maj7(C)
just to be with You, and to love You.
1.
B♭m7(Am)
2.
B♭m7(Am)
Fm(Em)
B♭m7(Am)
I live my
And here You know me,
Fm7/C (Em)
B♭m7(Am)
Fm7/C (Em)
and here You know me,
and here You know
B♭m7(Am)
Fm7/C (Em)
B♭m7(Am)
To end
Fm7(Em)
me,
and here I love You.

Through Jesus, therefore, let us continually offer to God a sacrifice of praise – the fruit of lips that confess His name.

HEBREWS 13:15

1329. I love You, Lord

(Joy)

Mt 5:14, 16

With a driving rhythm

John Ellis

Verse
D
1. I love You, Lord, I wor-ship You, I love You, Lord, al-ways.
A
D
So thank-ful Lord, You saved my life, You
saved my life to-day.
A
Chorus
Let me be a
G2
shin-ing light for You,
D
let me be a
G2
joy to You al - ways,
D
let me be a
G2
shin-ing light for You,
D
let me be a
G
joy to You
C
al-ways.
D

2. And Lord, I love to bring to You
The honour due Your name;
Just look at what You've done for me,
I'll never be the same.

1330. I love You more each day

Mt 6:21

Gently

Ken Riley

G/B C G/B C F C/E Dm C G/B
I
G/B C G/B C F C/E Dm C
love You more each day, with all my heart can
G/B C G/B C
give; wor - ship at Your feet,
F C/E Dm C G/B F C
lost with - in Your gaze. Just to know that You're near, my

F C Am D7
trea - sure is here, that You gave Your life to save
F G F C
me; how my heart sings with praise and
F C Am D7
calls on Your name, my Sav - iour, my Lov - er, my
F G F C
King. Come to me a - gain.

1331. Image of invisible God

Ps 36:9; 46:2-4; Is 9:6; Mk 10:45; Jn 15:15; Col 1:15-17; Heb 1:6

Stuart Townend
& J.K. Jamieson

Steadily, with majesty

Verse
B E B/D♯ F♯sus4 F♯
1. I - mage of in - vi - si - ble God,
2. Ho - ly One whom an - gels at - tend,
B E B/D♯ F♯sus4 F♯
Cre - a - tor and Su - stai - ner of all;
righ - teous King who calls me His friend;
B/D♯ E G♯m7 C♯9
the King who came to ran - som my soul,
the Prince who of - fers peace with - out end,
C♯m7 E/F♯ C♯m/B B
thank You for Your per - fect love.
thank You for Your per - fect love.
Chorus
And it's

B/D♯
E
You, O Lord, You're all that I could ask for, and in
You, O Lord, who gives me strength to fol - low, and in
B/D♯
C♯m7
You, O Lord, I find the deep - est joy:
You, O Lord, is grace for e - v'ry day:
Em6
B/D♯
G7
A/D
Foun - tain of life, o - cean of mer - cy and peace.
bound - less in love, full - ness of hea - ven on earth.
1.
E/F♯
And it's
2.
C♯m/F♯
B
C♯m/F♯
B

3. Therefore I will not be afraid,
Though mountains fall and rivers may rage;
I'm safe within the city You've made,
Thank You for Your perfect love.

1332. I'm calling out to You
(Passion for Jesus)

Capo 3(D)

Ps 119:145-46; Rom 8:13; Rev 2:4

Brian Houston

Steadily
Verse
F(D)
I'm call - ing out to You,
fied,
Dm7(Bm)
there must be some thing - more,
and my sin is put to death,
F(D)
some deep - er place to find,
and I can hear Your voice,
some se - cret place to
Your pur - pose is my
Dm7(Bm)
F/C(D)
C(A)
F(D)
hide
choice,
where I've not gone be - fore.
as na - tural as a breath.
1.
Where my soul is sa - tis -
2.
The love I knew be -

Gm7(Em)
F/A(D)
Gm7(Em)
fore, when You first touched my life,
F/A(D)
B♭(G)
F/A(D)
B♭(G)
I need You to re-store, I want You to re-vive.
Csus4(A)
Chorus
F(D)
B♭(G)
F(D)
Oh, place in my heart a pas-sion for Je-sus, a
My one de-si-re, my great-est pos-ses-sion, my
B♭(G)
F(D)
1.
B♭(G)
(A)
Csus4
C(A)
hun-ger that sei-zes my pas-sion for You.
on-ly con-fes-sion, my
2. Last time to Coda
C(A)
B♭sus2(G)
D.C.
Coda
F(D)
pas-sion for You. I'm call-ing out to You.

1333. I'm cradled

(Cradled)

Deut 33:27; Mt 11:28; 1 Pet 5:7

Dave Bilbrough

Gently

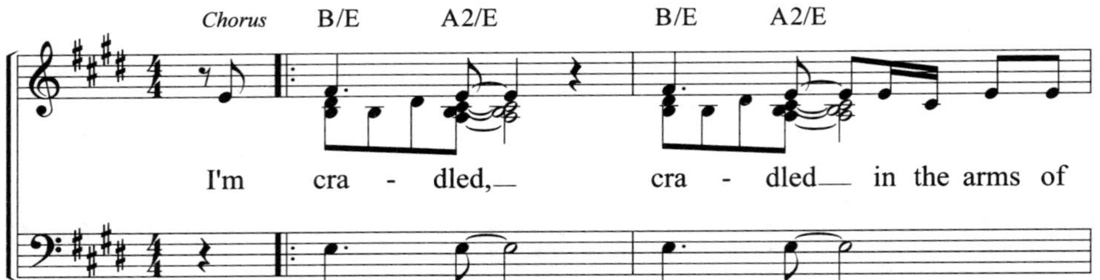

Chorus
B/E A2/E B/E A2/E
I'm cra - dled, cra - dled in the arms of

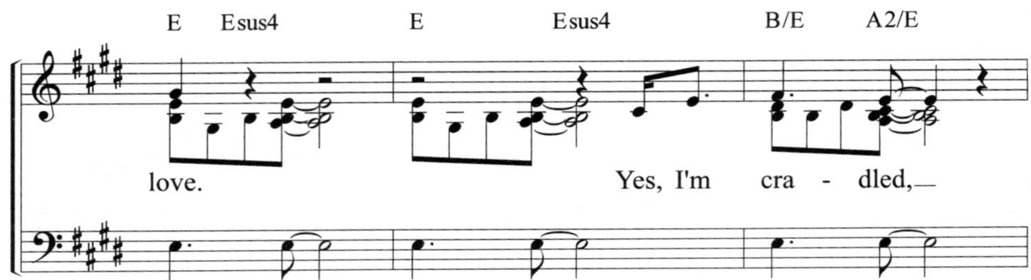

E Esus4 E Esus4 B/E A2/E
love. Yes, I'm cra - dled,

To mid section after v.2
B/E A2/E E Esus4 E Esus4
(Fine)
last time rit .....
cra - dled in the arms of love.

(v.2)
G♯m7 A2
Verse
1. My strug-gles for ap - pro - val

G♯m7 A2 F♯m7add4
were ne-ver meant to be. To know that I'm ac-
G♯m D B D.C.
cep-ted is Your de-sire for me. Be-cause I'm
Mid section B/E A2/E B/E A2/E B/E A2/E
love. In the arms of love,
B/E A2/E B/E A2/E B/E A2/E D.C. al fine
in the arms of Love. Yes, I'm

2. My fears about the future,
All my anxieties
Are calmed when I surrender
To the One who's holding me.

1334. I'm crying out

Jn 4:35; Acts 5:20; 1 Pet 2:4

Wayne Drain & Noel Richards

Strong 4
G G/F♯ Em7 A7
I'm cry-ing out, let ev-'ry-bo-dy hear this
D G G/F♯ Em7
mes-sage loud and clear. I'm cry-ing out, I
A7 D
want the world to know that Je-sus is my hope.
G Em7
I've cho-sen to be-lieve that God has cho-sen me
A/C♯ A C G
now at this time. He turned my life a-round,

Em7
A/C♯
A
I make a diff - 'rent sound, now I want to be a sign.
D
C
Har-vest fields are white,
Em7
C
wan-na do what's right, can't keep it to my-self,
Em7
A
D/A
A
D/A
G
got-ta go, got-ta tell ev-'ry-one, yeah.

1335. I'm drawn a little bit closer

(A little bit closer)

1 Cor 9:24; Heb 12:1; Jas 4:8

Geraldine Latty & Noel Robinson

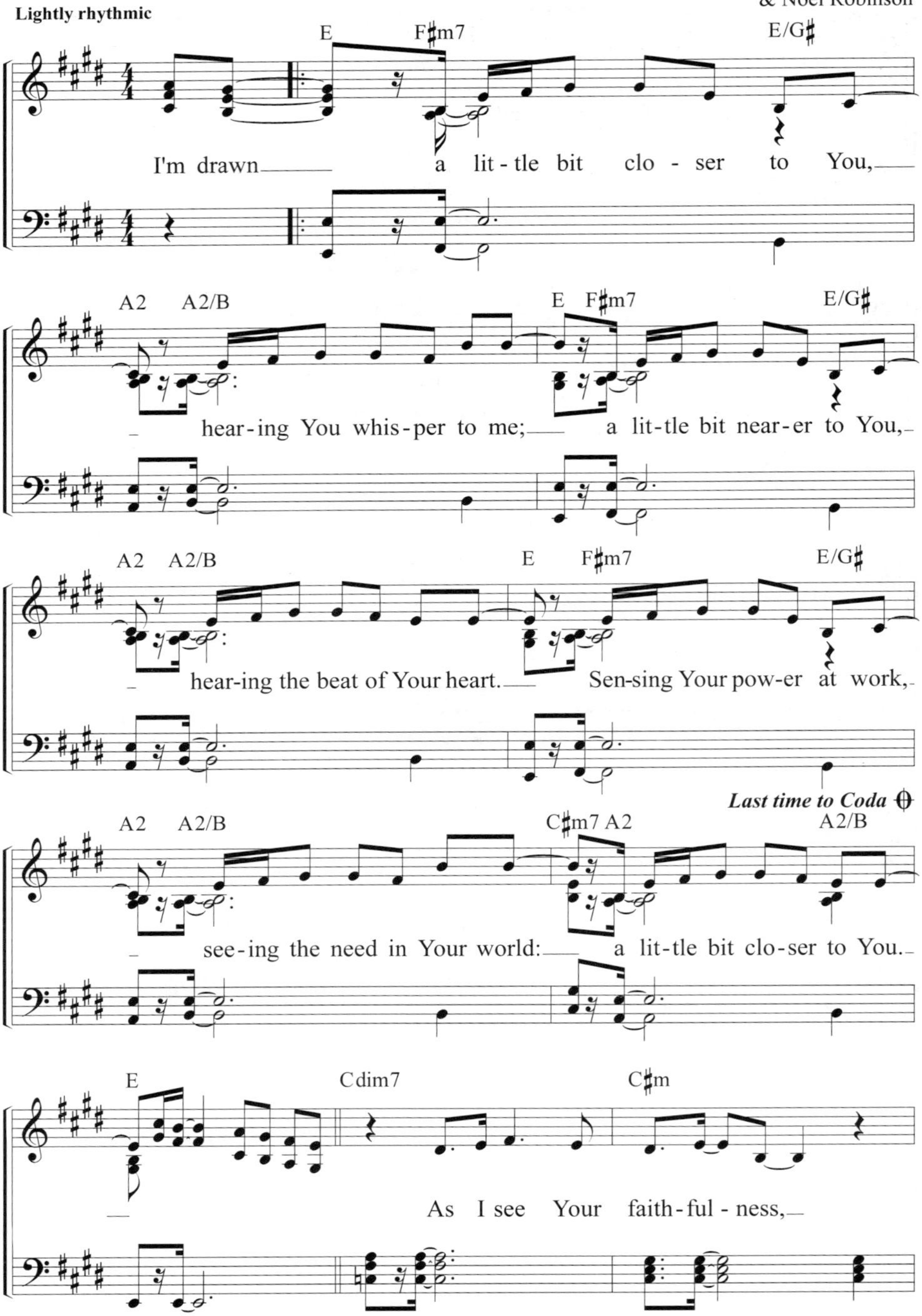

Lightly rhythmic

I'm drawn a lit-tle bit clo-ser to You,

hear-ing You whis-per to me; a lit-tle bit near-er to You,

hear-ing the beat of Your heart. Sen-sing Your pow-er at work,

Last time to Coda

see-ing the need in Your world: a lit-tle bit clo-ser to You.

As I see Your faith-ful-ness,

Cdim7
C♯m
F♯m7
as I fix my eyes on You, O Lord; as I run the
E2/G♯
A2
race You've run, ev-'ry day,
A/B
after repeat D.S. al Coda
Coda
E
Fine
ev-'ry day. I'm drawn

1336. I met You

(Glory)

Mt 28:20; Lk 19:10; Jn 8:12

Steadily

Ken Riley

E
Am
E
Verse
1. I met You when
You are the light

Am
D
You called my name, love sur-round-
that seeks to save: a burn - ing fire

G
C
ed and for - gave, and then You
of pur - est grace, show - er - ing the

Bsus4
B
1. E
filled my heart with praise.
world with

2.
E
Chorus
Bsus4
B
Bsus4
love.
And I will give glo - ry un-to You,
E
Bsus4
B
Bsus4
E
I will give glo - ry un-to You,
I give my-self
A
E/G♯
F♯m
F♯m/E
B
B/C♯
To verse
B
A
whol - ly, on - ly to you.
D.S to repeat chorus
B
Bsus4
To finish
B
A
E
And I will give

2. You stand beside me when I fail,
And carry me through times of pain:
For you are with me all the way.
And when my life begins to fade
You'll be the lamp to guide my way,
Shining to eternity.

1337. I'm forever in Your love

Eph 1:4; 2:8; Rev 17:14; 19:16

Doug Horley

Strong rock beat
Verse
E
B
I'm for - ev - er in Your love, I'm for-
e - ver trust in You, I'll for-
E
A
E
e - ver saved by grace, You have cho - sen me and
e - ver say You're good, You are King of kings and
1.
B
A
crowned me with Your love. I'll for -
2.
B
A
E
Chorus
I will wor - ship You. La la la la la
B
E
la, just want to thank You, la la la la la la, just want to praise

B
1.
– You, la la la la la la, that I can live like this for - e -
E
2.
to Coda
- ver.
La la la la la live like this for - e -
D
D.S. al Coda
ver.
I'm for -
Coda
D
A
E
- ver.

1338. I'm giving You my heart

(Surrender)

Phil 3:8

Marc James

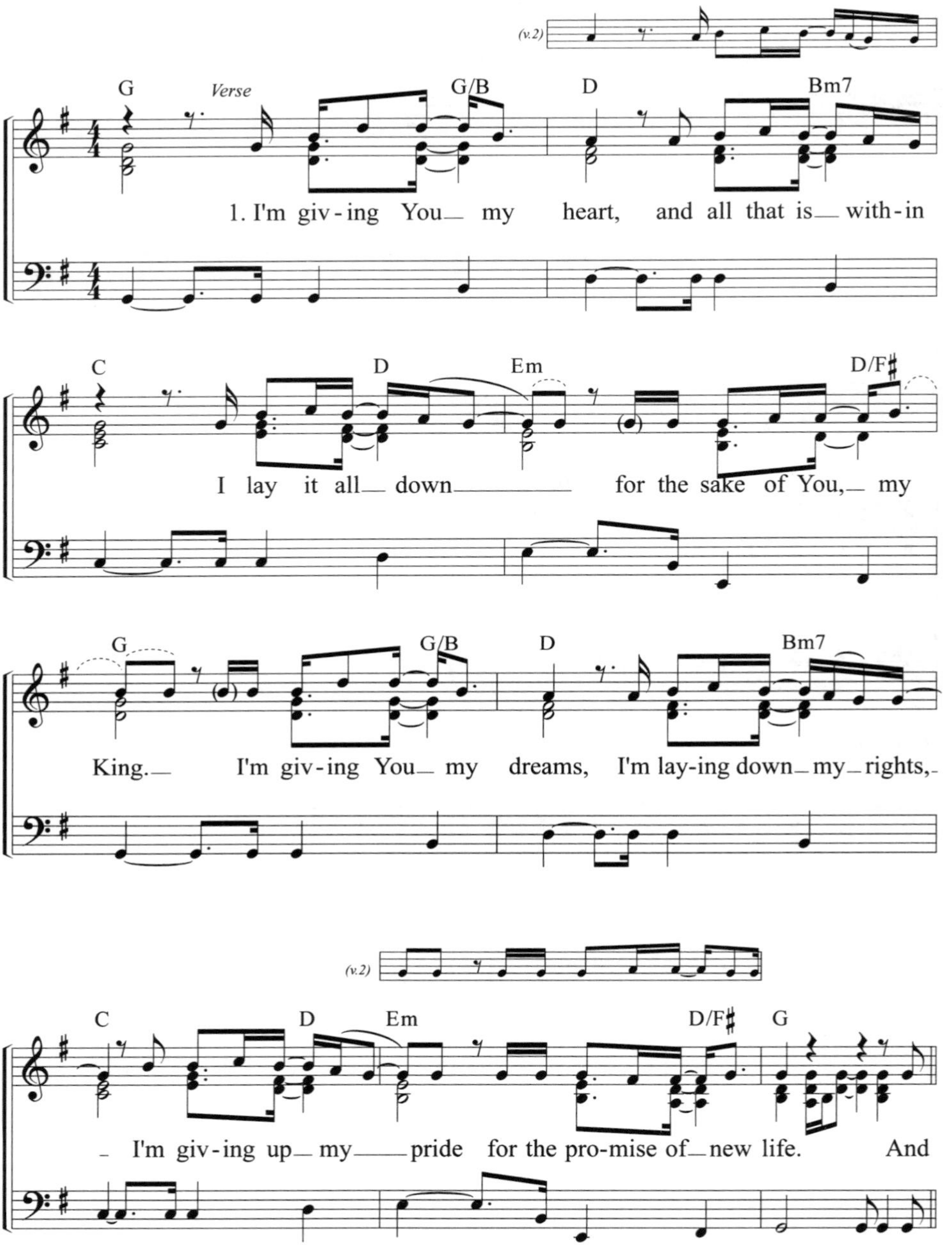

Slowly

Verse

G G/B D Bm7
1. I'm giv-ing You my heart, and all that is with-in

C D Em D/F♯
I lay it all down for the sake of You, my

G G/B D Bm7
King. I'm giv-ing You my dreams, I'm lay-ing down my rights,

C D Em D/F♯ G
I'm giv-ing up my pride for the pro-mise of new life. And

Chorus
Em
D/F♯
G
C
G
Em7
I surrender all to You, all to You.
D
Csus2
Em
D/F♯
G
C
And I surrender all to You,
G
Em7
D
Csus2
D.C.
To end
Gsus2
all to You.

2. I'm singing You this song,
   I'm waiting at the cross,
   And all the world holds dear,
   I count it all as loss.
   For the sake of knowing You,
   The glory of Your name,
   To know the lasting joy,
   Even sharing in Your pain.

1339. I'm gonna trust in God

(Gonna trust in God)

Zeph 1:14; Lk 21:28; Col 1:27; Heb 12:2; Jas 1:12

Steve Earl

Steady and bright
Verse
E
1. I'm gon-na trust in God, I'm gon-na trust in
Bsus4
Je - sus without shame and with-out
E
fear. I'm gon-na fix my eyes on the hope of
Bsus4
glo - ry, for His day is draw-ing
E D A
near.
Chorus
E B
How great is the love of

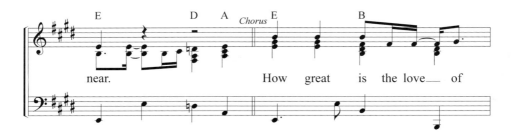

F♯m D/F♯ E/G♯ A E/G♯
God, how stea - dy is His hand to
F♯m7 Bsus4 B E B
guide me through this world. And though I am weak, in Him I
F♯m D/F♯ E/G♯ A E/G♯
stand, and you will hear me say to - day, in
F♯m Bsus4 B E
faith, I'm gon - na trust in God.

2. Now when the cares of life seem overwhelming,
And my heart is sinking down,
I'm gonna lift my hands to the One who'll help me,
To the One who holds my crown.

1340. I'm grateful

(Close to You)

Prov 18:24

Johnny Parks

Driving 4 in a bar

(v.2)

G Bm/F♯ Em C

1. I'm grate - ful for the way You look at me.

G Bm/F♯ Em C

I'm thank - ful that You don't give up.

G Bm/F♯ Em C

You're a friend who's smiled at me a thou - sand times.

G Bm/F♯ Em C(no3rd)

When I cause You pain, You bring me love.

A C A C

I've found a place where I'm free.

A
C
A
I'm dan - cing now,
'cause You love me,
C
D
G
D/F♯
You love me, You love me, You love me.
I
Em
C
G
D/F♯
Em
C
G
D/F♯
love You,
You know it's true.
And all
Em
C
G
D/F♯
Em
C
D7
G
to v2
I want is to be close to You.

2. When I've done the worst,
You've seen the best in me.
I was running away,
But You brought some rest to me.
My heart is Yours and I give it all to You.
And when it's tough, I know You'll pull me through.

1341. I'm learning to love You

(Learning to love You)

Deut 32:4; Ps 103:15-17; Rom 11:33

Paul Oakley

Bright and rhythmic
G
Am7
I'm learn - ing to love You, to love and to
to the words You have
G/B
C
G/B
trust You. I'm learn-ing to give You
spo - ken. I'm learn-ing to let go
C
D
G/B
1.3.
C
all that I am. I'm learn-ing to cling
my life in Your hands.
2.4. Last time to Coda
C
D
C/D
For You are faith-ful in all of your ways,
D
in wis-dom un - search-a - ble, and full of

C/D
D
grace.
Oh, You are beau-ti-ful
C G C G
be-yond words. I'm learn-ing to love You.
Am7
G/B
1.3.5.
C
2.6.
F
D.S.
4.
C
F2
2. So teach me to love
We are like
C
sha-dows that change with the day;

F2
C
and like the flow-ers our beau-ty will fade.
Cm/E♭
F
But Yours is the king-dom and the pow-er;
Cm/E♭
F
for-ev-er and ev-er Your glo-ry
G
D.S.S. to ad lib chorus
will al-ways re-main.
Coda
G
Fine.

2. So teach me to love You,
To love and to trust You,
And teach me to give You
All that I am.
And teach me to cling to
The words You have spoken,
Teach me to let go
My life in Your hands.

Love the Lord your God with all your heart and with all your soul and with all your strength.

DEUTERONOMY 6:5

1342. I'm making melody

(Making melody)

Ps 92:1-3

Matt Redman

Strong beat

E
D
I'm mak-ing me - lo-dy
in my heart to You.
E
D
I'm mak-ing me - lo-dy
in my heart to You.
C♯m
C♯m/B
A
Pour - ing out Your praise
with ev - 'ry-thing with - in.
Yours will al - ways be
the song I love to sing.
1.
E
D
2.
E
How can

A
B
E
hearts
not love Your
name?
How can
A
B
E
souls
not sing Your
praise?
A
A/B
A/C♯
A/B
Je - sus,
You
put
mu - sic
in
my
1.
E
D.C.
D
2.
E
soul.
soul.

1343.

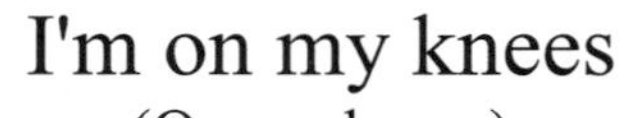

I'm on my knees
(On my knees)

Lk 18:13; Col 1:20

Slow 4

Dave Bilbrough

Verse

G D/F♯ Em7 C2 G Em7 C2 Dsus4 D G D/F♯ Em7 C2 G D

I'm on my knees at the cross, where Your blood was sa-cri-ficed; so a-mazed that there is grace e-nough for me. I don't deserve the love You bring, but I'm at that place a-gain, where I need You to for-give my fool-ish heart.

Last time to Coda
Chorus
G Gsus4 G Em7 Bm7 C2 Em7 D/F♯
Oh, what mer - cy, oh, what
G Em7 D/F♯ A
mer - cy, oh, what mer - cy
D D/C G/B D/A
D.S. al Coda
is mine to re-ceive. I'm on my knees
Coda
G

1344. I'm working out what it means

(The calculator song)

Lk 14:28, 33; Phil 2:12

Jim Bailey

Brightly

G C D G
I'm work - ing out what it means to fol - low Je - sus,

C D G
add - ing up what it costs to fol - low Him; count - ing the times that His

C D Em C D G
love is mul - ti - ply - ing, re - al - is - ing He took a - way my sin. He's

C G D
al - ways in my me - mor - y; He'll nev - er can - cel what He's

G G7 C G D/F♯ Em C D7
done for me. When I add it to-geth - er I cal-cu-late Je - sus is
Em C D7 G
great, Je - sus is great!
D G
Fine

1345. In awe of You

(You are near)

Ex 40:34-35; 2 Cor 3:18; Rev 5:13

Reuben Morgan

Flowing

E/G♯
Verse
D/F♯
A/E
In awe of You, we wor - ship

D/E
E/G♯
D/F♯
and stand a - mazed at Your great love.

A/E
E
E/G♯
We're changed from glo -

D/F♯
A/E
D/E
E/G♯
ry to glo - ry, we set our hearts

D/F♯
G
D/F♯
Esus4
E
on You, our God.
Now Your pre-
Chorus
A
E/A
D
A/E
sence fills this place,
be ex-al-ted in our praise.
Esus4
E
A
E/A
D
As we wor-ship I be-lieve You are near.
1.3.
A2
D2
D/E
2.
A2
D
D.C.
Now Your pre-
4.
A2
D2
E
Bles-sing and ho-nour and

E/F♯
F♯m7
A/D
A/E
E
glo - ry and pow - er for e - ver, for - e - ver.
Slower
E/G♯
D/F♯
A/E
Fine
In awe of You we wor - ship.

Look to the Lord and His strength; seek His face always.

1 CHRONICLES 16:11

1346. In Christ alone

Capo 1 (D)

Steadily

Is 53:5; Mt 27:42; Jn 1:5, 9; 10:28; 15:26; Acts 2:32-33; Rom 5:9; 8:1-2, 38-39; 1 Cor 15:28; Eph 2:20; 3:18; Phil 2:7-8; Col 1:27

Stuart Townend
& Keith Getty
A♭(G) E♭(D) A♭(G) B♭(A) E♭/G(D)
1. In Christ a - lone my hope is found, He is my
(G) (D) (Em) (G)
A♭ E♭/G Fm7 A♭/B♭ E♭(D) A♭(G) E♭(D) A♭(G)
light, my strength, my song; this Cor - ner - stone, this so - lid
B♭(A) E♭/G(D) (G) (D) (Em) (G)
A♭ E♭/G Fm7 A♭/B♭
Ground, firm through the fier - cest drought and
E♭(D) E♭/G(D) A♭(G) E♭/G(D) (A) (A)
B♭sus4 B♭ E♭/G(D)
storm. What heights of love, what depths of peace, when fears are
A♭(G) Cm7(Bm) (A) (A)
B♭sus4 B♭ A♭(G) E♭(D) A♭(G)
stilled, when striv - ings cease! My Com - for - ter, my All in

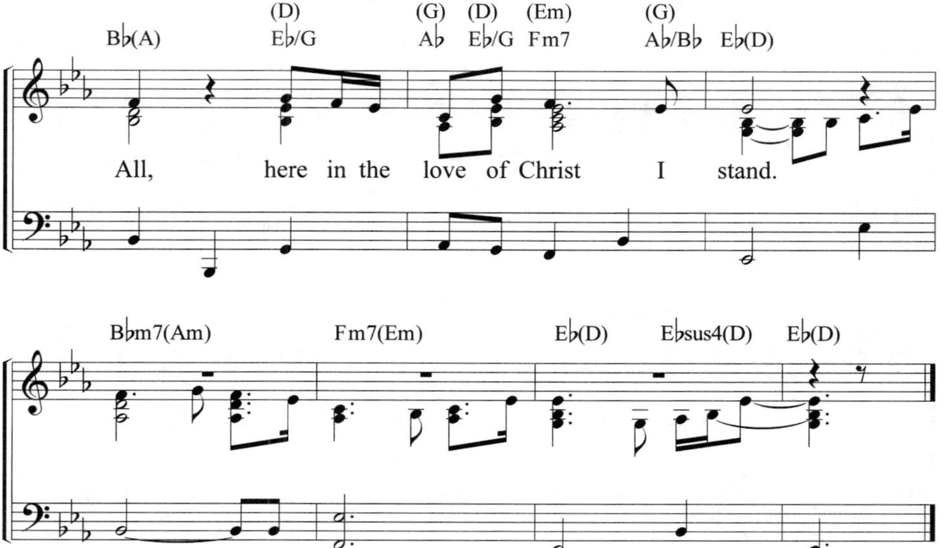
(D)
(G) (D) (Em)
(G)
B♭(A)
E♭/G
A♭ E♭/G Fm7
A♭/B♭ E♭(D)
All, here in the love of Christ I stand.
B♭m7(Am)
Fm7(Em)
E♭(D)
E♭sus4(D)
E♭(D)

2. In Christ alone! - who took on flesh,
   Fulness of God in helpless babe!
   This gift of love and righteousness,
   Scorned by the ones He came to save:
   Till on that cross as Jesus died,
   The wrath of God was satisfied -
   For every sin on Him was laid;
   Here in the death of Christ I live.

3. There in the ground His body lay,
   Light of the world by darkness slain:
   Then bursting forth in glorious Day
   Up from the grave He rose again!
   And as He stands in victory
   Sin's curse has lost its grip on me,
   For I am His and He is mine -
   Bought with the precious blood of Christ.

4. No guilt in life, no fear in death,
   This is the power of Christ in me;
   From life's first first cry to final breath,
   Jesus commands my destiny.
   No power of hell, no scheme of man,
   Can ever pluck me from His hand;
   Till He returns or calls me home,
   Here in the power of Christ I'll stand!

1347.

I need You
(Romance me)

Ps 61:4; Song 1:4; 2:6; Jn 4:14

Paul Oakley
& Martin Cooper

Steadily
A
Dmaj7
Verse
A
1. I need You like the summer needs the sun.
like a river needs the rain.
D
D/C♯
Bm7
I need You
I need You
E
to walk and to run.
to fill me again.
1.
I need You
2.
Bm7
With-out You
F♯m
F♯m/C♯
I run dry;

F♯m F♯m/C♯ Bm7
with - out You I won't e - ven sur - vive.
E E/B E
Chorus A
So wake me,
me,
take me with You, chase me where Your
clo - ser to You, lead me
D
ri - ver runs, ro - mance me till my heart be - longs to You.
in Your ways, en - chant me 'cause my life be - longs to You.
F♯m
D
1. Last time to Coda
2. D.S.
Oh, draw
2. I need You,

3.
Bm
Em-brace me, let me feel Your strength,
Dmaj7
F♯m
hide me in Your shade. You're my
E
D.S.S. al Coda
shel-ter in the rain. So wake
Coda
A
E/G♯
F♯m
D
me, clo-ser to You, lead me in Your ways, en-chant
A
E/G♯
D
A
me, 'cause my life be-longs to You.

2. I need You like the stars need the sky.
I need You to help me to shine.
I need You like a singer needs a song.
I need You, to carry on.
Without You, I run dry.
Without You, I won't even survive.

1348. I need You now
(Crying out to You)

Capo 1 (D)

Ps 38:15; Jn 20:22; 1 Cor 3:12; 2 Cor 4:7; Phil 2:17; Jude 21

Paul Oakley

Slow, strong in the chorus
Cm(Bm) B♭(A) E♭(D) Cm(Bm) B♭(A)
1. I need You now, my King, my Love;
I wait for You, my Hope, my Love,
E♭(D) Cm(Bm) B♭(A)
I am more aware this clay
because I've dreamed I'd see Your king-
E♭(D) A♭(G) 1.3. B♭(A)
than all Your pow'r within.
-dom come and I
2.4. B♭(A)
still believe. So come and
A♭/B♭(G) B♭(A)
breathe on me now, I am

A♭/B♭(G)
poured out for You.
B♭(A)
Come and
A♭/B♭(G)
re - lease Your pow'r.
B♭(A)
Last time to Coda
I'm cry-ing out
E♭(D)
Gm(F♯m)
to You, I'm cry-ing out
Cm(Bm)
to You.
A♭(G)
1.
B♭(A)
2.
Gm(F♯m)
Your pro - mise a - lone
Cm(Bm)
should be
A♭(G)
e - nough
B♭(A)
for me.
Gm(F♯m)
Still I'm cry - ing out,

Cm(Bm)
A♭(G)
B♭(A)
D.C. al Coda
'I need Your touch.'
Coda
E♭(D)
Gm(F♯m)
To repeat
Cm(Bm)
A♭(G)
to You. I'm cry-ing out to You. I'm cry-ing out
Last time
Cm(Bm)
A♭(G)
E♭(D)
Fine
to You.

2. What works have I?
   What fruit to show?
   I can hardly stand before Your grace,
   Yet I, I know
   Your love, Your grace
   Has lifted me,
   But I need You now so I can build
   With gold, pure gold.

But for you who revere My name, the sun of righteousness will rise with healing in its wings.

MALACHI 4:2

1349. In every day that dawns

(I know You love me)

1 Chron 29:11; Ps 17:8; 84:11

Kate Simmonds & Stuart Townend

With a steady rhythm

E D2+6 Asus2 B E D2+6 Asus2 B F♯m7 A B F♯m7 A

1. In ev - 'ry day that dawns, I see the light of Your splen - dour a - round me; and ev - 'ry - where I turn, I know the gift of Your fa - vour up - on me. What can I do but give You glo - ry, Lord? Ev - 'ry - thing good has come from You.

Bsus4 B E E2/D♯ C♯m7 E/B
_ I'm grate - ful for the air_ I breathe,_ I'm so thank-
F♯/A♯ F♯ B7sus4
ful for this life_ I live,_ for the mer-
E E2/D♯ C♯m7 E/B
cies that You pour_ on me,_ and the bless-
F♯/A♯ F♯ B7sus4
ings that meet ev - 'ry need._ And the grace_
F♯m7 E/A B
_ that is chang-ing me_ from a hope-less case_

F♯m7
E/A
B
to a child that's free, free to give You praise,
F♯m7
E/A
B
E
for in ev - 'ry - thing I know You love
D2+6
A2/C♯
B
me. I know You love
E
D2+6
A2/C♯
B
D.C.
me.
E

2. Through all that I have known,
I have been held in the shelter of Your hand;
And as my life unfolds,
You are revealing the wisdom of Your sovereign plan.
There are no shadows in Your faithfulness,
There are no limits to Your love.

1350. Infant holy

Lk 2:7-13

Capo 1 (G)
Tune: INFANT HOLY

From a Polish carol
Arr. A.E. Rusbridge (1917-69)

(G) A♭ (D) E♭ (G) A♭ (G) A♭/C (C) D♭ (D) E♭ (G) A♭
1. In-fant ho-ly, in-fant low-ly, for His bed a cat-tle stall;
(D) E♭ (G) A♭ (D) E♭ (G) A♭ (G) A♭/C (C) D♭
ox-en low - ing, lit-tle know - ing Christ the babe is
(D) E♭ (G) A♭ (C) D♭ (Am) B♭m (D) E♭
Lord of all. Swift are wing - ing an-gels sing - ing,
(Bm) Cm (Em) Fm (Am) B♭m (D) E♭ (G) A♭ (Am) B♭m
no-wells ring - ing, tid-ings bring - ing: Christ the babe is

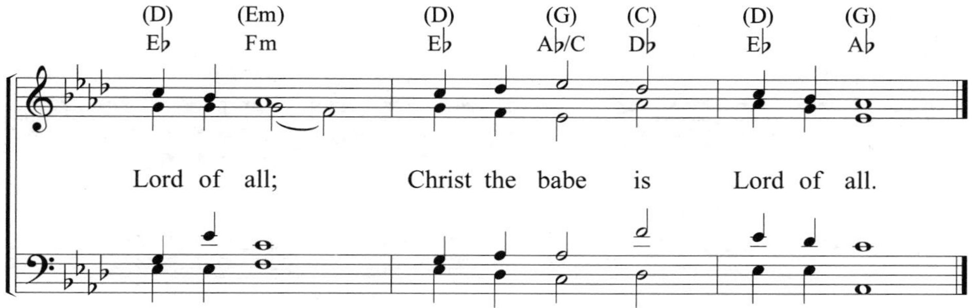
(D)
E♭
(Em)
Fm
(D)
E♭
(G)
A♭/C
(C)
D♭
(D)
E♭
(G)
A♭
Lord of all; Christ the babe is Lord of all.

2. Flocks were sleeping, shepherds keeping
Vigil till the morning new,
Saw the glory, heard the story,
Tidings of a gospel true.
Thus rejoicing, free from sorrow,
Praises voicing, greet the morrow:
Christ the babe was born for you!
Christ the babe was born for you!

Tr. E. M. G. Reed (1885-1933)

1351. In the shadow of the cross

Rom 8:37; Heb 2:18; 4:15; 1 Pet 2:21

Capo 3 (D)

Gently

Paul Oakley

Intro F(D)
B♭/D(G)
F/C(D)
B♭(G)
F(D)
Verse
B♭/D(G)
F/C(D)
1. In the sha - dow of the cross,
Je-sus Christ, my sac - ri - fice,
B♭(G)
F(D)
B♭/D(G)
Last time to Coda
E♭2 (C)
let ev-'ry-thing fall in - to place a -
how I need to find Your grace a -
B♭(no3rd)(G)
E♭2(C)
Chorus
B♭/D(G)
gain.
gain.
mf
And no-thing I can do could add
F2(D)
E♭2(C)
B♭/D(G)
to all You've done, so let my soul be sa - tis-fied.

SoF3

F(D)
E♭2(C)
B♭/D(G)
As I re-ceive Your fa - vour, I
F2(D)
Gm(add4)(Em)
will o - ver-come.
So in my life
E♭2(C)
B♭/C(G)
D.S. al Coda
be glo - ri - fied.
Coda
E♭2(C)
B♭(no3rd)(G)
F2(D)
B♭/D(G)
F/C(D)
pos - sess this peace.
B♭2(G)
F(D)

2. Jesus Christ, my perfect Priest,
How You understand my weaknesses.
Thank You for Your gift to me:
Through Your sufferings I now possess this peace.

1352. In this place we gather

Ps 84:1; 132:7

Stuart Plumb

Steadily
Verse
D
Dsus2/G
In this place we gather to worship You
to - ge - ther, to come be - fore You, ho - ly God.
A7sus4
Dsus4/G
D/F♯
Chorus
G
And as we seek Your face,
let this be Your dwell - ing place, we have come
Bm
Em
to wor - ship You. We come to give

G
D/F♯
G
our all,
it's at Your feet we fall,
Last time to Coda
1st time D.C.
Bm
G
Em D/F♯ G
we have come to praise You.
Em
D/F♯
G
We have come to wor - ship,
we have come
Asus4
Em
D/F♯
to wor - ship,
we have come to wor - ship
G
D.S. al Coda
Coda
D
You.

1353. In this stillness

Song 1:3-4; Is 6:3; 9:6; Jn 4:14; 15:15; 2 Cor 2:14; Jas 4:8; Rev 17:14; 19:16

Brooding

Paul Oakley

Em7 Verse Cmaj7 Em7
1. In this still - ness I will
I come run - ning, thirst - ing,
Cmaj7 Em7 Cmaj7 1. Em7
wor - ship, love You, Je - sus, I turn to-ward
long - ing for You, Je - sus,
Cmaj7 Em7 Cmaj7 Em7 Cmaj7
to kiss Your face.
2. Em7 Cmaj7 A
in the qui - et of this place.
Am Em Am Em Am
Draw me clos - er to You, Je - sus, I would

Em D/F♯ D G Chorus C
be with You.
Ris - en Heal - er,
G C Em7 C
con - quering Sa - viour, King of kings and Prince of
D C G C G
Peace.
Faith - ful Fa - ther, my Friend
C Em7 C D
for-e - ver, I will live to bring You praise.
D.C.
Last time
Em7 Cmaj7 Em
Fine

2. In Your presence I will bow down,
Join with the angels singing 'Holy is Your name'.
In this moment heaven's fragrance
Touches earth and I can feel Your kingdom come.
Draw me closer to You, Jesus,
I would be with You.

1354. In Your arms of love I sing

(Arms of love)

Capo 1(A)

Steadily

Deut 33:27; Mt 6:10; 16:24; 1 Cor 6:19; Phil 3:7-9

James Gregory

Verse
B♭(A)
1. In Your arms of love I sing, giving glo -
E♭sus2(D)
B♭(A)
ry to my King: I have come to seek Your face
E♭sus2(D)
F/A(E)
(v.2)
in this se - cret, se - cret place. And I will bow
Cm(Bm)
F(E)
Cm(Bm)
be - fore Your throne, for my life is not my own.

F(E) E♭sus2(D)
Chorus
F/A(E)
And I will
I will
E♭(D) F/A(E) Gm(F♯m) F(E)
praise You, ev-'ry day I'll come before Your throne.
give You all my hopes, my dreams I lay them down,
E♭(D) B♭/D(A) Cm(Bm) Fsus4(E)
1. F(E)
I am ho - ly un - to You. And
Lord, may I be found in You.
2. F(E) B♭(A)
1. to verse 2
D.C.
2.
2. I have ta -
And I will fol -
F/E♭(E) B♭/D(A) Cm(Bm)
low You, my Lord, for e - ver more

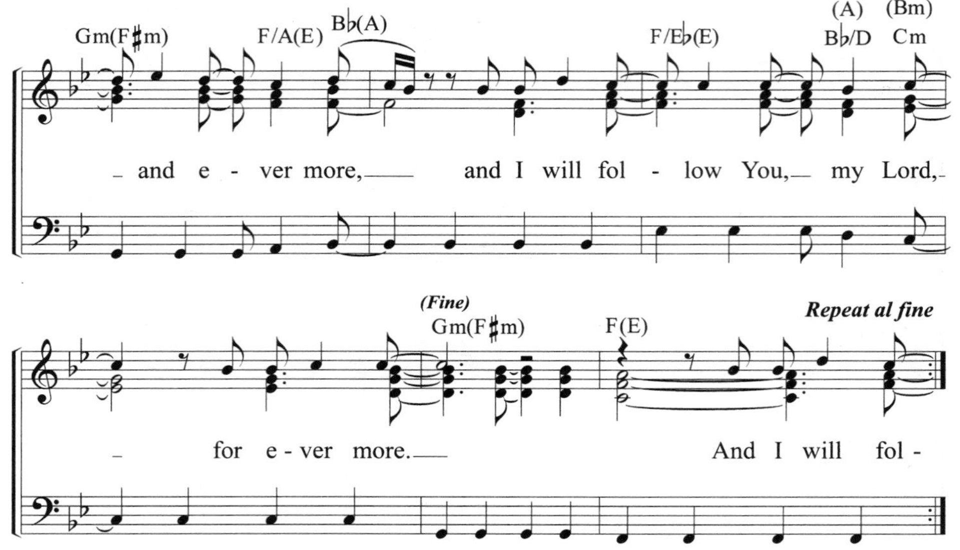
Gm(F♯m)
F/A(E)
B♭(A)
F/E♭(E)
(A)
(Bm)
B♭/D
Cm
and e - ver more,
and I will fol - low You, my Lord,
(Fine)
Gm(F♯m)
F(E)
Repeat al fine
for e - ver more.
And I will fol -

2. I have taken up my cross,
What was gain I've counted loss,
Father, let Your will be done
For I am broken by this love.
Send Your fire to purify,
Jesus, teach me how to die.

1355. In Your presence
(God is here)

Ps 16:11; Joel 3:10; Lk 4:18; Jn 10:10; 2 Cor 12:10

Lara Martin

Simply

Verse
Amaj7
Dmaj7
1. In Your pre - sence, there is full - ness of life,
Amaj7
Dmaj7
and heal - ing flow - ing for bo - dy, soul and mind.
Amaj7
Dmaj7
Amaj7
God of mi - ra - cles, God of the im - pos - si - ble is here,
Dmaj7
Asus2
A
Asus2
A
Chorus
God is here. God is here, let the

D
A
bro-ken-hear-ted je - joice.
(Lift up Your head.)
God is here,
D
E
let the sick say I am well.
(All suf - fi - cient One.)
A
D
God is here,
let the weak say I am strong.
A
F♯m7
God is here,
His
(Let the weak say I am strong.)
E
1.
D
won - ders to per-form.

2.
D
E
— Oh, His wonders, yes, His won-ders, His
D2
won-ders to per-form. Oh, His won-ders, yes, His won-ders,
E
1.
2.
A2
His won-ders to per-form. won-ders to per-form.
rall.......

2. In Your presence there is perfect peace;
In the stillness, I behold Your deity.
God of wonder, God of power is here,
God is here.

1356.

In Your presence there is joy

(God of glory)

Ps 16:11

Steadily

Libby Huirua

Verse
Gmaj9 A
In Your pre - sence there is joy, in Your
G/B Bm7 F♯m7 Gmaj7 A
pre-sence there is free - dom, but the great-est joy of all is to
Bm7 A/B Bm7 F♯m7 Gmaj9 A
know we've made You smile. In Your pre-sence there is life, in Your
G/B Bm7 F♯m7 Gmaj9 A2
pre-sence there is heal - ing, but the great-est joy of all is to
Chorus
Em7 F♯7aug5 Gmaj9 F♯7
know we've reached Your heart. God of glo - ry, we give You praise,

Bm
E7
Gmaj9
F♯m7
lift You up in this ho - ly place; our hearts are rea - dy, our lives made new, it's
Em7
F♯7aug5
Gmaj9
F♯7
all we long to do.
God of glo - ry, we give You praise, we
Bm
E7
Gmaj9
F♯m7
lift You up in this ho - ly place; our hearts are rea - dy, our lives made new,
Em7
D/F♯
Asus4
A
1.
Bm
E
God of glo - ry, we wor - ship
You.
Gmaj9
F♯aug5
2.
Bm
E7
G2
G/A
D
In Your
You.

1357. In You we live

With a light calypso rhythm

Graham Kendrick

E
B
E
E
B
E
In You we live, Jesus, in You we move.
B
E
In You we breathe, Jesus, in You we love.
A
B
E
C♯m
A
B
E
And we are Your body here, we are Your body here.
E
free touch - our hands, Your words - our voice,
You give - we share, You lead - we go,

A
Your way - our feet, Your tears in our eyes,
You send - we serve, You build and we grow.
E
Your Spi - rit is here.
Verse A
E
1. A - cross the world You're mov - ing; the sound of prayer
2. You are the light that's dawn - ing, You are the hope
A
is grow - ing strong - er, from e - v'ry tribe
trans - form - ing all things; free - ing the whole
E
1. A
and na - tion join - ing in one sal - va - tion song.
cre - a - tion to join in one sal - va - tion

2.
1st time D.S.
A
E
B
song, one song.
E
A/B
E
B
(One song.)
In You we live, Je-sus,
In You we breathe, Je-sus,
E
A/B
E
in You we move.
in You we love.
(One song.)

1358. I reach up high

2 Sam 6:14, 16, 21-22

Judy Bailey

Chorus
A
E
I reach up high, I touch the ground, I
F♯m
D
A
stomp my feet and turn a-round. I've got to (woo
E
A/E
Bm/E
A
E
woo) praise the Lord. I
A
E
jump and dance with all my might, I
F♯m
D
A
might look fun-ny, but that's all right, I've got to (woo

To verses
Last time
Fine
E A/E Bm/E A G♯ A
woo) praise the Lord.
D E/D C♯m7 F♯m7
Verse
1. I'll do a - ny - thing just for my God
Bm7 E7 A G/B A/C♯
'cause He's done e - v'ry - thing for me.
D E/D C♯m7 F♯m7 B7
It doe - sn't mat - ter who is look - ing on, Je - sus is the
E
D.C.
per - son that I want to please. I

2. May the whole of my life be a song of praise,
To worship God in every way.
In this song the actions praise His name,
I want my actions every day to do the same.

1359. I see the Lord

Is 6:1, 3, 5, 7; Heb 9:14

Capo 3 (D)

Paul Oakley

Smoothly
F(D)
C(A)
F(D)
1. I see the Lord, and He is high and lif - ted up, and His
B♭(G)
C7sus4(A)
F(D)
train fills the tem - ple. I see You, Lord, and You are
C(A)
F(D)
1.3.
B♭(G)
high and lif - ted up, and Your train fills the tem-
Csus4(A)
C(A)
Chorus
B♭(G)
F(D)
B♭(G)
F(D)
ple. And I cry ho - ly, ho - ly is the Lord,

B♭(G) F(D) Csus4(A) C(A) B♭(G) F(D)
ho - ly is the Lord most high. And I cry ho - ly,
Last time to Coda
B♭(G) F(D) B♭(G) F(D) Csus4(A) C(A)
ho - ly is the Lord, ho-ly is the Lord most high.
2. B♭(G) Csus4(A) C(A) B♭(G)
blood I come. Who am I that I should
C(A) Dm7(Bm) B♭(G)
gain the Fa - ther's love? Now my eyes have seen the King.
Csus4(A) C(A) B♭(G) C(A) Dm7(Bm)
Touch my lips that I may tell of all You've done:

Gm(Em)
C7sus4(A)
D.C. al Coda
fill — my heart — I cry, —
be glo - ri - fied! ——

Coda
Csus4(A)
C(A)
F(D)
Fine
— high.

2. I see Your holiness,
And light surrounds Your throne;
Who am I to come before You?
But now my guilt is gone,
My sins are washed away,
Through Your blood I come.

1360. I see You hanging there

(For the cross)

Ps 27:5; Is 53:5; Lk 23:44-46; Acts 10:40; 2 Cor 5:21; Eph 1:20-21; 2:6; 1 Pet 2:24; 1 Jn 3:8

Capo 3(D)

Michael Sandeman

With intensity
Verse
Gm(Em) D/F♯(B) Gm(Em)
1. I see You hanging there, nailed to a
And in those dark, dark hours, as life drained
D/F♯(B) E♭(C) B♭(G)
splin - tered wood - en beam, drink - ing pain and sor - rows,
from Your flesh and bones, I know my life had its be -
F(D) 1. C(A) 2. C(A)
breath - ing a - go - ny. And I
gin - ning at Your cross.
E♭maj7(C) F(D) E♭/G(C) F/A(D) F(D) Chorus B♭2(G)
thank You, thank You: For the cross, where You bled,
E♭2(C) B♭2(G) E♭2(C)
for the cross, where You died, for the cross,

B♭2(G)
Gm(Em)
E♭2(C)
E♭/F(C)
where You've bro-ken Sa-tan's back. For the cross,
Gm7(Em)
E♭2(C)
B♭2(G)
E♭2(C)
where You won, for the cross of vic-to - ry, for the cross,
B♭2(G)
E♭2(C)
F2(D)
E♭2(C)
To end
B♭(G)
where You paid the price for me.

2. You were my substitute
In laying down Your life for mine,
Being cursed and bearing
The wrath of God for me.
You were crushed by sin,
Your punishment has brought me peace,
And by the wounds You suffered
I'm alive and healed.
And I thank You, thank You:

3. Two days in the grave,
Then You rose up from the dead -
Now You reign in glory,
Rule in righteousness.
And I was raised with You,
Free at last from all my sin,
Safe forever in the shelter of my King.
And I thank You, thank You:

1361. I thank You for the cross

(Thank You for the cross)

Is 53:5; Mk 10:45; Rom 7:4

Ken Riley

Steadily

Verse

E

I thank You for the cross where all my shame was

A F♯m7

laid, bro - ken by Your pow - er, ba - nished to the

B7sus4 E

grave. You gave Your - self for me, a sin - ner for a

A F♯m7

King, of - fer - ing Your death and suf - fer - ing my

B7sus4
Chorus
A
B7sus4
sin. And I will give my life to You, Lord,
life for You, Lord,

C♯m7
A
F♯m7
for with grace You came to pay the ran -
You brought me back from death, in - to Your mer -
1.
Bsus4
E
E/D
som for my soul.
And I will live my
2.
(Fine)
Bsus4
E
Esus2+4 E
D.C.
cy on the cross.
I thank You for the

1362. It is good

Capo 3 (D)

Ps 92:1-4, 7, 12-14; 1 Thess 5:18; Heb 13:5

With a latin feel
Dan Adler
Chorus
F(D) B♭(G)
It is good, it is good it is
play on our in - stru - ments
Gm7(Em) C(A) F(D) B♭(G)
good to give thanks to the Lord on high,
sweet songs of praise for the things You do:
Gm7(Em) B♭(G) C(A) F(D) B♭(G)
to sing of Your faith - ful ness
It is good, it is good, it is
1. Gm7(Em) C7(A) F(D) B♭(G) (D) (Bm) Gm7(Em) (A)
F/A Dm C
and lov - ing kind-ness both day and night; to
After 2nd verse to mid section
2. Gm7(Em) C(A) F(D) B♭(G) Gm7(Em) C(A) F(D)
(Fine)
good to give thanks to You.

Verse
B♭(G) C(A) Dm(Bm) C(A) F(D) B♭(G)
1. For though the wick-ed spring up like the grass and are ev-'ry-where,
F(D) Dm(Bm) C(A) B♭(G) C(A)
soon they will pe - rish; but all those plant - ed in
Dm(Bm) Gm7(Em) C(A) B♭/D(G) C/E(A) C(A)
D.C.
Your house will grow with - out end. Sing it a-gain! It is
Mid section
F(D) B♭(G) C(A) F(D)
(Leader)
(All)
Why give Him praise? Be - cause He is wor - thy.
B♭(G) C(A) F(D)
(Leader)
(All)
Why should we sing? He loves you and me.

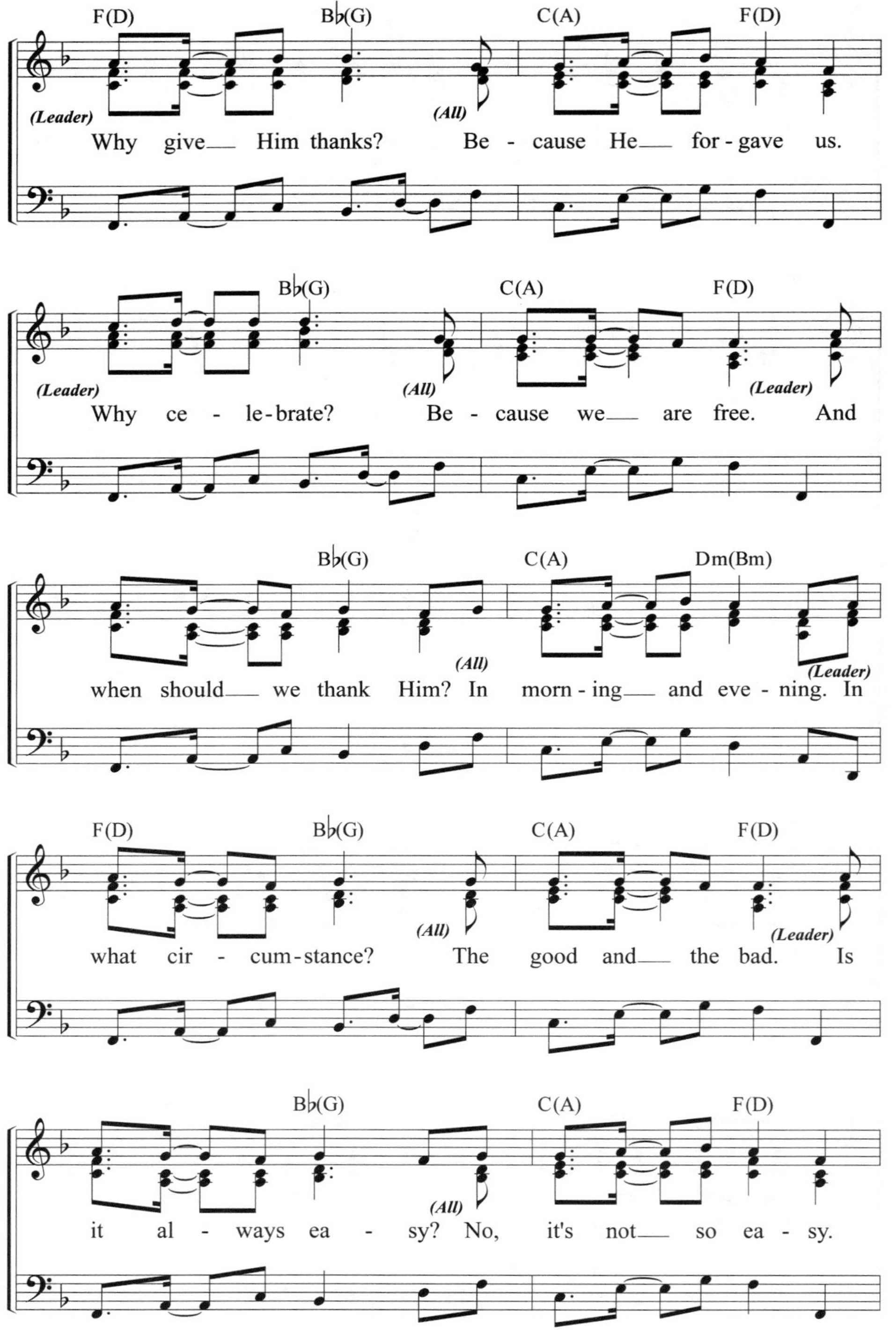
F(D) B♭(G) C(A) F(D)
(Leader) (All)
Why give Him thanks? Be - cause He for - gave us.
B♭(G) C(A) F(D)
(Leader) (All) (Leader)
Why ce - le - brate? Be - cause we are free. And
B♭(G) C(A) Dm(Bm)
(All) (Leader)
when should we thank Him? In morn - ing and eve - ning. In
F(D) B♭(G) C(A) F(D)
(All) (Leader)
what cir - cum - stance? The good and the bad. Is
B♭(G) C(A) F(D)
(All)
it al - ways ea - sy? No, it's not so ea - sy.

B♭(G)
(Leader)
But is it good?
(All)
Yes, it's good, it is good, it is
C(A)
D.C.
good.
It is

2. For though we struggle
And trials and troubles still come our way,
You won't forsake us;
Your word has told us
Your promises will never end.

1363. It is to You

Ps 34:3

Steadily
Duke Kerr
A2 D
It is to You I give the glo - ry, it is to You
A2 G2 D
I give the praise, be - cause You have done
A A♯dim7 Bm7 E7sus4 E7 Em7/A
so much for me, I will mag - ni - fy Your name.
A7 D/F♯ Gaug Em/G Gmaj7 G D/F♯
It is to You, ho - ly Fa - ther,
Em/C♯ F♯7 Bm7 Em7 Bm A2
no one else but You, and I will praise Your name,

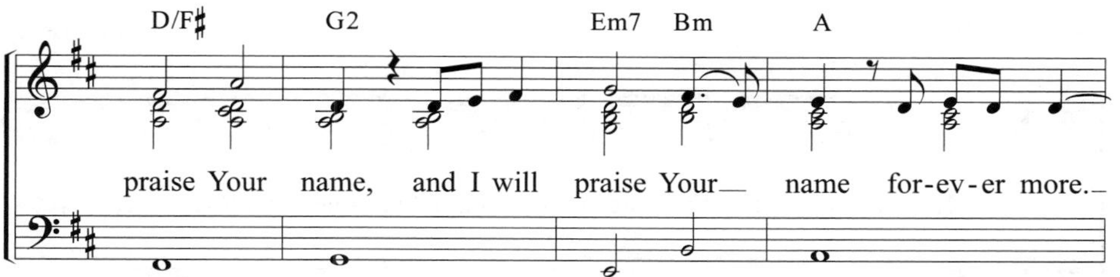
D/F♯
G2
Em7
Bm
A
praise Your name, and I will praise Your name for-ev-er more.

D

1364. I tremble in Your presence

(How I long for You)

Ex 40:34; Ps 42:1; Jn 15:15; 2 Cor 2:14; Rev 1:16

Rohn Bailey

Slow & steady
Verse
C2
Am7addD
1. I trem - ble in Your pre - sence, I am hum - bled that You came, yet I
F2
C/G
G
know it's all be - cause I choose to praise You. I re -
Csus 2 4
C
G/A
Am
cog - nise Your fra - grance, as Your glo - ry fills this place;
F2
C/G
G
F
C
Chorus
C/E
all I'd planned to say means no - thing now. Oh,
F2
Am
G
C
C/E
how I long for You. Oh,

F2
Am
G
C
C/E
– how I long for You. Oh,
F2
Am
G/B
Csus4
C
C/E
1.
F2
G
– how I long for You, oh. 2. I
2.
F2
G
Rit.
C

2. I shiver in Your presence,
I am frozen by my shame.
My heart is breaking
More than I can stand it.
Your radiance is blinding,
Yet You hug me like a friend;
I am overcome by Your mercy again.

1365. It was on a starry night

Lk 2:7-13

Capo 1 (D)

Joy Webb

Moderately

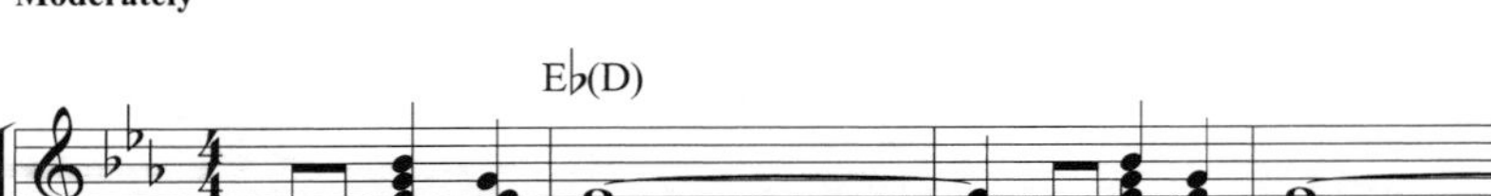
E♭(D)

Verse
(A)
B♭7/E♭
E♭(D)
A♭(G)
1. It was on a star - ry night
when the hills were bright,

(D)
E♭/G
(D)
E♭maj7/G
E♭6(D)
F7(E)
earth lay sleep - ing,
sleep - ing calm and

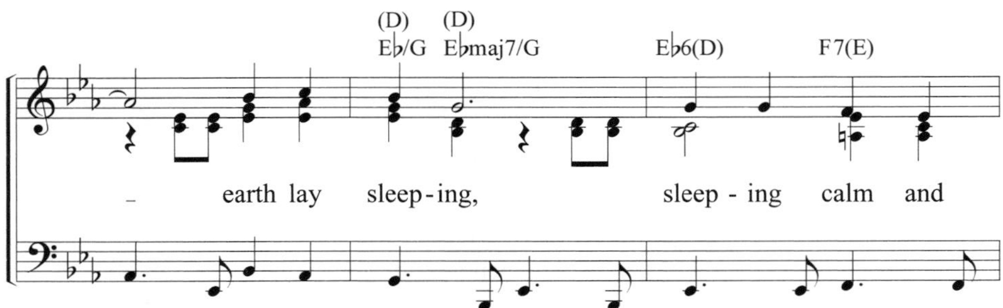
B♭7(A)
(A)
B♭7/E♭
E♭(D)
E♭7(D)
still;
then in a cat - tle shed,
in a

A♭(G)
E♭(D)
B♭7(A)
man - ger bed a boy was born, King of all the
E♭(D)
Chorus
B♭7/E♭(A) E♭(D)
world. And all the an - gels sang for Him,
E♭7(D)
A♭(G)
the bells of hea - ven rang for Him; for a boy was
E♭maj7(D)
B♭7(A)
1. E♭(D)
born, King of all the world. And all the an-gels
2. Last time to Coda
D.C. al Coda
E♭(D)
world.

𝄌 *Coda*

On a star-ry night,
on a star-ry night.

2. Soon the shepherds came that way,
Where the baby lay,
And were kneeling, kneeling by His side.
And their hearts believed again,
For the peace of men;
For a boy was born, King of all the world.

1366. I've come to meet with You

(Through the veil)

Ps 84:1; Is 53:5; 61:1; Mk 15:38; 2 Cor 3:16

Tim Beck

Fast, with energy
G
Verse
Cmaj7
D
Cmaj7
I've come to meet with You, my
to be with You, to know Your
D
Cmaj7
D
G
C
God, to bless Your heart, my King;
love, to give an of - fer - ing.
G
Chorus
C
D
And I will seek Your love-ly face, through the veil I'll
G
C
G
C
Last time to Coda
come, to love you in Your dwell-ing place,
D
Em
D/F♯
1.3.5.
G
to gaze up-on Your throne. And I will seek Your

2.
G
D.S.
4.
G
Bm
Bridge
A/C♯
Your
I know the pu - nish-ment
C
Am
Bm
Em
You took for me;
thank you, Sa-viour, for the cost,
C
Am
Am/G
D/F♯
D.S. al Coda
that set me free,
that set me free.
I've
Coda
D
G
C
G
Fine
to gaze up-on Your throne.

2. Your grace and love have come to me,
You've set this captive free.
This child of Yours, You have redeemed
For life eternally.

1367. I've filled my days with details

(Be still)

Ps 46:10; Mt 6:31; 11:28-30

Reflective

David Gate

E *Verse* B/E

1. I've filled my days with details and all the

A/E B/E E

choi - ces of the earth, car - ried the yoke of wor - ry,

B/E A/E

and all the burd - ens that it brings.

B/E E

And through the midst of all the rush - ing,

B/E
A/E
B/E
You whis - per to our hearts, and with Your

D
B
sweet voice
You say to us:
Chorus
E
To be still and know You are
A/C♯
E
God, to be still and
A/C♯
Last time to Coda
know You are God, just to
F♯m
1.
E
rest in Your arms,

2.
E
F♯m
arms,
just to
rest

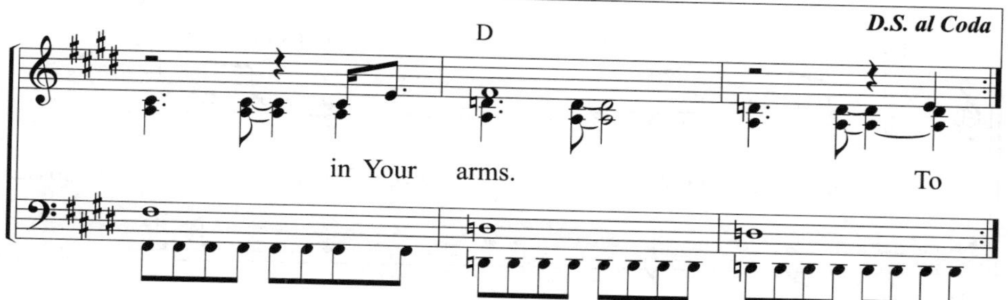
D
D.S. al Coda
in Your
arms.
To

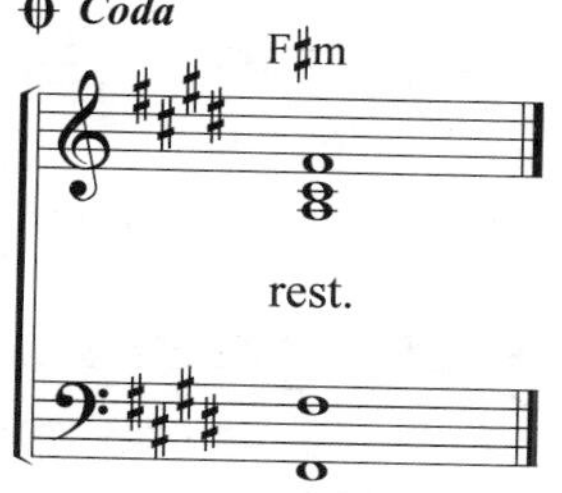
Coda
F♯m
rest.

2. So give me peace and wisdom
To know how to fill my time,
Where I can learn to keep You
At the centre of my life.
So through the midst of all the rushing
There is time to spend with You,
And my foundation will daily be:

1368. I've thrown it all away

(Take the world)

Mt 6:21; Mk 16:15; Phil 3:8; 1 Jn 4:4

Capo 3 (G)

Exuberantly

Matt Redman

Verse
Cm7 (Am7)
1. I've thrown it all away that I might gain
B♭/D(G) E♭(C) Cm7 (Am7)
a life in You. I've found all else is loss
B♭/D(G) E♭(C)
compared to the joys of knowing You. Your
F/A(D) E♭2 (C) B♭/D (G) E♭(C)
beauty and Your majesty are far beyond compare: You've
F/A(D) E♭2 (C) F (D) E♭(C) B♭(G)
won my heart, now this will be my prayer.

Chorus
E♭(C)
Gm(Em)
'Take the world but give me Je-sus!' You're the trea-sure in this life.
Now I've seen You as the Sa-viour, I will leave the rest be-hind:
C7/E (A)
E♭2 (C)
'Take the world but give me Je-sus!'
'Take the world but give me Je-sus!'
1.3.4.
4th time D.S. al fine
B♭2 (G)
is my cry.
2.5.
(Fine)
B♭2 (G)
is my cry.
2. In-

2. Into the world I'll go
That I might live this life of love.
I won't be overcome,
For You are in me and You are strong.
For time and for eternity
I know I'm in Your care;
You've won my heart,
Now this will be my prayer.

1369. I want to be before Your throne

(As I am known)

Ps 8:1; Song 6:3; Jn 3:14; Acts 17:28

Rocky

Paul Oakley

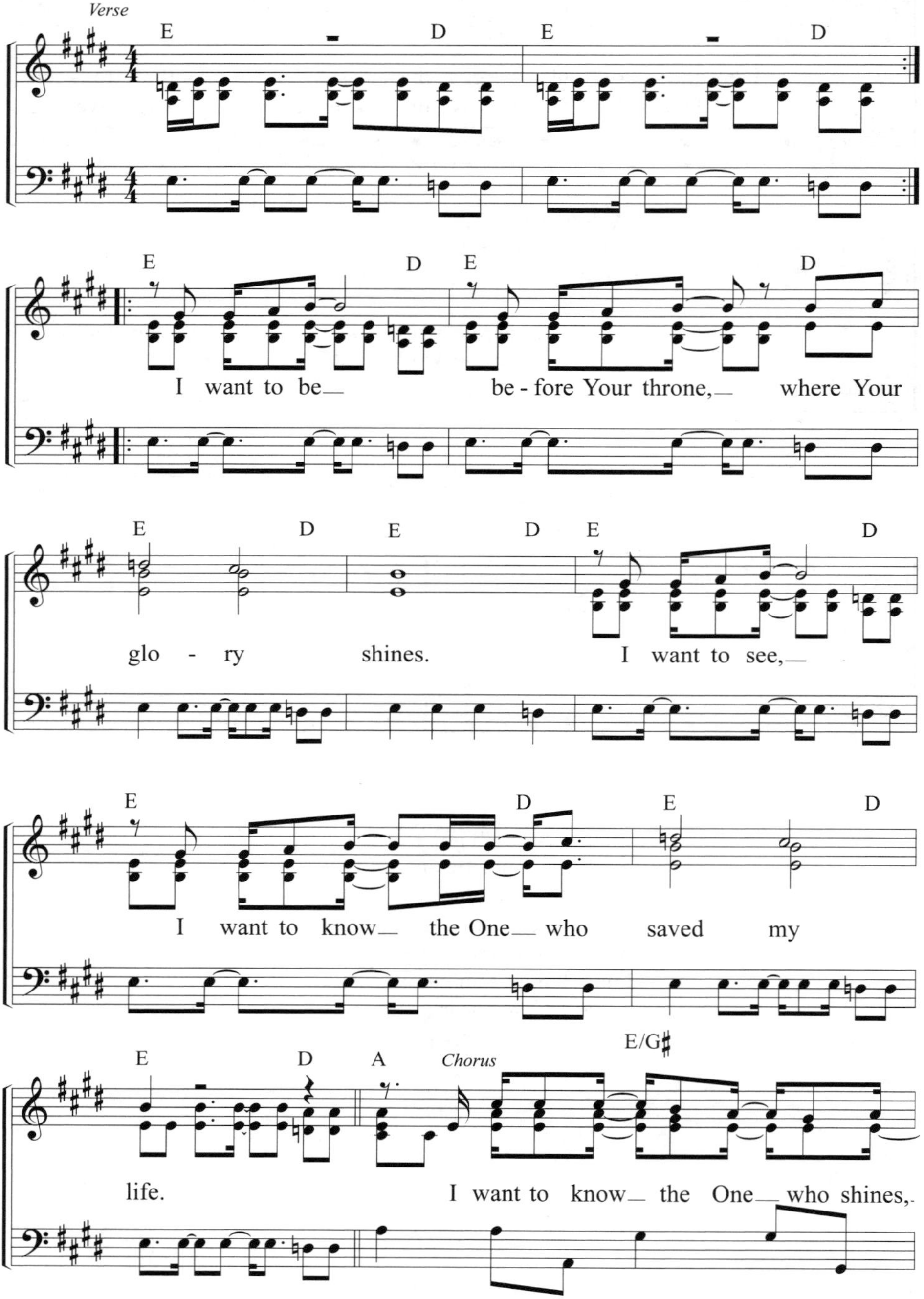

Verse

I want to be before Your throne, where Your glory shines.
I want to see, I want to know the One who saved my life.

Chorus

I want to know the One who shines,

F♯m E A E/G♯
the One en-throned a - bove the skies,
F♯m E D A/C♯
the One who gave his life, was
Bm Bm/A B7
cru-ci-fied, and lift-ed up on high.
E D E D E

2. I want to know as I am known,
In this space and time.
Now I am Yours, and in lover's words:
Jesus, You are mine.

3. In You I live, in You I move
And have my being.
It's You I love
It's You I choose to believe in.

1370. I will call upon the name of the Lord

(God of the breakthrough)

Gen 22:14; Ex 15:26; 17:15; Deut 6:4; Judg 6:24; Ps 18:2-3; 23:1; 31:16; Jer 23:6; Ezek 48:35; Mt 26:19; Jn 12:13

Robert Critchley

Strong rock beat
C
B♭
I will call up-on the name of the Lord, for
F
C
He is wor-thy to be praised. I will shout ho-san-na to
B♭
1.
F
Je-sus, my Rock. I-be-lieve He is the Migh-ty One who saves.
C
2.
F
He is the Migh-ty One, the
Unis
Csus4
C
Migh-ty One who saves. God of the break-through,

E♭
B♭
God of the break - through, all things are pos - si - ble with You.
F
C
Lord, I be - lieve You are the God of the break - through,
E♭
B♭
Last time to Coda
God of the break - through. Let Your love shine down on me.
1.
C
2.
C
You are the
O let Your
E♭
love shine down on me. Let Your
call on Your name, O Lord. I will
B♭
C
love shine down on me. Let Your
call on Your name, O Lord. I will

E♭
love shine down on me. Let Your
call on Your name, O Lord. I will
B♭
1.
C
2.
C
love shine down on me. And I will Je-sus!
call on Your name, O Lord.
E♭
B♭
C
Je-ho-vah E-
E♭
B♭
lo-him, the Lord is God. Je-ho-vah Nis - si, the
C
Lord is my ban - ner. Je-ho-vah Ro - phi, He is the

E♭
B♭
Lord who heals me. Je - ho - vah Ji - reh, the
C
Lord who provides. Je - ho - vah Tsid - kenu, the
E♭
B♭
Lord, our right - eous - ness. Je - ho - vah Sha - lom, He is the
C
Lord of peace. Je - ho - vah Ro - hi, the
E♭
B♭
Lord is my Shep - herd. Je - ho - vah Sham - mah, the
C
D.S. al Coda
Lord is here. He is the
Coda
C

1371.
I will come
(All)
Ps 42:2; Is 53:5; 55:1; Zech 12:10; Mt 11:28; 1 Cor 9:24; Rev 1:7, 14, 16
Capo 1 (D)
Tim Sherrington
Rhythmically, with anticipation
Verse
Cm(Bm)
A♭(G)
E♭(D)
1. I will come, come, come to the wa-ters and drink;
I will praise, praise, praise Your name a - gain.
(v.2)
I will rest, rest, rest, rest at Your feet,
for You have won my heart once a - gain.
1.
2.
Chorus
2. I will thirst
And You are God, with

E♭(D)
fire in Your eyes, and You are God,
A♭(G)
E♭(D)
adorned in radiant light.
A♭(G)
You are God whose hands were pierced for all:
E♭(D)
B♭/D(A)
Cm(Bm)
B♭(A)
what choice do I have, but to give You my ve-ry all.
E♭(D)

2. I will thirst, thirst, thirst
For all that You give;
And I will fall, fall, fall
Into Your arms again.
I will call, call, call
To You alone each day,
For You have won my heart once again.

3. I shall wait, wait, wait
At the cross where we meet;
And I will live, live, live,
By Your name I speak.
I will run, run, run
For Your face to seek,
For You have won my heart once again.

1372. I will enter Your house

(Blessed to be a blessing)

Ps 100:4-5; Mal 3:10; Jn 10:10; 1 Pet 1:8

Lara Martin

Very rhythmic
D C G/B D
I will en-ter Your house with thanks-giv-ing, I will sing of Your
C G/B G A
good-ness to me. For my heart is e - ter - nal - ly grate - ful,
G Em7
I am blessed a - bun - dant - ly. You have gi - ven me
Bm7 A G A Bm
life in all its full ness, and joy no words can de-scribe.
Em7 Bm7 A G
But I know it's for more than me, it's for those,

A
those You sent me to reach. I am
D
G
Em7
blessed, blessed to be a bless - ing, I am blessed, I
A
D
live un - der an o - pen hea - ven, blessed, that
G
Em7
1.
A
2.
A
all may see it's Christ, Christ in me. I am
D
C
G/B
C
D

Praise be to the God and Father of our Lord Jesus Christ, who has blessed us in the heavenly realms with every spiritual blessing in Christ.

EPHESIANS 1:3

1373. I will love You for the cross
(For the cross)

Capo 2 (Am)

Is 53:3-5; Mt 11:19; Rom 6:4; Col 2:2; 1 Pet 2:24; Rev 5:9

With a strong rhythm

Matt & Beth Redman

Verse
Bm(Am) A(G) G(F) Bm(Am) A(G) G(F)
I will love You for the cross,
You came into a world of shame,
Bm(Am) A(G) G(F) Bm(Am) A(G) G(F)
and I will love You for the cost:
and paid the price we could not pay:
A(G) G(F)
Man of sufferings, bringer of my peace.
death that brought me life, blood that brought me home.
Bm(Am) A(G) G(F) Bm(Am) A(G) G(F) A(G)
Death that brought me life,
G(F) D(C) F♯m7(Em)
blood that brought me home. And I love

Chorus
Bm(Am) G(F) A(G)
You for the cross, I'm o-ver-whelmed by the my-
G(F) Bm(Am) G(F)
ste - ry. I love You for the cost,
A(G) G(F)
that Je - sus, You would do this for me. When You
Bm(Am) G(F) A(G)
were bro - ken, You were beat - en, You were pun - ished, I
G(F) Bm(Am) G(F)
go free. When You were wound - ed and re-ject - ed, in-

Last time to Coda
A(G)
Gmaj7(F)
1.
Bm(Am) A(G) G(F) Bm(Am) A(G) G(F)
Your mer - cy, I am healed.
Bm(Am) A(G) G(F) Bm(Am) A(G) G(F)
2.
Bm(Am) G(F) F♯m(Em)
G(F)
D.S. al Coda
And I love
Coda
Bm(Am) G(F) F♯m7(Em) G(F)

2. Jesus Christ, the sinner's friend;
Does this kindness know no bounds?
With Your precious blood
You have purchased me.
O the mystery of the cross,
You were punished, You were crushed;
But that punishment has become my peace.
Yes, that punishment has become my peace.

1374. I will never be the same

Rom 1:16; I Cor 15:55; Heb 10:19

Growing in strength

Ian Hannah

A D/A A Bm E/G♯
I will ne - ver be the same now my eyes are o - pen wide.
A D/A E/A A
I have been for - e - ver changed through the
Bm A/E E (Fine) A C♯m D
po-wer of His blood. I will tri - umph in the cross
A C♯m D
that my Sa - viour bore for me. I will stand

F♯m
A/E
with con - fi - dence because of Je -
E
D
sus. I no lon - ger fear the grave, I'm a child
A
C♯m
D
D
of His grace. I no lon - ger feel a-shamed,
F♯m
A/E
E
D.C. al Fine
be-cause of Je - sus.

1375. I will never be the same

Is 53:5; Mt 27:45; 2 Cor 5:21

Meditatively

Paul Oakley & J.K. Jamieson

Bm
Bm/A
I will ne - ver be the same,
G
D/F♯
A
now that I have seen the cross;
Bm
Bm/A
and how You took up - on Your - self
G
Bm
the full - ness of the wrath of God.
Em7
G
And I may ne - ver un - der - stand

Em7
A
just what You suf-fered in my place;
Bm
Bm/A
Je - sus, You who knew no sin,
G
D
how You were made sin for us. And
Am7
C
Bm
oh, how fierce the Fa-ther's an - ger.
F#7
Am7
And though You were pierced,

C
D
all the pain could not com - pare;
C/D
Am7
C
so dark was the hour, when all
Bm
Bm/A
hea-ven turned its face a-way, turned its face a-way from You.
G
D/F♯
G
But how sweet is Your mer -
D/F♯
G
A7sus4
cy as it finds its way to me.
D

1376.
Jesus, all for Jesus
(All for Jesus)
1 Cor 10:21; 2 Cor 4:5; Gal 5:1
Jennifer Atkinson
& Robin Mark
Steadily
Verse
E A E Esus2 E
1. Je - sus, all for Je - sus; all I
(v.2)
B
am and have and ev - er hope to be.
(v.2)
1.3.
1st time Repeat v.1
2nd time v.2
C♯m B
2nd & Last time
(Fine)
Repeat v.2
E A2 E
be.
4.
E A2 E
Chorus
hands. For it's
A E
on - ly in Your will that I am free. For it's
A E B Bsus2 B
D.C.
on - ly in Your will that I am free.

2. All of my ambitions, hopes and plans,
I surrender these into Your hands.
(Repeat)

1377. # Jesus, be the Centre

Jn 1:4; 8:12; 14:6; Col 1:27

(Be the Centre)

Moderately

Michael Frye

Verse

D

1.4. Je - sus, be the Cen - tre,

A7sus4
G/B
4th time to Coda ⊕
be my source, be my light, Je - sus.

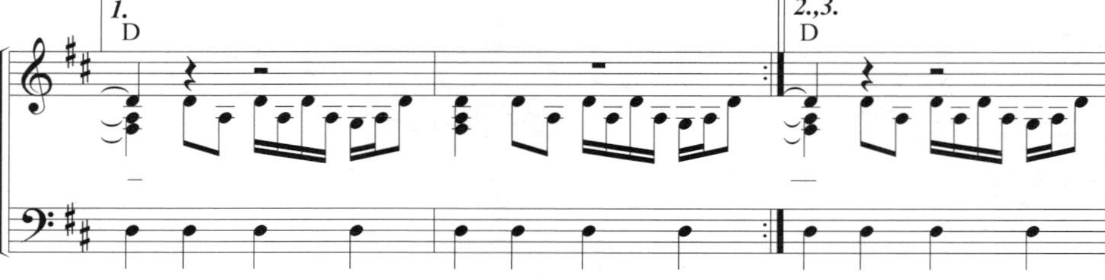

1.
D
2.,3.
D

Chorus
A7sus4
D
Be the fi - re in my heart, be the wind

A7sus4
D
A7sus4
in these sails; be the rea - son that I live,

Bm
A 7sus4
G/B
1.,2.
D
Je - sus,
Je - sus.
D.C.
Coda
D

2. Jesus, be the Centre,
   Be my hope, be my song,
   Jesus.

3. Jesus, be my vision,
   Be my path, be my guide,
   Jesus.

1378.
Jesus Christ
(All my love)
Capo 3(G)
Ps 42:7; Is 53:5; 1 Cor 13:12; 1 Tim 1:15; Titus 3:7; Heb 9:15
Noel Richards
Simply
B♭(G) F/A(D) E♭(C) B♭/D(G)
1. Je-sus Christ, You came in - to this world to re -
F(D) F/E♭(D) B♭(G) F/A(D)
- scue me. On the cross, my sin was
E♭(C) B♭/D(G) F(D) F/E♭(D) B♭(G)
laid on You, what a - go - ny. There Your
F(D) F/E♭(D) B♭/D(G) E♭(C)
pre - cious life - blood flowed so free. E-v'ry-

F(D) F/E♭(D) B♭/D(G) F(D)
drop that fell still clean - ses me.
All Your love, all Your love, all Your love, all Your love
All Your love, all Your love, all Your love, all Your love
All my love, all my love, all my love, all my love
B♭(G) Fsus4(D) F(D) B♭(G)
E♭(C) B♭(G) F/A(D) (Em) Gm (Bm) Dm/F E♭2(C) F(D) B♭(G)
pour - ing out for me like a flood.
sweep - ing o - ver me like a flood.
flow - ing out to You like a flood.
1.2. E♭/B♭ (C)
3. B♭(G)
2. I am
3. So I

2. I am safe
Upon the ocean of Your mercy.
I am loved
With all the passion of eternity.
It is deeper than the deepest sea;
Like a tidal wave it carries me.
All Your love...

3. So I stand
Upon Your promise of eternal grace.
I believe
That I will one day see You face to face.
I will worship You forever more
In ways I never have before.
All my love...

1379. Jesus Christ, Emmanuel

Is 7:14; 9:6; Mt 1:23; Jn 1:1, 3; Acts 4:12; Col 1:16; Phil 2:9-11; Heb 12:22; Rev 1:17; 5:11-12

Martyn Layzell

Quite slow, with a rock feel

G D/F♯

1. Je - sus Christ,— Em-ma - nu - el,—
2. Ho - ly one— up - on— the throne,—

Em C2

the Sa - viour of— the world;—
to You the an - gels sing:—

G D/F♯

Cre - a - tor of— the u - ni - verse,—
and here we join— their hea - v'nly song,—

Em C2

the true and liv - ing Word.—
pro-claim - ing You— as King.—

D C/E

Let ev - 'ry tongue— con - fess— Your name,—

D
Em
D/F♯
we bow the knee before Your hand of grace,
C
D
giv-ing You the high-est praise.
Chorus
Em7
D/F♯
G
C
You are, You are - the e-ver-last-ing Prince of Peace,
Em7
D/F♯
G
D/F♯
the First, the Last, in whom all things were made.
Em7
D/F♯
G
Asus4
A
You reign with love, Coun-sel-lor, Al-migh-ty God.

C2
D/F♯
Em
Asus4 A
Je - sus, You're the name by which we're saved,
1. C2
D/F♯
G
D/F♯
Je - sus, You're the name a-bove all names.
Em
C
2. C2
D/F♯
Je - sus, You're the name a-bove all names.
G
D.S. to chorus
3. C2
D/F♯
Je - sus, You're the name a-bove all names.
Em
A
C2
G/D
rit.
D/F♯
G
Je - sus, You're the name a-bove all names.

1380. Jesus Christ, holy One

Ps 3:3; Jn 14:6; 20:22; Rom 8:15, 37

Nathan Fellingham

Brightly
Verse
C G Am7
Je - sus Christ, ho - ly One, the lif-ter of
F C G
our heads, through You I come, con - qu'ring Son,
Am7 F G C/E
to my Fa - ther in heav'n. And I'm con - fi-dent
F C G C/E
that I be - long to You, as the Spi - rit tes - ti-fies.
F C G C/E F
I shall not fear, fear has

SoF3

C Dm C/E F G
no hold, so I cry 'Ab-ba Fa - ther!'
C Chorus G Am7
What mer - cies You have poured on me, with thank-
C/E F C
ful - ness I'll sing; I choose to fix my mind on
F F/G C
all the bles - sings You have gi - ven me. For You've re-vealed
G Am7 C/E
to me Your grace, the won - der of the cross;

F
C
F
You've breathed new life to me, and in Your vic - t'ry I
G
C
G
C
G
now stand to-day.
C

1381. Jesus Christ is waiting

Mt 14:36; Mk 1:17; 10:14; Lk 4:39; 9:58; Jn 2:15

Words: John L. Bell
Music: French Trad.
Arr. David Ball

Tune: NOËL NOUVELET

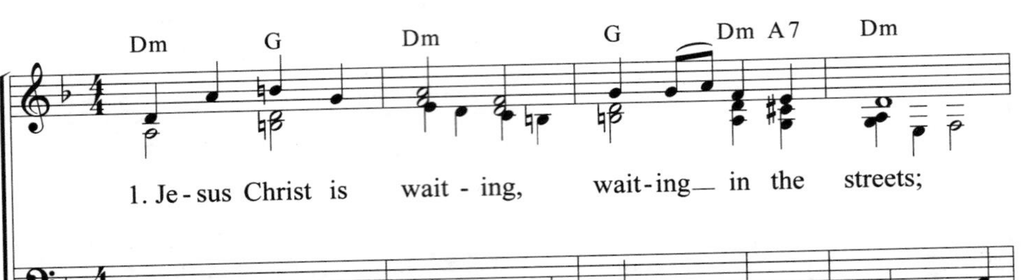

Dm G Dm G Dm A7 Dm
1. Je-sus Christ is wait - ing, wait-ing in the streets;

G Dm G Dm A7 Dm
no one is his neigh - bour, all a - lone he eats.

E7 A Dm7 G Csus2 C Asus4 A
Lis - ten, Lord Je - sus, I am lone-ly too:

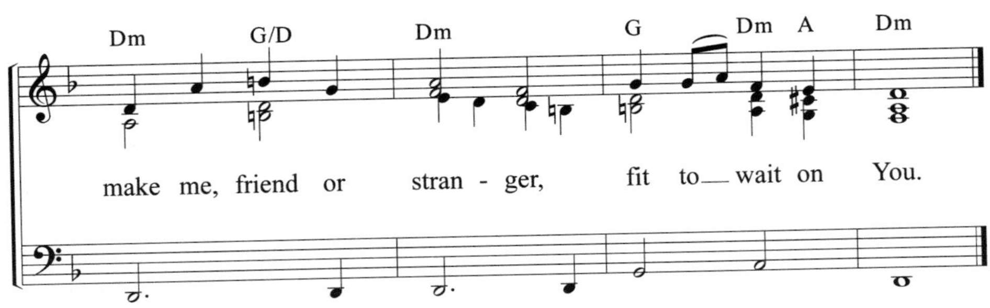

Dm G/D Dm G Dm A Dm
make me, friend or stran - ger, fit to wait on You.

2. Jesus Christ is raging,
Raging in the streets,
Where injustice spirals
And real hope retreats.
Listen, Lord Jesus,
I am angry too:
In the kingdom's causes
Let me rage with You.

3. Jesus Christ is healing,
Healing in the streets,
Curing those who suffer,
Touching those he greets.
Listen, Lord Jesus,
I have pity too:
Let my care be active,
Healing just like You.

4. Jesus Christ is dancing,
Dancing in the streets,
Where each sign of hatred
He, with love, defeats.
Listen, Lord Jesus,
I should triumph too;
Where good conquers evil
Let me dance with You.

5. Jesus Christ is calling,
Calling in the streets,
'Who will join my journey?
I will guide their feet.'
Listen, Lord Jesus,
Let my fears be few:
Walk one step before me;
I will follow You.

1382. Jesus, draw me ever nearer

(May this journey)

Ps 59:16; 143:8; Is 40:31; 1 Jn 3:2

Capo 1 (D)

Margaret Becker & Keith Getty

With feeling

(G)
E♭(D) A♭/E♭ E♭(D)
Verse
E♭(D)
(G)
A♭/E♭ E♭(D)
1. Je-sus,_ draw me e-ver near-er, as I

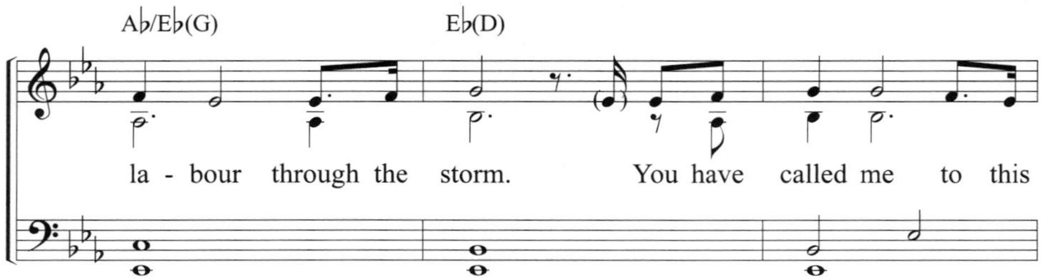

A♭/E♭(G)
E♭(D)
la-bour through the storm. You have called me to this

(G)
A♭/E♭ E♭(D)
A♭/E♭(G)
E♭(D)
Chorus
pas-sage, and I'll fol-low, though I'm worn. May this

B♭(A) E♭/B♭(D) B♭(A) E♭/G(D) A♭(G)
jour-ney bring a bless-ing, may I rise__ on wings of

D♭(C)
E♭(D)
(G)
A♭/E♭ E♭(D)
faith: and at the end of my heart's test - ing, with Your
A♭/E♭(G)
1.2.
E♭(D)
3.
E♭(D)
like - ness let me wake. 2. Je - sus wake.

2. Jesus, guide me through the tempest,
   Keep my spirit staid and sure.
   When the midnight meets the morning,
   Let me love You even more.

3. Let the treasures of the trial
   Form within me as I go.
   And at the end of this long passage,
   Let me leave them at Your throne.

1383. Jesus, God's righteousness revealed

(This kingdom)
Is 9:7; Lk 1:33; Rom 1:17; Col 1:15; 2:9-10
Geoff Bullock
Verse
D A2/C♯ F♯ Bm7
1. Je - sus, God's righ - teous - ness re - vealed,
Am7 D7 G D2/F♯
the Son of Man, the Son of God, His king - dom
Em7 G/A A Bm7 Am7 D9
comes. Je - sus, re - demp - tion's sa - cri -
Gmaj7 F♯m7 Em7 D/F♯ G2
fice, now glo - ri - fied, now ju - sti - fied, His king - dom
G/A A7 Chorus D
comes. And His king - dom will know no end,

A2/C♯ Bm7 F♯m/A
and its glo - ry shall know no bounds, for the
G A/G D/F♯ E/G♯
ma - je - sty and pow - er of this king - dom's King has come,
Asus4 A D A/C♯
and this king - dom's reign, and this king - dom's rule, and this
Bm7 F♯m/A G2 D/A Bm7
king - dom's pow - er and au - tho - ri - ty, Je - sus, God's
Em7 Asus4 A G D
right - teous - ness re - vealed.

2. Jesus, the expression of God's love,
The grace of God, the word of God, revealed to us;
Jesus, God's holiness displayed,
Now glorified, now justified, His kingdom comes.

1384.
Jesus, high King of heaven
Ex 15:11; Col 1:15-16; Heb 1:3; 13:8; Rev 22:13
Capo 3 (D)
Philip Lawson Johnston
Brightly
Chorus
B♭(G) F(D) B♭(G) F(D) C(A) F(D)
Je - sus, high King of hea - ven,
B♭(G) F(D) B♭(G) F(D) C(A) Csus4(A) C(A)
we bring our high praise to You.
B♭(G) F(D) B♭(G) F(D) C(A) Dm(Bm)
Je - sus, high King of hea - ven,
3rd time to Bridge
Last time to Coda
B♭(G) F(D) C(A) F(D) Fsus4(D) F(D)
to whom all high praise is due.
Verse
Dm(Bm) B♭(G)
1. Who can be com - pared to You, O Ho - ly One?

F(D)
C(A)
None in heav'n or earth is Your e - qual. You
Dm(Bm)
B♭(G)
will not share Your glo - ry with a - no-ther;
F(D)
C(A)
D.C.
⊕ Bridge
Am(F♯m)
Ho - nour to Your name. You are the
Dm(Bm)
B♭(G)
i - mage, the ra - di - ance of God's glo - ry. Through You the
F(D)
C(A)
Am(F♯m)
u - ni - verse was made. You are the

Dm(Bm)
Al - pha, O - me - ga, the First and Last, You
B♭(G) F(D) C(A) D.C. al Coda
are the Be - gin - ning and the End.
Coda
B♭(G) F(D) B♭(G) F(D) 1. C(A) F(D)
Je - sus, high King of hea - ven.
2. C(A) F(D)
hea - ven.

2. O Lord God Almighty, who is like You?
Yesterday, today and forever,
Power, mercy, faithfulness surround You;
Eternal is Your name.

"Who will fear You, O Lord, and bring glory to Your name? For You alone are holy. All nations will come and worship before You, for Your righteous acts have been revealed."

REVELATION 15:4

1385. Jesus, hope of the nations

Ps 18:2; Is 9:6; Mt 5:4; Lk 4:18; Jn 1:5, 9, 12; 8:12;14:6; Acts 2:32; Col 1:27

(Hope of the nations)

Brian Doerksen

Strong rhythm
Verse
A D/A A D/A F♯m E D E D A/C♯ Bm7 E
Je - sus, hope of the na - tions; Je - sus, com - fort for all who mourn, You are the source of hea - ven's hope on earth.
Je - sus, light in the dark - ness, Je - sus, truth in each cir - cum - stance, You are the source of hea - ven's light on earth.
1. 2.
In hi - sto - ry, You lived and died, You broke the chains, You rose to life. You are the Hope,

Chorus
A
D
– liv - ing in us,___ You are the Rock,_
– con - quer - ing fear,___ our Prince of peace,_
E
A
– in whom we trust.___ You are the Light,_
– draw - ing us near.___ Je - sus, our Hope,_
F♯m
D
E
– shin - ing for all___ the world__ to see.___
– liv - ing for all___ who will__ re - ceive,___
1.
D/E
2.
D
A
You rose from the dead,_ Lord, we__ be - lieve.___
D/A
A
D/A
A

1386. Jesus is exalted

Ps 40:3; 1 Cor 9:24; 13:12;
Eph 1:20-21; 1 Thess 4:17; 2 Thess 1:7; 1 Pet 2:9;
Heb 1:2-3; 12:1; Rev 11:15; 17:14; 19:7, 16; 22:5

With energy
Alan Rose
Verse
E B/D♯ A/C♯ E
1. Je - sus is ex - alt - ed to the high - est place,
A E Bsus4 B
seat - ed at the right hand of our God. He
A E A E
reigns in pow'r and glo - ry, He is God's ap - point - ed heir, He is
A E Bsus4 B E/G♯ Chorus
right - eous, He is ho - ly, He is Lord! Hal - le -
A E B C♯m7 A
lu - jah! He is King of kings. Hal - le - lu -

E
B
E/G♯
A
E
jah! He is the Lord. Hal-le-lu - jah! He is
B G♯/B♯ C♯m7
A
Last time to Coda
E
Bsus4
Je-sus Christ, reign-ing for - e-ver more,— e-ver more.
1.
B
2.
B
D
Bridge
A/C♯
2. The
The day is com-ing when He
E
G
D
will ap-pear,— His glo-ry shin-ing like the
Asus4
A
C
G
sun; and ev-'ry na-tion then will

D
C
G
see and fear the migh - ty and ex - alt - ed
Bsus4
B
D.C. al Coda
One. 3. So
Coda
Bsus4
B
E
more.

2. The throne of God will last for all eternity,
   We will reign with Him as those He has redeemed.
   For we are a chosen people,
   We will be the bride of Christ,
   He has chosen us to ever be with Him!

3. So let us throw aside all that would hinder us,
   And run as those who run to win the prize.
   For we will see His glory,
   We will see Him face to face,
   We will join Him as His glory fills the skies!

Let us rejoice and be glad and give Him glory! For the wedding of the Lamb has come, and His bride has made herself ready.

REVELATION 19:7

1387. Jesus is Lord

Mt 28:6; Lk 15:20; Jn 1:1; 6:51; 13:5; Acts 2:24; Rom 10:9; Gal 3:13; Eph 1:7; Phil 2:7, 10; 1 Thess 4:17; Rev 1:7

Stuart Townend
& Keith Getty

Majestically
D Em7 D/F♯ Bm Bm/A G D/F♯
1. 'Je-sus is Lord' - the cry that e - choes through cre -
Gmaj7 Asus4 A Bm A/C♯ Dsus4 Bsus2+4 Bm
a - tion: re - splen - dent pow'r, e - ter - nal
G Em7 Asus4 A D Em7 D/F♯ Bm Bm/A
Word, our Rock. The Son of God, the King whose
G D/F♯ Gmaj7 F♯/A♯ Bm A/C♯
glo - ry fills the hea - vens, yet bids us
D Bsus2+4 Bm G G/A D Em7
come to taste this liv - ing Bread.

D/F♯ G
Asus4 A
D
Fine

2. Jesus is Lord - whose voice sustains the stars and planets,
   Yet in His wisdom laid aside His crown.
   Jesus the Man, who washed our feet, who bore our suffering,
   Became a curse to bring salvation's plan.

3. Jesus is Lord - the tomb is gloriously empty!
   Not even death could crush this King of love!
   The price is paid, the chains are loosed, and we're forgiven,
   And we can run into the arms of God.

4. 'Jesus is Lord' - a shout of joy, a cry of anguish,
   As He returns, and every knee bows low.
   Then every eye and every heart will see His glory,
   The Judge of all will take His children home.

1388. Jesus, Jesus, Healer, Saviour

Ps 140:7; 1 Jn 4:14

David Fellingham

Gently

G D Am Am/D G

Je - sus, Je - sus,

C/G G C/G G C/G G B/F♯ Em

Heal - er, Sav - iour, strong De - liv er-er,

C G/D D Em G/B C G/D D G

how I love You, how I love You.

1389. Jesus, Jesus, Jesus

(Jesus, how I love Your name)

Ps 91:1

Dave Bilbrough

Simply
D A Bm F♯m/A G D Asus4 G/A D F♯
Je - sus, Je - sus, Je - sus,
Bm G/A D Em/A D (Fine)
how I love Your name. The sweet - est name on earth
Em7 G/A D B7 Em Gmaj7/D
will ne - ver be e - nough to tell the won - der of Your
A2 D G G/A
love. Come hide me in Your arms and calm my rest - less heart;
D.C. al fine
D B7 Em D Asus4 G/A
I hun - ger, Lord, for more of You.

The Lord will be king over the whole earth. On that day there will be one Lord, and His name the only name.

ZECHARIAH 14:9

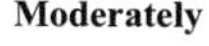

1390. Jesus, King of the ages

(Prophet, Priest and King)

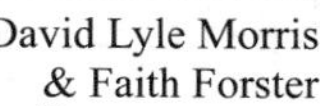
Mk 1:15; Lk 4:18; 7:22; Jn 1:1-2; 1 Cor 15:25; 2 Tim 2:12; Heb 4:16; 7:25-26; 9:5; 10:12-13; 1 Jn 2:2; Rev 15:3; 20:6

Moderately

David Lyle Morris
& Faith Forster

Chorus

E A B E A B
Je - sus, King of the a - ges, plead-ing our

E A F♯m7 Bsus4 B7
cause be - fore the throne of God.

E A B E A B
Je - sus, the liv-ing Word of God, our

A B C♯m A B
Pro-phet, Priest and King, our Pro-phet, Priest and

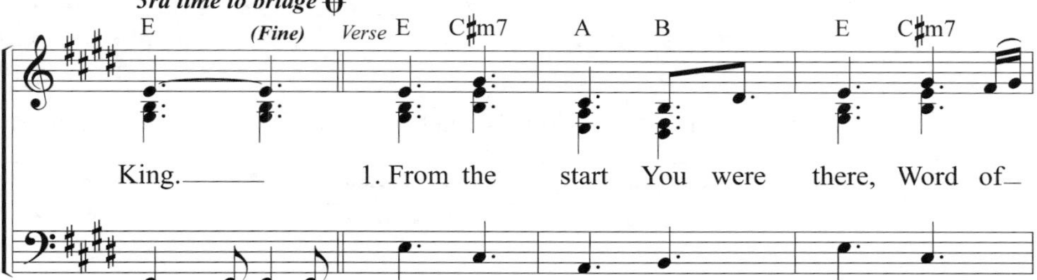

3rd time to bridge ⊕
E
(Fine)
Verse E C♯m7 A B E C♯m7
King.
1. From the start You were there, Word of

A B E C♯m7 A F♯m B
God, an-cient pro-mis - es You came to ful - fil;
G♯m A
You came re-veal - ing the Fa-ther's heart, His
F♯m F♯m/E B/D♯ C♯m
fa-vour, His pur-pose, His will: shar-ing His good news
D F♯m B D.C.
with the poor, de - clar - ing God's king-dom is here.
Bridge
C♯m D F♯m7 F♯m7/E
Je-sus shall reign at the Fa-ther's hand till all of His e - ne-mies

B/D♯
C♯m
D
cease: hell and de-struc - tion, di - sease and death— are
F♯m7
B
Amaj7
un-der His glo-ri-ous feet.— We will reign— with Christ, (we will
C♯m
reign— with Christ,) we will reign— with Christ, (we will
F♯m7
reign— with Christ,) we will reign— with Christ (we will
Bsus4
B
D.C.
reign— with Christ) for e - ver. With

2. At the cross You poured out costly blood,
Perfect sacrifice, atoning for sin,
So we may enter the holy place
To meet You, our faithful High Priest;
As we come to the mercy seat
We find grace in our time of need.

1391.

Jesus loves the church

(Can you hear Him singing?)

Capo 1 (D)

Song 4:9; Mt 16:18; Jn 15:16; Eph 2:21-22; 5:25, 27

With strength

Michael Sandeman

Eb(D) *Verse* Bb/Eb(A) Bbm7(Am)

1. Je - sus loves the church, He gave Him-self for His bride.

Ab2/C(G) Eb(D) Bb/Eb(A)

He knows what we will be, a con-quer-ing ar -

Bbm7(Am) Ab2/C(G) Ab(G)

my, an un-blem-ished peo - ple. We're ac - cep - ted, we're for -

Bb(A) Ab/C(G) Bb/D(A)

giv - en, we're u - ni - ted with Him; not re -

Ab(G) Bb(A) Ab/C(G)

jec - ted, not for - got - ten, not a - ban - doned in

(A)
B♭sus4 B♭(A) Chorus
E♭/G(D) A♭(G) E♭/G(D) A♭(G)
sin. Can you hear Him sing - ing, 'I love you, I love
E♭/G(D) B♭sus4(A) E♭/G(D) A♭(G) E♭/G(D) A♭(G)
you.' Can you hear Him call - ing, 'I want you, I have cho -
E♭/G(D) B♭sus4(A) A♭(G)
sen you to be Mine.'

2. Jesus loves the church,
His passion through the ages.
Hell will not prevail,
He builds us together,
A living temple.
We're accepted, we're forgiven,
We're united with Him,
Not rejected, not forgotten,
Not abandoned in sin.

1392. Jesus, melt my cold heart

Caroline Bonnett
& Steve Bassett

Moderately
Chorus
C
Fmaj7
Am7
1. Je - sus, melt my cold heart, break my sto - ny e - mo-tions.
Fmaj7
C
Fmaj7
Cos I've been play-ing with the waves when I should be swim-ming in the
Am7
Fmaj7
Chorus
Dm7
C
Dm7
C
Dm7
C
o-cean.
Take me deep - er, show me
G
Dm7
C
Dm7
C
Dm7
C
more.
It's all or no - thing, I give You e-v'ry thing, my Lord.
Gsus4
G
Last time
C

2. Jesus, show Your mercy,
I'm so sorry for waiting,
I should be running to Your heart,
But I know I've been hesitating.

1393.

Jesus, my desire

Capo 3 (D)
Energetic

Ps 40:2; 46:2;
Jn 15:4; 2 Cor 12:10

Martyn Layzell

C7sus4(A) Gm7(Em) B♭(G) Gm7(Em)
Verse
C7sus4(A) Gm7(Em) B♭(G)
1. Je - sus, my de - sire, I turn to - wards Your ways,
2. How can I stay pure, oh, how can I stay true?
Gm7(Em) C7sus4(A) Gm7(Em)
hun - gry for Your truth, I'm
By liv - ing as Your word and
B♭(G) Gm7(Em)
here to seek Your face.
dwell - ing on Your truth.
Bridge
Dm(Bm)
But in my weak - ness, I
B♭2(G) F/A (D) C7sus4(A)
cry out to You, on - ly You, to

Dm(Bm)
B♭2(G)
F/A (D)
be my strength when I am weak and do as You do.
C7sus4(A)
B♭(G)
Chorus
F/A (D)
With You, it all
B♭(G)
F/A (D)
seems so right, if the sun don't shine there's light
C7sus4(A)
F/A(D)
B♭(G)
in Your eyes, with You when moun-tains fall, I
F/A(D)
1.3.
C7sus4(A)
stand on the Rock and I'm safe in Your arms when I'm with

Gm7(Em)
B♭2(G)
C7sus4(A)
You,
when I'm with You.
Gm7(Em)
B♭2(G)
Gm7(Em)
1° D.C. to verse 2
2° D.S. to bridge
2.4.
D.S.S. to chorus
C7sus4(A)
in your arms with You.
5.
C7sus4(A)
in Your arms when I'm with
Gm7(Em)
B♭2(G)
C7sus4(A)
You,
when I'm with You.
Gm7(Em)
B♭2(G)
rit.
F(D)
Just to be with You.

1394. Jesus, my passion

(Above all else)

Phil 3:8

Worshipfully

Vicky Beeching

Verse
D
Je - sus, my pas - sion in life is to know
Je - sus, You've sho - wered Your good - ness on
Bm
You. May all o - ther goals bow down to this
me, gi - ven Your gifts so free - ly, but
Em
G
Asus4
D
jour - ney of lov - ing You more.
there's one thing I'm long - ing for.
Em7
D/F♯
G
Hear my heart's cry, and my pray'r for this life.

Asus4 A
D/G
Chorus
D/F♯
Em
A-bove all else,
a-bove all else,
A
G
D/F♯
a - bove all else,
Em
A
Last time to Coda
1.
D
give me Your - self.
D.C.
2.
D/G
D.S.
Coda
D
A-bove all else,

1395. Jesus, Name above all names

(The Jesus song)

Song 2:1; Mk 1:1; Jn 3:14; Acts 3:13; Phil 2:9; Rev 22:13, 16

Tenderly

Owen Hurter

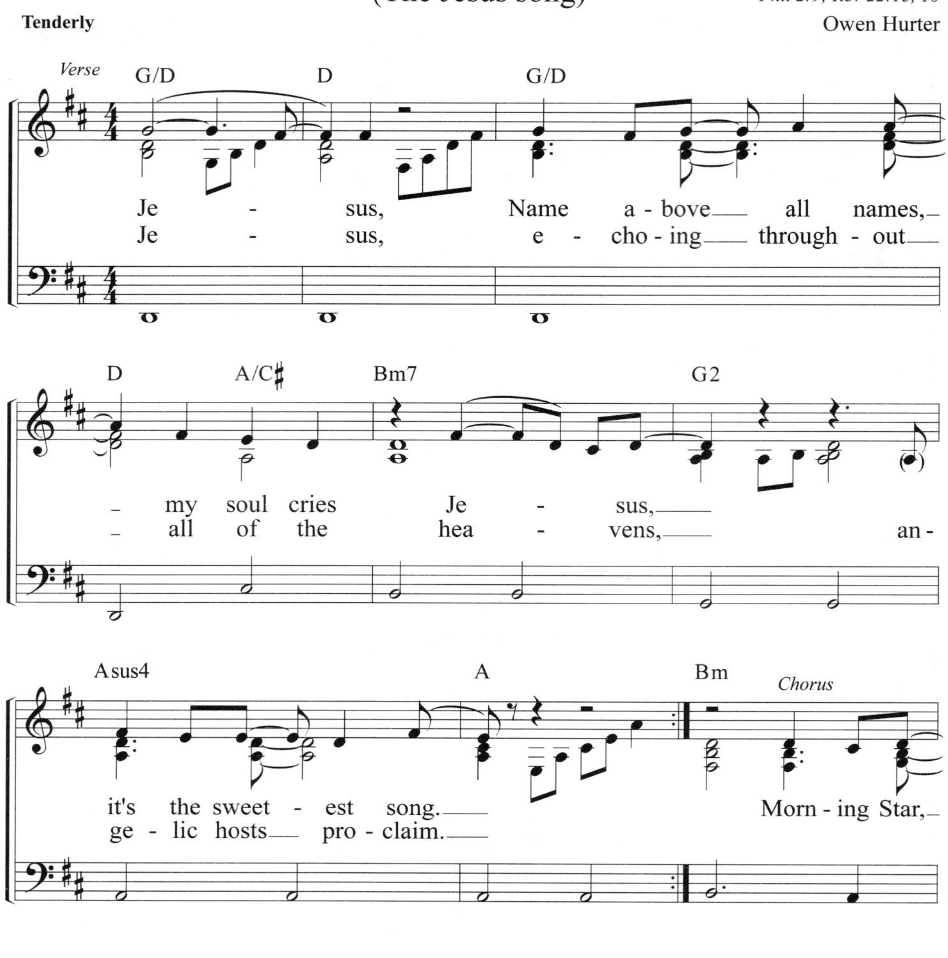

Verse
G/D D G/D
Je - sus, Name a - bove all names,
Je - sus, e - cho - ing through - out
D A/C♯ Bm7 G2
my soul cries Je - sus,
all of the hea - vens, an -
Asus4 A
it's the sweet - est song.
ge - lic hosts pro - claim.
Bm
Chorus
Morn - ing Star,

G Bm G Bm

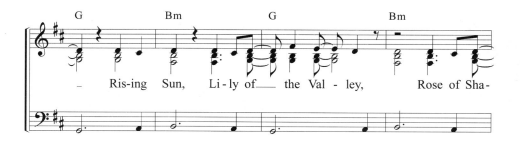

Ris-ing Sun, Li - ly of the Val - ley, Rose of Sha-

G
Asus4 A
Asus2 A
Bm
- ron, Son of God.
Lift - ed up,
G
Bm
G
glo - ri - fied,
praised through all the a - ges;
Bm
G
D/A
3
the First and Last, Be - gin - ning and End.
A
D.C.
To end
D

1396.

Jesus, Redeemer

Is 9:6; Col 1:14; Rev 15:3

(Redeemer)

Tim Hughes

Rhythmically
Verse
1. Je-sus, Re - deem-er, Friend and King to me.
My re-fuge, my comfort, You're ev-'ry-thing to me.
And this heart is on fire for You,
yes, this heart is on fire for You.
For
Chorus
You a-lone are won-der-ful, You a - lone are Coun-sel-lor,

A
E2/G♯
A
A/B
e - ver - last - ing Fa - ther, migh - ty in the hea - vens.
E
E2/G♯
Ne - ver to for - get the love You dis - played up - on a cross,
A
E2/G♯
A
A/B
Son of God I thank You, Prince of Peace, I love Your
E
E2/G♯
A
A/B
E
name.

2. Saviour, Healer,
Just and true are You.
Now reigning in glory,
Most high and living God.
And this heart is in awe of You,
Yes, this heart is in awe of You.

If you believe, you will receive whatever you ask for in prayer.

MATTHEW 21:22

1397. Jesus taught us how to pray

Mt 6:9-12

(Can I see heaven?)

Capo 4 (C)

With energy

James Gregory

E(C) F♯/C♯(D) G♯m7(Em)

Je - sus taught __ us how __ to pray: __
Would You give __ us what __ we need, __

E(C) F♯/C♯(D)

Fa - ther, hal - lowed be __ Your name. __
and for - give __ our fool - ish ways? __

B(G) C♯m(Am)

I know Je -

G♯m7(Em) F♯sus4(Dsus4) F♯(D)

sus on - ly prayed, __

E(C) B/D♯(G) C♯m7(Am)

Fa - ther, what __ You had __ or - dained. __

B/D♯(G)
E(C)
F♯/C♯(D)
3
B(G)
Let Your king-dom come on
A(F)
E/G♯(C)
F♯/A♯(D)
B(G)
earth, Lord, as we pray.
Let Your - will be done to
A(F)
E/G♯(C)
F♯/A♯(D)
G♯m7(Em)
glo-ri - fy Your name.
Let the king-dom that we
F♯/A♯(D)
B(G)
(G/B)
B/D♯
E(C)
E/D♯(C)
live for be re - vealed in us to - day.
Can I see
C♯m(Am)
C♯m/B (Am)
1.
F♯/A♯(D)
hea - ven,
can I see hea - ven here

E(C)
B(G)
A(F)
B(G)
_ on earth_ to - day?_
C♯m7(Am7)
2.
F♯/A♯(D)
E(C)
E/D♯(C/B)
C♯m(Am)
hea - ven,_ can I see hea - ven?_
C♯m/B (Am)
F♯/A♯(D)
E(C)
E/D♯(C/B)
Can I see hea - ven,_ can I see
C♯m(Am)
G♯m(Em)
F♯/A♯(D)
hea - ven?_ Can I see hea - ven_ here_
E(C)
_ on earth_ to - day?_

1398. Jesus, You alone

Heb 12:2; Rev 2:4

Capo 4(G)

Tim Hughes

Driving

Verse
B(G)
E(C)
1. Je - sus, You a - lone shall be my first love, my
B/F♯(G)
F♯(D)
B(G)
first love. The se - cret place and high - est praise shall be
E(C)
B/F♯(G)
F♯(D)
Bridge
E(C)
F♯(D)
Yours, shall be Yours. To Your throne I'll

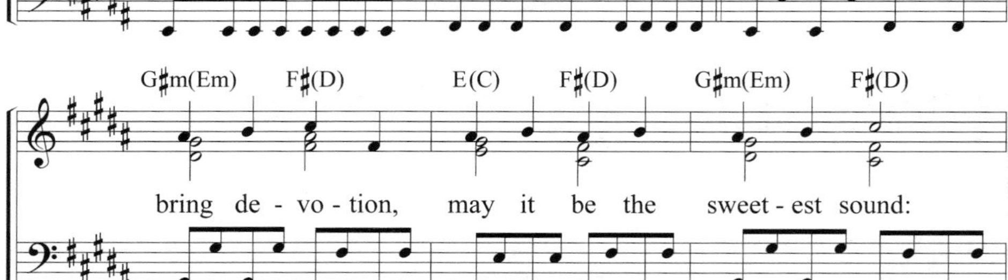
G♯m(Em)
F♯(D)
E(C)
F♯(D)
G♯m(Em)
F♯(D)
bring de - vo - tion, may it be the sweet - est sound:

E(C)
F♯(D)
G♯m(Em)
F♯(D)
E(C)
Lord, this heart is reach - ing for You now.

Chorus
B(G)
/A♯
/G♯
/F♯
So I'll set my sights upon You,
You alone will be my passion,
/E
/D♯
/C♯
F♯(D)
set my life upon Your praise;
Jesus, You will be my song:
B(G)
/A♯
never looking to
You will find me long-
1.
E(C)
F♯sus4(D)
another way.
2.
ing after You.
D.C. (Last time D.S.)
To end

2. Day and night I lift my eyes
To seek You, to seek You.
Hungry for a glimpse of You
In glory, in glory.

1399. Jesus, You are so precious

Jn 12:3; Heb 2:9

Nathan Fellingham

Gently
Verse
Em D/F♯ G C G/B Am Em D/F♯ G
1. Je - sus, You are so pre - cious to me; to be - hold You is
Seat - ed in glo - ry, now and for - e - ver, my Je - sus, my
C Dsus4 1. D 2. D
Chorus
Em Bm/D C2
all I de - sire.
Sa - viour, my Lord.
I wor - ship You,
C D Em D/F♯ G Gsus4 G D/F♯ Em Bm/D
I wor - ship You. Lord, I wor - ship
C2 C D Em D/F♯ G Gsus4 G
You, yes, I wor - ship You.

2. Jesus, You are so precious to me;
Your beauty has captured my gaze.
Now I will come and bow down before You,
And pour sweet perfume on Your feet.

1400. Jesus, Your beauty
(Holy river)

2 Chron 7:1; 2 Cor 2:14; Heb 10:19, 22; Rev 22:1

Sue Rinaldi & Caroline Bonnett

Steadily

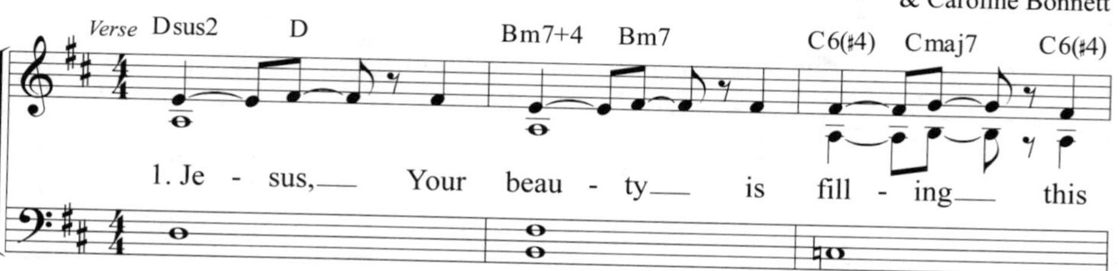

Verse
Dsus2 D Bm7+4 Bm7 C6(♯4) Cmaj7 C6(♯4)
1. Je - sus, Your beau - ty is fill - ing this

Gmaj7 G6 Dsus2 D Bm7+4 Bm7
tem - ple. Je - sus, Your fra - grance is

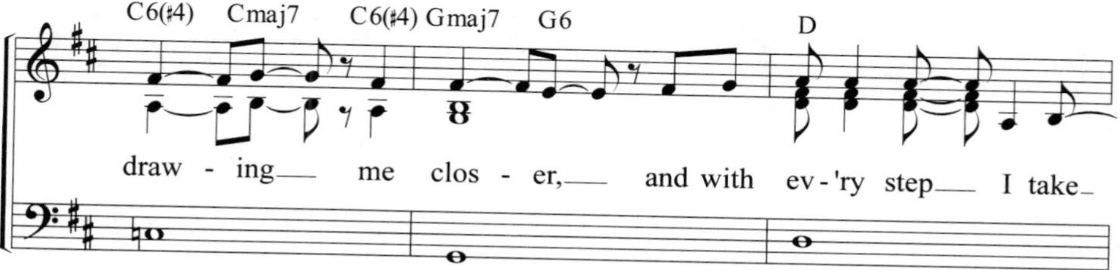

C6(♯4) Cmaj7 C6(♯4) Gmaj7 G6 D
draw - ing me clos - er, and with ev - 'ry step I take

Bm F♯m/C♯ D E/G♯
You lead me in - to this ho - ly place, and it wash - es me clean,

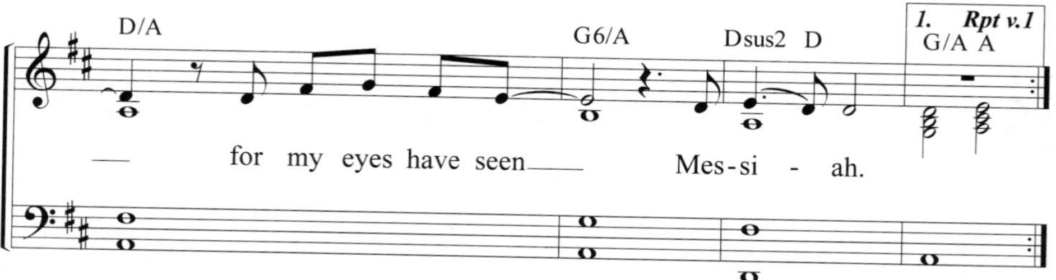

D/A G6/A Dsus2 D
1. Rpt v.1
G/A A
for my eyes have seen Mes - si - ah.

2.
G/A A Gmaj7/A A
Chorus
D
G/D D
And I will jump into the holy river, I will
F♯m Bm7
G D/A
D
lose myself to my Deliv'rer. I will jump into the
G/D D
F♯m Bm7
G D/A
holy river, I will lose myself to my Deliv'rer.
Em7+4
Em7 D/F♯ G2
In this holy place I can see Your face,
Last time to Coda
G6/A A Dsus2 D Bm7+4 Bm7 C6(♯4) Cmaj7 C6(♯4) Gmaj7 G6
D.C. v.2
Messiah.

Coda
Dsus2 D
Bm7+4 Bm7
C6(♯4) Cmaj7 C6(♯4) Gmaj7 G6
Dsus2 D
- si - ah.
Mes - si - ah.
Bm7+4 Bm7
C6(♯4) Cmaj7 C6(♯4)
F♯7/A♯
Bm7+4 Bm7
Mes - si - ah.
G6 G
C6(♯4) Cmaj7 C6(♯4)
F♯7/A♯
Bm7+4 Bm7
G6 G
Mes - si - ah.
C6(♯4) Cmaj7 C6(♯4)
F♯7/A♯
D
Fine
Mes - si - ah.

2. Jesus, Your passion is filling this temple.
Jesus, Your mercy is drawing me closer,
And with every step I take
You lead me into a world that aches,
And I cannot rest till all eyes have seen
Messiah.

1401. Jesus, You're all I need

Jn 4:14; Gal 2:20; Rev 5:9; 11:15; 17:7

Darlene Zschech

Steadily

F/C G/B C C/E

Je - sus, You're all I need, You're all

Fmaj7 G C F/C C

I need. Now I give my life to You
Lord, You gave Your-self so I

D/F♯ G Em7 1. Dm7 C B♭2 G/B

a - lone, You are all I need. Je - sus, You're all
could live,

2. Dm7 Dm7/G C *(Fine)* F

You are all I need. Oh, You pur - chased my sal - va -
You a - lone are

C/D Dm7 G Em7 B♭/C

tion, and wiped a - way my tears; now I
ho - ly, I'll wor - ship at Your throne; and

F
Dm7
D7 D7/C
1.
G/B
F/A
drink Your li - ving wa - ter, and I'll ne - ver thirst a - gain.
You will reign for - e - ver,
G
2. G/B
F/A
G
D.C.
For ho - ly is the Lord.

"Great and marvellous are Your deeds, Lord God Almighty. Just and true are Your ways, King of the ages."

REVELATION 15:3

1402. King Jesus, I believe

Ps 119:105; Is 61:1-3; Amos 5:24; Mt 5:6; 6:10; Lk 4:18; Jn 6:33; Rom 12:15; 2 Pet 3:12

Martyn Layzell

With energy
Am G Em7 Fmaj7
Verse
Am G Em7
1. King Je - sus, I be-lieve the words of life You breathe.
F2 Am G
You've spo - ken pro - mi-ses, a
Em7 F Am
guid - ing light for our feet. We fall down to
G Em7 F
our knees, and weep with those who weep: let jus-

Em
F
tice flow upon this earth, a never failing stream.
G
Chorus
C
C/B
I'm thirsty, longing just
Am
F
C
to see Your kingdom come. Praying that today
G/B
Am
F
C
Your love is shown. I'm hungry
C/B
Am
F
for the will of God to be made known, pray-

Last time to Coda
C
G/B
Am
F
D.C.
ing for the day of Your re-turn.
Dm
B♭maj7
C
We pray, we pray, we pray
Am
Dm
B♭maj7
for the king-dom. We pray, we pray.
G
1.
2.
D.S.
Coda
Am
Fmaj7
I'm

2. You have anointed us,
To bind the broken heart:
Proclaimed deliverance
For those enslaved in the dark.
You pour the oil of joy
All over my despair.
O Spirit of the Sovereign Lord,
Empower us once again.

1403.

King of history

(Redemption hymn)

Eph 3:18; 1 Tim 1:14; 1 Jn 3:1

David Gate

Fairly slow

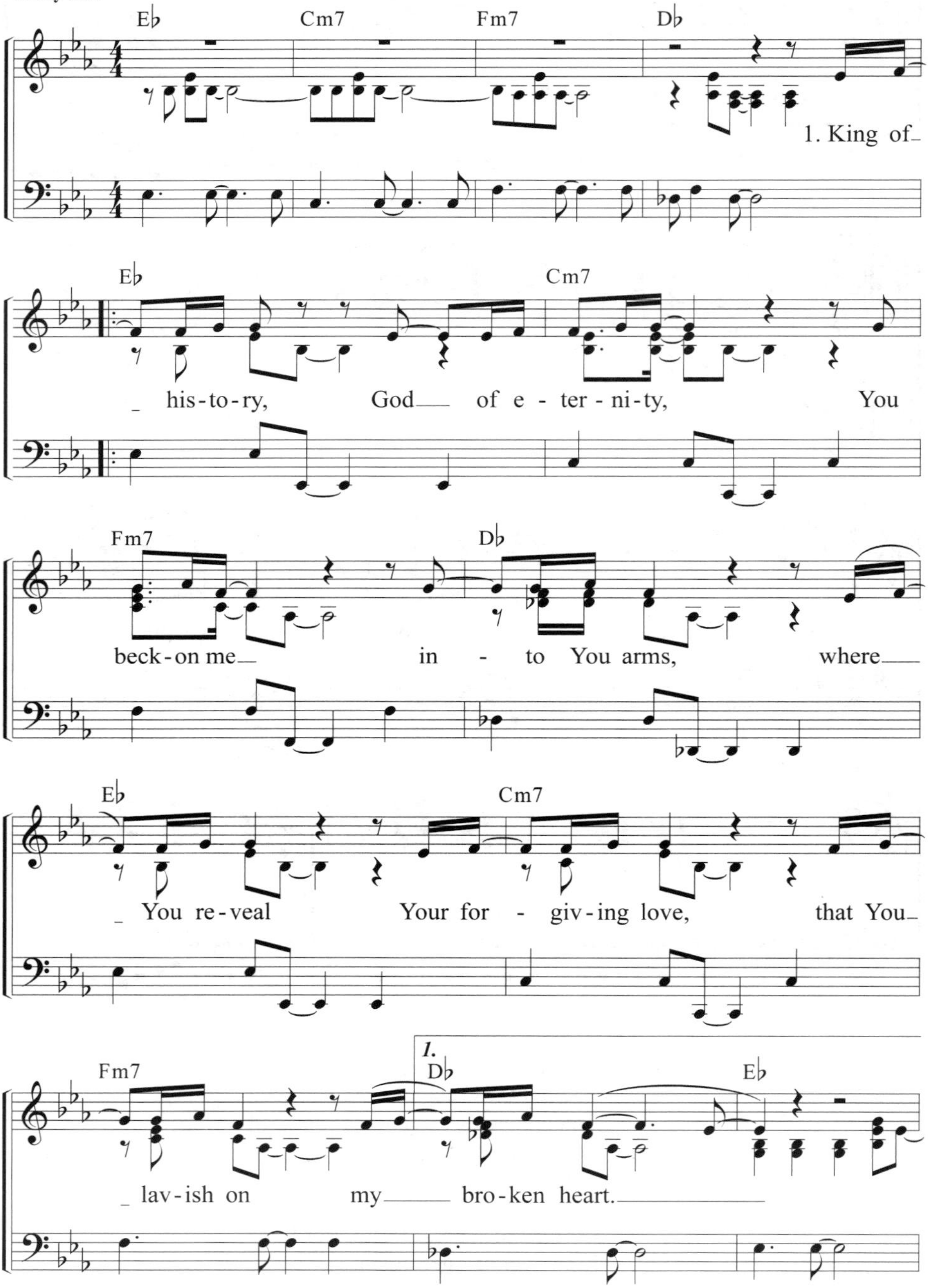

Eb Cm7 Fm7 Db

1. King of history, God of eternity, You beckon me into You arms, where You reveal Your forgiving love, that You lavish on my broken heart.

Cm7
Fm7
D♭
2. Such a -
2.
D♭
E♭
the cross
So I
thank You for Your
Cm7
Fm7
D♭
sav - ing love,
so I
E♭
Cm7
Fm7
D♭
thank You, for Your sav - ing love.

2. Such amazing grace that You pour on me,
And You freely give every day I live.
And I'll never know the depth of love
That You gave to me upon the cross.

1404. King of kings, Majesty

Jn 15:15; Col 1:27; Rev 5:9; 7:9; 22:13

Jarrod Cooper

Verse
A E/G♯ A
1.King of kings, Ma - je - sty, God of
D/A E/A A E/G♯
hea - ven liv - ing in me, gen - tle Sa - viour clo - sest
A A/C♯ D E F♯m
friend, strong De - li - v'rer, Be - gin - ning and End, all with-
Bm7 C♯m7 Dmaj7 D/E Chorus A E/G♯
in me falls at Your throne. Your ma - je - sty, I can but

F♯m A/E D A/C♯ Bm D/A E/G♯ D/E
bow. I lay my all be-fore You now. In ro-yal
A E/G♯ F♯m A/E D D/E E7
robes I don't de - serve I live to serve Your ma-je-
To repeat
A
sty. 2. Earth and
Last time
F♯m A/E D D/E E7 A
- sty, I live to serve Your ma-je-sty.

2. Earth and heaven worship You,
   Love eternal, faithful and true,
   Who bought the nations, ransomed souls,
   Brought this sinner near to Your throne;
   All within me cries out in praise.

1405. King of love

Deut 33:27; Jn 10:28

Capo 2 (D)

Steadily

Doug Horley

Chorus 1
E(D)
B(A)
C♯m(Bm)
King of love, praise You, King of love,
A(G)
E(D)
B(A)
Last time to Coda
wor-ship You, King of love, thank You, I'm
1.
C♯m(Bm)
A(G)
trea - sure in Your eyes.
2.
C♯m(Bm)
trea - sure in Your eyes.
A(G)
Verse
E(D)
B(A)
I know my heart will love You for e - ver,
C♯m(Bm)
A(G)
I know Your word, I'll al - ways be Your child.

E(D)
B(A)
C♯m(Bm)
_ I know my soul is safe for e-ter-ni-ty 'cause You hold_ me
A(G)
1st time D.C.
E(D)
B(A)
close in Your arms.
(2nd and 3rd time - Chorus 1 may be sung along with Chorus 2)
C♯m(Bm)
A(G)
Chorus 2
E(D)
Gon-na give You all the praise I can,
(2nd time) love
B(A)
1.,2.
C♯m(Bm)
gon-na give you all the thanks I can, in Your arms_ I_ will be,
praise
A(G)
3.
C♯m(Bm)
King of love,_ hold - ing me. King of love,_ King of love,_ I

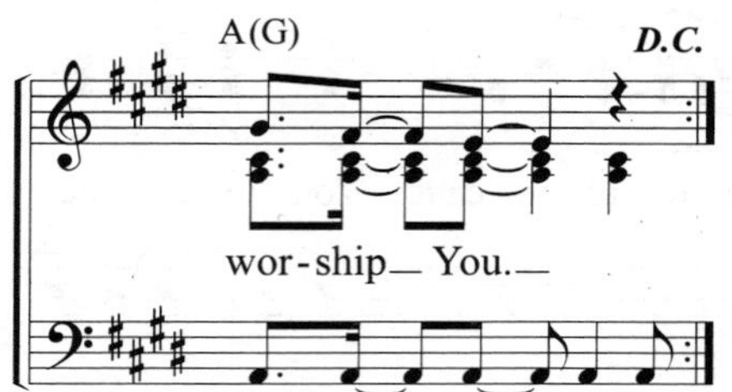
A(G)
D.C.
wor-ship You.

Coda
C♯m(Bm)
trea - sure in Your eyes.

A(G)
E(D)

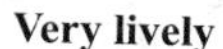

1406. King of our lives

Ps 51:10; 139:23; Mt 5:4-5, 8, 13-14; 6:33; Lk 2:14; 4:19; Jn 6:63; Phil 3:7; 4:19; Col 3:15; 1 Pet 5:7

Very lively

David Lyle Morris
& Nick Wynne-Jones

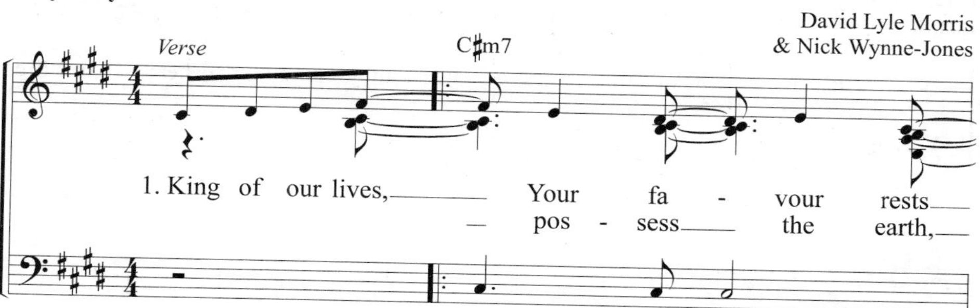

Verse
C♯m7
1. King of our lives, Your fa - vour rests
pos - sess the earth,

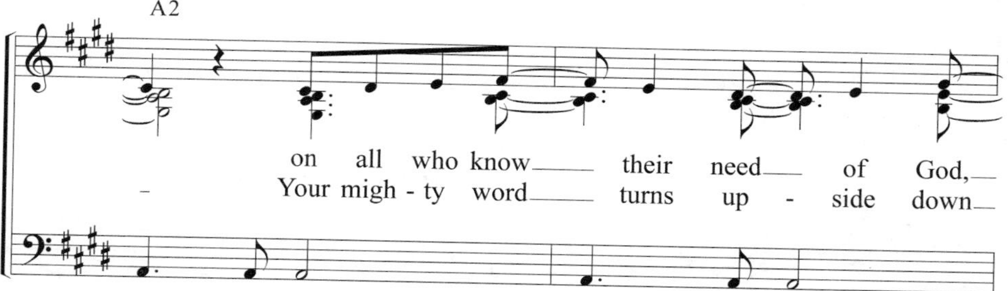

A2
on all who know their need of God,
Your migh - ty word turns up - side down

C♯m7
1.
Bsus2
and You will com - fort those who mourn.
all that this world con - si - ders great.

C♯m7
2.
Bsus2
The hum-ble meek

Chorus
E
A2
C♯m7
Je - sus, King of our lives, as once they came to hear Your life
A2
E
A2
sus - tain - ing words, we ga - ther now with hun - gry hearts
Last time to Coda
(D.S. for final chorus)
C♯m7
A2
B
A2
Your liv - ing truth a - lone can fill.
Bridge
F♯m7
E/G♯
Je - sus, we come sit at Your feet, yield You our lives
All of our cares we give to You, all that we need
A2
that we may be salt of the earth, light of the world.
our Fa - ther gives, so we will put Your king - dom first.

B
2° D.C.
Coda
E
King of our lives,
A
C♯m7
A
E
Tea - cher.
Sa - viour.
Mes - si - ah.
Rule in our hearts,
King of our lives,
Rule in our hearts,
A
C♯m7
A
B
E
Mas - ter,
Heal-er
and
friend.
A
E

2. King of our lives, the pure in heart
Will know the joy of seeing God,
So purify us deep within:
Our thoughts, our words, the things we do,
Your searching word turns inside out -
So touch our hearts and make us clean.

Final chorus.
King of our lives, as once they came
To hear Your life-transforming word,
We ask You now to rule our hearts
With living words, to do Your will.

1407. King of the ages

Jn 8:12; Acts 13:47; Col 1:27; Rev 1:7; 15:3-4

Majestically

Stuart Townend & Keith Getty

Chorus
C Dm7+4 C/E F G/F
King of the a - ges, Al - migh - ty God, Per - fect
Who will not fear You and bring You praise? All the
1. Dm G C F/G G
love, e - ver just and true.
2. Dm G (Fine) C Gm7 C7
na - tions will come to You.
Verse
Fmaj7 G/F Em7 Am7 Dm7 F/G G
1. Your ways of love have won my heart, and brought me
F/C C B♭/D C/E Fmaj7 G/F C/E Am7
joy un - end - ing. Your sav - ing pow'r at work in

Dm
F/G G F/G G
me, bring-ing peace and the hope of glo - ry.

2. Your arms of love are reaching out
To every soul that seeks You;
Your light will shine in all the earth,
Bringing grace and a great salvation.

3. The day will come when You appear,
And every eye shall see You.
Then we shall rise with hearts ablaze,
With a song we will sing forever.

1408. Knowing Your grace

(Child of the King)

Ps 17:8; 63:7; Is 6:7; Song 1:4; Mt 11:28; Jn 14:27; Gal 5:1; Eph 1:4-5, 8; Phil 1:6; 1 Jn 3:1

Terry Virgo
& Stuart Townend

Gently

Bm F♯m7 Em7 A7sus4
1. Know-ing Your grace has set me free, Lord. I'm
Bm F♯m7 Em7 Am7 D9
seek-ing Your face; I feel Your plea - sure, Your
Gmaj7 A/G F♯m7 Bm7
joy in the ones You have cho - sen by name. You've
1. Em7 C♯m7♭5 F♯7
lif-ted my bur - dens and cast off my shame.
2.3. Em7 A7sus4 Em/D D (Fine) F♯m7
I am a child of the King. You will fin - ish the work

Bm
Gmaj7
F♯m7
You've be - gun in me, I'm a - dop - ted, a son
C/D
D
Gmaj7
F♯m7
in Your fa - mi - ly! You've drawn me with kind -
Em7
F♯sus4 F♯
Em7
C2+6
D.C. al fine
A/C♯
ness and love in - to this ho - ly place.

2. Feeling Your touch
Gives me such peace, Lord.
I love You so much,
I know You'll lead me.
Wherever I go I'll be under Your wing,
For I am a child of the King.

3. What can I say?
Your lavish mercy
Turned night into day -
My guilt has gone now.
Forever I'll stand in Your presence and sing,
For I am a child of the King.

Because of the Lord's great love we are not consumed, for His compassions never fail. They are new every morning; great is Your faithfulness.

LAMENTATIONS 3:22-23

1409. Kyrie Eleison
(Lord, have compassion)

Ps 86:3; Lk 18:13

Taizé
Jacques Berthier (1923-1994)

G D Em Bm C D G D
Ky - ri - e, Ky - ri - e e - le - i - son. Ky - ri - e,
Lord, Lord, have com - pas-sion. Lord,
Em Bm C D G D
Ky - ri - e e - le - i - son.
Lord, have com - pas-sion.

1410.
Lamp unto my feet
(It is You)
Ps 51:17; 119:105, 127; Is 40:31; Mt 6:21
Steadily
Darlene Zschech
Verse
G D/G G D/G G2/B
1. Lamp un - to my feet, light un - to my path, it is
trea - sure that I hold, more than fi-nest gold, it is
C2
You,
You,
1. Em7 D/F♯ G
Je-sus, it is You.
2. This
Em7 D/F♯ G C2/G D/G
Je - sus, it is You.
Chorus
G Am7 G/B
With all my heart, with all my soul, I live to wor-
Em7 C D
- ship You and praise for-e - ver-more, praise

C/E D/F♯ G
for e - ver-more. Lord, e - v'ry day
Am7 G/B Em7
I need You more, on wings of hea - ven I will soar
Last time to Coda
C G/D D Em7 D/F♯ C/G
with You.
Verse
G D/G G D/G
3. You take my bro - ken - ness, call me
G G2/B C2 Em7 D/F♯
to Your-self, there You stand, heal - ing in Your hands.
G C2/G D/G
D.S. al Coda
Coda
G
Rit . . .

1411.
Laying aside everything
(Looking to Jesus)
1 Cor 13:12; 1 Tim 2:8; Heb 12:1-2
Capo 5 (Am)
With energy
David Fellingham
Dm(Am)
Lay-ing a-side ev - 'ry - thing that would hin -
C(G)
Bbmaj7(F)
- der us from com - ing in - to the pre - sence of our
Em7(Bm)
A7(E)
great and awe - some King; lift - ing up ho -
Dm(Am)
Cm7(Gm7)
- ly hands in faith, we long to see You face to face,
Bbmaj7(F)
Gm(Dm)
Em7(Bm)
G/A(D)
free - ly we come, free - ly we come.

A(E)
Dm(Am)
And we're-look-ing to Je - sus, the One who has saved
C(G)
Bb(F)
us, we're look-ing to Je - sus,
A7(E)
the One who can heal us. To the
Dm(Am)
Dm/C#(Am)
Dm/C(Am)
Em7/B (Bm)
Au-thor and the Fi - ni-sher of all that we be-lieve, free-ly we
Bbmaj7(F)
(Bm)
Em7b5
A7(E)
Dm(Am)
To repeat D.C.
A7+5 (E)
Last time
Dm(Am) Fine
come, free-ly we come.
(last time repeat)

Keep yourselves in God's love as you wait for the mercy of our Lord Jesus Christ to bring you eternal life.

JUDE: 21

1412. Lead us, heavenly Father

Ps 16:11; Mt 8:24-27; Jn 15:11; Acts 2:32; Eph 1:3; Heb 4:15

Capo 3 (G)

Words: James Edmeston (1791-1867)
Music: Geraldine Latty
4 part harmony
B♭(G) E♭(C) B♭/D (G) F(D) B♭(G)
1. Lead us, hea - v'nly Fa - ther, lead us through this
E♭(C) B♭/D (G) (Em) Gm/E F(C) B♭/D (G) E♭(C) B♭/D (G)
world's tem - pes-tuous sea; guard us, guide us, keep us,
F(D) Gm(Em) E♭(C) (Am) Cm F(D) B♭(D) (Am) (G) Cm B♭/D
feed us- You our on - ly help and plea; here pos - sess - ing e-v'ry
E♭(C) B♭/F (G) Gm(Em) F(D) B♭(D)
bless - ing if our God our Fa - ther be.

2. Saviour, by Your grace restore us
All our weaknesses are plain;
You have lived on earth before us,
You have felt our grief and pain:
Tempted, taunted, yet undaunted,
From the depths You rose again.

3. Spirit of our God, descending,
Fill our hearts with holy peace;
Love with every passion blending,
Pleasure that can never cease:
Thus provided, pardoned, guided,
Ever shall our joys increase.

1413. Let all mortal flesh

Is 6:2; Zech 2:13; Jn 1:5; 6:54; 8:12; Col 3:2; Rev 7:11; 17:14; 19:16

Capo 5 (Am)
Tune: PICARDY

17th cent. French carol melody

(Am) Dm (F) B♭ (C) F (Am) Dm (C) F7/C
1. Let all mor - tal flesh keep_ si - lence and with fear and
(F) B♭ (E) A (F) B♭ (C) F (Dm) Gm7 (Am) Dm
trem - bling_ stand; pon - der no - thing earth - ly - min - ded,
(C) F7/C (F) B♭ (C) F (A) D/F♯ (Dm) Gm
for with bles - sing in His_ hand Christ our God to earth de -
(Am) Dm (G) C (Am) Dm/F (Dm) Gm (G) C (Am) Dm
scen - deth, our full ho - mage to de - mand.

2. King of kings, yet born of Mary,
As of old on earth He stood,
Lord of lords, in human vesture,
In the body and the blood:
He will give to all the faithful
His own self for heavenly food.

3. Rank on rank the host of heaven
Spreads its vanguard on the way,
As the Light of light descendeth
From the realms of endless day,
That the powers of hell may vanish
As the darkness clears away.

4. At His feet the six-winged seraph;
Cherubim with sleepless eye.,
Veil their faces to the Presence,
As with ceaseless voice they cry,
Alleluia, alleluia,
Alleluia, Lord most high!

Liturgy of St James, c.4th cent.
Tr. Gerard Moultrie (1829-85)

1414. Let the poor man say, I am rich in Him

(Let the river flow)
Jn 3:3; 9:25; 2 Cor 8:9; Rev 22:2
Darrell Evans
With strength
Let the poor man say, I am rich in Him; let the lost man say I am found in Him:
Let the blind man say, I can see again; let that dead man say, I am born again:
let the river flow.
Let the river flow.
Let the river flow, let the river flow.

B
E
B
Ho - ly Spi-rit, come;
A
E/A
E/B
B
F♯m7
move in pow - er. Let the ri - ver flow. (Let the
1.
E
Esus4
E
Esus4
D.C.
ri - ver flow.)
2.3.
A
ri - ver flow.) Let the ri - ver flow. (Let the
F♯m7
Last time to Coda
ri - ver flow.) Let the ri - ver flow. (Let the

D.S. al Coda
A
B
ri - ver flow.) Let the ri - ver flow.
Coda
E
Esus4
E
ri - ver flow.)

Be joyful in hope, patient in affliction, faithful in prayer.

ROMANS 12:12

1415. Let there be joy

Mt 21:21; 28:19; Rom 1:17; 5:2; 14:17; Gal 5:1; Eph 6:14; Rev 1:7

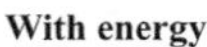
With energy

Bruce Napier

E A

Let there be joy, let there be peace, let there be pow -

G

er, let there be praise. Let there be joy, joy

D A

in the Ho - ly Ghost. It was for free -

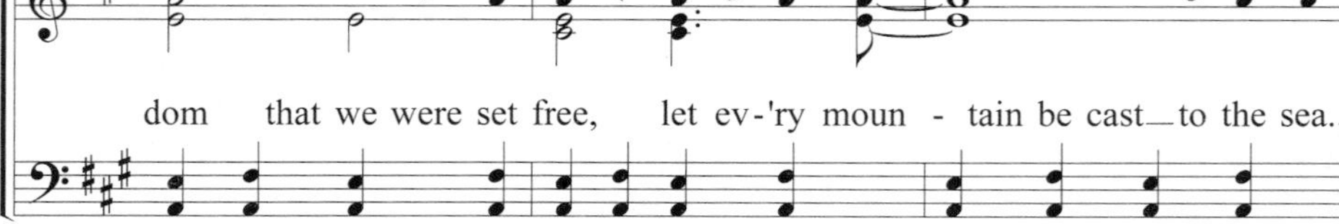
dom that we were set free, let ev-'ry moun - tain be cast to the sea.

G
D
A
Let there be joy, joy in the Ho - ly Ghost.

Last time to Coda
G
D
A
We will de-clare it to the hea - vens,
G
D
the righ-teous-ness of God in which we stand.
Esus4
E
G
D
We will pro-claim it to the na -
A
G
- tions; ev-'ry eye shall see, ev-'ry ear
D
Esus4
D.C. al Coda
E
shall hear, ev-'ry heart will un - der - stand.
Coda
A
Fine

1416. Let the weak say I am strong

(What the Lord has done in me)

Ps 18:16; Mt 21:9; Jn 9:25; 2 Cor 8:9; 12:10; Rev 5:12; 22:1-2

Steadily

Reuben Morgan

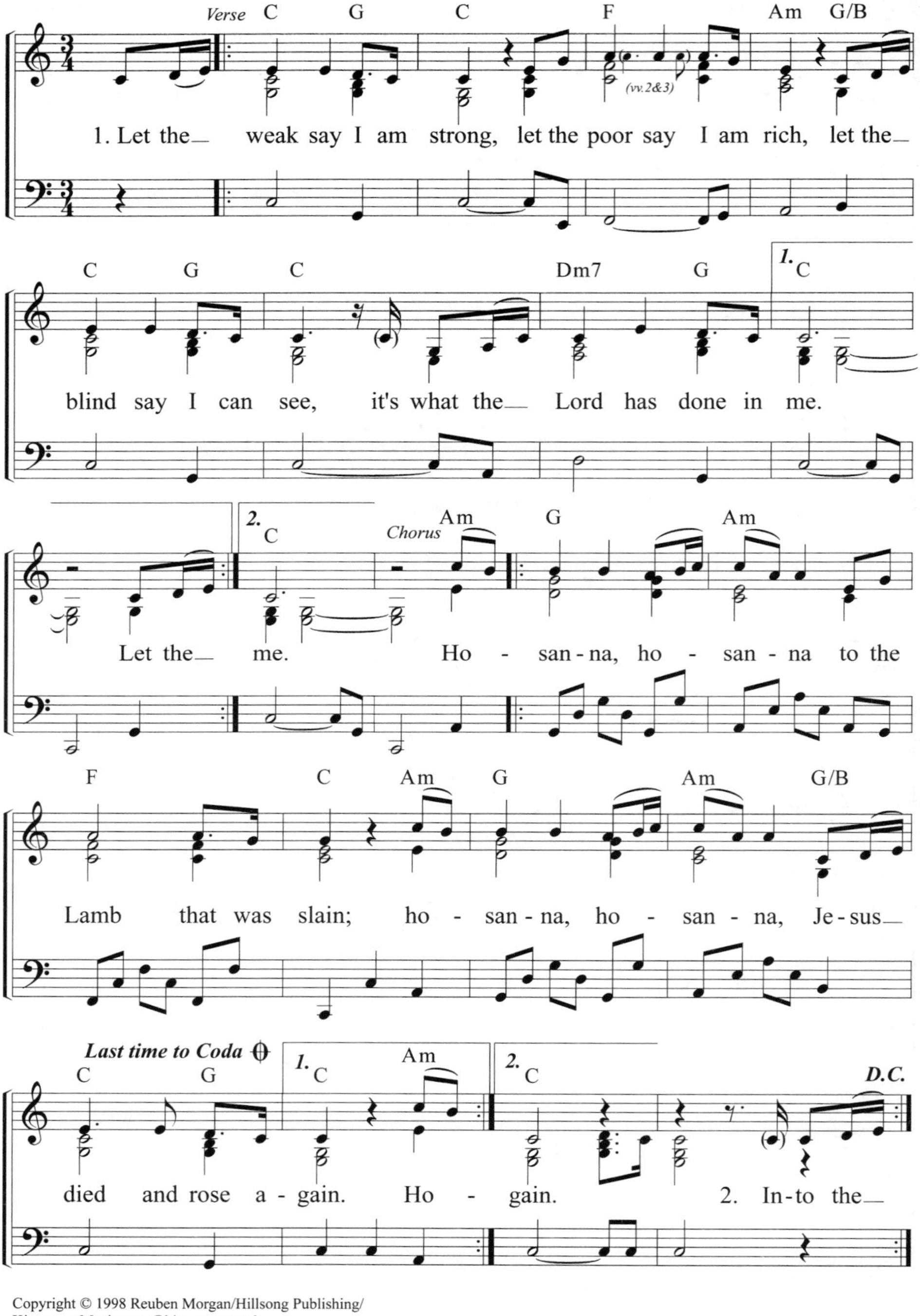

Verse C G C F Am G/B

1. Let the weak say I am strong, let the poor say I am rich, let the

(vv.2&3)

C G C Dm7 G 1. C

blind say I can see, it's what the Lord has done in me.

2. C *Chorus* Am G Am

Let the me. Ho - san-na, ho - san - na to the

F C Am G Am G/B

Lamb that was slain; ho - san-na, ho - san - na, Je-sus

Last time to Coda 1. C Am 2. C **D.C.**

C G

died and rose a - gain. Ho - gain. 2. In-to the

Coda
C G/B C G C G/B C G C
Fine
gain, Je-sus died and rose a - gain, Je-sus died and rose a - gain.

2. Into the river I will wade,
There my sins are washed away;
From the heavens mercy streams
Of the Saviour's love for me.

3. I will rise from waters deep
Into the saving arms of God;
I will sing salvation songs:
Jesus Christ has set me free.

1417. Let us run with perseverance

Jn 1:1-3; 1 Cor 15:56-57; Phil 1:6; Heb 12:1-3

Brightly
David Lyle Morris
Chorus
E B
Let us run with per - se - ve - rance the
F♯m7 E/G♯ A B C♯m
race set out be - fore us; let us fix our eyes on Je -
G♯m F♯m E/G♯ A A/B B7
- sus, the Au - thor and Per - fec - tor of our
E A/E E (Fine) Verse B E
(v.2&3)
faith. 1. In the be - gin - ning the
B E A E/G♯ F♯m
Word was with God, through Him all of us were

Bsus4
B
E
made; He be-gan a work in us, a
(v.2)
(v.2)
B
E
A
E/G♯
F♯m7
good work to per-fect un-til He re - turns a -
Bsus4
B
gain.

2. Since we are surrounded by heaven's cheering crowd,
   Let us throw off every chain:
   For all that opposes us, look to Jesus who endured
   So we'll not lose heart again.

3. For the joy before Him, He suffered the cross,
   He defeated death and shame,
   Now He reigns in glory at the right hand of God -
   He is calling us by name.

1418. Lift high the cross

Jn 12:32; Col 2:15; Heb 2:10; 1 Jn 2:2; Rev 7:9; 9:4

Tune: CRUCIFER

Sydney H. Nicholson (1875-1947)

Chorus (Unison)
C C/E Dm7 G7 F/A G/B C F/A C/G D7/F♯ Gsus4 G G7/B
Lift high the cross, the love of Christ pro - claim till
C G7/D C/E Dm/F Em/G F/A G/B F/A Em/G Dm/F Dm7 G7 Csus4 C
(Fine)
all the world a - dore His sa - cred name!
Verse (Harmony)
Em Am D G/B C B Em Am/C B Em
1. Come, bre - thren, fol - low where our Cap - tain trod, our
Am7 D G/B C Dsus4 D G
Dm 7/G Em/G
King vic - to - rious, Christ the Son of God.
(Org.)

2. Each new-born soldier of the crucified
Bears on His brow the seal of Him who died.

3. This is the sign which Satan's legions fear
And angels veil their faces to revere.

4. Saved by this cross whereon their Lord was slain,
The sons of Adam their lost home regain.

5. From north and south, from east and west they raise
In growing unison their song of praise.

6. O Lord, once lifted on the glorious tree,
As Thou has promised, draw men unto Thee.

7. Let every race and every language tell
Of Him who saves our souls from death and hell.

8. Set up Thy throne, that earth's despair may cease
Beneath the shadow of its healing peace.

G.W. Kitchen (1827-1912)
& M.R. Newbolt (1874-1956)

1419.
Light of the world
(Here I am to worship)
Capo 2(D)
Ps 95:6; Song 5:16; Jn 1:3, 11; 8:12; 9:25; 2 Cor 8:9; Phil 2:8-9
With feeling
Tim Hughes
Verse
E(D) Bsus4(A) F♯m(Em)
1. Light of the world, You stepped down in-to dark-ness,
E(D) Bsus4(A) A2(G) E(D) Bsus4(A)
o-pened my eyes, let me see beau-ty that made this
F♯m(Em) E(D) Bsus4(A) A2(G)
heart a-dore You, hope of a life spent with You.
Chorus
E(D)
So here I am to wor-ship, here I am to
B/D♯(A) E/G♯(D)
bow down, here I am to say that You're my God.

Asus2(G)
E(D)
And You're al - to - ge - ther love - ly, al - to - ge-ther
B/D♯(A)
E/G♯(D)
1. 3.
A(G)
3. To Coda
A2(G)
wor-thy, al-to-ge-ther won-der-ful to me.
2.
A(G)
Bridge
B/D♯(A)
E/G♯(D)
A(G)
And I'll ne - ver know how much it cost to see
B/D♯(A)
E/G♯(D)
1.
A(G)
2.
A(G)
my sin up-on that cross. And I'll ne - that cross.
Asus2(G)
D.S. al Coda
So here I am to
Coda
E(D)

2. King of all days,
Oh so highly exalted,
Glorious in heaven above;
Humbly You came
To the earth You created,
All for love's sake became poor.

1420. Like a fragrant oil

(Fragrant)

Capo 5(D)

Ps 141:2; Song 1:3; Jn 4:24; 12:3; Heb 13:15; Rev 5:12; 8:4

Paul Oakley

Tenderly

F(C) Verse C/E(G) Dm(Am)
1. Like a fra-grant oil, like cost-ly per-
B♭(F) F(C) C/E(G)
fume poured out, let my wor - ship be to You.
Dm(Am) B♭(F) F(C) C/E(G)
Like a fer-vent pray'r,
Dm(Am) B♭(F) F(C)
like in-cense ri - sing to Your throne, in spi-
C/E(G) Dm(Am) B♭(F) Chorus F(C)
rit and in truth. Je -

C/E(G) Dm(Am) B♭(F)
sus, You a-lone are wor - thy of my praise,
F(C) C/E(G) Dm(Am) B♭(F)
I owe my life to You.
F(C) C/E(G) Dm(Am)
Je - sus, You a-lone can
B♭(F) F(C) C/E(G) Dm(Am)
make me ho - ly, so I bow be-fore You.
B♭(F)
Last time
F(C)

2. Like a wedding vow,
'All I am I give to You,'
Let my sacrifice be pure.
Like the sweetest sound,
Like a lover's whisper in Your ear,
I've set my heart on You.

1421. Like the sunshine

Ps 19:1; 46:10; Zeph 3:17; Rom 8:6

Stuart Townend

Gently
E A2/C♯ E
1. Like the sun-shine af-ter rain-fall, like the gen-tle breeze;
A2/C♯ E A2/C♯
like the still - ness of the morn - ing,
E/B F♯/A♯ A6
like the ra - diant trees: these things I
E/G♯ A/C♯ E/B F♯ F♯/A♯ B
knew be - fore, but ne-ver have they spo-ken such life to me;
E A2/C♯ E/B A C♯m7
oh, the won - der of a Ma - ker whose heart de -

Bsus4
B
E
A2/C♯
E
lights in me.
Last time to Coda ⊕
A2/C♯
Bm7
A
E
The heav'ns de - clare His mag - ni - fi - cence,
Bm7
A
E
the earth re - sounds with His praise;
Bm7
A
E
F♯m7
be still, my soul, and be sa - tis - fied to wor - ship Him,
B7sus4
B
D.C. al Coda
Coda ⊕
E
to wor - ship Him.

2. Like the nurture of a baby
At its mother's breast;
Like the closeness of a lover,
Like two souls at rest:
These things I knew before,
But never have they spoken such peace to me;
Oh, the wonder of a Maker
Whose heart delights in me.

3. Like the vastness of a desert,
Like the ocean's roar;
Like the greatness of the mountains,
Where the eagles soar:
These things I knew before,
But never have they spoken such power to me;
Oh, the wonder of a Maker
Whose heart delights in me.

1422. Look to the skies

(Worship the King)

Is 9:6-7; Mt 1:23; 6:10; 28:19; Lk 2:13-14; Jn 1:5; 2 Pet 1:19; Rev 1:7

Graham Kendrick
Arr. David Peacock

Capo 3 (D)

Triumphantly

Verse

F(D) Dm(Bm) Gm7(Em) (A) Csus4 (A) C Dm(Bm) B♭(G) Gm7(Em) (A) Csus4 (A) C F(D) Dm(Bm) Gm7(Em) (A) Csus4 (A) C Dm(Bm) B♭(G) Gm(Em)

1. Look to the skies, there's a ce-le-bra-tion, lift up your heads, join the an-gel-song, for our Cre-a-tor be-comes our Sa-viour, as a ba-by born! An-gels a-mazed bow in a-do-ra-tion: 'Glo-ry to God in the high-est heav'n!' Send the good news out to e-v'ry na-tion, for our hope has

(A) (A)
Csus4 C
Chorus
Dm(Bm)
Gm(Em)
C(A)
come. Wor - ship the King, come see His bright-ness;
Dm(Bm)
B♭(G)
(A) (A)
Csus4 C
Dm(Bm)
wor - ship the King, His won-ders tell: Je - sus our King is
B♭(G) C(A) Gm7(Em)
B♭/C(G) C(A) F(D)
born to-day we wel-come You, Em - ma - nu - el!

2. Wonderful Counsellor, Mighty God,
Father for ever, the Prince of peace:
There'll be no end to Your rule of justice,
For it shall increase.
Light of Your face, come to pierce our darkness;
Joy of Your heart come to chase our gloom;
Star of the morning, a new day dawning,
Make our hearts Your home.

3. Quietly He came as a helpless baby -
One day in power He will come again;
Swift through the skies He will burst with splendour
On the earth to reign.
Jesus, I bow at Your manger lowly:
Now in my life let Your will be done;
Live in my flesh by Your Spirit holy
Till Your kingdom comes.

1423. Lord, hear the music of my heart

Eph 5:19

(Hear the music of my heart)

Matt Redman

Strong & rhythmic
Verse
Em
G
Lord, hear the mu - sic of my heart;
You've be-come the ru - ler of my heart;
G7/B
C
hear all the pour - ings of my soul.
You've be-come the lov - er of my soul.
1. 3.
Em
G
Songs tell - ing of a life of love:
F
C2
Jesus, this is all for You.
2. 4. Em
You've be-come the Sa-vi-our of
G
F
C2
this life: You are ev-'ry - thing to me. Oh now,

Chorus
Em
G
A7/C♯
Je-sus, Je-sus, I will pour my praise on You. Wor-ship, wor-ship
Cmaj9
Em
de-mon-strates my love for You. May I come to
G
A7/C♯
be a bless - ing to Your heart; Je - sus, Je - sus,
1. Cmaj9
Em
G
who can tell how won-der-ful You are, how won-der-ful You
A7/C♯
Cmaj9
D.C.
are.
2. Cmaj9
D.S.
Who can tell how won - der-ful.

3. Cmaj9
Em
Who can tell how won - der - ful You are,
G
A7/C♯
Cmaj9
how won-der - ful You are.
Em7
Em7/D
Gmaj9/B
Cmaj9
Last time
Em
O, how won - der - ful You are.

May the God of hope fill you with all joy and peace as you trust in Him, so that you may overflow with hope by the power of the Holy Spirit.

ROMANS 15:13

1424. Lord, I am not my own
(What I have vowed)

Jonah 2:9; Mt 6:21; 10:38; 1 Cor 6:19; 9:24; 2 Cor 4:2

Matt Redman

Tenderly

Verse
C
Em7
1. Lord, I am not my own, no long-er my own,
Am
Am/G
living now for You, and ev-'ry-thing I
Fmaj7
G6
Am
think, all I say and do is for You, my Lord.
1.
Am/C E7sus4/B
2.3.
Am/C E7sus4/B
Chorus
Em7
And what I have vowed I
F
C
Em7
will make good, ev-'ry pro-mise made will

F
C
Em7
be ful-filled,
till the
day I die,
ev-'ry
F
C
Am
Am2/G
Fmaj7
day I live
is for You,
is for You,
is for You,
is for
Am
Am2/G
Fmaj7
You,
is for You,
is for You.

2. Now taking up the cross,
   Walking on Your paths,
   Holding out Your truth,
   Running in this race,
   Bowing every day,
   All for You, my Lord.

3. Earth has nothing I desire
   That lives outside of You,
   I'm consumed with You.
   Treasures have no hold,
   Nothing else will do,
   Only You, my Lord.

1425.

Lord, I come

1 Cor 13:12; Eph 2:8; Heb 10:19

Slowly
Geraldine Latty
Verse
C F/C
1. Lord, I come, long-ing to know You, Lord, I come,
C Gsus4 G G/F C/E F
drawn by Your love; Lord, I come, long-ing to see
Gsus4 C Dm7 C/E F Gsus4 G
Your face, for You called me to come in-to the ho - li-est
1.,4. (4th time Fine)
Repeat v.1
2.,3.
C F2 G C
Chorus
place. 1. Lord I come place. What did I do
G/B F/A C C/E
to de-serve Your fa - vour, what did I do

G
F
C
C/E
– to de-serve Your grace? Called by my name
G/B
F/A
C/G
Dm7
– in - to Your pre - sence, un - de-served,
Gsus4
G
D.C.
ho - ly God. 2. Lord, I come

2. Lord, I come, because of Jesus,
Lord, I come, because He came;
Lord, I bow, as You reveal Your face,
You have called me to come into the holiest place.

1426. Lord, I come to You

(How can I do anything but praise You?)

Capo 3(D)

Driving

Colse Leung

Verse F(D)
C/E(A)
Lord, I come to You, bro - ken and lost,
Here I am a - gain, long - ing for more,
Dm(Bm)
Je - sus, be the high - est part.
wait - ing for Your pre - sence, here,
1. B♭2(G)
2. B♭2(G)
C(A)
Your pre - sence here. And

Chorus
F(D)
how can I do__ a - ny - thing but praise__ You,
Lord, You a - maze__ me__ with__ Your fa - vour,
Am7(F♯m)
how can I not__ wor - ship You,__
Lord, You a - stound__ me__ with Your love,
and
Dm(Bm)
F/C(D)
B♭(G)
how can I live__ my life__ with - out__ You, God?__
2nd time D.C.
To end
F(D)

1427. Lord, I'm grateful

(Grace)

Ps 63:3; Is 64:6; Rom 1:17; 5:19; 2 Cor 8:9; Eph 1:5; 2:8; 1 Tim 2:6; 1 Pet 1:18-19

Stuart Townend
& Fred J Heumann

With energy
Verse
A D A D
1. Lord, I'm grate-ful, a - mazed at what You've done.
A D G D
My fin-est ef-forts are fil - thy rags; but
A D A D
I'm made righ-teous by trust-ing in the Son:
A D G D Chorus
I have God's rich-es at Christ's ex-pense! 'Cause it's
A D A D
grace! There's no-thing I can do to make You love me

A D G D
more, to make You love me less than You do. And by
A D A D
faith I'm stand-ing on this Stone of Christ and Christ a -
A D G D
lone, Your righ-teous-ness is all that I need, 'cause it's
A (Fine) Mid 8 F♯m
grace! Grace loves the sin-ner, loves
D A E
all I am and all I'll e-ver be;

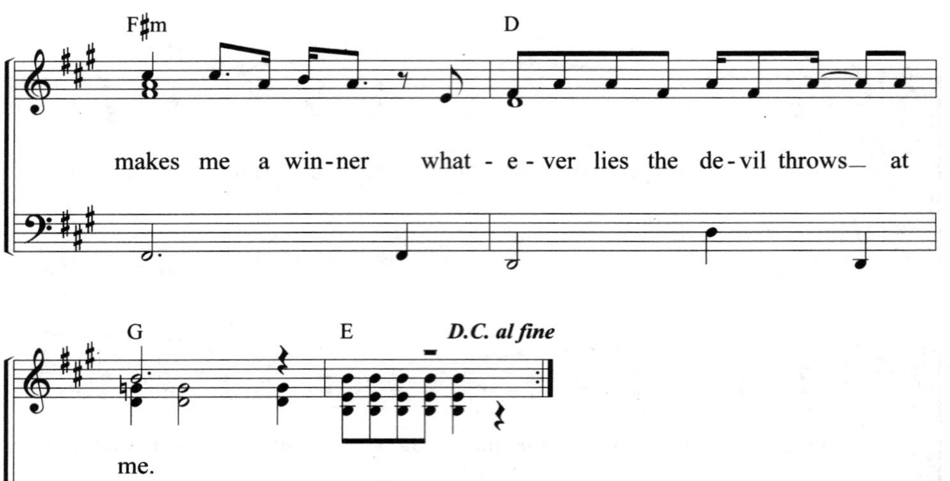
F♯m
D
makes me a win-ner what - e - ver lies the de-vil throws_ at
G
E
D.C. al fine
me.

2. Called and chosen when I was far away,
You brought me into Your family.
Free, forgiven, my guilt is washed away;
Your loving kindness is life to me.

3. Freely given, but bought with priceless blood,
My life was ransomed at Calvary.
There my Jesus gave everything He could
That I might live for eternity.

1428. Lord, I want to tell You

(Overflow of worship)

Slow and gentle

Marilyn Baker

D
G/D
D
Em7
Asus4
A
1. Lord, I want to tell You how much I love You; Your
D
G/D
D
Em7
Asus4
A
ten - der-ness and mer - cy have o - ver-whelmed my heart.
Bm7
Dmaj7/A
Gmaj7
Bm7
Dmaj7/A
Gmaj7
G6
Let my whole life be an o - ver-flow of wor - ship:
D/A
Bm7
Gmaj7
Asus4
D
all I have and all I am I give back, Lord, to You.

2. Lord, I want to tell You my heart's desire;
The love You've put within me will burn with holy fire.
Let my actions spring from an overflow of worship:
All I have and all I am I gladly give back to You.

1429. Lord Jesus, robed in splendour
(High over all)

Ps 19:1; 89:6; Hab 2:14; Acts 4:12; Heb 2:9

Strongly

Phil Lawson Johnston

Verse

C
Lord __ Jesus, robed in splendour, clothed in
Jesus, all resplendent, adorned in

F G
glory high over all. Lord Jesus, King Mes-
beauty, who can __ compare? Lord Jesus, You are

F C G 1. C
siah, mighty Saviour, high over all. Lord __
mighty, Your kingdom rules __ high over

2. C *Chorus* Am F
all. Yours is the name __ by which we are saved, the

C G Am
Name high ov - er all. Yours is the name which
F D G C F
(Last time)
we will pro-claim, for You are Lord of all. Je-sus, Lord,
C F G C F C F G C
(Last time) (Fine) D.C.
high ov-er, Je-sus, Lord, high ov-er all! The
B♭ C B♭ C B♭
hea - vens de - clare the glo - ry of God; the skies pro-
C F
claim the work of His hands. The

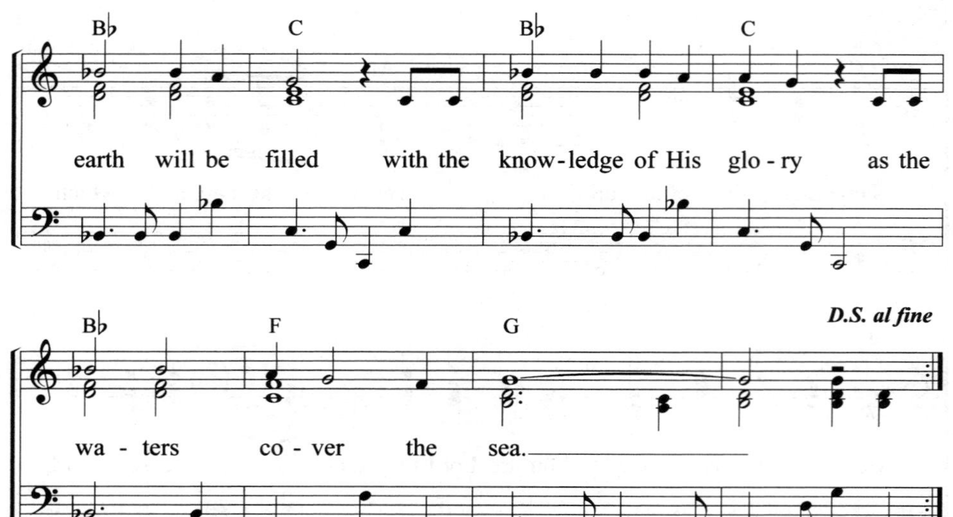
Bb C Bb C
earth will be filled with the know-ledge of His glo-ry as the
Bb F G
D.S. al fine
wa-ters co-ver the sea.

Lift up your heads, O you gates; be lifted up, you ancient doors, that the King of glory may come in. Who is this King of glory? The Lord strong and mighty, the Lord mighty in battle.

PSALM 24:7-8

1430. Lord, let Your glory fall

(You are good)

2 Chron 5:13-14; 7:1-3

Matt Redman

Steadily
D
Verse
Dmaj7
G2
1. Lord, let Your glo - ry fall
And as a sign to You
D/F♯
G2
as on that an - cient day;
that we would love the same,
Bm
Dmaj7/F♯
G2
songs of en - dur - ing love,
our hearts will sing that song:
Em7
G
1. D
Dsus2
2. D
(vv.2&3)
and then Your glo - ry came.
come.
God, let Your glo - ry
Dsus2
Chorus
D/F♯
You are good, You are good, and Your

G
D/F♯
love en - dures.— You are good, You are good, and Your
G
Bm
Dmaj7/F♯
love en - dures.— You are good, You are good, and Your
G
D
G
D.C.
Last time
D
love en - dures— to-day.—

2. Voices in unison,
Giving You thanks and praise,
Joined by the instruments,
And then Your glory came.
Your presence like a cloud
Upon that ancient day;
The priests were overwhelmed
Because Your glory came.

3. A sacrifice was made,
And then Your fire came;
They knelt upon the ground,
And with one voice they praised.
(Repeat)

One thing I ask of the Lord, this is what I seek: that I may dwell in the house of the Lord all the days of my life, to gaze upon the beauty of the Lord and to seek him in his temple.

PSALM 27:4

1431.

Lord, my request
(It's the way You walk with me)

Gal 2:20

Mark Baldry

Rhythmically
Verse
E B C♯m7
Lord, my re - quest, Lord, my de -
A2 E B
sire is to touch Your ve-ry heart through the
C♯m7 B A2 E
way I live my life. Je - sus, all I
B C♯m7 A2
seek, Sa - viour, all I want is a
E B C♯m7 B
pas - sion for Your ways and a heart that longs for

A2
C♯m7
B
A2
You, yes, a heart that longs for You.
Chorus
E
It's the way You walk with me, it's the way You
E/D♯
A/C♯
B/D♯
talk with me, and You sa - cri-ficed your all to give me life.
A
E
It's the way You took that cross with Your arms held
E/D♯
A/C♯
B/D♯
out in love, yes, You sa - cri-ficed Your all to give me life.

A2
1.
D.C.
2.
You gave Your
C♯m7
B
A2
C♯m7
B
all to give me life, You gave Your all to give me
A2
F♯m7
G♯m7
life, You gave Your all to give me
A2
F♯m7
G♯m7
A2
life, You gave Your all to give me life.
F♯m7
G♯m7
A2

1432. Lord of every heart

Is 43:19; Jn 4:14; Eph 5:18; Phil 3:8; Rev 4:10

Steady 4

Stuart Townend

Verse
Bm
F♯7
1. Lord of e-v'ry heart, I'm com-ing back to You. I'm stand-ing in the shal-
(v.2)
Gmaj7
Dmaj7
lows of what Your love can do; Re-mem-ber-ing the joy
Bm
F♯7
of laugh-ter in the rain, I'm call-ing from the de-
Chorus
Gmaj7
Dmaj7
Em7
sert, won't You fill me a-gain? Fill me a-gain, won't You

DaddE/F♯ Gmaj7
fill me a-gain? I'm tired and I'm thir - sty and I've
A/B B7 Em9
come to the end. Come cleanse me with fi - re, re-fresh
A/C♯ D Em9 Gmaj7 Bm
me with rain. O, Breath of the Spi - rit, come clo -
1. A 2. A
ser. 2. Lord of e - v'ry ser.

2. Lord of every deed,
Your promise is enough;
You're unreserved in mercy,
And unrestrained in love.
I'm casting down these crowns
Of all that I can do;
I'm trading my ambitions
For a touch of You.

1433. Lord of the Church

Tune: LONDONDERRY AIR

Lk 1:33; 15:21-22; Jn 4:10, 14; 17:17, 21; Acts 2:2-4; Eph 1:12, 22; Col 1:18

With feeling
Trad. Irish melody
Arr. Stuart Townend
G7 C F
1. Lord of the Church, we pray for our re - new - ing:— Christ o-ver
C Gsus4 G G7 C C7
all, our un-di-vi-ded aim;— fire of the Spi - rit, burn for our en -
F Fm C Dm G7 C G7
du - ing,— wind of the Spi - rit, fan the liv-ing flame! We turn to
C F G Am E7
Christ a - mid our fear and fail - ing, the will that

SoF3

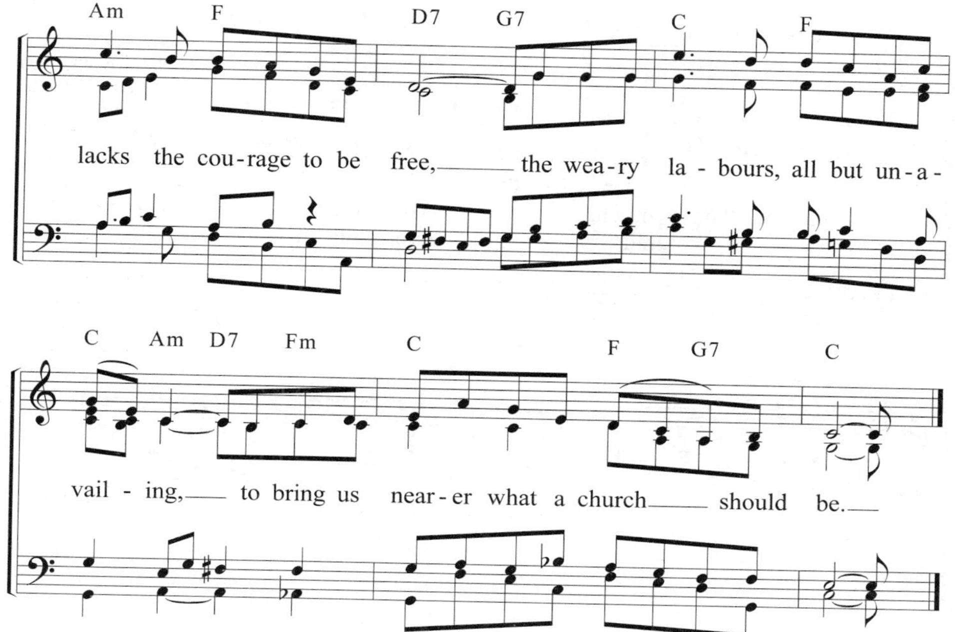
Am F D7 G7 C F
lacks the cou-rage to be free, the wea-ry la - bours, all but un-a-
C Am D7 Fm C F G7 C
vail - ing, to bring us near-er what a church should be.

2. Lord of the Church, we seek a Father's blessing,
A true repentance and a faith restored,
A swift obedience and a new possessing,
Filled with the Holy Spirit of the Lord!
We turn to Christ from all our restless striving,
Unnumbered voices with a single prayer -
The living water for our souls' reviving,
In Christ to live, and love and serve and care.

3. Lord of the church, we long for our uniting,
True to one calling, by one vision stirred;
Once cross proclaiming and one creed reciting,
One in the truth of Jesus and His word!
So lead us on; till toil and trouble ended,
One church triumphant one new song shall sing,
To praise His glory, risen and ascended,
Christ over all, the everlasting King!

Timothy Dudley-Smith

1434. 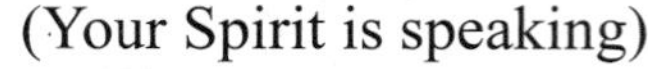

Lord of the Church

(Your Spirit is speaking)

Rev 1:20; 3:15, 22

David Lyle Morris
& Nick Wynne -Jones

Steady 4

Verse

D2 / Em9 / Gmaj9 / A7sus4

1. Lord of the Church, You hold us in Your hand, and know us through and through. You speak to us of love and faith and strength, and of our weakness too.

2. From love grown cold, faint faith that seems alive, from luke-warm lives and pride. We turn to You, that we may be revived, on fire with love renewed.

1st time only
A7

2.3.
A7

Chorus

Bm9

Your Spirit is speaking,

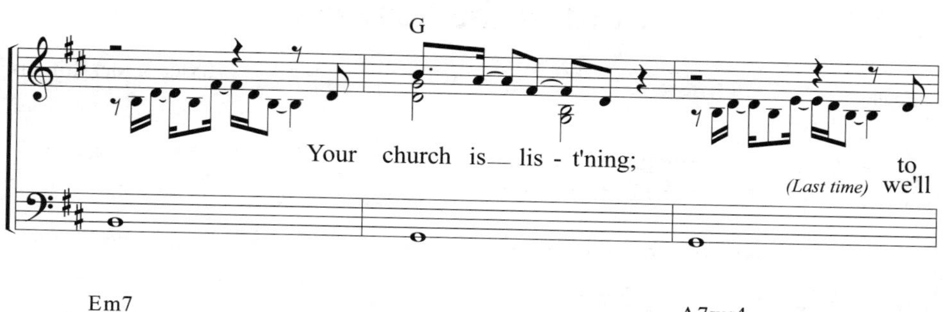
G
Your church is lis - t'ning; to
(Last time) we'll

Em7
A7sus4
hear, and to o-bey,
(Last time) we'll
1.2.
A7
D.C.
3.
A7
D2
3. From com - pro -
Lord of the church.

3. From compromise,
With all that is not true,
With all that is not pure,
We turn to You.
That we be full of faith,
Holy in all we do.

4. Lord of the Church,
Your Spirit speaks in love,
To call us back to You.
We ask You, Lord,
To share Your life with us,
And fill Your church with power.

1435. Lord of the heavens

Eph 1:7; 1 Jn 4:10

Shaun & Mel Griffiths

Steadily
D2
Verse
Lord of the hea - vens,
I bow my knee and
A/G
G2
wor - ship You;
D2
I stand be-fore You,
D2
and I am a - mazed.
G2
D2
I see Your beau - ty
Bm7
dis-played in ev-'ry -
C2
thing You do.
Asus4
A
Chorus
For You are my Sa - viour, Lord
A/C♯
a - tone - ment, sa -

G/D D A/C♯
and King, You are the on - ly One
- cri - fice: through His death re-demp - tion gives
G/D D A/C♯
for me; You are the on - ly One
new life, and I reach out, re - ceive
G/B
that I a - dore.
Your end - less love.
1. Asus4 A
In Your Son
2. Asus4 A D.C.
To end
D2

1436. Lord, to love You more

(To love You more)

Phil 4:19; Heb 10:22; 12:2

James & Hayley Gregory

Steadily
F
C7sus4(A)
F(D)
Lord, to love You more is all I want, to hear You speak-
Fix my eyes on You and draw me near, let all dis - trac -
C7sus4(A)
Dm(Bm)
Gm7(Em)
ing to my heart, to be con-sumed by You a-gain.
tions dis - ap - pear, I need You e - ven more to-day.
C7sus4(A)
B♭/D(G)
1. Gm7(Em) F/A(D)
2. Gm7(Em) F/A(D)
B♭(G)
For Je - sus, I am
hum-bled by the
C7sus4(A)
B♭(G)
o - ver-whelmed by all Your love has done,
grace of God, You meet my ev - 'ry need.

C7sus4(A) F/A(D) Gm7(Em) Dm(Bm)
– and all I want to say is that I a -
– And Je - sus, You will be al - ways my
Gm7(Em) F/A(D) Gm7(Em)
1. C7sus4(A) D.C.
2. B♭(G) B♭/D(G)
dore You, Lord. (I'm)
great - est love.
C7sus4(A) F/A(D) B♭(G) B♭/D(G) C7sus4(A) F/A(D) B♭(G) B♭/D(G)
I a -
C7sus4(A) F/A(D) Gm7(Em) F/A(D)
1. C7sus4(A) F/A(D)
2. C7sus4(A)
dore You, I a - dore You. dore
F(D) C7sus4(A) F(D)
You.

1437. Lord, we thank You for the promise

Martin Setchell (b.1939)

Tune: THE PROMISE

Unison

Gm F/A B♭ Gm

1. Lord, we thank You for the pro-mise seen in e-v'ry hu-man

Dsus4 D Gm F/A B♭ F/A

birth: You have planned each new be - gin - ning - who could

Gm7 C7 F Dm F7/C B♭ Cm/E♭

hope for great - er worth? Hear our pray'r for those we

Fsus4 F B♭/D F7/C Bdim7 Am7♭5 G/B Cm C♯dim7 D D/C

che-rish; claim our chil-dren as Your own; in the fer-tile ground of

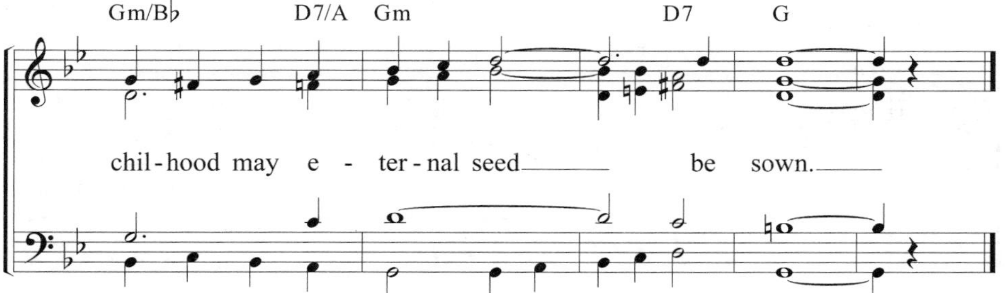
Gm/B♭
D7/A
Gm
D7
G
chil - hood may e - ter - nal seed
be sown.

2. Lord, we thank You for the vigour
Burning in the years of youth:
Strength to face tomorrow's challenge,
Zest for life and zeal for truth.
In the choice of friends and partners,
When ideas and values form,
May the message of Your kingdom
Be the guide, the goal, the norm.

3. Lord, we thank You for the harvest
Of the settled, middle years:
Times when work and home can prosper,
When life's richest fruit appears;
But when illness, stress and hardship
Fill so many days with dread,
May Your love renew the vision
Of a clever road ahead.

4. Lord, we thank You for the beauty
Of a heart at last mature:
Crowned with peace and rich in wisdom,
Well-respected and secure;
But to those who face the twilight
Frail, bewildered, lacking friends,
Lord, confirm Your gracious offer:
Perfect life which never ends.

Martin E. Leckebusch (b.1962)

1438. Lord, when I think of You

(Head over heels)

Rocky, not too fast
Ken Riley
(Fine)
Verse
G B Em C G B
1. Lord when I think of You,
Em C G B
and what I put You through, I'll nev - er un - der - stand Your
Em C G B
end - less mer - cy. To think You chose to come,
Em C G B
em - bod - ied in Your Son, to fall in - to the hands of
Em C Am G/B C
Your cre - a - ted. Oh, feel my heart ex - plode with praise,

D G Chorus B Em C (2°)
yeah.
(Well) I give You all my love,
And I know You burn with pas - sion
G B Em C G B
and I give You ev - ry - thing,
when I call on Your name,
You are the God
and Your love runs as
Em C 1. Am D
of heav - en, head o - ver heels with me.
a ri - ver,
2. Am D Am
wash - ing my shame a - way,
re - stor - ing my faith a - gain,
D C D.C.
yeah.

2. How did You look upon
The sight of Your own blood?
You even took the sin of those who nailed You!
For grace and justice meet
In Him who's chosen me
To walk the path that takes me on to heaven.

1439. Lord, You are my righteousness

Ex 17:15; Ruth 3:9; Ps 23:1; Jer 23:6; Lk 19:40;
Jn 15:13, 15; Phil 2:11; Col 3:3; Rev 17:14; 19:16

Steadily

Andrew Rogers

D
1. Lord, You are __ my right - eous - ness, __ the
2. Though You are __ the King __ of kings, __

G2
One who sanc - ti - fies __ my life, my Shep - herd and __ my __
yet You are my next __ of kin, and my near - est __

D
_ guide. __ Ban - ner of __ de - li - ve - rance, __
_ friend. __ Lay - ing down __ Your life __ for me, __

G2
war - ri - or __ and my de - fence, in Your se - cret place __ I hide. _
Your a - ma - zing grace I see, and Your love with - out __ an end. _

D
_ Ev - 'ry o - ther throne __ must fall
_ How can I __ keep si - lent, Lord?

G2
and pro-claim You Lord of all at the men - tion of Your
E - ven stones o - bey Your word and they give to You their
D
name; my sal - va - tion and my light.
praise. You're the Lord of ev - 'ry - thing,
G2
In Your pre-sence I a - bide and Your right-eous-ness I
all cre - a - tion's voi-ces sing of the glo - ry of Your
D F♯m G2 D F♯m G2 D
claim. Je - sus, Je - sus,
name.
F♯m G2 D F♯m G2 D
Je - sus, Je - sus.

1440.

Lord, You see me

(Where truth and mercy meet)

Rom 3:25; 5:8, 10; Col 1:20

John Hartley
& Gary Sadler

Slow 4

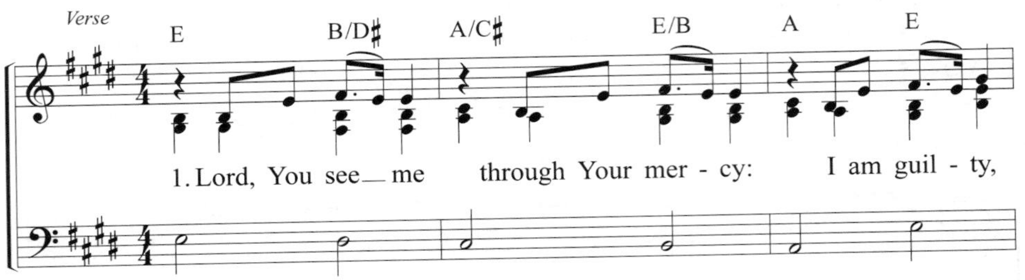
Verse
E
B/D♯
A/C♯
E/B
A
E
1. Lord, You see — me through Your mer - cy: I am guil - ty,

F♯m
D
A
E
B/D♯
A/C♯
E/B
(v.2)
still You love — me. In Your kind - ness there is jus - tice;

A
E
F♯m
D
A
through Your good - ness, You have brought — me

Chorus
A
B
E
B/D♯
here, where truth and mer - cy meet, — You tri - umph o - ver me, —
still I am so — a - mazed, — my guilt is washed a - way —

C♯m7
A
1.
E
B
Your love has won my heart a-gain. And
be - fore Your cross of peace,
2.
E
B
Last time to Coda
A
B
where truth and mer - cy meet.
A
B
D.C.
Coda
E

2. King of glory, Lord of mercy,
Risen Saviour, Perfect Wonder.
Through Your kindness
You have drawn me,
By Your suffering
You have saved me.

1441. Lord, You've been good to me

Ps 13:5-6; Lam 3:22-23

Graham Kendrick

Gently

D
Verse
Em7
A
1. Lord, You've been good to me all my life,
Em7
A
D
Em7
all my life; Your lov-ing kind-ness ne-ver fails.
G
Em7
A
I will re-mem-ber
D/F#
G
Em7
all You have done, bring from my
A
G/A
D
heart thanks-gi-ving songs.

G
Chorus
D
New e-v'ry morn - ing is Your love,
G
Em7
Asus4
filled with com-pas - sion from a - bove.
A
G
Em7
F♯m7
Grace and for-give - ness full and free,
G
A6
G6/A
D
Lord, You've been good to me.

2. So, may each breath I take
Be for You, Lord, only You,
Giving You back the life I owe.
Love so amazing,
Mercy so free.
Lord, You've been good,
So good to me.

1442. Love is patient
(Amazing love)

Jn 15:15; 1 Cor 13:4-9; Heb 7:25

Brightly

Stuart Townend

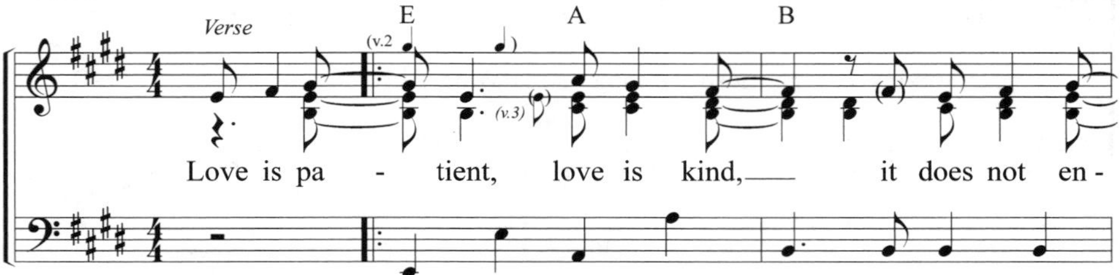

Verse
E
A
B
(v.2
(v.3)
Love is pa - tient, love is kind, it does not en -

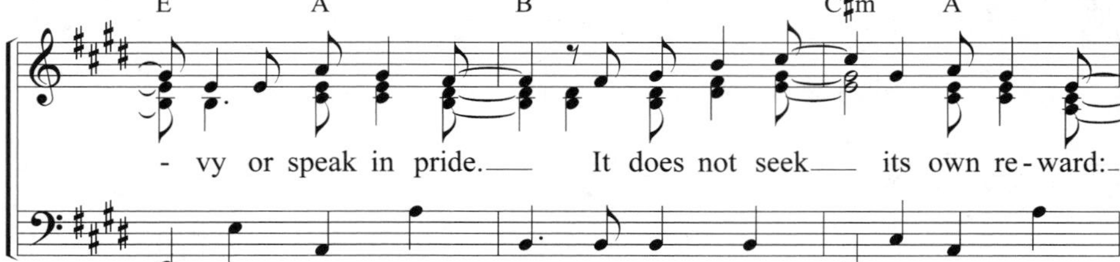

E
A
B
C♯m
A
- vy or speak in pride. It does not seek its own re - ward:

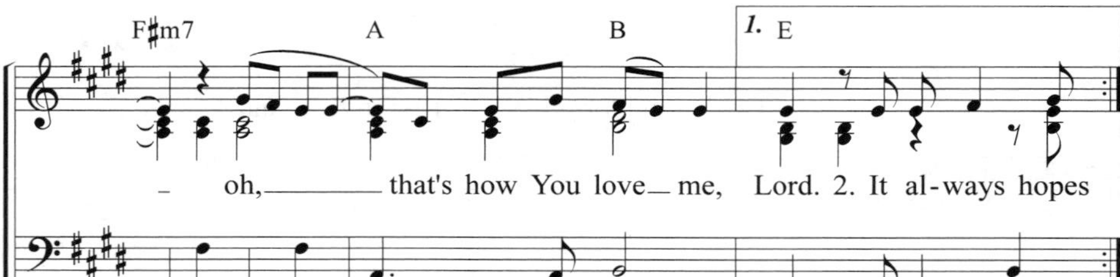

F♯m7
A
B
1. E
- oh, that's how You love me, Lord. 2. It al-ways hopes

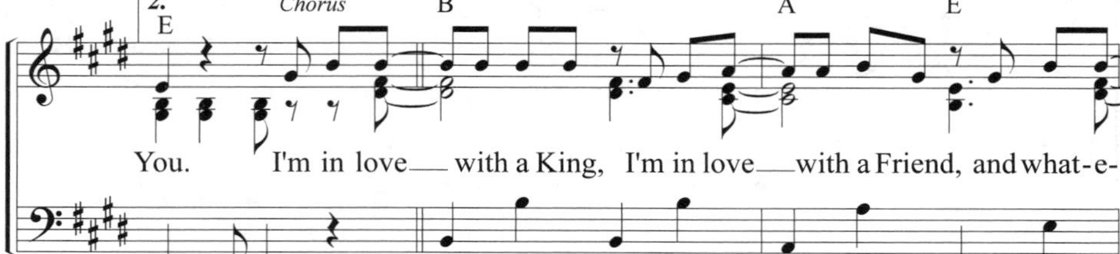

2. E
Chorus
B
A
E
You. I'm in love with a King, I'm in love with a Friend, and what-e-

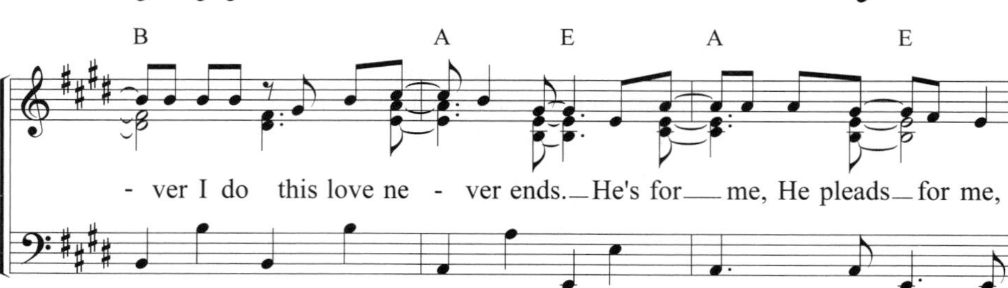

B
A
E
A
E
- ver I do this love ne - ver ends. He's for me, He pleads for me,

A E F♯m7 B
pours out His life__ for me; what more do__ I need?__ A-ma-zing love!__
E B E B E

2. It always hopes and perseveres,
It covers over a wealth of sins,
It shuns all evil, delights in truth:
Oh, I want to be like You.

3. There are tongues now, but they will cease;
There is knowledge - it's incomplete.
For what we know now, we know in part,
But what endures is a loving heart.

1443. # Love, joy, peace
(The fruit of the Spirit)

Rom 17:14; Gal 5:22-23, 25; 6:8

David Lyle Morris

Rhythmically
Chorus
G C G C C/E
Love, joy, peace and pa - tience, kind-ness, good-ness, faith-
D G/D G G/B C G
ful - ness, gen - tle-ness and self - con - trol:
1.
C C/E D G C C/E D
this is the fruit of the Spi - rit. We want the fruit of
G
the Spi - rit.
2.
C C/E D G
we will reap what we sow,
C C/E D G
we will reap what we sow.
Verse
G/B
1. We want joy

C/D G C C/E D G
— in the Spi - rit, we will re-joice in the Spi-rit of God.
C6 D7 G G G/B C/D G
There is peace ___ in the Spi - rit,
C C/E D G C6 D7 G D.C.
we want to rest in the Spi-rit of God.
Repeat x 4
G G/B C6 D G G/B C6
Walk - ing with the Spi-rit of Je - sus.
Liv - ing by the Spi-rit of Je - sus.
Re-joic - ing in the Spi-rit of Je - sus.
Rest - ing in the Spi-rit of Je - sus.
D6 G Fine

2. We want life in the Spirit,
We want to live by the Spirit of God,
Keep in step with the Spirit,
We will be led by the Spirit of God.

1444. Love like a jewel

(I will seek after You)

Mt 13:46; Heb 12:1-2

Sue Rinaldi
& Steve Bassett

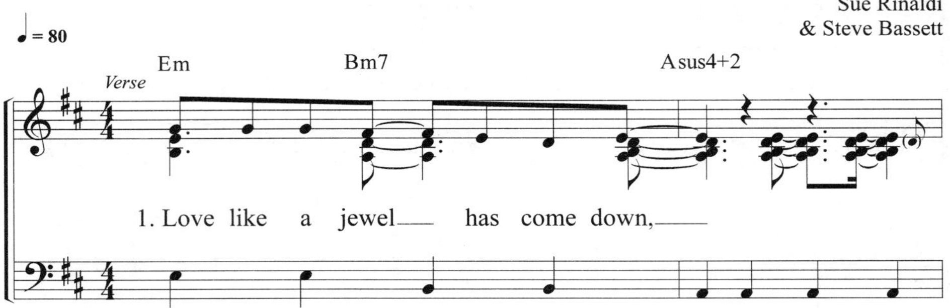
♩ = 80
Em
Bm7
Asus4+2
Verse
1. Love like a jewel has come down,

Em
Bm7
D2
most pre - cious gem in hea - ven's crown.

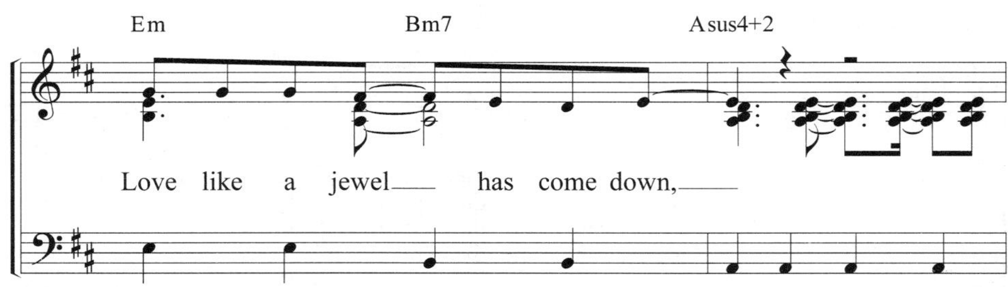
Em
Bm7
Asus4+2
Love like a jewel has come down,

Em
Bm7
D/A
Asus4
G
the great - est trea - sure that I have found. And

Chorus
D
D/C♯
Bm
Bm/A
I will seek af-ter You, for-sake e-v'ry thing that is
G
A
D
dis-trac-ting me from this search-ing, and
D/C♯
Bm
Bm/A
run to the place where my heart on-ly hears the beat
Gmaj7
F♯m/A
Em
Bm7
Asus4+2
of Your love for this world.
Em
Bm7
Asus4+2
(Fine)

2. Love like a jewel has come down,
You walk with the hurting,
You're a friend to the poor.
Love like a jewel has come down,
Our greatest treasure,
Where hope can be found.

1445. Magnificat

(Sing out, my soul)

Lk 1:46

Taizé
Music: Jacques Berthier (1923-1994)

Canon

1
2
Mag - ni - fi - cat, mag - ni - fi - cat, mag - ni - fi - cat a - ni - ma
Sing out, my soul; sing out, my soul. Sing out and glo - ri - fy the
G C Am7 D7 G G C Am7
3
me - a Do - mi - num. Mag - ni - fi - cat, mag - ni - fi - cat,
Lord who sets us free. Sing out, my soul; sing out, my soul.
D7 G G C Am7 D7 G
4
mag - ni - fi - cat a - ni - ma me - a!
Sing out and glo - ri - fy the Lord God!
G C Am7 D7 G

1446. Many are the words we speak

(Now to live the life)

Steadily

Amos 5:24; Mt 5:39, 41; Eph 4:1; Phil 3:10

Matt Redman

Bm
1.Ma-ny are the words we speak,
(v.2 we pray that)

Gmaj7
ma - ny are the songs we sing;

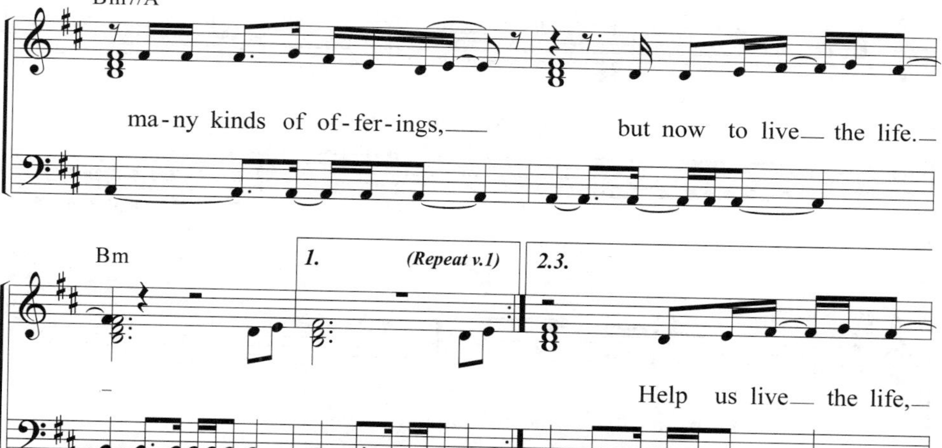

Bm7/A
ma-ny kinds of of-fer-ings,
but now to live the life.
Bm
1.
(Repeat v.1)
2.3.
Help us live the life,

D
Bm
help us live the life.

Gmaj7
All we want to do is bring You some - thing real,
bring You some - thing true.
1.
D
A
D.C.
2.
D
(2. We hope that)
A
D.S.
3.
D
A
Help us live the life.
Bm
Dmaj7
Now to go the ex - tra mile, now to turn the oth - er cheek,

Gmaj7
Dmaj7
Gmaj7
– and to serve You with a life.___ Let us share Your fel - low-ship,–
Dmaj7
Gmaj7
– ev - en of Your suf - fer ings;___ ne - ver let the pas - sion die.__
F♯7sus4
D
– Now to live__ the life,____
Bm
now to live__ the life,____
D
A7sus4
D
now to live_ the life,– - now to live the life.

2. (We hope that)
Precious are the words we speak,
(We pray that)
Precious are the songs we sing;
Precious all these offerings,
But now to live the life.

1447. # May my eyes see more of You

(You've captured my heart)

With feeling
Doug Horley
Verse
E G♯m7 F♯m
May my eyes see more of You, Lord; may my heart just
E B E G♯m
beat with Yours. May my hope be in Your good-ness,
F♯m E A G♯m7
may my life be pure. And ev-'ry day my
F♯m7 B A G♯m7
cry is just the same: Make me more like
F♯m7 B
Je-sus, Lord, I pray.
Chorus
Be-cause You've

E B A
cap - tured my heart, You have cap - tured my heart.
G♯m A
King of love, and King of glo - ry,
In Your throne room there will be no
G♯m F♯m7
Au-thor of cre-a - tion's sto - ry, I de-light in You, and
hi-ding place in pu - ri - ty, a life laid bare for all to see, O
B E
now and for - e - ver. You have
God, make me ho - ly. You have
cap - tured my heart,
B A G♯m
You have cap - tured my heart.
F♯m7 B E
I de-light in You, You've cap-tured my heart.

My soul glorifies the Lord and my spirit rejoices in God my Saviour.

LUKE 1:46

1448. May the mind of Christ my Saviour

Capo 1 (D) *1 Cor 2:16; Col 3:15-16; Heb 12:1-2*

Tune: ST LEONARDS Arthur C. Barham-Gould (1891-1953)

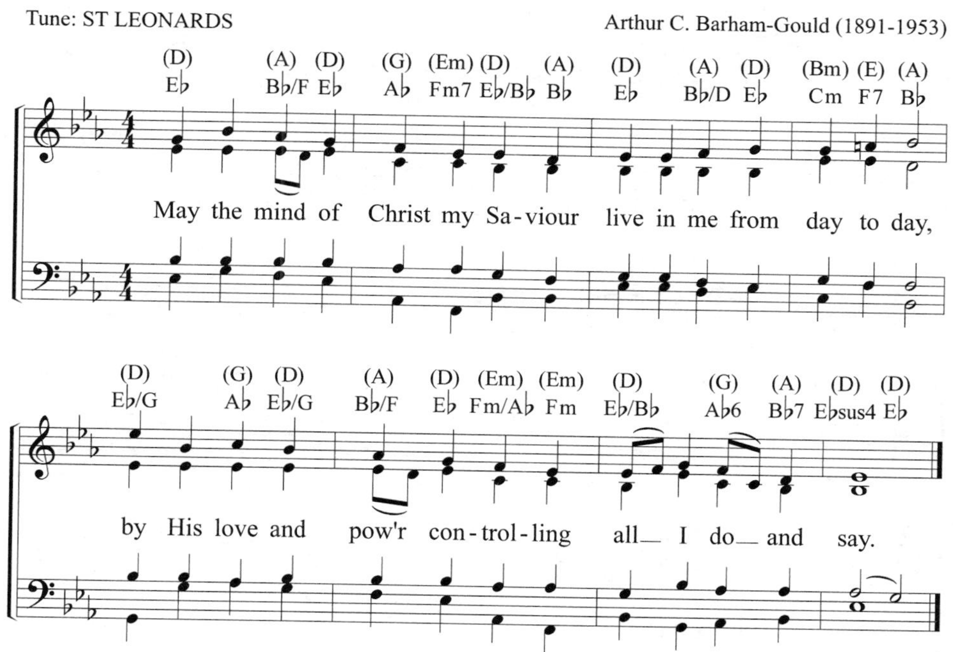

(D) Eb (A) Bb/F (D) Eb (G) Ab (Em) Fm7 (D) Eb/Bb (A) Bb (D) Eb (A) Bb/D (D) Eb (Bm) Cm (E) F7 (A) Bb
May the mind of Christ my Sa-viour live in me from day to day,
(D) Eb/G (G) Ab (D) Eb/G (A) Bb/F (D) Eb (Em) Fm/Ab (Em) Fm (D) Eb/Bb (G) Ab6 (A) Bb7 (D) Ebsus4 (D) Eb
by His love and pow'r con-trol-ling all — I do — and say.

2. May the word of God dwell richly
In my heart from hour to hour,
So that all may see I triumph
Only through His power.

3. May the peace of God my Father
Rule my life in everything,
That I may be calm to comfort
Sick and sorrowing.

4. May the love of Jesus fill me,
As the waters fill the sea;
Him exalting, self abasing,
This is victory.

5. May I run the race before me,
Strong and brave to face the foe,
Looking only unto Jesus,
As I onward go.

Kate B. Wilkinson (1859-1928)

1449. May the words of my mouth

Ps 19:14; Jn 8:12; 14:6; 1 Thess 4:1

Tim Hughes & Rob Hill

Steadily
C
Em7
Am
Am/G
F
C
G
1. May the
Verse
C
Em7
Am
Am/G
words of my mouth, and the thoughts of my heart bless Your
F
C
G
name, bless Your name, Je - sus: and the
C
Em7
Am
Am/G
deeds of the day, and the truth in my ways speak of
F
C
G
You, speak of You, Je - sus. For this is what

Chorus
C
F
I'm glad to do, it's time to live
Am
Am/G
D/F♯
G
a life of love that pleas - ses You. And I will give
my all to You, sur-ren - der ev -
'ry-thing I have and fol - low You, I'll fol-low You.
1.
F2
3
Fmaj7
2. Lord, will You.
2.
F2

(2.)
Am
G/B
1.2.3.
repeat and build
C
D
I will fol-low,
I will fol-low You.
4.
C
D
Dsus4 D
F2
D.S.
I will fol-low You.
For this is what
3.
C
You.

2. Lord, will You be my vision,
Lord, will You be my guide:
Be my hope, be my light and the way?
And I'll look not for riches,
Nor praises on earth,
Only You'll be the first of my heart.

1450. Merciful Lord

(Ouve Senhor)

Ps 86:6

With expression

Brazilian melody
Arr. David Peacock
Words: S. Montiero

Em
Am7
Mer-ci-ful Lord, In Your lov-ing - kind-ness,
Ou-ve Se - nhor, eu es-tou cla - man - do,
D
B7
Em
hear our pray'r, lis-ten to our in-ter-ces-sion. Mer-ci-ful
tem-pie - da - de de mim e me res-pon-de. Ou-ve Se-
Am7
Lord, in your lov-ing - kind-ness, hear our
nhor, eu es-tou cla - man - do, tem-pie-
D
B7
Em
pray'r, lis-ten to our in - ter - ces - sion.
da - de de mim e me res - pon - de.

1451. Mercy
(You have been patient)

Mic 7:18-19; Jn 13:34; Col 3:13

Lynn DeShazo & Gary Sadler

♩ = 76
G D/F♯ A D
Chorus
G/D D A D
Mer - cy, mer-cy, Lord, Your

G D G A G/D D
mer-cy is how we are re-stored; mer - cy, O

Last time to Coda
A Bm7 G D/F♯ A D
mer-cy, Lord, help us to show Your mer-cy, Lord.

G D/F♯ A Gsus2
Verse
G Bm
1. You have been pa - tient with our of-fen-

G D A
ces, You have for-giv - en all of our sins; we were de-serv-
Bm G
ing on - ly Your judge - ment, but Your great mer -
Em G A D.S.
cy tri-umphed a - gain.
Coda
G D/F♯ A D
Help us to show Your mer - cy, Lord.

2. Lord, You have taught us,
'Love one another,'
As You have loved us
So we must love;
Always forbearing,
Always forgiving,
Showing to others
The mercy we've known.

1452. More than I could hope or dream of

(One day)

Ps 84:10; Lk 2:14; 6:38

With energy

Reuben Morgan

A
F♯m7
More than I could hope or dream of,
G
D
A
You have poured Your fa-vour on me. One day in the
F♯m7
G
D
house of God is bet-ter than a thou-sand days in the world.
Esus4
A/D
E
So blessed,
C♯m7
F♯m7
A/D
E
C♯m7
F♯m7
I can't con-tain it, so much I've got to give it a-way.

A/D
E
C♯m7
F♯m7
G
Your love has taught me to live, now, You are
D
D/E
A
E
F♯m7
D
A
E
more than e-nough for me.
F♯m7
D
A
Asus4
Lord, You're more than e-nough
A
Asus4
D
D/E
for me, more than e-nough for me.
A

For in the day of trouble he will keep me safe in his dwelling; he will hide me in the shelter of his tabernacle and set me high upon a rock.

PSALM 27:5

1453. My Friend and King

Rom 5:7-8

James Taylor

Gently
Verse
G D/F♯ Em7 D/F♯ G D/F♯
My Friend and King, love sweet - er than a rose;
What can I do but bow down on my knees?
Em7 C2 G/B Am G Dsus4 D
You meet me where I am.
Your beau - ty blows my mind.
1. Dsus4 D
2. Chorus
Dsus4 D G C
Lord, I will call on-ly to You,
And I will live on-ly for You,
G D/F♯ Em7 C G/B
for You de-serve the high - est praise.
for You de-serve the high - est praise.
Dsus4 D Dsus4 D
D.C.
Last time
G

2. To be with You
Is all that I desire;
Lord, may You shine in me.
You gave me life
And sacrificed Your own;
Who else would die for me?

1454. My God is a Rock

Ps 18:2; 23:6

Capo 3 (Em)

Kate Simmonds
& Mark Edwards

With life

Gm7(Em)
Ab/Bb(F)
1. My God is a Rock! My feet are plan - ted and I'm
God is a Rock who can't be sha - ken, no, I
Ebmaj7(C)
Dm7(Bm)
(Am) Cm7
(Bm) Dm7
(C) Ebmaj7
(B) D7#9
Gm7(Em)
not gon - na stop prai - sing. This love is a-live!
won't e - ver stop prai - sing. This love is a-live
Ab/Bb(F)
Ebmaj7(C)
Dm7(Bm)
Good-ness and mer - cy all the days of my life.
with e - v'ry pro - mise writ - ten o - ver my life.
1.3.
(Am) Cm7
(Bm) Dm7
(C) Ebmaj7
(B) D7#9
2.4.
(Am) Cm7
(Bm) Dm7
(C) Ebmaj7
(B) D7#9
Gm7(Em)
Ab7(F)
2. My
And in Him I live, for He

Gm7(Em) A♭7(F) Gm7(Em) A♭7(F) Gm7(Em) D7(B)
lives in me, and in Him I move, and I have my be -
Gm(Em) Dm/F(Bm) E♭maj7(C) D7(B) Gm(Em) (Bm) Dm/F (C♯m♭5) Em7♭5 (C) E♭ (B) D7
ing. I'm held for - e - ver in Your hand.
(Rock so - lid, rock so - lid.)
Gm(Em) Dm/F (Bm) E♭maj7(C) D7(B) Gm(Em) Dm/F(Bm)
And now this ground on which I stand.
(is rock so - lid,
(C♯m♭5) Em7♭5 E♭(C) D7(B)
Last time
Gm7(Em)
My
it's rock so - lid.)

3. My God is a rock and my salvation,
   That's why I'll never stop praising.
   This love is alive! My strength and shelter
   All the days of my life.

4. My God is a Rock who never changes,
   How can I ever stop praising?
   This love is alive! Night and day
   He's watching over my life.

1455. My God is so big

Neh 9:6; Ps 147:4-5; Mt 19:26

Author unknown
Arr. Stuart Townend

Brightly
G
1. My God is so big, so strong and so migh - ty, there's
Am7 D G C/G G
no - thing that He can - not do. My God is so big, so
Am7 D
strong and so migh - ty, there's no - thing that He can - not
G G/B C C/E
do. The ri - vers are His, the moun - tains are His, the

G
Am7
D
G
stars are His han - di - work too. My God is so big, so
Am7
D
G C/G G
strong and so migh - ty, there's no - thing that He can - not do.

2. My God is so big, so strong and so mighty,
There's nothing that He cannot do.
My God is so big, so strong and so mighty,
There's nothing that He cannot do.
He's called you to live for Him every day,
In all that you say and you do.
My God is so big, so strong and so mighty,
There's nothing that He cannot do.

1456. My heart is captivated, Lord

(Divine exchange)

Is 61:1; Lk 4:18; 2 Cor 5:21; 8:9; Heb 12:28

Lara Martin

Gently
C2
My heart is cap - ti - va - ted, Lord, by You a-lone;
Am7
cap - tured by the awe - some-ness of You a-lone.
F
Melt - ed by the grace and mer - cy You have shown, I stand
G
in won - der.
C2
I reach to You, the One who makes the blind
Am7
eyes see, who breaks the chains of sick - ness with au - tho -

F
ri-ty. Re-stor - ing what was bro - ken, so it may
Am7/G G
C2
fly a-gain. I live to wor - ship You; I breathe
Am7
F
to wor - ship You. All of my days Your
G Am/G G
C2
face I will seek. For as I wor - ship You,
Am7
F
You lead me to that place, to that place of di-

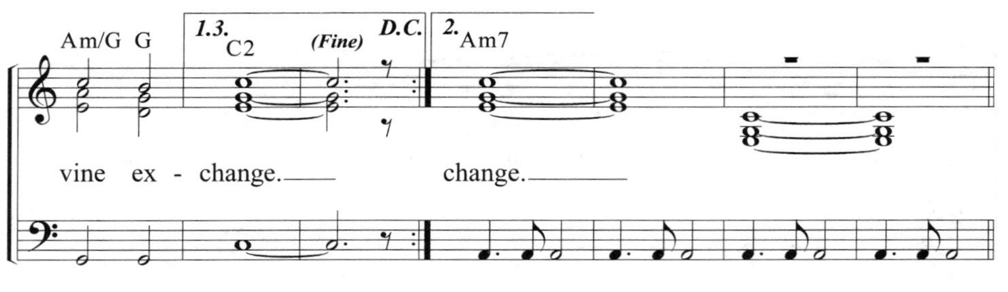
Am/G G
1.3.
C2
(Fine)
D.C.
2.
Am7
vine ex - change.
change.

Am7 G/B C2 Am7 G C2 Am7 G/B C
Je - sus, Je - sus. Je - sus,

Am7 G C G
D.S. al fine
Je - sus. I live

1457. My hope is in the Lord

Job 19:25-26; Is 40:31

Simply

Robin Mark

Verse
D
G
A
My hope is in the Lord who
has made heav'n and earth and
D/F♯
G
A
has re - newed my strength, when ev -
things seen and un - seen; what - e -
D
G
1.
Em7
G/A
- 'ry - thing seems sense - less, my hope is still in Him
- ver shade of pas - sing day, my hope
D
2.
Em7
G/A
D
Chorus
A
who is still in Him. My hope is
F♯m7
Bm7
1. - 3.
4.
D.C.
in You, Lord. My My

4. (2°)
G
A/G
For I know that my eyes shall
Em7
A
D
G
Em7
see You, in the lat - ter days to
Asus4
A
G
A/G
come. When You stand on the earth, with my lips
A
Bm7
G
I will con - fess that the hope of my heart
A
Bm7
G
is come, that the hope of my heart

1.
A
D
2.
A
– is come.
For I
– is come,

Bm7
G
that the hope
of my heart

A
D
– is come.

1458. My hope rests firm

1 Cor 13:12; Phil 1:23; 3:13-14; 1 Tim 2:6; Heb 12:1

With feeling

Keith Getty
& Richard Creighton

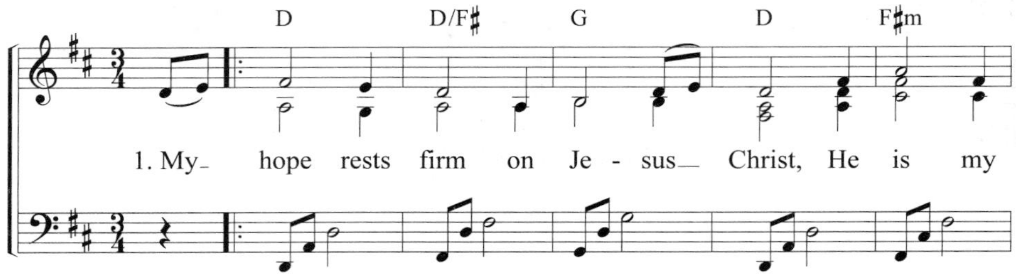
D
D/F♯
G
D
F♯m
1. My hope rests firm on Je - sus Christ, He is my

Bm
A
G
A
on - ly plea: though all the world should

D
D/F♯
G
Em
A
Bm
point and scorn, His ran - som leaves me free,

Em
A
D
G
Em9
His ran - som leaves me free.

Asus4
A
Last time
D
2. My

2. My hope sustains me as I strive
And strain towards the goal;
Though I still stumble into sin,
His death paid for it all,
His death paid for it all.

3. My hope provides me with a spur
To help me run this race:
I know my tears will turn to joy
The day I see His face,
The day I see His face.

4. My hope is to be with my Lord,
To know as I am known:
To serve Him gladly all my days
In praise before His throne,
In praise before His throne.

1459. My troubled soul

(Praise the mighty name of Jesus)

Ps 18:46; 42:5; Mt 6:27; 1 Pet 5:7

Robert Critchley

Capo 3(G)

Gently

Verse
B♭(G)
E♭(C)
1. My trou - bled soul, why so weighed down? You were not made
2. My an - xious heart, why so up - set? When tri - als come
B♭(G)
F(D)
to bear this hea-vy load. Cast all your bur-
how you so ea - si - ly for - get to cast your bur-
B♭(G)
E♭(C)
B♭(G) F(D)
dens up-on the Lord;
dens up-on the Lord:
Je-sus cares, He cares for you.
B♭(G)E♭/B♭(C)
B♭(G) B♭/D(G)
E♭(C)
Je-sus cares, He cares for you. And all your

B♭(G)
F(D)
wor-ry-ing won't help you make it through. Cast all your bur-
B♭(G)
E♭(C)
dens up-on the Lord. And trust a-gain
B♭(G)
F(D)
B♭(G)
E♭/B♭(C)
Chorus
B♭(G)
in the pro-mise of His love. I will praise the migh-ty
E♭(C)
B♭(G)
F(D)
B♭(G)
name of Je-sus, praise the Lord, the lift-er of my head. Praise the Rock of
E♭(C)
B♭(G)
F(D)
B♭(G)
E♭/B♭(C)
B♭(G)
(Fine)
my sal-va-tion, all my days are in His faith-ful hands.

1460. Name above all names

Ps 36:9; Is 40:31; Rom 5:8; Phil 2:9

Neil Bennetts

Capo 3(D)

Worshipfully
F(D) F/E(D) Dm(Bm)
1. Name a-bove all names, the Sa-viour for sin-
C7sus4 (A7sus4) F(D) F/E(D)
-ners slain. You suf-fered for my sake,
Dm(Bm) C7sus4(A7sus4) B♭/D (G)
to bring me back home a-gain. When I was lost
C/E (A) F(D) B♭/D(G)
You poured Your life out for me.
F(D) C(A) B♭(G) C7(A7)
Name a-bove all names, Je-sus, I love You.

1.2.
F(D)
F/E(D)
Dm(Bm)
C7sus4 (A7sus4)
Last time
F(D)

2. Giver of mercy,
The fountain of life for me.
My spirit is lifted
To soar on the eagle's wings.
What love is this
That fills my heart with treasure?
Name above all names,
Jesus, I love You.

3. High King eternal,
The one true and faithful God.
The beautiful Saviour,
Still reigning in power and love.
With all my heart
I'll worship You forever:
Name above all names,
Jesus, I love You.

1461. No longer just servants

Capo 4 (G)

Ps 23:1; Mt 22:8; 25:21; Jn 15:15; 1 Cor 2:9

Matt Redman

Steadily
Verse
B(G)
B/A♯(G)
1. No longer just servants in the house of the King, the
G♯m7(Em)
E2(C)
banquet is ready and You draw us in. You
B(G)
B/A♯(G)
G♯m7(Em)
E2(C)
call us to eat with You, and to be Your
(v.2)
friends, those who love You, Your
1.
2.3.
friends, those who know You. 2. A You. O

Chorus
F♯(D)
E2(C)
how can it be that I have be - come a
G♯m7(Em)
E2(C)
friend of the King af - ter all that I've done? A
F♯(D)
E2(C)
sin - ner in rags, now a child in Your care, You
G♯m7(Em)
E2(C)
showed me the cross and I met You there. Your
B(G)
B/A♯(G)
G♯m7(Em)
E2(C)
friend, one who loves You, Your

(Fine)
B(G)
B/A♯(G)
G♯m7(Em)
E2(C)
D.C.
friend,
one who loves
You.
3. And

2. A servant is trusted with some secret things,
   And so, how much more for the friend of a King.
   No eye has seen, and no ear has heard
   What You've prepared for those who love You,
   What You've prepared for those who know You.

3. And I'll sing a song for the One that I love,
   You captured my heart when I met with Your Son.
   And so I will live a life full of praise
   For You, Lord and Shepherd,
   For You, Friend and King.

1462. None other

Rev 5:12

Geraldine Latty

Worshipfully
Dmaj7
A♯°
None o - ther is more wor - thy, none o -
Bm7
Em7
D/F♯
G G♯° A13
ther is more de - serv - ing of our praise. None o -
Dmaj7
- ther is so ho - ly, sov - 'reign God
Em7
D/F♯
Gmaj7
G/A
Dmaj7
(Fine)
we come to You, we will give the glo - ry due Your name.
D.C.
None o -

1463. No scenes of stately majesty

Mt 8:20; 26:41; 27:29, 60; 2 Jn 1:6; Rev 8:4; 17:14; 19:16

Capo 3 (D)

Graham Kendrick

Steadily
F(D)
Bb(G)
1. No scenes of state - ly ma - jes - ty for the King of
F(D)
Bb(G)
Bb/C(G)
kings. No nights a - glow with can - dle flame for the King of
F(D)
(Em) (D)
Gm7 F/A C(A)
Dm(Bm)
(A) C/E
love. No flags of em - pire hung in shame for Cal - va - ry. No
Bb(G)
F/A(D)
Am7(F#m)
Bb(G)
(A) C
Bb/D (G)
F/C (D)
flow'rs per - fumed the lone - ly way that led Him
Bb(G)
F/A(D)
Bb(G)
C7(A)
F(D)
to a bor - rowed tomb for Eas - ter Day.

B♭(G)
F(D)

2. No wreaths upon the ground were laid
For the King of kings.
Only a crown of thorns remained
Where He gave His love.
A message scrawled in irony -
King of the Jews -
Lay trampled where they turned away,
And no one knew that it was the first Easter Day.

3. Yet nature's finest colours blaze
For the King of kings.
And stars in jewelled clusters say
'Worship heaven's King.'
Two thousand springtimes more have bloomed -
Is that enough?
O how can I be satisfied until He hears
The whole world sing of Easter love.

4. My prayers shall be a fragrance sweet
For the King of kings.
My love the flowers at His feet
For the King of love.
My vigil is to watch and pray until He comes;
My highest tribute to obey and live to know
The power of that first Easter Day.

5. I long for scenes of majesty
For the risen King.
For nights aglow with candle flame
For the King of love.
A nation hushed upon its knees at Calvary,
Where all our sins and griefs were nailed
And hope was born of everlasting Easter Day.

1464. Not by words and not by deeds

(You opened up my eyes)

Capo 3(Em)

Zech 4:6; 1 Cor 1:18; 2 Cor 12:9; Gal 5:1; Eph 2:5, 8

With strength

Martyn Layzell

Verse

Gm9(Em) Ebmaj7(C)

1. Not by words and not — by — deeds, — but by
strength and not — by — might, — but with

Gm9(Em) Ebmaj7(C) Gm9(Em)

grace we have — been — saved; — and it is the gift — of — God, —
pow - er from — on — high, — so that we can on - ly — boast, —

1. Ebmaj7(C) F2(D) Ebmaj7(C)

— the faith we need. — Not by

2. Ebmaj7(C)

— boast in You. —

F(D) Eb2(C) Bb(G)

Chorus

Eb(C)

For once I was — dead, now I'm a -

F(D) Eb(C) Bb(G)

live, — for free - dom I'm — set free; — and in Your great —

Eb(C)
F(D)
Eb(C)
Bb(G)
love, life do I find. You o-pened up my eyes.

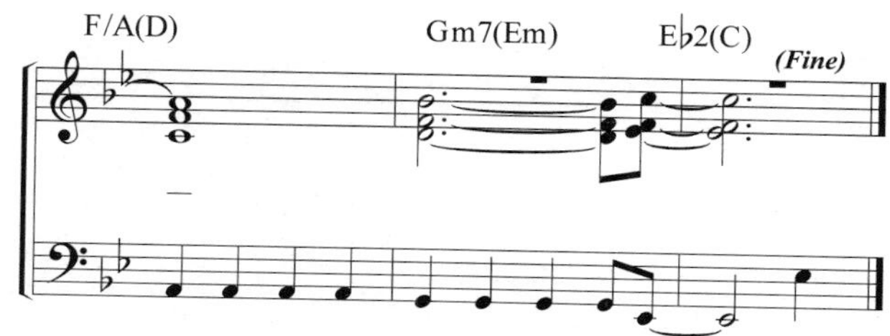
F/A(D)
Gm7(Em)
Eb2(C)
(Fine)

2. Not with eloquence or fame,
But in weakness and in shame,
For the power of Your strength is then revealed.
And the message of Your cross,
Seemed such foolishness to some,
But the mercy of Your grace is hidden there.

1465. Nothing in this world

Capo 1 (D)

Ps 84:10; 1 Cor 13:12; Phil 3:8

Tim Hughes

Tenderly
Verse
E♭(D)
E♭2/D(D)
1. No-thing in this world, no trea-sure man could
no-thing I want more than to spend my days with
A♭/C(G)
buy could take the place of draw-ing near to
You, dwel-ling in Your se-cret place of
B♭(A)
1.
E♭/A♭(D)
2.
E♭/A♭(D)
Chorus
You. There's
praise.
(And)
E♭(D)
B♭/D(A)
E♭/G(D)
A♭/C(G)
oh, how I need You.
Je - - - sus, I need You. You are the One

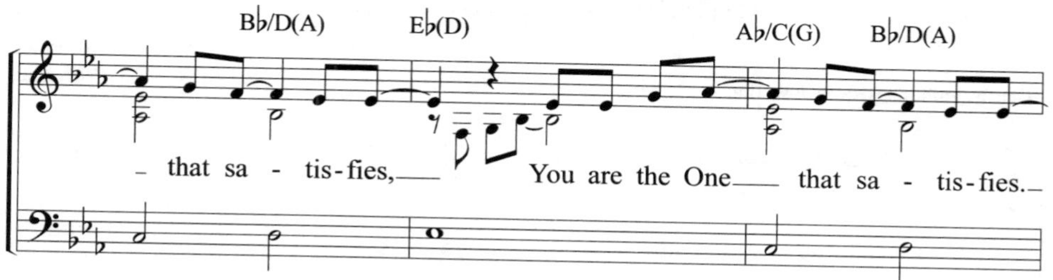
B♭/D(A)
E♭(D)
A♭/C(G)
B♭/D(A)
that sa - tis-fies, You are the One that sa - tis-fies.

E♭(D)
(Fine)
2. So

2. So place within my heart
A fire that burns for You,
That waters cannot quench
Nor wash away.
And let that fire blaze
Through all eternity,
Where one day I shall see You
Face to face.

1466. Nothing is too much to ask

Matt Redman
& Mike Pilavachi

Gently, building with each section
Am
G/B
No - thing is too much to ask
C
D2sus4
D2
Am
now that I have said I'm Yours,
Je - sus, take the whole of me
G/B
C
Last time to Coda
Dsus4
D2
un - re - serv - ed - ly.
Am
G2/B
C
Je - sus take me deep - er now
that I might go fur - ther too,
D2sus4
D2
Am
G2/B
I've re - ceived so much from You

C2
Dsus4
D
Am
un-de-serv - ed-ly.
I was made to love You, Lord,
G2/B
C
Dsus4
D
I was saved to wor - ship You.
Am
G2/B
C2
You will be the fo - cus of
all e-ter-
1. Dsus4
D
2. Dsus4
D
D.C.
- ni-ty.
- ni-ty.
Coda
Dsus4
Fine
ed-ly.

1467. Now has come salvation

(You are the One)

Rev 11:15

Mark Stevens

Strong 4
C2
Verse
D
Em7
C2
D
1. Now has come sal - va - tion,
now has come Your strength.
G2
C2
G/B
Dsus4
D
(vv.2,3)
And the king-dom of my God,
and the
C2
G/B
D
(v.3)
C2
D
pow - er of His Christ,
Je-sus, ho - ly One,
1st time D.C. (v.2)
D/E
D
C2
Dsus4
D
G2
Je - sus, ho - ly One.
Chorus
C2
D
G/B
C2
C/E
You are the One that I love, my Lord,
You are the One all of hea-

SoF3

D
Em
Em/D
C2
ven a - dores.
You are the One
who is high
D
D/F♯
Am7
C2
D
- o-ver all the earth.
Je-sus, my ri - sen Sa - viour,
Am7
C2
D
C2
D
Je-sus, my ri - sen Sa - viour.
D/E
D
C2
Dsus4
D
G2
D.C.(v.3)
(Fine)

2. Now has come Your mercy,
Now has come Your peace.
And the glory of Your presence,
And the greatness of Your name,
Jesus, holy One,
Jesus, holy One.

3. Now has come forgiveness,
Now has come Your grace,
And the precious Holy Spirit,
And the freedom that You gave
In Jesus, holy One,
Jesus, holy One.

1468. **Now in reverence and awe**

(Jesus, let me meet You in Your word)

Jer 23:29; Heb 4:12; 1 Pet 1:10-12

Graham Kendrick
Arr. Steve Thompson

Steadily

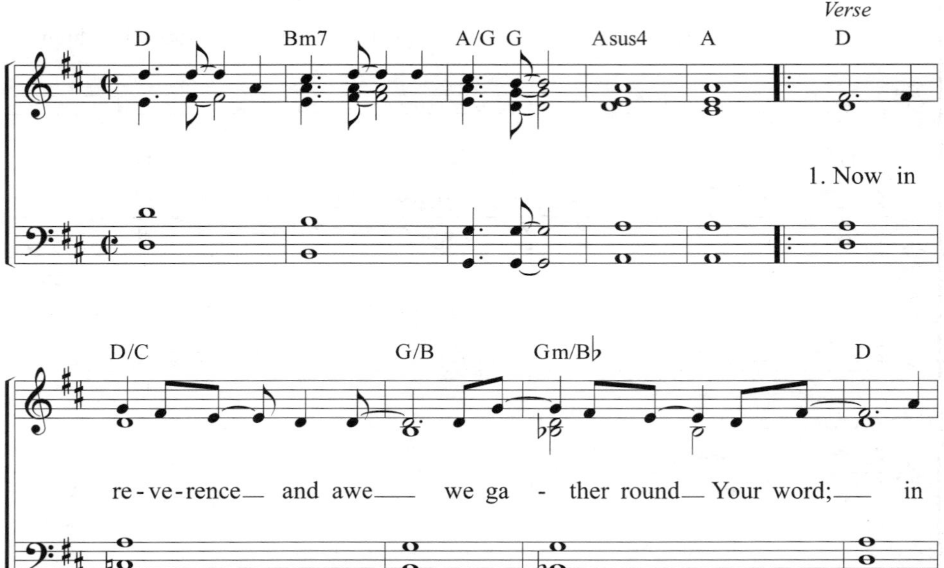

D
Bm7
A/G G
Asus4
A
Verse
D
1. Now in
D/C
G/B
Gm/B♭
D
re-ve-rence and awe we ga - ther round Your word; in

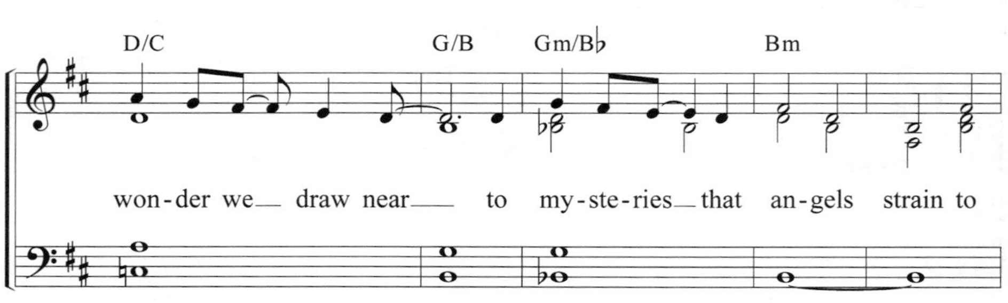

D/C
G/B
Gm/B♭
Bm
won-der we draw near to my-ste-ries that an-gels strain to

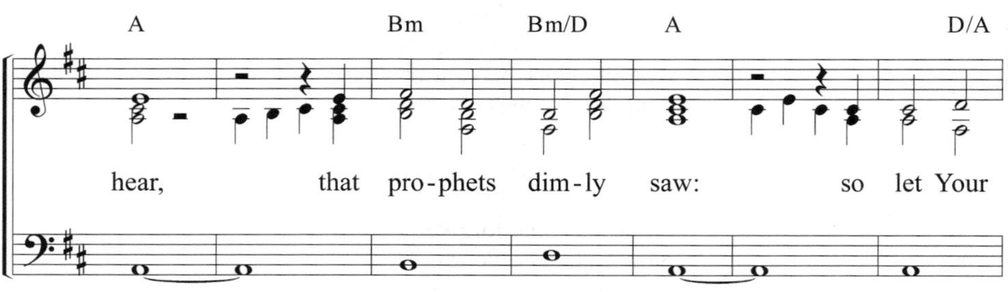

A
Bm
Bm/D
A
D/A
hear, that pro-phets dim-ly saw: so let Your

A7
A D/A A7
Chorus
Bm
A
Spi-rit shine up - on the page and teach me;
G
A
Bm
A
o - pen up my eyes, with truth to free me,
G
F♯m7
Em
G/A
D
light to chase the lies. Lord Je-sus, let me meet You in Your word;
Bm7
Em
G/A
D
(Fine)
Lord Je-sus, let me meet You in Your word.

2. Lord, Your truth cannot be chained;
It searches everything -
My secrets, my desires.
Your word is like a hammer and a fire,
It breaks, it purifies:
So let Your Spirit shine into my heart and...

1469. O changeless Christ

Mt 4:23; 8:24-27; 26:26-28; Mk 5:27-34; Heb 10:20; 13:8

Capo 1 (G)

George T. Smart (1776-1867)

Tune: WILTSHIRE

A♭(G)
(G) (D) (Em) (C) (G) (D)
A♭/E♭ E♭7 Fm D♭ A♭/E♭ E♭ A♭(G)
1. O change-less Christ, for e - ver new, who
(D)
E♭/G A♭(G) A♭/C A♭/E♭ E♭ E♭7 A♭(G) E♭7 A♭ A♭/C E♭
walked our earth - ly ways, still draw our hearts as
(G) (D) (G) (G) (D) (G) (C) (Am) (D) (D) (G)
A♭ E♭7/G A♭ A♭/E♭ E♭ A♭/C D♭2 B♭m E♭ E♭7 A♭
once You drew the hearts of o - ther days.

2. As once You spoke by plain and hill
Or taught by shore and sea,
So be today our Teacher still,
O Christ of Galilee.

3. As wind and storm their Master heard
And His command fulfilled,
May troubled hearts receive Your word,
The tempest-tossed be stilled.

4. And as of old to all who prayed
Your healing hand was shown,
So be Your touch upon us laid,
Unseen but not unknown.

5. In broken bread, in wine outpoured,
Your new and living way
Proclaim to us, O risen Lord,
O Christ of this our day.

6. O changeless Christ, till life is past
Your blessing still be given;
Then bring us home, to taste at last
The timeless joys of heaven.

Timothy Dudley Smith

1470. O dear God, we ask for Your favour

(By Your side)

Mt 6:10; Lk 4:19; 2 Cor 6:2

Steadily
Verse
G
Marty Sampson
1. O dear God, we ask for Your fa - vour,
G7
C
Em
come and sweep through this place. Oh, we de - si-
D
C
G
- re You.
I just want to be with You,
G7
C
be where You are, dwell in Your pre-sence, O God. Oh, I
Em
D
C
Chorus
want to walk with You.
And I

G
Dsus4
C
will climb this moun - tain,
Em7
Dsus4
and I step off the shore;
C
G
Dsus4
and I have cho - sen to fol-
Em
D
C
low, and be by Your side for-e - ver more.
1.
G
G7/F
G/E
G7/F
D.C.

2.
G
D
D.S.
Last time
G
And I
G7/F
G/E
G7/F
To end
G
G
2. Tell me what You want me to do, Lord God,
G7
C
Em
tell me what You want for my life. It's Yours, O God,
D
C
G
it's Yours. Do Your will,
G7
C
have Your way, be Lord God in this place. Oh, I
Em
D
C
D.S.
want Your will to be done. And I

1471. O for a closer walk with God

Capo 1 (D)

Words: William Cowper (1731-1800)
Adapted words & Music: Keith Getty

Thoughtfully
E♭(D)
E♭/G(D)
A♭(G)
1. O — for a clo - ser walk with God, — a
B♭/D(A)
E♭(D) A♭(G)
B♭(A)
E♭(D)
E♭/G(D)
calm and heav'n - ly — frame. — A — light that shines up - on the
A♭(G)
A♭/C(G)
E♭(D)
1.
B♭(A)
road, — lead - ing to the Lamb.
2. Where —
2.3.
E♭(D)
E♭/G(D)
A♭(G)
Cm7(Bm)
B♭/D(A)
E♭(D) E♭/G(D)
A — light to be my guide, — the Fa - ther's

A♭(G) Cm7(Bm) B♭/D(A) E♭(D) E♭/G (D) A♭(G) Cm7(Bm)
pre - sence at my side. In Your will my rest I
B♭/D(A) E♭(D) E♭/G(D)
find. O for a clo - ser walk with
A♭(G) A♭/C (G) E♭(D) A♭/E♭(G) E♭(D) (Fine) D.C.
God, lead-ing to the Lamb. 3. So

2. Where is the blessèdness I knew
When once I saw the Lord?
Where is the soul refreshing view
Living in His word?

3. So shall my walk be close with God
With all the hopes made new.
So purer light shall mark the road
Leading to the Lamb.

1472. **O God of love**
(How good it is)

Ps 100:5; 139:15-16; Mt 16:18; Rom 8:31; 2 Cor 12:10

Moderately

Louise & Nathan Fellingham

A Verse Bm7 D2 D/E
1. O God of love, I come to You a-gain,
A Bm7 D2 A Bm7
knowing I'll find mer-cy. I can't ex-plain
D2 D/E F♯m7 A/C♯ Bm7 A/C♯
all the things I see, but I'll trust in You. In
D A2/C♯ D
ev-'ry mo-ment You are there, watch-ing o-ver You hear
A/C♯ E Bm7 F♯m7
my prayer. You go be-fore me, You're be-hind me,

D E A Chorus Bm7
no-thing's hid - den from You. How good it is
D2 D/E A Bm7 D2 D/E
to be loved by You, how good it is.
A Bm7 D2 D/E A Bm7
How good it is to be loved by You, how good it is.
Last time to Coda
Mid 8
D2 D/E F♯m7 A/C♯ D
Who can stand a-gainst us? In my
F♯m7 A/C♯ D F♯m7 A/C♯
weak-ness You are strong. Your word is e - ver-last-

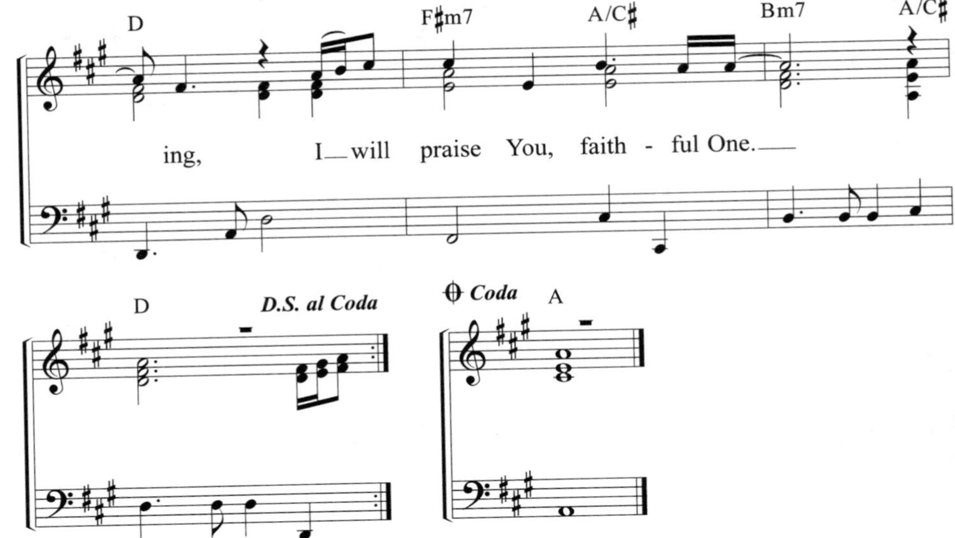
D
F♯m7
A/C♯
Bm7
A/C♯
ing, I — will praise You, faith - ful One. —
D
D.S. al Coda
Coda
A

2. O God of strength,
Your hand is on my life,
Bringing peace to me.
You know my frame,
You know how I am made,
You planned all my days.
Hand of mercy, hand of love,
Giving power to overcome.
If all beneath me falls away,
I know that You are God.

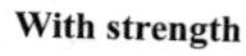

Oh fallen one
(Arise)

With strength

Ps 27:9; Is 60:1, 4, 10; 61:1; Mt 10:31; Col 3:4

James Gregory

F♯m7
Verse
E/G♯
Asus4
A
1. Oh fal - len one ___ co - vered now ___ in shame, ___

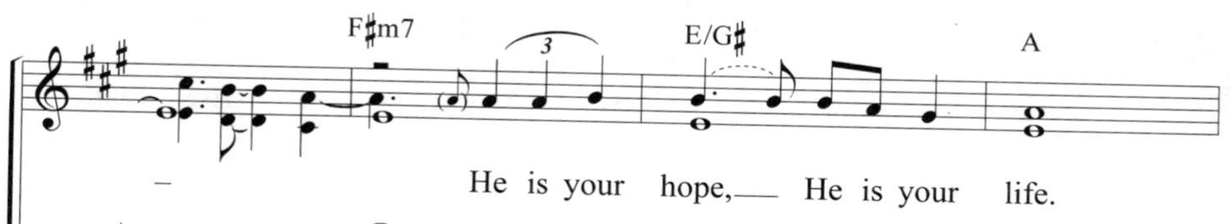
F♯m7
E/G♯
A
He is your hope, ___ He is your life.

F♯m7
E/G♯
Though He should judge, ___ His

Asus4
A
F♯m7
an - ger turns ___ a - way; ___ rise from the

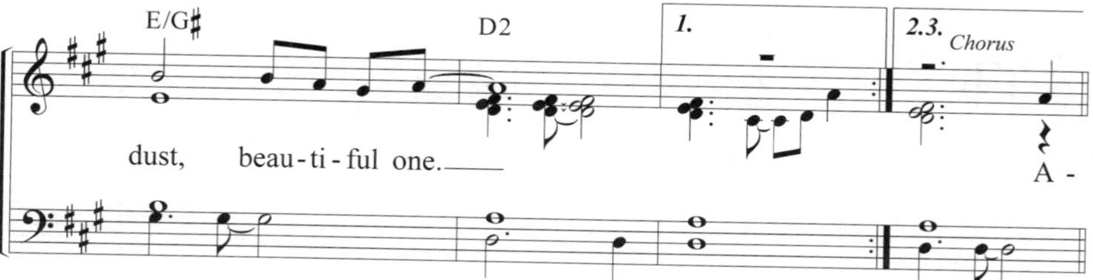
E/G♯
D2
1.
2.3.
Chorus
dust, beau - ti - ful one. ___ A -

D
E
A/C♯
D
E
A/C♯
D
rise and shine, your glo-ry has come, a - rise and
E
A/C♯
D
E
A/C♯
Bm7
shine, your glo - ry has come, a - rise and
F♯m7
D
E
shine, He is cal - ling you by name; though your walls
Bm
F♯m
3
D
D.C.
have fal - len down, He'll build you up a-gain.
E/G♯
F♯m7
D
E
E/G♯
F♯m7
So let Your sal - va - tion come, for Your glo - ry,

Dmaj7
E/G♯
F♯m7
D
Lord.
Set the cap - tives free, we
E
E/G♯
F♯m
Dmaj7
To end
Amaj7
pray; these souls are Your re - ward.

2. Don't be afraid,
   For you're not left alone;
   His heart of love is broken for you.
   Your Father cares
   For all your children now,
   Arise in His name, beautiful one.

3. Lift up your eyes,
   Many come to see
   The splendour your God has given to you.
   Could each of your saints
   Become a thousand saints?
   Rise up and praise, beautiful one.

1474. Oh kneel me down again
(Humble King)

Is 42:3; Jn 13:5; Phil 2:3, 8

Moderately

Brenton Brown

Verse
F♯m7
E/G♯
A2
B
Oh kneel me down a-gain, here at Your

E
F♯m7
E/G♯
feet; show me how much You love

A2
B
E
F♯m7
E/G♯
hu-mi-li-ty. Oh Spi-rit, be the star

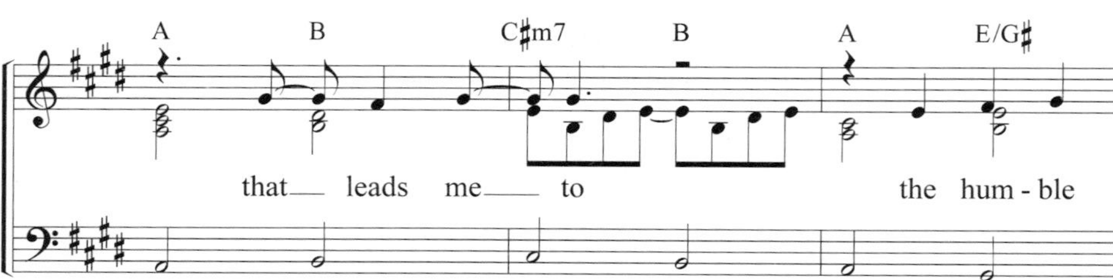

A
B
C♯m7
B
A
E/G♯
that leads me to the hum-ble

F♯m7
B7sus4
B7
E
heart of love I see in You.

Chorus
A2
E/G♯
('cause)You are the God of the bro - ken, the
F♯m7
B
A2
friend of the weak; You wash the feet of the wea-
E/G♯
F♯m7
B
ry, em - brace the ones in need. I want to be-
A2
E/G♯
F♯m7
like You, Je - sus, to have this heart in me.
B
F♯m7
E/G♯
You are the God of the hum - ble, You are

Last time to Coda
D.C.
A
B7
E
the hum - ble King.
Oh kneel me
Coda
E
F♯m7
E/G♯
You are the God of the hum - ble, You are
A
B7
E
the hum - ble King.

1475. Oi, oi, we are gonna praise the Lord

Ps 8:4

Moderately

Doug Horley

Chorus
G C D G
Oi, oi, we are gon-na praise the Lord. Oi, oi, we are gon-na
C D Em
praise the Lord. Oi, oi, we are gon-na
C D F
praise the Lord. He's an ex - cit-ing, po-wer-is-ing, c - co -
C D7 G
los-sal, hu-mun-gous-mun-gous God!
(Fine)
Verse
But it's
D
some-times hard to un-der-stand that the God who made the earth and man would

Em
point a fin - ger down from hea - ven and shout: "Hey
D
you! I love you. Hey You! I love you. Hey you, you! I
D.C. al fine
love you." But it's true! —

1476. O Jesus, Son of God

(Light of the world)

Capo 4 (G)

Jn 1:1-5, 9-11; 8:12; Col 1:16-17, 20; 1 Pet 1:10-12

Matt Redman

With a half time feel
Verse
B(G) F♯/A♯(D) G♯m(Em)
1. O Je - sus, Son of God, so full
up - on the earth, but who
F♯(D) B(G) F♯/A♯(D)
of grace and truth, the Fa - ther's sa - ving Word:
will un - der-stand? You came un - to Your own,
G♯m(Em) F♯(D) B(G)
so won - der - ful are You.
but who will re - cog-nise?
C♯m7(Am) B/D♯(G) E2(C)
The an - gels longed to see, and pro - phets
Your birth was pro - phe - sied, for You were
F♯sus4(Dsus4) C♯m7(Am) B/D♯(G)
searched to find the glo - ry we have seen re -
the Mes - siah, who came and walked up - on the

1.
E2(C)
2. 3.
E2(C)
(Dsus4)
F♯sus4
C♯m7(Am)
vealed. 2. You shone earth. Your glo - ry
B/D♯(G)
E2(C)
F♯sus4(Dsus4)
we have seen, the one and on - ly King,
C♯m7(Am)
B/D♯(G)
E2(C)
and now You're li - ving in our hearts.
Chorus
E(C)
Light of the world, Light of the world, Light of the world, You
B(G)
shine up - on us.

E(C)
Light of the world, Light of the world, Light of the world, You
shine up - on__ us.
B(G)
D.C.
C♯m7(Am)
B/D♯(G)
E2(C)
Light of the world, Light of the world, Light of the world, You
F♯sus4(Dsus4)
(x3)
To end
B(G)
shine up - on us.

3. In You all things were made, and nothing without You;
In heaven and on earth, all things are held in You.
And yet You became flesh, living as one of us,
Under the shadow of the cross,
Where through the blood You shed,
You have made peace again,
Peace for the world that God so loves.

1477. O Lord, I am devoted to You

(Devoted)

Martyn Layzell

Gently

Verse

E G♯m/D♯

O Lord, I am de - vo - ted to You, all that I am I
I am no - thing with - out You, all my hope is up - on You,

C♯m7 1. A B

give You, no - thing do I with - hold.
sim - ply tell - ing You I am

2. A F♯m

Yours, I am Yours.

A B E *Chorus* G♯m7/D♯

Je - sus, may my de - vo - tion be pleas - ing, ex -

C♯m7

pressed through this song I am sing - ing, pour - ing my heart out to

Am7+4
Am7
Bsus4/F♯
B7
E
You, on-ly You. You are the rea-son I'm liv-ing, I'm
G♯m7
F♯m7
breath-ing: my re-fuge, my strength and my heal-ing, so
Am7+4
Am7
Bsus4/F♯
B7
D.C.
To end
E
I give my heart un-to You, on-ly You.

2. Every earthly distraction
Fades away to the background,
I'm content just to be with You.
Jesus, You satisfy my longing,
To You do I cry, I'm coming,
Kneeling before Your throne,
At Your throne.

1478. O Lord, our Lord

Ps 8:1, 3-4; 18:6; Is 53:5; Phil 2:10-11; Col 1:15

Andrew & Shirley Rogers
Strong 4
Verse
D E7 G D E7 G D G A
Chorus
Em7 D/F♯ G D/F♯ Em7 A Em7 D/F♯ G D/F♯
mf
1. O Lord, our Lord, Your name is great and greatly to be praised. In heaven and the universe, Your glory is displayed.
Ev'ry knee must bow to You and ev'ry tongue confess: You are Lord, the Son of God, risen from the dead.
f
You're Jesus, Ruler of the universe. Majestic is Your

Em7
A
Bm
name in all the earth.
King-doms rise,
G
D
A
king-doms fall,
You are still the Lord of all.
Ma-
Bm
G
1. D
jes-tic is Your name here on earth.
2. D
Fine
earth.

2. When I see the moon and stars
Created by Your breath;
Why did You consider me
Worthy of Your death?
When I was the guilty one
You took away my shame:
When I called, You hid me in
The refuge of Your name.

I will extol the Lord at all times; His praise will always be on my lips. My soul will boast in the Lord; let the afflicted hear and rejoice. Glorify the Lord with me: let us exalt His name together.

PSALM 34:1-3

1479. O Lord, when I wake up

(Lift high)

Ps 92:1-2; Jn 12:32; 1 Cor 10:13; 2 Cor 4:8, 10

Brian Houston

Not too fast
Verse
E A E A A
1. O Lord, when I wake up in the morning, let my mouth be filled with praise for You. O Lord, that
when I go out in the evening, let my mouth be filled with praise for You,
F♯m A F♯m
all might know, yeah, and many might see yeah,
A E
that You're my Lord.
Bridge
F♯m C♯m
Fill me with a spirit of boldness, O my God,

F♯m
C♯m
and come and take all of my shame; that
F♯m
C♯m
I might see temp - ta - tion melt be - fore my eyes and watch the
F♯m
B
Bsus4
Chorus
de-mons flee in Je-sus' name. As we lift high the name. Lift high
E
A
B
Bsus4
the name of the Lord.
B
E
A
Lift high the name of the Lord.

B
F♯m
That ma-ny might know,
A
F♯m
A
that ma-ny might see
my Lord.
E
A
E
1.
A
2. O Lord,
2.
A
E

2. O Lord, when I'm stressed and feeling tired,
Let my mouth be filled with praise to You.
O Lord, when I'm pressed on every side,
Let my mouth be filled with praise to You.
That all might know and many might see
That You are Lord.

There is no-one holy like the Lord; there is no-one besides You; there is no Rock like our God.

1 SAMUEL 2:2

1480. O Lord, You are first in my life

(I am Yours)

Rom 12:1; Jas 4:8

Expressively

Jonathan James

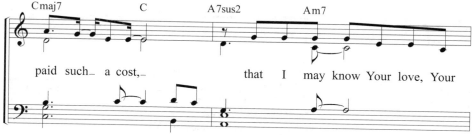

Verse
Cmaj7 C Cmaj7 C A7sus2 Am7
1. O Lord, You are first in my life; for You I live as a
A7sus2 Am7 F
sa-cri-fice, ho-ly in Your sight, pleas-ing to Your heart, as I
Gsus4 G Cmaj7 C
put my trust in You. 2. Pre-cious Je-sus, You
Cmaj7 C A7sus2 Am7
paid such a cost, that I may know Your love, Your

A7sus2
Am7
F
grace, Your touch; with e - v'ry - thing I am, I
Gsus4
G
want to know You more, my heart is o - pen to You.
Em7
D
C2
As I seek You, Lord, You draw me near-
Dsus4
D
G
Chorus
Em7
- er. I am Yours, Lord, I am Yours,
C2
D7sus4
G
com - plete - ly a - ban - doned to You. I am Yours,

Em7
C2
D7sus4
Lord, I am Yours,
wholly devoted to You.
Cmaj7
C
1.
Cmaj7
C
A7sus2
Am7
A7sus2
Am7
2.
Cmaj7
C
Cmaj7
C
Cmaj7
C
G
G/F♯
Em7
Dsus4
D
G
G/F♯
I am Yours, Lord,
Em7
1.-3.
Dsus4
Repeat x4
D
4.
D7sus4
D
rit.
C2
I am Yours, Lord,
Lord.

1481. O my soul, arise and bless your Maker

Ps 86:15; 139:18; Jn 6:48;
1 Cor 13:12; 2 Cor 12:10; Rev 5:9

Steadily

Stuart Townend

E F♯m7 E/G♯ Emaj7/G♯ A E/G♯ Bsus4 B E

1. O my soul, a - rise and bless your Ma - ker,
2. King of grace, His love is o - ver - whelm - ing;

E B7sus4/F♯ E/G♯ A E/G♯ Bsus4 B

for He is your Mas - ter and your Friend.
Bread of Life, He's all I'll e - ver need,

F♯m E/G♯ Bsus4 B C♯m Emaj7/B F♯/A♯ B7/A

Slow to wrath but rich in ten - der mer - cy;
for His blood has pur - chased me for - e - ver:

E/G♯ C♯m7 E/G♯ 1. F♯m7 B7sus4 E (Fine) 2. F♯m7 B7sus4 E

wor - ship the Sa - viour Je - sus. Je - sus. And
bought at the cross of

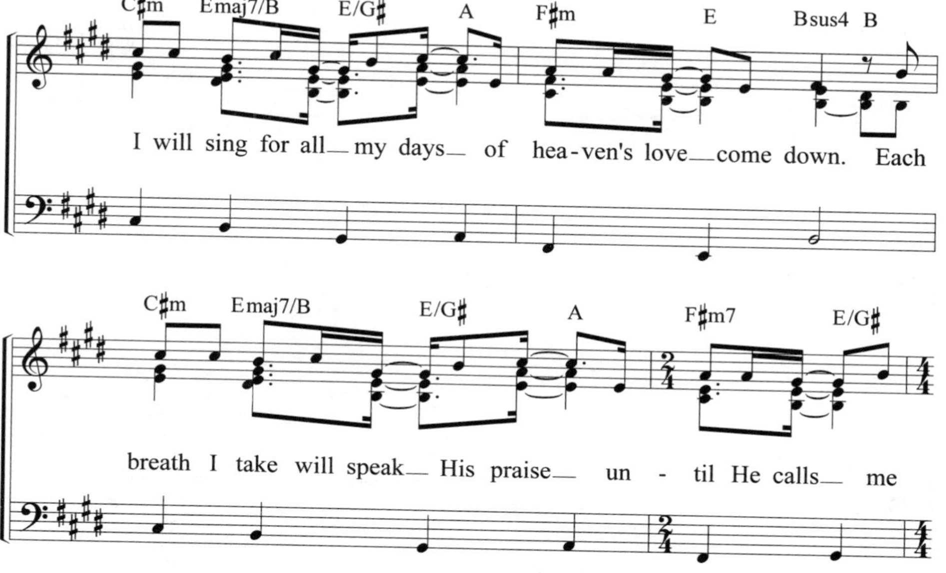
C♯m Emaj7/B E/G♯ A F♯m E Bsus4 B
I will sing for all my days of hea-ven's love come down. Each
C♯m Emaj7/B E/G♯ A F♯m7 E/G♯
breath I take will speak His praise un - til He calls me

Bsus4 B
D.C.
home.

3. When I wake, I know that He is with me;
When I'm weak, I know that He is strong.
Though I fall, His arm is there to lean on:
Safe on the Rock of Jesus.

4. Stir in me the songs the songs that You are singing;
Fill my gaze with things as yet unseen.
Give me faith to move in works of power,
Making me more like Jesus.

5. Then one day I'll see Him as He sees me,
Face to face, the Lover and the loved;
No more words, the longing will be over:
There with my precious Jesus.

1482. Once I was far away

(No height, no depth)

Rom 8:38-39; Eph 2:12; Phil 3:9; 1 Jn 3:1

Gently building

Kristyn Lennox
& Keith Getty

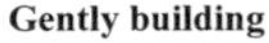

A
Verse
D
1. Once I was far a - way, but now my life is found in You.

(v.2)
A
Once I was with-out hope, but now I have a

D
F♯m
D
vi - sion of hea - ven. Fal - len from grace; by

F♯m
D
E
Chorus
F♯m
E/G♯
faith lif - ted up; now I be-lieve no height, no

A F♯m D E A A/C♯
depth can keep us from the love of Christ.
D E A F♯m D
No life, no death, no trial can tear us from the
E A D A D (Fine)
love of God in Christ.

2. How wonderful the love
Our Father God has given us,
That we should still be called
Children of God.

1483. One more step along the world I go

Tune: SOUTHCOTE

Jn 14:6; 16:33; Gal 5:25; Col 1:15; Rev 22:13

With a spring

Sydney Carter
Arr. Douglas Coombes

Verse

G D/F♯ D D7 G C G D7 G C/G G *Chorus* G/B C A D7 G D7 G C/G G

1. One more step a-long the world I go, one more step a-long the world I go, from the old things to the new, keep me tra-vel-ling a-long with You. And it's from the old I tra-vel to the new, keep me tra-vel-ling a-long with You.

2. Round the corners of the world I turn,
More and more about the world I learn.
And the new things that I see,
You'll be looking at along with me.

3. As I travel through the bad and good,
Keep me travelling the way I should.
Where I see no way to go,
You'll be telling me the way, I know.

4. Give me courage when the world is rough,
Keep me loving when the world is tough.
Leap and sing in all I do,
Keep me travelling along with You.

5. You are older than the world can be,
You are younger than the life in me.
Ever old and ever new,
Keep me travelling along with You.

1484. One sacrifice and I am free

Is 53:5; Lam 3:22; Mt 24:35; Eph 1:7

James Gregory

Brightly
E
Verse
One sa - cri - fice and I am free,
Je - sus, in death You set me free,
E/D♯
Asus2
the cross of Christ my vic - to - ry,
tak - ing the pun - ish - ment for me,
E
and on this grace I do be - lieve,
it is Your blood that co - vers me,
E/D♯
1.
Asus2
2.
Asus2
yes, I be - lieve.
yes, I be - lieve.
And be - cause
A
G♯m7
A
of what this love has done my heart is filled with praise.

F♯m11
E
Chorus
And so I lift my voice to You, pouring out all this love on You, what can I give for all You've done for me?
I know the Saviour lives today, heaven and earth may pass away, but I know Your love will never fail, no, no.
B
C♯m
G♯m7
C♯m
A
1.3.5.
E
B
2.4.6.
E
B
A
Last time to Coda
1.
F♯m11
D.C.

2.
F♯m11
E7
A
And e - v'ry day I live I vow
Am6
to fol - low You.
Repeat as required
E
E
D.S. al Coda
Coda
F♯m11
E
F♯m7
E2/G♯
A2
E/B
A2/C♯
B2/D♯
E
E2/G♯

1485. One thing I ask

Ps 27:4; Jn 15:15; Gal 3:13; Phil 3:8; Heb 6:19

Paul Oakley

With awe
Em7 Em9 Em7 Em9 Cmaj7 Cmaj7(♯11)
Cmaj7 Cmaj7(♯11) Em7 Em9
1. One thing I ask, one thing I seek,
To spend my days within the veil
Em7 Em9 Cmaj7 Cmaj7(♯11)
Cmaj7 Cmaj7(♯11) Em7 Em9 Em7 Em9
to see Your face, to gaze upon
Where purity and light pour o-
Cmaj7 Cmaj7(♯11) Cmaj7 Cmaj7(♯11)
Your beauty,
-ver me,
1.
Em/A D2/A
to search behind

Em/A D2/A Cmaj7 Cmaj7(♯11) Cmaj7
the eyes of love,
2.3.
C D E
and I am changed. I gaze on the One
C Am C
who so de - sired friend - ship with one as low as me.
G C Am
You left be - hind Your throne, so I'll
1. C D.C. for Verse
sing of Your love,
2. For alternative chorus
C
sing of Your love, sing of Your love,

Em
C
the King who be - came the - sac - ri - fice,
Am
C
G
bro - ken and cursed u - pon the tree, the Sav-
C
Am
1. C
- iour of my soul. Ha - le - lu - jah, ha - le - lu - jah.
2. C
Em
hal - le - lu - jah, Ha - le - lu - jah, Ha - le - lu - jah, Ha - le - lu - jah, Ha - le - lu - jah.

2. All I held close I now let go.
All else is loss
Compared to knowing You
And I am changed.

1486. # One thing I have been asking

(You're the desire)

Ps 27:4

Evan Rogers

Simply
Verse
G D Em7
1. One thing I have been ask-ing, one thing I am look-
Asus4 A G D
ing for: to see Your glo-ry and beau-ty,
Em7 C
Chorus
to know Your pre-sence, Lord. You're the de-
G D C
si-re of my heart, and You are all that I want;
D G D/F♯
You're the de-si-re of my heart, and You are

C
1.,3.
Last time to Coda
Dsus2
Dsus4
D
2.
Dsus2
D
all that I want.
Am7
G6/B
I am want - ing You, I am need - ing You much
F C F C
Am7
more, Lord. You have won my heart, You've
G/B
C
gi-ven me all that You've got, Your love was de - mon-stra - ted on the
D Dsus4 D
D.S. al Coda
Coda
G
cross. Thank You, Lord! You're the de -
p

2. You have all my attention,
You are the One I'm living for;
In You I find satisfaction,
You are mine and I am Yours.

1487. One voice
(Send a revival)

Is 7:14; 9:6; Mt 1:23; 3:3; 1 Pet 2:24; Rev 5:9; 14:6

Dave Bilbrough

Steady 4

Verse
A D2 E A D2 E
One voice, one mind, one will to
A D2 E A D D
see the heart of God re-vealed in pow'r.
A D2 E A
Let ev-'ry na-tion, tribe and tongue come
D2 D E
seek the Lord and His great love.
Chorus
Send a re-vi-
D2 A
val, send a re-vi-val, send-a re-vi-

D2
A
val, we pray. Send a re - vi -
D2
A
val, send a re - vi - val, send a re - vi -
D2
1.2.
A
3.
A
val we pray. 2. We

2. We will not cease, we will not rest
Until the Prince of Peace is seen.
As God with us, Emmanuel,
The hope of all humanity.

3. A vision burns within my soul
That all the world will come to know
The healing found at Calvary,
That place where truth and mercy meet.

4. I hear a sound across the earth;
It tells me that the time is near.
An anthem lifting up His name:
Make straight a path - prepare the way.

1488. Only You

(Nothing compares to You)

Ps 86:8; Hab 3:6, 10; Rom 8:32; 2 Cor 8:9

James Taylor

Medium pace

E
F♯m7
1. On-ly You can re - place rags for rich-
(2.) de - mons flee, moun - tains trem-
E/G♯
A
es pure as gold, and Your mer -
ble in Your sight, but You love
F♯m7
B
cy saved my soul, there's none like You.
me like a friend,
1.3.
E
B
2.4.
E
2. At Your name
Chorus
D
No - thing com - pares to You,

A
E
You're the one we love.
Send
D
A
Last time to Coda
E
down Your ho - ly fire o-ver all the earth.
1.3.
2.
No -
D.C.
Coda
3. You have paid

3. You have paid such a cost,
So much more than can be won:
God, You gave Your only Son,
There's none like You.

4. So we'll bow to the cross
Where the tears of heaven fall.
You have heard the sinner's call:
There's none like You.

Come near to God and He will come near to you.

JAMES 4:8

1489. Opening our hearts to You

(Highest praise)

Ps 86:12, 15

James Gregory

With energy
Verse
A D E F♯m7 D E F♯m7 D Bm7 E F♯m7 E/G♯
1. O-pen-ing our hearts to You,
fo-cus-ing our eyes on You,
lift-ing up our hands to You,
sing-ing out this song for You.
Prai-ses that will fill the skies,
rai-sing You o-ver our lives,
lift-ing up the Sa-viour high.

Chorus
A
E/G♯
F♯m7
We give You the high - est praise,
B7
D
Last time to Coda
E
1.
A
we give You the high - est praise.
D
E
2.3.
A
1st time D.C.
Mid section
E
All glo - ry, ho - nour, wor-
D
B/D♯
ship, praise, with hands held high and voi -
E
C♯7/E♯
F♯m
F♯m/E
D
ces raised, we of - fer up our hearts a-gain to You.

Esus4
1.
E
2.
D.S. (chorus)
E
All glo - _
Coda
A

2. You are so amazing, Lord,
A beautiful and mighty God,
Compassionate and merciful,
Glorious and powerful.
King over the universe,
Wonderfully in love with us,
Passionate about the earth.

1490. Open the eyes of my heart

2 Kg 6:17; Is 6:1, 3

Steadily
Paul Baloche
E
O - pen the eyes of my heart, Lord,
Emaj7
A/E
o - pen the eyes of my heart. I want to see You,
E
1.
2.
I want to see You. To see You
B
C♯m
A
high and lift - ed up, shin - ing in the light of Your glo -
B
C♯m
ry. Pour out Your pow'r and love, as we sing

A
B
E
ho-ly, ho - ly, ho - ly.
D.C.
B/D♯
Ho-ly, ho - ly, ho - ly,— ho-ly, ho - ly, ho-
A
3
E
ly,— ho-ly, ho - ly, ho - ly,— I want to see— You.—
(Fine)

1491. Open up the gates of heaven

Hos 6:3; Mal 3:10; Gal 5:24

Paul Oakley

Slowly
Asus2
Csus2
(x3)
O-pen up the gates of hea-ven.
Asus2
Csus2
O-pen up the gates of hea-ven, and
Em D Csus2 Em D
let Your ri - ver flow, and let new mer - cies fall
C Em D Csus2
like rain; oh, let me know Your pre-sence.
Dsus2 Csus2 Dsus2
You are all I need; let all earth - ly pas - sion

Csus2
D.C.
Em
D
fade a-way.
(cause) All I want is to know
Am9
Em
D
You more.
All I want is to meet
Am9
Em
D
with You in this place.
All I want is to be
Am9
Dsus2
Csus2
with You, to feel Your em-brace.
Last time
Em7
Fine

1492.
Open up the skies
(Kindness)
Ps 63:3; Hos 6:2-3; Rom 2:4
Chris Tomlin,
Louie Giglio & Jesse Reeves
Capo 1 (G)
Prayerfully
A♭ (G) E♭/G (D/F♯) Fm7 (Em7) E♭sus4 (Dsus4)
1.2. O - pen up the skies of mer - cy,
3. We can feel Your mer - cy fall - ing;
A♭ (G) E♭/G (D/F♯) Fm7 (Em7)
rain down the cleans - ing flood;
You are turn - ing our hearts back a - gain.
A♭ (G) E♭/G (D/F♯) Fm7 (Em7) E♭sus4 (Dsus4)
heal - ing wa - ters rise a - round us;
Hear our prais - es rise to heav - en;
D♭2 (C2)
hear our cries, Lord,
draw us near, Lord,
1. E♭sus4 (Dsus4)
let 'em rise.

2.3.
E♭sus4
(Dsus4)
let 'em rise. And it's Your
meet us here.
D♭
(C)
A♭
(G)
kind-ness, Lord, that
B♭m7
(Am7)
leads us to re-pen-tance; Your
D♭
(C)
A♭
(G)
fa-vour, Lord, is our de-sire.
B♭m7
(Am7)
It's Your
D♭
(C)
A♭
(G)
beau-ty, Lord, that
B♭m7
(Am7)
makes us stand in si-lence, and Your love,
D♭
(C)
Your
love is bet-ter than life.
1.
A♭
(G)
D.C.
2.
A♭
(G)

1493. O sacred King

Jn 15:15; Eph 3:9, 12; Heb 12:6

Matt Redman

With awe
G
Verse
C
G
O sa-cred King,
O sa-cred Friend,
O ho-ly
O ho-ly
C
Am7
Am/G
D/F♯
King,
Friend,
how can I ho-nour You right-ly,
I don't take what You give light-ly,
Am
Am/G
1.
D/F♯
ho-nour that's right for Your name?
friend-ship in-stead of dis-
2.
D/F♯
D
Chorus
G
grace.
For it's the mys-t'ry of the u-ni-verse,
Am
G/B
You're the God of ho-li-ness, yet You wel-come souls like

Cmaj7 C/D G
me. And with the bles - sing of Your Fa - ther's heart, You
Am G/B
dis - ci - pline the ones You love, there's kind - ness in your ma - jes - ty.
Cmaj7 Am Am/G D/F♯
Je - sus, those who re - cog - nise Your pow'r, know
Am Am/G D/F♯ D G
just how won - der - ful You are, that You draw near.

1494. O taste and see

(Taste and see)

Ps 34:8; Is 55:9; Jer 29:11; Mt 19:26; Phil 4:13

Dave Bilbrough

With a calypso feel
Chorus
(Fine)
G C D7 G C
O taste and see that the Lord is good.
D7 G
Verse
Em
He is a migh-ty God,
C Am D
His ways are high-er than ours;
G Em C
there's no-thing im-pos-si-ble for Him.
D C D G
The fu-ture is in His hands.

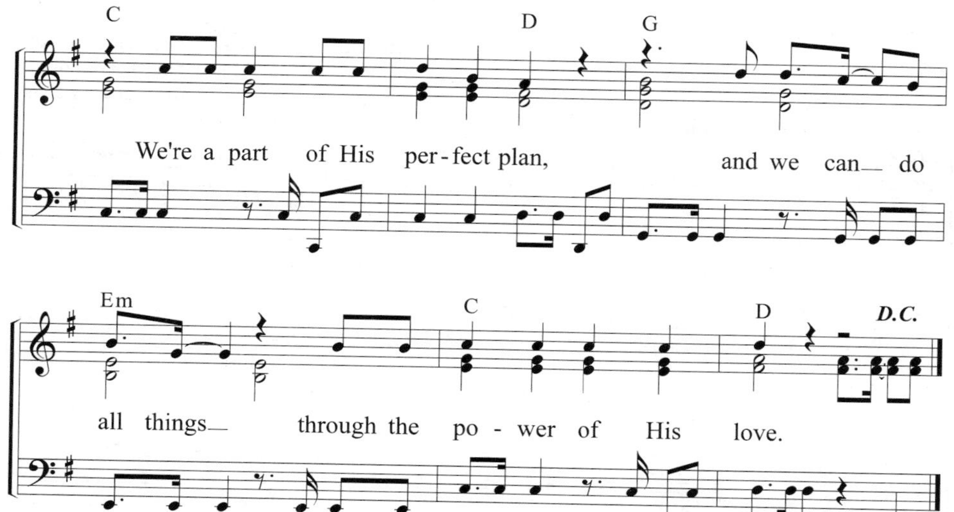
C
D
G
We're a part of His per-fect plan, and we can do
Em
C
D
D.C.
all things through the po - wer of His love.

1495. O, the love of God is boundless

Acts 5:30-31; Rom 3:25; Eph 3:18; Heb 4:9-10; 1 Jn 1:5

Words D.R. Edwards
Revised and adapted by Graham Kendrick
Music: Graham Kendrick
arr. Richard Lewis

Flowing

D Em7 A Bm D/F♯ G
1. O, the love of God is bound - less, per - fect, cause - less,—

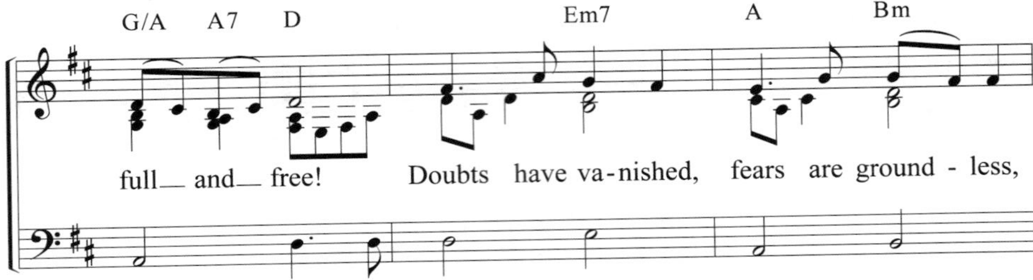

G/A A7 D Em7 A Bm
full— and— free! Doubts have va-nished, fears are ground - less,

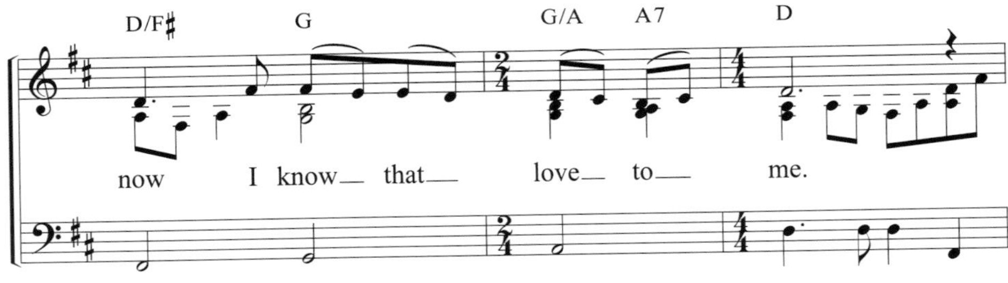

D/F♯ G G/A A7 D
now I know— that— love— to— me.

G A G/B A7/C♯ D D/F♯ Em7
Love, the source— of all my bless - ing, love that set— it -

G/A A D2 D G A G/B A7/C♯ D
self on me. Love, that gave the sin - less Vic - tim,
D/F♯ Em7 G/A A7 D
love, told out at Cal - va - ry.

2. O, the cross of Christ is wondrous!
There I learn God's heart to me;
'Midst the silent, deepening darkness
'God is light' I also see.
Holy claims of justice finding
Full expression in that scene;
Light and love alike are telling
What his woe and suffering means.

3. O, the sight of heaven is glorious!
Man in righteousness is there.
Once the victim, now victorious,
Jesus lives in glory fair!
Him, who met the claims of glory
And the need of ruined man
On the cross, O wondrous story!
God has set at His right hand.

4. O, what rest of soul in seeing
Jesus on his Father's throne!
Yes, what peace for ever-flowing
From God's rest in his own Son!
Gazing upward into heaven,
Reading glory in His face,
Knowing that 'tis He, once given
On the cross to take my place.

Holy, holy, holy is the Lord God Almighty; the whole earth is full of His glory.

ISAIAH 6:3

1496. Our God is strong and mighty

(Breaking out)

Rev 5:5; 7:9

Gary Sadler
& Stuart Townend

Capo 3 (D)

With energy

Intro
F7(D)
Bb/Eb(G)
Cm(Am)
Verse
1. Our God is strong and migh - ty, He's lift-ing up a shout.
It's rol-ling down like thun - der: can you
feel it shake the ground?
(G) (Dm)
Bb/Eb Fm7
Bb7(G)
And ev-'ry strong - hold trem-
bles as we hear the Li - on roar! He's break-ing out.
(The
Bb(G)
C(A)

Chorus
F7(D) B♭/E♭(G) Cm(Am) B♭/E♭(G) F7(D) B♭/E♭(G)
The Lord our God is
Lord our God is break-ing out.)
Cm(Am) B♭/E♭(G) F7(D) B♭/E♭(G) Cm(Am) B♭/E♭(G)
break-ing out.
(The Lord our God)
He's break-ing out!
Last time to Coda
F7(D) B♭/E♭(G) C7(♭9)(A) Dm(Bm)
O God of
B♭(G) F(D) C/E(A)
mer - cy, God of love, come show us the glo - ry of Your name.
Dm(Bm) B♭(G)
We're touched by the pas - sion of Your heart,

F(D)
C/E(A)
B♭(G)
and no-thing will e - ver be the same, nothing will e-
C(A)
B♭/D(G)
C/E(A)
ver be the same, don't let me e - ver be the same.
E♭2(C)
B♭2/D(G)
D.C.
Coda
F7(D)

2. He's rising in this nation,
He's coming into view;
Go tell it in the city
What Jesus' power can do.
We're losing our religion -
He's even greater than we thought!

3. Come do a work within me,
Let me see You as You are;
And make the cause of heaven
The obsession of my heart,
Till every tribe and nation
Bows in worship to the King.

1497. Our Master, our Saviour

Is 9:6; Rev 22:13

Gently

Viola Grafstrom

Verse
A F♯m D A
Our Ma - ster, our Sa - viour, You are Lord, our King.
E A F♯m D A
Our Ma - ster, our Sa - viour, we give our praise
E D E A A/C♯ D E
to our King, to our King.
1. A D E
Our Ma -
2. A (Fine)
Chorus E/G♯
You're the
F♯m D F♯m
e - ver - last - ing Fa - ther, the be - gin - ning and the end,

D
F♯m
D
— there is no— one— that can take Your place,— there is

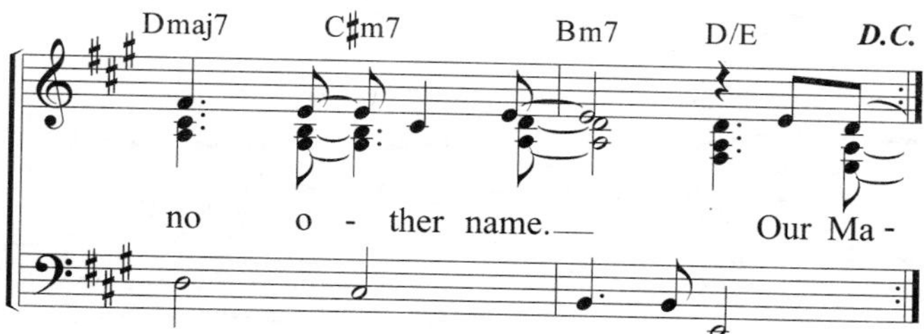
Dmaj7
C♯m7
Bm7
D/E
D.C.
no o - ther name.— Our Ma -

1498.

Over all the earth
(Lord, reign in me)

2 Cor 10:5; Col 3:15; Rev 11:15

Brenton Brown

Steadily
Verse
C G F G
1. Ov-er all the earth, You reign on high,
C G F G
ev-ery moun-tain stream, ev-ery sun-set sky.
Am7 G F G
But my one re-quest, Lord, my only aim
Dm7 F G F/G C
is that You'd reign in me a-gain.
Chorus
G C2/E F
Lord, reign in me,
G C G C2/E F G Am
reign in Your pow'r; ov-er all my dreams, in my dark-est hour.

G F G Dm7
Last time to Coda
You are the Lord of all I am, so won't You
F G F/G C
1. G F G Am7 G F
To verse 2
reign in me a-gain.
2. D.S. (to Chorus)
C G C2/E F
Lord, reign in me,
Coda F G Dm7
reign in me a-gain, won't You
F G F/G Dm7
F G C
Fine
reign in me a-gain, won't You reign in me a-gain.

2. Over every thought,
Over every word,
May my life reflect the beauty of my Lord;
'Cause you mean more to me
Than any earthly thing,
So won't You reign in me again.

1499.

Over, over
(The joy of the Lord)

Ps 30:5; Lk 6:38; Jn 15:11; Rom 15:13

Noel Robinson

Funky
C
G Am
C
O - ver, o - ver, the joy of the Lord is run-ning
G C
G Am
o - ver. O - ver, o - ver, the
C
G C
(Fine)
E♭
B♭
joy of the Lord is run-ning o - ver. Let me tell you of the su-per-
F
C F/C C
na - tural joy that you can find in Him, the man called

F/C
C
E♭
B♭
Je - sus. He'll take a - way the sor - row of this
F
F/G
life that brings so much sad - ness, give you o - ver - flow - ing joy that
Unis
Fmaj7
no man can e - ver, e - ver touch, yeah. Weep - ing may en - dure.;
Em7
1.
Dm9
Bm7(♭5)
E7(♯9) E7(♭9)
joy comes in the morn - ing.
2.
Dm9
D.C. al fine
F/G
joy comes!

1500. Peace, perfect peace

Jn 14:27; 15:11

Kevin Mayhew

Flowing

C Dm/C G/C C
1. Peace, per-fect peace, is the gift of Christ our Lord.
Am Dm7 G7sus4 G7 C C/E
Peace, per-fect peace, is the gift of Christ our Lord.
Fmaj7 Dm7 G C G/B
Thus, says the Lord, will the world know my friends.
A7sus4 A7 Dm Dm7 G7sus4 G7 C
Peace, per-fect peace, is the gift of Christ our Lord.

2. Love, perfect love, is the gift of Christ our Lord.
Love, perfect love, is the gift of Christ our Lord.
Thus, says the Lord, will the world know my friends.
Love, perfect love, is the gift of Christ our Lord.

3. Faith, perfect faith, is the gift of Christ our Lord.
Faith, perfect faith, is the gift of Christ our Lord
Thus, says the Lord, will the world know my friends.
Faith, perfect faith, is the gift of Christ our Lord

4. Hope, perfect hope, is the gift of Christ our Lord.
Hope, perfect hope, is the gift of Christ our Lord.
Thus, says the Lord, will the world know my friends.
Hope, perfect hope, is the gift of Christ our Lord.

5. Joy, perfect joy, is the gift of Christ our Lord.
Joy, perfect joy, is the gift of Christ our Lord.
Thus, says the Lord, will the world know my friends.
Joy, perfect joy, is the gift of Christ our Lord.

1501. Praise Him, you heavens

(Great in power)

Ps 25:6; 47:2; 138:5; 148:1-4; Dan 4:37; Nah 1:3; Eph 2:4

Russell Fragar

Steadily
Verse
D
Praise Him, you hea - vens and all that's a - bove.
Praise Him, the sun, moon and bright shin - ing stars.
Praise Him, you an - gels and hea - ven - ly hosts.
Praise Him, you hea - vens and wa - ters and skies.
G
Let the whole earth praise Him.
G/D D
Chorus
D A/D
Great in pow - er,
D
Bm A/B Bm
great in glo - ry,
G
great in mer - cy,
Bm Bm/A A
King of hea - ven.
D A/D
Great in

D Bm A/B Bm G
bat - tle, great in won - der, great in
Bm 1. D/A A D
Zi - on, King o-ver all. the earth.
D.C. 2. D/A A D.S.
all the earth.
3. D/A A D
all. the earth.
Fine

1502. Praises

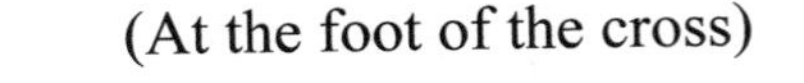

(At the foot of the cross)

Ps 13:6; Jn 5:24; 15:13; 1 Cor 15:3

David Gate

With strength

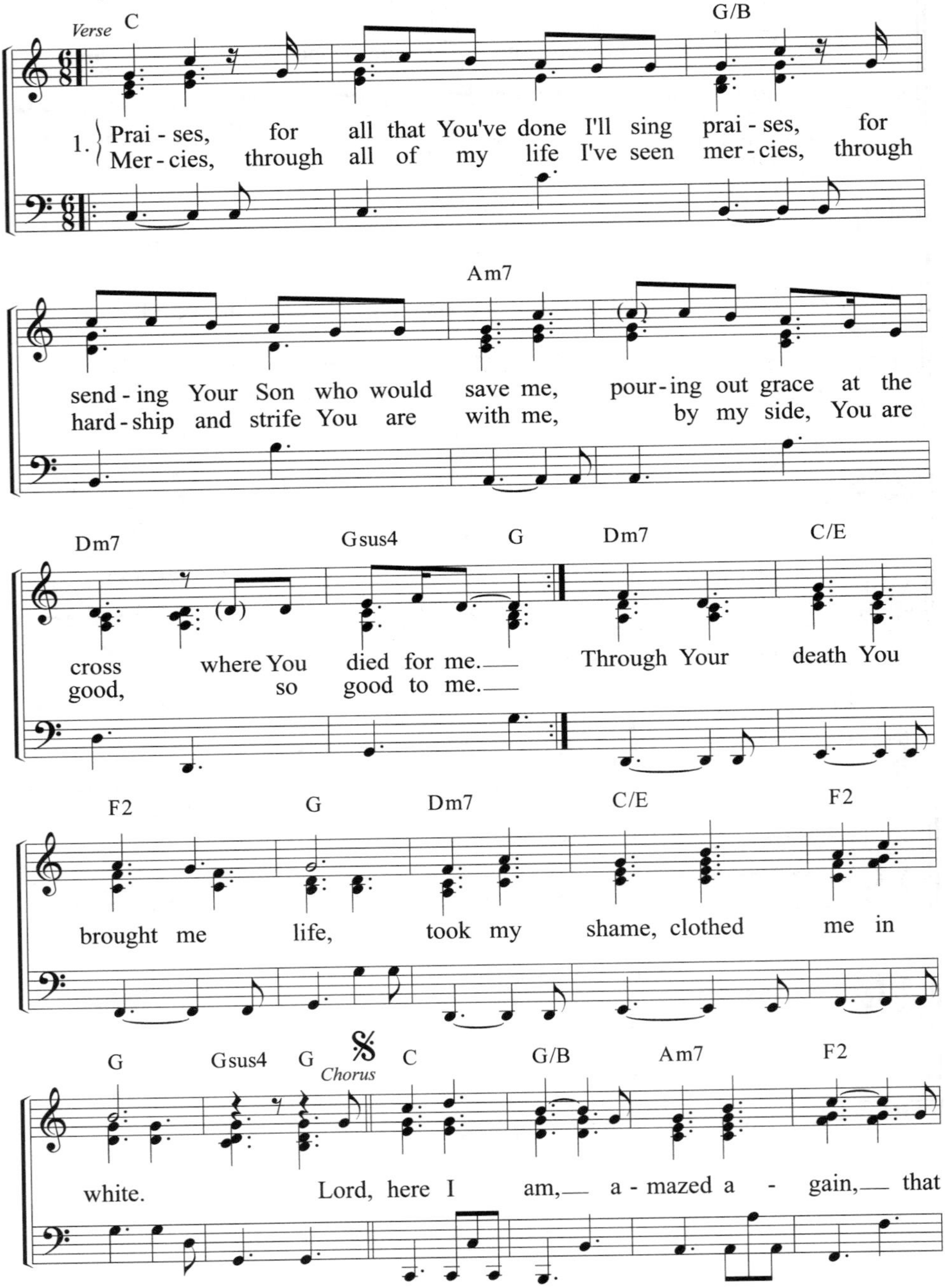

Verse
C
G/B
1. Prai - ses, for all that You've done I'll sing prai - ses, for
Mer - cies, through all of my life I've seen mer - cies, through
Am7
send - ing Your Son who would save me, pour - ing out grace at the
hard - ship and strife You are with me, by my side, You are
Dm7
Gsus4
G
Dm7
C/E
cross where You died for me.
good, so good to me.
Through Your death You
F2
G
Dm7
C/E
F2
brought me life, took my shame, clothed me in
G
Gsus4
G
Chorus
C
G/B
Am7
F2
white. Lord, here I am, a - mazed a - gain, that

C G/B Am7 F2 C G/B
You would die to save a friend. You clear my sin and
Am7 F Dm7 C/E F2
pay the cost, so on my knees I'll stay,
C G/B Am7
1. F
2. F
D.S.
at the foot of the cross.
Lord,
3. F C

2. Worship, day after day I will worship,
For glory and grace, and for goodness,
With all of my life I will be Your living praise.
And Jesus, I'll always look unto Jesus,
For guidance and strength and my focus,
Trying to live how You want Your child to be.

1503. Praise to Christ, the Lord incarnate

Is 53:3-5; Jn 1:14; 2 Cor 1:22; Gal 4:6; Eph 1:7, 13; Col 1:20; Heb 4:15; 7:25; 13:8

Steadily

Words: Martin E. Leckebusch
Music & words adapt. Graham Kendrick

Verse
F♯m7
B
F♯m7
E/G♯
1. Praise to Christ, the Lord in - car - nate, gift of God by hu - man
A
F♯m7
birth: He it is who came a - mong us, shared our
A2
E/G♯
A
life and showed our worth; ours the tur - moil He en -
E/G♯
A
E/G♯
Bsus4
B
E/G♯
coun - tered, ours the fight He made his own; now with -
F♯m(addB)
F♯m7
A2
C♯m7
in our hearts His Spi - rit makes His way of free - dom known.

C♯sus9
A
Chorus
B
C♯m
B
Praise to Christ our Sa - viour and our King.
A
B
F♯m7
A
1.,2.
Bsus4
Praise to Christ our King.
B
E/A
E/G♯
3.
Bsus4
B
E/G♯
E/B
D.S.
4.
Asus2
2. Praise to King.
King.
E/A
E

2. Praise to Christ, the Man of Sorrows,
Tasting death for our release:
His the cup of bitter anguish,
Ours the pardon, ours the peace;
His the blood that seals forgiveness,
Ours the weight of guilt He bore -
So by death and resurrection
Christ has opened heaven's door.

3. Praise to Christ, the Priest eternal:
Still for us he intercedes;
Still He sees our pains and problems -
How He understands our needs!
Yesterday, today, forever,
Always He remains the same:
Pledged to bring us to the Father,
Strong in grace, and free from blame.

1504. Prayer is like a telephone

(Prayer phone)

Eph 6:18; 1 Thess 5:17

Paul Crouch
& David Mudie

Brightly
Prayer is like a te-le-phone for us to talk to Je-sus.
Prayer is like a te-le-phone for us to talk to God. Prayer is like a
te-le-phone for us to talk to Je-sus. Pick it up and use it e-v'ry day.
(Fine)
We can shout out loud, we can whi-sper soft-ly,
we can make no noise at all. But He'll al-ways hear our call.

SoF3

1505. Prepare the way

Ex 15:11; Is 40:3; Mt 3:3; 28:18-19

Rhythmically

Dave Bilbrough

Em D/E Em D/E
Pre-pare the way of the Lord, pre-pare the
Em D/E Em D/E Em D/E
way of the Lord. Pre-pare the way of the
2° to Coda
Em D/E Em D/E Em
(Fine)
Lord, pre-pare the way of the Lord. Ma-
Am Em7
jes-tic in ho-li-ness, awe-some in glo-ry,
D/E D Em7
do-ing won-ders, this is our God.

D/E
Am
3
We will not be si - lenced from
Em7
3
D/E
D
C
speak - ing His word. We cry to the na - tions:
D.S. al Coda
Pre - pare the
Coda
Em E/D
Am
Lord All au - tho - ri - ty is in - ves - ted in the
Em Bm7 Em
D
name of Je - sus, and at the sound - ing of that name,

C
at the sounding of that name
He will a-
Em7 D/E
rise.
Em7 D/E
Em7 D/E
Em7 D/E
D.S. al fine
Pre-pare the

Speak to one another with psalms, hymns and spiritual songs. Sing and make music in your heart to the Lord.

EPHESIANS 5:19

1506. Rejoice in the Lord always

Phil 4:4

Capo 3 (C)

Evelyn Tarner

2 part round

Brightly

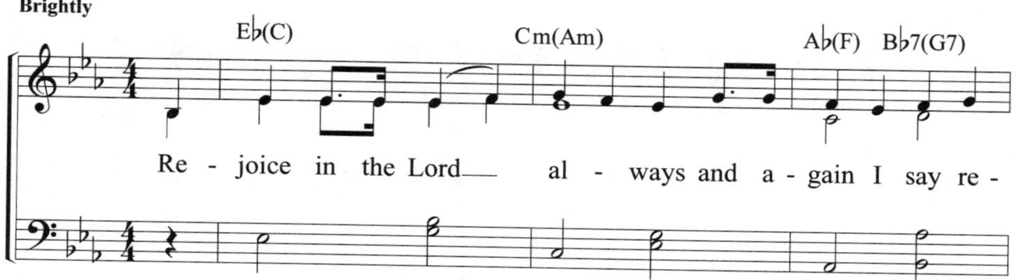

E♭(C)
Cm(Am)
A♭(F) B♭7(G7)
Re - joice in the Lord___ al - ways and a - gain I say re -

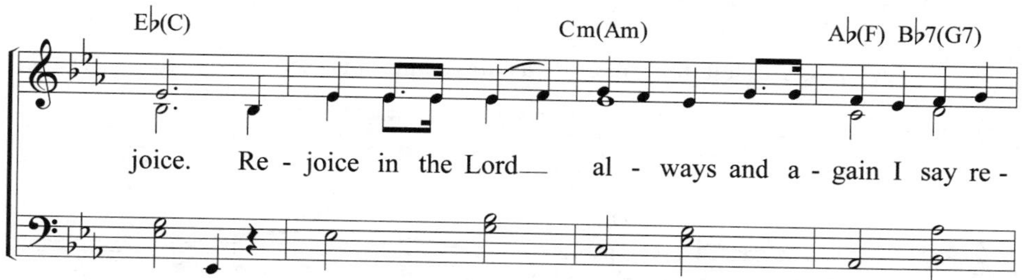

E♭(C)
Cm(Am)
A♭(F) B♭7(G7)
joice. Re - joice in the Lord___ al - ways and a - gain I say re -

E♭(C)
Cm(Am)
A♭(F) B♭7(G7)
E♭(C)
joice. Re - joice,___ re - joice,___ and a - gain I say re - joice. Re-

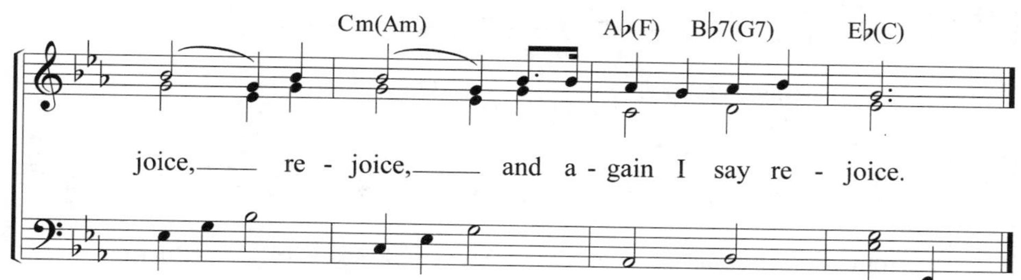

Cm(Am)
A♭(F) B♭7(G7)
E♭(C)
joice,___ re - joice,___ and a - gain I say re - joice.

1507.

Rock of Ages
(My Rock)

Ps 18:2; Zech 13:1;
Jn 19:34; Acts 4:12; 1 Cor 10:4;
Eph 2:8-9 1 Jn 1:7; Rev 5:6; 7:17

Graham Kendrick

Not too fast
D G6/A D G6/A D G6/A D
1. Rock of
Verse
D G6/D D G6 A D
A - ges, cleft for me, let me hide my-self in Thee. Let the
A D Bm7
wa - ter and the blood from Your wound-ed side which
Asus4 A D A Bm
flowed, be of sin the dou-ble cure, cleanse me
Last time to Coda
G F♯m7 Bm7 Asus4/E A G6/A
Chorus
D G6/D D
from its guilt and pow'r. My Rock (my Rock) my

Csus2 G D G/D D G6/D D G
Je - sus, my Rock. My Rock, (my Rock) my Je - sus, my
Csus2 G
Rock. 2. Not the
Coda B7sus4 B7 A/B
Thee. My
E A/E E Dsus2 A E A/E
Rock, (my Rock) my Je - sus, my Rock. My
E A/E E Dsus2 A 1. E A/E To end E
Rock, (my Rock) my Je - sus, my Rock. My Rock.

2. Not the labours of my hands
Can fulfil Your law's demands.
Could my zeal no respite know,
Could my tears for ever flow,
All for sin could not atone.
You must save and You alone.

3. Nothing in my hand I bring,
Simply to Your cross I cling.
Naked, come to You for dress,
Helpless, look to You for grace.
Foul, I to the fountain fly:
Wash me, Saviour, or I die.

4. While I draw this fleeting breath,
When my eyelids close in death,
When I soar to worlds unknown,
See You on Your judgement throne,
Rock of Ages, cleft for me,
Let me hide myself in Thee.

A.M. Toplady (1740-1778)
Revised and adpt. Graham Kendrick

1508. Sacred

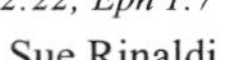
Dan 2:22; Eph 1:7

Sue Rinaldi
Caroline Bonnett & Steve Bassett

Gently

C C F
1. Sa - cred, ho - ly, pure,
Sa - cred ho - ly songs

C G C F
Lord of space and time, dwells — in per - fect light,
rise on wings of praise; all — cre - a - tion rings with

C Gsus4 1. C 2. C C
ra - di - ance sub - lime. — — And oh, — my
e - choes of Your grace. —

F (2°Am7) C F G 1. C 2. C
grate - ful heart re - joic - es at Your name. And name.

2. Sacred, risen Son,
Peerless Lamb of God;
Mercy, grace and peace
Rolling like a flood.
Promise forged in pain,
Forgiveness bought by blood;
Sealed with sacred words
From the mouth of God.

Salvation, spring up
(Salvation)

Josh 9:9; Is 64:1; Hab 3:2; Lk 15:20; Rom 8:22, 26

With excitement

Charlie Hall

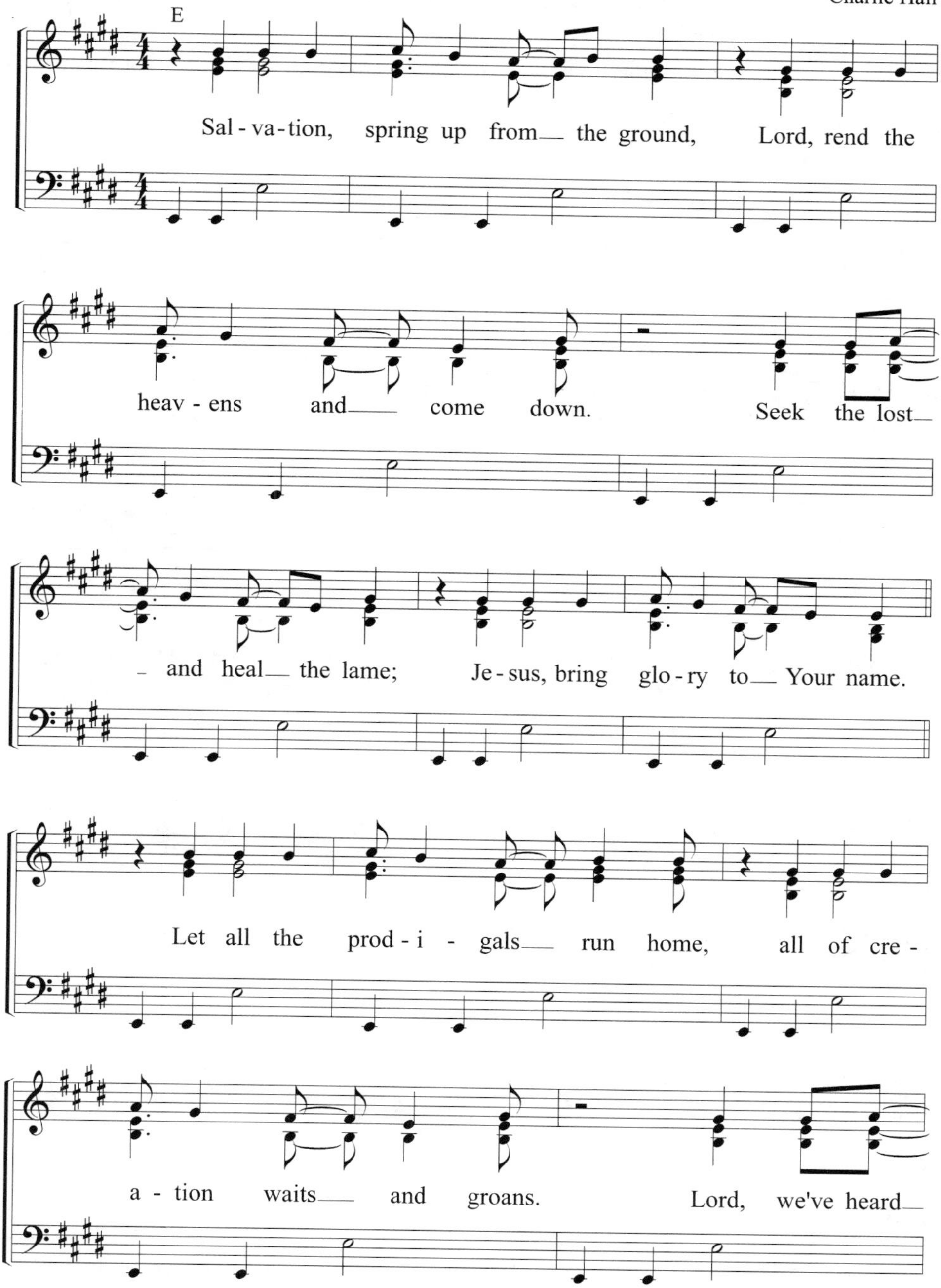

E

Sal - va - tion, spring up from the ground, Lord, rend the heav - ens and come down. Seek the lost and heal the lame; Je - sus, bring glo - ry to Your name.

Let all the prod - i - gals run home, all of cre - a - tion waits and groans. Lord, we've heard

(Fine)
of Your great fame; Fa-ther, cause all to shout Your name.
N.C.
B
C♯m
A
Stir up our hearts, O God;
B
C♯m
A
o - pen our spir - its to awe who You are.

B
C♯m
A2/C♯
E/B
Put a cry in us so deep in - side
A
E/G♯
Bsus4/F♯
E
A2
E/G♯
that we can - not find the words we need,
E
Cmaj7
E/G♯
A2
we just weep and cry out to You.
E/B
Cmaj7/E
Em9/F♯
Em/G
E/G♯
A2
E/B
1.
C2
2.
C2
D.C. al fine

1510. Search my soul

Ps 13:1; 38:22; 139:23; Mt 6:10; 1 Cor 3:18; Rev 1:14; 22:20

Tim Sherrington

Quietly, building to the chorus

Verse

D Dsus2 Dsus4 D Bm

1. Search my soul, and pierce my heart

D Dsus2 Dsus4 D

with a fire that burns from Your eyes.

Bm

(Last time fine)

G

And drive me on

D G D A/C♯

to the reason for living, that is just for You,

Bm
G
A
that is just for You.

D
Dsus2
Dsus4
D
2. How long must I wait for Your com - ing?
3. Come and break the chains that hold me back, Lord,
Bm
D
Dsus2
Come quick - ly, Lord,
from danc - ing in Your light
Dsus4
D
'cause You're the on - ly an - swer.
and being a fool for You.
Bm
G
D
And drive me on to the rea - son for liv - ing,
And I'm run - ning back to the rea - son for liv - ing,
G
D
A/C♯
that is just for You,
Bm

G
A
Chorus
that is just for You.
Let Your king -
D
D/C♯
Bm
- dom come,
let Your will
be done,
G
D
D/C♯
let Your rain
pour out
on my life.
Bm
G
D
Let Your king
- dom come,
D/C♯
Bm
G
let Your will
be done,
let Your rain
D
D/C♯
Bm
G
1st time D.S.
2nd time D.C. al fine
drench my life and do Your will.

1511. See how the Father

(To Jesus be glory)

Capo 3 (A)

Lk 3:22; Jn 1:29, 32; Rev 5:11-12; 22:2

Brightly, with strength

Robert Critchley

Verse
C(A) Bb(G) F(D) C(A)
1. See how the Fa - ther o - pens the hea - vens to ho - nour His Son.
F/A(D) Bb(G) C(A) Bb(G) F(D)
See how the Spi - rit de - scends like a dove
C(A) F/A(D) Bb(G) Eb(C)
up - on His be - lov - èd One. This is the Lamb
Ab/Eb(F) Eb(C) Ab(F) Bb(G)
of God who takes a - way the sins of the world.
C(A) Bb(G) F(D)
Grace has ap - peared to heal the na -

C(A)
Abmaj7(F)
Bb(G)
tions, Christ has been giv - en to set us free,
C(A)
Bb(G)
F(D)
C(A)
to Him be the glo - ry for-ev - er more.
F/A(D)
Bb(G)
Chorus
F(D)
C(A)
Bb(G)
F(D)
To Je - sus be glo - ry for-ev-er
C(A)
F/A(D)
Bb(G)
F(D)
C(A)
Bb(G)
F(D)
more. To Je - sus be glo - ry for-ev-er
C(A)
(Fine)
D.C.
Ab(F)
more. Can you hear the Fa-ther say - ing,

B♭(G)
C(A)
B♭(G)
F(D)
'I am so pleased just look at My Son,

C(A)
B♭(G)
F(D)
C(A)
B♭(G)
F(D)
C(A)
just look at My Son!'

D.S. al fine
F/A(D)
To

2. See how the Father opens the heavens,
Revealing His Son.
Angels and elders and saints without number
Worship the Risen One.
And with a shout they proclaim,
'Worthy is the Lamb that was slain;
To Him be all power and riches and wisdom,
To Him be all honour, dominion and praise,
To him be the glory forever more.'

1512. Send Your Spirit

Jn 8:12; 14:26; Acts 19:17

Dave Bilbrough

Capo 3 (Em)

Steadily
Gm7(Em) F/A(D/F♯) B♭sus2(G) C7sus4(A)
1. Send Your Spi - rit, send Your
dark - ness, light our
pow - er, move in
Gm7(Em) F/A(D/F♯) B♭sus2(G) C7sus4(A) Gm7(Em) F/A(D/F♯)
Spi - rit, send Your Spi - rit, O Lord,
dark - ness, light our dark - ness, O Lord,
pow - er, move in pow - er, O Lord,
B♭sus2(G)
Last time to Coda
C7sus4(A)
1. 2.
C(A)
we pray. 2. Light our
we pray. 3. Move in
we pray.
3.
C(A)
Cm7(Am)
For the ho-nour of Your name, for the ho-nour of Your name,

Dm7(Bm)
Ebmaj7(C)
for the ho-nour of Your name.
Cm7(Am)
For the ho-nour of Your name,
for the ho-nour of Your name,
Dm7(Bm)
C(A)
for the ho-nour of Your name,
Eb(C)
D.C.
O Lord.
1. Send Your
Coda
C(A)
Gm(Em)

1513. Shine Your light on us

(Shine)

Ps 18:28; 139:12; Mt 5:16; Jn 1:5; 8:12; 2 Cor 3:18; 4:6

Moderately

Marc James
& Tré Sheppard

Chorus

E Emaj7 A
Shine Your light on us that all may see Your good-
Am E Emaj7
-ness. Shine Your face on us that all

(Last time rit . . . .) (𝄐) *(Fine)*

A Am E E/G♯
may see Your glo - ry.

A Am E

Verse

1. An-swer me when

Emaj7/G♯ A Am7
I call. You are my on - ly pray'r.

E
Emaj7/G♯
A
When dark-ness is all a-round I know You will
Am7
C♯m
Bridge
A
be there. Ma-ny are ask - ing, who can show
E
F♯
C♯m
us some-thing real. Long-ing for hope
A
E
F♯
be - yond the pain of what they feel. So I
A
E
will go down on my knees and say: shine Your light

2. I wanna be close to You,
That my life would tell Your story.
I wanna be one with You,
Changed by the light of Your glory.

1514. Sing, praise and bless the Lord

(Laudate Dominum)

Ps 47:6-8; Rev 5:9; 7:9

Taizé
Music: Jacques Berthier (1923-1994)

Voices
Am E Am G
Sing, praise and bless the Lord. Sing, praise and bless the Lord.
Lau - da - te Do - mi - num, lau - da - te Do - mi - num,
Piano
C G 1. Am F Dm6 E 2. Am Dm E Am
Peo - ples! Na - tions! Al - le - lu - ia! Al - le - lu - ia!
om - nes gen - tes, al - le - lu - ia! al - le - lu - ia!
1.
2.

1515. Sing praises, all you peoples

(Laudate omnes gentes)

Capo 1 (D)

Ps 47:6-8; Rev 5:9; 7:9

Taizé
Music: Jacques Berthier (1923-1994)

Voices

Eb(D) | (G) Ab (D) Eb | (A) Bb (Bm) Cm (F♯) G | (Bm) Cm (A) Bb (D) Eb (G) Ab | Bb(A) Eb(D)

Sing prai-ses, all you peo-ples, sing prai-ses to the Lord. Sing

Lau - da - te om-nes gen-tes, lau - da - te Do-mi - num. Lau-

Piano

(G) (D) (A) (Bm) (A) (A)
Ab Eb Bb Cm Ab(G) Bbsus4 Bb Eb(D)
prai - ses, all you peo-ples, sing prai - ses to the Lord. Sing
da - te om-nes gen - tes, lau - da - te Do-mi - num. Lau -

1516. Sing praises to our God

Ps 47:1, 6-8; Rev 5:9; 7:9

David Lyle Morris

Rhythmically

Chorus

G C D
Sing prai - ses to our God, sing prai - ses.

Last time to Coda 𝄌

G C D
Sing prai - ses to the King, sing prai - ses. (For)

4th time to Mid section

Verse

C D G
God is King of all the earth, sing to Him a psalm of praise.

C D G
God reigns o - ver the na - tions, all our wor - ship we will raise.

C D G
He's King of all the earth, bring to Him a joy - ful song.

C D G C D D.C.
He's Lord of all cre - a - tion, seat - ed on His ho - ly throne.
Mid section
G D
Clap your hands, all you na - tions, shout to God with cries of joy, how
G C D G
awe - some is the Lord most high. Clap your hands, all cre-a - tion,
D G C
cry to God who made us all, the great King o - ver all the world.
D D.C. Coda G
sing prai - ses.

1517. Soldiers of our God, arise

(Save the lost!)

Mt 28:19-20; Jn 12:36; 1 Cor 9:25; Rev 12:12

Driving

Music: Trad. alt. Lex Loizides

Verse

A D E
1. Sol-diers of our God a-rise! The day is draw-ing near - er;

A D E
Shake the slum-ber from Your eyes, the light is grow-ing clear - er.

D A D A
Sit no long - er id - ly by while the heed - less mil-lions die. O,

D A/C♯ Bm7 A Bm7 E
lift the blood-stained ban-ner high, — and take the field — for

A
(1st time only)
Chorus
Je - sus.
Save the lost!
Save the lost!

E A E A

Spend your might for them; give Your life for them. Save the lost!

E A E

Save the lost! Don't back down on it; win your crown in it,

D E F♯m D E A

sol - diers of our God, sol - diers of — our God.

D.C.

2. See the brazen hosts of hell
Their art and power employing,
More than human tongue can tell
The blood-bought souls destroying.
See on ruin's hell-bound road
Victims groan beneath their load;
Go forward, O you sons of God,
And dare or die for Jesus.

3. Warriors of the risen King,
Great army of salvation,
Spread His fame, His praises sing
And conquer every nation.
Raise the glorious standard higher,
Work for victory, never tire;
O, forward march with blood and fire,
And win the world for Jesus.

Robert Johnson, alt. Lex Loizides

1518. Sovereign Lord

Song 2:6; Rev 1:16; 17:14; 19:6, 16

Martyn Layzell

Fairly slow

Verse
G
Em7
1. So - v'reign Lord, o - ver all,
C2 G D/F♯ G
You are reign - ing for - e - ver. Wor - ship flows
Em7 C2 G
from our lips, we have come for just one glimpse.
D/F♯ C2 D Em7 D/F♯ C2 D
And we sing hal - le - lu - ia, hal - le -
Em7 D/F♯ C2 D Em7 A7
lu - ia, hal - le - lu - ia.

Chorus
C2
G
Em7
Ma - je - sty, reign in me, Your right
D
C2
G
hand en-fold - ing me. Earth ap - plaud, hea - vens
Em7
D
1.
C2
C2
D.C.
sing at the sight of Christ the King.
2.
C2
D.S.
3.
C2
C/E
D/F♯
G
King. Ma - je - King.

2. Lord of lords, now enthroned,
Who can stand in Your presence?
Fire of love, holy One,
You burn brighter than the sun.

1519. Spirit, move on this land

Mt 5:16; 2 Pet 3:12

(Revival in our land)

Tim Sherrington

With a rock feel
F♯m A E
Spi-rit, move on this land,
F♯m A E
take Your peo - ple in Your hands.
F♯m E
We're wait - ing for the day,
F♯m E
the day You come a-gain.
Bm D C♯m
Your Spi-rit is com-ing to give to the poor;

Bm
D
so Fa-ther, take our lives and
A
E/G♯
F♯m
A
shine.
Re-vi - val in our land,
E
F♯m
won't rest un - til we see re - vi-
A
E
F♯m
val in our land.

The prayer of a righteous man is powerful and effective.

JAMES 5:16

1520. Spirit of the Lord

(Healing love)

Capo 3 (D)

Ezek 37:4-5; Rev 22:20

Ian White

Slowly

F(D) Gm7(Em) F/A(D) F(D)
1. Spi-rit of the Lord, come down a-mong us now; mi-ni-ster new
Gm7(Em) Csus4(A) C(A)
life to bones grown dry. Some-thing in our
(v.2)
F(D) Gm7(Em) F/A(D) F(D)
heart cries out to be made whole: the
Gm7(Em) Csus4(A) (A) C7sus4 (Fine) F(D) Fsus4(D)
touch of heal - ing love. 2. Give us just a

2. Give us just a glimpse of God, of Jesus' heart,
Open ears to hear the voice say, 'come':
Look up, look up, look up and see
The light of healing love.

1521. Standing on holy ground
(Isaiah 12)

Ex 3:5; Ps 28:7; 99:2; 1 Cor 13:12; Heb 10:20

With awe

Paul Oakley & Martin Cooper

A E B
Verse
Stand-ing on ho-
A E B
-ly ground, mer-cy and grace I've found.
C♯m D
I'm here be-fore Your throne now,
A Bsus4
by a new and liv-ing way.
Je-sus I come
A E B
to You, I lift up my eyes to You.

C♯m
D
How You've com - for - ted me,
A
Bsus4
how I long to see Your face.
Chorus
A
E
You are my strength, my song, You are my shield,
to You, beau - ti - ful things
A
E
A
my Re - deem - er. You are my hope, my sal - va -
You have done, great is Your name in Zi -
E
Bsus4
1.
- tion and my God. I'll al -
on, Ho - ly One.

A
E/G♯
Badd4
Asus2
- ways bring my praise to You, O God.
E
D.C.
2.
Bsus4
D.S.
3.
Stand-ing on ho -
So I will sing
I'll al-
A
E/G♯
B
A
E/G♯
ways bring my praise to You, I'll al - ways bring my praise
B
A
E/G♯
to You, I'll al - ways bring my praise
B
Asus2
E
A
E
to You, O God.

1522. Stay with me

Mt 26:38, 41

Tune: STAY WITH ME

Taizé
Music: Jacques Berthier (1923-94)

Dm Gm6/D Dm Gm6/D D C
Voice
Stay with me, re - main here with me, watch and
Piano
F C Dm Gm6/D Asus4 A
pray, watch and pray.

1523.
Surely our God
(Revealer of mysteries)
Capo 3 (D)
Dan 2:21-23, 47; Mt 11:25; Lk 1:52; 1 Cor 1:21; Col 2:2-3; Jas 4:6
Moderately
David Lyle Morris & Liz Morris
Chorus
F(D) Gm/B♭(Em) Dm(Bm) B♭2(G) C(A)
Sure - ly our God is the God of gods, and the Lord of kings, the re - veal - er of mys - te - ries. Sure - ly our God is the God of gods, and the Lord of kings, the re - veal - er of mys - ter - ies.
(Fine)
Verse
1. He chan - ges the times and the sea - sons, He gives rhy - thm to the tides; He

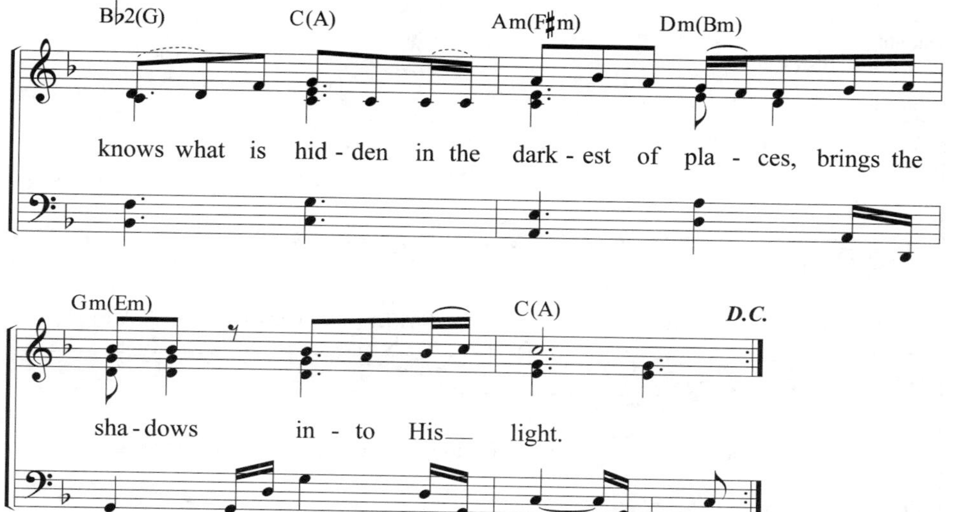
B♭2(G)
C(A)
Am(F♯m)
Dm(Bm)
knows what is hid - den in the dark - est of pla - ces, brings the
Gm(Em)
C(A)
D.C.
sha - dows in - to His light.

2. I'll praise You always, my Father,
   You are Lord of heaven and earth.
   You hide Your secrets from the 'wise' and the learnèd,
   And reveal them to this, Your child.

3. Thank You for sending Your only Son,
   We may know the mystery of God;
   He opens the treasures of wisdom and knowledge
   To the humble, not to the proud.

1524. Take me to Your sacred place

(Sacred place)

Ex 3:5; 1 Cor 13:12; Heb 10:19

Capo 1 (A)

Noel & Tricia Richards

Steadily
B♭2(A)
Verse
B♭(A) F/A(E)
1. Take me to Your sa-
E♭2/G(D) B♭(A) F/A(E) E♭2/G(D) F/A(E)
-cred place, how I long to see Your face.
B♭(A) F/A(E) E♭6/G(D) B♭(A)
I'll be lost in Your em-brace and be loved,
E♭6/G(D) F/A(E) B♭2(A)
Last time to Coda
and be loved by You.
Chorus
E♭2/G(D) F/A(E) E♭2/G(D) B♭(A) E♭2/G(D)
Draw me, draw me to Your sa-cred place.

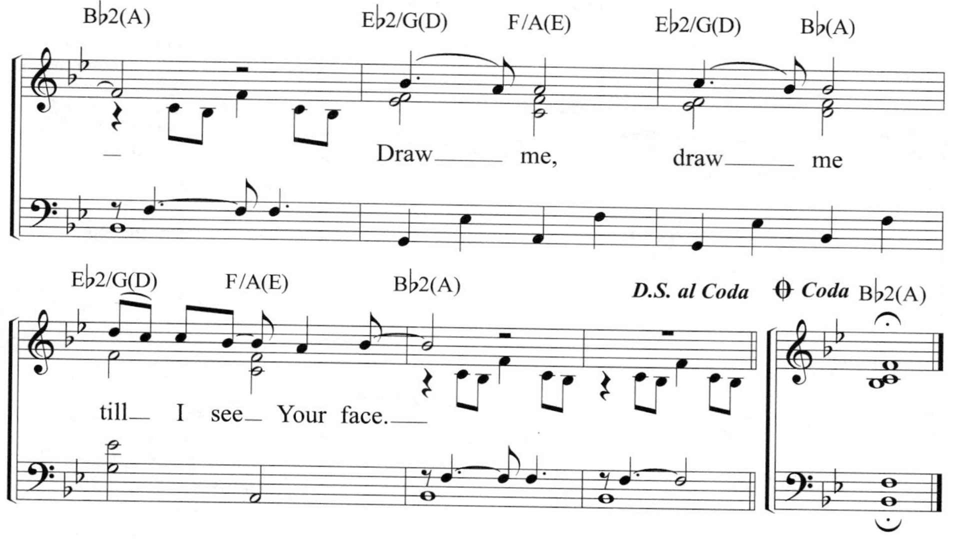

B♭2(A)
E♭2/G(D)
F/A(E)
E♭2/G(D)
B♭(A)
Draw me, draw me
E♭2/G(D)
F/A(E)
B♭2(A)
D.S. al Coda
Coda
B♭2(A)
till I see Your face.

2. Take me where Your glory shines,
Where Your holy fire burns.
Purify this heart of mine,
I surrender my life to You.

1525. **Take us to the river**

Ex 20:18; Ps 46:4; Is 61:1-2; Heb 4:16; 12:18; Jas 2:13; Rev 5:9; 7:2; 10:5; 22:2

Robin Mark

Steadily
Verse
(v.2)
(v.3)
(vv2.&3.)
D D/F♯ G D D/F♯ G A G D F♯m7 G D
1. Take us to the ri - ver, take us there in u-ni-ty to sing a song of Your sal - va - tion to win this ge-ne-ra - tion for our King. A song of Your for-give - ness, for it is with grace that ri-ver flows; take us to the ri - ver in the

A D
1. D.S.
2.3.
ci - ty of our God.
2. Take us to Your
For the
Chorus G A Bm
Spi - rit of the Sov - 'reign Lord is up - on us:
G D/F# Asus4 A
this is the year of the Lord.
1. Asus2 A
2. Asus2 A
D.S.
Last time Asus2 A D
Fine
The
3. Take us to the moun -

2. Take us to Your throne room,
Give us ears to hear the cry of heaven;
For that cry is mercy,
Mercy to the fallen sons of man:
For mercy it has triumphed,
Triumphed over judgement by Your blood;
Take us to the throne room
In the city of our God.

3. Take us to the mountain,
Lift us in the shadow of Your hands;
Is this Your mighty angel,
Who stands astride the ocean and the land?
For in his hand Your mercy
Showers on a dry and barren place;
Take us to the mountain
In the city of our God.

1526.
Teach me of Your ways
(Lord, have Your way)
Ex 33:13; Ps 25:4; Jer 18:6; Mt 5:16; Lk 22:42
Capo 2 (G)
Steadily
David Gate
Bm7(Am) E(D) Bm7(Am) E(D)
Bm7(Am) Verse E(D)
1. Teach me of Your ways,
Bm7(Am) E(D)
to hon - our You with all I have,
Bm7(Am) E(D)
and that I learn to say:
Bm7(Am) E(D) Chorus
'Not my will but Yours, my Lord.' O Je - sus,

A(G)
F♯m(Em)
B7/D♯(A)
be glo-ri-fied in all of my life. It's all a-bout You, the
D(C)
A(G)
wor-ship You're due. So help me to change,
F♯m7(Em)
B/D♯(A)
mould me like clay; Lord, have Your way,
1. D(C)
D.C.
2. D(C)
D.S.
Lord, have Your way with me. Lord, have Your way. O Je-sus,
3. D(C)
A(G)
Lord, have Your way with me.

2. Lord I long to be
A faithful child who honours You.
So Jesus, be in me,
Let Your light shine through me now.

1527. Tell the world

Mt 28:19-20; Lk 19:10; 1 Cor 2:9; Col 1:20; Heb 9:14; 1 Jn 2:2

With an African feel

Dave Bilbrough

Chorus
G D C D G D
Tell the world that Je-sus is ri-sen, let His praise en-
C D G D C D
cir-cle the globe; make it known a-mong all the na-tions that
C D
(Fine)
Je - sus is a - live!
G Verse D C D
1. From the cra-dle to the grave, from a sta-ble to a cross,
G D C D
His life was of-fered up in sa-cri-fice for us.

Em
C
D
He came from hea-ven's throne to seek and save the lost; to
C
D
D.C.
re-con-cile us back to God.
G
D
C
D
2. No eye has seen, no ear has heard what He's pre-pared;
G
D
C
D
His re-sur-rec-tion means His life is ours to share.
Em
C
D
The great-est mi-ra-cle of all has ta-ken place;
C
D
D.C.
Christ is ri-sen, He is Lord!

1528. Thank You for the cross, Lord

(Worthy is the Lamb)

Is 53:5; Phil 2:9; 1 Jn 1:7; Rev 5:12; 19:12

Moderately

Darlene Zschech

Verse
C G/B
Thank You for the cross, Lord; thank You for the
love, Lord; thank You for the
C Dsus4 D G D/E Em7
price You paid. Bear - ing all my sin and shame, in
nail - pierced hands. Washed me in Your cleans - ing flow, now
1. D C Am7 G/B Dsus4 D G G/B
love You came and gave a - ma - zing grace. Thank You for this
2. D C Am7 G/B Dsus4 D/F♯
all I know, Your for - give - ness and em - brace.

Chorus
G
D/F♯
Am7
G/B
Wor - thy is the Lamb, sea - ted on the throne;
C2
D
D/C
G/B
C
crown You now with ma - ny crowns, You
Am7
Am7/G
D
D/F♯
G
reign vic - to - ri - ous. High and lif - ted up,
D/F♯
Am7
G/B
C2
Je - sus, Son of God; the
D
D/C
G/B
C
Dar - ling of hea - ven, cru - ci - fied.

Dsus4
Am7
G/B
C
Wor-thy is the Lamb,
wor-thy is the
1.
Am7
G/B
D
D.C.
2.,3.
Am7
G/B
Lamb.
Thank You for the
Lamb.
Last time to Coda
Dsus4
Am7
G/B
C
Wor-thy is the Lamb,
wor-thy is the
Am7
G/B
1.,3.,4.
Dsus4
2.
D.S.
Dsus4
Lamb.
Wor-thy is the
Coda
Am7
G/B
D
G
Lamb.

1529. Thank You, Lord, for Your love to me

Capo 3 (D)

Intensely

Jn 8:32; Rom 3:24; Heb 10:19; 1 Jn 1:7

Paul Booth

Verse
F2(D) C/E(A) Gm(Em) B♭2(G)
mp
Thank You, Lord, for Your love to me.
F2(D) C/E(A) Gm(Em) B♭2(G)
By Your truth You have set me free.
F2(D) C/E(A) Gm(Em) B♭2(G)
Through the cross I can en - ter in.
F2/A(D) F2(D) Gm(Em) B♭2(G)
What seemed im-pos - si-ble till I let You wash a-way
F2(D) C/E(A) Gm(Em) B♭2(G)
my sin, take a-way all shame by the life-

F2(D) C/E(A) Gm7(Em) B♭(G)
- giv - ing blood of Je - sus, my Re-deem-er.
F(D) C(A)
Chorus
F(D) F/E(D) Gm7(Em)
f
Ho - ly, I stand be-
B♭2(G) F/A(D) C(A) Gm7(Em)
fore You, tru - ly, I am blame - less in Your sight.
B♭(G) F(D) F/E(D) Gm7(Em)
Right - eous, a roy - al robe I
B♭(G) F/A(D) C(A) Gm7(Em)
don't de-serve, yet You choose to clothe me still,

Last time to Coda
D.C.
B♭(G)
F2(D)
C/E(A)
Gm7(Em)
B♭2(G)
pre-cious mer-cy.
F(D)
F/E(D)
Gm(Em)
B♭(G)
Such mer - cy, such grace, such kind - ness to save
I'll love You, I'll serve You, I'll praise You for e - ver,
1.
F/A(D)
F/C(D)
Gm7(Em)
B♭(G)
e - ven a sin - ner like me.
2.
D.S. al Coda
F/A(D)
F/C(D)
Gm(Em)
B♭(G)
Thank You, Lord, for Your love to me.
Coda
F2(D)

1530. Thank You, Lord, You love us

Jn 15:15; Eph 5:19-20; Col 1:12, 14; Rev 17:14; 19:16

Words: Megamix Kids
Music: Paul Oakley

Lively
Verse
G
C
Thank You, Lord, You love us, thank You, Lord, You care.
G
Thank You, Lord, You made us,
D
G
thank You, Lord, You're there. Thank You for for-give-
C
G
ness, Your gift of life to me.
D
Thank You for Your faith - ful - nes, You're al-ways, al - ways, al-

Chorus
ways, al - ways good to me.
So we real-ly want to
G
C
say, 'we love You,' we real-ly want to shout, 'You're the best!'
D
We're gon-na bring our praise to You,
1.
2.
King of kings and my best friend. We want to best friend, oh yeah!
D.C.
Last time
G
F♯ F F♯
G
F♯ F F♯
G

1531. Thank You, thank You for the blood

(Thank You for the blood)

Eph 1:7; 3:12; Heb 10:20

Matt Redman

Rhythmically
C
Em7
Thank You, thank You for the blood that You shed,
Thank You, thank You for the bat - tle You won,
Am
F2
standing in its bles - sing we sing
standing in Your vic - t'ry we sing
C
Em
1.
F
2.
F
these free - dom songs.
we sing
sal - va - tion songs,
C
Em7
F
G
sal - va - tion's song.
You have
C
Em7
F2
3
o - pened a way to the Fa - ther, where be - fore we could ne - ver have

C
Em7
come. Je-sus, count us as Yours now for - e - ver, as we sing
Am
D7
G
1.
F2
D.C.
2.
F2
these free - dom songs. We
C
F
D/F♯
sing of all You've done, we sing of all You've done,
G
E/G♯
Am
Am/G
we sing of all You've done for us, won for us, paid
1. F
2. F
Last time to Coda ⊕
D.C.
Coda ⊕
C
for us. We for us.

1532. The birds don't worry

(You can depend on Him)

Ps 8:3; Mt 6:26-33

Brightly

Stuart Townend

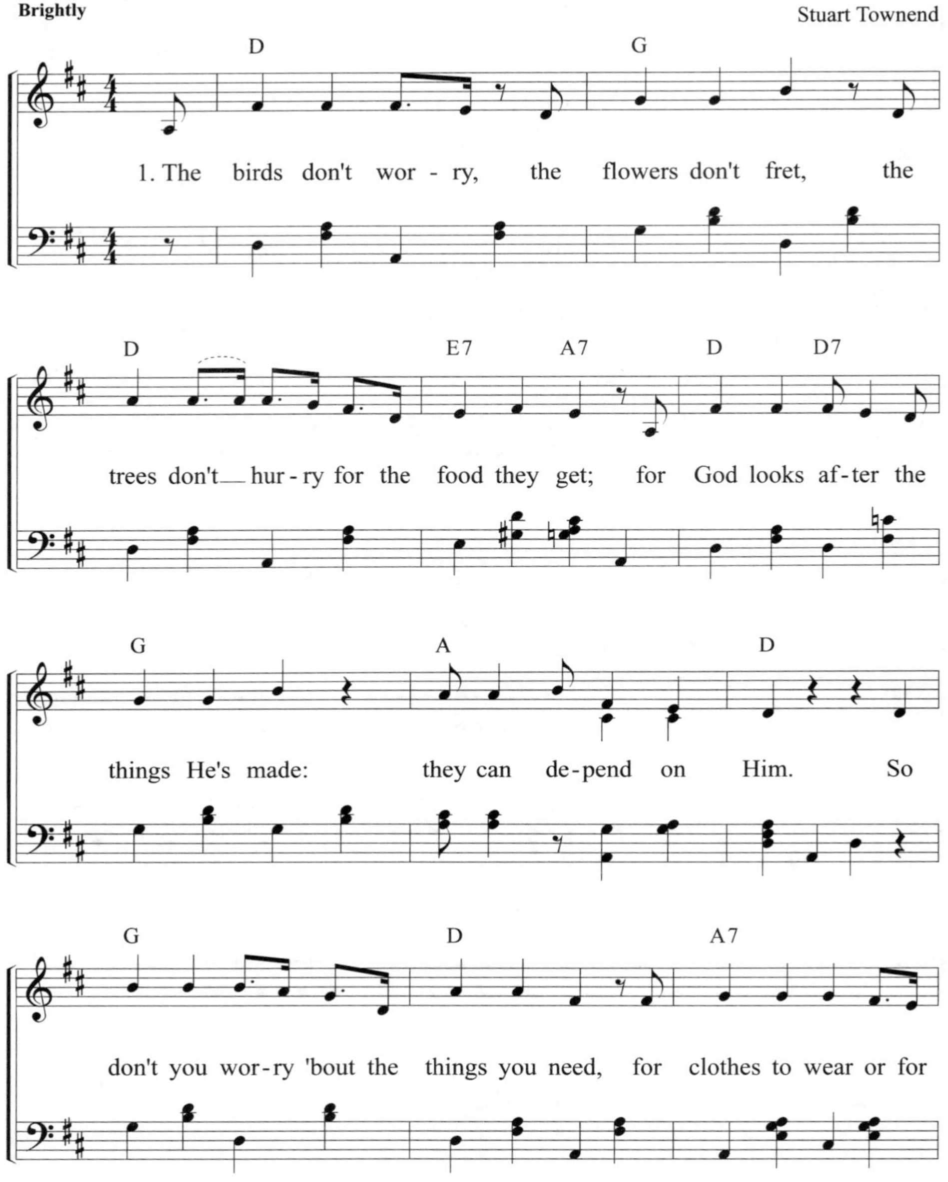

D
G
1. The birds don't wor - ry, the flowers don't fret, the
D
E7
A7
D
D7
trees don't hur - ry for the food they get; for God looks af - ter the
G
A
D
things He's made: they can de - pend on Him. So
G
D
A7
don't you wor - ry 'bout the things you need, for clothes to wear or for

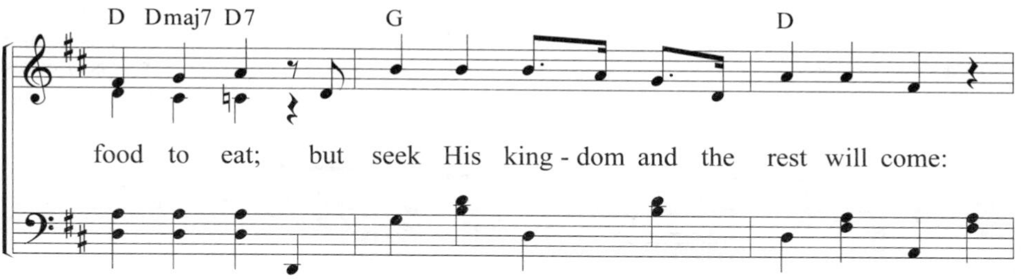
D Dmaj7 D7
G
D
food to eat; but seek His king - dom and the rest will come:

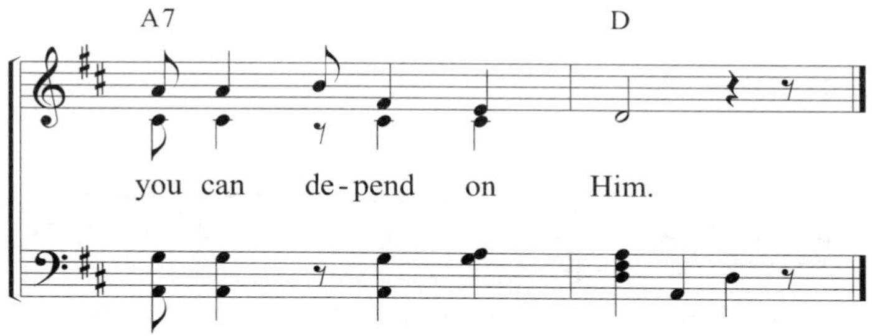
A7
D
you can de - pend on Him.

2. The hill's don't grumble, the stars don't cry,
The sun doesn't tumble from the big, blue sky,
For God has set everything in place:
They can depend on Him.

You can't live longer by worrying more,
You can't get taller than you were before;
So seek His kingdom and the rest will come:
You can depend on Him.

1533.

The cross before me

(Not to us)

2 Chron 7:1; Is 64:1; Hab 3:6; Lk 9:62

Chris Tomlin
& Jesse Reeves

With a strong rock beat

G
Verse
1. The cross before me, the world behind;
2. Our hearts unfold before Your throne,
Em7
no turning back, raise the banner high:
the only place for those who know:
Dsus4
C2
G
Gsus4 G
it's not for me, it's all for You.
it's not for us, it's all for You.
Let the heavens shake and split the sky,
Send Your holy fire on this offering,

Em7
let the peo - ple clap their hands and cry:
let our wor - ship burn for the world to see:
Dsus4
C2
G
Gsus4 G
it's not for us, it's all for You.
it's not for us, it's all for You.
F/C C
F/C C
Not to us, but to Your name be the glo - ry.
G
F/C C
Not to us, but to Your name be the glo -
1.
F/C C
G
G2
Cmaj7 C
F/C C
ry.

2.
F/C
C
G
- ry.
The earth is shak - ing, the
moun - tains shout - ing:
C6
C
it's all for You.
The
Em7
Dsus4
waves are crash - ing, the sun is ra - ging:
it's all for You.
The u - ni - verse
spin - ning and sing - ing:
it's all for You.
Your chil - dren dan - cing, dan -

Dsus4
C
cing, dan - cing: It's all for You, it's all for You,
Gsus4 G
Gsus4 G
C6 Cmaj7
C6 Cmaj7
E7sus4 Em7
my all for You.
Dsus4
C6 C
1.
C6 C
2.
C6 C
G
My all for You,
My all for You.

1534. The greatest thing in all my life

Phil 3:8

Steadily

Mark Pendergrass

D Bm Em
1. The great-est thing___ in all my life is know-ing You;___

Asus4 A7 Em Em7/A A7
_ the great-est thing___ in all my life is

Dsus4 D G/D D G G/A
know-ing You;___ I want to know You

Dmaj7 Em7 A7 D
more; I want to know You more. The

Bm
Em
A7sus4
D
great-est thing in all my life is know - ing You.

2. The greatest thing in all my life is loving You;
The greatest thing in all my life is loving You;
I want to love You more;
I want to love You more.
The greatest thing in all my life is loving You.

3. The greatest thing in all my life is serving You;
The greatest thing in all my life is serving You;
I want to serve You more;
I want to serve You more.
The greatest thing in all my life is serving You.

1535. The narrow pathway

(Faithful)

Is 42:3; Mt 6:10; 7:13; 19:24; Jn 4:35; Phil 1:29; Jas 4:6; Rev 19:9

David Ruis

With breadth
D
The nar - row path - way
G6/D
through the nee-dle's eye.
D
I'm step-ping for-
ward
G6/D
to the place I die.
Last time to Coda
G/D
G/B
For I know that You are faith - ful,
D

G/B
as we walk these fields of white.
D
G/B
To the wait - ing and the hum -
D
G/B
ble Your king - dom comes.
D
G6/D G/D
D.C.
Coda
G/D
D

2. The way of mercy
Takes me to the least.
Down the road of suffering
To the wedding feast.
For I know that You are faithful,
As we walk these fields of white.
To the weary and the hurting
Your kingdom comes.

Be patient, then, brothers, until the Lord's coming.

JAMES 5:7

1536. The people who walk in darkness

Is 9:2-4, 6-7

(He will be called Wonderful)

Dave Lyle Morris
& Jussi Miettinen
Brightly
Verse
G C G C Em C D
1.3. The peo-ple who walk in dark-ness will see a great light, for those who live in the land of the sha-dow of death, the light will shine.
2. You will en-large the na-tion, and in-crease their joy, so they de-light in Your pre-sence as they will re-joice at har-vest time.
1.
G C G C
2.3.
G Em D/F♯
For to us a Child is born, to

SoF3

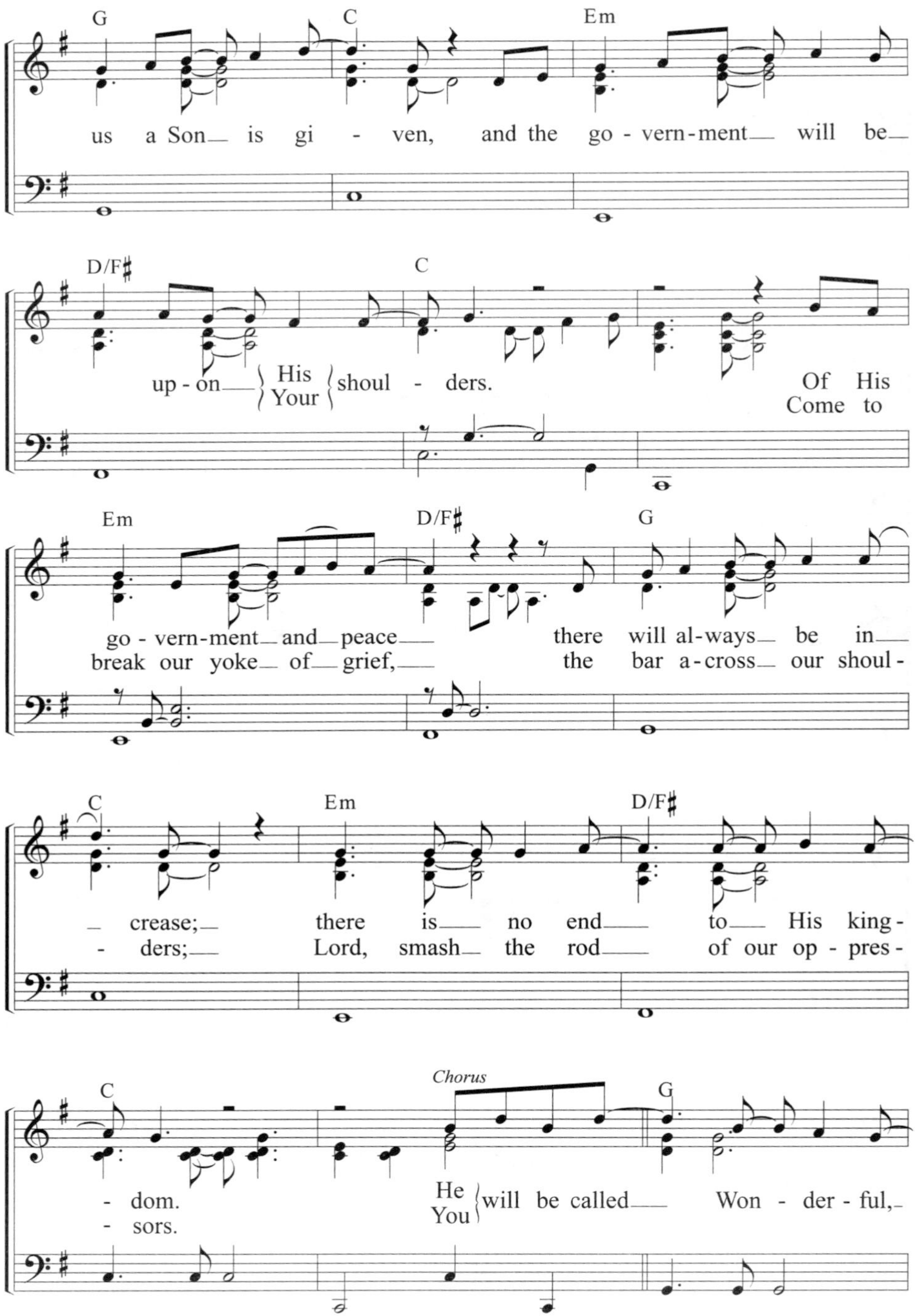
G C Em
us a Son is given, and the government will be
D/F♯ C
upon His / Your shoulders. Of His / Come to
Em D/F♯ G
government and peace there will always be in-
break our yoke of grief, the bar across our shoul-
C Em D/F♯
crease; there is no end to His king-
ders; Lord, smash the rod of our oppres-
C Chorus G
dom. He / You will be called Wonderful,
sors.

C G C
– Coun-sel - lor, Migh - ty God,
Em C D
E-ver - last - ing Fa - ther, Prince of Peace.
Chorus
G C
He
You
will be called Won - der-ful, Coun-sel - lor,
G C Em
Migh - ty God, E-ver - last - ing Fa -
C D
ther, Prince of Peace, the Prince of Peace.
G C G C G
D.C.
Fine
(3. The)

1537. The place where You dwell

Is 40:31; Phil 4:4; Rev 4:8; 5:12

Ed Pask

Gentle 3
D
A/C♯
G/B
1. The place where You dwell is where I want to be,
Asus4
D
A/C♯
G/B
it's where an-gels in splen-dour wor-ship the King.
Asus4
Bm
A/C♯
D/F♯
G
And to Je-sus in glo-ry each voice raised in song:
Em
D/F♯
G
Asus4
D
1.
ho-ly, ho-ly, ho-ly is the Lord.
Bm
A
2. Chorus
D/F♯
G
2. In the
It's all for You,

A
D/F♯
G
A
Je - sus, on - ly You, Je - sus.
Bm
A/C♯
D/F♯
G
You are my song and my rea - son to sing; You have
Em
D/F♯
G
A
set this heart free to rise on the wings of Your praise.
D
Bm
A/C♯
D.C.
To end
D

2. In the light of Your presence
I find perfect peace,
And my heart shall adore You
And in You rejoice.
And to Jesus victorious
I lift up my song:
Worthy, worthy, worthy is the Lamb.

1538. The power of Your love

Steadily
Gary Sadler
Chorus
E A F♯m7 Bsus4 E Bsus4 F♯m7 E
The pow'r of Your love is chang - ing me, chang-ing me, chang - ing me. O Lord,
change me by the pow'r of Your love.
Last time to Coda
1. B7sus4 E (Fine)
2. B7sus4 E
Verse A E/G♯ E A E/G♯ E
The
You've drawn me to Your side, and what else can I do? My
call - ing out for more; I'm ask - ing in Your name, that

1.
2.
A
C♯m7
F♯m7
Bsus4
E/G♯
B7sus4
E
B
Coda
D.C
heart is o - pen wide, my hands reach out to You.
by Your Spi - rit, Lord,
I'm
I will ne - ver be the same.
The
O Lord,
change me by the pow'r of Your love.
I'm
sing - ing out my praise, I'm pour - ing out my thanks, for the
lift - ing up my voice, I'm danc - ing in the joy, for the
pow - er of Your love is chang - ing me. (I'm)
pow - er of Your love is chang - ing me. (The)
(Repeat as required then D.C. al fine)

1539. There is a day

Rom 8:19, 21; 1 Cor 15:51-54; 2 Cor 4:17-18; 1 Thess 4:16-17; 1 Jn 3:2; Rev 21:4

Gently rhythmic
Nathan Fellingham
Verse
C2
Cmaj7
1. There is a day that all cre - a - tion's wait - ing for, a day of free - dom and li - be - ra - tion from the earth.
And on that day the Lord will come to meet His bride. And when we see Him, in an in - stant we'll be changed.
Am
F
1.
C/E
G
2.
C/E
G
Gsus4
(To verse 2)
C
Chorus
G
We will meet Him in the air and then we

Am
F
will be like Him, for we will see Him as He is,
C
G
C
oh yeah!
Then all hurt and pain will cease,
G
Am
and we'll be with Him for - e - ver, and in His glo-
F
C
G
Fmaj7
D.C. (v.3)
(Fine)
ry we will live. Oh yeah, oh yeah!

2. The trumpet sounds and the dead will then be raised
By His power, never to perish again.
Once only flesh, now clothed with immortality;
Death has now been swallowed up in victory.

3. So lift your eyes to the things as yet unseen,
That will remain now for all eternity.
Though trouble's hard, it's only momentary,
And it's achieving our future glory.

1540. There is a deeper love to know

Neh 8:10; Lk 6:38; Jn 8:12; Eph 3:18; Phil 2:10-11

With pace

James Taylor

Verse
E
F♯m7
There is a deep - er love to know, there is a high - er place where we
There is a free-dom at the cross, there is a light that shines for all
A
1.
B
2.
B
F♯m7
can go.
the world.
And I can't hold this
A
F♯m7
A
B
joy in - side, I'm jump - ing in Your arms of mer - cy.
Chorus
E
A
Ev - 'ry - bo - dy sing, ev - 'ry bo - dy shout, for the joy of the Lord

F♯m7
A
E
is our strength for-e-ver. Hey, ev-'ry-bo-dy sing, ev-'ry-
A
F♯m7
bo-dy shout, for the joy of the Lord is our strength.
1. 2.
2nd x D.S.
Bsus4
B
3.
D.S.S.
Bsus4
B
Last time
B
E
And

2. There is a brighter day to come,
When all the world will bow down to Your Son.
And all the broken will rejoice,
Even the kings will say 'You are the Lord.'

And we can't hold this joy inside,
We're dancing in Your arms of mercy.

1541. There is a higher throne

Rev 5:9, 12-13; 7:9; 21:4, 19

Keith Getty & Kristyn Lennox

Majestically
E
Verse
A/E
B/E
1. There is a high - er throne than all this
2. And there we'll find our home, our life be -
E
B/D♯
C♯m
A
world has known, where faith - ful ones from e - v'ry tongue
fore the throne; we'll ho - nour Him in per - fect song
F♯m7
Bsus4 B
E
A/E
will one day come. Be - fore the Son we'll stand,
where we be - long. He'll wipe each tear - stained eye,
B/E
E
B/D♯
C♯m
made fault - less through the Lamb; be - liev - ing hearts find
and thirst and hun - ger die; the Lamb be - comes our
A
F♯m7
Bsus4 B
E/G♯
Chorus
pro - mised grace: sal - va - tion comes. Hear hea - ven's
Shep - herd King: we'll reign with Him.

A B A/E E
voi - ces sing, their thun-d'rous an - them rings through
C♯m C♯m/B A A/G♯ F♯m7 B
em'-rald courts and sap-phire skies, their prai-ses rise.
E/G♯ E/A A B
All glo-ry, wis - dom, pow'r, strength, thanks and
A/E E C♯m7 C♯m/B A A/G♯ F♯m7 Bsus4 B
ho - nour are to God, our King who reigns on high, for - e - ver
E A/E E A/E D.C. E
more.

1542. There is a hope so sure

Mt 16:18; 1 Cor 6:19; Gal 2:20; Col 1:27-28; 2 Tim 2:11; 1 Jn 2:2

Graham Kendrick

Slowly
Verse
A2 E/G♯ A2 E/G♯
1. There is a hope so sure, a pro-mise so se-cure: the my-ste -
A B C♯m B E
ry of God at last made known. Trea-sures so
F♯m(addB) E/G♯ A2 C♯m
vast ap-pear, all wis-dom, know-ledge here: it's Christ in
A E/G♯ F♯m7 B E
Chorus
A/E E
us, the hope of glo - ry! And the life that I now live, no lon-ger
A/E E B/E C♯m7 A
is my own, Je - sus lives in me, the hope of

B E/G♯ A E A E/G♯ F♯m7
glo-ry. And each day I live, no lon-ger is my own, Je-sus
A B C♯m A2 B
1.,2.,4.
E A2
lives in me, the hope of glo - ry.
E/G♯ A B C♯m B E
(Fine)
D.C.
2. There is a
3.
E
D.S. Chorus rpt.
ry. And the life that

2. There is a life so true,
A life of love so pure,
For all our sin a perfect sacrifice.
And when that life was nailed,
On cruel cross impaled,
Our sinful flesh with Him was crucified.

3. There is a life so strong,
That a whole world of wrong
And all the powers of hell could not defeat.
For Jesus rose again,
And if we died with Him,
With Him we'll rise to share His endless life.

1543. There is a name
(High over all)

Jn 1:1, 11; Rom 8:34; Phil 2:9; Col 1:15; Heb 7:25

Nathan Fellingham

With energy

A
C♯m7
Verse
1. There is a name

Bm7
A
that's high o - ver all.

C♯m7
Bm
A
There is a King seat - ed on the throne.

D
E
F♯m7
C♯m/E
And He's in - ter - ced - ing for me,

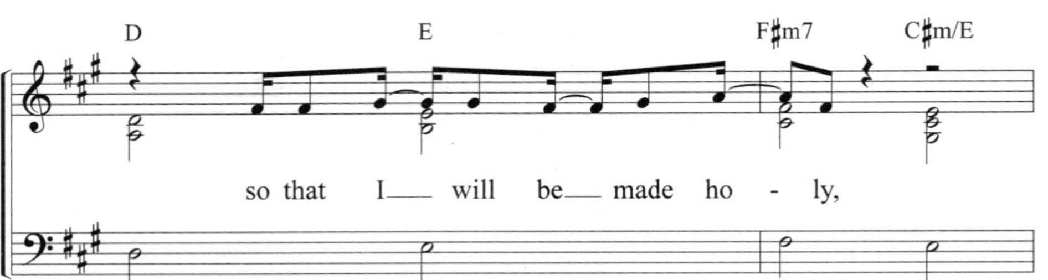

D
E
F♯m7
C♯m/E
so that I will be made ho - ly,

D E F♯m7 C♯m/E Bm7
and I know that in His love I will stay.
A/C♯
Chorus
D E A D E A/C♯
What a Saviour is my Jesus,
How I love You, oh my Jesus,
D E A Bm7 D E
1st time D.C.
2nd time D.S.
He came down so that I may go free.
You came down so that I may go free.
Last time
A

2. There is a Man who walked on the earth,
The Word of God made known to us.
He's the image of the Father,
The Firstborn over creation,
Yet He suffered at the hands of those He saves.

1544. There is a passion
(Lifted into Your presence)

David Fellingham
& Kim Morgan

Tenderly

G
C2
Em
D
There is a pas - sion deep in my heart to know You,
G/B
C
G
C2
Je - sus. There is a hun - ger deep in my soul
Em
D
C2
G/B
C
on - ly You can sa - tis - fy. I hear You cal - ling, draw -
D
C
G
ing me clo - ser, I can't re - sist Your grace.

G/B
C
D
Am7
Al-migh-ty pow'r and love so free, draw me to Your side.
Dsus4 D
G
C/G
G
D/F♯
G
C
D
And I'm lif-ted in-to Your pre-sence, lif-ted in-to Your
Bm7
Em
G
C/G
G
D/F♯
Em7
arms of love. Lif-ted in-to Your pre - sence,
C
Dsus4
D
Em7
C
Dsus4
D
now has my soul found rest, now has my soul found
G
Gsus4
1.
G
Gsus4
2.
G
D/C
C
G/B
rest. I see Your face,

D/C
C
G/B
D/C
I feel Your touch; re - ceive
C
Em
C
D
G
(2nd time fine)
Your love, I wor - ship You. (I)

Humble yourselves before the Lord, and He will lift you up.

JAMES 4:10

1545. There is a voice that must be heard

(Jesus, Friend of sinners)

Ps 34:3; 148:4; Prov 18:24; Mt 11:19; Jn 14:27; Acts 4:12; Rom 8:38-39

With energy

Paul Oakley

Verse
A
Asus4
1. There is a voice that must be heard,
There is a treasure more than gold,
A
Asus4
there is a song that must be sung;
there is a King upon the throne;
F♯m
1.
D
E
there is a name that must be lifted high.
there is one whose praise
2.
D
E
will fill the skies.
Chorus
A
D
His name is Jesus, Friend of

A
D
A
sin - ners,
Je - sus,
Je - sus,
D
F♯m
E
1.
D
D.C.
(Fine)
2.
D
D.S.
Friend of
mine.
His name is
3.
D
Bm
E
When I was cap - tive to my fears,
Bm
E
Bm
You were the one who came to me,
E
F♯m
E
D
x3
You set me free.
D.S. al fine
His name is

2. There is a peace that calms our fears,
There is a love stronger than death;
There is a hope that goes beyond the grave.
There is a Friend who won't let go,
There is a heart that beats for You;
There is one name by which we are saved.

1546. There is no other name

Mt 11:28; Lk 4:18; Acts 4:12; 1 Pet 2:24

Steadily
Robin Mark
Chorus
G D Em C
There is no o-ther name by which men can be saved, there is
G D C G/B Am7 G
no o-ther name un-der hea-ven. There is
D Em C
rest for my soul and the wound-ed made whole, and the
Last time to Coda
G D 1. C G/B Am7 G
cap-tives set free and for - gi-ven. There is
2. C G/B Am7 G
Verse
C D G
gi-ven. Such love as I had ne-ver known,

C D G Bm/F♯ Em
I've found in the grace that flowed to me in my un-
C Am
right-eous-ness; this is why my
D D.C.
heart and soul and tongue con-fess. There is
Coda
C G/B Am7 G
-gi-ven.

1547. There must be more

(Consuming fire)

Ps 27:14; 38:15; 130:5; Is 61:1; Acts 2:1-3; Heb 12:29

Tim Hughes

Verse
Em7 D/F♯ G C
1. There must be more than this: O Breath of God,
Em7 D/F♯ C Em7 D/F♯
come breathe within. There must be more than this:
G C Em7 D/F♯ C
Spirit of God, we wait for You.
Am7 G/B D Am7 G/B
Fill us anew, we pray; fill us anew, we pray.

D
Chorus
G
D/F♯
Con-sum-ing fire, fan in-to flame a
Em7
C
G
pas - sion for Your name. Spi-rit of God, fall in this
D/F♯
D/F♯
place. Lord, have Your way, Lord, have Your way with us.
C
D.C.
G

2. Come like a rushing wind,
Clothe us in power from on high.
Now set the captives free;
Leave us abandoned to Your praise.
Lord, let Your glory fall;
Lord, let Your glory fall.

1548. There's a call

(We will go)

Num 33:53-54; 1 Sam 17:47; Is 6:8; Mt 9:37; 28:19-20; Lk 1:79; Jn 4:35; 6:63; 8:12; 1 Cor 11:23-26; 2 Cor 12:9-10; Rev 5:9

Stuart Townend

With life
D Verse G/D
1. There's a call to the peo-ple of Zi-on,
We have stayed long e-nough on this moun-tain,
D G/D Em7
to a-rise and pos-sess the land;
now we're called to new realms of faith;
ev-'ry town has its
we are more than a
Bm7 A
heirs to the pro-mise,
tem-ple of wor-ship,
1. Em7 Bm7 A G/A
ev-'ry na-tion its sons of light.
2. Em7 A7sus4 D
we're an ar-my of praise!
We will go to ev-'ry place,
G/D D G/D G A
sharing mer-cy and preach-ing grace, for the

Bm
F♯m7
Em7
Bm7
Em7
A7sus4
fields are white for har - vest, and la - bour - ers are few.
D
G/D
No place too dark, no soul too lost for the pow -
D
G/D
G
A
Bm
F♯m7
Em7
er of the cross; for His light will shine in dark -
Bm7
Em7
A7sus4
ness, and ma - ny will be - lieve, so we will go.
2nd time D.C.
Last time only
D
G/D
Bm7
Em7
G/A
D

2. We have drunk of the wine of His presence,
We have feasted upon His word;
Now we're hungry for works of power,
Now we're thirsty to share His love.
He will give us the ground that we walk on,
For the battle belongs to God;
Do not fear, for His grace is sufficient,
When we're weak, He is strong!

1549. There's a calling to the nations

(All over the world)

Ps 30:11; Mt 11:29; Jn 1:1; 14:6; 17:17; Acts 2:17, 21; Heb 12:2; 2 Pet 3:12; Rev 14:15

Rock feel

Ken Riley

Verse
G C
1. There's a cal - ling to the na - tions to make rea -
G C Am
dy in Your name, to take up the yoke of Je -
D G C
- sus and pro-claim the com-ing day. There's a pour -
G C G
ing of Your Spi - rit as our old men dream Your dreams;
C Am D
- pro-phe-sy through sons and daugh - ters, come en-vi -

G
C
Bridge
Am
C
D
sion us a-gain. You're the Word and the Word is Truth,
Am
C
D
You're the Pro - mise that was born in You, and a wave
Am
C
G
F
D/F♯
of ex - pec-ta - tion fills my soul!
G
Chorus
D
G/B
All o-ver the world we're sing-ing, all o-ver the world
C
Am
Em/G
there's praise to the King of our sal-va - tion, and the Au-

F
D/F♯
G
D
thor of our faith.
All o-ver the world we're dan-cing,
G/B
C
Am
all o-ver the world there's joy, we've called up-on Your name
Em/G
1. F
D/F♯
G
C2
and we are saved.
G
C2
2. F
D/F♯
G
2. Can it be saved.
All o-ver the world.

2. Can it be this generation
That will hear revival's song?
As Your Spirit of creation
Comes awakening the lost.
Let the four winds blow Your justice,
Come and harvest of the earth;
Turn our mourning into dancing
As we herald Your return.

1550. There's a new song upon my lips

Ps 40:3; Phil 4:13

(God of great things)
Rhythmically
Johnny Parks
B E B E
1. There's a new___ song up - on my lips,___ a
fi - re burn-ing in my heart,___ a
B E B E B
song I al - ways knew.___ Thank___ You___ for
fire of faith___ in You.___ I be - lieve___ all___ the
A
all___ that___ You do.___
things___ we___ can do.__
1.
B E B E
There is
2.
B E
G♯
You're the God of___
C♯m G♯ C♯m
great___ things,___ You're the God of___ great___ things.___ I___ won't___

G♯m/B Amaj7 G♯m/B B
– hold back my thanks to You.
E Emaj7/B A
Thank You, thank You, hey, Je-sus, I
B E Emaj7/B
– a - dore You. Thank You, thank You,
A B 1. E B E
hey, Je-sus, I live for You.
B E B E 2. E
2. There's a –

2. There's a beat pounding through my feet,
A new dance of thanks to You.
I'm tasting the joy found in You.
There is courage building in my heart;
A strength that comes from You.
I'm going to live my life for You.

1551. There's a pageant of triumph in glory

(Let God arise)

Ps 68:1, 4; Acts 2:24; 1 Pet 3:19; 1 Jn 2:2; Rev 5:12

Capo 3 (Em)

David Fellingham

With a latin feel

Verse

Gm(Em) Dm(Bm) Cm(Am) Dm(Bm)

1. There's a pageant of triumph in glory, as

Gm(Em) Dm(Bm) Cm(Am) Dm(Bm)

Jesus the King takes His throne. The

Gm(Em) Dm(Bm) Cm(Am) Dm(Bm)

shame of the cross is exchanged for a crown, and

Gm(Em) Dm(Bm) Cm(Am)

heaven applauds the King. The

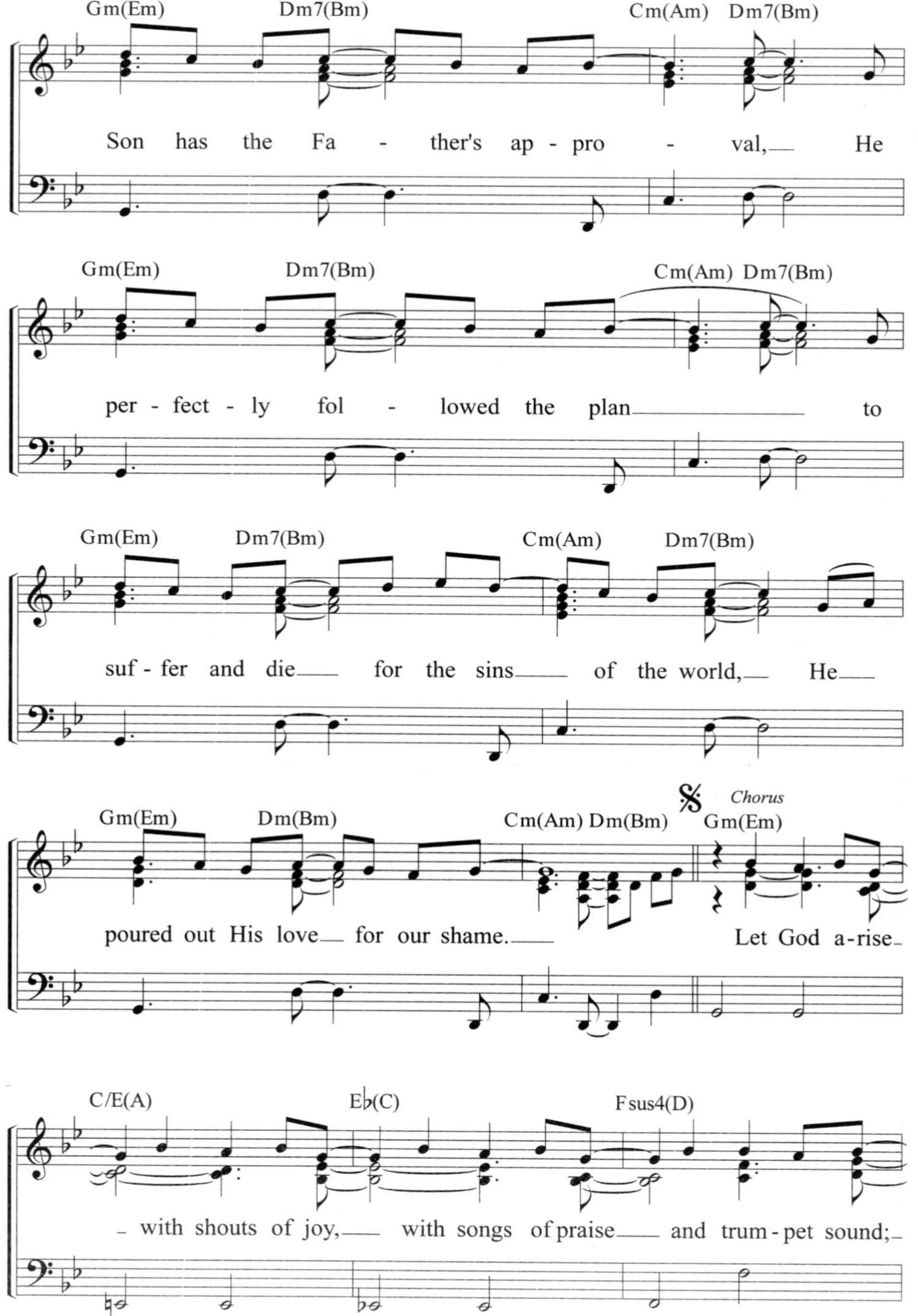

Gm(Em) Dm7(Bm) Cm(Am) Dm7(Bm)
Son has the Fa - ther's ap - pro - val, He
Gm(Em) Dm7(Bm) Cm(Am) Dm7(Bm)
per - fect - ly fol - lowed the plan to
Gm(Em) Dm7(Bm) Cm(Am) Dm7(Bm)
suf - fer and die for the sins of the world, He
Gm(Em) Dm(Bm) Cm(Am) Dm(Bm)
poured out His love for our shame.
Chorus
Gm(Em)
Let God a-rise
C/E(A) E♭(C) Fsus4(D)
with shouts of joy, with songs of praise and trum - pet sound;

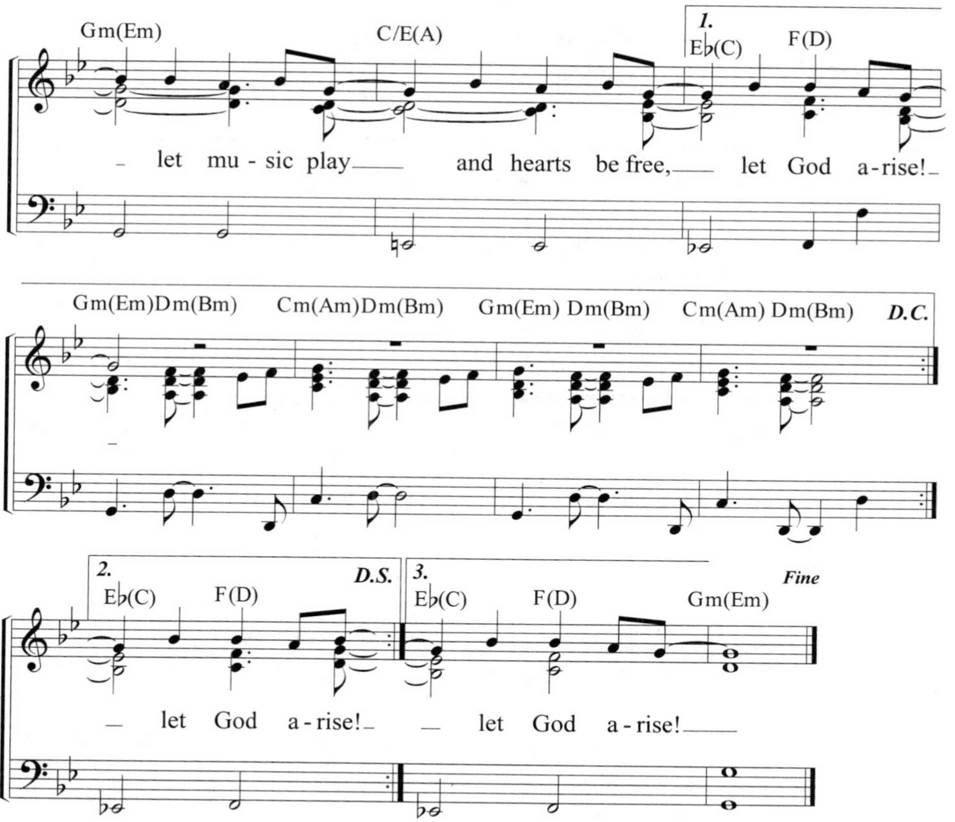
Gm(Em)
C/E(A)
1.
E♭(C)
F(D)
let mu - sic play
and hearts be free,
let God a-rise!
Gm(Em)Dm(Bm)
Cm(Am)Dm(Bm)
Gm(Em) Dm(Bm)
Cm(Am) Dm(Bm)
D.C.
2.
E♭(C)
F(D)
D.S.
3.
E♭(C)
F(D)
Gm(Em)
Fine
let God a-rise!
let God a-rise!

2. Death could not keep Him in prison,
He burst through the shackles of hell;
He's settled the score with the evil one,
And heaven applauds the King.
The fullness of Christ is my treasure,
I've cast off the past with its shame.
The power of the Father has raised me to life,
I'm a son, I'm forgiven and free.

1552. There's a people
(Oh, that we might see Your glory)

Is 51:11; 61:1; Mk 10:45; Jn 14:27; 15:11; 1 Cor 13:12; Eph 1:4; 5:18; 1 Thess 4:17

Rhythmic slow 4

Terry Virgo
& Stuart Townend

Verse

D G/D D G/D D Bm A
1. There's a peo - ple God has cho - sen from the na - tions, He has ran - somed from the pri - sons for His joy, for His — de - light.

D G/D D G/B D/A G A7sus4 D D/F♯ G
He has known — them from be - fore He made the hea - vens, and His love has spanned the a - ges, how He longs to bring — them home!

Chorus

A D/F♯ G A D/F♯ G
(Men) Oh, that we — might see Your glo - ry, — Lord. —
(Women) Oh, that we — might see Your face.

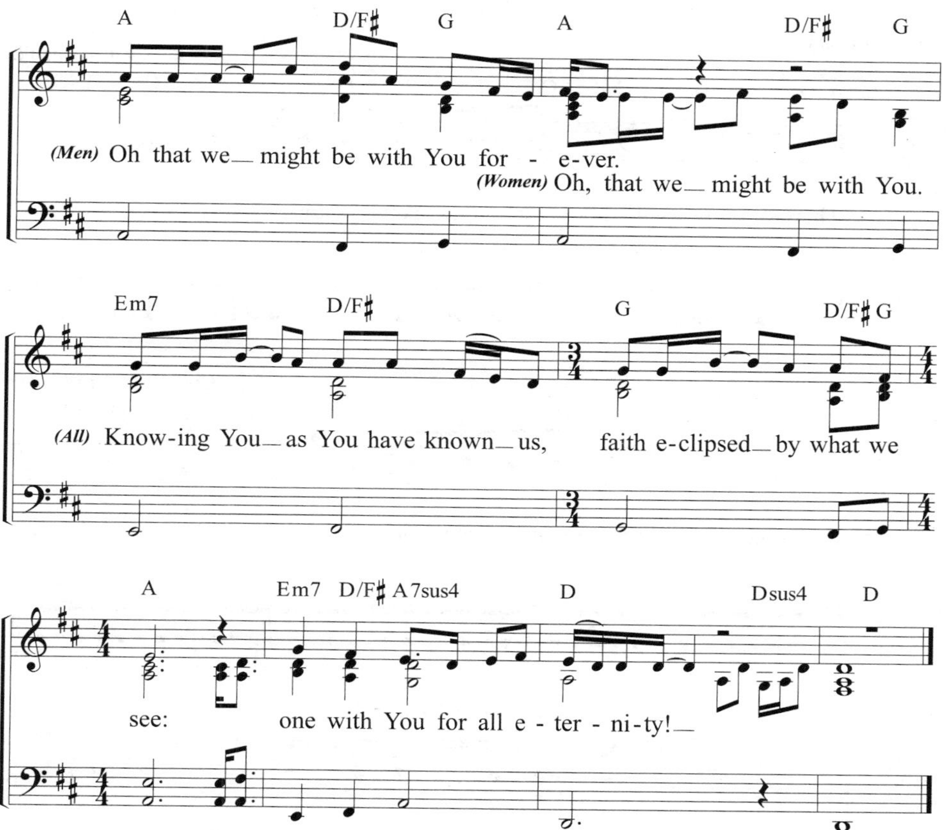
A D/F♯ G A D/F♯ G
(Men) Oh that we — might be with You for - e-ver.
(Women) Oh, that we — might be with You.
Em7 D/F♯ G D/F♯ G
(All) Know-ing You — as You have known — us, faith e-clipsed — by what we
A Em7 D/F♯ A7sus4 D Dsus4 D
see: one with You for all e - ter - ni-ty! —

2. We're that people
You have rescued from our blindness,
You have come to live within us,
To share Your peace, to share Your joy.
Come and fill us,
Flood our spirits with Your fullness,
Let us taste the wine of heaven,
Only You can satisfy.

1553. There's no love greater than Your love

*Ps 30:11;
Eph 3:18; Phil 2:10-11*

Driving rhythm

James Taylor

Chorus
G C/G G C/G G C/G G D/G
There's no love great-er than Your love,
G C/G G C/G G C/G G D/G
After v.2 D.S. to Bridge
(Fine)
there's no love great-er than You.
G
Verse
Am
I want to hear it sung a - round the world that
Want to see the day when all will know that
C G
Je-sus, You are Lord of all. And our
Je-sus, You are Lord of all. And we'll

Am
C
prais-es ring that You are King of all the hea-vens and the earth.
hear the songs of free-dom sound up-on the lips of young and old.
G
Am
And at Your name we bow,
And ev-'ry knee shall bow,
Em
Am
C
D.C.
You've turned our mourn-ing in-to danc-ing.
let all the earth re-joice with glad-ness.
Bridge
C
G/B
D
You came with love bright-er than the day.
C
G/B
Who can de-ny the won-der of Your

D
C
name?
Don't let me fall,
Em7
Am7
G
D
I was born to be with You: there's no love like You.
G
C/G
G
D/G
D.C. al fine

1554. There's no one like our God

Ps 8:1; 61:3; 86:8; 113:9; Gal 4:27; Eph 2:6; Phil 2:8; 1 Jn 4:10

Vicky Beeching
& Steve Mitchinson

Steadily

Chorus

A2 E B
There's no one like our — God, no one at — all.

A2 E B
He gave His Son for — us, Je - sus the — Lord.

A2 E B D2
And who can love us like — He does? No one at — all. —

Last time D.C. then to Coda

A A2 E
Oh, how we love You, Lord.

B A2 E B

E2
Verse
(v.2)
D2
1. You are high a - bove all na - tions,
A
E/B
Your glo - ry shines a - bove the hea - vens;
E2
D2
hum-bled Your-self to love and save us:
1.
A
F♯m7
be praised through end - less ge - ne - ra - tions.
D2
D.C.
2.
A
she'll dance for joy like the
F♯m7
D2
D.C.
mo - ther of chil - dren.

Coda
A2
E
B2
4th time
D2
Lord.
Oh, how we love You,
Lord.

A
E

2. You lift the needy from the ashes,
And seat them high up with the princes.
You give the barren woman healing;
She'll dance for joy like the mother of children.

1555. The Spirit lives to set us free

(Walk in the light)

Lk 19:10; Jn 10:10; 11:43-44; 14:16; Rom 8:2; 2 Cor 1:3; 1 Pet 2:24; 1 Jn1:7

Steadily

Music: Anon

Verse
G Bm C G C D G C/D D7
1. The Spi-rit lives to set us free, walk, walk, in the light; He
G Bm C G C D G
binds us all in u-ni-ty, walk, walk in the light.
Chorus
G G7/B C D D/C B7
Walk in the light, walk in the light,
Em Em/D C Am7 D D7 G
walk in the light, walk in the light of the Lord

2. Jesus promised life to all,
Walk, walk in the light;
The dead were wakened by His call,
Walk, walk in the light.

3. He died in pain on Calvary,
Walk, walk in the light;
To save the lost like you and me,
Walk, walk in the light.

4. We know His death was not the end,
Walk, walk in the light;
He gave His Spirit to be our friend,
Walk, walk in the light.

5. By Jesus' love our wounds are healed,
Walk, walk in the light;
The Father's kindness is revealed,
Walk, walk in the light.

6. The Spirit lives in you and me,
Walk, walk in the light;
His light will shine for all to see,
Walk, walk in the light.

Damian Lundy

1556. The voice of God

Mt 28:19-20; 1 Tim 1:15; Rev 5:9, 12; 7:9; 8:4

With strength
Dave Bilbrough
Verse
G
1. The voice of God is call - ing with
Em
C2
words that roar and rage; the pas - sion of the Fa - ther's heart
G
Dsus4 D
re - sounds through e - v'ry age.
G
Em
Mul - ti - tudes are wait - ing for this go - spel we pro - claim;
C2
Christ Je - sus came a - mong us that

SoF3

F
D
Chorus
G
G/F♯
all men might be saved. Show Your glo - ry, show Your
Em7
G/D G/C C Am
glo - ry, show Your glo - ry o - ver all the
Dsus4 D G G/F♯ Em7
earth. Show Your glo - ry, show Your glo - ry,
G/D G/C C C/D G
(Fine) D.C.
show Your glo - ry o-ver all the earth. (3. With)

2. This is our commission, to fill the air with praise
And to tell the people of this world the glory of His name.
With thousands upon thousands from every tribe and tongue
We cry 'worthy is the Lamb once slain, for He has overcome!'

3. With tears of intercession, through the prayers of all the saints,
We long to reach the nations with humility and grace.
Come touch this generation and use us, Lord, we pray;
Fill our hearts with boldness to do the things You say.

1557. The wonder of forgiveness

(All I want to say)

Ps 139:17; Phil 3:8, 14; Heb 10:20; Jas 2:23

Stuart Townend & Gary Sadler

Gently rhythmic

D
G/B
1. The won - der of for - give - ness,
2. I'm lay - ing down my trea - sures
D/A
Gmaj7
the com - fort of Your love,
to claim the per - fect prize.
Bm7
Gmaj7
the all - sur - pas - sing plea - sure
I'm pul - ling back the cur - tain
C2
G/B
Gmaj7/B
to be a friend of God.
to look in - to Your eyes.

Em
D/F♯
Your thoughts to me are end - less,
You know my in - hi - bi - tions,
Gmaj7
Asus4
Bm
this joy will ne - ver end. All I want to say is 'I love
but You can meet me here.
F♯m7
Gmaj7
Dmaj7
You,' all I want to give is my heart. All I want to
Bm
F♯m7
G
do is be near You, and to walk in Your ways.
Asus4
Bm
F♯m7
Rest-ing in the peace of Your pro - mise, trust-ing in the

Gmaj7
Dmaj7
Bm
cross that You bore, looking for the day when I see
F♯m7
Gmaj7
F♯m7
Em
A
You, Lord, I thank You for Your faith - ful-ness to me.
D
G/B
D/A
G
D

1558. The wonder of Your mercy

(Covenant of grace)

2 Cor 12:10; Eph 2:4; 2 Tim 2:13; Heb 10:19, 22

Don Wallace

Steadily

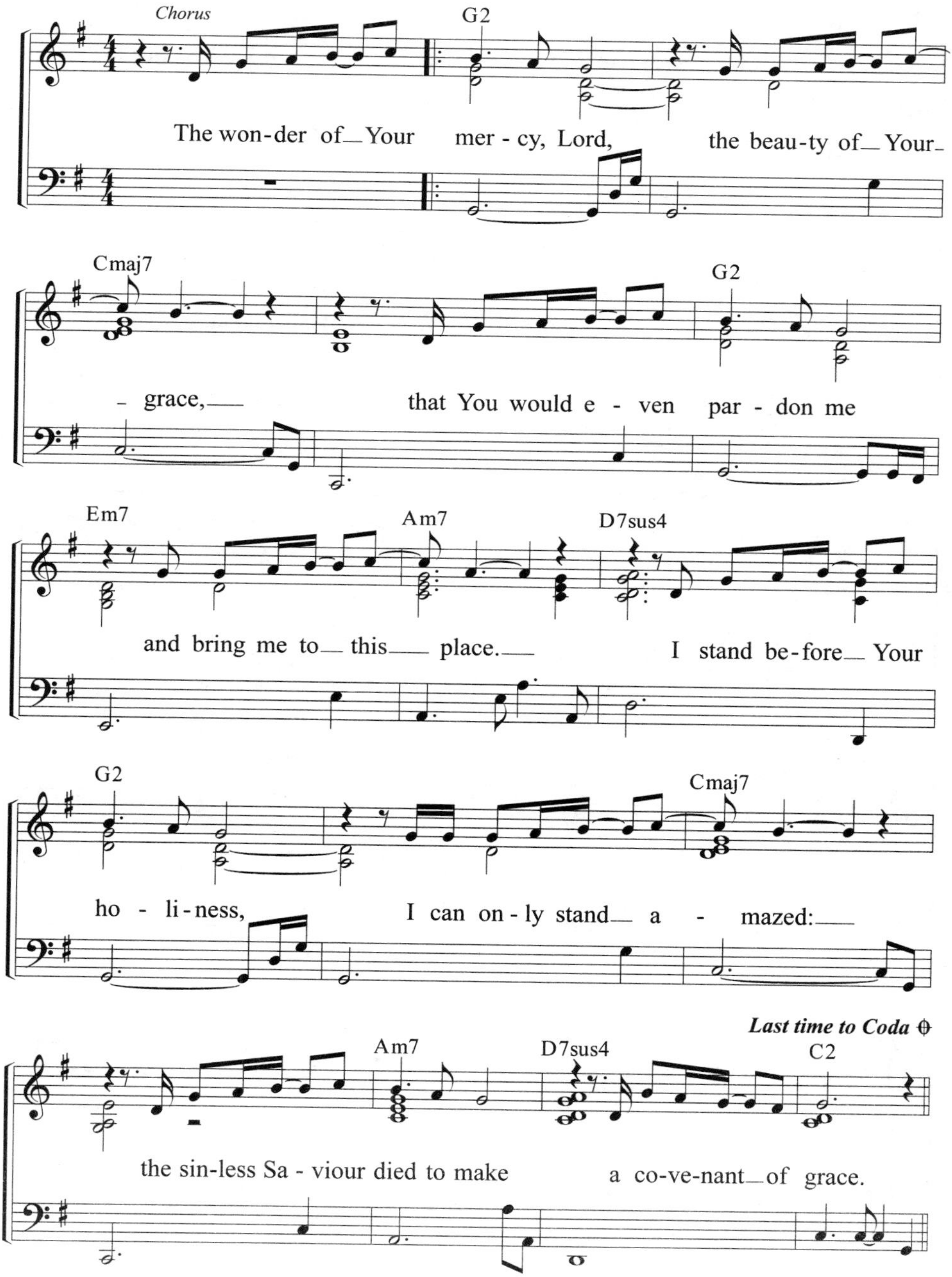

Chorus

The wonder of Your mercy, Lord,
the beauty of Your grace,
that You would even pardon me
and bring me to this place.
I stand before Your holiness,
I can only stand amazed:
the sinless Saviour died to make
a covenant of grace.

Last time to Coda

C2 Verse G C
1. I on-ly want to serve You, bring ho-nour to Your
G C Em
name, and though I've of - ten failed You,
Am D7sus4 C2
Your faith-ful-ness re - mains. I'll glo-ry in my
G C2 Em
weak-ness, that I might know Your strength. I will
Am7 G/B
live my life at the cross of Christ, and raise a

D.C. al Coda
Coda
Fine
C
Dsus4
C2
G2
ban - ner to pro-claim: the won-der of Your

2. You welcome us before You,
Into this holy place;
The brilliance of Your glory
Demands our endless praise.
The One, the only Saviour
Has opened heaven's doors;
We can enter in, free from all our sin,
By Your cleansing sacrifice.

1559. This Child

Lk 1:52-53, 78-79; Jn 1:9

Graham Kendrick

Calypso
D
G
A7
D
1. This
Verse
D
G
A7
Child, se-cret-ly comes in the night, O this Child, hid-ing a hea-
D
G
ven - ly light, O this Child, com-ing to us like a stran-ger,
A7
D
Chorus
G
this hea - ven-ly Child. This Child, hea-ven come down

D
A7
D
_ now to be with us here, hea-ven-ly love___ and mer - cy ap -
G
D
Asus4
pear, soft-ly in awe___ and won - der come near -
A
1.2.
D
3.
D
D.S.
to this hea - ven-ly Child. 2. This Child. This
4.
D
Child.

2. This Child, rising on us like the sun,
   O this Child, given to light everyone,
   O this Child, guiding our feet on the pathway
   To peace on earth.

3. This Child, raising the humble and poor,
   O this Child, making the proud ones to fall;
   O this Child, filling the hungry with good things,
   This heavenly Child.

1560. This is love
(Solid ground)

Jn 14:27; Acts 2:24; Rom 8:1; 2 Cor 5:7; Phil 2:7-8; 1 Jn 4:10

Keith Getty
& Kristyn Lennox

Brightly

Verse

D A G D A
1. This is love, not that we loved Him, but that He first loved

G D A G
us. Left be-hind glo-ries of hea-ven;

D A G Em
took on the shame of the cross. But in the place where

A Em A
love was poured death could not hold our ri-sen Lord.

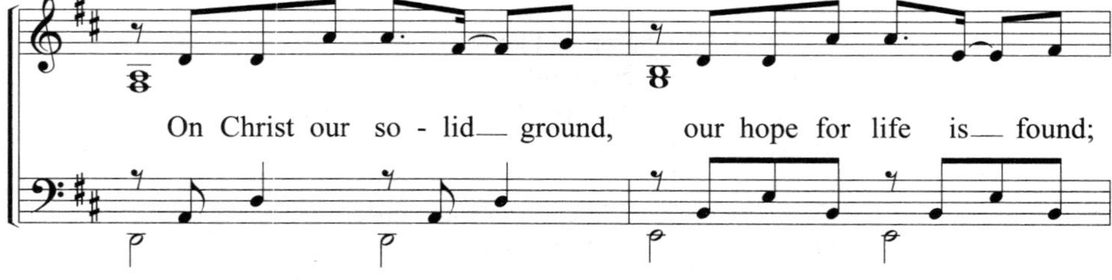
Chorus
D
Em
On Christ our so - lid ground, our hope for life is found;

D/F♯
G
D
the joy of our sal - va - tion on Christ our so - lid ground,
Em
D/F♯
G
our hope for life is found. There is no con - dem - na - tion.
Em
D/F♯
A
D
A
G
There is no con - dem - na - tion.
D
A
G

2. This is peace,
Not as the world gives,
But the true peace of Christ.
You have claimed
Our hearts for heaven;
Living by faith, not by sight.
Strengthen our faith in You alone
Until we stand before Your throne.

1561. This is my desire
(I give You my heart)

Reuben Morgan

Steadily

Verse
G
D/F♯
Em
C/G
G
D/F♯
This is my_ de - sire,_ to hon - our You:
All I have_with - in_ me,_ I give You praise:

Em
D/F♯
G
1.
Fsus2
F
Lord, with all_ my heart_ I wor-ship You._
all that I_ a - dore_ is in You._

C
C/D
2.
Fsus2
F
C
C/D
G
Chorus
Lord, I give You my heart,_

D/F♯
Am7
C/D
_ I give You my_ soul;_ I live for You a-lone.

G
D/F♯
Ev - 'ry breath that I take, ev - 'ry mo - ment I'm a - wake,
Am7
1.
C/D
Cmaj7
D/C
D.C.
Lord, have Your way in me.
2.
C/D
D.S.
3.
C/D
G
have Your way in me. have Your way in me.

1562. This is the air I breathe

(Breathe)

Mt 6:11; Jn 6:58

Steadily

Marie Barnett

Asus2
Dsus2/A
This is the air I breathe,
This is my dai - ly bread,

Asus2
Dsus2/A
A
E/G♯
this is the air I breathe:
this is my dai - ly bread:
Your ho-ly pre -
Your ve-ry word

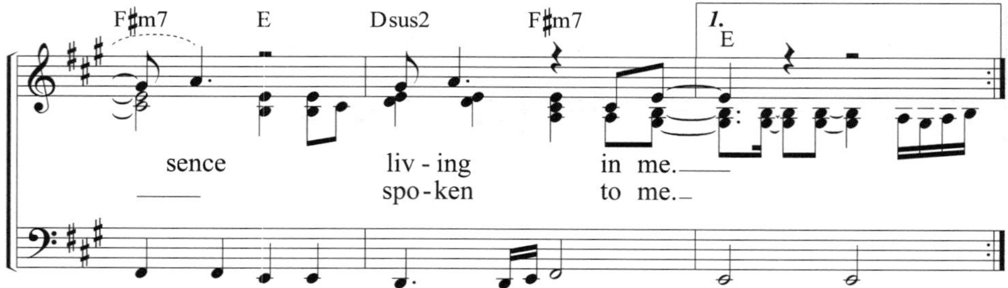

F♯m7
E
Dsus2
F♯m7
1.
E
sence
liv - ing
in me.
spo-ken
to me.

2.
E
A
E/G♯
F♯m7
E
And I,
I'm des-perate for

Dsus2
F♯m7
E
A
E/G♯
You.
And I,
F♯m7
E
Dsus2
F♯m7
To repeat
Esus4
E
I'm lost with-out You.
Last time
Esus4
E
Asus2

1563. This is the best place

(Worshipping the living God)

Capo 3 (D)

Heb 10:19, 22, 24-25

Ian White

Steadily

Verse
(v.2)
F(D)
(v.2)
1. This is the best place, this is the right place, and we have

(v.2)
(v.2)
Gm7(Em)
C(A)
F(D)
con-fi-dence now to en - ter: let us draw near_now, with hearts sin-

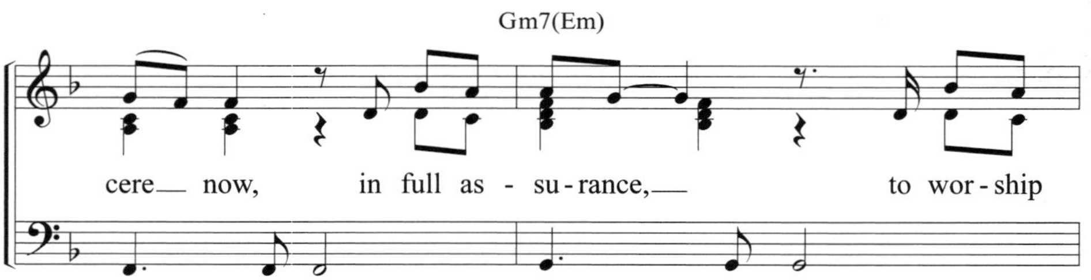

Gm7(Em)
cere_ now, in full as - su-rance,_ to wor-ship

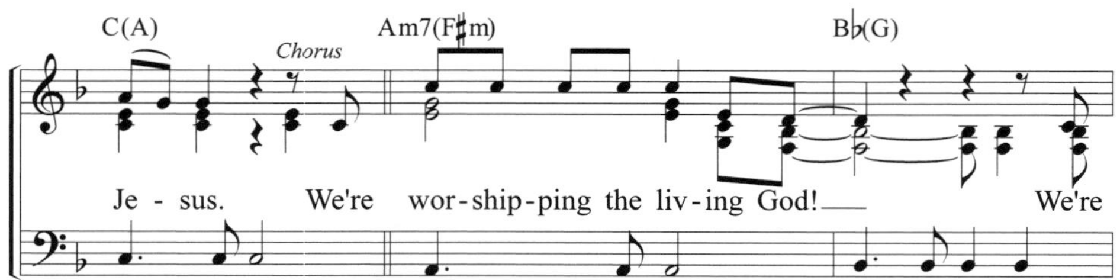

C(A)
Chorus
Am7(F♯m)
B♭(G)
Je - sus. We're wor-ship-ping the liv-ing God!_ We're

F(D)
C(A)
wor - ship - ping the liv - ing God!
We're
Am7(F♯m)
B♭(G)
wor - ship - ping the liv - ing God!
We're
F(D)
To verse
C(A)
wor - ship - ping the liv - ing God!
2. Let us con-
To end
C(A)
F(D)
The liv - ing God!

2. Let us consider,
For one another,
The way to love more,
As the day approaches.
Let us draw near now,
With hearts sincere now;
Let's meet together
To worship Jesus.

1564. This means I love You

Mt 16:24; Jn 15:5; Rom 7:4

Matt Redman
Worshipful
Chorus
E E/D♯ C♯m7 B
This means I love — You, sing-ing this song; — Lord I
A2 C♯m A2 B
don't have the words, — but I do have the will. — And
E E/D♯ C♯m7 B
this means I love — You, that I take up my cross, I will sing
Last time to Coda
A Bsus4 B
1. E
2.3. E
Verse
as I walk out this love. — —
2. For
C♯m7 B E
1. Je - sus, this life, — is for You, —
these are the plans — of my heart, — yet

C♯m7
B
E
ev - 'ry - thing, Lord, that I do;
of - ten I'm miss - ing the mark;
C♯m7
B
A2
A/C♯
deeds that are pleas - ing, and ways that are pure,
see my de - si - re to live in your truth,
F♯m7
Bsus4
B
E
D.C. al Coda
Lord, may my life bear this fruit.
this sure - ly means I love You.
Coda
E
Fine

1565.
Though trials will come
(Consider it joy)
Is 60:4; Jas 1:2-4, 12
Graham Kendrick
Steadily, with a gospel feel
Verse
1. Though trials will come, don't fear, don't run.
2. Though trials will come, won't fear, won't run.
Lift up your eyes, hold fast, be strong.
We'll lift up our eyes, hold fast, be strong.
Have faith, keep on be-liev - ing. Lift up your
Have faith, keep on be-liev - ing. We'll lift up our
eyes for God is at
eyes for God is at
work in us,— mould-ing and
(verse 3) trust - ing Him,— rea - dy for
shap-ing us— out of His love for us,— mak-ing us
a - ny-thing,- till we're com - plete in Him,— in ev - ery-thing

SoF3

C/D D C/D D C/D D Dsus4
Chorus
D7
G Am/G G
more like Je - sus.
more like Je - sus.
Con - si - der it joy, pure joy
C G C/D G G♯°7 Am7
when trou - bles come.
Ma - ny trials will make
Am7/D G Gsus4 G Am/G G C G
you strong. Con - si - der it joy, pure joy and stand your ground,
Last time to Coda
G♯°7 Am7 Am7/D
1. Csus2
then at last you'll wear a crown.
Dsus4 C/D
3. G B7 D.S.
2. G
3. Pa - tient - ly

C D Em D C D Em D
Joy, pure joy, con-si-der it joy, pure joy.
D.S.S. to Chorus
C D Em D C D Em D/F♯
Joy, pure joy, con-si-der it joy, pure joy. Con-si-der it
Coda
C/D D G Dm/F E7(♯9) G♯°7 Am7 C/D D G Dm/F
a crown, then at last you'll wear a crown,
E7(♯9) G♯°7 Am7 C/D Csus2
then at last you'll wear a crown.
Dsus4 C/D G

1566. Through all the changing scenes of life

Capo 1 (A)
Tune: WILTSHIRE

2 Kings 6:17; Ps 34:3-4; Eccles 12:13; Gal 6:14; 1 Pet 5:7

George Thomas Smart (1776-1867)

(A) B♭ (A) B♭/F (E) F (F♯m) Gm (D) E♭ (A) B♭/F (E) F (A) B♭
1. Through all the chang - ing scenes of life, in
(E) F/A (A) B♭ (E) Fsus4 (E) F (E) F7 (A) B♭ (E) F7 (A) B♭ (E) F
trou - ble and in joy, the prai - ses of my
(A) B♭ (A) B♭/F (E) F (A) B♭/D (D) E♭ (Bm) Cm (E) F (A) B♭
God shall still my heart and tongue em - ploy.

2. Of His deliverance I will boast,
Till all that are distressed
From my example comfort take,
And charm their griefs to rest.

3. O magnify the Lord with me,
With me exalt His name;
When in distress to Him I called,
He to my rescue came.

4. The hosts of God encamp around
The dwellings of the just;
Deliverance He affords to all
Who on His succour trust.

5. O make but trial of his love;
Experience will decide
How blest are they, and only they,
Who in His truth confide.

6. Fear Him, ye saints, and you will then
Have nothing else to fear;
Make you His service your delight,
He'll make your wants His care.

N. Tate (1652-1715)
& N. Brady (1659-1726)
New version, 1696 based on Psalm 34.

1567. Through days of rage and wonder

(Days of rage and wonder)

Rom 2:16; 1 Cor 11:23-26; 14:25; Heb 12:1-2; 1 Jn 4:18; Rev 21:2

Steadily
Graham Kendrick
Verse
1. Through days of rage and wonder we pursue the end of time, to seize the day eternal, the reign of love divine.
2. Fixing our eyes on Jesus, we will press on day by day. This world's vain passing pleasures are not our destiny.
1st time only
Chorus
Our ancient rites of passage still are the bread and wine:
E A B7 E C♯m7 B7 E A B7 E C♯m7 B7 E A E/G♯ A E/G♯ F♯m E/G♯ A

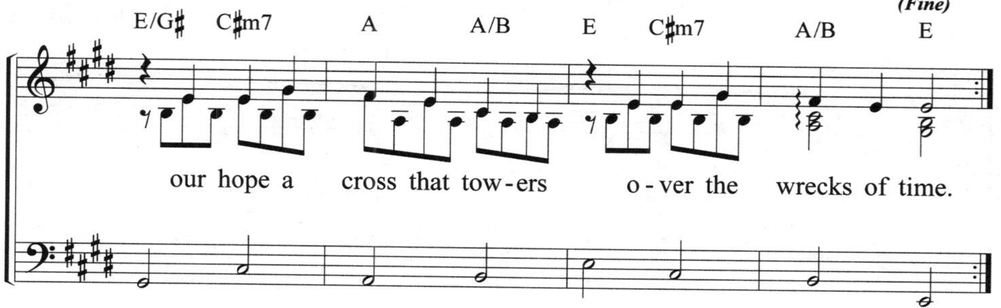
(Fine)
E/G♯ C♯m7 A A/B E C♯m7 A/B E
our hope a cross that tow-ers o-ver the wrecks of time.

3. Through days of rage and wonder, by the awesome power of prayer
   God will shake every nation, secrets will be laid bare.
   And if His light increasing casts deeper shadows here,
   Safe in His holy presence, love will cast out our fear.

4. Through days of rage and wonder, You will give us strength to stand
   And seek a heavenly city not built by human hands.
   Now is the only moment within our power to change:
   To give back in obedience while life and breath remain.

1568. Time is too short

(King of this heart)

Song 3:1-2

Matt Redman

With feeling
Verse
F♯m7
G2
1. Time is too short to say it's o-kay, to
think I can live this way, for just a-no-ther day. So I'll
search through the night for the One my heart loves, won't
stop 'til I've found You, for Lord I need to hold You close.
Chorus
A2
G
D
Be the King of this heart a-gain, be the

A2
G
D
3
A2
Lord of this life. In my soul there's a cry
G
D
Em7
D/F♯
to-day: be the King of this heart, be the
Last time to Coda
1.
G2
D.C.
2.
G2
G
King of this heart.
2. I've
Be the
F♯m7
G
light for my eyes, be the strength for my feet, be the
F♯m7
G
love of my soul, be my ev - 'ry-thing. Be my

F♯m7
G
day and my night, when I wake, when I sleep, un-di-
F♯m7
G
D.S.
Coda
G2
D
vi-ded my heart will be. Be the
al-ways
verse 2
F♯m7
G2
I've stood in the de-sert and thirs-ted for You, I've
F♯m7
G2
run through the ci-ty now I won't let go: I'm
F♯m7
G2
throw-ing my-self on Your mer - cy, O God, You
F♯m7
G2
say it's all or no-thing I'm say-ing: 'Je-sus have it all.' Be the

If we confess our sins, He is faithful and just and will forgive us our sins and purify us from all unrighteousness.

1 JOHN 1:9

1569. To Him we come

Tune: LIVING LORD

Mk 16:15; Jn 1:1; 14:6; 15:15; Acts 17:28; Phil 3:8; 4:13; 1 Pet 2:4; 1 Jn 3:2

Patrick Appleford

D G/A A7 D D/F♯ D7 G Em7
1. To Him we come - Je - sus Christ our Lord,
A A/G D/F♯ Bm E9 Asus4 A7
God's own liv - ing Word, His dear Son:
G A D/F♯ Bm G A F♯m B7
in Him there is no east and west, in Him all na - tions shall be blest;
Em Gm/E D/A B7 Em A7 D
to all He of - fers peace and rest - lov - ing Lord!

SoF3

2. In Him we live -
Christ our strength and stay,
Life and Truth and Way,
Friend divine:
His power can break the chains of sin,
Still all life's storms without, within,
Help us the daily fight to win -
Living Lord!

3. For Him we go -
Soldiers of the cross,
Counting all things loss,
Him to know;
Going to every land and race,
Preaching to all redeeming grace,
Building His church in every place -
Conquering Lord!

4. With Him we serve -
His the work we share
With saints everywhere,
Near and far;
One in the task that faith requires,
One in the zeal that never tires,
One in the hope His love inspires -
Coming Lord!

5. Onward we go -
Faithful, bold and true,
Called His will to do
Day by day
Till, at the last, with joy we'll see
Jesus in glorious majesty;
Live with Him through eternity -
Reigning Lord!

James E. Seddon (1915-83)

1570. # To walk with You
(All I ask of You)

Capo 3 (D)

Lev 11:45; Mic 6:8; Mt 5:16; Jn 10:3; Jn 13:34; Gal 2:20

Matthew Bridle

Steadily
Verse
C(A)
F(D)
To walk with You, to know You near me,
C(A)
F(D)
to know Your voice, to hear You call me;
F/A(D)
B♭(G)
F/A(D)
C(A)
this is all I ask of You.
B♭/C(G)
C(A)
F(D)
To be Your son, to feel You hold me,
Dm(Bm)
C(A)
F(D)
to know Your grace, to know You love me;

F/A(D) B♭(G) F/A(D) C(A)
This is all I ask of You.
Chorus
F(D) B♭(G) C(A)
To be Your joy, to give You glo - ry;
B♭/C(G) F(D) B♭(G) C(A)
to live with You, for-ev - er with me.
Am7(F♯m) Dm7(Bm) Gm7(Em) C(A)
To love You, Lord, as You have loved me, is
B♭(G) Gm7(Em) F/C(D) C(A) F(D)
all I ask of You, all I ask of You.

2. To love Your ways, to see Your beauty,
To seek Your face with all that's in me;
This is all I ask of You.
To worship You, to be Yours only,
To cry Your name, my Lord Almighty;
This is all I ask of You,
This is all I ask of You.

3. To live Your life, to serve You justly,
To tell Your word, to show Your mercy;
This is all I ask of You.
To bring Your light to those who know me,
To be like You, as You are holy;
This is all I ask of You,
This is all I ask of You.

1571. To You, King Jesus

Ps 104:1; Mt 28:18; Jn 1:1; Acts 2:4; 1 Cor 9:24; Eph 1:20; Heb 2:9; Rev 1:14-18; 5:9; 7:9; 21:9

Nathan Fellingham
Strongly, with a half time feel
Verse
E C D
1. To You, King Je - sus, we sing our song,
E C D
the First and the Last, the liv - ing One.
Am7 Em7 D/F♯
With eyes like fire, and feet like bronze, Your face shines brigh-
G Am7 Em7 Dsus4
ter than the sun, all cre - a - tion speaks Your name.
D Chorus G D/G Em7
Je - sus, Son of God, You stand in all au-

C
Em7
Dsus4
D
tho - ri - ty, and at Your name dark - ness flees. Oh,
G
D/G
Em7
Je - sus, liv - ing Word, reign - ing at the
C
G/B
Em7
C
Fa - ther's right hand, and You're clothed with ma - je - sty and
Last time to Coda
Am7
G/B
Dsus4 D
Bridge
C
pow - er. And we now stand at Your side,
Em7
C
a peo - ple cho - sen as Your bride. You've filled us with

Em7
D/F♯ G
C
the Spi - rit's pow'r, this is the hour. So in Your strength
Em7
I'll run this race, co-vered by Your dai - ly grace,
C
G/B
pres-sing on to win the prize, till the day
C
that You re - turn, and e-v'ry tribe and e - v'ry tongue
D.S. al Coda
G/B
Dsus4
D
will sing:
Coda
E

2. To You, King Jesus, we give our hearts,
For You have come to us with Your great love.
You suffered death, went to the grave,
But now You're crowned with glory.
All Your people speak Your name.

1572.
To You, O Lord
Ps 25:1-8
Capo 3 (D)
Graham Kendrick
Gently
Verse
F(D) C/F(A) B♭/F(G) F(D)
1. To You, O Lord, I lift up my soul,
C/F(A) B♭(G) F(D) C/F(A)
in You I trust, O my God. Do not let me
B♭/F(G) F2(D) 3rd time to Coda F(D) C/F(A)
be put to shame, nor let my e-ne-mies
B♭(G)
tri-umph o-ver me.
Chorus
F(D) C/F(A) B♭/F(G) B♭/C(G) C(A)
No one whose hope is in You will e-ver be put to shame;

F(D)
C/F(A)
B♭maj7(G)
C7sus4(A)
C(A)
that's why my eyes are on You, O Lord.
Dm(Bm)
Dm/C(Bm)
Dm/B(Bm)
Sur-round me, de-fend me, O, how I need You.
B♭(G)
Gm7(Em)
B♭/C(G)
C7(A)
To You I lift up my soul, to You I lift up my soul.
F(D)
C/F(A)
B♭/F(G)
F(D)
C/F(A)
B♭/F(G)
D.C.
To end
Fine
F(D)
Coda
F(D)
C(A)
B♭2(G)
or my re-bel-li-ous ways.

Ac-cord-ing to Your love, re -
B♭/F(G) F(D)
B♭(G)
mem - ber me, ac-cord-ing to Your love,
D.S al Fine
Gm7(Em)
C7sus4(A) C7(A) C7sus4(A) C7(A)
for You are good, O Lord.

2. Show me Your ways and teach me Your paths,
Guide me in truth, lead me on;
For You're my God, You are my Saviour,
My hope is in You each moment of the day.

3. Remember, Lord, Your mercy and love
That ever flow from of old.
Remember not the sins of my youth
Or my rebellious ways.

1573. # Ubi caritas

(Living charity)

1 Jn 4:8

Taizè
Music: Jacques Berthier (1923-1994)

F C Dm B♭ D G C
U - bi - ca - ri - tas et a - mor,
Liv - ing cha - ri - ty and stead - fast love,
F C Dm Gm C F
u - bi - ca - ri - tas De - us i - bi est.
liv - ing cha - ri - ty shows the heart of God.

1574. Unto us a boy is born

Is 9:6; Mt 2:16; Lk 2:7; Rev 1:8

Tune PUER NOBIS

German carol melody
Arr. Geoffrey Shaw (1879-1943)

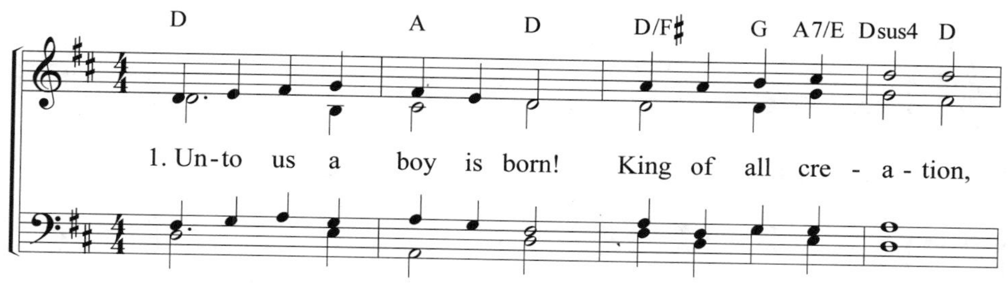
D A D D/F♯ G A7/E Dsus4 D
1. Un-to us a boy is born! King of all cre - a - tion,

D/F♯ G A Bm G A F♯m Bm D/F♯ G D/A A7 Bm Em
came He to a world for-lorn, the Lord of e-v'ry na - tion, the

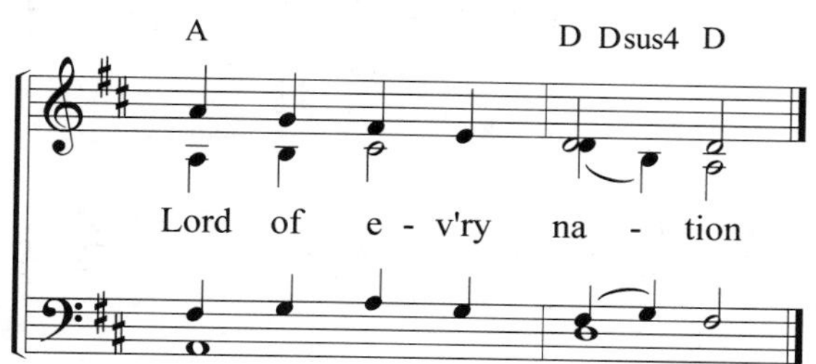
A D Dsus4 D
Lord of e - v'ry na - tion

2. Cradled in a stall was He
With sleepy cows and asses;
But the very beasts could see
That He all men surpasses,
That He all men surpasses.

3. Herod then with fear was filled:
'A Prince,' he said, 'in Jewry!'
All the little boys he killed
At Bethlem in his fury,
At Bethlem in his fury.

4. Now may Mary's Son who came
So long ago to love us,
Lead us all with hearts aflame
Unto the joys above us,
Unto the joys above us.

5. Alpha and Omega He!
Let the organ thunder,
While the choir with peals of glee
Doth rend the air asunder,
Doth rend the air asunder!

Latin (15th cent.)
Tr. Percy Dearmer (1867-1936)

1575. Wait for the Lord

Lk 21:28, 36

Taizé
Music: Jacques Berthier (1923-1994)

Voices
Piano
p
f
Em C Am6 B
Wait for the Lord, whose day is near.
Em D G Am B Em
Wait for the Lord: keep watch, take heart.

1576. We are called to be prophets to this nation

Capo 3 (G)

(Miracle in my heart)

Steadily

Mt 5:13, 16; Lk 4:18; Rom 12:1

Brian Houston

Verse
B♭(G)
E♭(C)
1. We are called to be pro - phets to this na - tion,
to be the word of God in ev - 'ry si - tu - a - tion; change my
Cm(Am)
F(D)
heart, change my heart to - day.
Who'll be the salt if the
salt should lose its fla - vour? Who'll be the salt if the salt

E♭(C)
Cm(Am)
should lose its fla - vour? Change my heart, change my
F(D)
B♭(G)
E♭(C)
B♭(G)
heart to - day.
Bridge
Dm(Bm)
E♭(C)
Dm(Bm)
Lord, loose the chains of op - pres - sion; Lord, set the cap - tives
E♭(C)
Dm(Bm)
E♭(C)
free. Lord, fill my heart with com - pas - sion:
F(D)
Fsus4(D)
F(D)
Fsus4(D)
shine Your light, shine Your light,
F(D)
Fsus4(D)
F(D)
Chorus
shine Your light through me. Work a

B♭(G)
E♭(C)
mi - ra - cle in my heart, work a
B♭(G)
E♭(C)
mi - ra - cle in my heart, work a
Gm(Em)
Dm(Bm)
E♭(C)
F(D)
mi - ra - cle in my heart, O Lord,
Fsus4(D)
F(D)
B♭(G)
E♭(C)
to - day.
B♭(G)
E♭(C)
D.C.
Last time
B♭(G)
Fine

2. Lord, take all my lies, and take all of my greed;
Let me be a sacrifice for those who are in need.
Change my heart, change my heart today.
Lord, without Your power it's all just good intentions;
Lord, without Your grace who could find redemption?
Change my heart, change my heart today.

1577. We are heirs of God Almighty

(Trinity hymn)
Capo 3 (G)
Deut 32:9-10; Mt 5:14; Jn 14:16; 15:5; Gal 5:22; Eph 1:4, 13-14; Phil 1:6, 10-11; 3:10; Titus 2:11-12
Tune: AUSTRIA
Franz Joseph Haydn (1732-1809)
Triumphantly
E♭(C) B♭(G) E♭(C) B♭7(G) E♭(C) A♭(F) E♭/G (C) B♭ (G) E♭(C)
1. We are heirs of God Al - migh - ty, ap - ple of the
(Dm) Fm F7(D) B♭(G) E♭(C) B♭(G) E♭(C) B♭7(G) E♭(C)
Fa - ther's eye; free, for - gi - ven, loved, ac - cep - ted,
A♭(F) E♭(C) B♭(G) E♭(C) (Dm) Fm F7(D) B♭(G)
clothed in righ - teous - ness di - vine. Cho - sen to be
E♭(C) B♭(G) Gm(Em) Cm(Am) F7(D) B♭(G)
pure and blame - less from be - fore the world be - gan;

SoF3

E♭(C) A♭(F) E♭(C) A♭(F) B♭(G) E♭(C) B♭(G) E♭(C) A♭(F)
grace for e - v'ry si - tu - a - tion, shel - tered in the

E♭(C) B♭7(G) E♭(C)
Fa - ther's hand.

2. We have Christ at work within us,
Shaping us to be like Him;
Resurrection power sustaining
Freedom from the snares of sin.
Saying no to flesh desires,
Saying yes to righteous ways;
Filled with passion and with power,
Lights that burn in darkened days.

3. We've the Spirit without measure,
Helper, Comforter and Guide;
One who brings the gifts of heaven,
One who comes to walk beside.
Taste of heaven's endless pleasure,
Guarantee of what's to come;
Causing fruit to grow in action,
Bringing glory to the Son.

Stuart Townend

1578. We are joined by angels

Rev 4:8; 15:4

(Joined by angels)

Lara Martin

Gently
Emaj7
Verse
Esus4
Emaj7
3
1. We are joined by an - gels, our pur-pose the

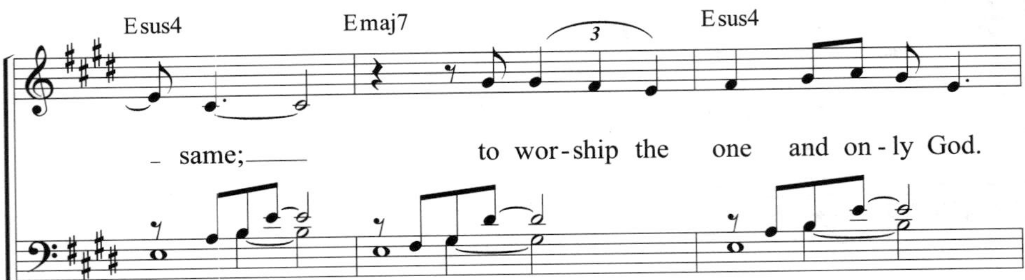
Esus4
Emaj7
3
Esus4
same; to wor-ship the one and on-ly God.

(v.2)
3
Emaj7
Esus4
A lit-tle piece of hea-ven is in this place.

Chorus
A
E
And we cry to-ge-ther: Ho-ly, ho - ly,

A
E
for there is no o-ther like You, Lord.
A
C♯m7
We de-clare to-ge-ther: You are awe - some,
A2 A
You are to be feared, ho-noured and re-vered,
F♯m7
1.
E
2.
E
for You are the Lord.
the Lord.

2. We are joined by angels,
With one voice we sing,
As we lift our hands to honour You,
In worship, the angels extend their wings.

1579. We bow our hearts

(Give us clean hands)

Capo 1 (G)

Deut 7:5; Ps 24:3-4; 119:37; Is 17:7; Phil 2:3, 10

Charlie Hall

Prayerfully

A♭ (G)
E♭ (D)
A♭/C (G/B)
We bow our hearts, we bend our knees;
D♭ (C)
A♭ (G)
D♭/E♭ (C/D)
A♭ (G)
O Spir-it, come make us hum-ble. We turn our eyes
E♭ (D)
A♭/C (G/B)
D♭ (C)
from e-vil things; O Lord, we cast down our i-
A♭ (G)
dols. Give us clean hands, give us pure hearts;
E♭ (D)
A♭ (G)
let us not lift our souls to an-

D♭
(C)
A♭
(G)
oth - er. Give us clean hands, give us pure hearts;
E♭
(D)
Fm
(Em)
E♭
(D)
let us not lift our souls to an -
A♭
(G)
oth - er. And O God, let us be a gen - er - a - tion that seeks,
E♭
(D)
Fm
(Em)
E♭
(D)
that seeks Your face, O God of Ja -
A♭
(G)
- cob. And O God, let us be a gen - er - a - tion that seeks,

E♭
(D)
Fm
(Em)
E♭
(D)
D♭
(C)
that seeks Your face, O God of Ja - cob.
A♭
(G)

1580.
We come in Your name
(You have been lifted)
Eph 2:6, 8; Phil 2:9; Col 1:16; Rev 4:8-9, 11; 5:12; 17:14; 19:16
Kate Simmonds & Mark Edwards
With energy
G
Verse
G
We come in Your name, for all things
that was slain for our sins
C/G
Em7
You have made, and by Your word all
lives to reign, the Lord of all, Name
Bm7
C
1.
things You sus - tain. The Lamb
a - bove all names.
2.
G/B
We have been saved by faith in - to Your glo -
C
Em7
G2/B
rious Name, and this a gift of God, free-ly gi - ven us.

C
Am7
G/B
Now all our sins are gone, de-fea - ted at
C
Em7
the cross, and we now live in You, raised
Em7/D
Cmaj7
Dsus4
D
G
Chorus
C/G
with You by the-pow - er of God. You have been lif-
G
Em7
Am
ted to the high - est place, and You now live and rule
E7/B
Am/C
C
G
C/G
for-e - ver. We come to bring
G
Em7
Am
to You the high - est praise, for You are King of kings

E7/B
Am/C
G/D
D♯dim
Em
– for - e - ver: Son of God,
F
C
1.
2.
G
Je - sus! We come Holy is
D/F♯
Em7
Am7
– the Lamb, wor - thy of glo - ry,
G/B
C
G
wor - thy of ho - nour. High and lif-
D/F♯
Em7
Am7
ted up, and sea - ted in ma-
G/B
C
G/D D
G
je - sty, Your throne will last for - e - ver more.

1581. We could watch You from afar

Heb 12:21, 28

(Rejoice with trembling)

Moderately
Matt Redman
Verse
Bm7(♭5) E Am
1. We could watch You from a-far, and for-e-
D/F♯ G A7/C♯
-ver be a-mazed at how glo - ri-ous You are.
D Bm7(♭5) E
Yet You've drawn us close to You,
Am D/F♯ G
where the won - der's great - er still, and You o-
A7/C♯ D C2
ver-whelm us, God.
Chorus
And we re-joice

G
D/F♯
Bm7(♭5)
with trem - bling in our hearts, bring
C/E
C
C/B
Am7
G/B
C2
You a song of re - ve-rence and love. Je - sus,
how good, how great You are, and
Am7
G/B
D.C.
we re-joice with trem-bl-ing be-fore Your throne.

2. Who could fully voice the praise
Of the God of endless days,
Tell a fraction of Your worth?
For we only sing in part
Of the grace of who You are;
Just an echo, just a glimpse.

1582. We fall down

Rev 4:8, 10

Intensely
Chris Tomlin
Verse
E B C♯m A2
mf
We fall down, we lay our crowns at the feet of Je-
F♯m addB E B C♯m
-sus. The great-ness of mer-cy and love, at the feet
A2 A/B B E2/G♯ A E/G♯ F♯m7 E2/G♯
Chorus
f
of Je - sus. And we cry ho - ly, ho - ly, ho - ly. And we cry
A E/G♯ F♯m7 E/B B A E/G♯
ho - ly, ho - ly, ho - ly. And we cry ho - ly, ho - ly, ho-
F♯m7 Bsus4 1. E Esus4 E Esus4/D 2. E
-ly is the Lamb.

1583. We have a gospel to proclaim

Mt 28:6, 19-20; Lk 2:7; Jn 1:11, 14; Acts 2:33; Rom 5:8; 10:9

Capo 3 (G)
Tune: FULDA

From W. Gardiner's *Sacred Melodies,* 1815

(G) Bb (D) F (Em) Gm (C) Eb (G) Bb/F (D) F7 (G) Bb (G) Bb/D (D) F/C (A) C/Bb
1. We have a go - spel to pro - claim, good news for
(D) F/A (Bm) Dm (G) Bb (D) F/C (A) C (D) F (D7) F7/A (G) Bb (D) F7/C
all through - out the earth; the go - spel of a
(G) Bb/D (C) Eb (A7) C7/E (D) F (D♯dim) F♯dim (Em) Gm (Am) Cm/Eb (G) Bb/F (D) F7 (G) Bb
Sa - viour's name: we sing His glo - ry, tell His worth.

2. Tell of His birth at Bethlehem,
Not in a royal house or hall
But in a stable dark and dim:
The Word made flesh, a light for all.

3. Tell of His death at Calvary,
Hated by those He came to save;
In lonely suffering on the cross
For all He loved, his life He gave.

4. Tell of that glorious Easter morn:
Empty the tomb, for He was free.
He broke the power of death and hell
That we might share His victory.

5. Tell of His reign at God's right hand,
By all creation glorified;
He sends His Spirit on His Church
To live for Him, the Lamb who died.

6. Now we rejoice to name Him King:
Jesus is Lord of all the earth;
This gospel-message we proclaim:
We sing his glory, tell His worth.

Edward Joseph Burns

1584. We have this treasure in jars of clay

Mt 5:16; 2 Cor 2:14; 4:7-8; Phil 2:15

Doug Horley

Rhythmically
D
Verse
D/C♯
mf We have this trea - sure in jars of_ clay._
Bm7
A7sus4
For all our fra - il - ty, You have en - trus - ted us
D
D/C♯
Bm7
to shine Your good - ness_ and life through - out the na - tions.
A7sus4
D
D/C♯
We may be pressed hard from e - ve - ry side,_
Bm7
A7sus4
but we will not be crushed, Your hope will streng - then us.

D
D/C♯
And when the hard times squeeze so_ tight,_
Bm7
A7sus4
may they re-lease more of the fra-grance of Je-sus. And
Chorus
D
D/C♯
Bm7
f let Your glo-ry shine,_ O let Your glo-ry shine._
A7sus4
D
D/C♯
_ O let Your glo-ry shine_ through our lives,_
Bm7
A7sus4
Last time to Coda
D
_ by Your grace,_ may we o - ver-flow with Je - sus.

D/C♯
Bm7
A7sus4
D
May we shine like,
C2
1.-3.
G
D
may we shine like, may we shine like stars in the dark-ness.
4.
G
D
D.S. al Coda
Coda
D
may we shine like stars. And

1585. Well, I call upon my Father

(Creator)

Jn 13:8; Eph 2:8

Ken Riley

Steadily
A
E
B
B2
1. Well, I call
Verse
upon my Father in the name
of Christ Your Son,
let the streams
of Your forgiveness come upon
me as a flood.
Chorus
I give my love

E
B
Bsus4
B
to my Cre-a - tor,
re-veal my
A
E
B
Bsus4
heart
un-to my
God,
I bring my
A
E
B
life
be-fore the Heal - er,
Bsus4
F♯m7
E
for I know in You my shame will be thrown
B
down.
1.2.
A
E
B
A
E

B
2. For with sin
3. A
You're wash-ing me down,
E
B
A
E
Last time to Coda
B
You're wash ing - me down,
I feel You, Lord,
A
wash - ing me down.
Coda
B
A
E
B
I give my love
to my Cre - a - tor.

2. For with sin there's separation,
Yet by grace through faith I'm saved;
Can You hear my spirit crying,
'Come and wash my sin away.'

3. Well, I call upon my Father
In the name of Christ Your Son,
Now I've tasted Your forgiveness;
My redemption through Your blood.

1586. We look to You, Almighty God

Capo 3 (D)

Is 6:1; Mt 6:10; Jn 17:22; Rev 11:15; 22:16

With energy

Alan Rose

F(D) *Verse* Gm7(Em)

1. We look to You,__ Al - migh - ty God,__ You are high_

Csus4(A)

_ and lif - ted up,__ You are sov - 'reign o - ver all_

Gm7(Em) C(A) F(D)

_ that You__ have made.__ O - ver king-

Gm7(Em)

doms and__ their kings,__ You are Lord__ of ev - 'ry - thing,_

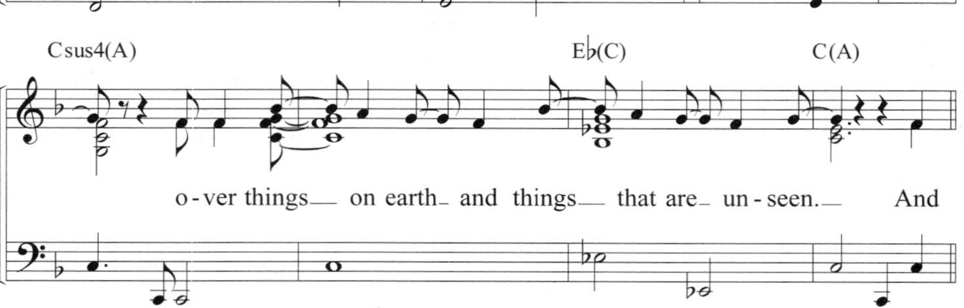
Csus4(A)
Eb(C)
C(A)
o - ver things__ on earth_ and things__ that are_ un - seen.__ And

Chorus
F(D)
F/A(D)
B♭(G)
F/A(D)
we re - joice in You,— we put our trust in You,— and
Gm(Em)
Gm/F(Em)
C(A)
with one voice we give— You praise.—
Sing-ing,
F(D)
F/A(D)
B♭(G)
F/A(D)
let Your king-dom come,— and let Your will be done,— and
Gm(Em)
Gm/F(Em)
C(A)
F(D)
through Your peo-ple make— Your glo - ry known.

2. Lord, we come to seek Your face,
Let Your glory fill this place,
We are hungry for Your presence in this hour.
To behold You as You are,
Heaven's bright and morning Star,
Let our hearts be changed,
And let Your kingdom come!

1587. We're gonna sing like the saved

(Sing like the saved)

Ps 66:1; 100:4; Eph 5:20; 1 Thess 5:18

Matt Redman

Energetic and funky
D7
G7
We're gon - na sing like the saved.
We're gon - na sing like the saved.
We're gon - na sing like the saved.
Last time to Coda
We're gon-na sing like the saved.
It is our du-
ty and our joy,
in ev - 'ry time and ev - 'ry place,

E7
A7
Your gates we'll en - ter to give thanks,
E7
A7
G
Your courts we'll run in - to with praise.
D.C.
Coda
D7

2. A joyful noise we will make . . .

3. You put Your joy in our hearts . . .

4. We're gonna dance like the saved . . .

Before they call I will answer; while they are still speaking I will hear.

ISAIAH 65:24

1588. We're longing for Your presence

(Open the heavens)

Capo 3 (D)

Is 64:1; Hos 6:2-3; Heb 10:20; 12:27

Stuart Townend

Steadily
Verse
F(D)
(Men - We're long-ing for_Your pre - sence, (we're long-ing for_Your pre-sence,) we're
Women echo) tas - ted of_Your good - ness, (we've tas - ted of_Your good-ness,) we've
B♭/F(G)
wait - ing on_ Your pro - mise, (we're wait - ing on_ Your pro - mise,) that
wad - ed in_ Your ri - ver, (we've wad - ed in_ Your ri - ver,) yet
F(D)
You will flood_ the na - tion (that You will flood_ the na - tion) with
still the streets_ are de - serts, (yet still the streets_ are de - serts,) and
B♭/F(G)
mer - cy and_ with jus - tice. (with
men cry out_ in hun - ger. (and
1.
mer-cy and_with jus-tice.) We've
2.
men cry out_ in hun - ger.) Let
C(A)
sin - ners find_ for - give - ness, (Let

B♭(G)
sin-ners find for give-ness,) the lone-ly find a fa-mi-ly; (the
C(A)
lone ly find a fa-mi-ly;) cause lips that mock and curse You (cause
E♭(C)
lips that mock and curse You) to sing of Your sal-va-tion. (to
B♭/D(G)
C(A)
F(D)
Chorus
sing of Your sal-va-tion.)
(All)
O-pen the hea-
B♭(G)
F(D)
Csus4(A)
C(A)
B♭(G)
-vens and come down.
F(D)
B♭(G)
F(D)
Csus4(A)
Come in Your glo-ry and Your pow'r.

C(A)
Gm7(Em)
C(A)
Send Your re - vi - val rain:
Gm7(Em)
E♭maj7(C) C/E(A) B♭(G) F(D)
re - plen - ish this land / heart a - gain!
O - pen the hea -
B♭(G)
F(D)
Csus4(A)
C(A)
B♭(G)
- vens and come down,
come
F(D)
down!

2. We want a way of living *(Men - Women echo)*
That ushers in Your kingdom:
Faith, purity and passion,
And love without condition.
Come shake the ground on which we stand,
Till all we need is found in You;
Then pour the fire into our hearts
To do the work that You would do.

1589. Were you there?

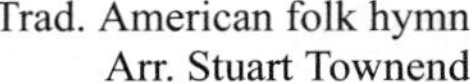
Jn 19:18, 42; Acts 2:32

Trad. American folk hymn
Arr. Stuart Townend

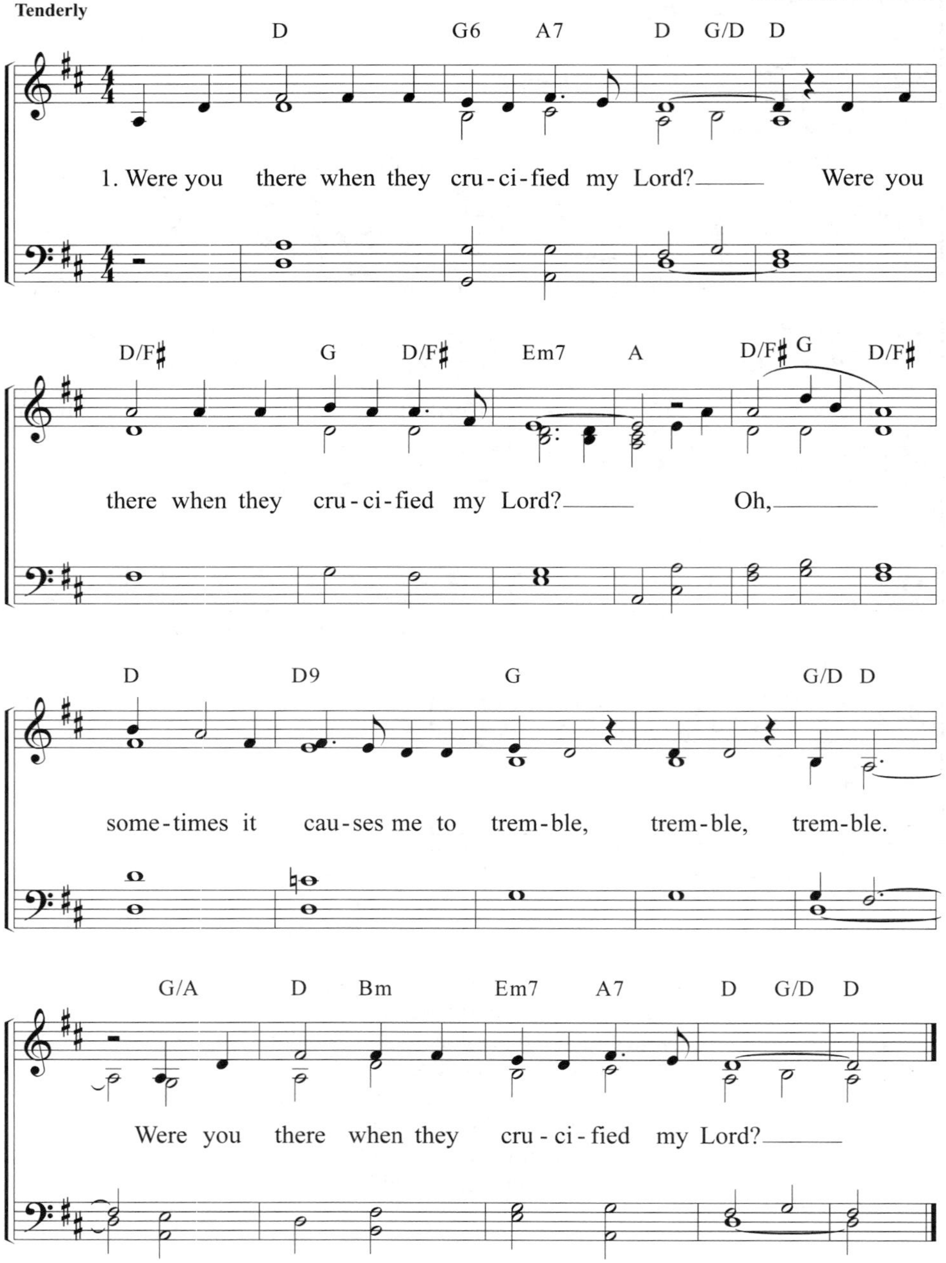

Tenderly

1. Were you there when they cru-ci-fied my Lord?
Were you there when they cru-ci-fied my Lord?
Oh,
some-times it cau-ses me to trem-ble, trem-ble, trem-ble.
Were you there when they cru-ci-fied my Lord?

2. Were you there when they nailed Him to the tree?
Were you there when they nailed Him to the tree?
Oh, sometimes it causes me to tremble, tremble, tremble.
Were you there when they nailed Him to the tree?

3. Were you there when they laid Him in the tomb?
Were you there when they laid Him in the tomb?
Oh, sometimes it causes me to tremble, tremble, tremble.
Were you there when they laid Him in the tomb?

4. Were you there when they raised Him from the dead?
Were you there when they raised Him from the dead?
Oh, sometimes it causes me to tremble, tremble, tremble.
Were you there when they raised Him from the dead?

1590. We see the Lord
(Everything cries holy)

Is 6:1, 3; Rev 4:8, 10; 5:6

Robin Mark

Steadily

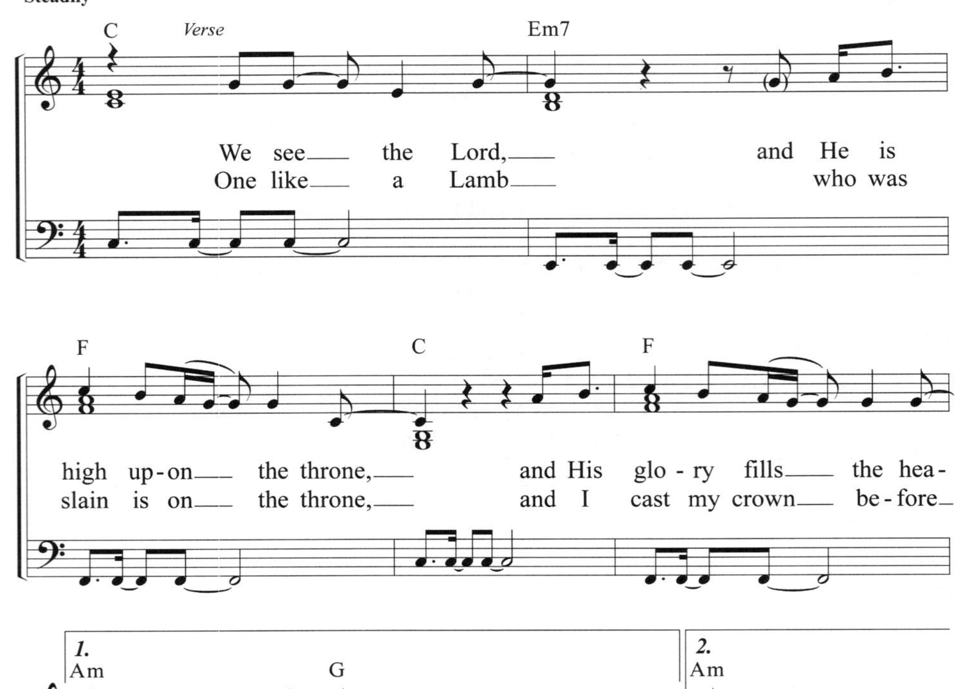

C
Verse
Em7
We see the Lord, and He is
One like a Lamb who was
F
C
F
high up-on the throne, and His glo-ry fills the hea-
slain is on the throne, and I cast my crown be-fore

1.
Am
G
2.
Am
-vens and the earth.
You, and bow

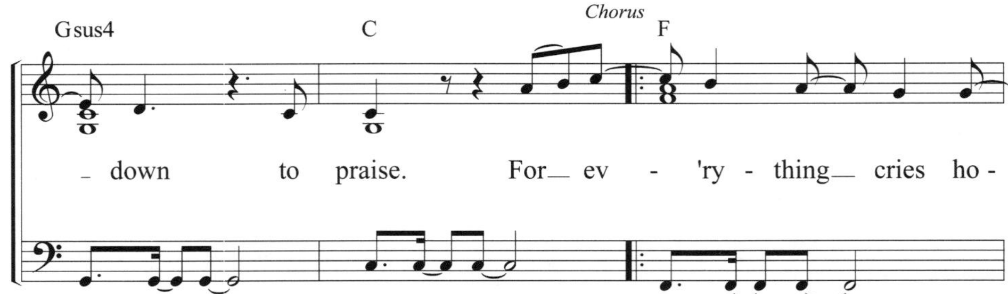

Gsus4
C
Chorus
F
down to praise. For ev-'ry-thing cries ho-

C/E
Dm7
C/E
ly, oh — ev - 'ry - thing — cries ho - ly, oh — ev-
F
Am7
Gsus4
'ry - thing — cries ho - ly to You, — Lord.
1.
G
2.
G
D.C.
3.
C
Oh — ev -

1591. We've come to praise You

Rom 8:32; Rev 19:11

Capo 3(D)
Gospel feel
Kate Simmonds
& Stuart Townend
F7(D) B♭(G) F7(D)
We've come to praise You, 'cause You're wor - thy.
B♭(G) F7(D)
No - bo - dy like You in Your glo - ry.
B♭(G) E♭(C)
We love to praise You, 'cause You're ho - ly,
B♭/D(G) E♭(C) F7(D)
awe - some, won - der - ful, migh - ty God.
(repeat 1st time only)
(Fine)
F7(D) B♭/F (G) F(D)
Dm(Bm) B♭(G)
And e - v'ry - thing that You do comes from a heart

E♭(C)
– of love and a hand of mer - cy;
F(D)
Dm(Bm)
G7sus4(E)
for You are faith - ful and true, work-ing all things
G7(E)
B♭(G)
F/A(D)
B♭(G)
Gm7(Em)
1.
D.C.
– for good for those who love You.
2.
A♭maj7(F)
E♭maj7(C)
– For if God in love did not spare His Son, but He gave
A♭maj7(F)
E♭maj7(C)
– Him up for His cho - sen ones, how much more

B♭maj7(G)
Fmaj7(D)
Dm7(Bm) Am7(F♯m) Gm7(Em)
will He free-ly give to us who call up-on His name,
Dm7(Bm) Am7(F♯m) Gm7(Em)
who call up-on His name, who
Dm7(Bm) Am7(F♯m) Gm7(Em)
Dm7(Bm) Gm7(Em) B♭/C(G)
call up-on His name, who call up-on His name?
D.C. al fine

1592. We will seek Your face, Almighty God

(Touching heaven, changing earth)

2 Chron 7:14; Ps 126:5; Lk 9:62; Jn 4:38; 1 Cor 9:24

With enegy

Reuben Morgan

Intro
G C Em D G C Em D
Verse
G C D G C
1. We will seek Your face, Al-migh - ty God,
D Em C D
turn and pray for You to heal our land.
Em C D G C D
Fa-ther, let re-vi - val start in us,
G C D Em C
then ev-'ry heart will know

Chorus
D
Em
Dsus4 D G/B C
C
Your king - dom come.
Lift-ing up the name
D
Em7
C
D
Em7
of the Lord
in
pow-er
and
in
u - ni - ty,
Last time to Coda
C
D
Em7
C
G/B
D
we will see the na - tions turn,
touch-ing hea - ven, chang-
Em7
D
C
G/B
D
ing earth,
touch - ing
hea - ven,
chang -
1.
G
C
Em7
D
D.S.
ing earth.

2.
Am7
G/B
C
Send re - vi - val, send re - vi - val, send re - vi-val to
1. G
D
Am7
2. Dsus4
D
D.S.S.
us. Send re - us.
Coda
C
G/B
D
Em7
Repeat as required
touch - ing hea - ven, chang - ing earth,
C
G/B
D
G
touch-ing hea - ven, chang - ing earth.

2. Never looking back, we'll run the race;
Giving You our lives, we'll gain the prize.
We will take the harvest given us,
Though we sow in tears, we'll reap in joy.

The Spirit of the Sovereign Lord is on me, because the Lord has anointed me to preach good news to the poor.

ISAIAH 61:1

1593. What a day to be alive

(This is our time)

Ps 34:8; 2 Cor 6:2

Lara Martin

Gently, with pace
D
A/C♯
What a day to be a-live,
what a time to live my
Bm7
Bm/A
G
life,
to have a de - sti - ny and call,
A7sus4
A
and see it day by day un - fold.
What a day to know You,
D
A/C♯
Bm7
Lord,
to live and walk with - in Your love,
Bm/A
G
to see the won - drous things You've done,

A7sus4 A
and know there's great-er things to come. And we sense
G A Bm7 G
the won - der of it all, we feel the ur - gen-cy;
A Bm7 G A Bm7
there's not a day to be was - ted. God, help
G Asus4 A
Your church, help us to see.
D G D
This is our time, this is our day; now's not the time to hold back

G
D/F♯
Em7
G
or de-lay.
Dreams can live a-gain,
faith
and hope re-stored.
Em7
G
A
D
Taste and see that the Lord is good;
this is the day of sal-va-
G
D
G
D/F♯
tion,
a time to break free from con-tain - ment.
Em7
A
G
Peo - ple need,
peo - ple need the Lord.
D
D.C.

1594. What can I say?

Is 6:1; Rev 15:3

Capo 3(D)

Neil Bennetts

Steadily

Verse
F(D)
B♭/F(G)
What can I say, but 'I love You'? What can I
do, but to bow down? What can I
F(D)
B♭/F(G)
Gm7(Em)
say, but 'I praise You'? As the train of Your robe fills this tem-
do, but to wor - ship? On - ly You are the One who is wor-
C(A)
1. Gm7(Em)
C7sus4(A) C(A)
ple, as the sound of Your voice fills this place. What can I
thy, on - ly
2. Gm7(Em)
Chorus
B♭/C(G)
C(A)
You are the One who is Lord. Great is the Lord,

F(D) A(F♯) Dm(Bm) Dm7(Bm) Gm(Em)
so great is the Lord, right-eous and true God, ho-ly and pure.
Csus4(A) B♭/D(G) C/E(A) F(D) A(F♯)
I fall on my knees, con-fess-ing my need
Dm(Bm) Dm7(Bm) Gm7(Em) B♭/C(G) C7(A) F(D)
for more of Your pre - sence, Lord.

1595. What child is this?

Mt 2:11; Lk 2:5-9; Jn 1:1, 14; 19:34; Rev 17:14; 19:16

Tune: GREENSLEEVES

English trad. melody
Arr. John Stainer (1840-1901)

Em D/F♯ G D Em Am/C
1. What child is this, — who, laid to rest — on Ma - ry's lap — is
B Em D/F♯ G D
sleep - ing: whom an - gels greet — with an - thems sweet, — while
Em Am B Esus4 Em Bm G
shep - herds watch — are keep - ing? This, this — is
D Em Am/C B
Christ the King, — whom shep - herds guard — and an - gels sing:

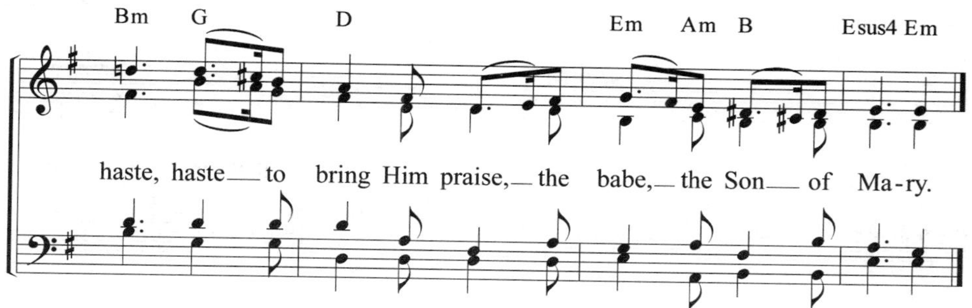

Bm G D Em Am B Esus4 Em
haste, haste — to bring Him praise, — the babe, — the Son — of Ma-ry.

2. Why lies He in such mean estate,
Where ox and ass are feeding?
Good Christian fear, for sinners here
The silent Word is pleading.
Nails, spear shall pierce Him through,
The cross be borne for me, for you.
Hail, hail the Word made flesh,
The babe, the Son of Mary.

3. So bring Him incense, gold, and myrrh,
Come, peasant, king, to own Him;
The King of kings salvation brings,
Let loving hearts enthrone Him.
Raise, raise a song on high,
The virgin sings her lullaby.
Joy, joy for Christ is born,
The babe, the Son of Mary.

William Chatterton Dix (1837-98)

1596. What love is this?

(I surrender)

Is 53:5; 61:1; Lk 4:18

Dave Bilbrough

Slow and intense

Verse

G Em7 C2 G/D Dsus4 D G Em7 C Dsus4 D

1. What love is this, that took my place? Instead of wrath, You poured Your grace on me. What can I do but simply come and worship You?

Chorus

G C2 G Em7 C2 G C2 G

I surrender, I surrender, I surrender

C2
D
1.2.
3.
G
all to You. 2. What love is this

2. What love is this
That comes to save?
Upon the cross
You bore my guilt and shame.
To You alone
I give my heart
And worship You.

3. A greater love
No man has seen;
It breaks sin's power
And sets this prisoner free.
With all I have
And all I am,
I worship You.

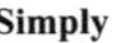

1597. What love is this?

Mt 5:16; Jn 15:15; 1 Jn 4:10; Rev 22:16

Doug Horley & Steve Whitehouse

Simply

Verse
D
G/D D
1. What love is this? The love of Je-sus, that gave its

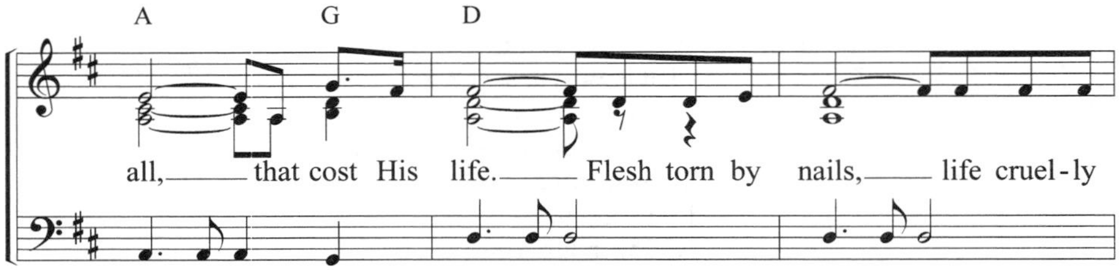
A
G
D
all, that cost His life. Flesh torn by nails, life cruel-ly

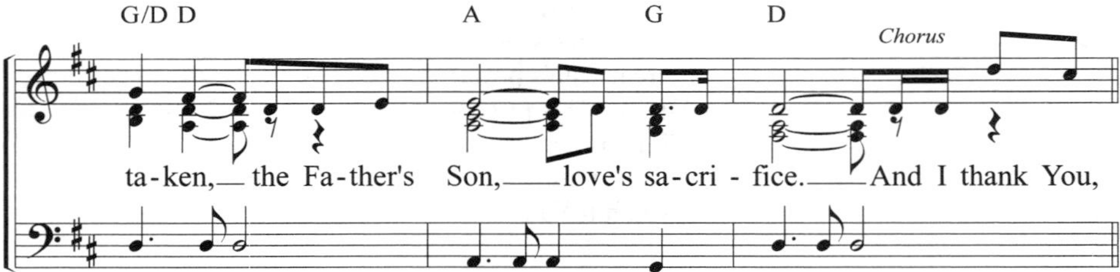
G/D D
A
G
D
Chorus
ta-ken, the Fa-ther's Son, love's sa-cri - fice. And I thank You,

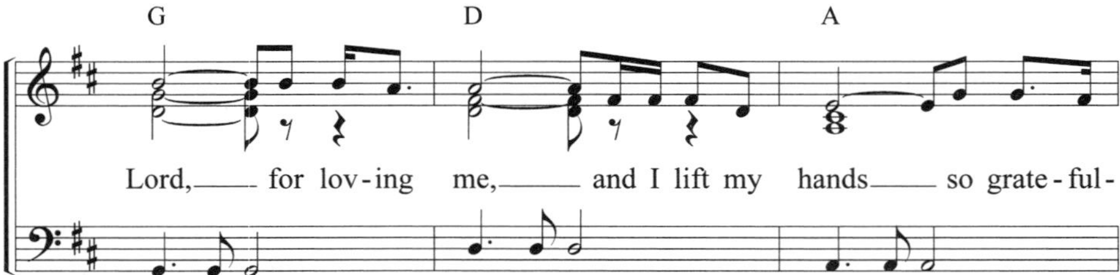
G
D
A
Lord, for lov-ing me, and I lift my hands so grate-ful-

D
G
D
ly. And I thank You, Lord, that I can be a child of

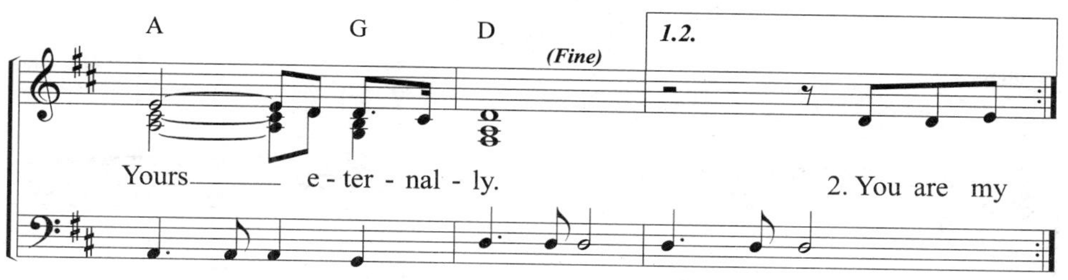
A
G
D
(Fine)
1.2.
Yours___ e - ter - nal - ly.
2. You are my

2. You are my King, You are my Saviour,
You'll always be a friend to me.
Safe in Your arms now and forever
Your love shines bright, my morning star.

3. Now let Your power rain down upon me;
Such peace and joy cascading down.
May Your love touch all those around me;
I'll shine for You, I'll shine for You.

1598. What to say, Lord?

(Every day)

Mt 5:14, 16; Gal 5:25

With life

Joel Houston

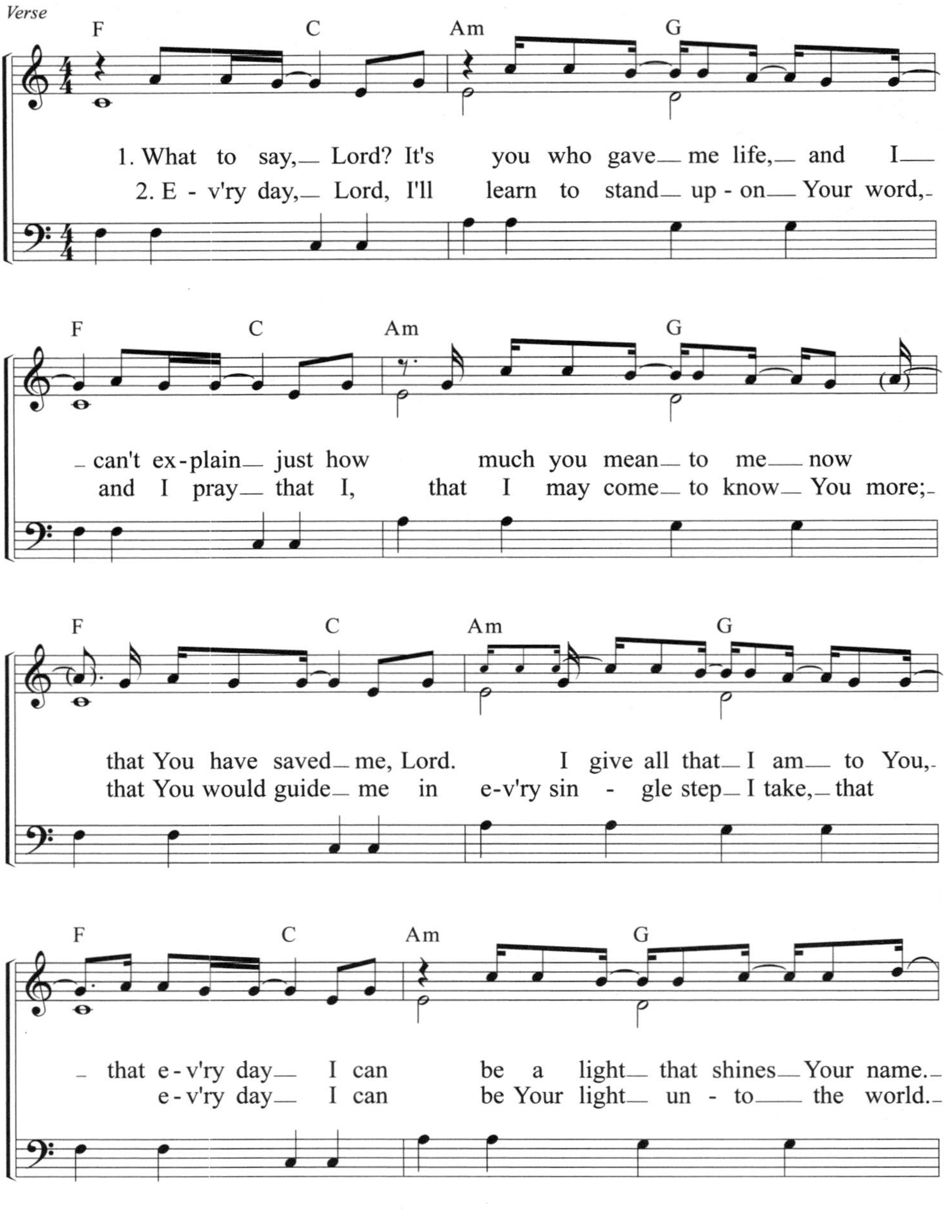

Verse

F C Am G

1. What to say, Lord? It's you who gave me life, and I can't explain just how much you mean to me now that You have saved me, Lord. I give all that I am to You, that e-v'ry day I can be a light that shines Your name.

2. E-v'ry day, Lord, I'll learn to stand up-on Your word, and I pray that I, that I may come to know You more; that You would guide me in e-v'ry sin-gle step I take, that e-v'ry day I can be Your light un-to the world.

1.
F C Am G F C Am G F C
2. Chorus
C F Am G C F
Ev-'ry day, it's You I'll live for, ev-'ry day, I'll
Last time to Coda
Am G C F Am G
fol-low af-ter You. E-v'ry day, I'll walk with You, my
C F Am G
Lord. (It's)
Bridge
C F
You I live for, e-
Am G C F Am G
-v'ry day, it's You I live for e-v'ry day, it's

D.S. al Coda

C F Am G C F Am G
You I live for, e - v'ry day.
Coda
Am G N.C.
walk with You, it's You I live for e - v'ry day.

1599. What wisdom once devised the plan?

(The wonder of the cross)

Steadily

Rom 1:17; 3:21, 24-25; 1 Cor 1:23-24; 2:9; Phil 3:8; 1 Pet 1:19

Bob Kauflin

Verse
A
C♯m
1. What wis - dom once de - vised the plan where

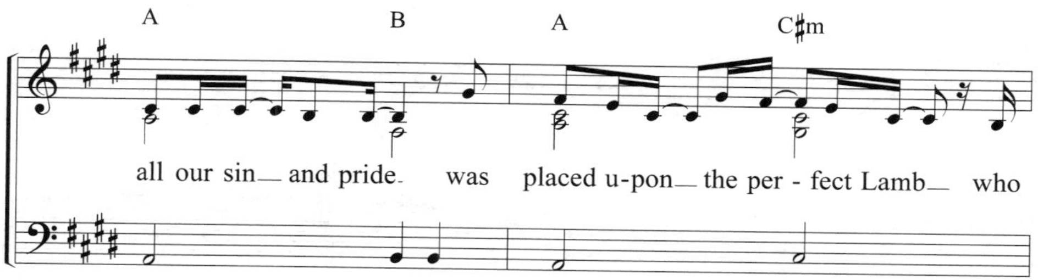
A
B
A
C♯m
all our sin and pride was placed u - pon the per - fect Lamb who

A
B
E
F♯m7
E/G♯
suf - fered, bled, and died? The wis - dom of a sov - 'reign God whose

Amaj7
Bsus4
B
great - ness will be shown, when

A
C♯m
A
B
those who cru - ci-fied Your Son re - joice a-round Your throne.
E
Chorus
B
C♯m
And oh, the glo - ry of the cross,
E
B
F♯m7
that You would send Your Son for us.
Amaj7
B
C♯m
I glad - ly count my life as loss
E
B/D♯
A
F♯m7
that I might come to know the glo-ry of, the

A
C♯m
To repeat
A B
Last time
A B
Fine
glo - ry of the cross.
2. What

2. What righteousness was there revealed
That sets the guilty free,
That justifies ungodly men
And calls the filthy clean?
A righteousness that proved to all
Your justice has been met,
And holy wrath is satisfied
Through one atoning death.

3. What mercy now has been proclaimed
For those who would believe?
A love incomprehensible,
Our minds could not conceive.
A mercy that forgives my sin
And makes me like Your Son.
And now I'm loved forever more,
Because of what You've done.

1600.

What wonder of grace

(My desire)

Ps 27:4; 85:10; 100:4; Mt 6:11; 2 Cor 12:9; Eph 1:7-8; Phil 4:12

Stuart Townend

Not too fast
D
A/C♯
1. What won - der of grace is this, what
Bm7
Em7
A7sus4
D
sto-ry of pas - sion di-vine, where judge-ment and mer-
A/C♯
F♯m7
Bm7
E/G♯
A7sus4 A7 D/F♯
cy kiss, where pow-er and love are en-twined?
G
D/F♯
Em7
G/A
No tongue can speak this glo-ry, no words ex-press the joy You
Bm7
A7sus4
A7
bring as I en - ter the courts of the King.

D
Em7
F♯7
Bm7
My de-sire is to come to this place, my de-sire
Am7
D7sus4
D9
Gmaj7
G6
is to look on Your face, per-fect in beau-ty, in truth
D2/F♯
D/F♯
Gmaj7
G6
D2/F♯
Bm7 Am7
and love, Your glo-ry shines o-ver all the earth;
Gmaj7
G6
D2/F♯
Bm7
Em7
G/A
the King who la-vi-shes grace on us is here.
Last time
D

2. Your will is my daily bread,
Enough for my plenty and need;
I'll live by the words You've said,
And follow wherever You lead.
And though my flesh may fail me,
You prove Your grace in all I do,
Lord, my heart is devoted to You.

Therefore, my dear brothers, stand firm. Let nothing move you. Always give yourselves fully to the work of the Lord, because you know that your labour in the Lord is not in vain.

1 CORINTHIANS 15:58

1601. When a knight won his spurs

Eph 6:16-17

Tune: STOWEY

English traditional melody
Arr. David Ball

With a gentle lilt

G C A D D7
1. When a knight won his spurs in the sto-ries of old, he was
G C Dsus4 D7sus4 G
gen-tle and brave, he was gal-lant and bold; with a shield on his
D/F♯ Em D D7 G C
arm and a lance in his hand, for— God and for va-lour he
Dsus4 D7 G
rode through the land.

2. No charger have I, and no sword by my side,
Yet still to adventure and battle I ride,
Though back into storyland giants have fled,
And the knights are no more and the dragons are dead.

3. Let faith be my shield and let joy be my steed
'Gainst the dragons of anger, the ogres of greed;
And let me set free, with the sword of my youth,
From the castle of darkness, the power of the truth.

Jan Struther (1901-53)

1602. When deep calls to deep

Ps 42:7; Lk 10:34; Rev 3:18

Paul Oakley

Quietly
D
Bm9
When deep calls to deep there a stir-ring in-side of me, a
thirst in my soul just to meet with You, God, I'm
Gmaj 9
D2/F♯
feel-ing that words won't des-cribe, like I'm
feel-ing the pull of Your love, like the
D
Bm9
hear-ing Your song touch-ing my spi-rit,
crash of Your waves, like the roar of Your wa-ter-falls,
Gmaj 9
1.
D
C2
cal-ling me deep-er with You. And the
draw-ing me on in-to You.
2.
D
C2
G/B
And all I know is it's You.

D
C2
G/B
And I cry out to You.
A7sus4
D
Give me oil for my wounds, give me
salve for my eyes, give me
C
G
wine for my heart, give me strength for to - day, and I
truth for the lies, give me love in my life and I
1.
Gm/B♭
2.
Gm/B♭
A7sus4
will stand. Give me
will run with You.
D.C.
To finish
D2
(When)

1603. When I come face to face

(I am in love)

Deut 6:5

Drew Land

Worshipfully
A E F♯m
p
When I come face to face with the One the angels
A D A
praise, I'm in awe, I'm a-mazed with a God
D E 𝄋 A
full of grace. It's the love You have shown
E F♯m A
that al-lows me at Your throne to a-dore,
Last time to Coda
D A D Esus4
and how I do: Fa-ther, I'm in love with You.

E A E
mf
Here I am with lift-ed hands, I give You praise
F♯m A D
and I ex-alt Your ho-ly name with all I have,
A D E
with all the strength that I can raise. And here I am
A E F♯m
once a-gain, I lift my voice with all the an-
A D A
gels 'round Your throne. I a-dore and I wor-

D
Esus4
1.
E
D.C.
ship You a-lone.
When I come
2.
E
A
E
f I am in love,
I am in love
F♯m
A
D
with all my heart, with all my soul, and all my mind
with the King and with His Son, the One who loved
A
D
1.
E
with all the strength I've e - ver known.
I am in love,
with His life and with His blood.
2.
Esus4
E
D.S. al Coda
It's the love
Coda
Esus4
rit. . . .
E

1604. When I needed a neighbour

(Were you there?)

Tune: NEIGHBOUR

Mt 25:35; Lk 10:36-37

Sydney Carter

Verse
B7/F♯
Em
Em/D
Cmaj7
Bm
1. When I need-ed a neigh-bour, were you there, were you there? When I
C2
Am7
Em
Chorus
D7/F♯
need - ed a neigh - bour were you there? And the
G
Bm
Em/G
Am
B7
Em
creed and the co-lour and the name won't mat-ter, were you there?
(I'll be there.)

2. I was hungry and thirsty,
Were you there, were you there?
I was hungry and thirsty,
Were you there?

3. I was cold, I was naked
Were you there, were you there?
I was cold, I was naked
Were you there?

4. When I needed a shelter
Were you there, were you there?
When I needed a shelter
Were you there?

5. When I needed a healer,
Were you there, were you there?
When I needed a healer,
Were you there?

6. Wherever you travel
I'll be there, I'll be there,
Wherever you travel
I'll be there.

1605. When I sing my praise

(When I worship You)

Rev 5:11

Noel & Tricia Richards

Gently
Intro
C♯m/E B/E A/E B/E E
Last time to Coda
Verse
1. When I sing my praise to You, I am lift-ed up to high-er ground.
2. Hea-ven is where I be-long, where the an-gels sing be-fore Your throne.
A E A B
E A E
Some-thing hap-pens in my soul when I lift my voice to wor-ship You.
I am caught up in their sound, when I lift my voice to wor-ship You.
B E B/E E B/E E
Feels like sun-shine on my face,
From be-yond where eyes can see,
(Vs.2
A E/G♯ A B
a cool breeze in a de-sert place.
love is pour-ing o-ver me.

Chorus
Emaj7
When I wor - ship You,
(I will wor - ship You,
Amaj7
A/B
hea - ven comes to me, hea - ven comes to me.
hea - ven come to me, hea - ven come to me.
Emaj7
When I wor - ship You,
I will wor - ship You,
Amaj7
A/B
D.C.
hea - ven comes to me, hea - ven comes to me.
hea - ven come to me, hea - ven come to me.)
Coda
E2

1606. When I survey
(The wonderful cross)

Mk 15:17; Rom 12:1; Phil 3:7

Words: Isaac Watts (1674-1748)
Refrain lyrics: Chris Tomlin & J.D. Walt
Arr. Jesse Reeves & Chris Tomlin

With strength
D
1. When I sur - vey the won - drous cross
on which the Prince of Glo - ry died,
my rich - est gain I count but loss,
and pour con - tempt on all my pride.
1.
2.3.
crown? Oh, the
G
won - der - ful cross,
D/F♯
oh, the

G
D/F♯
G
won - der - ful cross bids me come and die and find
D/F♯
A
that I may tru - ly live. Oh, the
G
D/F♯
G
won - der - ful cross, oh, the won - der - ful cross,
D/F♯
G
D/F♯
all who gath - er here by grace draw near and bless
A
1.
D.C.
2.
D
Your name.

2. See from His head, His hands, His feet,
Sorrow and love flow mingled down;
Did e'er such love and sorrow meet,
Or thorns compose so rich a crown?

2. Were the whole realm of nature mine,
That were an offering far too small.
Love so amazing, so divine,
Demands my soul, my life, my all.

Yet to all who received Him,
to those who believed in His name,
He gave the right to become children of God

JOHN 1:12

1607. When I was lost

(There is a new song)

Capo 3(D)

Ps 40:2-3, 5; Zeph 3:17; 2 Cor 5:17; Col 3:3; Heb 4:16

Kate & Miles Simmonds

Gospel feel
Verse
F(D)
Eb/Bb(C)
Bb(G)
1. When I was lost, You came and res-cued me;
You know all the things I've e-ver done,
F(D)
Eb/Bb(C)
Bb(G)
Bb/A(G)
reached down in-to the pit and lif-ted me.
but Je-sus' blood has can-celled e-v'ry one.
Gm(Em)
F/A(D)
1.
C/E(A)
F(D)
O Lord, such love, I was as far from You as
O Lord, such grace to qua-li-
Bb/D(G)
C7sus4(A)
2.
C/E(A)
F(D)
F/A(D)
Bb(G)
I could be.
fy me as Your own.
Bb/C (G)
Chorus
F(D)
F7/A(D)
F/Bb(D)
Bb(G)
There is a new song in my mouth, there is a
stand firm on this Rock, my life is-

C(A) C7/E(A) (Em) Gm/F F(D) A7/E(F♯) Dm(Bm) Dm7(Bm)
deep cry in my heart, a hymn of praise to Al-
hid - den now with Christ in God. The old has gone and the
Gm(Em) 1. C7sus4(A)
migh - ty God, hal - le - lu - jah! And now I
new has come, hal - le - lu -
2. C7sus4(A) Last time to Coda 1. F(D) F7/A(D) B♭(G) E♭/B♭(C)
jah! Your love has lif - ted me.
F(D) F7/A(D) B♭(G) E♭/B♭(C) D.C. 2. B♭(G) Mid section
me. Ma - ny are the won - ders You
B♭/C(G) B♭(G)
have done, and ma - ny are the things that You

B♭/C(G)
B♭(G)
have planned.
How beau - ti - ful the grace that gives
Dm7(Bm)
Gm(Em)
to us
all that we don't de - serve,
all that we can -
F/A(D)
B♭/C(G)
D.S. al Coda
not earn,
but is a gift of love.
There is a
Coda
B♭maj7(G)
B♭/C(G)
(Fine)
F(D) B♭/F(G) F(D)
A7♯5(F♯)
me.
Your love has lif-ted me.
Your love has lif-ted

2. Now I have come into Your family,
For the Son of God has died for me.
O Lord, such peace,
I am as loved by You as I could be.
In the full assurance of Your love,
Now with every confidence we come.
O Lord, such joy
To know that You delight in us.

1608. When Love came down

Is 53:5; Mt 11:19, 28; Lk 1:52; Jn 15:11; 1 Pet 5:7

Stuart Townend

Tenderly
Verse
E E/G♯ A B
1. When Love came down to earth and made His home with
E E/G♯ A B
(v.2) (v.3)
men, the hope-less found a hope, the sin-ner found a
E E/G♯ A B
friend. Not to the pow - er - ful but to the poor He
C♯m7 E/G♯ A B
(v.2)
came, and hum-ble, hun-gry hearts were sa-tis-fied a-
E E/G♯ Amaj7 B6 C♯m7 B6 Amaj7 B6 C♯m7 B6
Chorus
gain. What joy, what peace has come to us! What

Amaj7
B6
C♯m7
B6
Amaj7
To repeat
E/G♯
hope, what help, what love!
2. When ev-'ry un-clean
Last time only
E
D/E
C♯m/E
x3
E
Fine
what love!

2. When every unclean thought,
And every sinful deed
Was scourged upon His back
And hammered through His feet.
The Innocent is cursed,
The guilty are released;
The punishment of God
On God has brought me peace.

3. Come lay your heavy load
Down at the Master's feet;
Your shame will be removed,
Your joy will be complete.
Come crucify your pride,
And enter as a child;
For those who bow down low
He'll lift up to His side.

1609. When my heart is faint

Rom 8:15; Eph 2:6; Heb 7:25; Rev 1:5; 5:12

Steadily

Alan Rose

Em7
Verse
D
C
D
1. When my heart is faint within me,
and my troubles multiply,
I will lift my head to see You
seated at the Father's side.
You have triumphed over Satan,

Em7 D C D Em7 D
You're the first born from the grave.
You are al-ways in-ter-ced-
C D Em7 D A7
-ing,
You are a-ble now to save.
C D Chorus Em G A7
You are Je-sus Christ, faith-ful One, ri-sen King,
C D Em G
Cham-pi-on. You de-serve the high-est praise, the
A7 C D Em
Lamb of God, who once was slain for our sin.

2. In my heart I am persuaded
As the Spirit testifies,
And with glory and rejoicing
'Abba, Father' is my cry.
You have raised me up with Jesus
And in Him I am Your son,
So I glory in Your goodness,
In the things that You have done.

1610. When my heart runs dry

Lk 15:18; Rev 2:5

With feeling
Matt Redman
Verse
E2
1. When my heart runs dry and there's no
soul's de - sire, You are the
B
E
song to sing,— no ho - ly— me - lo - dy,—
hope with - in,— You bring my— heart to life,—
sim.
B
no words of— love with - in,—
You make my— spi - rit sing.—
I re-
G♯m7
B2
G♯m7
call the height from which this fra - gile heart has
E2
Chorus
B
F♯
slipped. And I'll re - mem - ber You, I will turn

G♯m
E
B2
back and do the things I need to do for the
F♯
B
love of You. Lord, I'll re - mem - ber You,
F♯
G♯m
E
I will turn back and do the things I need to
B
F♯
1.3.
E2
do for the love of You.
B
(Fine)
D.C.
2.
D.S.
F♯sus4/E
F♯
2. You are my
And I'll re -

1611. When the darkness fills my senses

(Your unfailing love)

Ps 13:5; 119:41; 139:23; Jn 9:11

Not too fast
Verse
Reuben Morgan
G
1. When the dark-ness fills my sen-ses, when my
bur-den keeps me doubt-ing, when my
blind-ness keeps me from Your touch,
mem-'ries take the place of You,
C
Cmaj7
Je-sus come.
Je-sus come.
1.
G2
2. When my
2.
G2
Gsus4 G G2
Chorus
G
Em7
And I'll fol-low You there,
C2
Em7
C2
to the place where we meet, and I'll

Em7
C2
Em7
lay down my pride as You search me a - gain.
C2
G
C2
G
Your un - fail-ing love, Your un - fail-ing love,
C2
G
C2
Your un - fail - ing love o - ver me a-gain.
G2
1.
C2
D.S.
2.
C2
G2
1. When the

1612. When the road is rough and steep

Prov 18:24; Jn 10:28; 15:15; 1 Cor 1:8; Heb 12:2

Brightly

Norman J. Clayton

C Em F C G7 C Gaug5
When the road is rough and steep, fix your eyes up-on Je - sus.
C Em F C G7 C
He a - lone has pow'r to keep, fix your eyes up - on Him.
E7 A7 D7 G Gaug5
Je - sus is a gra - cious friend, one on whom you can de - pend,
C Em F C G7 C
He is faith - ful to the end, fix your eyes up - on Him.

1613. When we turn our hearts to heaven

Capo 3(G)

(Dreamers of Your dreams)

Mal 3:7; 4:6

Quietly rhythmic

Noel Richards
& Ken Riley

B♭(G) F/A(D) Gm7(Em7)
When we turn our hearts to hea - ven and bow down,
E♭2(C2) B♭(G) F/A(D)
we'll see fa - thers and the chil -
Gm7(Em7) E♭2(C2) F(D)
dren re - con - ciled. We'll be the drea -
E♭2(C2) B♭2(G2)
mers of Your dreams.

F(D)
E♭2(C2)
B♭2(G2)
We'll be the drea - mers of Your dreams.
B♭/A(G/F♯)
When Your fi - re falls from hea - ven, we will rend
Gm7(Em7)
E♭2(C2)
B♭(G)
our hearts to You. We will tell it to our chil-
B♭/A(G/F♯)
Gm7(Em7)
E♭2(C2)
dren, all the won - ders You have done. And in e-
B♭(G)
B♭/A(G/F♯)
Gm7(Em7)
v'ry ge - ne - ra - tion, we will sing of Your great love.

E♭2(C2)
B♭(G)
B♭/A(G/F♯)
When Your fi - re falls from hea - ven we'll re - turn
Gm7(Em7)
E♭2(C2)
F(D)
to You a - gain!
We'll be the drea -
E♭2(C2)
B♭2(G2)
mers of Your dreams.
F(D)
E♭2(C2)
B♭(G)
We'll be the drea - mers of Your dreams.

1614. When words are not enough

Capo 1 (D)

Is 42:3; Phil 2:10; Heb 13:15

Martyn Layzell

Meditatively, with a gentle lilt

E♭(D) B♭/E♭(A) Fm7+4(Em) E♭/G(D)
1. When words are not e-nough to tell
A♭(G)
(vv 2&3
E♭/G(D) B♭7sus4(A) B♭7(A) E♭/G(D) A♭(G) E♭/G(D)
of all You've done, I bow the knee, let si-
Fm7(Em) E♭/G(D)
1.
A♭(G)
lence speak, and gaze up-on Your ma-jes-ty.
B♭7sus4(A) B♭7(A)
2.
A♭(G) B♭7sus4(A)
You, our of-fer-ing of praise.
B♭7(A) E♭/G(D) A♭(G)
And I sur-ren-der all,

B♭7sus4(A) B♭7(A) E♭/G(D) A♭(G) B♭7sus4(A)
and I sur-ren - der all; un-veil my heart to see
Cm7(Bm) A♭(G) B♭7sus4(A)
the won - der of your worth, as I sur-ren - der all,
Fm7+4(Em) A♭(G) B♭7sus4(A)
as I sur-ren - der all.
Fm7+4(Em) A♭(G)
D.C.
Last time
B♭7sus4(A) E♭(D)
(Fine)

2. These songs could not convey
A picture of Your love;
And knowing this, my life I give
To You, an offering of praise.

3. The worship You require
Is brokenness of heart;
So here I stand with open hands,
Surrendered to Your love and power.

1615. When You prayed beneath the trees

Tune: KELVINGROVE

Is 53:7; Mk 14:32, 43, 50, 61; 15:5, 21, 25, 33, 37; Lk 22:41-44; 23:46; Jn 18:3; 19:17; Acts 2:24; Rom 8:31

Unhurried

Scottish trad. melody
Arr. David Peacock

G D/F♯ Em C G/B Am C/D G

1. When You

G D/F♯ Em C G/B Am Am/C Am7/D D7

prayed be-neath the trees, it was for me, O Lord;___ when You

G D/F♯ Em C G/B Am C/D G

cried up-on Your knees, how could it be, O Lord?___ When in

Am C Bm7 Em

blood and sweat and tears___ You dis - missed Your fi - nal

Am7
D7
G
D/F♯
Em
Bm
C
G/B
fears, when You faced the sol - diers' spears, You stood for
Am
C/D
1.-3.
G
4.
G
me, O Lord.
Lord.

2. When their triumph looked complete,
It was for me, O Lord;
When it seemed like Your defeat,
They could not see, O Lord!
When You faced the mob alone
You were silent as a stone,
And a tree became Your throne;
You came for me, O Lord.

3. When You stumbled up the road,
You walked for me, O Lord,
When You took Your deadly load,
That heavy tree, O Lord;
When they lifted You on high,
And they nailed You up to die,
And when darkness filled the sky,
It was for me, O Lord.

4. When You spoke with kingly power,
It was for me, O Lord,
In that dread and destined hour,
You made me free, O Lord;
Earth and heaven heard You shout,
Death and hell were put to rout,
For the grave could not hold out;
You are for me, O Lord.

Christopher Idle

1616. Where can I go?

Capo 3 (D)

Rock style

Deut 1:30; Ps 28:7; 121:5; 139:7; Is 40:31; Mt 11:30

Brian Houston

F(D)
Bbmaj7(G)
Where can I go without You, Lord?
F(D)
Bbmaj7(G)
What can I do, how can I stand?
(G) Bb/A
Gm(Em)
C(A)
You are my com - fort and my strength.
Gm(Em)
You are my shield and my right hand.
C(A)
Bb(G)
And You pour out heal-ing on me,

F(D)
pour out heal-ing. And You make my spi-rit soar,
B♭(G)
and You make my burden light, and You soothe
Gm7(Em)
B♭(G)
me in the storm, and You go be-fore me in
B♭/C(G)
F(D)
B♭(G)
the fight.
Fight.
Gm(Em)
Gm7(Em)
C(A)
F(D)
Fight.
Fight.

1617. Where could I find someone like You?

(Secret place)
Ps 139:15-16
Robin Mark
Gently
D
A
Em7
1. Where could I find some-one like You?
G
D
A
Em7
(v.3)
(v.3)
Un - bound - ed love in all You do.
G
Bm7
A
Bm7
So I'll seek to know You more, I'll press in-to Your word a-gain,
A
Bm7
A
4
and draw-ing on Your Spi-rit's pow'r, and drink-ing from that
D/A
1.
A
2.3.
A
Chorus
well a - gain. For hea-ven and earth hand. And You
gain.

G D G D G D
knew — me in the se-cret — place — as my be-ing formed, You be-held — de-creed —
A G D G D
— my — days. And You know me — now, — You know all my — ways, — no-thing's
G D A7 1. 2. D
hid from You, I'm with You — al-ways. — 3. My weak-est

2. For heaven and earth are in Your hands,
This universe within Your plans.
Dust of life no eye can see,
They only stir when You command.
Some divine permission give,
Empowered by Your mighty hand.

3. My weakest means, my poorest words
To tell this world of Your redeeming love,
By Your Holy Spirit's power
Is articulation given,
Message to the poor in heart,
That Jesus Christ is risen again.

1618. Who can compare?

Ps 89:6; Jn 15:4; Rev 19:11

Gareth Robinson

Steadily
E A B E A B E
Verse
1. Who can com-pare with You, my Fa-ther; lo-ving and kind,
faith-ful and true? When You for-give my heart that is bro-ken, I
grate-ful-ly sing my love to You.
Chorus
I wor-ship You, I love You:
F♯m E/G♯

A B E F♯m E/G♯ A B
all that I am sings this song of
1. E A B E A B E
praise.
2. E D A E
praise. And I a-bide in You.
D A E (Fine)
I a-bide with You. And

2. Here I will dwell in the arms of my Father,
Knowing Your grace, hearing Your voice;
Trusting Your word, feeling Your peace,
Resting in You and in Your love.

1619. Who can stand before the Lord?

Ps 24:3-4; Jn 1:29;
Heb 6:20; 9:12, 24; 1 Jn 1:7

Steadily

Carey Luce
& Geraldine Latty

Verse
G
D/F♯
C/E
1. Who can stand be-fore the Lord in His ho-ly place, who can
G
D/F♯
C/E
walk up-on the hill of the Lord? On-ly
Am7
G/B
C
G/D
he whose hands are clean, on-ly he whose heart is pure can
C/E
D/F♯
G
Chorus
C
G
D
Em
stand be-fore the Lord. I will stand, I will come

C G D C G
be-fore the pre - sence of the King:
for His blood
D Em C D
1. G
2. G
wa-shes me from sin,
I en-ter in.
2. There is

2. There is One who stands for me
In the holy place,
And He walked the lonely hill to the cross.
And I know His hands are clean,
And I know His heart is pure,
He is Jesus Christ the Lamb.

1620. Who could offer us abundant life?

(Only Jesus)

Is 9:6; Jn 1:5, 14; 4:10; 6:48; 8:12, 58; 10:10; 14:6; Acts 4:12; 10:40-41; Phil 2:6, 9; 3:9; 1 Jn 4:10; Rev 1:16; 17:14; 19:16

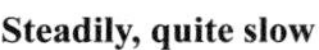

Steadily, quite slow

Evan Rogers

Em7 *Verse* D/F♯ G

1. Who could of - fer us a - bun - dant life?

Em7 D/F♯ G

Who could be the on - ly way?

C C/B Am7

Who could be the pur - est sac - ri - fice, who could have the pow -

C Am7 **1.** D **2.3.** D *Chorus*

- er to rise from the grave? (It's) On - ly Je -

G C D Am7 C

- sus shines like the sun.

D G Em7 D/F♯ D
On-ly Je - sus, the King of kings,
Em C D D/F♯ G C
the Ho - ly One. (It's) On - ly Je - sus,
D Em C D D/F♯
the Son of God, the Son of man. On - ly Je -
G C D Em C D D.C. (Fine)
sus, the Prince of Peace, the great I Am.
C/E D/F♯ G
Now on - ly I can of - fer up my life;

C
G/B
Am7
G
there's no - thing less that I could give
C/E
D/F♯
G
to Him who gave up all His heav'n - ly rights
D.S. al fine
Am7
C
D
so that I might live. (It's) On - ly Je

2. Who could be our only righteousness?
Who could be the One who saves?
Who could be the God who became flesh?
Who could have the Name above every name?

3. Who could give us living water?
Who could be the Bread of Life?
Who could overcome the darkness?
Who could be the Truth, our shining light?

The sun will no more be your light by day, nor will the brightness of the moon shine on you, for the Lord will be your everlasting light, and your God will be your glory.

ISAIAH 60:19

1621. Who is like You?

Ex 15:11; Ps 147:5; Jer 10:6-7; Eph 2:4; Phil 2:6-7

Joannah Oyeniran

Slowly
Verse
C
Am7
Who is like___ You, Lord Al - migh - ty?
God of jus - tice, rich in mer - cy.
C
Am7
Crowned in splen - dour, robed in ma - je - sty.
Grace that flows___ from awe - some glo - ry. the
1. G
Am
2. G
Am
Ho-ly is Your___ name.___
won-der of Your___ ways.___ Migh-ty in
F
G
Am
F
G
po - wer, per-fect in so-v'reign-ty, the re-ve - la - tion, You laid it a-
Am
E
Am
side for me and bore a hu - man frame___ in

F
G
Chorus
C
Je - sus. So I exalt You, God of all
Am
F
G
glo - ry, and I will wor - ship the Lord of e - ter - ni - ty. King of the -
C
Am
na - tions, my won - der - ful Sa - viour, God our Cre -
F
G
a - tor, my hea - ven - ly Fa - ther. I wor - ship on - ly
C
Am7
C
Am7
D.C.
To end
C
You.

1622. Who is there like the Lord our God?

Ex 15:11; Ps 96:11-12; 135:13; Eph 5:2

Neil Bennetts

Lilting
(v.2)
G
Verse
Dsus4
Am7
1. Who is there like the Lord our God,
C2
G
D
Am
faith - ful be - yond all com - pare?
C2
G
D
Am7
C2
Glo - ri - ous in such ho - li - ness,
Em7
D/F♯
C2
with po - wer to heal and to save. And

Chorus
G
D
Am7
C
You shall be called the Sa - viour e-ter - nal, there is
G
D
Am7
C2
grace in Your heart, and Your name. And
G
D
Am7
You shall be known through all ge-ne-ra-
C
G
D
Am7
tions as the hope for the life that re-ceives.
Last time to Coda
C2
D.C.
G/B
Em7
D
A love be-yond rea - son, this gift of life;

C2
G/B
Em7
D
the mer - cy of God in Your sa - cri - fice.
The foun - tain of truth that can sa - tis - fy, and it's
Am7
C
found in You, Je - sus, and it's found in
You, Je - sus, and it's found in You, Je -
D.S. al Coda
Coda
G
sus. And

2. Let heaven rejoice, You are wonderful;
Creation sings out to Your praise.
You are the Lord, You are beautiful;
Each work of Your hand shall proclaim.

1623. Whom have I but You?

Ps 46:2; 73:25

David Ruis

Gently
Chorus
Em7
D/F♯
G
Whom have I but You?
Em7
D/F♯
G
(Fine)
Whom have I but You?
Am
Verse
G
D
D/F♯
1. Though the moun - tains fall, they
Am
G
D
fall in - to the sea.

2. Though the coloured dawn
May turn to shades of grey.

3. Though the questions asked
May never be resolved.

1624. Who put the colours in the rainbow?

Gen 1:1; Job 38:4

J.A.P. Booth
Arr. Douglas Coombes

Brightly
D
Em/G A7
1. Who put the co - lours in the rain - bow?
Who put the hump up - on the ca - mel?
Em/G A7 D D/C♯ D7/C
Who put the salt in - to the sea? Who put the cold in - to the
Who put the neck on the gir - raffe? Who put the tail up-on the
G/B G A7 A7/C♯ D
snow - flake? Who made you and me?
mon - key? Who made hy - e - nas laugh?
D/F♯ D/A D7 G
Who made whales and snails and quails? Who made hogs and

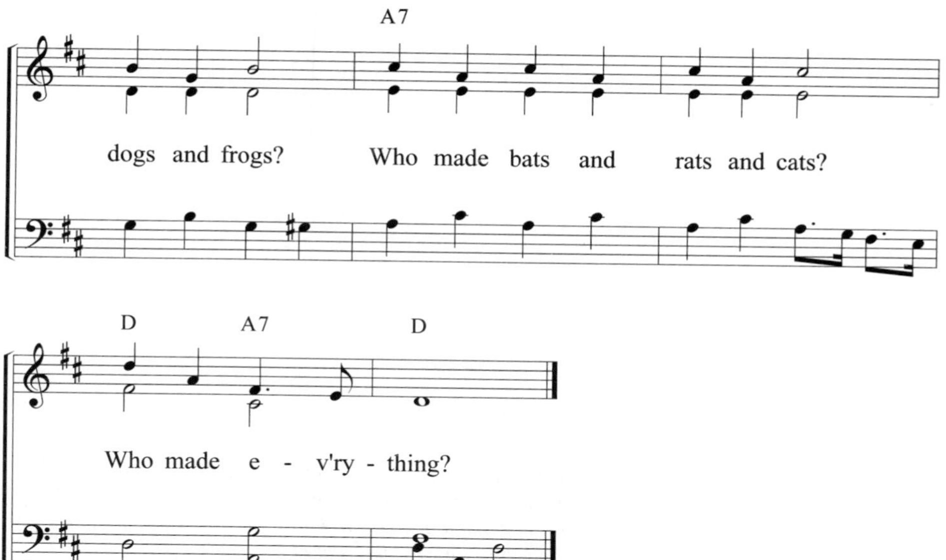
A7
dogs and frogs? Who made bats and rats and cats?
D A7 D
Who made e - v'ry - thing?

2. Who put the gold into the sunshine?
Who put the sparkle in the stars?
Who put the silver in the moonlight?
Who made Earth and Mars?
Who put the scent into the roses?
Who taught the honey bee to dance?
Who put the tree inside the acorn?
It surely can't be chance!
Who made seas and leaves and trees?
Who mad snow and winds that blow?
Who made streams and rivers flow?
God made all of these!

Through him all things were made; without him nothing was made that has been made. In him was life, and that life was the light of men.

JOHN 1:3-4

1625. Who's the king of the jungle?

Col 1:17

Annie Spiers
Arr. Andy Silver

Brightly
G
Who's the king of the jungle? Who's the king of the
D
D7
sea? Who's the king of the universe and
G C/E D7/F♯ G
who's the king of me? I'll tell you J-E-S-U-S is,
D
D7
He's the King of me, He's the King of the
G
universe, the jungle and the sea.

1626. Who's the only light?

(It's all about Jesus)

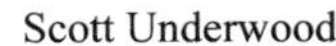
Jn 1:1, 3; 8:12; 14:6

Scott Underwood

Steadily

Verse

E E/D♯
1. Who's the on - ly light__ that shines and ne-ver fades?__
C♯m7 A2
The Light__ of the world,__ Je-sus.
E E/D♯
Who's the on - ly light__ that drives the dark__ a-way?__
C♯m7 A2
The Light__ of the world,__ Je - sus. It's all__ a-bout

Chorus

E E/D♯ C♯m7
Je-sus,__ Je - sus, it's all__ a-bout Je-sus,__

1.
A2
D.C.
2.3.
A2
E
Je-sus.
Je - sus.
It's all a-bout
Je-sus,
E/D♯
Last time to Coda
C♯m7
A2
Je-sus,
it's all a-bout
Je-sus,
Je-sus.
You're the
Amaj9
B/A
Amaj9
1.
Way,
the Truth,
and the Life.
You're the
2.
D.S. al Coda
B/A
Coda
A2
E
It's all a-bout
Je-sus.

2. Who's the only Word that made all things?
The Word was God, Jesus.
He's the only truth, the fullness of the Lord,
The Son of God, Jesus.

1627. With a prayer

(Love incarnate)

Is 53:5, 7; 58:7; Mk 1:25, 41; 8:34; 10:21; 14:22; Lk 8:24; 9:16; 23:34; Jn 1:10, 14; 11:43; 12:32; 1 Jn 1:2; Rev 12:11

Stuart Townend

Intro
D
G Asus4 A
Bm
G Asus4 A
1. With a
Verse
D
D/F♯
G A
Bm
D/F♯
pray'r You fed the hun-gry, with a cry You stilled the
Asus4 A
Em7
D/F♯
storm; with a look You had com - pas - sion on the
G
Asus4 A
G/B
de-sp'rate and for - lorn. With a touch You healed the
D/A
D
Bm
G
C
le - per, with a shout You raised the dead; with a word ex-pelled the

G/B
Em7
A7sus4
D
de - mons, with a bles - sing broke the bread.
Chorus
Gmaj7
A
Bm
Dmaj7/A Gmaj7
A/G
Love in - car - nate, love di - vine, cap - ti - vate this heart of
D/F♯
G
Asus4
A
D
G
mine till all I do speaks of You.
Asus4 A
Bm
G
1.2.
Asus4 A
3.
Asus4 A
D
2. As a
rall........

2. As a sheep before the shearer
You were silent in Your pain;
You endured humiliation
At the hands of those You'd made.
And as hell unleashed its fury
You were lifted on a tree,
Crying 'Father God, forgive them,
Place their punishment on me.'

3. I will feed the poor and hungry,
I will stand up for the truth;
I will take my cross and follow
To the corners of the earth.
And I ask that You so fill me
With Your peace, Your power, Your breath,
That I never love my life so much
To shrink from facing death.

1628. With His hands He made me

Ps 16:11; 36:8; 42:2; 57:1; Song 2:6; Is 53:5; Jn 1:10-11; 2 Cor 4:6; 1 Tim 1:15; 2 Tim 1:6; Heb 13:15

Stuart Townend

Gently

Verse
E B/D♯ E A E/B
1. With His hands He made me, breathed His life with - in me;
In His love He sought me, came to earth to save me;
E B/D♯ E
1. A Bsus4 B
with His heart He loved me, yet I turned a-way.
pun - ished my re - bel - lion
2. A Bsus4 E
with His sa - cri - fice.
Chorus
A B B/D♯
I'll come to the Gi -
rest in the shade
E/G♯ A F♯m7 B B/D♯
- ver of life, I'll drink from His well
of His wings, I'll feast on the plea -

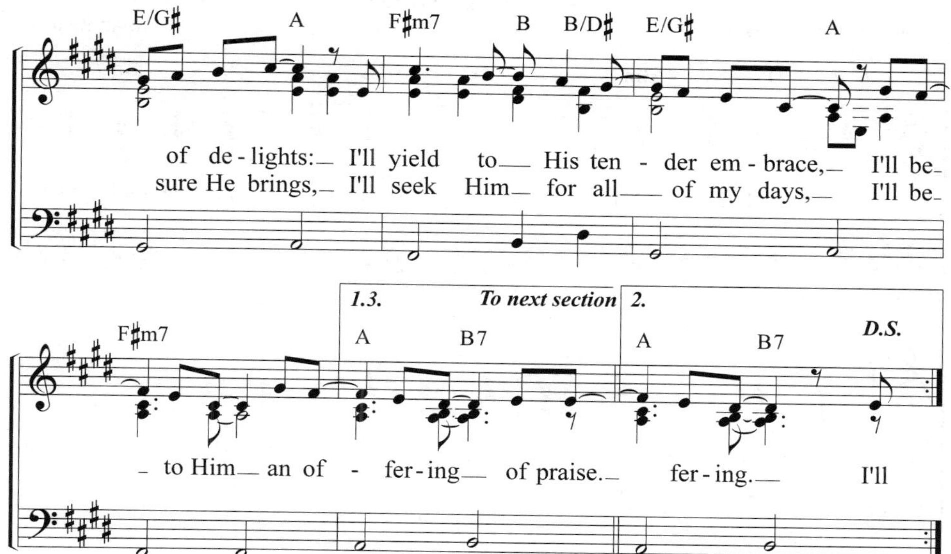
E/G♯
A
F♯m7
B
B/D♯
E/G♯
A
of de - lights: I'll yield to His ten - der em - brace, I'll be-
sure He brings, I'll seek Him for all of my days, I'll be-
F♯m7
1.3.
To next section
2.
A
B7
A
B7
D.S.
to Him an of - fer - ing of praise. fer - ing. I'll

Last time to Coda
D.C.
E
B/D♯
E
A/C♯
E/B
E
B/D♯
E
A/C♯
Bsus4

Coda
A/C♯
Bsus4
E
Fine

2. Here I stand before You,
Needing Your forgiveness,
Thirsting for Your Spirit,
Longing for Your touch.
Let the flame within me
Grow into a fire,
Banish all my darkness
With Your piercing light.

1629. With the choir of angels singing
(Hallelujah song)

Phil 2:10; Rev 8:4; 17:17; 19:4, 16

Steadily, building

Matt Redman

Verse
D Bm7 G A D Bm7
1. With the choir of an-gels sing-ing, and the realm of
G A D Bm7 G A
heav-'nly hosts; as those el-ders humb-ly bow, I'd
C G
love to come to Your throne with a sim-ple song. (Mmm
1.
D Bm7 G A
)
2.3. Chorus
D Bm7 G A
Hal - le - lu - jah, Je-sus,
D Bm7 G A D Bm7 G A
hal - le - lu - jah, hal-le - lu. Hal - le - lu - jah, Je-sus,

1.
2.3.
1st time D.S.
Last time to Coda
D Bm7 G A G A
pour - ing out my heart to You. heart to You. (And)
D Bm7 G A D Bm7
who can tell the a - dor - a - tion that will rise up
G A D Bm7 G A
to Your throne? Ev - 'ry knee that day shall bow to the
Cmaj9 G
D.S.
King of kings, the Ho-ly-One, the on-ly One. We'll all be sing-ing...
Coda
D
Hal - le-lu - jah.

2. With the living creatures speaking
Praise and praise and praise again;
With the company of heaven,
I'd love to come to Your throne
With a song of love.

3. I would bring this praise like incense
Rising to Your throne above,
Fill the air with heart-filled songs
In harmony and melody to the One I love.

1630. Wonderful grace

Lk 23:34; Rom 2:4; Eph 2:4-5; 2 Pet 3:9; 1 Jn 1:7

John Pantry

Smoothly
A D A D
1. Won-der ful grace, that gives what I don't de-serve,
E/G♯ A B7 D/E E
pays me what Christ has earned, then lets me go free.
A D A D E/G♯
Won-der-ful grace, that gives me the time to change, wash-es a-
A B7 D/E E D/E E A
Chorus
way the stains that once co-vered me. And all that I have I
C♯/E♯ F♯m F♯m/E D A/C♯
lay at__ the feet of the won-der-ful Sa-viour__ who

D/E
E
A
D/E
E
A
D/E
E
Last time
A
loves
me.

2. Wonderful love, that held in the face of death,
   Breathed in its latest breath
   Forgiveness for me.
   Wonderful love, whose power can break every chain,
   Giving us life again,
   Setting us free.

1631. Wonderful Redeemer

Ps 45:4; Eph 1:7; Phil 2:10

Ashton Gardner

Pulsing
Em(no3rd) C Am7 Em(no3rd) C Am7
Verse
Em(no3rd) C
(v.2)
1. Won - der - ful Re - dee - mer of my life,
2. Right-eous and ma - jes - tic King of Truth,
Em(no3rd) C
thank You for the grace You have shown to me:
all man - kind will one day bow the knee to You.
Em(no3rd) Am
no - thing can com - pare to Your heart of love, I have
May our lives re - flect the heart of You, O Lord, we will live
Bm7 Cmaj7 Chorus Em7 D/F♯ Am
Your eyes. Sing to the Lord our God,
for You.

C2 D Gsus4 G Em7 D/F♯
lift up His name and ex - alt Him. Your ho-li-ness is im-mense,
Am C2 D Gsus4 G
and we, Your peo-ple, will wor - ship
C2 1. D Em(no3rd) C Am7 Em(no3rd)
Your name for e - ver.
C Am7 D.C. 2. D Em(no3rd) C Am7
for e - ver.
Em(no3rd) C Am7 Em9(no3rd)

1632. Wonderful, so wonderful

(Beautiful One)

Ps 19:1; 36:7; 1 Cor 2:9

Tim Hughes

Verse
G A D/F♯
1. Won - der-ful, so won - der-ful is Your un-fail - ing
G A Bm7
love; Your cross has spo - ken mer - cy o - ver me.
G A D/F♯
No eye has seen, no ear has heard, no heart could ful - ly
G A D
know how glo - ri - ous, how beau - ti - ful You are.
Chorus
G A G
Beau - ti - ful One, I love You, beau - ti - ful One, I a -

To Coda
1.
D.C.
(Fine)
A
G
A
D
dore, beau-ti-ful One, my soul must sing.
2.
D.S.
3.
Bridge
G
Beau-ti-ful
You o - pened my eyes to Your won -
A
G
A
ders a-new, You cap - tured my heart with this love, 'cause no -
1.
G
A
D
thing on earth is as beau - ti-ful as You.
2.
G
A
D
D.S. al Coda
- thing on earth is as beau - ti-ful as You.
Beau-ti-ful

Coda
G
A
My soul, my soul must sing, my soul,
G/B
A/C♯
G
my soul must sing, my soul, my soul must sing,
A
D
D.S. al fine
3
beau - ti - ful One.
Beau - ti - ful

2. Powerful, so powerful,
Your glory fills the skies,
Your mighty works displayed for all to see.
The beauty of Your majesty
Awakes my heart to sing
How marvellous, how wonderful You are.

The Word became flesh and made His dwelling among us. We have seen His glory, the glory of the One and Only, who came from the Father, full of grace and truth.

JOHN 1:14

1633. Worship the Lord

1 Chron 16:29; Ps 23:6; 57:9; 68:34; 145:3; 146:5; Is 6:7-8; Col 1:9; 3:12; Heb 4:16

Louise Fellingham

Rock feel
D
C/D
G/D
C/D
To end
D
Verse
D
G/D
C/D
1. Wor - ship the Lord, see the splen - dour of His ho - li - ness. Give to the Lord all the glo - ry due His name.
Come and a - dore, come and lay Your hearts be - fore Him. With thank - ful - ness and love, come and shout a - loud Your praise.
G/D
D
G/D
1. Am7
G/B
2. Em7
D/G
Asus4
Chorus
A
Bm
G
De - clare His glo - ry a - mong all the na -

D/A A
- tions. De - clare His ma - je-sty, His
Bm
G A Bm
splen - dour and pow'r. Pro - claim sal-va - tion, His
G D/G D/A A
good - ness and mer - cy; for great is the Lord
Bm G Em7 D D.S.
- and most wor - thy, wor - thy of praise.

2. We are His people, belonging to our Father,
Set apart for truth, we are chosen by God.
With confidence we come, we are free and we're forgiven.
Blessed are the ones who put their hope in God.

3. Please come upon us now, we want to see Your face, Lord.
Soften our hearts, take us deeper into You.
Spirit, fill our minds with the knowledge of Your wisdom.
Come and touch our mouths, help us tell of all You've done.

1634. Worthy, You are worthy

1 Chron 16:25; Ps 42:5; 113:4; Rev 5:12

Matt Redman

With a 'half-time' feel
B C♯m7 B/D♯ E2
1. Wor-thy, You are wor-thy, much more wor-thy than I've known,
(v.2)
I can-not i-ma-gine just how glo-ri-ous You are.
F♯ E2 B/D♯ E2
I can-not be-gin to tell how deep a love You bring;
Lord, my ears have heard of You but now my eyes have seen.
E2 F♯2
2nd time to Chorus 2
Chorus 1
You're wor-thy, You're wor-thy, You're

B/D♯
E2
B
C♯m7
wor - thy,
You're
wor - thy
to
be praised,
for -
1.3. B/D♯
E2
2.4. B/D♯
E2
(Fine)
D.C.
e - ver and a day.
You're
e - ver and a day.
Chorus 2 ⊕
E2
B
C♯m7
You're
wor - thy,
You're wor - thy,
You're
glo - ry,
Your glo - ry,
Your
B/D♯
E2
B
C♯m7
wor - thy
You're
wor - thy
to
be praised,
for -
glo - ry,
Your
glo - ry
reach - es
high,
so
B/D♯
E2
B
C♯m7
e - ver and a day.
You're
wor - thy,
You're wor - thy,
You're
high a - bove the heav'ns.
Your
glo - ry,
Your glo - ry,
Your

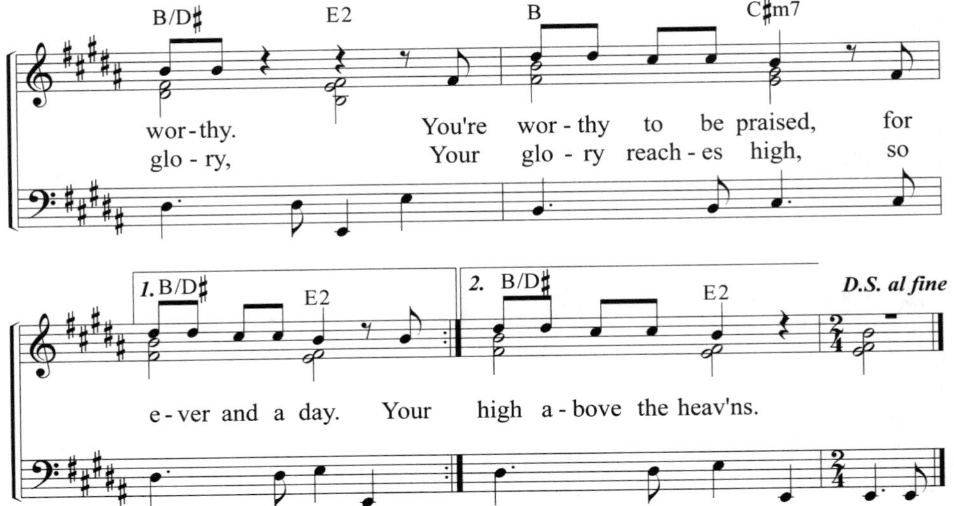
B/D♯
E2
B
C♯m7
wor - thy. You're wor - thy to be praised, for
glo - ry, Your glo - ry reach - es high, so
1. B/D♯
E2
2. B/D♯
E2
D.S. al fine
e - ver and a day. Your high a - bove the heav'ns.

2. Glory, I give glory to the One who saved my soul.
You found me and You freed me from the shame that was my own.
I cannot begin to tell how merciful You've been;
Lord, my ears have heard of You, but now my eyes have seen.

Yet a time is coming and has now come when the true worshippers will worship the Father in spirit and truth, for they are the kind of worshippers the Father seeks.

JOHN 4:23

1635. Woven together

(Psalm 139)

Ps 139:1-7, 13-17

Capo 3 (G)

Stuart Townend

Gently rhythmic

Verse

F(D) Gm7(Em) C(A) Dm/C(Bm) C(A) Gm7(Em) Dm7(Bm) C(A)

1. Wo - ven to - ge - ther with - in the womb, fear - ful - ly, won - der - f'lly made; You know me bet - ter than I know my - self, and still You look on with plea - sure.

Where can I go from Your Spi - rit, Lord? Where can I hide from Your gaze? O - cean to o - cean and shore to shore, Your hand rea - ches out to guide me.

F(D)
Chorus
Gm7(Em)
It's all too won - der - ful for me to know;
The care You show to those who love Your name;

F/G(D) C(A)
it's all too mar - vel - lous
it's all too won - der - ful,
1.
Gm7(Em)
for me to at - tain.
2.
Gm7(Em)
it's all too won-
F(D)
(A)
C/F F(D)
(Fine)
Dm7(Bm)
der - ful for me.
(instr.)
(F♯m)
Am7
Gm9(Em)
(F♯m)
Am7
Dm7(Bm)
(F♯m)
Am7
2nd time D.S. al fine
Gm7(Em)
C(A)

2. Lord, You have searched me, You know me well,
For nothing is hidden from You;
And even before there's a word on my tongue,
You know it completely, Lord.
How precious to me are Your thoughts, O God,
How great is the depth of Your love;
I know that You've numbered the sum of my days,
I'll rest in Your perfect wisdom.

1636. Yes, I thank You

Kevin Simpson

Caribbean style
C F G C F G C F C/G G
1. Yes, I thank You, O Lord. Yes, I thank You, O Lord.
C/G Dm7 C/E F
Look-ing back in my life I see ma-ny things You have done for me, I
C/G G C F G
1.-3.
C F G
4.
C
thank You, O Lord.
2. Yes, I
3. Yes, I
F Dm7
Ha - le - lu - jah, hal - le - lu - jah, glo - ry to Your

Gm7
C7
F
name.
Hal - le - lu - jah,
hal - le - lu - jah,
Dm7
F/G G7
1. C
F G
C
F G
D.S.
2. C
glo - ry to Your
name.
4. Oui, je
name.

2. Yes, I love You...

3. Yes, I praise You...

4. Oui, je te remercie, Seigneur.
Oui, je te remercie, Seigneur.
En arrière dans ma vie je vois
Toutes choses que tu as fait pour moi.
Je te remercie, Seigneur.

1637. Yesterday, today and forever

(Forever You're the same)

Ps 119:105; Mt 28:18; Rom 8:37; 2 Cor 1:20; 10:4; Heb 4:12; 13:8

Marilyn Baker

Brightly
Verse
C F/C C
1. Yes - ter-day, to - day and for-e - ver You're the
F/C Am7 Em7 F
same, all the pro-mis-es of God find their 'yes' in
G C F/C
You. De-mons flee, strong - holds fall, they must
C F/C Am7
bow be-fore Your name, no au - tho - ri - ty, no
F G C F/C Chorus C
pow-er is high - er than You. Let's sing our
Let's dance for

Dm7
G7
C
praise to the Lord, thank You for the great things You have done.
joy to the Lord, for You have washed our sins a - way.
Dm7
G7
Let's sing with all of our hearts, there's no Fa - ther like
We're more than con - quer - ors, with You close by our
C
F/C
C
You.
side.

2. Yesterday, today and forever You're the same,
We need never fear to put all our trust in You.
For Your word is a rock and a light to show the way,
And a sword that will pierce through the darkness each day.

1638. Yet will I praise Him

Gen 22:14; Hab 3:17-19; Jn 8:12, 58; 2 Cor 12:10

Geraldine Latty

Brightly
Chorus
D G Bm7 A
Yet will I praise him, I will lift my hands to my Cre-a-tor.
D G Em7 A
Yet will I praise him, my Sa-viour and my God.
D G Bm7 A
Yet will I praise him, I will put my trust in my Pro-vi-der.
Em7 G/F♯ G A
Yet will I praise him, Lord Je-ho-vah, Sov-'reign God.

D
(Fine)
Verse
Bm7
F♯m/A
1. Though the fig tree does - n't blos - som and no
G
F♯m7
Em7
Bm7
F♯m7
ri-pened grapes ap-pear, though the har-vest fails and fields pro-vide no food;
G
Bm7
F♯m/A
I'll be joy - ful in my Sa - viour, the
G
F♯m7
Em7
Bm7
F♯m7
Lord who is my strength; He will keep my ways and lead me in His truth.
G
G/A
D.C.

2. When the night is overwhelming
   And the day is far from clear,
   When my heart is restless for the peace of God;
   Let Your song, Lord, through the ages,
   Through the prophets You have given;
   Lift my mind and heart
   To gaze upon You, Lord.

3. Be the strength, Lord, in my weakness,
   Let Your song be in my night;
   Be my rock when all around is sinking sand.
   Be the light, Lord, in my darkness,
   Be the vision of my eyes:
   In my passing days You are the great 'I Am'.

Lord, I will praise You,
I will lift my hands to my Creator.
Lord, I will praise You,
My Saviour and my God.
Lord, I will praise You,
I will put my trust in my Provider.
Yes, I will praise You,
Lord Jehovah, Sovereign God.

1639. You are all I want

Is 53:5; Jn 13:10; Gal 2:20

Gareth Robinson

Brightly

Verse
G
D
Em
1. You are all I want, You're all I need to be set free.
Bm7
C
G/B
Am
D
Your cross of death gives life to me, Your sa-cri-fice
G
C
D
G
brings li-ber-ty. No one else could take
D
Em
B
my place but You, the per-fect One, the ho-ly God,
C
G/B
Am
D
G
re-vealed as man in Je-sus Christ.

D
C
B
Chorus
On - ly You could take my sin, so I love
C
G/B
Am
D
G
You, yeah, I love You, Je - sus.
B
C
G/B
Am
D
(And) I love You, yeah, I love You, Je -
G
D
D.C.
G
sus.

2. I will give to You my everything,
Abandon all my selfish dreams
To live for You and do Your will every day.
You have touched my heart and made me whole,
You've made me clean, so I will give
My offering of love to You,
All my life lived just for You, 'cause...

1640. You are forever in my life

(Through it all)

Deut 33:27

Steadily

Reuben Morgan

Verse
G
D/F♯
Em
You are for - e - ver in my life, You see
co - ver me with Your hand, and lead
Cmaj7
C6
1.
Dsus4
D
2.
Dsus4 D
Dsus2
me through the sea - sons; - eous - ness. And I
me in Your right -
Bm7
C
Bm7
C
Dsus4
look to You, and I wait on You. I'll
Chorus
G2
G
Cmaj7
C6
sing to You, Lord, a hymn of love for Your

D Em C Dsus4 G2 G
faith - ful - ness to me. I'm car - ried in e - ver - last -
Last time to Coda
1.
Cmaj7 C6 D/F♯ Gsus4 G C D
ing arms; You'll ne - ver let me go, through it all.
2. D.S.
3.
G C Dsus4 D C D
I'll through it all.
G2 G Em9 Em Cmaj7 C6 Dsus4 D
Bridge
G2 G Em9 Em Cmaj7 C6 Dsus4 D G2 G
Hal - le - lu - jah, hal - le - lu - jah, hal - le -

Em9 Em Cmaj7 C6
1. Dsus4 D
2. D.S. al Coda Dsus4 D
lu - jah, hal - le - lu - jah. lu - jah. I'll
Coda
C D G2 G Em9 Em Cmaj7 C6
through it all.
Dsus4 D G

1641. You are God in heaven

(Let my words be few)

Matt & Beth Redman

Steadily
G
G+
1. You are God in hea - ven, and here
2. The simpl-est of all love songs I want
Em7
C2
G
am I on earth; so I'll let
to bring to You; so I'll let
G+
Em7
C2
Am7
G/B
my words be few: Je - sus, I am so
my words be few: Je - sus, I am so
C2
D7
G
G
in love with You And I'll stand in awe
in love with You
F2
Em7
A2
C2
G
of You, yes, I'll stand in awe

F2
Em7
C2
Am7
Em7
of You.
And I'll let my words be few:
C
C2
Am7
G/B
C2
D7sus4
G
Je - sus, I am so in love with You.
To repeat
C2
To end
G/F
Em7
C2
G2
Fine

1642. You are holy

2 Sam 7:22; Ps 84:10; Rev 4:8

Reuben Morgan

Slowly
Am6/E E D♯dim7 G♯7 C♯m7
You are ho - ly, ho - ly,
F♯m7 E Dmaj9 A/B
Lord, there is none like You. You are
Am6/E E D♯dim7 G♯7 C♯m7 F♯m7 A/B B
ho - ly, ho - ly, glo-ry to You a - lone.
1. E A/B
2. E A/B
E B/E
I'll sing Your prais - es for - e -
E/A A6 E/G♯ F♯m7 Bsus4 B
ver, deep - er in love with You.

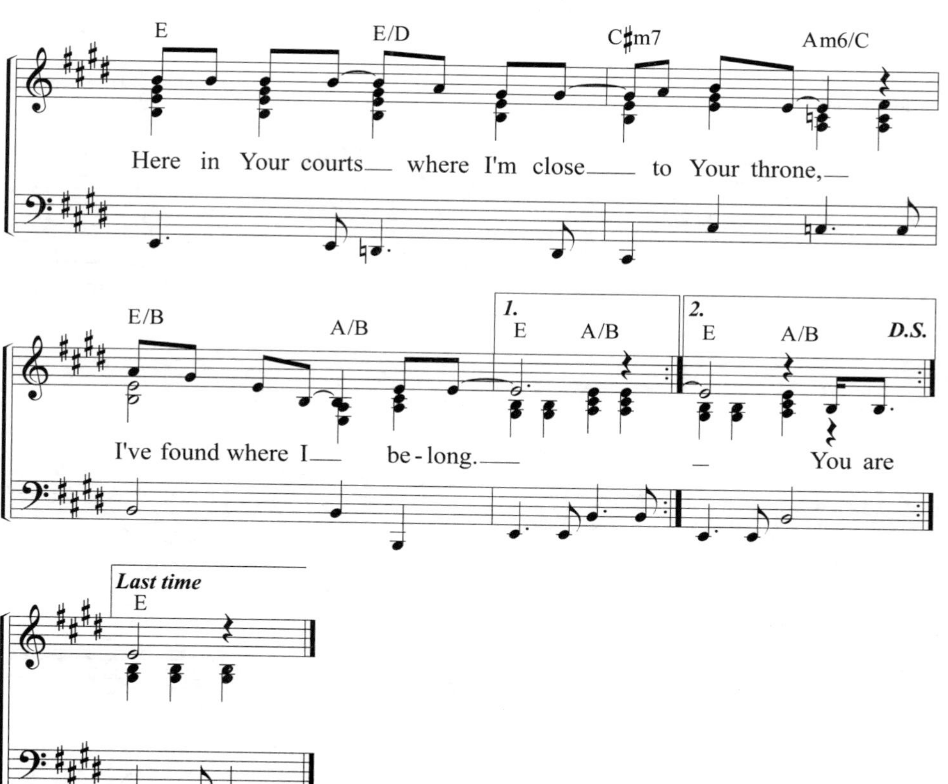
E
E/D
C♯m7
Am6/C
Here in Your courts where I'm close to Your throne,
E/B
A/B
1.
E
A/B
2.
E
A/B
D.S.
I've found where I be-long. You are
Last time
E

1643. You are holy

Rom 8:31

Tré Sheppard

With strength

Chorus
A
F♯m7
Last time to Coda
You are ho - ly, You are mer - cy, You are won -
- ful, You are gra - cious, You are love -
Dmaj7
1.
A
2.
A
- der, You are love. You are faith -
- ly, You are God.
F♯m
Verse
D
F♯m
1. I o - pen my eyes so I see Your love -
D
F♯m
D
li - ness. I o - pen my life so I

F♯m
D
A
D.C.
know Your ho - li - ness. You are ho -
Coda
Dmaj7
A
ly, You are God.

2. If You are for us who could
   Stand against us?
   Surely You are with us,
   Surely You are with us.

3. Surely You are with us,
   Surely You are with us,
   Surely You are with us,
   Surely You are with us.

1644. You are known as the Rock of Ages

(Rock of Ages)

Ps 18:2; Dan 7:9, 13, 22; Jn 1:14; Heb 12:6

Rhythmically

Robin Mark

Verse
E
1. You are known as the Rock of A - ges, and the holy Ancient of Days. Men of old who saw Your face, Lord, would not e - ver be the same. When You
came as God in - car - nate, walked this earth, Your glo - ry veiled, those who knew You and who loved You would not e - ver be the
A
E
1.3.
F♯m
B
2.4.
F♯m
A/B

E
Chorus
A
E
same. For I have seen You, Rock — of A-ges, and I will
A
E
A
ne-ver be — the same. Oh, — I love You, Rock — of
E
A
B
A-ges, and I will al-ways love — Your name.
1.
2.
E
2. Will You

2. Will You hide me, Rock of Ages,
In Your secret place of peace?
Can I feel Your burning glory,
Can I hear You when You speak?
Will You chasten me and mould me?
Will You hold me in Your will?
Oh, to know You, love and serve You
And Your purposes fulfil.

1645. You are Lord, You are Lord

Is 6:1

Neil Bennetts

Simply
G2 D/F♯ Em Em7/D
You are Lord, You are Lord, and Your glo - ry fills this
C G2 Bm7 Am7
tem - ple. You are Lord, You are Lord, and Your glo - ry fills this
C/D D7 Cmaj7 G/B
place. In Your pre - sence I will ho - nour, as I
Am7 C/D D7 G2
bring my praise to You. You are Lord, You are
D/F♯ Am7 C/D D7 G
Lord, and Your glo - ry fills this place.

1646.

You are my anchor

(The Father's embrace)

Ps 27:1-6, 11-14

With a steady rock feel
Stuart Townend
Verse
A
1. You are my an - chor,
my light and my sal -
E/G♯
va - tion.
You are my re - fuge,
F♯m7
F♯m
my heart will not fear.
Esus4
E
A/C♯
Though my foes
D
sur - round me on ev - 'ry
A/C♯
hand,
A
A/C♯
they will stum -
D
ble and fall while in grace
A/C♯
I stand.
E
A/C♯
In my day

D
F♯m7
G
D/F♯
of trou - ble, You hide me and set me a-bove
Esus4
E
A
Chorus
D
to sing this song of love:
One thing I will ask
Esus4
E
A
D
of You, this will I pray:
to dwell in Your house,
Esus4
E
F♯m
B/D♯
E/D
A/C♯
O Lord, e-ve-ry day;
to gaze u-pon
Your love - ly face,
D
A/C♯
Bm7
D/E
and rest in the Fa - ther's em-brace.

(Fine)
A
E/G♯ F♯m E
D/E
A
E/G♯ F♯m E
(D/E)
D.C. al fine
2. Teach me Your way,

2. Teach me Your way, Lord,
Make straight the path before me.
Do not forsake me,
My hope is in You.
As I walk through life, I am confident
I will see Your goodness with every step,
And my heart directs me to seek You in all that I do,
So I will wait for You.

1647. You are my foundation

(Hallelujah to the King)

Neh 8:10; Ps 61:2-3; Is 40:31; Heb 4:16

Capo 3 (G)

Mark Stevens

Gently, with pace
Verse
B♭2(G)
E♭(C)
You are my foundation,
You are my protection,
B♭2(G)
E♭(C)
You are my salvation, a
You are my resurrection, a
Gm7(Em)
(Em) Gm/F
E♭(C)
(D) Fsus2+4
(D) F
very present help in times of need.
higher place is where You're taking me.
E♭(C)
B♭/D(G)
E♭(C)
I get lifted up on eagles' wings, You lift me up

E♭/F(C)
F(D)
E♭/F(C) F(D)
B♭(G)
E♭(C)
and so I sing.
Ha - le - lu - jah,
B♭(G)
E♭(C)
B♭/D (G)
E♭(C)
Last time to Coda
F(D)
ha - le - lu - jah,
ha - le - lu - jah to the King.
E♭(C)
F sus4(D)
2nd time D.C.
Coda
B♭2(G)

2. You are my Redeemer,
You are my Healer,
A promise given, one of liberty.
You are my Restorer,
You are my strong Tower,
The joy of the Lord will be my strength.

1648. You are my King

(I am changed)

Song 1:4; 2 Cor 3:18; Gal 5:25

Mark Stevens

Driving
Verse
(v.2)
C
F
1. You are my King, I live to know You.
Am
G
Oh, to walk in the full - ness of Your Spi - rit.
I'll a - bide in You and You in me,
I'll see Your de - sire ful - filled with - in me.

Chorus
F/G
C
F
I am changed by You, into to Your i - mage.
Am
G
F
I am changed by You, I be - come the same.
C/E
I am changed by You, like my Fa -
F
F/G
Last time to Coda
C
F
C
ther God, King of hea - ven, King of hea - ven.
1.
D.C.
2.
F/A
G/B
C/E
F
2. You
Glo - ry to glo - ry to glo - ry, Lord,

G7sus4
Am
we will ne - ver be the same.
F/A
G/B
C/E
F
C/E
Glo - ry to glo - ry to glo - ry, Lord,
Oh, we will
Dm
Dm7
F/G
D.S. al Coda
ne - ver,
ne - ver be the same.
I am changed by You
Coda
F
C
F
C
King of hea - ven,
King of hea - ven,
Slower
F
Dm/G
C
King of hea - ven.

2. You placed in me a fire when I met You,
And the flame, it just burns brighter and brighter.
I'm coming after You with all that's in me,
I need You more and more each time I wake.

1649.

You are my Shepherd
(You are in control)

Ps 23:1-4; Jer 29:11; Rom 8:28

Scott Underwood

With a steady rhythm

D
You are my Shep-herd, I have no needs. You lead me by

G
A7sus4
peace-ful streams, and You re-fresh my life.

D
You hold my hand and You

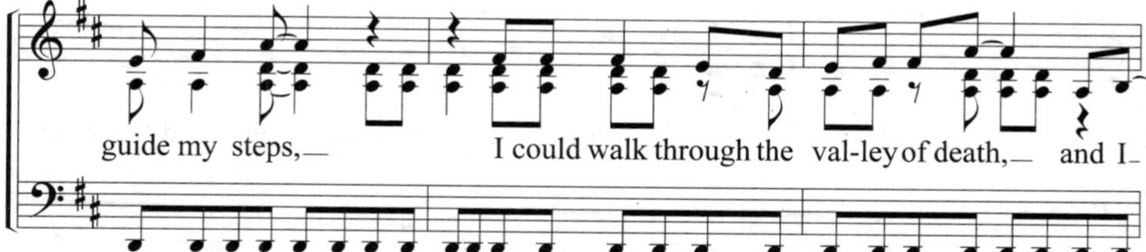
guide my steps, I could walk through the val-ley of death, and I

G
A7sus4
D
won't be a-fraid.

G
A7sus4
D
Be-cause You are in con-trol.
x3
G
A7sus4
D
You are in con-trol.
1.
D.C.
2.
C
You cause ev-'ry-thing to
G
D
C
G
D
work to-geth-er, You tru-ly have a sov-'reign plan, and You know
Em7
D2/F♯
G2
who I am,

Em7
D2/F♯
and You made who I am,
G2
Em7
D2/F♯
and You love who I am.
G2
1.
2.
You know
Be-cause You
G2
A7sus4
D
(Repeat as required)
are in con-trol.
You
G2
A7sus4
D
are in con-trol.

1650. You are mystical

Gen 2:2; Ps 30:5; 121:4; 139:7-10; Is 49:15

Shuffle
Brian Houston
G
1. You are my - sti - cal and deep.
- fer long, but Your pa - tience waits.
Bm
You take Your rest, but ne - ver sleep.
Your judge - ment al - ways he - si - tates.
C
(And) You watch me like a mo -
Your an - ger stays a mo -
1.
Bm
Am
D7sus4
- ther does, e - v'ry scar and e - v'ry tear and fall.
G
Gsus4
G
You suf -

2.
Bm
Am
- ment, yet Your fa - vour lasts a whole life long.
G
Bridge
And I
D
C
can-not stand si - lent-ly when faced with so much grace.
G
D
My chest is pound - ing with the need to
ce - le-brate You, God, and the mi-ra-cle of Your love.

Chorus
G
For You're e - v'ry-where, in e - v'ry place, in e -
Bm
C
v'ry time, in e - v'ry space, and e - v'ry breath that
G
I take You lend. You're the on -
C
Bm
Am
ly One who sa - tis-fies, the on - ly One who makes my life make
G
1.
2.
sense. 2. For

2. You are generous and kind,
So intimate and close at times,
Yet You reveal Your beauty in the twilight
And the summer evening rain.
You're in the rainbow and the dawn,
You steal my breath and then You're gone,
Yet when the morning sun breaks through,
I look for You and You are here again.

1651. You are the fountain of my life

Ps 36:7, 9

(Your love reaches me)

Capo 3 (D)
With anticipation
Darren Clarke
Verse
Bb2/D(G)
Bb(G)
You are the foun - tain of my life,
F(D)
Csus4(A)
C(A)
Bb2/D(G)
and in your light I find my rea -
Bb(G)
F(D)
Csus4(A)
C(A)
son, 'cause Your love reach -
Bb2/D(G)
Bb(G)
F(D)
Csus4(A)
es to the stars, e - ven the great deep.
C(A)
Bb2/D(G)
And Your love reach - es to this heart,

Chorus
B♭(G)
F(D)
Csus4(A)
F(D)
and it makes me sing.
Your love
B♭(G)
Gm7(Em)
(G) B♭/C
rea-ches me: it's what I need, it's what I need.
F(D)
3rd time to bridge
B♭(G)
Your love reach-es me: it's what I need,
1. Gm7(Em)
F(D)
D.S.
2. Gm7(Em)
it's what I need.
it's what I need,
C(A)
B♭2/D(G)
B♭(G)
Last time to Coda
it's what I need, Lord.

F(D)
Csus4(A)
C(A)
D.C.
You are the foun-
Bridge
B♭(G)
what I need,
Gm7(Em)
what I need. O
B♭(G)
Lord, how price - less
F(D)
is Your
Dm7(Bm)
un - end - ing love.
B♭(G)
Both high and low
F(D)
find re - fuge in Your sha - dow.
B♭2/D(G)
1.
B♭(G)
O
2.
B♭(G)
dow.
D.S.
Coda
B♭2(G)

1652. You are the King of glory

Lk 1:37; 18:27; Rom 8:31;
2 Cor 6:2; 1 Tim 2:1; Heb 1:8; 4:16

Steadily

Liz Fitzgibbon

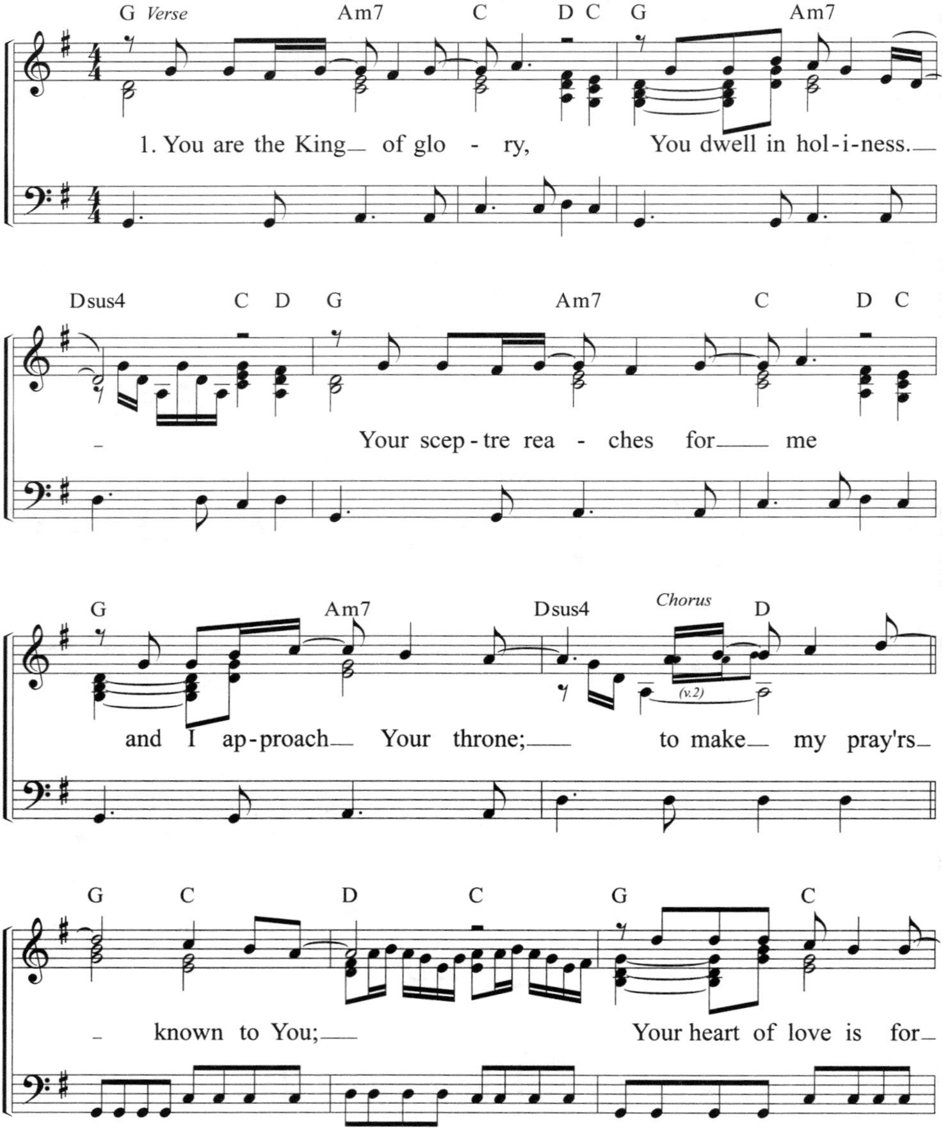

Verse

1. You are the King of glory, You dwell in holiness.
Your sceptre reaches for me
and I approach Your throne;

Chorus

to make my pray'rs known to You;
Your heart of love is for

D C G C
me. With bold-ness I draw near
D B7 C Dsus4 D/F♯ (Fine) G Am7
to Your throne, O God, to Your throne. La la la la la
D.C. (al fine)
C D C G Am7 C2 D C
la. La la la la la la.

2. You show Your favour to me,
My faith just grows and grows.
Nothing's too hard for my God,
No prayer too hard for You.

I will make my prayers . . .

1653. You are the Lord
(Famous One)

Ps 8:1; 19:1; Hag 2:7; Rev 22:16

Chris Tomlin & Jesse Reeves

With excitement
Chorus G
G/B
C2
You are the Lord, the fa-mous One, fa-mous One;
Em7
D
C
great is Your name in all the earth. The
G
G/B
C2
hea - vens de-clare You're glo-ri-ous, glo-ri-ous;
3rd time to Coda
Em7
D
G
great is Your fame be-yond the earth.
G/B
F2
C2

Verse
Am7
G/B
1. And for all You've done and yet to do,
C
G
with e - v'ry breath, I'm prais-ing You.
Am7
G/B
De - sire of na-tions and e-v'ry heart,
C
Dsus4
You a - lone are God, You a - lone are God.
1. D.C.
2. D.C. al Coda
Coda
G
the earth.

2. The Morning Star is shining through,
And every eye is watching You.
Revealed by nature and miracles,
You are beautiful, You are beautiful.

1654. You are the Lord
(Glorious)

Dan 7:9, 13, 22; Phil 2:9; Rev 5:9, 14; 7:9; 22:13, 16

Eoghan Heaslip & Mick Goss

Steadily

A
Verse
Bm7
Dsus2
E
You are the Lord, the King of hea - ven
Be - fore Your throne the el - ders fall,

A
Bm7
Dsus2
E
and all the earth, You'll reign for - e - ver.
and an - gels sing: 'Al - migh - ty God.'

A
Bm7
1.
Dsus2
E
A
Bm7
First and the last, You are glo-ri-ous,
Bright Mor - ing Star,

Dsus2
E
2.
Dsus2
E
D
You are glo - ri-

E
D
E
ous, You are glo - ri - ous. To
Chorus
A
E/G♯
You, the na - tions will come, e - v'ry
Bm7
D
E
A
tribe, e - v'ry tongue and wor - ship be - fore You, the
E/G♯
Bm7
An - cient of Days, the Name a - bove all names, who is
D
E
F♯m7
D
E
wor - thy of all our praise. You are glo - ri - ous.

1.
D.C.
A Bm7 Dsus2 E A Bm7 Dsus2 E
Yeah, You are glo - ri - ous.
Last time
A Bm7 Dsus2 E A Bm7 Dsus2 E A
Glo-ri-ous.
Rit.....
Glo-ri-ous.

1655. You are the One I love

Ps 119:105; Is 43:1

Sue Rinaldi
& Caroline Bonnett

With feeling

Chorus
D
You are the One I love, You are the One that I
A7
Asus4 A7
1.
a - dore.
To end
D (Fine)
2.
A
Verse
G
D/F♯
1. For You've called me by name, drawn me close
Em7
D/F♯
G
to Your heart, washed a - way all my shame
D/F♯
Asus4
A
G
with Your tears. For the rest of my days,

D/F♯ Em7 Bm7 G
I will of - fer my life in thanks-giv - ing and praise
D/F♯ Asus4
To repeat
A
Last time
A
D
to my King. Such pre -
A7 Asus4 A7
cious, pre - cious love.
1.
2.
Asus4 A
D.C. al fine
You have won me with Your

2. Now with You I will stay,
For Your word is my light,
And Your peace can allay all my fears;
And my victory song
Is the song of the cross,
You have won me with love so divine.

1656. You are the song that I sing

(My inspiration)

Ps 119:97

Lara Martin

Gently rhythmic

G
Verse
Am7
G/B
Am7
1. You are the song that I sing,
2. You are the light of my life,

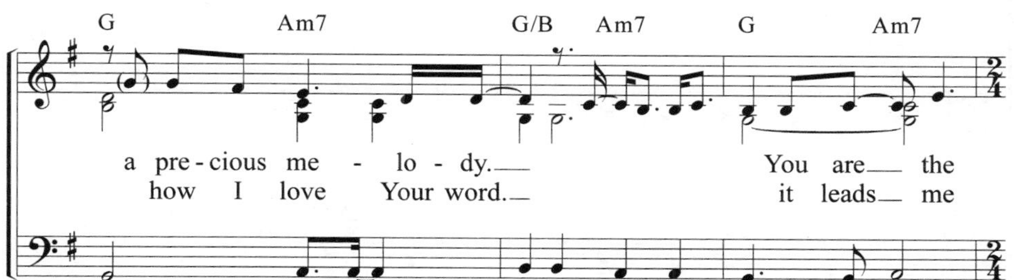
G
Am7
G/B
Am7
G
Am7
a pre-cious me-lo-dy.
how I love Your word.
You are the
it leads me

G/B
Csus2
(Chorus)
theme of my heart,
clo-ser to You.
You are my

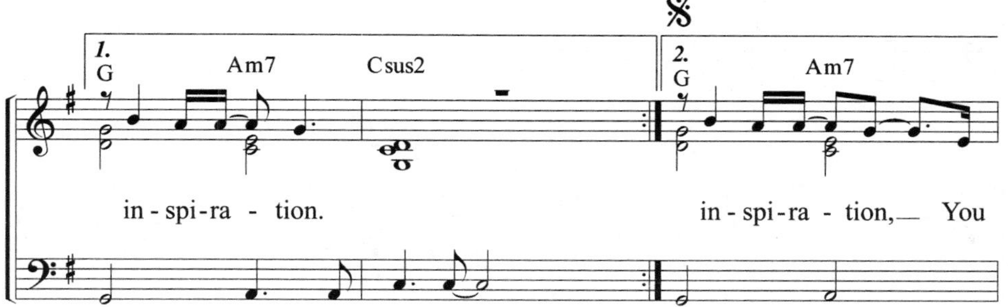
1.
G
Am7
Csus2
2.
G
Am7
in-spi-ra-tion.
in-spi-ra-tion, You

Lara Martin (Abundant Life Ministries, Bradford, England)

Csus2
G
Am7
cause me to sing. You are my in - spi - ra - tion, the
C
G
Am7
rea - son I live. You are my in - spi - ra - tion, I'm
2nd time to Coda
Csus2
G
Am7
C2
(Fine)
glad I'm a - live. You are my in - spi - ra - tion.
G
Am7
G/B
Am7
Verse
3. Your great - ness cre - a - tion di - splays,
G
Am7
G/B
Am7
G
Am7
such won - ders to be - hold. In awe I,

G/B
Csus2
D.S. al Coda
I live my days.
You are my
Coda
C2
D/F♯
Em7
D
Csus2
D/F♯
tion.
How then can I be si - lent,
Em7
D
Csus2
D
when my heart is so full?
Em7
D
C2
G/B
Csus2
In You I have di-sco - vered the se-cret of true love.
Dsus4
D (stop)
D.S. al Fine
And I want the world to know that You are my

1657. You are the sovereign 'I Am'

(Your name is holy)

Jn 8:58; Eph 6:13; 1 Pet 1:19; Rev 5:12

Brian Doerksen

With energy
E Bsus4 C#m7
You are the sov - 'reign 'I Am', Your
You are the Al - migh - ty One, Your
A2 E Bsus4
name is ho - ly. You are the pure, spot - less
name is ho - ly. You are the Christ, God's own
Last time to Coda
C#m7 A2 1. E Bsus4
Lamb, Your name is ho - ly.
Son, You name is ho - ly.
C#m7 A2 2. E
In Your name
E/G# A A/C# B C#m7 B/D#
there is mer - cy for sin, there is

E E/G♯ A2 F♯m7 Bsus4
safe - ty with - in, in Your ho - ly name.
B E/G♯ A A/C♯
In Your name there is strength to re - main,
B C♯m7 B/D♯ E E/G♯ A2 F♯m7
to stand, in spite of pain, in Your
E/B B D.C.
ho - ly name.
Coda
E Bsus4
C♯m7
To repeat
A2
Your name is ho - ly.
To end
A2 E
name is ho - ly.

1658. You call us first
(One thing)

Ex 20:3; Mk 12:30

Capo 5(C)

Tim Hughes

Worshipfully

Dm7(Am)
Verse
C/E(G)
F(C)
1. You call us first to love Your name,
2. Your ho - nour, Lord, Your name's re - nown
Dm7(Am)
C/E(G)
B♭2(F)
Dm7(Am)
C/E(G)
to wor - ship You.
To please Your heart
we long to see.
So let the glo -
F(C)
Dm7(Am)
C/E(G)
B♭2(F)
our one de - sire,
O Lord.
ry of Your name
be praised.
F(C)
Chorus
C/E(G)
Dm7(Am)
B♭(F)
F/A(C)
If there's one thing we are called to do, it's to love You, to a -

B♭(A) C7sus4(G) F(C) C/E(G) Dm7(Am)
dore You. We will bring our all and wor-ship You, bow be-
Last time to Coda
B♭(F) F/A(C) B♭(F) C7sus4(G) Am7(Em)
fore You, as we love You. I will ce-le-brate this
B♭2(F) F(C) C/E(G) Dm7(Am)
love, Je-sus, You are ev-'ry-thing to me.
Am7(Em) B♭2(F)
For what more, Lord, can I do? I will give this heart, this
D.S. Coda
F(C) C/E(G) Dm7(Am) B♭2(F)
life to You.
B♭(F) C7sus4(G) F(C)
love You, Lord.

1659. You came into my life

(While today is still today)

Ps 25:2, 4-5; Rom 12:1; Heb 13:5

Tim Hughes

With energy
D
Verse
A
1. You came in-to my life, a Sa-viour to my soul;
Bm
G
A
You set a hope with - in this heart of mine.
D
A
You said that I am Yours, that You will ne - ver leave
Bm
G
A
me, now I sur - ren - der all I am to You.
G
Bridge
A
I will ne - ver know why You chose me, God,
G
A
G
but You did. I will ne - ver know

A
G
why You took that cross, but You did,
A
D
Chorus
yes, You did.
While to-day is still to-day
A
Bm
I'll live just for Your praise, a liv-ing sa-cri-fice;
G
A
D
A
hold-ing out to be faith-ful un-to
Bm
G
D/F♯
G
D.C.
You, so in my life be glo-ri-fied, I pray.
Last time
D
Fine

2. In You, O Lord, I trust,
In You, O Lord, I live;
Do not let me stray from Your commands.
Guide me in Your way,
Protect me in Your truth,
Teach me what it means to follow You.

1660. You can have my whole life

(I want to go Your way)

Deut 10:12; Eph 2:8

Capo 3 (D)

Worshipful

James Taylor

F(D)
Bb/F (G)
C(A)
You can have my whole life, You can come and have it all:
Bb(G)
Gm7(Em)
C(A)
I don't want to go my own way now.
F(D)
I love to feel Your pre-
Dm(Bm)
C(A)
Bb2(G2)
-sence and I know Your sav-ing grace, I am no-
Gm7(Em)
C(A)
F(D)
-thing when You're se-cond place.

Am7(F♯m)
B♭(G)
I've been born to give You praise,
F(D)
Am7(F♯m)
not to yearn and strive for world - ly things.
Dm(Bm)
B♭(G)
F/A(D)
I've been born to love Your ways,
take my pride
Am7(F♯m)
Gm7(Em)
and let me al-ways say:
I want to go
C(A)
1.
F(D)
2.
F(D)
Your way now.
now.

1661. You chose the cross

(Lost in wonder)

Lk 4:18; 22:42; Jn 19:2; Acts 10:41; Phil 2:8; Heb 12:2

Capo 3 (G)

Martyn Layzell

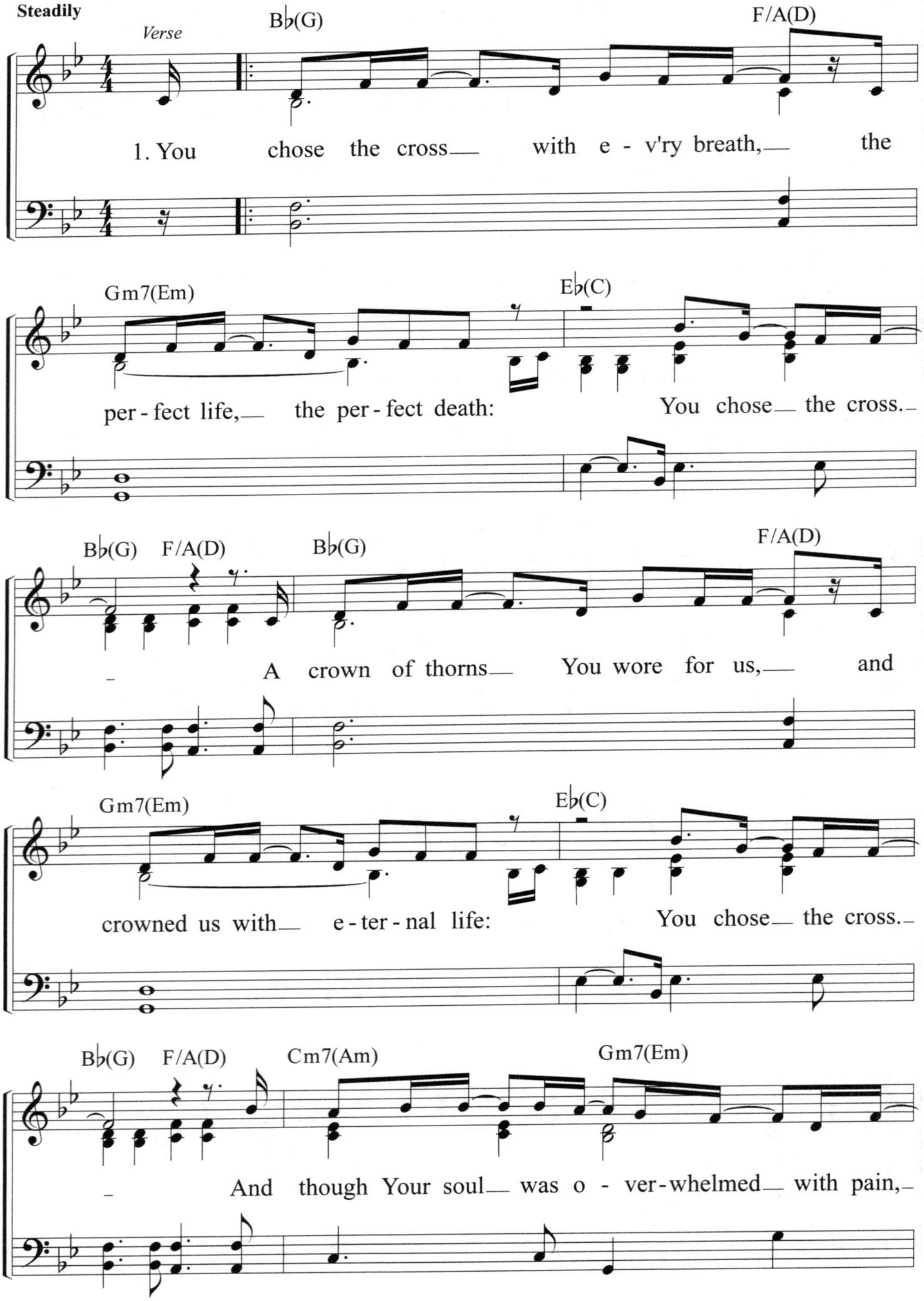

Steadily

Verse

Bb(G) F/A(D)

1. You chose the cross with e - v'ry breath, the

Gm7(Em) Eb(C)

per - fect life, the per - fect death: You chose the cross.

Bb(G) F/A(D) Bb(G) F/A(D)

A crown of thorns You wore for us, and

Gm7(Em) Eb(C)

crowned us with e - ter - nal life: You chose the cross.

Bb(G) F/A(D) Cm7(Am) Gm7(Em)

And though Your soul was o - ver - whelmed with pain,

F(D) B♭/D(G) Cm7(Am) B♭/D (G) F(D)
Chorus
– o - be-di-ent to death You o - ver - came. I'm lost in
B♭(G) F/A(D) Gm7(Em) E♭(C)
won - der, I'm lost in love, I'm lost in praise for - e-ver more.
F(D) B♭(G) F/A(D) Gm7(Em)
Be-cause of Je - sus' un-fail-ing love, I am for-
E♭(C) F(D) Fsus4(D) B♭(G)
Fine
gi - ven, I am re-stored. 2. You

2. You loosed the cords of sinfulness
And broke the chains of my disgrace:
You chose the cross.
Up from the grave victorious
You rose again so glorious:
You chose the cross.
The sorrow that surrounded You was mine,
'Yet not My will but Yours be done!' You cried.

1662. You confide in those who fear You

(The friendship and the fear)

Is 6:5; Jn 15:14-15; Rev 5:5

Matt Redman

Quite slow
Verse
G
C2/G
You con-fide in those_who fear_You, share the se-crets of_Your heart,_
friend-ship give to those_who seek_to ho-nour You with ev - 'ry part._
Am7
G/B
Though I'm one of un - clean lips,_Lord, I am cry-ing: 'woe_is me,'_
try-ing now to rid_my-self_of all the things that hin - der me_from
Chorus
Em7
Gmaj7/B
C2
know - ing You, hear-ing You

C2
Em7
Gmaj7/B
C2
G/B
speak, see-ing You move my-ste-rious -
Am7
Em7
Gmaj7/B
ly. Your whi - sper -
C2
Em7
Gmaj7/B
C2
ings in my soul's ear:
Em7
Gmaj7/B
C2
G/B
Am7
I want the friend - ship and the fear
G
C2/G
of know-ing You.

G
1.
C2/G
Last time
G
Fine

2. There is one thing You have spoken,
There are two things I have found;
You, O Lord, are ever loving,
You, O Lord, are always strong.
I am longing to discover
Both the closeness and the awe,
Feel the nearness of Your whisper,
Hear the glory of your roar, just . . .

I consider everything a loss compared to the surpassing greatness of knowing Christ Jesus my Lord

PHILIPPIANS 3:8

1663. You gave Your only Son

(Praise You)

Is 53:5; Rom 5:9; Jn 14:6; 1 Jn 4:10

Martyn Layzell

Steady 4
Verse
G
D
1. You gave Your on - ly Son, came down from heav'n a-bove,
Em7
C2
en-dured the cross, so I might know
G
D
this love that reached for me, a love that sets me free,
Bridge
Em7
C2
Em7
D/F♯
Your sa - cri-fice has saved my soul. To-day I'm re-
G
C2
Em7
D/F♯
mind - ed of Your grace; al - ways liv-ing

G
C2
D
C
now to sing Your praise, Your praise.
Chorus
G
Em7
C
Praise You, Je-sus, I praise You, I lift my hands and sing.
D
C
G
Em7
Em - brace You, I will em - brace You, my
C
D
C
Sa - viour and my King, my King.
G

2. I could not earn this love,
Such undeserved love;
Jesus, I know You are the way.
You paid the price for me,
Your blood was shed for me,
And in Your mercy took my place.

1664. You have given me new life

(Over me)

Jn 4:14; 1 Jn 1:7

David & Nathan Fellingham

Lively

Verse
A
E/G♯
F♯m7
D2
1. You have giv - en me new life;
now my heart is sa - tis-fied.
I'm
(v.2)
A2/C♯
Bm7
tast - ing the pow - er of the age to come,
E
I'm liv-ing in the glo - ry of the re-sur-rect - ed Son.
A/C♯
I'm walk-ing in the light and all that I now do

E
D2
A/C♯
Bm7
Esus4 E
is for You.
Chorus
A
D
E
Pour - ing o - ver me, ev - er - last - ing love
Pour - ing o - ver me, a - bound - ing grace
D/F♯
A
D
1.3.
E/G♯
and mer - cy, o - ver me in a flood of pow'r.
so free, o - ver me Your un -
Bm7
2.
E
Bm7
D.C.
end - ing love.
Last time
E
Bm7
A
Fine
end - ing love.

2. I've never had a friend like You;
All that You've promised You will do.
I'm drinking from the fountain that will never run dry,
I'm living in the joy of a heart that's purified.
I'm walking now with You, and all I have is Yours,
Take my life.

1665. You have laid Your hand on me

Jn 15:15; Phil 3:8

(How can I live?)

Noel Richards

Steady 4

G2
Verse
C
1. You have laid Your hand on me, I am changed for - e -
2. Help me ne - ver to for - get what I used to be.

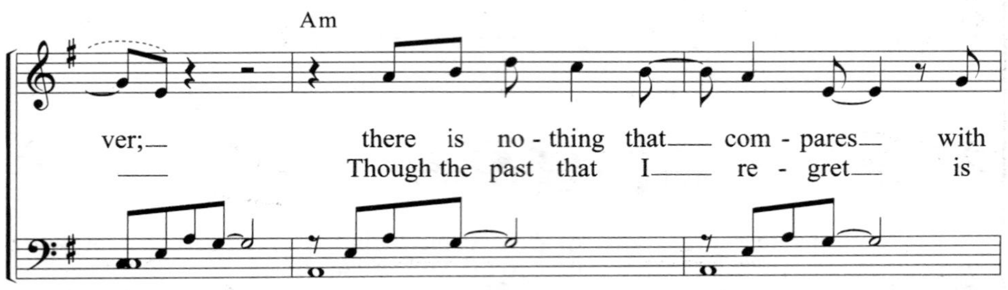
Am
ver; there is no - thing that com - pares with
Though the past that I re - gret is

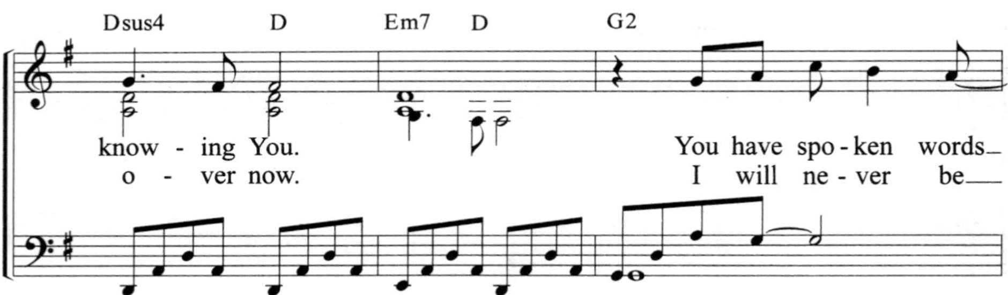
Dsus4
D
Em7
D
G2
know - ing You. You have spo - ken words
o - ver now. I will ne - ver be

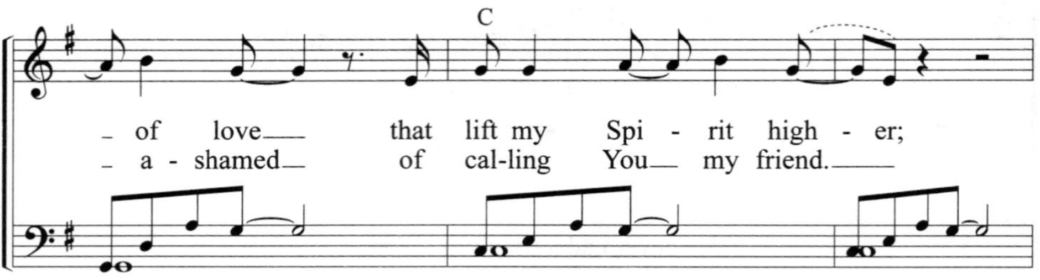
C
of love that lift my Spi - rit high - er;
a - shamed of cal-ling You my friend.

Am
D
Em7
Je-sus Christ, my dear - est friend, I'm ne-ver let-ting go.
I no lon-ger hide from You, I'm run-ning to Your side.
D/F♯
Chorus
C
G/B
How can I live, how can I live, how can I live
C
G
C
with-out Your love? How can I live, how can I live,
Last time to Coda
G/B
Am
1. D
Dsus4 D
how can I live with-out Your love?
2. D
C/E
All the rich-es I pos-sess are

Em7
C
mean-ing - less to me;
Your love is the great -

D.S. al Coda
D
C/E
D/F♯
est gift, the ve-ry air I breathe. How can I live

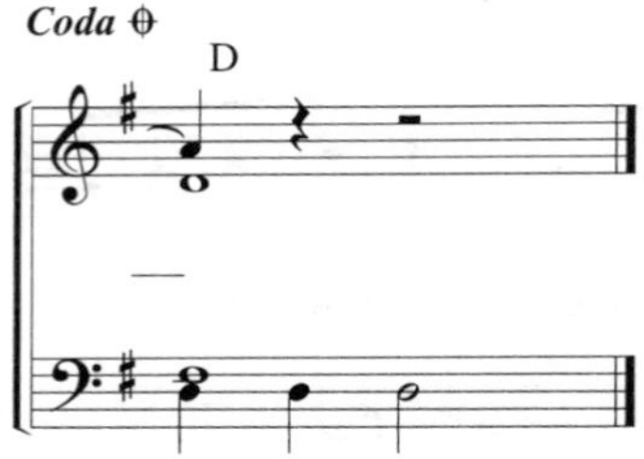
Coda
D

He gives strength to the weary and increases the power of the weak. Even youths grow tired and weary, and young men stumble and fall; but those who hope in the Lord will renew their strength. They will soar on wings like eagles; they will run and not grow weary, they will walk and not faint.

ISAIAH 40:29-31

1666. You led me to the cross

(Jesus, keep me near the cross)

Jn 9:25; 20:1, 6

Matt Redman

Capo 1(G)

Thoughtfully

A♭(G)
E♭/G(D)
Fm(Em)
1.You led me to the cross, and I saw Your face of mer-cy in that
D♭(C)
A♭(G)
E♭/G(D)
place of love. You o-pened up my eyes to be-lieve Your
Fm(Em)
D♭(C)
sweet sal - va - tion, where I'd been so blind.
B♭7/D(A)
D♭(C)
A♭(G)
Now that I'm liv - ing in Your all for-giv - ing love,
E♭(D)
B♭7/D(A)
D♭(C)
E♭/G(D)
my e - ve - ry road leads to the cross.

Ab(G)
Chorus
Eb/G(D)
Fm(Em) Fm/Eb(Em)
Je - sus, keep me near the cross,
Bb7/D(A)
Db(C)
Ab(G)
I won't for - get the love You've shown. Sa - viour,
Eb/G(D)
Fm(Em) (Em) Fm/Eb Bb7/D(A)
teach me of the cross, I won't for - get the love,
Db(C)
Ab(G) Absus4(G) Ab(G)
I won't for - get the love You've shown.

2. And there's an empty tomb,
That tells me of Your resurrection
And my life in You.
The stone lies rolled away,
Nothing but those folded grave clothes
Where Your body lay.
Now that I'm living as a risen child of God,
My every road leads to the cross.

1667. You pour out grace

Is 42:3; Lk 4:18; 2 Cor 12:10

Gareth Robinson
& Joannah Oyeniran

With a rocky feel

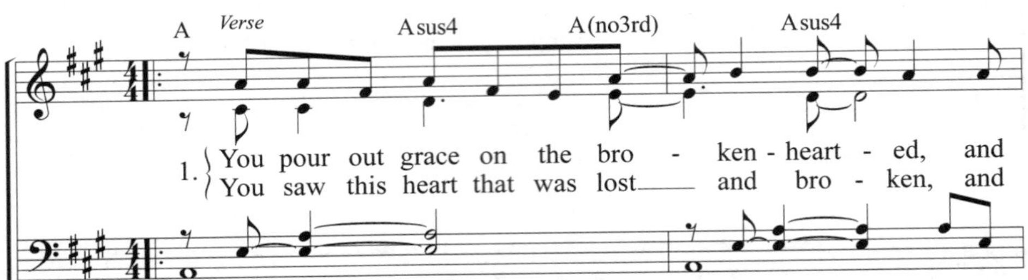
A
Verse
Asus4
A(no3rd)
Asus4
1.
You pour out grace on the bro - ken - heart - ed, and
You saw this heart that was lost and bro - ken, and

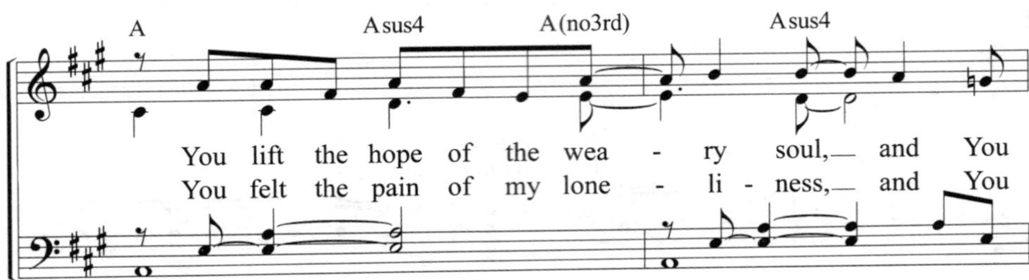
A
Asus4
A(no3rd)
Asus4
You lift the hope of the wea - ry soul, and You
You felt the pain of my lone - li - ness, and You

G
1. D
stretch out Your hand with Your lov - ing mer - cy.
be - friend - ed me and re - stored

A
Asus4
A(no3rd)
Asus4
2. D
my dig - ni - ty.

Chorus
A Asus4 A(no3rd) Asus4 A
You alone revealed the love of God to me, and
E Bm D
You alone have given ev'rything for me;
A E Bm
and You alone deserve the highest praise, Jesus.
D A E Bm A/C♯ D A Asus4

(Fine)
A(no3rd) Asus4
Bm
A/C♯
D
E
And You have gi - ven me great sal - va - tion,
and You have gi-ven me hope e-ter - nal, and ev'-ry day I will look
to give You all the glo-ry that's due Your name.
D.S. al fine

2. You demonstrated the life of love to me,
And how it was that You wanted me to live:
Heart of compassion and hands of healing.
I need Your Spirit to help accomplish this:
Abundant grace and Your strength in weakness,
And the steady hand of the Father holding me.

1668. You're the One who gave His Son

(God is still for us)

Rom 8:28, 31-32, 35, 38-39

Simply

Johnny Parks

Verse
E
Amaj7
1. You're the One who gave His Son, who will
E
Amaj7
C♯m7
free-ly give us all things, and no-thing can be a-gainst
Amaj7
E
Amaj7
us if God is still for us. And
E
Amaj7
E
all things work for good for those who love the Lord,
Amaj7
C♯m7
Amaj7
and no-thing can be a-gainst us when You are still

E
Amaj7
A
for us. And we're con - vinced that nei-ther death
C♯m7
B
E
A
nor life, an-gels or de - mons, height, nor depths, nor
C♯m7
B
what's to come can cut us off from the love of God.
A
E
E/D♯
God is still for us, God is still for us, God is
C♯m7
A
E
still for us, turn a-round. He is still for us, God is

E/D♯
C♯m7
1.
A
still for us, God is still for us, turn a-round.
2. When
2.
A
E2
E/D♯
C♯7sus4
C♯m7
Turn a-round,
turn a-round,
A
E
turn a-round.

2. When hardship or danger comes,
We know that God gave His only Son.
So as a body we are assured
That God is still for us.
We look to You, Lord, we stand on Your word;
We're holding on to the promise You've made -
That nothing can be against us
When You are still for us.

1669. You're the Word of God the Father

(Across the lands)

Ps 96:11; Lk 8:24; 9:16; 19:10; Jn 1:1, 3; Eph 4:8; Col 1:16-17; Heb 7:25; Rev 7:9

With a lilting feel

Stuart Townend
& Keith Getty

Verse

D G
1. You're the Word of God the Father, from be -

D A G G6 D/F♯
fore the world be - gan; e-v'ry star and e - v'ry pla-net has been

Em G D G
fash-ioned by Your hand. All cre - a-tion holds to - ge-ther by the

D A G G6 D/F♯
po-wer of Your voice: let the skies declare Your glo-ry, let the

Em G Asus4 A Chorus G
land and seas re - joice! You're the Au - thor of cre -
D D/F♯ G A2 Bm Bm/A
a - tion, You're the Lord of e - v'ry man; and Your
G G/A Bm7 A 1.2. 3.
cry of love rings out a - cross the lands. 2. Yet You

2. Yet You left the gaze of angels,
Came to seek and save the lost,
And exchanged the joy of heaven
For the anguish of a cross.
With a prayer You fed the hungry,
With a word You stilled the sea;
Yet how silently You suffered
That the guilty may go free.

3. With a shout You rose victorious,
Wresting victory from the grave,
And ascended into heaven
Leading captives in Your wake.
Now You stand before the Father
Interceding for Your own.
From each tribe and tongue and nation
You are leading sinners home.

1670. Your hand, O God, has guided

Eph 4:4-6

(One church)

Capo 3 (D)

Steadily

Music: Keith Getty

(Bm) (A) (Bm) (A)
Dm C/D Dm C/D
(Bm) (A) (Bm) (A)
Dm C/D Dm C/D
Verse
Dm(Bm)
C/D(A) Dm(Bm)
1. Your hand, O God, has gui - ded Your

B♭(G) C(A) Dm(Bm)
C(A) Dm(Bm)
church from age to age, the tale of love is writ - ten for

B♭(G) C(A) F(D) B♭sus2(G)
Dm7(Bm) Dm2(Bm)
us on e - v'ry page. Our fa - thers knew Your good - ness, and

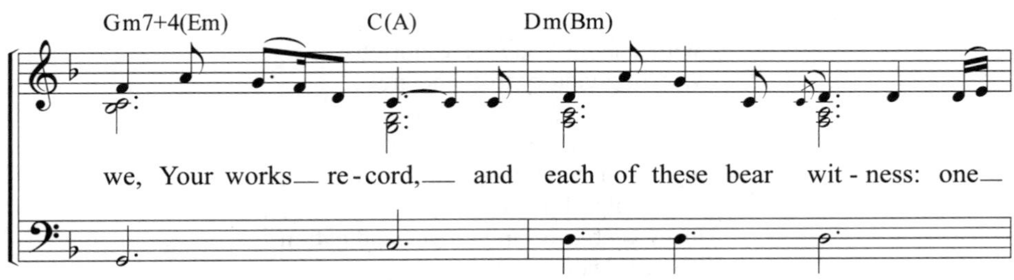
Gm7+4(Em) C(A) Dm(Bm)
we, Your works re - cord, and each of these bear wit - ness: one

Gm7(Em) Am7(F♯m) (G) B♭sus2 C7(A)
Chorus
F(D) C/F(A) (G) B♭sus2/D F(D)
church, one faith, one Lord.— One church, one faith, one Lord of life, one
B♭(G) F/A(D) C(A) F(D) C/F(A) Dm7(Bm) F(D)
Fa-ther, one Spi-rit, one Christ.—One church, one faith, one Lord of Life, one
B♭(G) F/A(D) (Bm) Dm (A) C/D (Bm) Dm (A) C/D
hea - ven-ly King, Lord of all.
1. Dm(Bm) (A) C/D Dm(Bm) (A) C/D
Last time Dm(Bm)
2. Your—

2. Your mercy never fails us, or leaves Your work undone;
With Your right hand to help us, the victory shall be won.
And then with heaven's angels Your name shall be adored,
And they shall praise You, singing: one church, one faith, one Lord.

E. H. Plumptre (1821-91) adapt. Keith Getty.

1671. Your kindness

(Wonderful, beautiful, merciful)

Zeph 3:17; Jn 14:6

Brightly

James Gregory

G
Verse
Bm
1. Your kind - ness o - ver - whelmed me, the love that cap -
You led me to the Fa - ther, and in - tro - duced
Em
C
C/B
Am
tured me. You helped me to be - lieve that You
us there, the Spi - rit poured out grace, and filled
F
F/E
Dsus4
D
(1st & 3rd times)
Chorus
de - light in me. You are won -
me with Your praise.
G
B7
Em
C
der - ful, beau - ti - ful, mer - ci - ful, and all my life

SoF3

G
1.
D
G
and my heart be-longs to You.
Dsus4
D
(Fine)
2.
D
G
B7
You are won - be-longs to You.
Em
C
D
Dsus4
D
C

2. Your plans for me are greater
Than I had ever thought,
You're daily changing me,
Revealing more to me.
My love for You is growing,
And as I reach for You,
Your Spirit pours out grace
And fills me with Your praise.

1672. Your kingdom generation

(Here to eternity)

Ps 57:5; Eccles 3:11

Darlene Zschech & David Moyse

Steadily
G
C/G
G
Your king - dom ge - ne - ra - tion de - clares Your ma -
We see Your Spi - rit mov - ing, we burn with ho -
C/G
C D+4
C
D+4
- je - sty, and our lives are re - sound - ing with Your praise.
ly fi - re. Your glo - ry is seen through all the earth.
1.
G
2.
G
C2
You set e - ter -
Dsus4
Em7
G/B
C2
ni - ty in my heart, so I'll live for You,
Dsus4
C2/E
D/F♯
for You.

G
Hal - le - lu - jah, hal - le - lu - jah,
ho - nour and praise for - e - ver.
we'll take our place in hi - sto - ry.
Em7
We'll shout a vic - to - ry cry
We'll shout Your awe - some love
C2 G/B C G/B Am7 D7sus4
from here to - e - ter - ni - ty.
F
D.C.
To finish
G

1673. Your light
(This is how we overcome)

Ps 30:11; 61:2

Reuben Morgan

Steadily
Fmaj9 Verse G Am7 Fmaj9
1. Your light broke through my night, re - stored ex-ceed-ing joy.
Your grace fell like the rain, and made this de - sert live.
1. G Am7 2. Gsus4 G
Chorus C F/A Gsus4 G
You have turned my mourn-ing in-to
Am7 F/A Gsus4 C F/A Gsus4 G
Last time to Coda
dan-cing. You have turned my sor-row in-to
1. F G D.C. 2. F Gsus4 D.S. 3. F
joy. joy. You have joy.
G Fmaj9 G Am7 Fmaj9 G Am7

Fmaj9
G
Am7
Fmaj9
G
Am7
This is how we o - ver - come.
Fmaj9
G
Am7
Fmaj9
G
Am7
This is how we o - ver - come.
F
F/E
F/D
F/C
G
Am7
1.-3.
F
F/E
F/D
F/C
G
Am7
This is how we o - ver - come. This is how we o - ver - come.
4.
F
NC
D.S. al Coda
This is how we o - ver - come. You
Coda
F
G
Fmaj9
joy.

2. Your hand lifted me up,
I stand on higher ground.
Your praise rose in my heart,
And made this valley sing.

1674.

Your love
(Pour over me)

Hos 6:3; Joel 2:23; Mt 11:28; Jn 15:11; 1 Pet 5:7

Stuart Townend

Steadily
Verse
D G/B A A/C♯
1. Your love, shin-ing like the sun, pour-ing like the
D G/B A A♯dim Bm Gmaj7
rain, rag-ing like the storm, re-fresh-ing me a - gain. Ooh,
A G/A D G/B 1. A/C♯ G2/B
I re - ceive Your love. 2. Your
2.3. A G/A
Chorus
D/F♯ G D/A G/B
Pour o - ver me, pour o - ver me,
D/A Bm E/G♯ A A/G D/F♯ G
let Your rain flood this thirs-ty soul. Pour o-ver me

D/A
G/B
D/A
G/B
D/A
A7sus4
To repeat
D
Your waves of love, pour o - ver me.
To end
D
Bm
G2
D
Bm
A7sus4
D
Bm
G2
C6
D
Fine

2. Your grace frees me from the past,
It purges every sin,
It purifies my heart
And heals me from within,
I receive Your grace.

3. I come and lay my burden down
Gladly at Your feet,
I'm opening up my heart,
Come make this joy complete;
I receive Your peace.

1675. Your love has captured me

(Be glorified)

With energy

Chris Tomlin, Jesse Reeves & Louie Giglio

G Verse C2 F2 C2/E G C2
Your love has cap-tured me, Your grace has
D G C2 F2 C2/E
set me free; Your life, the air I breathe:
Am7 D G C2 F2 C2/E
Be glo-ri-fied in me.
G C2 F2 C2/E C2 Chorus
You set my feet to danc - ing,
G C2
You set my heart on fire. In the pres-ence of a thou - sand kings, You

G
C2
are my one de - sire. And I stand be-fore You now with
Em
D
C2
Last time to Coda
trem-bling hands lift - ed high. Be glo-ri-fied.
1. G
C2
F2
C2/E
G
C2
F2
C2/E
2. G
G/B
C
D
G/B
C
Be glo - ri-fied in me, be glo - ri-fied
D
G/B
C
D
G/B
C
in me, be glo - ri-fied in me, be glo - ri-fied.

1.
G/B
C
2.
D.S. al Coda
Be glo - ri - fied
Coda
G
C2
F2
C2/E
G
C2
F2
C2/E
G

Give thanks to the Lord, for He is good. His love endures forever.

PSALM 136:1

1676. Your love is amazing

(Hallelujah)

Brenton Brown
& Brian Doerksen

Steadily
G2/B
1.(3.) Your love is a-maz - ing, stea-dy and un-chang-
Csus2
Dsus4
- ing; Your love is a moun - tain firm be-neath my feet.
Csus2
G2/B
Your love is a mys - t'ry, how you gent - ly lift
Csus2
Dsus4
me; when I am sur-round - ed, Your love car - ries me.
Csus2
Chorus
G
Dsus4
Hal-le-lu - jah, hal-le-lu - jah, hal-le-lu-

Em7
Csus2
G
- jah, Your love makes_ me sing. Hal-le-lu - jah, hal-le-lu-
Dsus4
Em7
Csus2
Last time to Coda
jah, hal-le-lu - jah, Your love makes_ me sing.
1.2.
D.C.
3.
D
Em7
2. Your love is_ sur-pri-
3. Your love is_ a-maz-
Yes, You make_ me_ sing,
D/F♯
Csus2
D
Lord, You make_ me_ sing, sing,_ sing, how You make_ me_
Em7
D/F♯
D.S. al Coda
_ sing. Hal - le - lu

Coda
C Csus2♯4 C2
C Csus2♯4 C2
C Csus2♯4 C2
Lord, You make me sing,
C Csus2♯4 C2
C Csus2♯4 C2
G
how You make me sing.

2. Your love is surprising,
I can feel it rising,
All the joy that's growing deep inside of me.
Every time I see You,
All your goodness shines through,
And I can feel this God song
Rising up in me.

1677. Your love is better than wine

(Draw me after You)

Song 1:2-4

Robert Critchley

Worshipfully

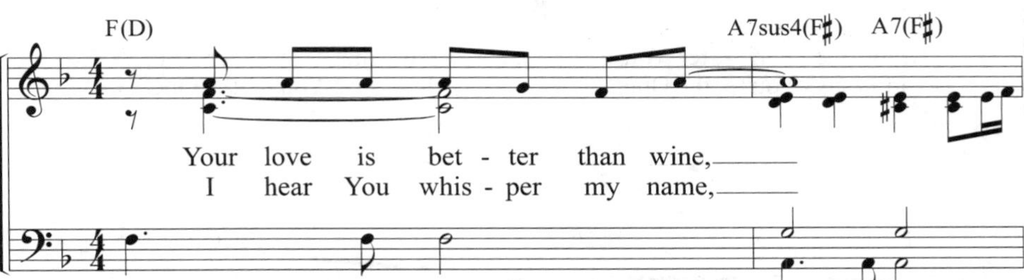
F(D)
A7sus4(F♯) A7(F♯)
Your love is bet - ter than wine,
I hear You whis - per my name,

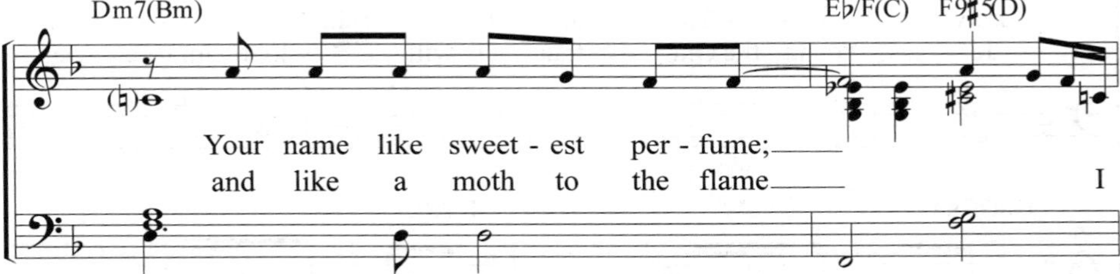
Dm7(Bm)
E♭/F(C) F9♯5(D)
Your name like sweet - est per - fume;
and like a moth to the flame
I

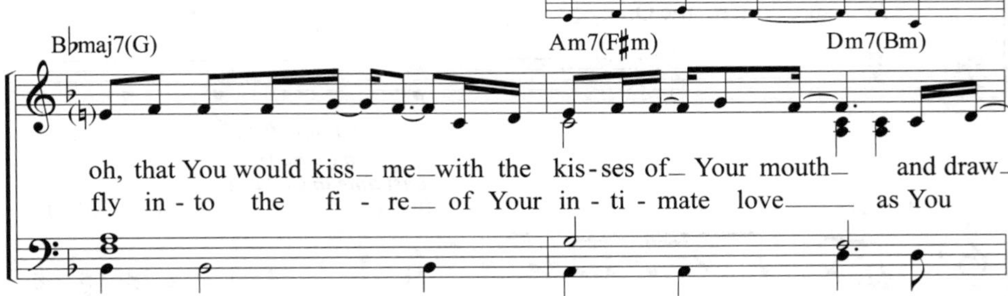
B♭maj7(G)
Am7(F♯m)
Dm7(Bm)
oh, that You would kiss me with the kis - ses of Your mouth and draw
fly in - to the fi - re of Your in - ti - mate love as You

Gm7(Em) B♭/C(G)
1. F(D) B♭/C(G)
2. F(D) B♭/C(G)
me, draw me af - ter You.
(Come and draw me deep - er)
draw me, draw me af - ter You.

F(D)
Gm7(Em)
Draw me af - ter You, draw me af - ter You,
Je - sus, You're the One, Je - sus, You're the One,
F/A(D)
B♭2(G)
(F♯+5) (F♯)
B♭/C (G) A+5/C♯ A7/C♯
draw me af - ter You and let us run to - ge - ther.
Je - sus, You're the One that I will love for - e - ver.
Dm7(Bm)
F/A(D)
Draw me af - ter You, draw me af - ter You,
Je - sus, You're the One, Je - sus, You're the One,
1st time D.C.
2nd time D.S.
Last time to Coda
B♭2(G)
B♭/C(G)
Dm(Bm) G7(E)
draw me af - ter You and let us run to - ge - ther.
Je - sus You're the One that I will love for - e - ver more.
B♭/C(G) F(D) Dm7(Bm) G7(E) B♭/C(G) F(D) Dm7(Bm) G7(E)
So a - maz - ing, so di - vine, I am Yours and

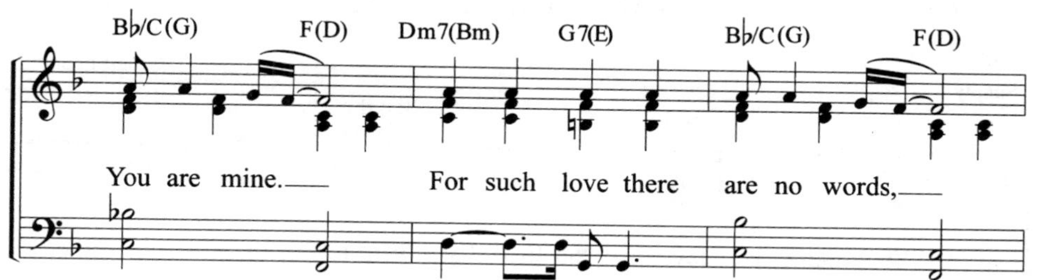
B♭/C(G)
F(D)
Dm7(Bm)
G7(E)
B♭/C(G)
F(D)
You are mine.
For such love there are no words,

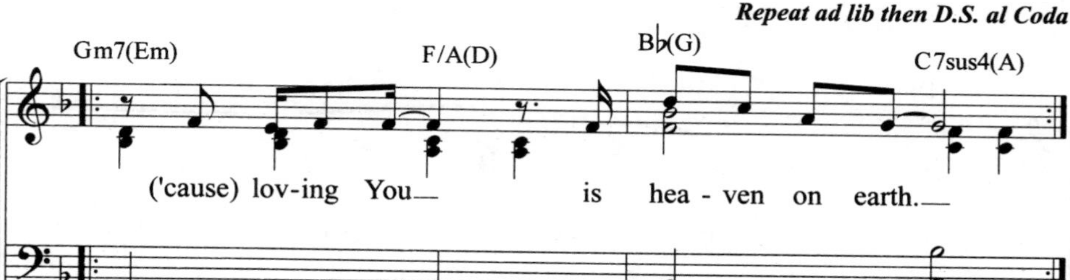
Repeat ad lib then D.S. al Coda
Gm7(Em)
F/A(D)
B♭(G)
C7sus4(A)
('cause) lov-ing You
is hea - ven on earth.

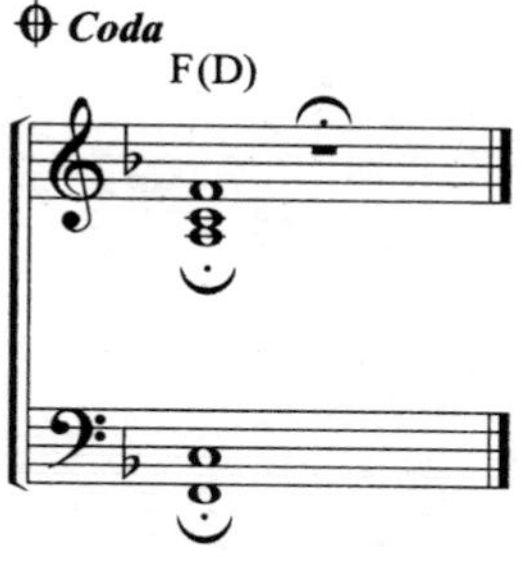
Coda
F(D)

1678. Your name is love

Capo 3 (D)

Mt 11:19; Jn 8:32; Phil 2:9; Rev 5:12

Greg Shepherd

Simply

Verse
F(D)
Bb(G)
1. Your name is love, the love that went to the cross. Your name is
F(D)
Bb(G)
peace, You've ta - ken my sins a - way, and how I
C(A)
Bb(G)
1.
F(D)
love all that You are, Your name is Je - sus.
Bb(G)
Bb/C(G)
2.,3.
F(D)
Chorus
2. Your name is Je - sus. Je - sus, Name
C(A)
Bb(G)
F(D)
C(A)
Bb(G)
a - bove all names, I will e - ver more pro - claim:

F(D)
C/E(A)
Dm(Bm)
Dm/C(Bm)
'wor - thy is the Lamb to re - ceive all pow'r,
B♭(G)
B♭/C(G)
1.,3.
F(D)
2.
F(D)
to re - ceive all praise.' Je - sus, Name
B♭2(G)
F(D)
B♭2(G)
D.C.
4.
F(D)
3. Your name is

2. Your name is truth,
The truth that sets me free.
Your name is hope,
Hope for eternity,
And how I love
All that You are,
Your name is Jesus.

3. Your name is Lord,
I gladly bow the knee.
You are a friend,
A friend of sinners like me,
And how I love
All that You are,
Your name is Jesus.

1679. Yours is the kingdom

Mt 25:1; 1 Cor 15:52; 1 Thess 4:16

Dave Bilbrough

Brightly
Chorus
G
Yours is the king-dom, the pow'r and the glo-ry, for
C/G
Am7
e-ver and e-ver, for e-ver and e-ver, a-
Last time to Coda
G
C
D
Em
Verse
men! 1. A trum-pet blast will
C
A
D
he-rald the day of Your re-turn:
B
Em
Your glo-ry and Your splen-dour will be

C
D
C
seen in all the earth! And oh, what a day,
G
oh, what a day that will be, when the
C
A
D
earth joins with hea-ven in wor-ship and praise to Je - sus!
D.C.
Coda
C
D
G
A - men!
C
D
G
C
D
G
A - men! A - men!

2. The time is drawing nearer,
I believe it's coming soon,
When we will rise to greet You
As a bride to meet her groom.

1680. Your voice

(Awesome God)

Ps 29:4

With a strong rhythm
Vicky Beeching
Em
C/E
G
Your voice is the voice that com-mand-ed the u-
D
Em
C/E
ni-verse to be. Your voice is the voice that
G
D
Am7
G/B
is speak-ing words of love to me:
C
Am7
G/B
C
Chorus
G
how can it be? Awe-some God,
C
Em
C
ho-ly God, I wor-ship You in won-der.

G
C
Awe - some God,
ho - ly God,
as
Em
C
Am7
You draw near I'm hum - bled
by Your ma - jes - ty
C
D
and the my - ste - ry
of Your great love for me.
Em
C/E
Em7
D
D.C.
To end
Em

2. Your arms are the arms that
Hung shining stars in deepest space.
Your arms are the arms that
Surround me in a warm embrace:
Amazing grace.

1681. Your whisper to my soul

Is 53:5; Mt 28:2; 1 Pet 1:18

Brian Houston

Country rock feel
A7 Verse D
Your whis - per to my soul
You took me as I am,
Bm
when I was like a child, lift - ed off the yoke,
You knew what I had done, still You took my shame.
F♯m G D D/A
plan - ted fields of hope in this heart of mine.
and You called my name, I was o - ver - come.
D Bm F♯m
When You broke the bonds of how I used to be,
G
You rolled a - way the stone, You set the cap - tive free.

A
D
Chorus
I wan - na thank You, You're the
A
Bm
G
God of mer-cy; I wan-na thank You, Lord, for giv-ing me peace.
D
A
I wan - na thank You, You're the God who loved me;
Bm
G
I wan - na thank You, You're the God who res-cued me.
D
A
Em7
G
8
(God who res-cued me.)

Last time to Coda
1.
D.C.
D
A
Em7
G
2.
Em
G
Bridge
F♯m
You co - vered all my sin, re-
G
D
A
G
stored to me my youth a - gain. And I am sa - tis - fied,
F♯m
G
Em7
for You have healed me and re - deemed me,
G
A7
crowned my head with end - less beau - ty,
D.S. al Coda
Coda
G
D
end - less beau - ty.

1682. You said

2 Chron 7:14; Is 11:9; 60:3; Mt 7:7; Jn 4:35

Reuben Morgan

Steadily
Verse
A/D E F♯m7 E/G♯ A/D E
1. You said: 'Ask and you will re-ceive what-e-ver you need.'
(v.2)
F♯m7 E/G♯ A/D E F♯m7 E/G♯
You said: 'Pray, and I'll hear from hea-ven,
(v.2)
1.
A/D E F♯m7 A/D E F♯m7 E/G♯
and I'll heal your land.'
A/D E F♯m7 E/G♯
2.,3.
A/D E
har-vest is here, the
F♯m7 E/G♯ A E
king-dom is here.' You said: 'Ask, and I'll give the na-

F♯m7
D
A
E
D
E
tions to you.' O Lord, that's the cry of my heart.
A
E
F♯m7
D
A
E
Dis-tant shores and the is - lands will see Your light as it ri-
1.,3.
D
E
2.
D
E
A/D
E
- ses on us. You said: - ses on us.
F♯m7
E/G♯
A/D
E
F♯m7
E/G♯
D.C.
4.
D
E
D.S.
- ses on us. You said:
5. (Last time)
D
E
A/D
E
F♯m7
E/G♯
- ses on us. O Lord, I ask for the na - tions.

1.,2.
A/D
E
F♯m7
E/G♯
3.
A/D
E
F♯m7

2. You said Your glory will fill the earth,
Like water the sea.
You said: 'Lift up your eyes,
The harvest is here,
The kingdom is here.'

1683. You set me apart

(Dwell in Your house)

Ps 23:6; 25:4-5; 46:1-2

Paul Ewing

Steadily
Verse
A/C♯ D2 F♯m7 E
1. You set me a-part, gave me a new heart,
A/C♯ D2 F♯m7 E
filled with com-pas - sion to share Your great love.
A/C♯ D2 F♯m7 E
Show me Your ways, I want to know You.
A/C♯ D2 F♯m7 E
Guide me in truth, my hope is in You.
Chorus
A/D E F♯m7
That I may dwell in Your house for-e - ver,

Last time to Coda
A/D
E
F♯m7
1. A/D
lift-ing up Your name;
dwell in Your house
E
F♯m7
E
D
D/E
for-e-ver more.
That I may
2. A/D
E
F♯m7
E
D2
1.
dwell in Your house for-e-ver more.
D.C.
2.
D2
E
F♯m7
2. I'll
Ho-ly Spi-
E
A/C♯
D2
rit, have Your way.

F♯m7
E
A/C♯
Sweet a - noint - ing teach our hearts, our lives,
D2
Esus4
E
D.S. al Coda
we pray. That I may
Coda
A/D
E
F♯m7
E
D2
dwell in Your house for - e - ver more.

2. I'll hold on to You,
   My Strength and my Refuge.
   Whom shall I fear?
   I know You are near.
   All of my days
   I live for You, Lord.
   Establish my path,
   There's one thing I ask.

1684. You shaped the heavens

(Maker of all things)

Ps 19:1; Dan 7:9, 13, 22; Col 1:16-17; Rev 22:13

Tim Hughes

Strongly
C2
Verse
G2
D
1. You shaped the hea - vens and the earth,
re-vealed Your splen - dour. You spoke Your life
in-to our hearts, so we be-long to You.
Chorus
You are the Mak - er of all things,
G
First and the Last; cre - a - tion sings praise

D G C2
to You, God. You're reign-ing in glo-
D G C2 D C2
ry, An-cient of Days; Your peo-ple sing praise
D G C2
1.3. (Fine) 2.
to You, God. And
D/F♯ G C2
earth joins with hea-ven, de-clar-ing Your glo-ry; pro-
D/F♯ 1. Em7 C2
claim-ing the works of Your hands. Yes,

2.
Em7
C2
D.S. al fine
works of Your hands.
You are the

2. Creator God, in You all things
Now hold together,
Working Your wonders day by day,
You'll reign forever.

1685. You spread out the skies

(Wonderful Maker)

Gen 1:3, 31; Job 26:14; Col 1:15

Matt Redman
& Chris Tomlin

Verse
C
Em7
1. You spread out the skies o-ver emp-ty space, said 'Let there be light' - to a
C
D
G/B
dark and form - less world Your light was born.
C
2. You spread out Your arms o - ver emp - ty hearts,
(3.) eye has ful - ly seen how beau - ti - ful the cross, and
Em7
said 'Let there be light' - to a dark and hope - less world Your Son was
we have on - ly heard the faint - est whis - pers of how great You
C
D
Am7
G/B
born. You made the world and saw that is was
are.

C2
Am7
G/B
C
good. You sent Your on-ly Son, for You are good.
D/F♯
Chorus
C2
What a won-der-ful Ma - ker, what a won-der-ful Sa-
Em7
C2
viour. How ma-jes-tic Your whis - pers,
D/F♯
G
G/B
and how hum-ble Your love. With a strength like no o-
C2
Em7
ther, and a heart of a Fa - ther,

C2
How ma - jes - tic Your whis - pers,
D/F#
1.
G
2.3.
Am7 G/B
what a won-der-ful God.
3. No
(2nd time instrumental)
C
Am7 G/B
C
What a won-der-ful God,
what a won-der-ful God.
Am7 G/B C
1.
D
D.S. al fine
2.
Am7 G/B C
Fine
What a won-der-ful Ma -

1686. You take me by the hand

Lam 3:22

(Carry me)

Dave Bilbrough

Steadily
D/F♯ A G D/F♯
You take me by the hand, and
G D/F♯ Em Asus4 A D A
though there are times I don't un-der-stand, Your love will ne-
G D/F♯ G A D D/F♯
ver fail, and my heart be-longs to You. E-ven when the
G A D G A
rain clouds break and the cold wind blows
Bm7 A
all a-round me, I will

G A D G D/F♯
not be put to shame; Lord, my hope is in Your name.
A7sus4 A G D/F♯ Em A7sus4 A7
You will car-ry me on Your shoul - ders and lead me
D A D/A A
home. Car-ry me o-ver trou-bled wa - ters, car-ry
G D/F♯ A
me o-ver stor-my seas. When the skies are dark and hea-
D/A A G D/F♯ A
vy, by Your grace You'll car - ry me.

G A D
Though the way can seem un-cer - tain be-cause the time
G A Bm7 G D/F♯
of change has come, 3 You will car-ry me on Your shoul-
Em A7sus4 A7 D
ders and lead me home.

1687. You've placed a hunger in my heart

(Come to us)

1 Kings 19:12; Mt 11:12; Jas 2:13; 1 Pet 2:5

Quickly, with energy

Stuart Townend

A/E
Verse
E
B7sus4
1. You've placed a hun - ger in my heart to see Your glo-
E
A/E
E
ry, You've caused a thirst that I can - not
B7sus4
A/E
E
ig - nore; You've stirred a pas - sion that will drive
B7sus4
E
A/E
me to Your pre - sence, and I won't rest
E
B7sus4
E
un - til You've heard me cry for more.

Chorus
A E A E A E C♯m B A E A E A E
Come as a migh - ty tor - rent, come as a ra - ging fire, come as a hur - ri - cane that drives the heat of my de - sire.
Come in the smal - lest whis - per, come as the qui - et dew:
we don't care how You come, as

B7sus4
E
D.C.
To finish
long as You come__ to us.__

2. Though people mock the church and curse the One who made them,
   Your kingdom is advancing every day;
   Like living stones we're being built into a temple,
   We've seen the glory and we cannot turn away.

3. Is this the summer that will see a mighty harvest?
   A sense of expectation fills the air;
   Though sin abounds, Your love is streaming to the nations,
   Let mercy triumph over judgement everywhere.

Come to the politician, come to the refugee,
Come to the victim of respectable society;
Come to the mighty fallen, come to the poor oppressed:
We don't care how You come, as long as You come to them.

1688. You've placed a song within my heart

(I will bless the Lord at all times)

Ps 34:1; Is 7:14; Mt 1:23; Rom 8:31; Phil 4:4; 1 Thess 5:18

Lara Martin

Strong beat
G
Am7
G/B
You've placed a song within my heart, and this song
Am7
G
Am7
will bless You. Your praise is always on my
G/B
Am7
G
Am7
lips. Whatever life may bring, I know
G/B
Am7
G
Am7
that You are God; So I can trust in You and
G/B
Am7
C2
D
Em
sing. Immanuel, God with us, Immanu-

C2 D Em7 C2 D Em Em/D
nu - el, You are near. Im - ma - nu - el, my God is for
C2 Am7 D
me, my God is for me. So I will
G D C D G D
bless the Lord at all times, I will bless the Lord at all times.
C2 G/B Am7 C2
In e - v'ry si - tu - a - tion, I will give You praise;
Am7 C2 D
I will re - joice in You al - ways. I will

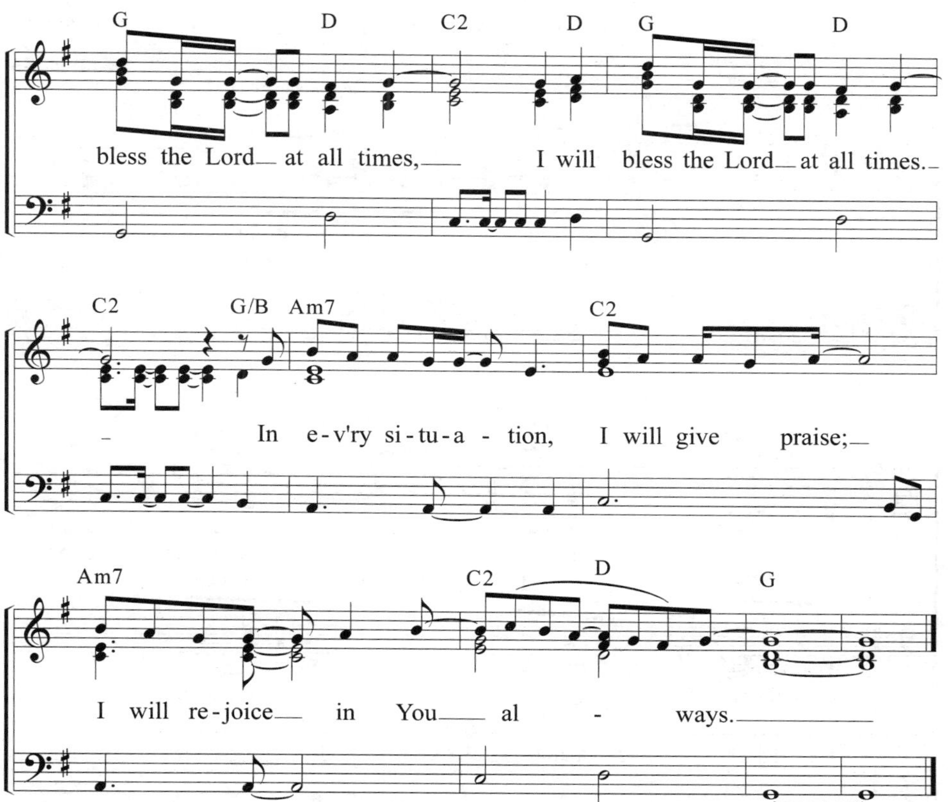
G
D
C2
D
G
D
bless the Lord at all times, I will bless the Lord at all times.
C2
G/B
Am7
C2
In e-v'ry si-tu-a-tion, I will give praise;
Am7
C2
D
G
I will re-joice in You al-ways.

1689. You've put a new song in my mouth

(Justice and mercy)

Ex 22:22; Ps 40:3; 68:5; Is 58:6; Zech 7:9

Matt Redman

Chorus
D2
F♯m7
G
Asus4
Last time to Coda
You've put a new song in my mouth;
Jus - tice and mer - cy are its theme,
it is a hymn of praise to You.
and I will live
1.
2.
G2
it back to You.
A
B♭2
1.2.
To verse
3.
To bridge
I

Bm7
Verse
F♯m7
1. The kind of fast You've cho - sen, Lord,
2. Lord, I won't bring an emp - ty song;
G2
G
Asus4 A
Bm7
it must reach out to bro - ken lives
it's mean - ing - less with - out com - pas -
F♯m7
G2
G
Asus4 A
and to the poor: so change me, Lord.
sion in my life, and ho - li - ness.
I
Bridge
D/F♯
G
D/F♯
know You are the or - phan's hope, I know You are the
Fa - ther where no fa - ther lives and to the lone - ly
1. G
2. G
Bm7
wi - dow's song; You're You're a friend. O Lord, You're

F♯m7
Em7
Asus4
A
D.C.
show-ing me what's on Your heart.
Coda
Em7
F♯m7
G
Asus4
D2
Fine
And I will give it back to You.

1690. You've touched my heart

Is 42:3; Col 1:27; Rev 17:14; 19:16

Neil Bennetts

Simply

E/G♯
Verse
A
Bsus4
1. You've touched my heart with
E/G♯
A
E/G♯
Bsus4
words of Your mer - cy and thoughts of Your beau - ty.
E/G♯
A
Bsus4
E/G♯
A
Your pre-sence, God, has cap-tured me now with the
E/G♯
Bsus4
F♯m7(+4)
F♯m7
E/G♯
Bsus4
hope of Your glo - ry. You've o-pened my eyes to see
F♯m7(+4)
E/G♯
Bsus4
B
You're all that this heart can need.

Chorus
E
B
C♯m7
For what is wor - thy of the King of kings, but a
A
E/G♯
F♯m
Bsus4
heart that is sa - tis-fied in lov - ing You?
E
B
C♯m
Yours is the song, Yours is the praise I'll bring, with a
A
E/G♯
F♯m
Bsus4
E
pas-sion for the won-der of see-ing Your glo - ry here.

2. This song I'll bring
Is my song of love from
A heart that's been broken.
It's what You've done,
For I've been set free by
The life that You've given.
Faithful and holy One,
Forever I live to sing.

Thematic Index

The following index is designed to help church leaders, worship leaders and musicians find songs and hymns appropriate for various themes, settings or occasions. It should be noted that this is by no means an exhaustive listing, and many of these inevitably overlap. If looking for a particular theme, therefore, it is recommended that one looks at several associated categories, rather than just one.

The "seasonal" section has deliberately been kept short. Apart from Easter and Harvest (Christmas songs and carols can be found under the "Jesus: Nativity" section), most other occasions in the church calender will be covered by themes already listed below.

A. GOD THE FATHER

1. General

2. Creation

3. God's love and faithfulness

4. Salvation and protection

5. God's grace and mercy

6. Forgiveness

7. Thirst for God

8. His presence

B. JESUS

1. Kingship

2. Nativity

3. The cross and redemption

4. Sacrifice (the Lamb), the blood of Jesus

Song no.

5. Second coming

6. His name

7. Resurrection

C. HOLY SPIRIT

1. Love

2. Joy

3. Peace

4. Holiness, passion and the fire of God

5. Faith

6. Hope

7. Power and anointing

8. Guidance

9. Refreshing and the river

D. CHURCH

1. General

2. Call to worship

3. Praise and thanksgiving

4. Proclamation and evangelism

5. Worship, love and adoration

6. Confession and repentance

7. Communion

8. Commission and revival

9. Commitment

10. Unity

11. Healing and personal renewal

12. Spiritual warfare and deliverance

13. Justice

14. Prayer

15. Church eternal

Index of Tunes

A more extensive selection of tunes is available in the first Songs of Fellowship Music edition (Songs 1 – 640).

GUITAR CHORD CHART

The following chord diagrams show the fingering for many of the guitar chords in this songbook.

Key

o = *play open string*
x = *don't play string*
1 = *thumb*
2 = *index finger*
3 = *middle finger*
4 = *ring finger*
5 = *little finger*
[bar symbol] = *index finger bar*
3 = *fret number*

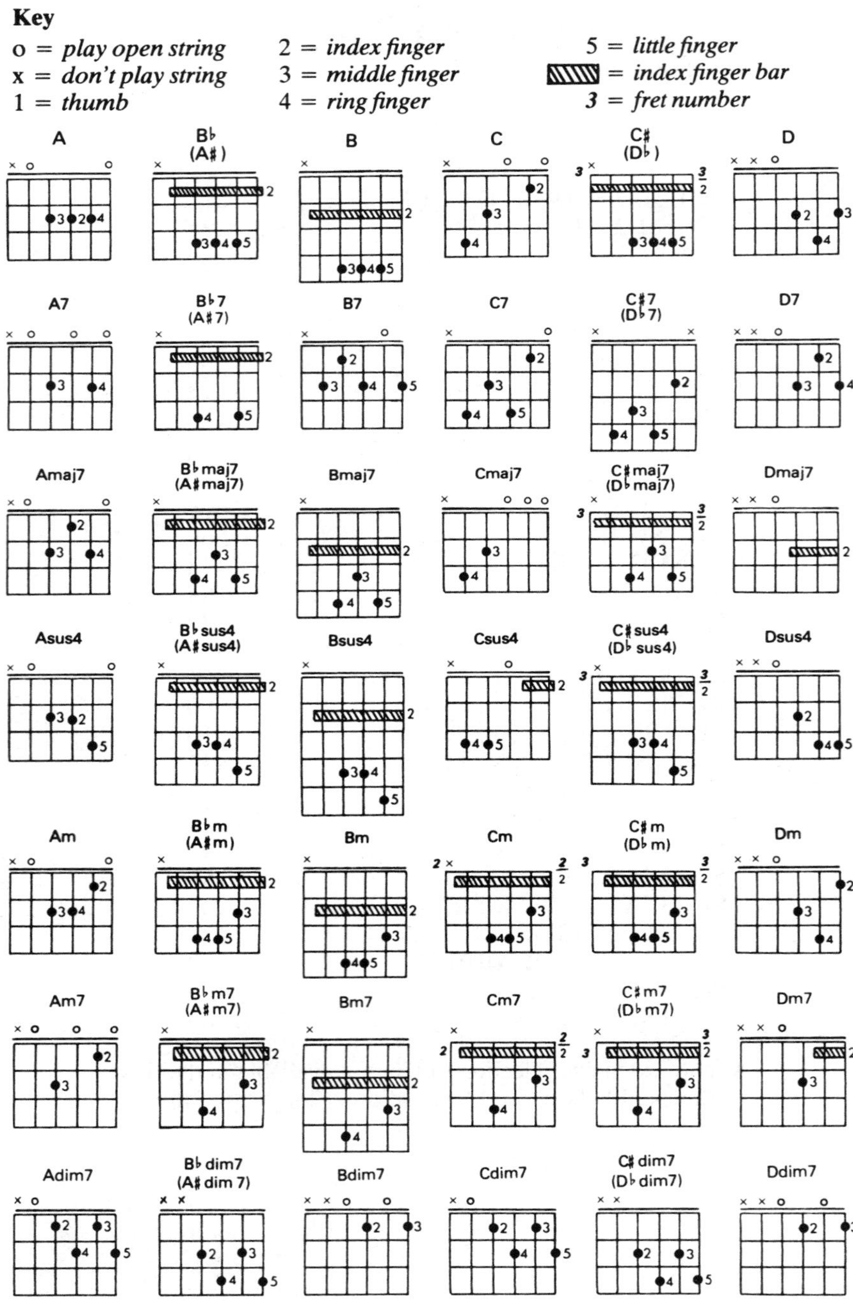

A
B♭ (A♯)
B
C
C♯ (D♭)
D
A7
B♭7 (A♯7)
B7
C7
C♯7 (D♭7)
D7
Amaj7
B♭maj7 (A♯maj7)
Bmaj7
Cmaj7
C♯maj7 (D♭maj7)
Dmaj7
Asus4
B♭sus4 (A♯sus4)
Bsus4
Csus4
C♯sus4 (D♭ sus4)
Dsus4
Am
B♭m (A♯m)
Bm
Cm
C♯m (D♭m)
Dm
Am7
B♭m7 (A♯m7)
Bm7
Cm7
C♯m7 (D♭m7)
Dm7
Adim7
B♭dim7 (A♯dim 7)
Bdim7
Cdim7
C♯dim7 (D♭dim7)
Ddim7

The chords which have been used throughout the book have been carefully chosen with the elementary guitarist in mind. Capo markings, in the left hand corner of many of the songs, allow simple chord shapes to be played with a capo in position. *Capo 3 (C)*, for example, means place the capo at the third fret and play the simple chords in brackets, which you will find are in C rather than E♭. If you use these capo markings you will find that you are able to play almost all of the songs using just ten chords: C, D, Dm, E, Em, F, G, A, Am, B7. If you do see a chord which you don't know, you will probably find that it is playable by mentally stripping it of all its 'extras' e.g. Gmaj7, just play G; Dm9, just play Dm; Csus4, just play C.

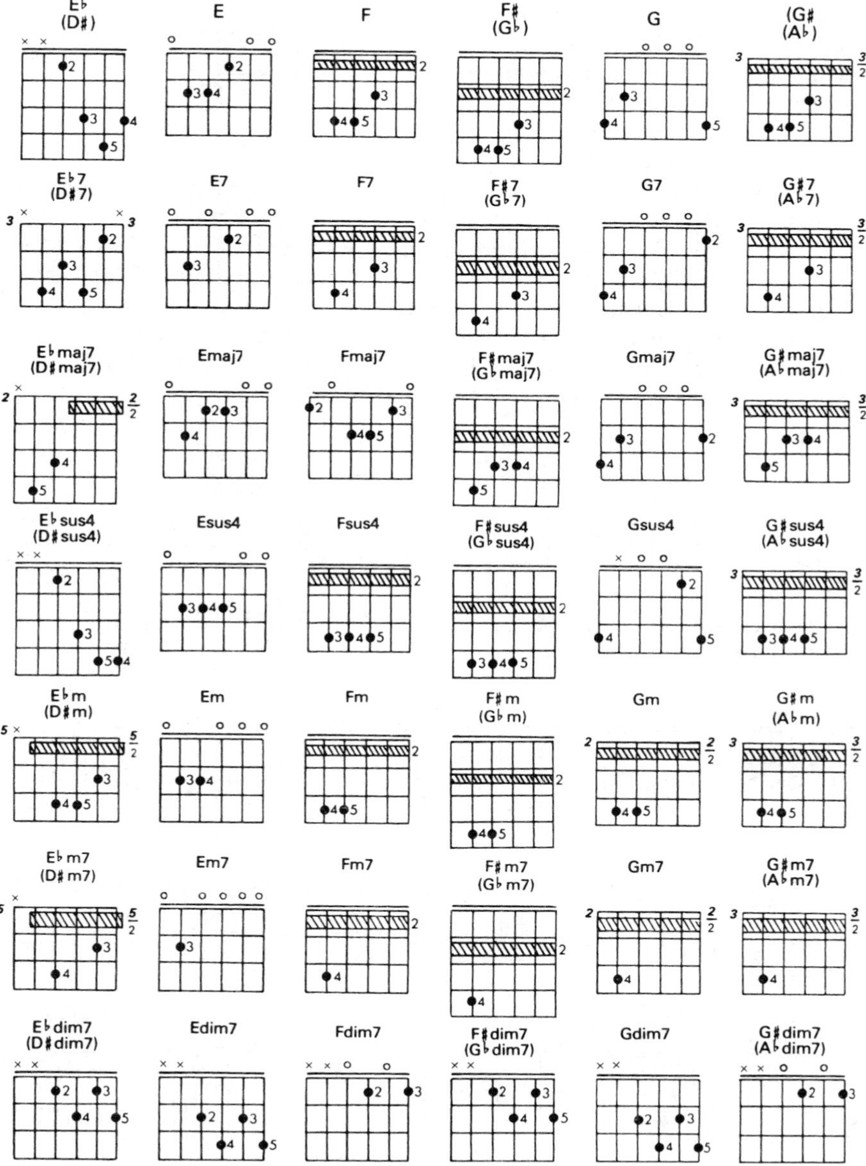
E♭ (D♯)
E
F
F♯ (G♭)
G
(G♯ (A♭)
E♭7 (D♯7)
E7
F7
F♯7 (G♭7)
G7
G♯7 (A♭7)
E♭maj7 (D♯maj7)
Emaj7
Fmaj7
F♯maj7 (G♭maj7)
Gmaj7
G♯maj7 (A♭maj7)
E♭sus4 (D♯sus4)
Esus4
Fsus4
F♯sus4 (G♭sus4)
Gsus4
G♯sus4 (A♭sus4)
E♭m (D♯m)
Em
Fm
F♯m (G♭m)
Gm
G♯m (A♭m)
E♭m7 (D♯m7)
Em7
Fm7
F♯m7 (G♭m7)
Gm7
G♯m7 (A♭m7)
E♭dim7 (D♯dim7)
Edim7
Fdim7
F♯dim7 (G♭dim7)
Gdim7
G♯dim7 (A♭dim7)

More unusual chords

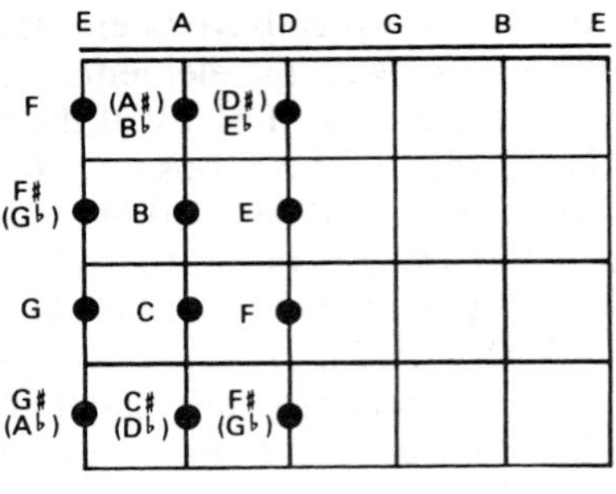
E A D G B E
F
(A♯) B♭
(D♯) E♭
F♯ (G♭)
B
E
G
C
F
G♯ (A♭)
C♯ (D♭)
F♯ (G♭)

In this songbook you will come across some more unusual chords—mainly chords with different bass notes. If you see D/A, for example, this means play the chord of D with the note A in the bass. For a guitarist who is strumming, this bass note isn't too important and he can just play an ordinary chord of D, but the A bass note is useful for bass and keyboard players, and for guitarists who are picking and want to add colour to their playing.

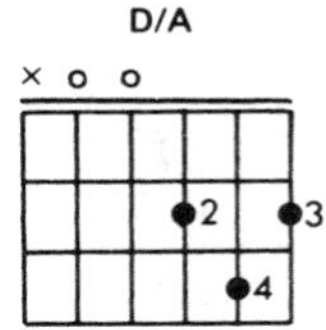
D/A

The diagram on the right above shows the position of bass notes on the guitar for those who want to learn them. Looking at the diagram you can work out that a D/A is simple (see second diagram).

As already stated, when *strumming,* the bass note (as long as it is a note from the chord) isn't too important as it doesn't sound above the other guitar strings. Because one requires as loud and full a sound as possible when strumming it is best to play chords which use all six strings. This can be achieved by incorporating a different bass note. Use the following full sounding versions of common chords when strumming. For—

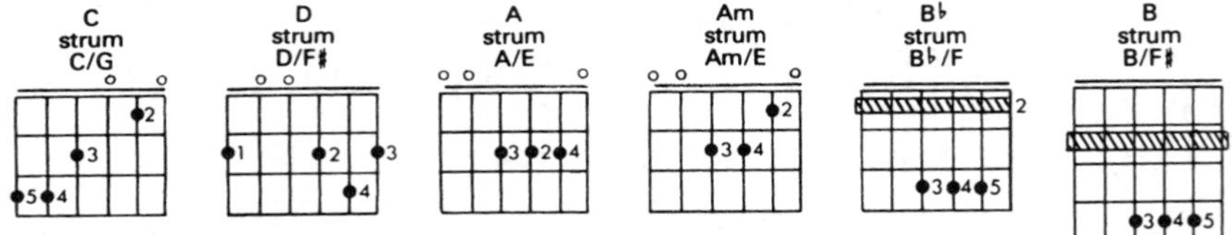
C strum C/G
D strum D/F♯
A strum A/E
Am strum Am/E
B♭ strum B♭/F
B strum B/F♯

The following are some of the more complex chords you will find in the songbook:

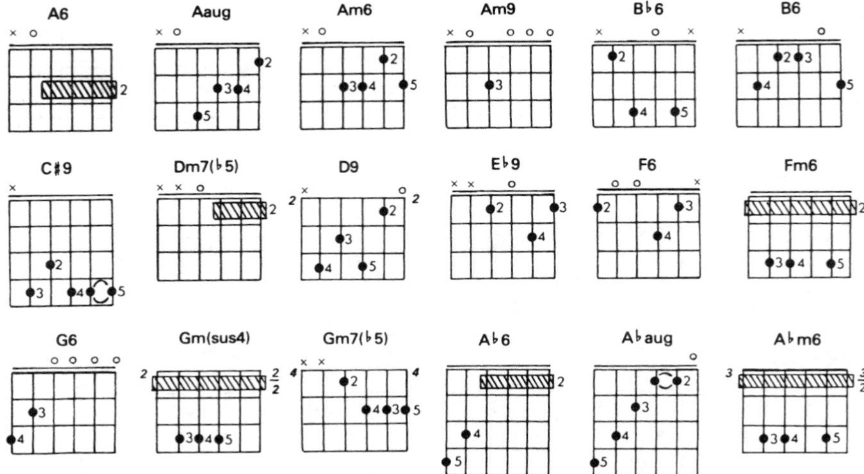
A6
Aaug
Am6
Am9
B♭6
B6
C♯9
Dm7(♭5)
D9
E♭9
F6
Fm6
G6
Gm(sus4)
Gm7(♭5)
A♭6
A♭aug
A♭m6

Scripture Index

This index lists Bible passages quoted or echoed in the songs. While not exhaustive, it provides a biblical background for many of the ideas expressed.

Matthew *(cont.)*

Mark

Mark *(cont.)*

Luke

Ephesians *(cont.)*

Philippians

Philippians *(cont.)*

Colossians

Colossians *(cont.)*

1 Thessalonians

2 Thessalonians

1 Timothy

2 Timothy

Index of Titles and First Lines

Authors' titles, where different from first lines, are shown in *italics*.

DISK USERS - PLEASE READ NOW!

Enclosed is your Songs of Fellowship 3 words CD. This contains the words to all the songs in this book. They are laid out simply and clearly, one to a page, and are ideal for 1) printing on to OHP acetates; 2) making your own customised church songbook; or 3) incorporating in service sheets.

Please note, files have been scanned for all current known viruses.

IMPORTANT NOTE: Purchasing this songbook does not grant the purchaser the right to reproduce the words from the CD. Any church or individual wishing to reproduce a song for church use must hold a current CCL licence for the territory in which the words are to be used. Permission to reproduce a song (or any part of it) must be gained from the individual song copyright holder (addresses given at the bottom of each song in the songbook). Any unauthorised usage is illegal.

To find out more about obtaining a licence, please contact CCLI at info@ccli.co.uk or by using the details shown on the Bibliography page at the front of the book.

REQUIREMENTS AND USAGE
The CD should auto-run on inserting it into your CD Rom drive. If the CD does not load up automatically, then you can start the program in the following way:
1) Click on the 'start' button on your task bar. (bottom left of the screen)
2) Click on 'run...'
3) Type in 'd:\menu.exe' (assuming that <d:> is your CD Rom drive letter)
4) The menu should now run allowing you to open the text files as required.

If this menu will still not load, the files are stored on the root of the CD which you can see by selecting your CD drive in 'My Computer'

PC Users
The words are saved as Rich Text Format (.rtf) files. You will be able to open or import the files if you have Microsoft Word™ or almost any other word processor.

Macintosh™ Users
Please double-click on the text files in the 'Mac' folder. Alternatively, you should be able to import the rtf files into your word processor.

IN CASE OF DIFFICULTY
If you encounter problems using the disk, please email us at support@kingsway.co.uk
Problems with using your word processing package should be referred to your software provider's technical support line.